HELLENISTIC CULTURE AND SOCIETY

General Editors: Anthony W. Bulloch, Erich S. Gruen, A. A. Long,
and Andrew F. Stewart

Poetic Garlands

Poetic Garlands

Hellenistic Epigrams in Context

Kathryn J. Gutzwiller

UNIVERSITY OF CALIFORNIA PRESS

Berkeley   Los Angeles   London

University of California Press
Berkeley and Los Angeles, California

University of California Press, Ltd.
London, England

Library of Congress Cataloging-in-Publication Data

Gutzwiller, Kathryn J.
    Poetic garlands : Hellenistic epigrams in context / Kathryn J. Gutzwiller.
       p.   cm. — (Hellenistic culture and society : 28)
    Includes bibliographical references and index.
    ISBN 0-520-20857-9 (cloth : alk. paper)
      1. Greek poetry, Hellenistic—History and criticism. 2. Epigrams,
Greek—History and criticism. 3. Books and reading—Mediterranean
Region. 4. Meleager—Knowledge—Literature. 5. Callimachus.
Epigrams. 6. Literary form. I. Title. II. Series.
PA3123.G88   1998
888.'0108–dc21   97-5676
                                          CIP

Printed in the United States of America
9 8 7 6 5 4 3 2 1

For Bob and Charlie

CONTENTS

PREFACE

In the Foreword to his commentary on Hellenistic epigrams, A. S. F. Gow remarks that he took up the *Greek Anthology* because he had been "constantly reminded how inadequate was the provision of signposts for those who strayed into that labyrinth." The image of the maze seems particularly apt in describing the various woven and unwoven strands that make up our Byzantine anthologies of Greek epigrams. The commentary of Gow and Page remains an essential guide in matters of chronology, diction, and text, and one now supplemented in important ways. Sonya L. Tarán has reprinted in two volumes a number of earlier German monographs that provide crucial information about the ancient anthologies through which Hellenistic epigrams passed into the Byzantine tradition. In addition, Alan Cameron has recently issued a detailed history of the *Greek Anthology*, which builds upon these earlier discoveries and adds a wealth of information derived from papyri and his own study of the Byzantine texts. What remains to be attempted, however, is a specifically literary study of Hellenistic epigrams. The poems themselves have, apparently, seemed too brief and the labyrinth of the *Anthology* too uncharted to accommodate lengthy studies concerned with interpretation rather than the *realia* of textual transmission. But the problem has seemed to me, in literary terms, to be one of failure to account fully for context; I have thought that, if we could uncover to any degree at all the original settings in which these epigrams were read, we would have a basis for understanding the literary meaning the poems held for ancient readers.

The significance of the term *context* in my title is twofold. On the one hand, it refers to the specific physical context in which an epigram is read. Verses inscribed on grave monuments or accompanying dedications take on meaning in relation to their site of inscription. During the Hellenistic era epigrams were sometimes recited as entertainment for friends, a context that produced different types of epigrams—erotic, satiric, and sympotic—as well as different responses. Within the third century B.C. epigrams were also collected into poetry books, where even the briefest of poems could acquire broader meaning by juxtaposition with other epigrams. By the beginning of the first century B.C. these epigram collections were being excerpted and rewoven into anthologies, like Meleager's *Garland*, where the grouping of poems by multiple authors on a single theme contextualized the history of the form. In the course of time even these contexts were remolded as the ancient anthologies were plucked apart to form the great Byzantine compendia based on different principles of arrangement. One goal of this book is to show how changed context produces changed meaning.

Because readers tend to privilege the poetic contexts established by authors, I have concentrated on studying the way in which Hellenistic epigrams may have functioned in their original collections. I am under no delusion that the scope or order of these lost poetry books can be reestablished. Meleager clearly used earlier epigram collections, but he thoroughly redistributed their contents throughout his anthology. In addition, he probably excerpted only a small percentage of published Greek epigrams and may have selected from a given poet certain types of epigrams over others. But it is also likely that he tended to anthologize key poems from earlier collections, those on themes unique to a certain author and those that foster an impression of the poetic persona controlling the collection. Although I believe that in certain instances enough evidence exists to justify speculation about a poem's position within a collection, usually as an opening, closing, or transitional poem, my order of discussion, both of individual poems and of poems in groups, is more often designed to illustrate similarities and so interconnections, not to suggest an original order. The exception is Meleager's *Garland*, for which I have been able to build upon earlier, and largely unknown, scholarship in order to establish the major structure of his various sections. The patterns of arrangement that can now be reconstructed for this anthology are so complex and fascinating that they no doubt represent a culmination in the Hellenistic process of weaving poetic garlands.

Because I concentrate in this diachronic continuum on the synchronic moment of the author-issued epigram collection, the term *context* acquires a further reference to the social and historical matrix in which the author composed. These are not poems written by scholars in ivory towers, with an eye only to earlier Greek literature or contemporary literary quarrels. The individuals presented in the epigrams are, for the most part, either historically real or fictioned as like persons of the poet's own day. The dominating themes I identify for the epigrammatists discussed here are connected to the personal positions they occupied in the fragmented and shifting world of Hellenistic culture. Anyte and Nossis write from the perspective of women dwelling in communities far from the centers of literary culture and political power. Leonidas, who characterizes himself as a poor wanderer, presents a more sympathetic identification with the underclass figures in his epigrams than with the wealthy and aristocratic ones, those who would be more likely to appreciate, and patronize, his art.

Asclepiades, Posidippus, and perhaps Hedylus as well eschew bonds of tradi-
tional aristocratic affiliation in favor of an individually chosen philosophical
perspective. Antipater of Sidon and Meleager, both eastern Greeks inhabiting
a world increasingly dominated by Rome, employed techniques of varying the
earlier epigrammatic tradition as a way of marking their right to belong to
the historical trajectory of Greek culture. These contexts too, the social and
historical ones, have been obscured by the long process of anthologizing.

None of the scholars who have seriously examined the evidence have ques-
tioned the existence of epigram books from as early as the third century B.C. Not
only do we have ancient references to such collections, but traces of these poetry
books have been identified on papyri and even in the manuscript tradition.
More important, it is no longer the case that all Hellenistic epigram books are
essentially lost. After I had begun work on this project, there came to light a
papyrus of the late third century B.C. containing about one hundred epigrams, at
least two of which were known compositions of Posidippus. I regret that, as my
book goes to press, the papyrus as a whole has yet to be published. But the future
editors have published the texts of twenty-five epigrams, and I have information
about the arrangement of the papyrus both from published reports and from pri-
vate correspondence. The Milan papyrus is clearly an exciting discovery, which
provides important information about early epigram collections. Scholars were,
for instance, surprised to learn that a collection of this early date was divided
by headings into epigram types, in the manner of Meleager's *Garland*. It remains
to be seen whether the epigrams within the sections are linked associatively by
theme or key word, as in that later anthology. But I caution against taking the
new Posidippus collection as a model for all epigram books. Such collections
were likely structured in a variety of ways. We do not even know if the sylloge in
Milan was arranged by the author himself or by a posthumous editor.

Because few readers will bring to this book a thorough familiarity with
Hellenistic epigrams, I have printed the texts of many of the poems I discuss.
Whenever possible, these are cited from Gow-Page's *Hellenistic Epigrams*, but a
variety of other editions needed to be used as well. The edition from which the
text was drawn will be indicated by the first reference given in the citation. In a
fair number of instances I have felt compelled to edit the epigram, either because
the earlier editor (often Gow-Page) has printed a clearly corrupt text in daggers
or because the reading in my source, most often an emendation, seems to me
unlikely to be correct; such changes are indicated in a note. The translations are
my own, though I have borrowed at times from earlier translators.

In working over a number of years on a book of this complexity, I have
developed a good many debts. Opportunity for research and writing on this
project was afforded by the Semple Classics Fund, which awarded me a series
of summer research grants, and the University of Cincinnati, which provided
a period of sabbatical leave in 1990–91 and again in 1994–95. Preliminary
versions of various parts of the book were presented as lectures at Case Western

Reserve University, the University of Cincinnati, Emory University, Ohio State University, the Classical Association of the Middle West and South, and the American Philological Association. I am grateful for various comments and encouragements offered by all these audiences. In response to requests from editors, a portion of Chapter 3 was published, in an earlier form, as "Anyte's Epigram Book," *Syllecta Classica* 4 (1993) 71–89, and another portion of that same chapter has been adapted as a part of "Genre Development and Gendered Voices in Erinna and Nossis," in *Dwelling in Possibility: Women Poets and Critics on Poetry*, edited by Yopie Prins and Maeera Shreiber (Ithaca, 1997) 202–22. I have benefited from discussion about epigrams with several scholars, in particular Peter Bing and Alan Cameron, and I appreciate information about the Milan papyrus provided by Guido Bastianini. Those who read the book in manuscript have been helpful in suggesting various improvements: Ann Michelini, who is a good enough friend to read practically everything I write, and the kind readers for the press, Diane Rayor and David Sider, whose detailed comments were a great aid in final editing. Shannon Leslie proofread much of the manuscript for me and saved me from several mistakes. I am grateful as well to Erich Gruen, who solicited the manuscript for this series, and Mary Lamprech, who waited patiently for its completion.

Cincinnati
July 1997

ABBREVIATIONS

AP	*Palatine Anthology.*
APl	*Planudean Anthology.*
BKT	*Berliner Klassikertexte.* Berlin, 1904–39.
CA	Powell, John U., ed. *Collectanea Alexandrina.* Oxford, 1925.
CEG	Hansen, Peter Allan, ed. *Carmina epigraphica Graeca saeculorum VII–V a. Chr. n.* Berlin, 1983.
CEG²	Hansen, Peter Allan, ed. *Carmina epigraphica Graeca saeculi IV a. Chr. n.* Berlin, 1989.
CGF	Kaibel, Georg. *Comicorum Graecorum fragmenta.* Berlin, 1899.
EG	Page, D. L., ed. *Epigrammata Graeca.* Oxford, 1975.
FGE	Page, D. L., ed. *Further Greek Epigrams.* Cambridge, 1981.
GLP	Page, D. L., ed. *Greek Literary Papyri* I. Cambridge, Mass., 1942.
Gow	Gow, A. S. F., ed. *Theocritus.* 2 vols. 2nd ed. Cambridge, 1952.
G-P	Gow, A. S. F., and D. L. Page, eds. *The Greek Anthology: Hellenistic Epigrams.* 2 vols. Cambridge, 1965.
G-P, *Garland*	Gow, A. S. F., and D. L. Page, eds. *The Greek Anthology: The Garland of Philip.* 2 vols. Cambridge, 1968.
GV	Peek, Werner, ed. *Griechische Vers-Inschriften I: Grab-Epigramme.* Berlin, 1955.
M.-W.	Merkelbach, R., and M. L. West, eds. *Hesiodi fragmenta selecta.* 3rd ed. Oxford, 1990.
PCG	Kassel, R., and C. Austin, eds. *Poetae comici Graeci.* Vols. 2–5, 7. Berlin, 1983–.
Pf.	Pfeiffer, Rudolf, ed. *Callimachus.* 2 vols. Oxford, 1949–51.
PLF	Lobel, Edgar, and Denys Page, eds. *Poetarum Lesbiorum fragmenta.* Oxford, 1955.
PMG	Page, D. L., ed. *Poetae melici Graeci.* Oxford, 1962.
P.Oxy.	*The Oxyrhynchus Papyri.* London, 1898–.
RE	Pauly, A., G. Wissowa, and W. Kroll, eds. *Real-Encyclopädie der klassischen Altertumswissenschaft.* Stuttgart, 1893–1978.
SH	Lloyd-Jones, Hugh, and Peter Parsons, eds. *Supplementum Hellenisticum.* Berlin, 1983.
SVF	Arnim, Hans von. *Stoicorum veterum fragmenta.* 3 vols. Leipzig, 1903–21.
W	West, M. L., ed. *Iambi et elegi Graeci ante Alexandrum cantati.* 2 vols. 2nd ed. Oxford, 1989.

CHAPTER ONE

Introduction

The epigram, as its name indicates, is a written form, often a verse inscription. From the eighth or seventh century B.C. epigrams, among our earliest examples of writing in the Greek alphabet, were chiseled on grave monuments to commemorate the dead and on votive offerings to explain the act of dedication.[1] Numerous verbal and metrical parallels show that epigrams, composed first in hexameters and later primarily in elegiac couplets, drew from the same

1. Pre-Hellenistic verse inscriptions have been collected by Peter A. Hansen, *Carmina epigraphica Graeca saeculorum VII–V a. Chr. n.* (Berlin, 1983) and *Carmina epigraphica Graeca saeculi IV a. Chr. n.* (Berlin, 1989). For a survey of the earliest inscriptions, down to 650 B.C., see Barry B. Powell, *Homer and the Origin of the Greek Alphabet* (Cambridge, 1991) 123–80. No comprehensive edition of verse inscriptions, including those from later antiquity, has appeared since Georg Kaibel, ed., *Epigrammata Graeca ex lapidibus conlecta* (Berlin, 1878), but sepulchral epigrams through the late period may be found in Werner Peek, ed., *Griechische Vers-Inschriften* I (Berlin, 1955) and, selectively, in *Griechische Grabgedichte* (Berlin, 1960). The reader is cautioned, however, that Peek includes many epigrams preserved in manuscript and perhaps never intended for inscription. A comprehensive book on ancient epigram is yet to be written, but general discussions may be found in R. Reitzenstein, "Epigramm," *RE* 11 HB (1907) 71–111; J. Geffcken, "Studien zum griechischen Epigramm," *NJA* 39 (1917) 88–117, reprinted in shortened form in *Das Epigramm: Zur Geschichte einer inschriftlicher und literarischen Gattung*, ed. Gerhard Pfohl (Darmstadt, 1969) 21–46; Hermann Beckby, ed., *Anthologia Graeca* (Munich, 1957) I 9–99; and, for the later Greek period, R. Keydell, "Epigramm," *Reallexikon für Antike und Christentum* 5 (1962) 539–77. Two more recent books go some way toward filling this gap. Marion Lausberg, *Das Einzeldistichon: Studien zum antiken Epigramm* (Munich, 1982), though ostensibly concerned only with two-line poems, surveys much of the history of Greco-Roman epigram as well as the history of scholarship on epigram. Pierre Laurens, *L'abeille dans l'ambre: célébration de l'épigramme* (Paris, 1989) covers literary epigrams from the beginning of the Hellenistic age through the Renaissance, but with a concentration on the Latin poems.

traditional language found in epic and elegy.[2] Although some scholars, by associating writtenness with literature, have placed epigram at the head of the western literary tradition and others have compared inscribed verse to the occasional poetry of the oral period,[3] it is my own view that early Greek culture granted to epigram, in comparison with the major poetic forms of epic, elegy, and lyric, an aesthetic value like that of "craft to art."[4] It was the writtenness of the epigram, as its essential feature, that for centuries confined it to the ranks of the minor arts, to the category of the decorative and the trivial. During this period literary works of higher rank obtained written form only for mnemonic purposes, to be preserved for the next oral performance.[5] The epigram, on the other hand, unlike any other archaic or classical poetic form, was intended

2. For these parallels, see Paul Friedländer with Herbert Hoffleit, *Epigrammata: Greek Inscriptions in Verse from the Beginnings to the Persian Wars* (Berkeley, 1948) 65–70; A. E. Raubitschek, "Das Denkmal-Epigramm," *L'épigramme grecque* in Entretiens sur l'antiquité classique 14 (Geneva, 1968) 3–26; and B. Gentili, "Epigramma ed elegia," *L'épigramme grecque* 39–81. On the change to elegiac in the sixth century, see M. B. Wallace, "The Metres of Early Greek Epigrams," in *Greek Poetry and Philosophy: Studies in Honour of Leonard Woodbury*, ed. Douglas Gerber (Chico, 1984) 303–17.

3. For celebration of epigram's position in western literature, see Raubitschek 5 and, more elaborately, Helmet Häusle, *Einfache und frühe Formen des griechischen Epigramms* in Commentationes Aenipontanae 25 (Innsbruck, 1979). For the comparison of epigram to oral song, see G. B. Walsh, "Callimachean Passages: The Rhetoric of Epitaph in Epigram," *Arethusa* 24 (1991) 79 and J. W. Day, "Rituals in Stone: Early Greek Grave Epigrams and Monuments," *JHS* 109 (1989) 26, who likens the role of the epitaph reader to that of a praise poet.

4. In his use of this phrase, Friedländer 1 seems to have in mind the essential merit of inscribed verse, while I am referring only to ancient aesthetic evaluation.

5. See, in general, B. M. W. Knox, "Books and Readers in the Greek World: From the Beginnings to Alexandria," *The Cambridge History of Classical Literature* I, ed. P. E. Easterling and B. M. W. Knox (Cambridge, 1985) 4. On the rarity of books in the fifth century, see E. G. Turner, *Athenian Books in the Fifth and Fourth Centuries B.C.* (London, 1952); H. R. Immerwahr, "Book Rolls on Attic Vases," in *Classical, Medieval, and Renaissance Studies in Honor of B. L. Ullman* I, ed. C. Henderson, Jr. (Rome, 1964) 17–48, where the use of scrolls for oral recitation is evident; and William V. Harris, *Ancient Literacy* (Cambridge, Mass., 1989) 84–88. On the existence of written poetic texts in the "song culture" of ancient Greece, see John Herington, *Poetry into Drama: Early Tragedy and the Greek Poetic Tradition* (Berkeley, 1985) 45–47, 201–6. Important studies on the change from a predominantly oral to a predominantly literate culture include: Eric Havelock, *Preface to Plato* (Oxford, 1963), *The Literate Revolution in Greece and Its Cultural Consequences* (Princeton, 1982), and *The Muse Learns to Write: Reflections on Orality and Literacy from Antiquity to the Present* (New Haven, 1986); J. Goody and I. Watt, "The Consequences of Literacy," in *Literacy in Traditional Societies*, ed. Jack Goody (Cambridge, 1968) 27–68; Walter J. Ong, *Orality and Literacy* (London, 1982). These works should be read in conjunction with the revision in the theoretical approach to orality and literacy put forth by, e.g., Ruth Finnegan, *Oral Poetry: Its Nature, Significance, and Social Context* (Cambridge, 1977) and Rosalind Thomas, *Oral Tradition and Written Record in Classical Athens* (Cambridge, 1989) and *Literacy and Orality in Ancient Greece* (Cambridge, 1992).

not for public recitation but for private reading whenever a passerby, whose curiosity was piqued by a monument or dedication, paused briefly to peruse the inscription.[6] Although the solitary reading of an epigram does anticipate the experience of later book readers, within this cultural context verse inscriptions were valued more for their practical function of praise and commemoration than purely as literary objects. The literariness of an inscription was further limited because the reader's aesthetic experience involved visually perceived objects as well as discourse—it was based on the shape of the letters as much as the poetic quality of the verse and on the relationship of the inscription to the crafted object of which it was a part.[7] As long as the epigram was confined to its monument, it was excluded from the arena of oral discourse where poetry could obtain rank and status by performance, and reperformance, before a collective audience.

Only at the beginning of the Hellenistic age did epigrams emerge as fully literary forms; in fact, they became a favorite of those on the cutting edge of literary development.[8] Certain authors, like Posidippus and Leonidas, were known primarily or exclusively as epigrammatists, while poets better known for their work in other genres, like Callimachus and Theocritus, also composed significant quantities of epigrams. Epigram is in some ways the most characteristic of Hellenistic poetic forms. Because of its inherited brevity and conciseness, its necessary concern with the personal and the particular, it conformed well

6. Jesper Svenbro, *Phrasikleia: An Anthropology of Reading in Ancient Greece*, trans. Janet Lloyd (Ithaca, 1993) 44–63 has argued that an inscription was normally read by a single reader to a group of auditors, but he produces a doubtful text of a single epigram (108 *CEG*) as his only evidence for this custom. While such a "performance" of an epigram may sometimes have taken place, surely it was also common, we may suppose more common, for an epigram to be read by a single reader. Nor should we assume that inscriptions were always read aloud. While B. M. W. Knox, "Silent Reading in Antiquity," *GRBS* 9 (1968) 433–34, has shown that silent reading was not unusual in the fifth century, there is no reason to doubt that it was accomplished at an even earlier date.

7. For the dependence of an epigram's meaning upon its relationship with its monument, see Raubitschek 3 and Häusle 88–105. Christoph W. Clairmont, *Gravestone and Epigram: Greek Memorials from the Archaic and Classical Period* (Mainz, 1970) is concerned with the relationship between stone and inscription in the narrower sense of what the verse reveals about the figures represented on the monument.

8. M. Puelma, "Ἐπίγραμμα—*epigramma*: Aspekte einer Wortgeschichte," *MH* 53 (1996) 123–39 has recently argued that epigram was not canonized as a poetic genre until the time of Martial. His argument is primarily a semantic one, based on the fact that the word ἐπίγραμμα does not appear in the texts of Hellenistic epigrammatists. Though the poets themselves do use a variety of terms to refer to their short poetry, ample evidence shows that ἐπίγραμμα was a standard designation for short verse in the third century B.C.; see Chapter 2. As with other new Hellenistic poetic forms, such as pastoral, the genre itself was practiced by poets before the terminology to designate the genre became fixed. Praxis preceded canonization.

to the Callimachean aesthetic preference for the miniature, the intricate, and the fragmented. The term later used by Philip of Thessalonica to designate the brevity characteristic of the epigram (ὀλιγοστιχίην, 1.6 G-P, *Garland* = *AP* 4.2.6) echoes Callimachus' programmatic term for his own short poetry (ὀλιγόστιχος, fr. 1.9 Pf.).[9] The illusion of inscription maintained in many literary epigrams may also have boosted the genre's appeal to this bookish age, concerned with the visual as well as the more strictly literary aspects of the written word.[10]

But the admission of the epigram to the status of a fully literary kind resulted most directly from its new similarity to other, "higher" forms of poetry. Epigrams continued to be composed for inscriptional purposes, but they were increasingly found also in settings where literary discourse was conventionally presented. Terse elegies, resembling epigrams in their brevity, and parodies of inscriptions, probably recited at symposia, are known already from the fifth and fourth centuries.[11] But Asclepiades was apparently the first person to devote himself to the composition of sympotic epigram, which derives its themes from the elegies traditionally performed in the symposium setting. Richard Reitzenstein argued a century ago that Asclepiades and his circle composed their epigrams for performance at Hellenistic banquets.[12] Antipater of Sidon's reputation as an improviser indicates that even ostensibly inscriptional epigrams were recited on

9. It was after Callimachus, however, and after Meleager's *Garland* as well, that epigram-matists began to impose severe limitations on their compositions. See Parmenion 11.1–2 G-P, *Garland* = *AP* 9.342.1–2, φημὶ πολυστιχίην ἐπιγράμματος οὐ κατὰ Μούσας εἶναι, "I tell you that the epigram of many lines does not accord with the Muses"; Cyrillus *AP* 9.369.1, πάγκαλόν ἐστ' ἐπίγραμμα τὸ δίστιχον, "An epigram of two lines is a beautiful thing"; and with a different emphasis, Leonidas of Alexandria *AP* 6.327.2, οὐ γὰρ ἔτι στέργω τὴν δολιχογραφίην, "I no longer care for writing at length." For theoretical considerations of brevity as the essential characteristic of epigram, see Lausberg 20–101.

10. For references in poetry to reading and the appearance of writing on the page, see Peter Bing, *The Well-Read Muse: Present and Past in Callimachus and the Hellenistic Poets* in Hypomnemata 90 (Göttingen, 1988) 10–48.

11. See Ulrich v. Wilamowitz-Moellendorff, *Hellenistische Dichtung in der Zeit des Kallimachos* (Berlin, 1924) I 129–32; B. Gentili 40–43.

12. *Epigramm und Skolion: Ein Beitrag zur Geschichte der alexandrinischen Dichtung* (Giessen, 1893) 87–96. Although Reitzenstein understood well that these poems were also placed in books, he considers them first and foremost "Lieder beim Gelage" (96). Reitzenstein's thesis has recently been revived by Alan Cameron, *Callimachus and His Critics* (Princeton, 1995) 71–103, who argues that epigram was the "new sympotic poetry of the age" (76). I agree with Cameron that the epigram books of the third century probably incorporated poems originally recited to friends and likely included short poems in nonelegiac meters. But I resist his implication that the collection of these epigrams onto papyrus scrolls was a mere afterthought and so without specific literary intent ("publication of epigrams in book form must have been secondary, a way of preserving the best of the new epigrams rather than the factor that gave birth to them," 78). My study will show that at least in some instances Hellenistic epigrams were composed to occupy key positions in poetry books.

similar occasions.[13]   Epigram became virtually indistinguishable from shorter elegy or extracts from longer elegy not only because both were now performed but also because both were now encountered by readers in books. Scholars have pointed to the precedent set by the *Theognidea*, a collection of elegiac passages suitable for recitation at symposia, and to an edition or editions of epigrams attributed to Simonides, gathered both from stone and from the anecdotal tradition.[14] Although both collections underwent evolution in form throughout the Hellenistic period, recent studies dated the prototypes to the end of the fourth century.[15]   In all likelihood, then, the formation of these sylloges was precedent to the earliest epigram books rather than coincidental with them. The epigrammatists themselves count among their forerunners the elegists Mimnermus and Antimachus and certain lyric poets (Sappho, Anacreon, and Bacchylides, as well as Simonides) whose preserved works include a number of epigrammatic poems.[16]   At the same time that scholarly editions of these poets were being formed, Hellenistic epigrammatists began to collect their own compositions and to publish them in the form of epigram books. Even if Hellenistic poets sometimes composed for the stone and sometimes recited their

13. Cic. *De Or.* 3.194. The practice was still familiar in the first century A.D.: Martial (2.1.9–10) pictures the proper setting for a reading of his epigrams to be a banquet and Leonidas of Alexandria, of Neronian date, assumes that his isopsephic distichs will offer symposium entertainment (*AP* 6.322). Yet within their published form such statements represent an established fiction about epigram performance rather than the author's expectation for the use of his poetry. Leonidas' play with the numerical sums of the letters in his lines of verse could hardly be appreciated orally; for the fictionality of such reference in Martial, see D. P. Fowler, "Martial and the Book," *Ramus* 24 (1995) 31–58.

14. The basic study on the Simonidean sylloge is Marcus Boas, *De epigrammatis Simonideis* (Groningen, 1905); see also D. L. Page, ed., *Further Greek Epigrams* (Cambridge, 1981) 119–23, who accepts only 6 *FGE* (= Hdt. 7.228.3) as genuinely Simonidean.

15. Martin L. West, *Studies in Greek Elegy and Iambus* (Berlin, 1974) 57 dates the core of the *Theognidea*, that which he calls the "florilegium purum" (lines 19–254), to about 300 B.C. Page (1981) 123 places the core of the Simonides collection "quite early in the Hellenistic period" or, alternatively (210), "in the latter part of the fourth century." This dating assumes that the collection was supplemented with clearly spurious epigrams throughout the third and second centuries, resulting in a much expanded collection used by Meleager; see D. L. Page, ed., *Epigrammata Graeca* (Oxford, 1975) v–viii. John H. Molyneux, *Simonides: A Historical Study* (Wauconda, Ill., 1992) 13–15, who perhaps exaggerates the inconsistency in Page's stated positions, finds credible the hypothesis of an original fourth-century collection.

16. Posidippus (9 G-P = *AP* 12.168) claims inspiration from Mimnermus, Antimachus, Homer, and Hesiod, while Asclepiades' praise of Antimachus' *Lyde* (32 G-P = *AP* 9.63) suggests a similar literary heritage. In listing the epigrammatists anthologized in his *Garland* (1 G-P = *AP* 4.1), Meleager mentions a number of pre-Hellenistic poets: Sappho, Simonides, Bacchylides, Anacreon, Archilochus, and Plato. For epigrams on lyric poets, see S. Barbantani, "I poeti lirici del canone alessandrino nell'epigrammatistica," *Aevum Antiquum* 6 (1993) 5–97.

epigrams to friends at social gatherings,[17] they were nevertheless self-consciously aware that their epigrams would ultimately reside with other poetry in a written context.

Study of the literary art of the Hellenistic epigram is inescapably concerned, then, with epigram as book poetry. But the book epigrams of this era have been preserved for us not in their original collections but by means of successive anthologies compiled from the late Hellenistic period through the Byzantine era.[18] This anthologizing has strongly affected the hermeneutical approaches applied to Greek epigrams, which tend to be read either as isolated poems or as part of a sequence of poems designed to display the skill of successive poets at the art of variation.[19] While such methods of interpretation often make valuable contributions to our understanding of the poems, scholars have sometimes translated the brevity of epigram into a limited potential for meaning and have assessed the variation of themes as an artistic sterility developing over the course of time.[20] To comprehend more fully the appeal of epigram for Hellenistic readers, we need to reconstruct the historical contexts in which these poems were read—above all, the collections compiled or approved by the authors themselves. Toward this goal, the next chapter will survey what can be known about specific editions and what the manuscript and papyrological records tell us

17. Although some epigrams were likely improvised on the spot, others were probably composed in advance and then recited at an opportune moment. In either case, we are dealing with drafts that were presumably improved before circulation in written form.

18. The standard commentaries on Hellenistic epigrams are A. S. F. Gow and D. L. Page, eds., *The Greek Anthology: Hellenistic Epigrams*, 2 vols. (Cambridge, 1965) and *The Greek Anthology: The Garland of Philip*, 2 vols. (Cambridge, 1968). Manuscript epigrams omitted by Gow-Page have been edited by Page (1981). There are also a number of important editions of the *Greek Anthology*, which preserves most of the surviving Hellenistic epigrams: Friedrich Jacobs, *Anthologia Graeca*, 13 vols. (Leipzig, 1794–1814) and, with a fuller text of P, *Anthologia Graeca ad fidem codicis olim Palatini nunc Parisini*, 4 vols. (Leipzig, 1813–17); Hugo Stadtmüller, ed., *Anthologia Graeca epigrammatum Palatina cum Planudea*, 3 vols. (Leipzig, 1894–1906), which stops at 9.563; W. R. Paton, ed. and trans., *The Greek Anthology*, Loeb Classical Library, 5 vols. (Cambridge, Mass., 1916–18); Pierre Waltz *et al.*, eds., *Anthologie grecque*, 13 vols. (Paris, 1928–94); Beckby, 4 vols. (1957–58).

19. The study of Hellenistic epigrams as isolated entities is exemplified by the numerous publications of Giuseppe Giangrande, who examines linguistic usage and thematic convention within the poems; see, for example, "Gli epigrammi alessandrini come arte allusiva," *QUCC* 15 (1973) 7–31. For focus upon a sequence of epigrams linked by variation of a theme, see W. Ludwig, "Die Kunst der Variation im hellenistischen Liebesepigramm," *L'épigramme grecque* 299–334; Sonya L. Tarán, *The Art of Variation in the Hellenistic Epigram* (Leiden, 1979); and Laurens 76–96.

20. See, for instance, the comments of A. W. Bulloch, "Hellenistic Poetry" in *The Cambridge History of Classical Literature* (1985) I 616–17: "The epigram is always particularly concerned with stock themes and variation within the genre, and even poems which strike an apparently intimate note are also written with a view to displaying a literary conceit or figure, or a witticism. For all its fecundity the epigram was never more than a minor form."

about the principles of order and design in those editions. With this information as a guide, we will then be in a position to apply a new interpretive strategy to individual Hellenistic epigrams—to read them *as if* we knew their place in historical collections. But first, we will consider here, more theoretically, the general effects that accrue from placing epigrams in a literary context.[21]

In form, epigrams preserved in manuscript do not differ from those found on stone. The inscribed poems of the Hellenistic era often display the same level of poeticity in diction and imagery as the anthologized poems, some of which must themselves have been composed for inscription.[22] The literariness of the Hellenistic epigram depends, then, not upon some "bookish" element in form, style, or theme (though many poems do seem unlikely candidates for inscription), but upon the context in which the poem is found. When an author or editor transfers an epigram from its site of inscription to a papyrus roll, it is signaled by cultural convention that a more literary form of interpretation is now expected of the reader. The poem is no longer an "epigram" in the original sense of an inscription but a representation of such an "epigram." The monument adorned by the epigram is no longer visually present but, like the banqueting hall as the site of sympotic epigram, must now be reconstructed in the reader's imagination. When Gow surmises time and again that certain epigrams were composed to accompany pictorial representations, he points unwittingly to the imaginative process—the mental filling-in of information—that book epigrams commonly evoke. A Pompeian wall painting illustrating an epigram by Leonidas carries this response to the extreme point of re-creation in a visual medium.[23] The painter who represented in fresco Leonidas' scene of three brothers—a fowler, a hunter, and a fisherman—dedicating nets to Pan created a pictorial version of the numerous literary imitations composed by later epigrammatists.

21. For a general discussion of the effects of collection on reading, see N. Fraistat, "Introduction," *Poems in Their Place: The Intertextuality and Order of Poetic Collections*, ed. Neil Fraistat (Chapel Hill, 1986) 3–17 and D. Fenoaltea, "Preface," *The Ladder of High Designs: Structure and Interpretation of the French Lyric Sequence*, ed. Doranne Fenoaltea and David Rubin (Charlottesville, 1991) vii–x. For literary study of an epigram collection, see Ann B. Coiro, *Robert Herrick's "Hesperides" and the Epigram Book Tradition* (Baltimore, 1988).

22. On the heightened poeticity of Hellenistic inscribed verse, see Peek (1960) 37. For discussion of certain epigrams from the *Anthology* that have also been found as inscriptions, see G. Pfohl, "Inschriften in der Anthologia Graeca," *Euphrosyne* 2 (1968) 155–60. On the problem involved in making a strong differentiation between inscribed and literary epigrams, see Lausberg 96–97.

23. 46 G-P = *AP* 6.13. Gow-Page (1965) II 342, 356 seem uncertain whether the fresco was composed for the inscription or vice versa. But the fact that it is one of four sets of painted illustrations of inscriptions argues against the priority of the fresco, since it is highly unlikely that all the inscriptions, with distinct origins, were composed to accompany paintings. For discussion of the paintings and identification of the inscriptions, see Carl Dilthey, *Epigrammatum Graecorum Pompeis repertorum arias* (Diss. Turici, 1876).

As Wolfgang Iser has taught us, the process of imaginatively re-creating the experiential world suggested by the text is a fundamentally literary response to the act of reading.[24]

So too, the placing of an epigram in a book grants the referents of that poem a certain indeterminacy of meaning.[25] The reader of an inscription assumes the persons or events mentioned to be historically real; clearly false or fictional information would disrupt the bonds of trust established by convention between author and reader. But whether the reader of a book epigram knows the referents of the poem to be historical or fictive, or is uncertain of the choice, makes little difference in terms of the expected literary response.[26] Of course, readers may dissect epigrams for the historical information they contain; but in doing so they, as readers, are not fulfilling the role anticipated by the author or editor who gave those epigrams a literary context. The epigram placed in a book, whatever its intended purpose at the time of composition, gives meaning to its referents through exemplification: its subjects become types, presented, gemlike, through brief but specific details.

In an epigram collection, as in any poetry book, the reader encounters a tension between the book as a whole and the poems placed within it. The act of reading is a process of weighing the boundaries of single poems against evidence for cohesiveness of design—formal and thematic similarities, patterns of arrangement, significant placement. Although the privileging of part over whole, or whole over part, is often determined by a reader's own expectations, the epigram book has by its very nature a strong centrifugal force pulling the reader's focus to the isolated poem. Because of its origin as inscribed verse, the epigram form possesses what Barbara Herrnstein Smith has called "maximal closure."[27] As a statement that must define its subject for all time, and in a form short enough to be engraved on stone, the epigram developed the distinctive traits not only of brevity and restraint but also of appearing to have the last word. The reading of an epigram book is a process of continually seeing its subjects briefly but whole, of ending and ending again. Recognizing that satiety comes quickly for the reader of epigrams, Martial limits the length of his books to about a hundred poems (1.118; cf. 2.1, 4.89, 11.108, and 12.5) and encourages

24. *The Act of Reading: A Theory of Aesthetic Response* (Baltimore, 1978). For the process in relationship to epigram, see P. Bing, "Ergänzungsspiel in the Epigrams of Callimachus," *A&A* 41 (1995) 115–31.

25. For a good discussion of determinate and indeterminate meanings in literary works, see Barbara Herrnstein Smith, *On the Margins of Discourse: The Relation of Literature to Language* (Chicago, 1978) 137–46.

26. For this reason, the attempts of Wilamowitz to distinguish between epigrams composed for inscription and those composed for books has proved ultimately fruitless and futile. For his position that epigrams should be taken as historical unless clearly shown to be fictive, see (1924) I 121.

27. *Poetic Closure: A Study of How Poems End* (Chicago, 1968) 197.

the impatient reader to shorten the book even further by selective reading (10.1; cf. 14.2). But in all likelihood, earlier Greek epigrammatists sometimes compiled longer editions, since Hellenistic poetry books had a maximum length of about two thousand lines in comparison with the Roman limit of slightly over one thousand lines.[28] In fact, the new Posidippus collection on the Milan papyrus (P.Mil.Vogl. inv. 1295) is apparently incomplete at one hundred poems, and books of Meleager's *Garland* may have contained as many as three hundred epigrams. Given the brevity of each epigram and the large number of poems in some collections, Greek epigram books, by nature if not also by design, would tend to display a discontinuity of structure that was a hallmark of the Hellenistic literary aesthetic.

Scholars have commonly stressed diversity of arrangement—the Greek ποικιλία or the Latin *variatio*—as the primary principle of ordering developed in the early Hellenistic period and handed on to the Romans.[29] Since in other contexts ποικιλία can refer, concretely, to embroidery or, more abstractly, to intellectual subtlety, it suggests, with reference to literary arrangement, the craft and the intricacy of pattern that is characteristic of Hellenistic poetry and art.[30] But ποικιλία alone would produce collections without structure or unity, and we find in surviving Hellenistic and Roman poetry books that poets employed a number of techniques to weld their diverse poems into a cohesive whole.[31] If

28. Theodor Birt, *Das antike Buchwesen in seinem Verhältniss zur Litteratur* (Berlin, 1882) 291–99 set the average length for both Greek and Roman poetry books at 700 to 1,100 lines and attempted to explain the longer books of Apollonius and Lucretius as early aberrations. But papyrological evidence for Hellenistic scholarly editions plus additional information about Hellenistic poetry books suggests that books between 1,000 and 2,000 lines were the norm for Greek poets; see J. Van Sickle, "The Book-Roll and Some Conventions of the Poetic Book," *Arethusa* 13 (1980) 8–12.

29. The classic studies of variety as a principle of poetic arrangement are Wilhelm Kroll, *Studien zum Verständnis der römischen Literatur* (Stuttgart, 1924) 225–46 and W. Port, "Die Anord- nung in Gedichtbüchern der augusteischer Zeit," *Philologus* 35 (1926) 280–308, 427–68. In rhetorical theory the terms ποικιλία and *variatio* are applicable, not just to arrangement, but to every level of composition, from sounds to words to tropes to the ordering of subject matter; for discussion and references, see Michael Roberts, *The Jeweled Style: Poetry and Poetics in Late Antiquity* (Ithaca, 1989) 44–65.

30. See Barbara H. Fowler, *The Hellenistic Aesthetic* (Madison, 1989) 5–22.

31. Matthew Santirocco, *Unity and Design in Horace's "Odes"* (Chapel Hill, 1986) 7, 11 has argued that *variatio* has been overemphasized at the expense of unifying devices. On the techniques of cohesion in the *Aetia*, see Nita Krevans, *The Poet as Editor: Callimachus, Virgil, Horace, Propertius and the Development of the Poetic Book* (Diss. Princeton, 1984) 230–300. On the structure of the *Iambi*, see C. M. Dawson, "The *Iambi* of Callimachus," *YCS* 11 (1950) 142–43 and D. L. Clayman, *Callimachus' "Iambi"* (Leiden, 1980) 48–49. A summary essay on Augustan poetry books is provided by W. S. Anderson, "The Theory and Practice of Poetic Arrangement from Vergil to Ovid" in Fraistat 44–65; additional details in Helena Dettmer, *Horace: A Study in Structure* (Hildesheim, 1983).

the unifying principles of an epigram book can be grasped even by a selective reader, as Martial suggests, that is an advantageous circumstance for the project at hand, since we must deal with the debris of Hellenistic collections. The evidence from papyri and manuscripts adduced in the next chapter will show that Hellenistic editors employed various means of creating cohesion in their collections—grouping by length of poem or by topic, linking poems associatively by verbal repetition or thematic similarity. The poems on the Posidippus papyrus are organized by fairly specific topics (such as stones, omens, shipwrecks), each category given its own heading; and we have strong evidence for complicated sequencing in Meleager's multi-authored anthology as well as evidence that associative bridging within sequences appeared already in earlier single-authored collections. We may justifiably assume, then, that the striking similarities sometimes found between the epigrams attributed to one poet were used in collection for poetic effect. Since one epigram may often do the work of another, we will make no attempt to establish the exact order in these lost collections. Yet even editors with a minimal sense of design may choose to place at points of opening, transition, and closing epigrams that convey specialized, usually programmatic, meaning.[32] Examples are offered by the placement of hymns at the opening of scholarly editions of the archaic poets (such as Sappho, Alcaeus, and Theognis), by the poetic statements within the prologue and epilogue of Callimachus' *Aetia*, by opening and closing poems in many Roman poetry books. In the course of analyzing Hellenistic epigrams from the point of view of their original context, we will find numerous examples of poems whose significance is altered or deepened when their programmatic function within a collection is determined or surmised. The arrangement of a poetry book should be conceptualized, then, as a balance between unifying cohesion and pleasing variety, each a necessary ingredient of an artistically designed collection.

Another effect of reading an epigram in a literary context is an increased awareness of the poet who composed the poem. In inscribed epigram the poet remains anonymous, his persona effaced by the objectivity of the style. In earliest times, when the inscription consisted of a single hexameter or elegiac couplet, the composer may often have been the very person who commissioned the monument or the artisan who designed and constructed it.[33] Later when the

32. See, for instance, J. Van Sickle, "Poetics of Opening and Closure in Meleager, Catullus, and Gallus," *CW* 75 (1981) 65–75 and, for discussion of the opening and closing poems of the Anacreontic anthology, Patricia A. Rosenmeyer, *The Poetics of Imitation: Anacreon and the Anacreontic Tradition* (Cambridge, 1992) 126–37.

33. For the commissioner of the monument as the composer, see Florence A. Gragg, "A Study of the Greek Epigram before 300 B.C.," *Proceedings of the American Academy of Arts and Sciences* 46 (1912) 12–13 and Wilamowitz (1924) I 126–27. For sculptors as composers of epigrams, see Clairmont 10; M. Wallace 308–11; Lausberg 121; and Ute Ecker, *Grabmal und Epigramm: Studien zur Frühgriechischen Sepulkraldichtung* (Stuttgart, 1990) 132–49.

poems grew more complex, we may assume that a professional poet, perhaps the local epigrammatist, was more often hired for the task. Although the purpose of early inscriptions was largely encomiastic, to preserve the dedication or the deceased in honorific memory,[34] the epigrammatist, unlike the praise poet, never took up the custom of vocalizing his own participation in the praise. Even when the tombstone or the deceased, the votive offering or the recipient deity speaks or holds a conversation with a passerby, the human presence behind the voice or voices of inscribed epigram is understood to be the person erecting the monument or making the dedication. The proper stance of the epigrammatist, as mere spokesman, is to have no stance at all, to avoid any personal perspective or sentiment. It is first in the fourth century, and then only rarely, that we find poets breaking with this tradition of self-effacement to name themselves as composers of epigrams. The authorial disengagement later associated with epigrammatic style is, then, an inheritance from the traditional objectivity of earlier inscribed verse.

But in the early Hellenistic age the persona of the epigrammatist fully emerged—as a direct result of the collection of epigrams into books. The roots of this phenomenon may lie in symposium recitation of "epigrams," whether intended by their reciters as short elegies or imitations of inscriptions, since performed poetry is necessarily associated with the known characteristics of the performer. An additional factor was, in all likelihood, the scholarly editing of older poets, which must have revealed to Hellenistic epigrammatists the possibilities of the poetry book as a literary form. Readers of poetry books tend to bestow upon similarities of theme, form, and tone the constructed persona of a speaker. The gathering of the poetry attributed to such figures as Sappho, Theognis, and Simonides made evident to the reader of their collected works the thematic and stylistic traits characteristic of each poet. We will find in our analysis of Hellenistic epigram books that the poetic personae of the epigrammatists fall into two categories, one more naturally associated with sympotic and erotic epigram and the other with sepulchral and dedicatory epigram. When the voice speaking within individual poems can be closely identified with the poet, as in sympotic-erotic epigram, the collection may present itself as autobiographical narrative or as a series of personal statements revealing the poet's beliefs and values. When a different voice speaks from poem to poem, as commonly in collections of ostensibly inscriptional verse, the reader may nevertheless fashion a poetic creator responsible for the overall design; the presence of that persona is revealed, amid the multiplicity of voices, through thematic repetition, formal cohesiveness, and uniformity of subject and tone. While in the latter type of collection the reader can usually distinguish the poet's persona from the impersonated voices in the various epigrams, even in

34. On the encomiastic purpose of epigram, see Svenbro 64–79 and Day.

the sympotic-erotic type the reader may perceive a certain distance between the voice of the poet speaking within the epigrams and the seemingly less involved, more controlled persona of the poet who orders the collection and thus the experiences revealed within it.[35]

The reader tends to synthesize a collection's themes, tonalities, and principles of order into a conception of the author's poetic message, heard in no one poem but perceivable by reading across the boundaries of individual poems. The example of the *liber Catulli*, which readers commonly interpret as a history of an unhappy love affair despite the fact that the majority of the poems do not concern Lesbia at all and despite continuing uncertainties about the extent to which Catullus participated in the editing of his collection,[36] indicates that collections including poems of different types on a variety of subjects may yet be synthesized by the reader into a controlling poetic focus. By encountering Hellenistic epigrams only in anthologies, readers have been deprived of the opportunity to hear the larger messages that were surely suggested by at least some of the original collections.[37] The study at hand will reveal that Hellenistic epigram books encouraged a variety of interpretive approaches: as indices of poets' conceptions about their personal experiences and social relationships; as a means of focusing on certain classes of individuals and modes of living so as to make ideological statements; as vehicles for conveying a poet's literary personality and for placing a poet's achievements within the context of literary tradition. Once we recognize that such larger messages may be conveyed by the briefest of poems when gathered into collections, we can see that part of the attraction of the epigram book for early Hellenistic poets was to rival in length

35. An example of this distinction between the poet within and the poet without the collection may be found in Horace's *Sermones*, where J. E. G. Zetzel, "Horace's *Liber Sermonum*: The Structure of Ambiguity," *Arethusa* 13 (1980) 59–77 has identified an ironic tension between the artistry of the ordering poet and the intellectual failures of his moralizing persona.

36. For the currently popular view that Catullus is responsible for the order of the entire *liber*, see M. B. Skinner, "Aesthetic Patterning in Catullus," *CW* 81 (1988) 337–40. Fundamental to the acceptance of this view has been the work of Kenneth Quinn, *Catullus: An Interpretation* (London, 1972) 9–53 and T. P. Wiseman, *Catullan Questions* (Leicester, 1969) 1–31. For a recent argument in favor of a posthumous editor for much of the collection, see T. K. Hubbard, "The Catullan Libellus," *Philologus* 127 (1983) 218–37. Paul A. Miller, *Lyric Texts and Lyric Consciousness* (London, 1994) 52–77 has now offered a reading of the Catullan book as a complex set of dialogical relationships between individual poems. For a discussion of how the author Catullus has been constructed from the heterogeneity of his poetry, see William Fitzgerald, *Catullan Provocations: Lyric Poetry and the Drama of Position* (Berkeley, 1995) 19–33.

37. The thematic unity of early Greek epigram books finds reflection in later parallels, such as Strato's Μοῦσα Παιδιϰή devoted to pederastic themes (preserved in *AP* 12.1–11, 175–258, excluding 230, 232–33, 256–57) and some of Martial's books—*de spectaculis* on wonders of the amphitheater, Book 11 organized around the theme of Saturnalian license, Books 13 and 14 on gifts. See N. M. Kay, *Martial, Book XI: A Commentary* (London, 1985) 5–6; J. P. Sullivan, *Martial: The Unexpected Classic* (Cambridge, 1991) 217–21; and D. Fowler.

and function traditionally longer works while yet working within a genre of brief compass and low rank.

In considering the types of messages that were likely delivered by epigram books, we should look to the reasons that epigram, both in isolation and in collected form, appealed so strongly to Hellenistic writers and readers. Epigrams focus on individuals, in their particularity, in their personal relationships with family, friends, and deities, in the crucial moments of their professional and personal lives. In the cosmopolitan world of the Hellenistic era, individual subjectivities were no longer shaped by allegiance to a particular class or an independent political unit. Cities were mixtures of Greeks and non-Greeks, and the Greeks within them were of diverse origins and status, forming allegiance to an autocratic monarch for reasons of personal advantage or necessity rather than because of common political goals. By their focus on the personal and the particular, epigrams could reflect these new bonds—shifting, local, and pragmatic, and much altered from the earlier, inescapable and unquestionable, webs of relationship that enmeshed individuals in the cultural myths of their own polis. Epigram was a traditional poetic form that could yet avoid without excuse the larger social, religious, and political themes dominating earlier Greek literature. As a minor form elevated to major status, a marginal type brought to the center, epigram, matching form to content, could represent individuals as they now were—marginal, drifting, fragmentary and fractured selves.

So too, epigram books, inasmuch as they lacked the unified and balanced structures of earlier literature, as discontinuous and fragmented entities without organic requirements of length or form, were effective representations of the changeable and unpredictable patterns of affiliation that linked Hellenistic individuals one to another.[38] We will find that the epigram books of the third and second centuries were themselves individualized, differentiated from each other through thematizations that are often local, gender-specific, reflective of personal choice rather than social given, expressive of unique tonalities and philosophies. These Hellenistic epigram collections are among (if they do not in fact constitute) the earliest poetry books in the western literary tradition, and for that reason alone are worthy of more attention than they have received in the past. But far from being randomly or haphazardly constructed, or organized through simple or pedantic techniques, what we can know of them suggests that their very fragmented structures were organic to their messages. Yet the coherent unity of each individual epigram also encouraged the shifting of these texts into new contexts, where they formed affiliations that reflected new matrices

38. On cultural affiliation as a substitute or replacement for biological filiation, see Edward W. Said, *The World, the Text, and the Critic* (Cambridge, Mass., 1983) 16–24. In an illuminating study of *Idylls* 2, 14, and 15, Joan B. Burton, *Theocritus's Urban Mimes: Mobility, Gender, and Patronage* (Berkeley, 1995) has shown the importance of mobility and internationalism in Theocritus' poetry.

of meaning. As Alan Cameron has recently commented, "The epigram was in fact destined by its very nature to be *anthologized*."[39] By grouping old with new, known with unknown, the poet-editors of epigram anthologies fashioned a literary context for historical intertextuality. In such anthologies the aesthetics of editing, important even for the earliest epigram books, came to the forefront to rival the aesthetics of composition. For an anthologist like the Syrian Meleager, who owed his Greekness to the process of colonization, the ability to project a personal style while maintaining through variation the tradition of Greek literature may have become the new message.

39. *The Greek Anthology from Meleager to Planudes* (Oxford, 1993) 4.

CHAPTER TWO

Hellenistic Epigram Books:
The Evidence from Manuscripts
and Papyri

The great majority of Hellenistic book epigrams were preserved through Meleager's Στέφανος, or *Garland*. This anthology, compiled about the beginning of the first century B.C.[1] collected the works of more than forty-seven epigrammatists, including the editor himself. Meleager's *Garland* was not only the primary vehicle through which Hellenistic epigrams were transmitted to later centuries, but it also served as a model for collections of post-Meleagrian epigrams: principally, the *Garland* of Philip, compiled during the Julio-Claudian era, and the *Cycle* of Agathias, in which the epigrams of the Justinian period were gathered.[2] Early in the tenth century A.D. Constantinus Cephalas, the protopapas of the palace at Constantinople in 917 A.D., drew upon these and other ancient collections to

---

1. Gow-Page (1965) I xiv–xvi place the outer limits for the publication of the *Garland* between the death of Antipater of Sidon (which they set about 125 B.C. but which is probably later, even as late as the 90s) and the publication of Philodemus' epigrams (about 80 B.C.) and decide, since the lemmatist on *AP* 4.1 assigns Meleager's *floruit* to the reign of the last Seleucus (96/95 B.C.), upon "the early years of the first century B.C." (xvi) as the most likely date. T. B. L. Webster, *Hellenistic Poetry and Art* (London, 1964) 208 and Beckby I 63 date the collection as late as 70 or 60 B.C. But Alan Cameron, who earlier ("The *Garlands* of Meleager and Philip," *GRBS* 9 [1968] 323, n. 1) sought to push back the date a couple of decades into the second century because of the likelihood that the *Garland* was known to the "circle" of L. Lutatius Catulus, has now (1993) 49–56 dated the *Garland* and its Latin imitations between 102 and 90 B.C. Similar conclusions may be found in Laurens 159–81.

2. On these and other ancient anthologies, see L. Schmidt with R. Reitzenstein, "Anthologia," *RE* 2 HB (1894) 2380–91; Waltz I ix–xxv; Beckby I 62–68; A. Meschini, "La storia del testo" in *Antologia Palatina* I, ed. Filippo Maria Pontani (Turin, 1978) xxxi–xxxvi, and especially Cameron (1993) 1–43. On the *Garland* of Philip, see Cameron (1968) 331–49, "The *Garland* of Philip," *GRBS* 21 (1980) 43–62, and (1993) 56–65; he argues against the usual date in the reign of Gaius in favor of a date in the reign of Claudius or Nero. On the *Cycle*, see A. and A. Cameron, "The *Cycle* of Agathias," *JHS* 86 (1966) 6–25 and Averil Cameron, *Agathias* (Oxford, 1970) 12–29.

compose a comprehensive anthology. From Cephalas' collection derives our *Greek Anthology* in two principal manuscripts of overlapping content: the Codex Palatinus of the later tenth century, to which the *Palatine Anthology* (*AP*) owes its name, and the Codex Marcianus 481 dated to 1301 A.D., the autograph of Maximus Planudes known as the *Planudean Anthology* (*APl*), which, although shorter than the *AP*, preserves almost 400 epigrams (printed as Book 16 of the *AP*) not in the *Palatine Anthology*.[3]

It is generally agreed that Meleager culled the epigrams comprising his *Garland* from collections of earlier epigrammatists. The purpose of this chapter is to examine the direct evidence for the existence and character of these earlier epigram books. Evidence of three types can be found: (1) statements in ancient sources documenting the existence of such collections, (2) groups of epigrams found on papyri, and (3) sequences of epigrams preserved in manuscript that seem to derive from single-authored collections. The second category includes the newly discovered collection of about one hundred epigrams by Posidippus, while the third category includes a collection of twenty-two epigrams ascribed to Theocritus. The existence of epigram books from as early as the third century cannot, then, be doubted, and even the poetic design of these collections can sometimes be glimpsed from the tattered remains on papyri and in manuscripts.

"IN THE EPIGRAMS OF ..."

At least some, if not most, Hellenistic epigram books bore the simple title Ἐπιγράμματα with the name of the author following in the genitive case. A surviving example appears on P.Petrie II 49 a, which is headed σύμμεικτα ἐπιγράμματα, *Miscellaneous Epigrams*, and preserves a portion of Posidippus' name. But since these titles, like Callimachus' Ἴαμβοι, are simply descriptive of content, references in ancient sources to the Ἐπιγράμματα of a given poet are not conclusive proof for the existence of an epigram book. To cite something a poet said "in his epigrams" might mean only that the citation comes from one of his epigrams, and to quote a poem found "among the epigrams of ..." might indicate only a sequence of epigrams in a collection of mixed poetic types. References to the ἐπιγράμματα of a poet must, then, be used cautiously in conjunction with other information when determining whether Meleager knew a collection of epigrams by a given poet.

It is possible that the epigrams of some early Hellenistic poets appeared in collections also containing other forms of verse. Philetas of Cos was a

---

3. On the Cephalan and Planudean collections and their derivatives, including some minor sylloges not mentioned here as well as the apographa of the principal codices, see Waltz I xxv–xxxiv; Beckby I 68–73; Gow-Page (1965) I xxxiii–xlv; A. S. F. Gow, *The Greek Anthology, Sources and Ascriptions* (London, 1958); Franz Lenzinger, *Zur griechischen Anthologie* (Zurich, 1965); Meschini xxxvii–xliii; and Cameron (1993).

highly influential figure, the first to be called both scholar and poet and a model for the slender but erudite style labeled Μοῦσα λεπταλέη by Callimachus (fr. 1.24 Pf.). Although Stobaeus twice cites the ἐπιγράμματα of Philetas (*Flor.* 124.11 = 12 *CA*, *Flor.* 59.5 = 13 *CA*),[4] Meleager makes no mention of him in his preamble and so did not include him in the *Garland*.[5] To complicate the situation, Stobaeus also preserves two elegiac excerpts from Philetas' *Paignia*, one of which can be interpreted as a complete, if playful, epigram (*Flor.* 81.4 = 10 *CA*) and the other of which (*Flor.* 124.10 = 11 *CA*) has plausibly been joined to the following excerpt, itself cited as one of the "epigrams," to form one of the most poignant of all Hellenistic epitaphs.[6] This confusion in the citations works against the possibility that Philetas' elegiac couplets circulated in an edition entitled *Epigrammata*. Quite probably, *Paignia* was the general title for a miscellaneous collection which included short elegiac poems that could be descriptively called ἐπιγράμματα. Aratus, the author of the astronomical *Phaenomena*, may have produced a similarly mixed collection. Although only two of his epigrams survive in the *Anthology*, Meleager includes Aratus in his preamble (1.49–50 G-P = *AP* 4.1.49–50); the reference to Aratus' "first-born shoots" (1.50) suggests that the epigrams were among his early works. Evidence from the *Suda* (*s. v.* Aratus) indicates that Aratus published these epigrams with a dedication to Phila, the wife of Antigonus Gonatas (συνέταξε ... ἐπιγράμματα εἰς Φίλαν), and so apparently in a poetry book issued some time after the marriage about 276 B.C.[7] A problem arises, however, because Macrobius (*Sat.* 5.20.8) ascribes one of Aratus' two surviving epigrams to a *liber Elegion*, "book of elegies."[8] While Macrobius may have been using the term *elegy* loosely to refer to a book of epigrams composed in elegiac couplets, it is also possible that the poetry book for Phila included both epigrams and longer elegiac pieces on the order of Philetas' *Paignia*. So too, the *Suda*'s reference to the early third century Moero (*s. v.* Μυρώ) as a poet of epic, elegiac, and melic verse suggests that her two

---

4. Cf. the *Suda* *s. v.* Philetas: ἔγραψεν ἐπιγράμματα, καὶ ἐλεγείας καὶ ἄλλα.

5. But epigrams attributed to a Philetas of Samos occur in a Meleagrian context; on the problem, see Gow-Page (1965) II 476.

6. See Wilamowitz (1924) I 115–16, who discounts the possibility of a book of epigrams by Philetas, and Wilhelm Kuchenmüller, *Philetae Coi reliquiae* (Borna, 1928) 66–67.

7. As usual, however, the reference to the ἐπιγράμματα is not entirely unambiguous. It seems best to interpret ἐπιγράμματα εἰς Φίλαν as a single title on the model of ὕμνους εἰς Πᾶνα or ἐπικήδειον πρὸς Θεόπροπον, although it is just possible we are dealing with two works, one entitled ἐπιγράμματα and another εἰς Φίλαν (cf. εἰς Θεόπροπον and εἰς Ἀντίγονον cited by the *Suda*).

8. It has been suggested that the epigrams were gathered with other pieces into a comprehensive collection known as the Κατὰ λεπτόν (Strab. 10.5.3); see Jean Martin, *Histoire du texte des Phénomènes d'Aratos* (Paris, 1956) 179 and W. Ludwig, "Aratos," *RE*, Suppl. 10 (1965) 29–30. Perhaps a specific book of epigrams or elegiac poems formed part of a multi-book collection known as Κατὰ λεπτόν.

surviving epigrams may have come from a collection of mixed poetry. The *Suda* tells us as well that Simias of Rhodes, another early epigrammatist represented in the *Anthology*, composed four books of ποιήματα διάφορα, "diverse poems." Although Theocritus is a difficult case because of the complicated history of his text, it is a credible hypothesis that those genuine epigrams ascribed to him were originally included in a third-century edition entitled εἰδύλλια, "little types," a term used by ancient sources for both hexameter and melic poems.[9]

But references to the ἐπιγράμματα of other poets more certainly indicate collections consisting solely of epigrams. The firmest evidence of this sort comes from scholium A on *Iliad* 11.101. On the reading βῆ ῥ' Ἴσον, the scholiast comments:

> Ζηνόδοτος ἔξω τοῦ ρ "βῆ Ἴσον" μὴ ἐμφέρεσθαι δέ φησιν ὁ Ἀρίσταρχος νῦν ἐν τοῖς Ποσειδίππου ἐπιγράμμασι τὸν "Βήρισον," ἀλλ' ἐν τῷ λεγομένῳ Σωρῷ εὑρεῖν. εὔλογον δέ φησιν ἐξελεγχόμενον αὐτὸν ἀπαλεῖψαι.

> Zenodotus wrote βῆ Ἴσον without the ρ. But Aristarchus says that, though Βήρισον does not now appear in the *Epigrams* of Posidippus, he found it in the so-called *Soros*. He says it is probable that, when the reading was questioned, he [Posidippus] expunged it.

In his edition of Homer, Zenodotus had rejected the reading Berisus in favor of the simpler name Isus and had made evident his interpretation by also omitting the *rho*. Aristarchus in examining the scholarly history of the controversy had found evidence for earlier acceptance of the rejected reading in Posidippus' use of the name Berisus in a poem that appeared in the *Soros* but not in the *Epigrams*. Aristarchus' suggestion that Posidippus expunged the name or the poem containing it indicates that he considered the *Soros* chronologically prior to the *Epigrams*. Reitzenstein argued that the *Soros*, or "Heap," was an anthology, a songbook of sympotic epigrams by Asclepiades, Posidippus, and Hedylus.[10] But until we have more certain evidence for the existence of multi-authored anthologies before the time of Meleager, we should not assume that the *Soros* was anything other than an earlier edition of Posidippus' epigrams, imaginatively named to reflect a harvest of poetry. In fact, I later argue that

9. On this third-century edition, see K. Gutzwiller, "The Evidence for Theocritean Poetry Books," *Theocritus*, Hellenistica Groningana 2, ed. M. A. Harder, R. F. Regtuit, and G. C. Wakker (Groningen, 1996) 119–38. *Id.* 29, a melic παιδικά, is labeled an εἰδύλλιον in K.

10. Reitzenstein (1893) 89–102. Reitzenstein's theory has found a certain amount of acceptance, as, for instance, by W. Peek, "Poseidippus von Pella," *RE* 43 HB (1953) 431. But others, such as H. Lloyd-Jones, "The Seal of Posidippus," *JHS* 83 (1963) 96 and P. M. Fraser, *Ptolemaic Alexandria* (Oxford, 1972) I 560, have found no reason to assume that the *Soros* was an anthology. Yet the authority of Reitzenstein's position is so strong that even those who recognize the fatal flaws in his argument seek to maintain his thesis of a joint edition, if only in modified form; see Cameron (1993) 4–5, 369–76.

the "reaping" imagery in one of Posidippus' surviving poems suggests that his erotic epigrams were once included in this *Soros* collection. In the Homeric scholium ἐπιγράμματα also functions as a title for a collection: if the term were used generically to indicate that Aristarchus somehow searched through all the epigrams of Posidippus no matter where published, it makes no sense to say that Aristarchus found Berisus in the *Soros*, which contained epigrams, but not in the "epigrams." No doubt, then, in the second century B.C. Aristarchus had at his disposal an authoritative edition of Posidippus' *Epigrams*, for which the poet had made such editorial decisions as the omission of a problematic poem. For reasons given below, the Posidippus collection on the new Milan papyrus does not seem synonymous with this comprehensive edition.

The various ancient allusions to Callimachus' *Epigrammata* also refer, in all likelihood, to a collection of epigrams edited by the poet himself. Some time after 246 B.C. Callimachus published the four books of the *Aetia* and issued a carefully ordered collection of his *Iambi*. Since it is clear that the *Iambi* followed the *Aetia* in a multi-volume edition, the probability exists that late in life Callimachus published his complete oeuvre, ordered and divided into books.[11] That the epigrams appeared in book format either then or at an earlier time is indicated by commentaries written on them, one by a certain Archibius of the late second or first century B.C. (*Suda s. v.*) and another by someone named Hedylus (*Et. Magn. s. v.* ἀλυτάρχης), who is quite possibly the third-century epigrammatist.[12] Evidence for an edition of Hedylus' own epigrams comes from Athenaeus 8.344f–45b, where a series of three poems on gluttons is cited from Hedylus' catalogue in his epigrams. Elsewhere (10.412d, 415b) Athenaeus preserves a similar group of poems on gluttons from Posidippus' epigrams. Since the new Posidippus papyrus divides its epigrams into sections on the basis of specific topics (though gluttons are not in evidence), it appears that these two sets of epigrams also come from epigram books so divided.

In regard to other poets, judgment about the publication of an epigram book is more difficult, depending largely upon the weight granted to inclusion or exclusion from Meleager's *Garland*. Ancient sources cite poetic texts from the epigrams of Theodoridas and Nicaenetus.[13] Both are mentioned in Meleager's preamble, and a number of epigrams by each (nineteen by Theodoridas and four by Nicaenetus) survive in the *Anthology*. A date in the second half of the third century for both poets increases the likelihood that we are dealing with the remains of epigram collections. To Apollonius, who is not mentioned

---

11. See Dawson 144–48 and Rudolf Pfeiffer, *Callimachus* I (Oxford, 1949) 125.

12. For other references to Callimachus' *Epigrammata*, see Diog. Laert. 1.79, Achilles Tatius *Vita Arati* 4 = fr. 460 Pf., *Suda s. v.* Callimachus and Marianos. Both Martial 4.23 and Pliny *Epist.* 4.3.3–4 imply that a collection of Callimachus' epigrams was widely known.

13. The citation to Theodoridas ἐν ἐνίοις ἐπιγράμμασι comes from *Et. Gud.* p. 355.35 Sturz κυρβασία = 740 *SH*; for the citation of Nicaenetus' *epigrammata*, see Ath. 15.673b.

by Meleager, only one epigram is ascribed (*AP* 11.275), and that a possibly spurious invective against Callimachus. We would never suspect his authorship of an epigram book if Antoninus Liberalis (23) did not speak of a reference · Apollonius made in his epigrams. Since of the hundred or so epigrams on the new Posidippus papyrus very few were preserved also in the manuscript, we should be cautious in assuming that slight remains argue against the earlier existence of a collection. Meleager clearly had a wealth of material to choose from, and he limited his collection to certain types of epigrams, largely omitting satirical epigrams such as the one attributed to Apollonius.

In sum, we may conclude that a reference in an ancient or Byzantine source to the epigrams of a given poet is not by itself sufficient proof of the existence of an epigram book. The epigrams may have belonged to a collection of mixed poetic types, especially if the poet comes from the first half of the third century, or may even have been transmitted through another type of source. Yet with substantiating evidence we may feel confident that references to the ἐπιγράμματα of a poet indicate an authorially compiled epigram book.

ON PAPYRI

Any analysis of the papyrological sources for Hellenistic epigram collections must take into account the nature of the book in the Hellenistic era.[14] We have evidence from the late fifth century for booksellers who catered to a new interest in reading for entertainment.[15] But we should not imagine that official or authorially sanctioned editions issued by a bookseller were the only or even the primary form in which literature was known to Hellenistic readers. The composition of one or more epigrams, especially inscriptional epigrams, as a gift for a friend was surely a widespread practice in antiquity.[16] As it became more and more common for epigrams to be divorced from inscriptional purposes, the

14. A dated list of these "anthologies" appears in Roger A. Pack, *The Greek and Latin Literary Texts from Greco-Roman Egypt*, 2nd ed. (Ann Arbor, 1965) 90–94. My discussion concerns only papyri containing epigrams written between the beginning of the Hellenistic age and the compilation of Meleager's *Garland*. For discussion of later epigram anthologies, see G. Guidorizzi, "Gli epigrammi papiracei di epoca imperiale," *Atti del XVII congresso internazionale di papirologia* II (Naples, 1984) 313–17.

15. Frederic G. Kenyon, *Books and Readers in Ancient Greece and Rome*, 2nd ed. (Oxford, 1951) 21–22; Turner (1952) 18–23; J. A. Davison, "Literature and Literacy in Ancient Greece," *Phoenix* 16 (1962) 156, 219–21; Knox (1985) 8–10; R. Johne, "Zur Entstehung einer 'Buchkultur' in der zweiten Hälfte des 5. Jahrhunderts v. u. Z.," *Philologus* 135 (1991) 50–51. ·

16. Birt 342–48 has demonstrated that even in Roman times circulation of a literary work among friends often preceded or replaced publication through a bookseller. On the Greek period, see Knox (1985) 14 and P. E. Easterling, "Books and Readers in the Greek World: The Hellenistic and Imperial Periods," *The Cambridge History of Classical Literature* I 19–20.

presentation of epigram collections to friends, like Meleager's Diocles (see 1.3–4 G-P = *AP* 4.1.3–4), and to royal patrons, like Aratus' Phila, became a logical extension of the standard practice.[17]   In addition, individuals, both scholars and more casual readers, often copied or had copied works of literature or selections from them for private use.   The great Library at Alexandria was actually two libraries, an inner one for the use of the scholars associated with the Museum and an outer one from which the general public borrowed books for reading and copying.[18]   The epigrammatists working in Alexandria, so we may assume, provided the Library with editions of their epigrams arranged with a view to public scrutiny and literary immortality.   For epigrammatists working elsewhere, the Library copies may have been obtained more haphazardly, in whatever form they reached Alexandrian collectors.[19]   These official copies are probably the ones that authors refer to with the "in the epigrams of . . ." phrase.   Since epigrams so lend themselves to selection and rearrangement, it is natural that they circulated in many formats—some issued by the authors to acquaintances, some compiled by authors or editors for the reading public, but many selected and copied by individual readers in accordance with their own tastes and interests.[20]

   To show the practical uses from which epigram books developed, we begin with third-century papyri that clearly do not represent epigram books in any literary sense.   It is questionable whether any epigram at all, strictly speaking, is found on P.Berol. 270, written before 280 B.C. and found at Elephantine in Egypt; it contains portions of at least four rather cryptic scolia and a ten-line elegy prescribing proper behavior at a symposium.[21]   The editors suggested that the papyrus was a private copy brought to Elephantine by a soldier, who likely performed the songs in social gatherings attended by his companions. The papyrus thus provides striking confirmation of Reitzenstein's theory that in the Hellenistic age epigrams came to function at symposia as elegy and scolia

---

17. On Martial's practice of presenting to patrons *libelli* that were later incorporated into his longer published books of epigrams, see P. White, "The Presentation and Dedication of the *Silvae* and the *Epigrams*," *JHS* 64 (1974) 44–48.

18. Edward A. Parsons, *The Alexandrian Library: Glory of the Hellenic World* (London, 1952) 108–19; Rudolf Pfeiffer, *History of Classical Scholarship from the Beginnings to the End of the Hellenistic Age* (Oxford, 1968) 99–102; Fraser I 323–24; Rudolf Blum, *Kallimachos: The Alexandrian Library and the Origins of Bibliography*, trans. Hans H. Wellisch (Madison, 1991) 104–6.

19. Galen, *Epidemics* 3 (17.1.606 Kühn) reports that Ptolemy III Euergetes confiscated all the books on board ships landing at Alexandria, had them copied, and returned the copies to the owners. Books were of course acquired through more legitimate channels as well.

20. On authors' lack of control over the recopying and excerpting of their works, see Easterling 19–20. For an extreme view of the elite nature of the reading audience, see Harris 126.

21. *BKT* 5.2 (1907) 56–63, ed. Schubart-Wilamowitz; Lyr. adesp. 16–21; *CA* (pp. 190–92); 86 and 103 *GLP*; Adesp. Eleg. 27 W.

had in earlier centuries. Preservation for inscription rather than performance is illustrated by two epitaphs for the Indian hound Tauron, one in elegiacs and one in iambics, composed by a poet of some merit for Zenon, who superintended a Fayum estate for Apollonius, the financial minister of Ptolemy Philadelphus (P.Cair.Zen. 59532).[22] We assume that one or both of the poems were intended for inscription on Tauron's tomb, to honor the hound for saving his master from a boar. The two poems are separated by the word ἄλλο, which sometimes appears between concurrent epigrams on tombstones and commonly separates epigrams by a single author or on a repeating topic in papyri and manuscripts.[23] This papyrus thus represents a stage in between inscription and book epigram, illustrating, like the Elephantine papyrus, the traditional practice of writing for mnemonic purposes, to preserve a literary work until, as here, it reaches its site of inscription or, as commonly, acquires an occasion for performance.

An example of epigrams preserved for personal reading, rather than for inscription or recitation, is provided by the Firmin-Didot papyrus, which contains passages from Euripides, Aeschylus, and a comic poet, as well as two epigrams by Posidippus on Ptolemaic monuments—the lighthouse at Pharos (11 G-P) and the temple of Aphrodite-Arsinoe at Zephyrium (12 G-P).[24] The epigrams are entitled [Ποσ]ειδίππου ἐπιγράμματα and separated by ἄλλο. D. J. Thompson has studied the literary extracts as a personal anthology preserved by the two sons of a Macedonian soldier resident near Memphis. While finding much personal relevance in the dramatic extracts, she concludes that the epigrams had probably been studied in school as patriotic literature and had appealed to the papyrus owner as a reminder of his Hellenic heritage preserved by the Ptolemaic rulers.[25] Two other highly literary epigrams—one on a fountain decorated with a statue of Arsinoe II or III and another on a temple dedicated to Homer by Ptolemy IV Philopator—did in fact form part of a school notebook (P. Cair. inv. #65445).[26] While E. G. Turner cautions that many of the anthologies found on

22. C. C. Edgar, "Selected Papyri from the Archives of Zenon," *ASAE* 19 (1920) 101–4; 109 *GLP*; anon. 146 *FGE*; 977 *SH*. Discussion in Fraser I 611–12, II 863–64 and literary analysis in I. Cazzaniga, "Pap. Zenon 59532," *Eirene* 11 (1973) 71–89.

23. On the use of ἄλλο, see Gow (1958a) 29 and Fraser II 863, n. 427.

24. Published by M. Henri Weil, *Un papyrus inédit de la bibliothèque de M. Ambroise Firmin-Didot* (Paris, 1879). For discussion of the poems, see also Fraser I 568–69, II 810–12; F. Chamoux, "L'épigramme de Poseidippos sur le phare d'Alexandrie," *Le monde grec: Hommages à Claire Préaux*, ed. Jean Bingen, G. Cambier, and G. Nachtergael (Brussels, 1975) 214–22.

25. "Ptolemaios and the 'Lighthouse': Greek Culture in the Memphite Serapeum," *PCPhS* 33 (1987) 113, 116. For a discussion of the brothers who compiled the extracts on the papyrus, see Naphtali Lewis, *Greeks in Ptolemaic Egypt* (Oxford, 1986) 69–87.

26. O. Guéraud and P. Jouguet, *Un livre d'écolier du IIIe siècle avant J.-C.* (Cairo, 1938) 20–26; 105 *GLP*; anon. 151 (a) and (b) *FGE*; 978, 979 *SH*. For discussion, see Fraser I 609–11, II 860–63.

papyri may be school texts,[27] it is important to keep in mind that such educative compilations may be copies of professionally edited manuscripts or, at least, mimic the practices common in them.

Likewise, those papyri that appear to be the working notes of scholars provide valuable information about the nature of epigram collections. To this category may belong P.Petrie II 49 b of the third century B.C., which contains a series of epigrams on plays by various dramatists—perhaps Aristophanes, then Aristarchus, Astydamas, and Cratinus.[28] Hugh Lloyd-Jones and Peter Parsons suggest that the series, apparently in alphabetical order, was being prepared by a scholar to head copies of the plays.[29] But in the late third century B.C., Dioscorides wrote five epigrams on dramatists, two of which (on Aeschylus, 21 G-P = *AP* 7.411, and Sositheus, 23 G-P = *AP* 7.707) seem to refer to two others (on Thespis, 20 G-P = *AP* 7.410, and Sophocles, 22 G-P = *AP* 7.37, respectively) as if they were intended to be read in sequence,[30] and a series of epigrams on authors and their works eventually found its way into the *Anthology* (*AP* 9.184–214). So it is quite possible that the Petrie papyrus preserves a single-authored collection of epigrams on plays,[31] or, alternatively, it may illustrate the kind of scholarly document that offered a model for sequences such as that of Dioscorides.

Another third-century document that is not itself an epigram collection but provides information about one is the unpublished P.Vindob G 40611, containing epigram incipits divided by headings (εν τηι β βυβλωι, εν τηι δ βυβλωι) into four or more books. In a preliminary report, H. Harrauer has identified only one incipit, from an epigram by Asclepiades (15 G-P = *AP* 12.46), although he notes that the name Kallistion found in another (l. 114) appears in three known epigrams— by Callimachus (16 G-P = *AP* 6.148), by Posidippus (8 G-P = *AP* 12.131), and by

27. *Greek Papyri: An Introduction* (Oxford, 1968) 91. For the connection between school texts and the development of literary anthologies, see Guéraud and Jouguet xxiv–xxxi with the supplementary remarks of J. Barns, "A New Gnomologium," *CQ* 44 (1950) 132–37, 45 (1951) 1–19.

28. *The Flinders Petrie Papyri* II, ed. John P. Mahaffy (Dublin, 1893) 158–59; anon. 178 *FGE*; 985 *SH*.

29. Lloyd-Jones and Parsons (1983) 502. Alphabetization developed as a scholarly tool in Alexandria during the era of the first two Ptolemies, although influence from the Peripatetic tradition remains a distinct possibility; see Lloyd W. Daly, *Contributions to a History of Alphabetization in Antiquity and the Middle Ages* (Brussels, 1967) 15–44. For other examples of alphabetized lists of author's names, see Blum 60, 155, 185–87.

30. Wilamowitz, *Sappho und Simonides: Untersuchungen über griechische Lyriker* (Berlin, 1913) 231 argued that the epigrams were accompanied by illustrations in Dioscorides' book, but Gow-Page II (1965) 254 are content to assert that "D. wrote a series of epigrams on dramatic poets connected only by their related themes." See also the discussion in Mathäus Gabathuler, *Hellenistische Epigramme auf Dichter* (St. Gallen, 1937) 82–90.

31. Cf. Cameron (1993) 8.

Hedylus (3 G-P).[32] It is unclear, then, whether the papyrus documents a collection of mostly unknown epigrams by Asclepiades (who may also have written about a Kallistion) or an anthology by more than one author. The fact that the Milan papyrus contains about a hundred epigrams by Posidippus, at least two of which were preserved elsewhere, increases the likelihood of the first alternative. Peter Parsons, who collaborated on the papyrus, has indicated that the collection included a variety of meters,[33] and Harrauer's report that one poem consisted of twenty-one lines clearly indicates a nonelegiac meter. Two other relatively long poems, of forty and fifty-two lines, are also reported by Harrauer. The purpose of the incipit list, like a later one listing epigrams by Philodemus and others (P.Oxy. 3724 from the late first century A.D.),[34] is also unclear. Harrauer thinks of notes for a future edition, while Cameron assumes that we have a list of epigrams needed for the purpose of checking the accuracy of a scholarly text.[35] This point will need further clarification before we can establish whether the sums given for epigrams and lines reflect the entire contents of completed books or only some portion of them. The sum for the first book is 83 epigrams in 344 lines (averaging 4.15 lines per poem) and for another book 33 epigrams in 264 lines (averaging eight lines per poem). These totals would produce books somewhat shorter than Martial's and considerably shorter than the books of Meleager's *Garland*, which contained well over four thousand lines organized by epigram type into four books. The difference in average length for the two books for which totals are preserved suggests that the length of individual poems was one criterion for organization, a possibility strengthened by a run of thirteen single-couplet epigrams (l. 225). In short, this papyrus provides important evidence for a third-century epigram collection of considerable scope, whether an anthology by various hands or a collection of epigrams by Asclepiades.

32. "Epigrammincipit auf einem Papyrus aus dem 3. Jh. v. Chr. P. Vindob G 40611: Ein Vorbericht," *Proceedings of the Sixteenth International Congress of Papyrology*, ed. Roger Bagnall *et al.* (Chico, 1981) 49–53.

33. "Poesia ellenistica: testi e contesti," *Aevum Antiquum* 5 (1993) 14.

34. David Sider, "Looking for Philodemus in P. Oxy. 54.3424," *ZPE* 76 (1989) 229–36, *The Epigrams of Philodemus: Introduction, Text, and Commentary* (Oxford, 1997) 203–25, and, more cautiously, M. Gigante, "Filodemo tra poesia e prosa," *SIFC* 7 (1989) 129–51 have argued that many of the unknown epigrams may also be by Philodemus. For discussion of the list, see Cameron (1993) 379–87, who argues that the incipits represent a list made for a personal selection of epigrams rather than an index to a preexisting book. Also to be compared with the third-century incipit list are the thirteen incipits, two of them identifiable as dedicatory epigrams of Leonidas (25 G-P = *AP* 9.322, 46 G-P = *AP* 6.13), written on an ostracon of the second century B.C. (U. Wilcken, *Griechische Ostraka* 1488 = 976 *SH*). Ernst Nachmanson, *Der griechische Buchtitel: Einige Beobachtungen* (Göteborg, 1941; reprinted Darmstadt, 1969) 37–52 discusses the use of incipits as a supplement to or substitute for titles and derives the practice from Callimachus' cataloging techniques; cf. Blum 147, 156–57.

35. Cameron (1993) 10.

Direct evidence for a third-century epigram book of high literary quality is provided by P.Petrie II 49 a, thought to have been written about 250 B.C. On the recto is a twenty-four line elegiac epithalamium for Arsinoe, who is either the first or second wife of Ptolemy Philadelphus; the introductory poem, and one assumes the collection itself, thus dates no later than 274 B.C. The verso preserves a title, σύμμεικτα ἐπιγράμματα (*Miscellaneous Epigrams*), followed after a space by Ποσειδίπ[που].[36] Although F. Lasserre claimed that the names of other poets were included here as well, they are not now visible,[37] and it seems possible that the collection consisted solely of the works of Posidippus. Whether the title was provided by the owner or the editor, the word σύμμεικτα appears during this period in titles of single-authored works, such as the σύμμικτα συμποτικά of Aristoxenus of Tarentum (Ath. 14.632a).[38] We may wonder as well whether Tzetzes' remark about the "mixed" (συμμιγεῖς) and "unmixed" (ἀμιγεῖς καὶ ἁπλοῖ) books in the Alexandrian Library (Kaibel, 1 p. 19 Pb 4ff. *CGF*) is relevant here. Although the meaning of the terms has been disputed, it seems likely that "mixed" rolls were those containing more than one literary work, whether by one or more authors.[39] The term σύμμεικτα, like the term ἐπιγράμματα, may, then, be technical and descriptive. But in a culture in which scholars and poets are one and the same, the term may also carry poetic significance, by referring to the variety, or ποικιλία, characteristic of certain Hellenistic poetry books. In one such book, Callimachus' *Iambi*, the term σύμμεικτον (fr. 203.18) refers to the poet's freedom in mixing dialects, just as the Diegesis employs the term πολυείδεια, "use of many forms," (Dieg. 9.34; cf. εἰδύλλια, "little types") to describe his ability to compose in diverse genres.

Papyri containing epigrams attributed to a single poet are of special interest as compilations perhaps arranged by the author. By far the most important of these is the new Posidippus papyrus, P.Mil.Vogl. inv. 1295. Unfortunately, at the

36. First published by Mahaffy, *The Flinders Petrie Papyri* II (1893) 157 and revised by H. J. M. Milne, ed., *Catalogue of the Literary Papyri in the British Museum* (London, 1927), no. 60; now 961 *SH*. Although titles were usually written on a parchment tag at this period, Turner (1952) 14 discusses a fifth-century illustration of a papyrus with a label written on the back of the roll.

37. Lasserre, "Aux origines de l'anthologie: I. Le papyrus P. Brit. Mus. Inv. 589," *RhM* 102 (1959) 222–47 found traces of the names Hedylus, Leonidas, and Anyte. But neither T. C. Skeat, who examined the papyrus for Fraser (II 858, n. 403), nor Lloyd-Jones and Parsons (1983) 465 have been able to observe more than ink stains. Even so, Lloyd-Jones and Parsons point out that the space after the title and before the poet's name functions like a colon and so suggest that other names, now lost, did follow.

38. For the significance of such titles within the Callimachean poetic program, see Mario Puelma Piwonka, *Lucilius und Kallimachos: Zur Geschichte einer Gattung der hellenistisch-römischen Poesie* (Frankfurt am Main, 1949) 198–202.

39. See Fraser I 329 with the literature cited in II 485, n. 171; Blum 107–8.

present time the papyrus has not been fully published. I owe the information presented here to two advance publications by its editors, Guido Bastianini and Claudio Gallazzi,[40] and to a number of private correspondences for which I acknowledge my gratitude. The papyrus was used as mummy cartonnage, together with five documents from the reign of Ptolemy V Epiphanes, one of which bears the date of 183/82 B.C. The literary papyrus is older, however, and the editors assign it to the fourth quarter of the third century B.C. It contains a collection of about one hundred epigrams, reportedly unknown except for an epigram on Lysippus' portrait of Alexander the Great transmitted in the *Anthology* under the name of Posidippus (18 G-P = *AP* 16.119) and an epigram on a snake stone preserved by Tzetzes (20 G-P = *Chil.* 7.660–69).[41] The lack of authors' names between any of the epigrams indicates that the papyrus contains the works of only one poet, so that we apparently have a collection of epigrams by Posidippus alone. The original extent of the collection cannot now be known, but it was considerable, exceeding the six hundred verses preserved on the papyrus. Yet the editors point out that it was apparently not a complete collection of Posidippus' epigrams, since known epigrams (such as his poems on shipwrecks) are missing from the sections where we would expect to find them.

The collection is organized by subject matter into sections, each with its own heading. To date twenty-five of the epigrams have been published, but in a nondiplomatic text that lacks the usual markings for doubtful readings and contains the editors' supplements without brackets.[42] Except for a few epigrams printed in an earlier article, it is also impossible to know with certainty the distribution of the epigrams among the sections, since the epigrams seem only partially printed in an order that corresponds to the reported sequence of the sections. The topics of the sections are as follows:

(i) stones, particularly carved gemstones. One charming poem describes a stone of lapis lazuli, commissioned as a gift for a "dark-haired" girl in exchange for a "tender kiss" (1). Other epigrams that apparently fall in this section concern a Pegasus engraved in chalcedony (2), a piece of beautiful

40. "Il poeta ritrovato," *Rivista 'Ca' de Sass'* 121 (1993) 28–39; *Posidippo: epigrammi* (Milan, 1993).

41. L. Lehnus, "Posidippo Ritorna," *RFIC* 121 (1993) 364 reports to have learned through the courtesy of the editors that the *dracontias* epigram has been identified on the papyrus, although this information is not provided in their publications.

42. Bastianini and Gallazzi 1993b. The numbering system used below is from this publication, but I caution the reader that the text is preliminary and likely to differ somewhat in the definitive edition.

but commonplace rock crystal (3), and a snake stone carved with a tiny chariot.[43]

(ii) omens obtained from the observation of birds (title of section, according to the editors), though auspices derived from dreams appear here as well. In one epigram a warrior who believes he is accompanied into battle by a divine spirit because he dreamed of wedding Athena is killed by Ares due to his arrogance toward the gods (7). Other poems include an advertisement for a seer (4), an epitaph for a bird-diviner who aided Alexander the Great against the Persians (5), and the report of an ill omen that preceded the death of a warrior in battle (6).

(iii) dedications, three of which commemorate gifts to Arsinoe II. One of these, on a statue of the queen dedicated by the nauarch Callicrates in Arsinoe's sanctuary at Zephyrium (20), is paralleled by two previously known Posidippan epigrams on the same sanctuary (12, 13 G-P).

(iv) funereal epigrams. One tender epitaph describes a mother of five living children, who tends her sixth infant on her knees in Hades (11), while other published epitaphs concern young girls who died before marriage (8, 9, 10). The editors give a varied list of subjects for this rather lengthy section—"young and old, maidens and mothers, masters and slaves."

(v) sculpture. The epigram on Lysippus that appears in the *Anthology* occurs here.

(vi) equestrian epigrams, composed to celebrate victories of illustrious persons at Olympia, Delphi, Nemea, and Corinth. Literary treatments of this topic, known from inscriptions, were previously rare.[44] One epigram presumably from the section describes an artistic depiction of the victorious horse winning the crown at Nemea for his master (23).

(vii) shipwrecks. Deaths at sea are placed in a separate section, distinct from the general epitaphs. In one particularly poignant poem the shipwrecked person offers thanks to the stranger who gave him burial (13).

(viii) cures for diseases and afflictions. In one remarkable epigram a deaf man reports that he was healed by Asclepius so as to hear even words through bricks (18). Other poems that apparently belong here include a dedication of a silver saucer to Asclepius (17) and a prayer to the same deity for "moderate wealth" and "health," two conditions that are named the "high acropolis" of human existence (16).

---

43. For discussion of the Pegasus and snake stone poems as parallels for an epigram by Asclepiades on an amethyst ring engraved with a figure of Methe (44 G-P = *AP* 9.752), see K. Gutzwiller, "Cleopatra's Ring," *GRBS* 36 (1995) 385–89.

44. See Joachim Ebert, *Griechische Epigramme auf Sieger an gymnischen und hippischen Agonen* (Berlin, 1972). For equestrian epigrams preserved in books, see *AP* 6.49, 6.246; Maria L. Lazzarini, *Le formule delle dediche votive nella Grecia arcaica* (Rome, 1976) 139–46, 295–302. A. Cameron, "Two New Poems of Posidippus," *ZPE* (forthcoming) discusses one of these equestrian epigrams, on an Olympian victory by Berenice, presumably the wife of Soter.

(ix) τρόποι or "manners." A surprising category that includes an epitaph for a Cretan of few words, who berates passersby for inquiring into his identity (25).

Though the papyrus breaks off at this point, traces of another column indicate that the text continued with one or more additional sections. Some of the sections correspond to divisions found in Meleager's *Garland* and the later anthologies: Meleager, Philip, and Agathias devote major sections or books to epitaphs and dedications, and the poems on sculptures recall another major section of these anthologies, the epideictic. Meleager also groups shipwreck poems together, though as a subsection within the larger division of epitaphs. But Posidippus' other categories—stones, omens, equestrian epigrams, cures, and "manners"—are more surprising. Their presence indicates that Meleager, in limiting his anthology to certain types of epigrams, has strongly affected our later perception of the variety of epigram subjects that existed in the earlier Hellenistic period. We cannot know whether the papyrus also included any of Posidippus' erotic epigrams, some of which are preserved in Meleager's amatory section. Against the possibility is the fact that all the preserved epigrams are ostensibly inscriptional rather than sympotic.

The Milan papyrus is an exciting find, one which establishes beyond doubt the existence of epigram collections in the third century B.C. I caution, however, against the assumption that it is typical of all epigram books from that period. Not only do epigrams lend themselves to a variety of arrangements, but the papyrus, written a generation or more after the death of Posidippus, may well have been compiled by a posthumous editor rather than the poet himself. The editors have declared the possibility of assemblage after Posidippus' death the "more likely" ("più verosimilmente") alternative.[45] Although the collection shows evidence of an advance plan, this plan may reflect the practicalities of editing more than the aesthetic considerations of artistic design. Until the publication of the complete papyrus, we will not know the ordering of the epigrams within sections, and so I am unable to determine whether there are any patterns of linkage between poems. Bastianini has reported no sign of poems of introduction, conclusion, or transition on the papyrus.[46]

But even if the editor did little to create cohesiveness beyond organizing the epigrams into sections, the reader may yet find a unifying focus in the peculiarities of the author's style and tone. A number of the epigrams were clearly not intended for inscription, and we should not imagine a collection consisting solely of pieces commissioned by patrons. To give an example, a meditation on a crystal washed down from the mountains by an Arabian stream concerns the human folly of placing little monetary value on the rock's beauty because of its lack of rarity (3). The philosophical tone betrays the author's

---

45. Bastianini and Gallazzi (1993b) xix.
46. Private correspondence dated April 10, 1995.

personality rather than a patron's interest in the object. So too, an epitaph for a warrior who foresaw his own demise when his servant stumbled as he was bringing his master's armor from indoors (6) seems designed to undercut the military pretentiousness of the "important hero" (βαρὺν ἥρω) who is brought back from battle as only "a bit of ash" (ὀλίγην σποδιήν). This ironic tone is improbable in a geniune inscription. Other poems also turn on a central verbal contrast or play with words. An example is this epitaph ostensibly designed for a cenotaph:

τέτρακι βούλευσαι, ὃ καὶ ἐν τότε κῦμα πλοΐζου,
    μὴ ταχὺς Εὐξείνου γίνεο ποντοπόρος,
τοῦτον ἰδὼν κενεὸν Δώρου τάφον, ὃν πάρα μίμνων
    τῆλ' ἐμοῦ εἶ, καὶ μ' αἱ θῖνες ἔχουσιν ἁλός.

(14)

Take thought four times, even you who in the past have sailed the waves,
    so that you not too quickly become a sea-traveler of the Euxine,
As you look at this empty tomb of Dorus. If you remain here beside it
    you'll be far from me, imprisoned in the sandy depth of the sea.

Here the commonplace irony that the deceased speaks from an empty tomb to name his own absence is converted to a warning to the passerby to remain beside the stone (τάφον, ὃν πάρα μίμνων) far from the body of the deceased (τῆλ' ἐμοῦ) and so to avoid the dangers of sea travel. Another epitaph for a shipwrecked person gains interest as well from a play with words. A stranger who buried a corpse despite his own haste to continue his journey earns "great" gratitude from the deceased: ἀποδοῦναι Λεωφάντῳ μεγάλην Μίκκος ἐγὼ χάριτα (13). The contrast between μεγάλην ("great") and Μίκκος ("Piccolo" as the editors translate it) reinforces the suggested message that we are all made equal in death, since even a traveler with an aristocratic-sounding name like Leophantus may offer the service of burial to an unknown person, who turns out to bear a lowly name like Miccus. The reader is likely to recognize the same artistic personality behind the play on words in Posidippus' epigram describing a Pegasus carved in a gemstone:

εὖ τὸν Πήγασον ἵππον ἐπ' ἠερόεσσαν ἴασπιν
    χεῖρά τε καὶ κατὰ νοῦν ἔγλυφ' ὁ χειροτέχνης·
Βελλεροφόντης μὲν γὰρ ἀλήϊον εἰς Κιλίκων γῆν
    ἤριφ', ὁ δ' εἰς κυανῆν ἠέρα πῶλος ἔβη,
οὕνεκ' ἀνηνιόχητον ἔτι τρομέοντα χαλινοῖς
    τοῦτον ἐν αἰθερίῳ τῷδ' ἐτύπωσε λίθῳ.

(2)

With skill and design the craftsman carved well
    this horse Pegasus on sky-blue chalcedony.
Bellerophon fell into the Aleian plain of the Cilicians,
    but his horse climbed up into the dark blue sky.

To show this he depicted the horse without a rider,
  still trembling from the bit, on the skylike stone.

The poet compliments the artisan as he interprets his miniature work of art,
by explaining the exact mythical moment represented on the stone. In doing
so, he suggests that the beauty of the stone is enhanced by a connection between
the artistic medium and the subject: the sky-blue (ἠερόεσσαν) chalcedony is an
appropriate choice for the depiction of a winged horse flying up into the dark blue
aether (κυανῆν ἠέρα). The phrase ἐν αἰθερίῳ τῷδ' . . . λίθῳ in the final line pulls
together the connection between the cloudy blue background of the chalcedony
and the heavenly region it depicts. Although the editor of the Milan papyrus
seems to have approached the task of arrangement in a fairly mechanical fashion,
readers may yet reconstruct the thematic similarities and stylistic tendencies they
perceive into a unifying focus for the collection as a whole.

Another but much less significant papyrus of the third century B.C., P.Berol.
9812 (= 974 *SH*), may also belong to the category of single-authored collections,
since there is little room for author names in the spaces separating its poems.[47]
It preserves portions of three quatrains, at least two of them dedicatory and
two on artworks. The first (*AP* 6.3), on the dedication of a club to Heracles,
was previously known; in the *Anthology* the poem is ascribed to a "Dionysius"
(5 G-P), which is also the name of the dedicator. The two other poems, unknown
from elsewhere, both concern artworks—a statue of a wrestler (as it seems) and
Apelles' painting of Aphrodite Anadyomena. Since justifiable doubts about
the attribution of the first epigram to "Dionysius"[48] suggest that it came into
the *Anthology* anonymously, we are left without any means of determining the
authorship of these poems. Although the sequence is too brief to draw firm
conclusions, the epigrams do display continuity in length and in type, whether
the class was considered dedicatory or epideictic. Two other papyri also seem
to contain compilations of epigrams perhaps by one author. In P.Harris 56
(= 981 *SH*), dated to the middle of the second century B.C., the one legible
poem, another unknown epigram on the painter Apelles, is followed by ἄλλο,
indicating that the next poem was an epigram by the same author or on the
same subject.[49] P.Petrie inv. O(2) (= 986 *SH*), dated to about 100 B.C., contains

47. The papyrus was published by Wilamowitz (*BKT* 5.1.77–78) as a single long epigram, but
the first four lines were identified as a complete epigram by M. Gronewald, "Ein Epigramm-
Papyrus," *ZPE* 12 (1973) 92–98. J. Ebert, "Zur Epigramm-Anthologie P. Berol. 9812," *APF*
24–25 (1976) 47–54, who has published revised readings based on examination of photographs
of the papyrus, reports a space between the first and second epigram but none between the
second and third; he suggests (54, n. 21) the possibility of a change in author or the notation of
a subject change (for which, cf. P.Oxy. 3725).

48. Gow-Page (1965) II 234.

49. For discussion, see C. H. Roberts, "A Hellenistic Epigram Recovered," *JJP* 4 (1950)
215–17; anon. 158 *FGE*.

two apparently sepulchral epigrams;[50] the heading of the first, ἄλλο ἐπίγραμμα, suggests, again, that we may be dealing with a grouping of epigrams of a single type by a single author, although the word ἐπίγραμμα just possibly points to a collection of mixed poetic kinds. These three papyri indicate that the sort of collection found on the Milan papyrus, consisting of epigrams by one author arranged by formal type or subject matter, was commonplace in the Hellenistic era.

P.Köln 5.204 more certainly comes from a single-authored collection. Dating from the second century B.C., the papyrus bears the heading Μνασάλκου and contains six epigrams, one of which has been transmitted under that poet's name (9 G-P = *AP* 7.488). Although the fourth epigram is remarkably similar to an epigram ascribed to Hegesippus (3 G-P = *AP* 6.226), M. Gronewald, who edited the papyrus, concludes that the copyist intended to assign all the epigrams to Mnasalces.[51] The sequence of subjects is as follows: dedication of a shield won in an athletic competition, epitaph for a warrior, epitaph for an unmarried girl, dedication of an Artemis statue by a maiden, epitaph for an unknown female, an epigram on a poet that may be an epitaph. The editor finds associative bridging between the shield dedication and the second poem, where he detects a possible mention of a shield in the first line.[52] But another, more comprehensive technique for providing both unity and diversity is also at work here. Conformity in length to four lines as well as the limitation to ostensibly inscriptional types provides the sequence with a formal coherency. Within this overall similarity, variety and linkage are simultaneously achieved by the manipulation both of inscriptional type, dedication versus epitaph, and of gender, male versus female: at no point do two epigrams of the same formal type and concerning persons of the same sex occur consecutively, and yet either the type or the subject of each epigram corresponds to that of its successor. This delightful and intricate pattern strongly suggests that the papyrus, though apparently written out for private use rather than the book trade, preserves a copy of Mnasalces' own epigram book, either ordered by the poet himself or at the very least by an editor conscious of poetic design.

P.Oxy. 3324, datable perhaps to the Augustan era, contains four epigrams by Meleager. The papyrus is quite possibly a remnant of an edition of Meleager's

50. Published by E. G. Turner, "Two Greek Epigrams," *JJP* 4 (1950) 235–38.

51. "Epigramme des Mnasalkes," *Kölner Papyri* V, ed. Michael Gronewald, K. Maresch, and W. Schäfer (Opladen, 1985) 23. Gronewald 30 offers two explanations for the similarity of the surviving portion of the fourth epigram, apart from the change of a name, to Hegesippus 3 G-P: either the epigram, like many others in the *AP*, was variously ascribed or Mnasalces composed a close variation of Hegesippus' poem, just as he closely varied (17 G-P) Asclepiades' epitaph for Ajax (29 G-P = *AP* 7.145). Cameron (1993) 4, in supporting the second suggestion, argues that a reference may have been made in the form of a lemma to Mnasalces' variation of Hegesippus.

52. Gronewald (1985) 23.

own poetry. Cameron has recently argued that it is an extract from the *Garland*, on the basis of another papyrus (*BKT* 5.1.75), which shows that amatory epigrams in the *Garland* were later dispersed to Books 5, 9, and 12 of the *AP*.[53] While it is true that all four poems on the papyrus likely appeared in the erotic section of the *Garland*, it does not have the normal characteristics of a mechanical extract. The reversal of the order of *AP* 5.190 and 5.152 speaks strongly against selection from the *Garland*, and the sequencing of the poems on the papyrus indicates artistic design rather than selection from an anthology:

τρισσαὶ μὲν Χάριτες, τρεῖς δὲ γλυκυπάρθενοι Ὧραι,
   τρεῖς δ' ἐμὲ θηλυμανεῖς οἰστροβολοῦσι Πόθοι·
ἢ γὰρ Ἔρως τρία τόξα κατείρυσεν ὡς ἄρα μέλλων
   οὐχὶ μίαν τρώσειν, τρεῖς δ' ἐν ἐμοὶ κραδίας.[54]

(74 G-P = AP 9.16)

Triple are the Graces, and three are the sweet maidenly Seasons,
   and three Passions of woman-madness goad me forth.
For Eros drew three bows as if he were going to wound
   not one heart, but three hearts in me.

κῦμα τὸ πικρὸν Ἔρωτος ἀκοίμητοί τε πνέοντες
   ζῆλοι καὶ κώμων χειμέριον πέλαγος,
ποῖ φέρομαι; πάντη δὲ φρενῶν οἴακες ἀφεῖνται·
   ἢ πάλι τὴν τρυφερὴν Σκύλλαν ἐποψόμεθα;

(64 G-P = AP 5.190)

O briny wave of Love and sleepless blasts of jealousy
   and stormy sea of wine and song,
Where am I borne? Everywhere my mind's rudders are loosened.
   Will I ever set eyes again on that delicate Scylla?

Κύπρις ἐμοὶ ναύκληρος, Ἔρως δ' οἴακα φυλάσσει
   ἄκρον ἔχων ψυχῆς ἐν χερὶ πηδάλιον·
χειμαίνει δ' ὁ βαρὺς πνεύσας Πόθος, οὕνεκα δὴ νῦν
   παμφύλῳ παίδων νήχομαι ἐν πελάγει.

(119 G-P = AP 12.157)

The Cyprian is my captain, and Eros guards my tiller,
   holding the end of my soul's rudder in his hand.

---

53. Cameron (1993) 27.
54. In line 2 I print οἰστροβολοῦσι found in P and Pl in place of οἰστοβολοῦσι preferred by Gow-Page. Line 3 contains Guyet's correction of κατήρισεν; I have also preferred Ἔρως to the manuscript τοι which remains in most modern editions.

Passion with its stormy blasts rages about me, because now
   I swim in a sea of boys from many nations.

πταίης μοι κώνωψ ταχὺς ἄγγελος, οὔασι δ᾽ ἄκροις
   Ζηνοφίλας ψαύσας προσψιθύριζε τάδε·
"ἄγρυπνος μίμνει σε, σὺ δ᾽ ὦ λήθαργε φιλούντων
   εὔδεις." εἶα πέτευ, ναὶ φιλόμουσε πέτευ·
ἥσυχα δὲ φθέγξαι, μὴ καὶ σύγκοιτον ἐγείρας
   κινήσῃς ἐπ᾽ ἐμοὶ ζηλοτύπους ὀδύνας.
ἢν δ᾽ ἀγάγῃς τὴν παῖδα, δορᾷ στέψω σε λέοντος,
   κώνωψ, καὶ δώσω χειρὶ φέρειν ῥόπαλον.

(34 G-P = *AP* 5.152)

Fly for me, my mosquito, swift messenger, and grazing
   the tip of Zenophila's ear whisper this:
"He lies awake waiting for you, but you sleep forgetful
   of your lovers." Now fly, yes fly, lover of song.
But speak softly and don't wake her bed companion
   so as to stir up the pain of jealousy against me.
If you bring the girl, I'll drape you with a lion skin,
   mosquito, and give you a club to carry in your hand.

The series is unified by the poet's consistent stance as the victim of passion and
varied by the sequence of love objects: three female loves, one female love, a
sea of boy loves,[55] Zenophila. Although four epigrams constitute a small sample,
it appears that the ordering principle of the sequence was alternation of multiple
with single loves. In addition, 64 and 119 are linked by the sea-of-love theme, a
connection enhanced by verbal repetition (πνέοντες ... χειμέριον; χειμαίνει
... πνεύσας). Verbal linkage of this sort has been identified as a characteristic of
the *Garland*, and, as we will see in Chapter 6, these two poems probably stood
close together in the amatory section of Meleager's anthology. Since we do not
seem to be dealing with a selection from the *Garland*, it becomes not unlikely
that the papyrus preserves an author-edited compilation of Meleager's erotic
verse, from which the poet carried over certain principles of ordering to his
multi-authored anthology. But more generally, we may say that the Mnasalces
and Meleager papyri give evidence that Hellenistic epigram collections, both
the votive-sepulchral and the amatory types, were ordered to display pleasing
diversity amid unifying constraints.

   Cameron has recently argued that, contrary to common assumption, Melea-
ger's *Garland* is the earliest known epigram anthology, in the sense of a collection
of epigrams by multiple hands designed for publication as a literary text.[56] It

---

55. Although παίδων in 119.4 is not given grammatical gender, Meleager's use of the word
elsewhere (e.g., 78.2 G-P = *AP* 12.256.2) indicates a specific reference to boys rather than boys
and girls. The alternation of multiple and single lovers remains in any case.

56. Cameron (1993) 5–12.

is true that, to my knowledge, all the papyri clearly containing anthologies of epigrams written by more than one author date to the first century B.C. or later, that is, are post-Meleagrian, although those to be discussed here, namely the ones containing poems of earlier epigrammatists, could conceivably be copies of anthologies compiled before the *Garland*. It would be dangerous to conclude that anthologizing was unknown before Meleager, but it does appear that in the post-Meleagrian era anthologies increased in popularity as a means of pre- serving the best of earlier Greek epigrams. Since in multi-authored anthologies diversity was necessarily present through change in authorship, juxtaposition of poems on similar topics offered a mode of coherency. P.Freib. 4 of the first century B.C. contains remnants of six epigrams:[57] the first, possibly the model for or copy of *AP* 16.293, on Homer;[58] the second, an epigram on the enigma of Homer's fatherland;[59] the fourth, Theodoridas 17 G-P = *AP* 9.743 on twelve bronze cows fashioned by the sculptor Phradmon;[60] the sixth, Posidippus 18 G-P = *AP* 16.119 on a sculpture of Alexander by Lysippus (which, interestingly, appears also on the Milan papyrus). The identifiable epigrams are all epideictic and concern famous literary or artistic craftsmen. On the other hand, the epi- grams in P.Tebt. 1.3 of the same century—a poem on an artistic representation of Phaethon's death, Alcaeus 17 G-P = *AP* 9.588 on a bronze figure of a famous athlete, Posidippus (?) 24 G-P on a literary artist, and Asclepiades (?) 47 G-P on a cowardly Spartan killed by his mother—are less clearly connected by any similarity of subject matter; they might yet be classed together as epideictic poems.[61] Both these may of course be privately compiled rather than published anthologies.

A papyrus of Augustan date, P.Oxy. 662, presents a sequencing of epigrams to demonstrate variations on a single theme—the principle of arrangement so common in Meleager's *Garland*. It contains: epitaphs for Prexo by Leonidas (70 G-P = *AP* 7.163), by Antipater of Sidon (21 G-P = *AP* 7.164), and by Amyntas

57. Wolf Aly, ed., *Mitteilungen aus der Freiburger Papyrussammlung* I (Heidelberg, 1914) 58–59; 973 *SH*. Albert Wifstrand, *Studien zur griechischen Anthologie* (Diss. Lund, 1926) 30–33, reprinted in *The Greek Anthology* I, ed. Sonya L. Tarán (New York, 1987) has shown that the papyrus is not a copy of Meleager's *Garland* but either an independent anthology or a collection excerpted from Meleager.

58. So Wifstrand 31–32; but for other possibilities, see Aristoxenos D. Skiadas, *Homer im griechischen Epigramm* (Athens, 1965) 20, n. 3.

59. Edited and discussed by Page, anon. 159 *FGE*; the epigram also appears on an ostracon of the second century B.C. (*BKT* 5.1.78).

60. On this epigram, see Gerda Schwarz, *Die griechische Kunst des 5. und 4. Jahrhunderts v. Chr. im Spiegel der Anthologia Graeca* (Diss. Graz, 1971) 41–44.

61. Bernard P. Grenfell, A. S. Hunt, and J. G. Smyly, eds., *The Tebtunis Papyri* I (London, 1902) 10–12; 988 *SH*. Only the final part of the names of the poets for the last two epigrams are preserved; and, as Gow-Page (1965) II 151 point out, Hegesippus and Dosiadas remain rival claimants.

(1 *FGE*); an epigram on Philopoemen by Amyntas (2 *FGE*); epigrams describing Glenis' rustic dedications by Leonidas (51 G-P) and by Antipater (48 G-P); and the beginning of another poem by Leonidas.[62] Wifstrand has argued that P.Oxy. 662 represents an anthology formed, perhaps by Amyntas himself, before Meleager's *Garland* but on the same variation principle.[63] Support for his position comes from the ascription of [Samius] 2 G-P = *AP* 6.114 to Amyntas by the corrector (C) of the Palatine manuscript.[64] This poem, on a dedication of a wild bull killed by Philip V of Macedon (238–179 B.C.), appears in the *AP* in a good Meleagrian sequence together with two other epigrams on the same theme, one by Antipater of Sidon (47 G-P = *AP* 6.115) and one by Philip's contemporary and friend Samius (1 G-P = *AP* 6.116). The last epigram is surely the original, while the poems by Amyntas and Antipater appear to me to be independant variations. If, as it appears, Amyntas was included in the *Garland*, then the anthology found on P.Oxy. 662 would likely either predate Meleager's or be roughly contemporary with it. It does appear that Amyntas is at least slightly posterior to Antipater since his variation of the Prexo theme is situated on the papyrus as an imitation of Antipater's imitation of Leonidas' composition. The sequence of terminology for Prexo's age at death—Leonidas' straightforward "twenty-two," Antipater's "twice eleven," and Amyntas' "thrice seven plus one"—confirms the chronological sequence. But if our *terminus post quem* for Amyntas is the lifetime of Antipater, that could still allow him to be a contemporary of Meleager or even slightly older. Whatever the date of Amyntas, it would be rash to assert that grouping of variations on a single theme was the invention of Meleager, since poets had been composing such variations (e.g., Posidippus' imitations of Asclepiades) from the early third century. Scholars are generally agreed that *BKT* 5.1.75, from a tiny book of the first century A.D., preserves extracts of amatory poems by various authors from the *Garland*.[65] The papyrus offers important evidence that the Meleagrian erotic epigrams in *AP* 5, 9, and 12 formed a single section in the original anthology.

It is instructive that almost every one of the papyri containing sequences of epigrams displays some principle of design. In the single-authored sequences continuity of authorship and normally of epigram type provides a built-in

62. On Amyntas, see Page (1981) 5–10.

63. Wifstrand 33–39.

64. See G. Luck, Review of Gow/Page, *Hellenistic Epigrams*, *GGA* 219 (1967) 38–39. Cameron (1993) 11–12 argues, on the basis of the ascription of *AP* 6.114 to Amyntas, that he lived during the rule of Philip, but the ascription does not date Amyntas to the lifetime of that monarch at all. Cameron 28 also asserts, mistakenly, that P.Oxy. 662 contains "an unbroken sequence of seven funerary poems" in order to argue that the papyrus is an excerpt from the funereal section of Meleager's *Garland*. But the Glenis epigrams are clearly dedicatory, not funereal like the Prexo epitaphs, and it is unlikely that we are dealing with excerpts from two different books of Meleager's anthology—the dedicatory and the sepulchral.

65. See Wifstrand 10–13, Gow (1958a) 15–16, and Cameron (1993) 11.

cohesiveness. In multi-authored anthologies the opposite is true: diversity is mandated through the continual change in authorship so that unifying forces need to be developed by grouping epigrams through similarity of topic or even as variations one of another. That the patterns of arrangement we have observed in papyri are far from accidental will be confirmed by evidence from sequences of epigrams preserved in manuscripts.

IN MANUSCRIPT

The very instrument through which most Hellenistic book epigrams were preserved—Meleager's *Garland*—has also become the main obstacle to discovering the poetic design of Hellenistic epigram books. Scholars of the *Palatine Anthology* have identified and examined sequences of epigrams that seem to come from the *Garland*, in some instances relatively intact.[66] Carl Radinger has shown that Meleager's method of ordering his anthology was to use the epigrams of one or two poets (Leonidas and Callimachus for the dedicatory and sepulchral sections, Asclepiades and Posidippus for the amatory sections) as the "Grundstock" around which were grouped epigrams by other poets on the same or similar themes.[67] Albert Wifstrand has further demonstrated that epigrams in the *Garland* were linked thematically, by subject matter or by verbal repetition.[68] In plotting his artistic design, Meleager so intertwined author with author, as plant with plant, that he effectively erased all trace of the principles of order structuring the collections that were his sources.

But runs of three or more epigrams by the same Meleagrian author occur at certain points within the *Anthology*. At least some of these, particularly the longer groups, can be shown not to descend from the *Garland* and so may offer evidence for ancient editing practices that are not Meleagrian. The passages of most relevance here are *AP* 6.134–157 and 7.507b–529, the parallel nature of which becomes clear when their respective contents are aligned in columns:

---

66. Gow-Page (1965) I xxv summarize the sequences identified by Stadtmüller and by Rudolf Weisshäupl, *Die Grabgedichte der griechischen Anthologie* (Vienna, 1889), reprinted in *The Greek Anthology* I, ed. Sonya L. Tarán (New York, 1987). Crucial to identifying the longer sequences left relatively undisturbed by Cephalas are the refinements presented by Lenzinger 2–30 with Taf. I and Cameron (1993) in his Table.

67. *Meleagros von Gadara: Eine litterargeschichtliche Skizze* (Innsbruck, 1895) 100–107, reprinted in *The Greek Anthology* II, ed. Sonya L. Tarán (New York, 1987).

68. Wifstrand 14–29. Radinger 100–001 has effectively refuted the statement of the Palatine lemmatist on 4.1 that Meleager ordered his *Garland* alphabetically. Additional confirmation has come from Axel Mattsson, *Untersuchungen zur Epigrammsammlung des Agathias* (Diss. Lund, 1942), reprinted in *The Greek Anthology* II, who showed that Agathias modeled his techniques of ordering through association on Meleager. Although Beckby I 63–64 follows older scholars in crediting the lemmatist, Gow-Page (1965) I xvii–xviii and Cameron (1968) 324–26, (1993) 19–33 accept the overwhelming evidence for a less mechanical arrangement.

6.134–145	Anacreon	7.507b–516	Simonides
6.146–150	Callimachus	7.517–525	Callimachus
6.151–154	Tymnes, Agis,	7.526	Nicander
	Anyte, and Leonidas		
6.155–157	Theodoridas	7.527–529	Theodoridas

The same rough chronological order in the grouping of poets is observable in each case: a pre-Hellenistic poet, Callimachus, solitary epigrammatists probably all of the third century, and then Theodoridas, who belongs to the second half of the third century.[69] These passages are further parallel in that they both occur at the end of long Meleagrian sections (6.110–157 and 7.406–529; see Table I). Since grouping by author rather than theme runs counter to the principles of order preferred by Meleager, it seems reasonable to assume that these passages were not part of Meleager's original anthology.[70] Direct evidence for this assumption is provided by the repetition of 6.146 after 6.274, where it fits thematically into a long sequence of Meleagrian authors; this second manuscript position, not the grouping with other Callimachean poems, clearly preserves Meleager's arrangement. It is also unlikely that Cephalas himself culled them from another collection, since the following sections of the *AP* seem to consist of Cephalan supplements and are derived from Philip and Agathias as well as Meleager with a quite different method of ordering.[71] In all likelihood, then, 6.134–157 and 7.507b–529 were supplements attached, probably in antiquity, to the ends of the dedicatory and sepulchral books of Meleager's *Garland*. Their source would be either single-authored editions or a multi-authored anthology in which epigrams were grouped by author.[72]

As evidence for the design of Hellenistic poetry books, these sequences are comparable to the papyrological extracts from the books of Mnasalces and Meleager or the new Posidippus papyrus, except that we must allow for the possibility that certain epigrams have been removed because they were already anthologized in the *Garland*. Even so, general principles of arrangement are again discernible. The first nine poems of the Anacreontic segment (6.134–142) and the first seven poems of the Simonidean segment (7.507b–513) are in alphabetical order.[73] Denys Page has pointed out that 6.133 by Archilochus,

---

69. The alternative ascription of 6.154 to Gaetulicus is unlikely; see Gow-Page (1965) II 393. For the date of Theodoridas, a contemporary of Euphorion and Mnasalces, see Wilhelm Seelbach, *Die Epigramme des Mnasalkes von Sikyon und des Theodoridas von Syrakus* in Klassisch-philologische Studien, 28 (Wiesbaden, 1964) 1–2 and Gow-Page (1965) II 537.

70. For this view, see Weisshäupl (1889) 26; Page (1981) 121, n. 2; Cameron (1993) 2.

71. See Lenzinger 7, 13.

72. The poems without companion pieces by the same epigrammatist (6.151–54 and 7.526) may either derive from some heterogeneous section in an ancient source or be a later intrusion.

73. *AP* 7.507 is a conflation of two epigrams and bears an ascription in P (the manuscript of the *AP*) to Simonides. Planudes, however, has only 7.507a with an ascription to Alexander,

beginning with an α, may belong to the same alphabetic series as the poems by Anacreon.[74] We may conclude that the epigrams by Archilochus, Anacreon, and Simonides were added to Meleager's *Garland* from an anthology of pre-Hellenistic epigrammatists, in which the poems were ordered alphabetically. This alphabetical ordering is a likely editorial practice for a scholarly edition.[75] I have argued elsewhere that alphabetization was the ordering principle for the first book of Theocritus' bucolic poems, probably edited in the late third or second century B.C. (an order reflected in the Laurentian family of manuscripts), and Alan Cameron has proposed that Philip later turned alphabetization into an art form by arranging epigrams thematically under the rubric of each letter.[76] But for this edition of pre-Hellenistic epigrammatists, which may have its roots (like the alphabetical sequence in P.Petrie II 49 b) in the scholarly collecting of the third century B.C., alphabetization provided a practical rather than an artistic approach to arrangement.

The Callimachean sequences present a different situation. Alphabetization is to some degree present, in four of the five poems from *AP* 6 (146–149) and in five of the nine poems from *AP* 7 (518–522). But the question arises whether these alphabetical sequences are significant, since chance alphabetization will inevitably occur in any such anthology. Given that ancient alphabetization was by first letter alone, it has been argued that alphabetical sequences of four or five epigrams are probably meaningless.[77] And even if these alphabetical sequences do reflect editorial design, should we assume that they were excerpted from a scholarly edition of Callimachus' epigrams or that they formed part of Callimachus' own epigram book? I would point out that Callimachus, the quintessential scholar-poet, was fond of extending his scholarly habits to his

---

who is apparently Alexander Aetolus, a Meleagrian author. As Page points out (1981) 4, the ascription to Simonides in P was probably transferred from the second couplet at the time of conflation, while the ascription of the first couplet to Alexander in Pl (the Venetian manuscript of *APl*) "is certainly not a guess and is not likely to be a corruption." Even though 7.507a, beginning with an α, would fit within the alphabetical Simonidean sequence, I think it more likely a poem by Alexander Aetolus occurring toward the end of the Meleagrian book of epitymbia, where it is thematically suited (see Chapter 6).

74. Page (1981) 147–48.

75. The *Dithyrambs* of Bacchylides are preserved on papyrus in alphabetical order by title; see Herwig Maehler, ed., *Bacchylidis carmina cum fragmentis* (Leipzig, 1970) ix. According to Edgar Lobel, Σαπφοῦς Μέλη (Oxford, 1925) xv, the odes in certain books of Sappho were likely arranged alphabetically. For additional examples of alphabetization of literary works by title or first word, see Daly 23–25, 41–44 and Blum 191–93.

76. Gutzwiller (1996a) 126–27; Cameron (1968) 331–349 and (1993) 33–43.

77. See Wifstrand 7; Gow-Page (1965) I xviii, n. 3. Luck (1967) 51–52 has suggested that brief alphabetical sequences of Meleagrian authors may be an indication of the original ordering principle, perhaps in the edition from which Meleager selected, but Cameron (1993) 20–21 argues that these sequences, in which epigrams tend to begin with the same word, are actually thematic arrangements, with a resulting appearance of alphabetization.

poetic pursuits. It is certainly within the realm of possibility that the aesthetic application of "scholarly" alphabetization found in Philip's *Garland* had a model in Callimachus' own collection.

Whether or not the alphabetization has any significance here, we should notice that another principle of arrangement, based on the voice speaking in the poem, seems to be at work as well.[78] *AP* 6.146 and 147 are addressed to the recipient deity by the dedicator, while 6.148 and 149 are spoken by the dedicatory object itself. Grouping in accordance with speakers is again found in the sepulchral epigrams. In 7.517–519 the first person plural verbs (ἐθάπτομεν, ἀεισόμεθα, ἐθάπτομεν) indicate that the speaking voice represents the community of mourners—an unusual phenomenon in grave inscriptions. The next series shows a perhaps meaningful variety:

7.520   tombstone (or poet?) speaks
7.521   tombstone speaks
7.522   passerby speaks
7.523   tombstone speaks
7.524   tombstone and passerby hold a dialogue

The couplet preserved as 7.523 is commonplace, and so rather inconsequential for the literary reader:

οἵτινες Ἀλείοιο παρέρπετε σᾶμα Κίμωνος,
    ἴστε τὸν Ἱππαίου παῖδα παρερχόμενοι.

(39 G-P)

Whoever walks past the tomb of Elian Cimon,
    know that you pass by the son of Hippaeus.

We may wonder why Callimachus published it, unless it was simply to hold a place in the final sequence of three, consisting of address to the stone, address to passersby, and then dialogue between the two. This sequence, constructed through a removal of 7.523 from its more logical grouping with 520 and 521, may deliberately highlight the dialogue in 7.524:

– ἦ ῥ᾽ ὑπὸ σοὶ Χαρίδας ἀναπαύεται; – Χ. εἰ τὸν Ἀρίμμα
    τοῦ Κυρηναίου παῖδα λέγεις, ὑπ᾽ ἐμοί.
– ὦ Χαρίδα, τί τὰ νέρθε; Χ. πολὺ σκότος. – αἱ δ᾽ ἄνοδοι τί;
    Χ. ψεῦδος. – ὁ δὲ Πλούτων; Χ. μῦθος. – ἀπωλόμεθα.
Χ. οὗτος ἐμὸς λόγος ὕμμιν ἀληθινός, εἰ δὲ τὸν ἡδύν
    βούλει, Πελλαίου βοῦς μέγας εἰν Ἀίδῃ.

(31 G-P)

---

78. That voice was a recognized means of creating variety in poetic arrangement is confirmed by Servius *ad Ecl*. 3.1, who in asserting the necessity of *variatio* in bucolic poetry differentiates three forms of address—narrative, dramatic, and mixed; see also Proleg. D to the bucolic scholia.

– Does Charidas rest under you? – If you mean
   the son of Cyrenaean Arimmas, he does.
– Charidas, what is below? Ch. Much darkness. – And what about return?
   Ch. A lie. – And Pluto? Ch. A myth. – We are lost.
Ch. I'm telling you the truth. But if you prefer a pleasant lie,
   a large ox can be had for only a Pellaean in Hades.

Here the passerby speaks through the stone to the deceased and so discovers the
truth about death, that despite popular belief it is in fact nothingness. Is this a
message that Callimachus himself finds congenial and so places in a position
of final emphasis within his collection? It is a question to which we will return in
a later chapter.

The possibility that the sequence is not haphazard, but constructed with
aesthetic design, is increased by the fact that the final poem, 7.525, is a fictional
epitaph for Callimachus' father, concluding with a statement of the Muse's favor
for the poet himself:

ὅστις ἐμὸν παρὰ σῆμα φέρεις πόδα Καλλιμάχου με
   ἴσθι Κυρηναίου παῖδά τε καὶ γενέτην.
εἰδείης δ' ἄμφω κεν· ὁ μέν ποτε πατρίδος ὅπλων
   ἦρξεν, ὁ δ' ἤεισεν κρέσσονα βασκανίης.
οὐ νέμεσις, Μοῦσαι γὰρ ὅσους ἴδον ὄμματι παῖδας
   μὴ λοξῷ πολιοὺς οὐκ ἀπέθεντο φίλους.

(29 G-P)

You who carry yourself past my tomb, know that
   I am both son and father of Cyrenean Callimachus.
You would know both of them. One commanded his country's
   arms, while the other sang beyond envy.
No wonder, for those children whom the Muses look upon with eyes not aslant
   they do not abandon as friends even when aged.

The final couplet, which is repeated in the Prologue to the *Aetia* (fr. 1.37–38 Pf.),
is inappropriate in a true epitaph but provides a meaningful conclusion to a
poetic sequence. In both form and substance it should be compared to the two
concluding lines of *Idyll* 9 (35–36), which probably ended an early collection
of "Theocritean" pastorals, and to the self-epitaph that likely closed Leonidas'
collection (93 G-P = *AP* 7.715). While the traces of contrived arrangement here
uncovered indicate that both 6.146–150 and 7.517–525 derive, though probably
with omissions, from Callimachus' own epigram book, the presence of the
epitaph for the poet's father with its programmatic reference to the Muses
suggests that the second sequence may preserve the conclusion to Callimachus'
collection or at least to the sepulchral portion of it.[79]

79. Wilamowitz (1913) 299 suggested that this poem stood in the collection beside Cal-
limachus' self-epitaph (30 G-P = *AP* 7.415). Since the self-epitaph appears in the *AP* in a

Before leaving these *Garland* extracts, we should comment briefly on the three poems by Theodoridas that conclude each supplement to Meleager's *Garland*. Although our sample is small, the poems do appear to be arranged by topic. *AP* 6.155 and 156 are both dedications of hair by boys, while 7.527 and 528 both concern premature deaths—of a young man before marriage and a young woman during the birth of her first child. The parallelism of the two sequences as a whole, as well as the internal pairing of poems by topic, suggests that these epigrams of Theodoridas may descend from a collected format.[80]

One single-authored epigram book survives intact in manuscript form—the Theocritus collection preserved in the Ambrosian family of manuscripts. By all indications, however, this assemblage of epigrams attributed to Theocritus— some falsely as universally agreed—was compiled by a posthumous editor, not by the author himself. Theocritus' epigrams were apparently unknown to Meleager, who would surely have mentioned so famous a poet in his preamble if he had included any of his epigrammatic compositions in the *Garland*. His omission of the Theocritean epigrams is confirmed by the fact that those epigrams attributed to Theocritus in the *Anthology* tend to be outside of or on the fringes of the Meleagrian sequences. The early decades of the first century B.C. is thus the earliest possible date for a publicly issued compilation of Theocritus' epigrams, and it was about 70 B.C. that Artemidorus gathered "the previously scattered bucolic Muses" (26.1 Gow = *AP* 9.205.1)—that is, the poetry of Theocritus and perhaps other bucolic poets—into one comprehensive edition.[81] Since in this period the bucolic genre was marked, not by rustic content, but by the identification of the poet with a βουκόλος, "cowherd,"[82] there is no reason to suppose that Artemidorus excluded epigrams or selected only those on rustic themes.[83] But whether or not Artemidorus included Theocritus'

Meleagrian sequence, it seems likely that Meleager anthologized only that poem and then later for another compilation the epitaph for Callimachus' father was excerpted as part of a sequence taken in order (with omissions for poems already excerpted) from the original Callimachean collection.

80. For a discussion of Theodoridas' epigrams, see M. Gigante, "Teodorida di Siracusa nella storia dell'epigramma ellenistico," *A&R* 23 (1988) 123–42; for commentary on the individual poems, see Seelbach 65–127.

81. See Wilamowitz, ed., *Bucolici Graeci*, (Oxford, 1905) iii–v; *Die Textgeschichte der griechischen Bukoliker* (Berlin, 1906) 124–26.

82. See Carlo Gallavotti, ed., *Theocritus quique feruntur bucolici Graeci*, 3rd ed. (Rome, 1993) #13; Kathryn J. Gutzwiller, *Theocritus' Pastoral Analogies: The Formation of a Genre* (Madison, 1991) 177–79.

83. As assumed by Robert J. Smutny, "The Text History of the Epigrams of Theocritus," *University of California Publications in Classical Philology* 15.2 (Berkeley, 1955) 69, who limits Artemidorus' edition to epigrams 1–6. The citation of Theocritus' "epigrams" in a Homeric vita (Thomas Allen, *Homeri opera* [Oxford, 1912] *vita* VI, p. 250) offers no evidence at all for a collection of Theocritus' epigrams. Since the phrase ἐν τοῖς ἐπιγράμμασιν is omitted in one of the two manuscripts, it is likely an interpolation, and perhaps a misunderstanding of the

epigrams in his edition, Vergil's imitation of the first epigram both at the beginning of the first *Eclogue* (1.7–8) and at the opening of the rustic song in the third (3.62–63) gives evidence that the collection existed more or less as we have it by circa 40 B.C.[84]

The artistic unity of the sequence of twenty-two epigrams preserved in the bucolic manuscripts indicates that it was compiled by an editor working in the tradition of Hellenistic epigram books. The compilation falls into three distinct sections: epigrams on bucolic themes (1–6), dedicatory and sepulchral epigrams (7–16), and epigrams in diverse meters (17–22).[85] The compromises that had to be made in order to create a cohesive whole from an inherited and motley body of poetry are illustrated by the presence of 20—an epitaph for a Thracian nurse in hendecasyllables and Archilochians—not among the sepulchral epigrams, but among the poems in diverse meters, which otherwise all concern literary greats. Yet even this apparent inconsistency in topic contributes to the organic unity of the collection, for, by the placement of the Cleita poem, the first and third sections come to balance each other in length, each consisting of six epigrams. These two most distinctly Theocritean sections then surround a larger core of inscriptional epigrams less marked by authorial individuality.

While the division into three parts has been observed by others, the editor's skillful ordering within sections has been inadequately appreciated. The opening poem, generally explained as an ecphrastic description for a relief or painting, clearly substitutes for the traditional invocation to the deities who inspire poetry:[86]

---

reference (to *Id.* 7.47?). But even if original, the phrase may refer to a group of epigrams known from any sort of collection, not necessarily from an epigram book.

84. For the significance of the imitations with reference to dating the collection, see K. Gutzwiller, "Vergil and the Date of the Theocritean Epigram Book," *Philologus* 140 (1996) 92–99. For a later dating to the imperial period, see G. Tarditi, "Per una lettura degli epigrammatisti greci," *Aevum Antiquum* 1 (1988) 46–47 and A. Porro, "L'epigramma XI della silloge teocritea: problemi di cronologia," *Aevum Antiquum* 2 (1989) 238–43.

85. Although it is conceivable that 23, 24, or (less likely) 25 Gow, all preserved in the *Anthology* but not in the Theocritean manuscripts, originally came from the same epigram collection, the evidence from transmission does not speak in favor of it. The confusion in ascription between Theocritus and Leonidas in *AP* 7.654–65 is a thornier problem. W. C. Helmbold, "The Epigrams of Theocritus," *CP* 33 (1938) 47–54 argued that 9, 15, and 16 Gow were not by Theocritus and came into the sylloge from the *Anthology*. But both Gow (1952) II 525–27 and Smutny 72–77 have offered convincing refutation of the theory. In fact, a comparison of the order of the twenty-two epigrams in the bucolic manuscripts with the order of the same poems in the *AP* provides an excellent example of the method by which epigram collections were dismembered and distributed in the *Anthology*; see Smutny 63–65, Gow-Page (1965) II 525.

86. For the theory that the epigram is an ecphrastic description, see Wilamowitz (1906) 120; Gow (1952) II 527–28; Gow-Page (1965) II 528. But on the prooemial use of the epigram, see Tarditi 47. The first four poems in the *Theognidea* (1–18)—two prayers to Apollo, one to Artemis, and another to the Muses and Graces—provide a parallel for the placement of such

τὰ ῥόδα τὰ δροσόεντα καὶ ἁ κατάπυκνος ἐκείνα
  ἕρπυλλος κεῖται ταῖς Ἑλικωνιάσιν·
ταὶ δὲ μελάμφυλλοι δάφναι τίν, Πύθιε Παιάν,
  Δελφὶς ἐπεὶ πέτρα τοῦτό τοι ἀγλάϊσεν·
βωμὸν δ' αἱμάξει κεραὸς τράγος οὗτος ὁ μαλός
  τερμίνθου τρώγων ἔσχατον ἀκρεμόνα.

(1 Gow = 5 G-P = *AP* 6.336)

These dewy roses and that thick creeping thyme
  are dedicated to the Heliconian Muses.
These dark leaves of laurel are for you, Pythian Apollo,
  since they grow in abundance on your Delphic rock.
This white, horned goat will bloody your altar,
  the one gnawing the tips of the terebinth branch.

The use of vegetable symbolism in a preamble to characterize the collected epigrams seems to go back to the third century B.C. The epigram that apparently introduced Nossis' collection alludes to the Sapphic identification of poetry with roses (1 G-P = *AP* 5.170), and we may legitimately wonder if Posidippus' *Soros* did not take its title from a listing of grains or similar materials at the opening of that collection. Post-Meleagrian readers would easily interpret the roses and thyme offered to the Muses and the laurel offered to Apollo as symbols of the poems within the collection, just as the plants mentioned in Meleager's preamble stand for the epigrammatists in his anthology. The sacrificial goat, on the other hand, points to the author's identification with a herdsman and prepares the way for the bucolic epigrams that follow. Once we recognize that the first Theocritean epigram draws on a tradition of literary symbolism, derived both from other epigram collections and from bucolic poetry, we must question the circumstances under which the epigram was composed. I do not believe it was written by Theocritus, both because of its programmatic position in a collection not edited by the author and, more subjectively, because it seems unworthy of him. Was it, then, composed by the editor of the collection to serve as a preamble, just as the spurious *Idylls* 8 and 9 were apparently written to conclude a posthumous collection of Theocritus' pastoral *Idylls*?

The entire first section displays a linear arrangement that progresses by thematic linkage from poem to poem. The second epigram is, like the first, a dedication, but in subject—Daphnis' offering to Pan—it looks forward to 3, where Pan and Priapus attempt an assault on Daphnis. The fourth poem moves the sexual theme from the gods to the world of a herdsman, who prays for relief from his passion for Daphnis. Music-making with Daphnis is the theme of 5, again narrated by a rustic. The imitation of *Idyll* 1 in the fifth epigram (λῇς ποτὶ

---

appropriate material at the head of a collection by a Hellenistic editor; on which, see West (1974) 42. Cf. as well the four poems on deities that head the series of Attic scolia preserved by Athenaeus (15.694c–d = 884–87 *PMG*).

τᾶν Νυμφᾶν, 5.1 and spoken by Thyrsis in *Id.* 1.12) prepares for 6, which features, not now Daphnis, but Thyrsis mourning the loss of a kid. Not only does the elegiac theme act as a closure device for the bucolic section, but it also provides a bridge to 7, an epitaph for Eurymedon that heads the inscriptional group.

This second section is ordered, like the epigram sequence from Mnasalces' book, by varying both inscriptional type and gender of subject. The relevant information may be presented schematically: 7, epitaph; 8, dedication; 9, epitaph; 10, dedication; 11, epitaph; 12, dedication by male; 13, dedication by a female; 14, a trade sign for a banker; 15, epitaph for male; 16, epitaph for female. The editor has cleverly provided variety to eliminate the tedium that can take hold when reading a sequence of inscriptions on unknown persons. The simple alternation of epitaph and dedication slides at 12 into a different pattern, in which dedications for a male and a female (12, 13) and epitaphs for a male and a female (15, 16) surround the one unusual inscription, the trade sign.[87] In addition, we may observe that 11, in which the epigrammatist himself is mentioned (χὐμνοθέτης, 11.4), falls at the end of the collection's first half and is suggestively surrounded by epigrams on a musician's dedication to the Muses and a choral victor's dedication to Dionysus.

The last section in diverse meters is more simply organized, two pairs of epigrams on statues (17 and 18, 21 and 22) surrounding a pair of epitaphs (19 and 20). The penultimate poem, on Archilochus, includes a reference to the Muses and Apollo (21.4) and so harks back to the opening epigram. We may wonder, then, why the epigram on Pisander was chosen to close the collection. The editor may have considered Pisander, who wrote an epic on Heracles, a suitable surrogate for Theocritus, who also celebrated Heracles as an ancestor of the Ptolemies (*Id.* 17.20–33, *Id.* 24). Another factor may have been the appropriateness of closing the collection with a reference to a bronze statue of a poet. The editor of the epigram collection, limited in his choice of a closing poem to those handed down under the name of Theocritus, placed at the end the one that suggested, even if only by metonymy, the everlasting fame of his epigrammatist. In doing so, he may, again, be following the precedent of earlier epigram collections. The self-epitaph that probably closed Leonidas' collection ends with a claim to poetic immortality (93 G-P = *AP* 7.715), and we may also think of the conclusion of Horace's third book of *Odes*, where he claims to have erected "a monument more lasting than bronze" (*exegi monumentum aere perennius*, 3.30.1).

We find within the three sections of the Theocritean collection patterns of arrangement that are simultaneously orderly and varied—patterns perhaps derived from earlier epigram books known to the compiler. The first section, ordered by associative bridging, presupposes the reader's knowledge of the

---

87. Cf. the advertisement for an omen-taker found on the new Posidippus papyrus (4).

epigrammatist's literary persona, his identification with a βουκόλος, or cowherd. It finds parallels in single-authored epigram books that projected a distinct literary personality as the creative force behind the collection. The second section shows the same kind of organization, with variation by gender and epigram type, that we found in the Mnasalces extract. The final section of epigrams in diverse meters has a parallel in the thirteenth book of the *AP*, a collection of thirty-one epigrams in nonelegiac meters. Since all its epigrams except one, the opening dedication to Aphrodite by Philip, are attributed to authors who preceded Meleager, the collection probably dates to the Julio-Claudian period.[88] It is not far distant in date, then, from the collection of Theocritean epigrams.

In the early decades of the third century B.C., poets began to modify their craft by combining literary composition with editorial technique. While poetry was still composed for the occasion or, in the case of some epigrams, for inscription, the secondary audience of readers had in the course of the fourth century become as important as, if not more important than, the primary audience of listeners or observers. As a result, the poets of this era, some of whom had honed their skills as editors of the great literature of the past, turned their scholarly practices to artistic purpose and invented the poetry book. Among the earliest of these poetry books were, in all likelihood, collections of epigrams. The collection entitled *Miscellaneous Epigrams*, dedicated to Arsinoe, proves that epigram books existed as early as the 280s or 270s. While Philetas and Theocritus seem not to have published their epigrams in separate books, the surviving epigrams of Asclepiades, Anyte, Leonidas, and Nossis, all probably working in the first quarter of the century, indicate that their innovations, which served as models for epigrammatists in centuries to come, could only have taken place within the context of epigram collections. The Milan papyrus now provides us with an example of an epigram collection, though perhaps not an author-ordered one, produced before the end of the third century B.C.

In preparation for reading these epigrams as book poetry, we have examined the papyrological and manuscript record to determine the principles of arrangement and techniques of significant placement that were used in Hellenistic epigram books. For scholarly editions of earlier poetry, practicality determined the criteria for arrangement, and we know of editions ordered on the principles of meter, occasion, and alphabetization. But for books of their own poetry,

---

88. P. Wolters, "De Constantini Cephalae anthologia," *RhM* 38 (1883) 110–13 and, in more detail, G. Morelli, "Origini e formazione del tredicesimo libro dell'*Antologia Palatina*," *RFIC* 113 (1985) 257–96 argue for an earlier version of the collection in the second half of the second or the first half of the first century B.C. For the view that *AP* 13 was first formed in the imperial period, see B. M. Palumbo Stracca, "Le note metriche di *A. P.* XIII e la genesi del libro," *BollClass* 5 (1984) 76–78 and Cameron (1993) 143.

Hellenistic epigrammatists developed much more imaginative designs. The surviving sequences from the epigram books of Callimachus and Mnasalces show the presentation of individual epigrams, each of which is by nature specific and final, not as a repetitive catalogue, but in associative patterns that point up similarities and contrasts and so encourage the reader to extract larger poetic meanings. At the present time we know that the Posidippus collection on the Milan papyrus was organized into sections by topic, but we cannot yet tell whether the editor employed any more interesting techniques of arrangement. The complexity of pattern evident in the Theocritus collection, its multiple strategies for achieving unity amid diversity conceived by a nonauthorial editor, indicate that in the course of the Hellenistic period artistic design had become an expected part of editorial practice.

Despite several papyri containing epigrams by more than one poet, there is no certain proof of a publicly issued, artistically constructed anthology before Meleager's *Garland*. The papyri that are certainly from anthologies all date to the first century B.C. or later, while neither of the third-century papyri possibly from multi-authored collections—*Miscellaneous Epigrams* (P.Petrie II 49 a) and the unpublished list of incipits (P.Vindob G 40611)—can be definitely shown to contain epigrams by more than one poet. But it is unlikely that Meleager invented the epigram anthology and much more probable that he synthesized to a new artistic whole techniques of arrangement developed from as early as the third century B.C. It appears that in multi-authored anthologies variety was achieved by change in authorship from poem to poem while cohesion resulted from similarity of formal type, from grouping epigrams on the same subject (as in the new Posidippus collection), or from juxtaposing poems that varied a single theme. Meleager's success lay in the sophistication with which he employed these preexisting techniques.

CHAPTER THREE

The Third Century:
From Stone to Book

In the archaic and classical ages inscribed epigrams were an integral part of the monuments and votive offerings that served to commemorate the praiseworthy acts of individuals. The Greek society accustomed to enjoy poetic compositions in a public or private act of oral performance showed little or no curiosity about the authors of verse inscriptions. But toward the end of the fifth century and throughout the fourth, a period of time during which written documents came to be valued for their contents as well as for their symbolic meaning,[1] epigrams were sometimes copied from their sites of inscription and quoted within various kinds of documents. In these new contexts, separated from the physical locations where they performed their functions of commemoration and praise, epigrams began to be perceived as literary texts, objects of aesthetic worth,[2] composed by authors with individual and distinct styles and beliefs.

The history of the word ἐπίγραμμα points to the process by which epigrams were incorporated into the canon of literary texts. In authors of the fifth century an ἐπίγραμμα was simply an inscribed text, often a verse inscription. Herodotus (5.59–61, 7.228) and Thucydides (6.54, 6.59) quote metrical dedications and epitaphs, not for their intrinsic literary worth, but as historical evidence or to commemorate significant events. The direct denotative link between ἐπίγραμμα and physical inscription is suggested by Thucydides' use of the alternative term τὸ ἐλεγεῖον, "elegiac couplet," to designate a couplet inscribed by Pausanias on a tripod at Delphi but later erased by the Spartans (1.132); a verse that no longer possessed a site of inscription was more properly described by its metrical form

---

1. See Thomas (1989) 45–94.
2. For the process of change in aesthetic evaluation, see Jan Mukarovsky, *Aesthetic Function, Norm and Value as Social Facts*, trans. by Mark E. Suino (Ann Arbor, 1979) and Barbara Herrnstein Smith, *Contingencies of Value: Alternative Perspectives for Critical Theory* (Cambridge, Mass., 1988).

than as an epigram.[3] Nor did the use of this terminology change significantly in the fourth century. Plato (*Phdr.* 264c–d) quotes an "epigram" that obviously circulated orally, yet designates it as the one "they say is engraved (ἐπιγεγράφθαι) over the Phrygian Midas." So soon, the orators offer ἐπιγράμματα as evidence in court cases (Dem. *De Cor.* 289, *Lept.* 112; Aeschin. *In Ctes.* 190) precisely because inscription on stone lends credibility to their testimony of past events. But half a century later the term ἐπίγραμμα no longer had a strict connection with actual inscription; it could then apply to any short poem that mimicked in some way the typical qualities of inscribed verse. Concrete evidence for this change in meaning is provided by the title σύμμεικτα ἐπιγράμματα attached to a collection of poetry that is to be dated no later than 274 B.C. (P.Petrie II 49 a). From the next decade we have an inscription (*IG* 9².I.17.24) designating Posidippus an ἐπιγραμματοποιός, a term constructed in parallel to words like ἐλεγειοποιός or μελοποιός referring to composers of literary forms.

The conceptualization of epigram as a literary kind, documentable for the first half of the third century, had its roots in a growing interest in the authorship of epigrammatic compositions traceable throughout the fourth century. While the great majority of inscribed epigrams continue to be anonymous, we do find fourth-century instances of author's names attached to verse inscriptions.[4] At a Letöon near the city of Xanthus in Lycia, two hexameter inscriptions honoring the Lycian ruler Arbinas, engraved shortly after 400 B.C., are followed by two-line verse signatures, naming as the composers the seer Symmachus from Pellana (*CEG*² 888.18–19) and a gymnastic trainer whose name is now lost (889.7–8).[5] In the second half of the fourth century, Ion of Samos, an otherwise unknown poet, composed two elegiac epigrams that were added to statues erected by Lysander at Delphi after his victory at Aegospotami.[6] In one epigram Ion names himself in the first line (*CEG*² 819.5), while he attached to another a metrical signature (ἐξάμο ἀμφιρύτας τεῦξε ἐλεγεῖον Ἴων, "Ion from sea-girt Samos composed the elegy," 819.13). This cluster of author's names on stone confirms our impression that during the fourth century epigrams came to be viewed as aesthetically valued texts for which the composers wished to be known and remembered.

---

3. This interpretation of the passage is supported by Pl. *Hipparch.* 228d, where τὸ ἐλεγεῖον clearly refers to the metrical form of an inscription. On the relationship between elegy and epigram, see West (1974) 2–21 and R. L. Fowler, *The Nature of Early Greek Lyric* (Toronto, 1987) 97–100.

4. For poetic signatures in addition to those discussed below, see Hansen, *CEG*² ad 888ii.

5. It seems significant that the poem by Symmachus was inscribed as an offering of the poet himself some time after the death of Arbinas, who dedicated the monuments; see J. Bousquet, "Arbinas, fils de Gergis, dynaste de Xanthos," *CRAI* (1975) 147.

6. For the dating on epigraphical grounds, see Russell Meiggs and David Lewis, *A Selection of Greek Historical Inscriptions*, 2nd ed. (Oxford, 1988) 288 and Hansen (1989) 224 with scholarship cited there.

During the same time period anonymously inscribed epigrams began to be assigned to specific authors, because of a perceived fit with historical circumstance or personal character. While Meleager later included in his *Garland* epigrams attributed to a number of pre-Hellenistic poets, the principal figure whose poetry was recovered from stone was Simonides. Already in the fifth century Herodotus had quoted an epitaph that Simonides set up as a mark of friendship for the seer Megistias who died at Thermopylae (7.228). Although the term used by Herodotus, ὁ ἐπιγράψας, indicates merely the commissioning of the verses' inscription, Simonides was in all probability the author of the epigram.[7] Since accurate memory for a span of more than three generations is unlikely, in the fourth century and later there occurred many false ascriptions of epigrams on the basis of historical reference and style to famous poets like Simonides and Anacreon. The time frame for the beginning of this process is indicated by the Archedice epitaph ("Sim." 26a *FGE*), quoted anonymously by Thucydides (6.59) but attributed to Simonides by Aristotle (*Rh.* 1.9.20, 1367b). Similarly, an epigram that had been preserved in the Corinthian temple to Aphrodite since the Persian Wars ("Sim." 14 *FGE*) was first quoted by Theopompus, apparently anonymously, and then in the early third century attributed to Simonides by Timaeus.[8] Another example of the process by which epigrams became attached to the name of Simonides is provided by an inscription for an Olympian victor anonymously cited by Aristotle directly before his attribution of the Archedice epigram to Simonides ("Sim." 41 *FGE*). The later claim of Simonidean authorship for the epigram on the athletic victory surely derives simply from its proximity in Aristotle's text.

Another source for the assignment of epigrams, both inscriptional and non-inscriptional, to an author like Simonides was Peripatetic literary biography. These biographies, existing from the late fourth century, consisted largely of anecdotal information substantiated by quotations of memorable remarks or passages from literature. Chamaeleon, who dates to the late fourth and early third centuries, quoted extemporized poetic verses in his biographical treatise on Simonides (Περὶ Σιμωνίδου; see Ath. 10.456c, 14.656c–d). Likewise, the second-century scholar Callistratus quotes a six-line poem expressly termed an epigram that Simonides supposedly improvised at a symposium (Ath. 3.125c–d = "Sim." 88 *FGE*). The poem, a pointed comment made when a servant offered others ice for their wine but neglected the poet's cup, is almost certainly a Hellenistic product. As a further example, Page surmises that two Simonidean epitaphs preserved in the *Anthology* ("Sim." 84 *FGE* = *AP* 7.516, 85 = *AP* 7.77)

7. Page (1981) 196 attributes Herodotus' knowledge of the epigram to the Spartan oral tradition about the battle at Thermopylae; see also S. West, "Herodotus' Epigraphical Interests," *CQ* 35 (1985) 287–89.

8. For excellent discussion of the complicated evidence for the early ascription of this epigram to Simonides, see Boas (1905) 47–70; cf. Page (1981) 207–10.

were composed by some biographical source "to add colour and verisimilitude to an anecdote about a famous man":[9] Simonides' life was supposedly saved when the ghost of a shipwrecked man he had buried warned him about sailing on a doomed ship. Another example of spurious epigrams preserved or promoted through biography is Diogenes Laertius' quotation of several erotic epigrams by Plato from a work called περὶ παλαιᾶς τρυφῆς, "On Ancient Luxury," authored by a certain Aristippus (3.29–32). This Aristippus, whose name is perhaps a pseudonym suggesting a connection with the hedonistic philosopher, supported his claims for Plato's various erotic relationships through his quotation of epigrams attributed to the philosopher.[10] We clearly have moved a long way from the anonymity of earlier inscriptional verse when in the course of the Hellenistic period authors came to compose spurious epigrams in an attempt to illustrate the personal habits and character traits of individual poets.

This brings us to the question of the so-called *sylloge Simonidea*, a collection of Simonidean epigrams gathered from stone or literary texts, which Reitzenstein placed in the fourth century.[11] The date of the collection is important for the project at hand, because the Simonidean sylloge has been cited as a model for the earliest Hellenistic epigram books edited by the authors themselves. Later scholars have cast doubt on Reitzenstein's early dating. Boas argued that Timaeus' citation of the Corinthian epigram is our earliest evidence for this sylloge, which he then dates to about 310 B.C.[12] Page has since pointed out the large number of Hellenistic compositions among the ninety or so poems assigned to Simonides; he concludes that either the sylloge was formed somewhat later in the Hellenistic period or a collection existing at the beginning of the third century was supplemented by later compositions assigned to Simonides.[13] To my mind, the most likely scenario is an evolving collection or collections, perhaps initiated in the fourth century, more certainly edited and ordered by third-century Alexandrian scholars, and gathering accretions throughout the third and second centuries. Such a concept of evolution helps to account for complicated patterns of imitation that have been observed: third-century epigrammatists sometimes seem to be influenced by classical models and sometimes seem themselves to provide the models for epigrams spuriously ascribed to pre-Hellenistic poets.[14]

9. Page (1981) 299; for a thorough discussion of the sources, see Boas (1905) 98–101.

10. On Aristippus, see Page (1981) 126–27.

11. Reitzenstein (1893) 116.

12. Boas (1905) 73–74.

13. In his later discussion, Page (1981) 122–23 inclines to the latter alternative, although earlier, in *Epigrammata Graeca* (Oxford, 1975) vi–vii, he preferred a dating in the third or even the second century for the sylloge.

14. While Reitzenstein (1893) 135 claimed that the Peloponnesian school had imitated the Simonidean sylloge, Boas (1905) 208–22 showed that most of the Simonidean epigrams in question were Hellenistic compositions and so actually imitations of the Peloponnesian

No one seriously doubts that Meleager, who cites Simonides among the forty-seven epigrammmatists included in his *Garland*, drew his Simonidean epigrams from a collection. How much earlier did the sylloge exist? There is no reason to assume, with Boas, that Timaeus' ascription of the Corinthian epigram to Simonides (Ath. 13.573c–d) presupposes the existence of a collection. Because of the erotic symbolism of the epigram ("Sim." 14 *FGE*)—Corinthian women, either matrons or prostitutes, ask Aphrodite to inspire their men with *eros* to combat the Persians—the attribution could easily have come from one of those Peripatetic researchers who assigned epigrams to Simonides in anecdotal contexts. But I do believe that a *terminus ante quem* for the Simonidean collection is provided by the explication of Aristophanes of Byzantium on the rare word ἄσιλλα (Eust. *Od.* 1761.25), found in an epigram on an Olympian victory cited anonymously by Aristotle (41 *FGE*) but known as Simonidean to Aristophanes.[15] A writer of commentaries on major Greek poets and a pupil of Aristarchus, Aristophanes was no doubt commenting on the text of a Simonidean sylloge edited by third-century Alexandrian scholars.[16] Since epigram had acquired the status of a recognized literary category by at least the 270s, we may safely assume that epigrams attributed to Simonides would have been sought out and properly ordered no later than the time of Callimachus' *Pinakes*. While epigrams attributed to Simonides were to be found quoted in various texts by this time, the Alexandrians may also have had access to compilations made directly from stone. A parallel is provided by Philochorus' *Attic Epigrams* (*Suda s. v.* Φιλόχορος), formed sometime between the late fourth century and about 260 B.C.

The alphabetical sequences of epigrams attributed to Anacreon and Simonides in *AP* 6 and 7 are, in all likelihood, remnants of the Alexandrian editions from which Meleager selected.[17] As we saw in the last chapter, they are not sequences from the *Garland* but, more probably, supplements to it constructed from the unanthologized portions of Meleager's source. The dates of the epigrams in these sequences may, then, provide evidence for the period in which the collections were formed. The alphabetical sequence attributed to Anacreon (6.134–42) consists, apart from the initial poem, of single couplets which celebrate dedications in the austere style typical of the archaic and early classical eras. But the first poem (6.134)—an ecphrastic quatrain describing three Bacchae—is almost certainly a Hellenistic composition. Only by explaining its inclusion in the alphabetized sequence as an accident of its position can

---

epigrammatists. In a satirical epitaph (15 G-P = *AP* 13.21) Theodoridas criticized Mnasalces for bombastic, even "dithyrambic," imitations of Simonides.

15. An ἄσιλλα was a yoke set on the shoulders with baskets hanging to the right and left for carrying such items as fish; see Page (1981) *ad loc.*

16. So Boas (1905) 70.

17. Page (1981) 121, 279 refers to the Simonides sequence in 7.507b–516 both as "Meleager's source" and, more explicitly, as the "*Sylloge Simonidea.*"

we make a case for a fourth-century compilation of the Anacreon collection. No such special pleading can place the Simonidean sequence (7.507b–513) before the third century. A memorial erected by a deceased's friend (7.509) and an epitaph for Tegean warriors (7.512) are perhaps genuine inscriptions of the fifth or fourth centuries, while the first-person statement of mourning in 7.511 is likely detached from an elegiac *threnos*, perhaps of the classical era. Page assigned both 7.507b, on a young man who died before marriage, and 7.510, on a Chian who perished at sea, to the Hellenistic age,[18] but arguments for an earlier date are not out of the question. The insipid 7.513, containing a son's dying words, however, is almost certainly an imitation of a much better epigram by Anyte (7 G-P = *AP* 7.646). In addition, 7.508, an epitaph for a doctor named Pausanias, clearly dates the sequence to a period after the fourth century. Diogenes Laertius (8.60–61) attributes the same epigram (with the nonepitaphic wording ἔθρεψε Γέλα replacing ἔθαψε Γέλα) to Empedocles, who was supposedly the lover of this Pausanias. Page, following Boas, has persuasively argued that the epigram, whose first line echoes the opening of Empedocles' *On Nature*, was originally composed to illustrate the life of Empedocles; it was derived both by the compiler of the Simonidean sylloge (who converted it to an epitaph to fit the poetic persona of Simonides) and by Diogenes' source (Satyrus) from "a biographical essay written in the fourth century B.C. (or early in the third)."[19] The Pausanias epigram is firmly embedded in the alphabetical sequence even to the extent that its final hemistich (Φερσεφόνης θαλάμων, changed from the Φερσεφόνης ἀδύτων of the Empedocles version) echoes the conclusion of the previous epigram (Φερσεφόνης θάλαμον). We may conclude, then, that the alphabetical sequences attributed to Anacreon and Simonides came from scholarly editions formed no earlier than the first half of the third century B.C. That smaller, less formal compilations lay behind this alphabetical one is highly likely, but not provable through existing evidence.

Toward the end of the fourth century and at the beginning of the third, epigrams began to be conceptualized as a literary kind, as aesthetic products produced by specific authors whose individuality was conveyed by the style or sentiment of the poems. Anonymous inscriptions found their way into literary texts, where, often through a process of quotation and requotation, they were attributed to a known poet of an earlier era. Eventually, the epigrams ascribed to Simonides and Anacreon were gathered into editions,[20] where the individualizing traits of the authors, those that were often the basis for

18. Page (1981) 293, 298.

19. Page (1981) 152–53; cf. Boas (1905) 124–29.

20. Epigrams attributed to other pre-Hellenistic poets included in Meleager's *Garland*— such as Archilochus, Sappho, and Bacchylides—were probably edited in an anthology of various poets or grouped with other types of poetry in the editions of these authors; cf. West (1974) 20.

ascription, could be construed by the reader as a poetic persona. It was against this background that Hellenistic epigrammatists began to compose epigrams, not solely for inscriptional purposes, but as sophisticated vehicles for literary expression. Given the ease with which epigrams move from context to context, we may assume that these more "bookish" epigrams circulated in a variety of ways, including small, private compilations as well as more formal collections consisting either solely of epigrams or of epigrams in combination with other types of poetry. The attribution of actual inscriptions to poets like Simonides and Anacreon and the composition of spuriously ascribed epigrams was surely an important influence upon the development of Hellenistic epigram as a literary type; but, as I have argued, the advent of the poetry book likely involved more than imitation of a Simonidean sylloge. We should think instead of a creative interaction between scholarly practice and poetic originality.

The three epigrammatists treated in this chapter—Anyte, Nossis, and Leonidas—participated in the process of remaking the briefest of poetic forms into high art by refocusing it, away from its traditional subjects, toward marginal figures and themes.[21] This refocusing became possible only with the development of personalized personae for the individual epigrammatists. Anyte gave meaning and coherency to her innovative choice of subject matter—children, women, animals, inhabitants of isolated country districts—by presenting herself as a woman from Arcadia. Nossis also created within her epigram book a distinct poetic world specific as to gender, class, and place, and she did so, like Anyte, by self-definition, by presenting the limited perspective that she herself held as a female aristocrat from Epizephyrian Locri. In his one hundred or so surviving epigrams, Leonidas exhibits a clear preference for working-class subjects and advances a philosophy of life that commends simplicity and self-sufficiency. Whatever were the historical realities of Leonidas' life, within his collection he projects the poetic persona of a man who, sadly separated from his native Tarentum, shares the poverty-stricken existence of his favorite subjects. As our discussion of these epigrammatists will illustrate, the birth of the epigram book was occasioned by the social and political realities of the third century, a time when individuals found stability in local allegiance, in commonality of gender and class, in affiliations based on friendship rather than family—in short, in whatever fragile bonds could be formed by rootless and decentered selves.

21. Anyte, Nossis, and Leonidas were associated by Reitzenstein (1893) 121–23 as members of the so-called Peloponnesian school; for the characteristics of this school, see Beckby I 20–25 and E. Degani, "L'epigramma" in *Lo spazio letterario della Grecia antica* I.2, ed. G. Cambiano, L. Canfora, D. Lanza (Rome, 1993) 207–12. While I resist the notion that these poets formed any kind of school on the basis of either geographical location or poetic ideology, I group them because they worked only with inscriptional types of epigrams—that is, they did not draw as well upon the tradition of sympotic elegy, as did certain epigrammatists concentrated in Alexandria.

ANYTE

A native of Tegea in Arcadia, Anyte belongs to the first generation of Hellenistic poets.[22] She may have been a lyric poet as well as an epigrammatist,[23] but only her epigrams survive—all dedicatory, sepulchral, or descriptive in type. Several factors indicate that Anyte issued her epigrams in book format, whether as a collection consisting solely of epigrams or in combination with lost lyric poems.[24] Certain of her epigrams could scarcely have been inscriptional, and her sophisticated use of language in even her most traditional poetry indicates a high degree of poetic self-consciousness.[25] In addition, the fairly large number of epigrams preserved for us (twenty-four, of which I consider 1–20 G-P to be genuine)[26] suggests that Meleager had at his disposal a collection from which he anthologized. The fact that all but one of these are composed as quatrains suggests that Anyte employed uniformity in length as a means of providing formal coherency. We have already observed that Anyte's most faithful imitator, Mnasalces (writing perhaps as early as 250 B.C.) appears to have issued an epigram collection in quatrains that skillfully intermingled sepulchral and dedicatory epigrams through associative bridging and variation of subject and type. Such techniques of arrangement may well descend from the collections of earlier epigrammatists, among them, prominently, Anyte.

Anyte is most famous for her descriptive epigrams, which introduced rural or, from a later perspective, pastoral themes into the genre, and as a composer of

22. Tegea is named as Anyte's homeland by both Pollux 5.48 and Stephanus Byzantinus, *s. v.* Τεγέα (where the manuscript reading Αὐγή is commonly changed to Ἀνύτη). The early dating of her *floruit* to about 300 B.C. is based primarily on her style and the apparent imitation of her poetry by Nicias and Mnasalces, pointed out by Reitzenstein (1893) 123–27. Confirmation for this dating comes from the report of Tatian, *Or. ad Graecos* 33 that Euthycrates and Cephisodotus made statues of her. Discussion of the evidence for her homeland and date may be found in Gow-Page (1965) II 89–90, and texts of the testimonia are cited in D. Geoghegan, *Anyte: The Epigrams* (Rome, 1979) 181–82.

23. Anyte is designated μελοποιός by the lemmata to 4, 5, 7, 8, 12, and 16 G-P and λυρική by the lemma to 9. I am not entirely convinced that these descriptive labels reflect actual knowledge of lyric poetry written by her rather than the general tendency to conceive all female poets in Sapphic terms; so Gow-Page (1965) II 89 ascribe the ethnic Μιτυληναία preceding 23 G-P to "the belief that all poetesses, were, or should be, compatriots of Sappho."

24. An epigram collection issued by Anyte was considered certain by Reitzenstein (1893) 135 and Geffcken (1917) 102–5.

25. For details about Anyte's refined style, see Geoghegan 9–14, who points out that the phrase θῆλυν Ὅμηρον (Antip. Thess. 19.3 G-P, *Garland = AP* 9.26.3) may have been applied to Anyte (though some construe the appositive with Sappho rather than Anyte) because "almost every line of the epigrams embodies a reminiscence of Homer" (9).

26. Of the remaining four 21 G-P = *AP* 7.232, ascribed to Antipater by the corrector of the Palatine and to Anyte by Planudes, and 23 G-P = *AP* 7.492, ascribed to Anyte by the corrector of P and without ascription in Planudes, are quite possibly compositions by Anyte.

tender epitaphs for dead animals.[27] Yet little attempt has been made to relate these two topics one to the other, or to the themes found in the remaining epigrams. Scholarly assessment of Anyte has been influenced by Wilamowitz's claim that there is nothing "personal" or "womanly" in her poetry, that it has "no definite tone."[28] I assert, on the contrary, that Anyte may have been the first epigrammatist to project a distinct literary persona, and that she did this by setting herself, as a woman and an inhabitant of largely rural Arcadia, in opposition to the anonymous composer of traditional epigram. While the anonymous composer appears at first glance to be characterized by having no characteristics at all, that impression is in fact false. In order to remain self-effacing, the traditional epigrammatist must reflect without individualizing deviation the values of the society for which he writes, a society that during the sixth, fifth, and fourth centuries was essentially the male-governed polis. Anyte, by her dominating interest in women, children, and animals and by the attention she paid to the landscape and its inhabitants, defined her literary self by her deviation from the standard imposed upon the traditional epigrammatist, that of celebrating upper-class, masculine achievements and values. While the characteristics that define her persona do not emerge from any single epigram (and Wilamowitz apparently read the poems as separate inscriptions),[29] they become evident upon a contextual reading, one that assumes the surviving epigrams to be the remains of a designed group. Of course, the epigrams that survive are a select group, representing what Meleager or others chose to preserve, but they may nevertheless be characteristic of the

27. Reitzenstein (1893) 130–33 posited that the Peloponnesian school, composed of Anyte and her imitators, was concerned with "bucolic" themes and that a tradition of Arcadian pastoral derived from Anyte's lyric poetry. Under the influence of Reitzenstein, Gerhard Herrlinger, *Totenklage um Tiere in der antiken Dichtung* (Stuttgart, 1930) 57 connected Anyte's writing of the first animal epitaphs with the development of Peloponnesian bucolic. Although there are points of similarity between Anyte's descriptive epigrams and Theocritus' rustic *Idylls*, we should be careful to avoid an anachronistic assumption of a generic link, since the ancients formed a conceptualization of the bucolic genre only after and in consequence of Theocritus' poetry about herdsmen.

28. Wilamowitz (1924) I 136. The effect of his depreciatory attitude may survive in the recent survey by G. O. Hutchinson, *Hellenistic Poetry* (Oxford, 1988), where Anyte receives not a single mention. Even M. B. Skinner, "Nossis *Thelyglossos*: The Private Text and the Public Book" in *Women's History and Ancient History*, ed. Sarah B. Pomeroy (Chapel Hill, 1991) 21 cites with approbation Wilamowitz's comments and characterizes Anyte's verse as "conventional." Other feminist scholars have now started to revise Wilamowitz's view, however, and to assert Anyte's worth as an innovative and influential poet. Jane M. Snyder, *The Woman and the Lyre: Women Writers in Classical Greece and Rome* (Carbondale, Ill., 1989) 77 questions the early twentieth-century view of Anyte as a "masculine" writer, a "virgin huntress," and S. Barnard, "Anyte: Poet of Children and Animals" in *Rose di Pieria*, ed. Francesco de Martino (Bari, 1991) 165–76 has connected Anyte's interest in children and animals with her feminine nature.

29. See Wilamowitz (1924) I 136 with notes 5 and 6, 137 with note 1.

whole collection, anthologized as those that defined Anyte's uniqueness for her readers.

For some of her poems, Anyte apparently found precedents in epigrams circulating under the names of Simonides and Anacreon. The strongest evidence that Anyte was familiar with epigrams attributed to Simonides is her use of the phrase εὐρύχορος Τεγέα, "Tegea of wide spaces," (2.2 G-P = *AP* 6.153.2) in the same line position in which it appears in an epigram found in the alphabetical section of the Simonidean sequence from *AP* 7 (53.2 *FGE* = *AP* 7.512.2).[30] Other parallels, some less precise, suggest as well that Anyte was familiar with epigrams published under the name of Anacreon. An apparently early incorporation of the common prose signature of an artisan into a dedicatory epigram is the type of inscription from which Anyte's dedication of a cauldron evolves:

Πραξαγόρας τάδε δῶρα θεοῖς ἀνέθηκε, Λυκαίου
    υἱός, ἐποίησεν δ᾽ ἔργον Ἀναξαγόρας.

("Anacreon" 10 *FGE* = *AP* 6.139)

Praxagoras, the son of Lycaeus, offered these gifts
    to the gods, and Anaxagoras was the artist.

βουχανδὴς ὁ λέβης· ὁ δὲ θεὶς Ἐριασπίδα υἱός
    Κλεύβοτος, ἁ πάτρα δ᾽ εὐρύχορος Τεγέα·
τἀθάνᾳ δὲ τὸ δῶρον, Ἀριστοτέλης δ᾽ ἐπόησεν
    Κλειτόριος, γενέτᾳ ταὐτὸ λαχὼν ὄνομα.

(Anyte 2 G-P = *AP* 6.153)

The cauldron is as large as an ox. The dedicator is Eriaspidas' son,
    Cleubotus; his countryland is wide-spaced Tegea.
The gift belongs to Athena, and Aristoteles made it,
    the one from Cleitor who shares his father's name.

Likewise, this simple commemoration of a dedicated shield provides our best pre-Hellenistic parallel for Anyte's shield poem:

ῥυσαμένα Πύθωνα δυσαχέος ἐκ πολέμοιο
    ἀσπὶς Ἀθηναίας ἐν τεμένει κρέμαται.

("Anacreon" 12 *FGE* = *AP* 6.141)

The shield that saved Python from the woes of war
    hangs in the precinct of Athena.

ἕσταθι τᾷδε, κράνεια βροτοκτόνε, μηδ᾽ ἔτι λυγρόν
    χάλκεον ἀμφ᾽ ὄνυχα στάζε φόνον δαΐων,

30. Page (1981) 279 dates the epigram broadly to the fifth or fourth century. Because the parallel between Anyte 2 G-P and "Simonides" 53 *FGE* refuted Boas's argument (1905) 208–22 that only Mnasalces, and not Anyte, imitated the Simonidean sylloge, he later posited, in an article entitled "Anyte und Simonides," *RhM* 62 (1907) 61–63, that Anyte knew the epigram through Tegean tradition.

ἀλλ' ἀνὰ μαρμάρεον δόμον ἥμένα αἰπὺν Ἀθάνας
ἄγγελλ' ἀνορέαν Κρητὸς Ἐχεκρατίδα.

(Anyte 1 G-P = AP 6.123)

Stay here, murderous staff, and no longer drip
enemy blood around your baneful bronze cusp.
But rather, lying in the lofty marble house of Athena,
announce the manliness of the Cretan Echecratidas.

That the name Ἐχεκρατίδα appears in the same line position as Ἐχεκρατίδας in "Anacreon" 13 *FGE* (= *AP* 6.142), another probably early inscription, increases the likelihood that Anyte found models for her dedicatory poems in epigrams attributed to Anacreon as well as those deemed Simonidean.

The dedication of a cauldron could commemorate victory in athletic competition, success in war, or achievement of political power,[31] while the dedication of a spear validates the same class of behavior—the competitive endeavors of men. It may rightly be asked, then, how these two poems could contribute to Anyte's poetic identity if that identity were defined by its rejection of traditional masculine values. Anyte likely gathered into her poetry book a variety of epigrams composed over the course of time, without regard to absolute consistency in tone, type, or theme, and in collections characterized by diversity and fragmentation, as epigram books undoubtedly were, poetic identity was determined by those poems that were unique or dominating. The λέβης poem belongs in any collection of Anyte's works simply because of its remarkable artistic merit, its deceptively simple arrangement of phrasing and pattern of sound. But beyond that it could serve to identify the epigrammatist as a Tegean and an Arcadian, proud that native sons of her town and district could manufacture and dedicate a cauldron of such size.[32] The spear epigram is ostensibly a celebration of Echecratidas' manliness, but there may also be read in it a womanly dislike of war through the command issued to the "murderous" weapon to retire from active service (μηδ' ἔτι ... στάζε φόνον δαΐων). In the imitations of the poem by Nicias (1 G-P = *AP* 6.122), by Mnasalces (5 G-P = *AP* 6.128), and by the probably Hellenistic composer of "Simonides" 61 *FGE* = *AP* 6.52,[33] the voices of the male

---

31. For examples of all three causes of celebration, see *AP* 6.6, 6.7, and 6.8. Geoghegan 33 imagines that the occasion for Cleubotus' dedication was victory in athletic competition.

32. Geoghegan 37 argues that the epigram served *falsely* to identify Anyte as a Tegean, that is, that Pollux derived his assumption the poet was a native of Tegea from this poem alone. But since her rural themes fit so well with an Arcadian homeland, it seems excessively cautious to reject the evidence of Pollux (given in reference to another poem), especially when confirmed by Stephanus Byzantinus.

33. Although Reitzenstein (1893) 123–24 and Gow-Page (1965) II 92 judge Anyte the imitator of this Simonidean epigram, Boas (1905) 208 and Page (1981) 283 persuasively argue that it is a Hellenistic composition and so necessarily absent from the Simonidean sylloge as known to Anyte.

epigrammatists more neatly coalesce with the voices of the dedicators. Both poems by Anyte powerfully illustrate how a woman poet must be fluent in the conventional speech forms of her male-controlled society in order to find her own voice from within those forms.[34]

Anyte's orientation toward female concerns comes through more strongly in her human epitaphs. While in archaic and classical inscriptions the deceased is most commonly a young man and the mourner most commonly his father, only one of Anyte's epitaphs follows that pattern:

ἦ ῥα μένος σε, Πρόαρχ᾽, ὅλες᾽ ἐν δαΐ, δῶμά τε πατρός
   Φειδία ἐν δνοφερῷ πένθει ἔθου φθίμενος,
ἀλλὰ καλὸν τοι ὕπερθεν ἔπος τόδε πέτρος ἀείδει
   ὡς ἔθανες πρὸ φίλας μαρνάμενος πατρίδος.[35]

(4 G-P = *AP* 7.724)

Your fighting spirit destroyed you in battle, Proarchus, and you by dying
   cast the house of your father Phidias into black grief.
But the stone above you sings this lovely song,
   that you died fighting for your countryland.

All the others concern a young woman who died before marriage, and in each case the mourning for her emanates from a female presence:

πολλάκι τῷδ᾽ ὀλοφυδνὰ κόρας ἐπὶ σάματι Κλείνα
   μάτηρ ὠκύμορον παῖδ᾽ ἐβόασε φίλαν,
ψυχὰν ἀγκαλέουσα Φιλαινίδος, ἃ πρὸ γάμοιο
   χλωρὸν ὑπὲρ ποταμοῦ χεῦμ᾽ Ἀχέροντος ἔβα.

(5 G-P = *AP* 7.486)

Cleina, the mother, often mourning here at the tomb
   of her daughter, cried out for her child who died too soon,
Calling upon the soul of Philaenis, who before marriage
   crossed over the pale stream of the river Acheron.

παρθένον Ἀντιβίαν κατοδύρομαι, ἇς ἐπὶ πολλοὶ
   νυμφίοι ἱέμενοι πατρὸς ἵκοντο δόμον
κάλλευς καὶ πινυτᾶτος ἀνὰ κλέος· ἀλλ᾽ ἐπιπάντων
   ἐλπίδας οὐλομένα Μοῖρ᾽ ἐκύλισε πρόσω.

(6 G-P = *AP* 7.490)

I mourn the maiden Antibia, for whom many bridegrooms
   came eagerly to her father's house,

34. On this often misunderstood aspect of women's literature, see J. Winkler, "Gardens of Nymphs: Public and Private in Sappho's Lyrics," in *Reflections of Women in Antiquity*, ed. Helene P. Foley (New York, 1981) 68–69.

35. The text of the epigram's first line is quite uncertain. I have printed the readings of Stadtmüller. For other possibilities, see Geoghegan 57–60 and Barnard 172–73.

Following the fame of her beauty and discretion. But
   destructive Fate rolled the hopes of all out of reach.

λοίσθια δὴ τάδε πατρὶ φίλῳ περὶ χεῖρε βαλοῦσα
  εἶπ' Ἐρατὼ χλωροῖς δάκρυσι λειβομένα,
῏Ω πάτερ, οὔ τοι ἔτ' εἰμί, μέλας δ' ἐμὸν ὄμμα καλύπτει
  ἤδη ἀποφθιμένας κυάνεος θάνατος.

(7 G-P = AP 7.646)

Erato spoke these last words as she threw her arms
   about her father and wept pale tears,
"Oh father, I am no more, and the deep blackness
   of death covers my eyes as I die."

ἀντί τοι εὐλεχέος θαλάμου σεμνῶν θ' ὑμεναίων
  μάτηρ στᾶσε τάφῳ τῷδ' ἔπι μαρμαρίνῳ
παρθενικὰν μέτρον τε τεὸν καὶ κάλλος ἔχοισαν,
  Θερσί, ποτιφθεγκτὰ δ' ἔπλεο καὶ φθιμένα.

(8 G-P = AP 7.649)

Instead of a happy marriage chamber and holy wedding rites
   your mother has placed upon this marble tomb
A maiden's statue having your form and beauty,
   Thersis, and you, though dead, have been saluted.

While we may conjecture that Anyte as a female poet was more often asked
to write epitaphs for women than for men, the inclusion of these five epitaphs
within a collection (assuming of course that they are typical of that book) suggests
a world of female grief that stands as a counterpart to the predominantly male
perception of death we find in the corpus of earlier epitaphs.

Although we have no knowledge of the position of these epigrams within
the collection, as a group they display a perhaps deliberate variety in terms
of the narrating or dramatic voices employed in each. While all the forms of
address displayed here find parallels in actual inscriptions, the absence of the
inscriptional setting in favor of the written page makes it more difficult for the
reader to determine the source of the speaking voices. As a result, there is a
tendency to synthesize the voices into one controlling intellect, which either
speaks directly to the reader or ventriloquizes those voices that are identifiable.
So while 5 may presuppose a relief depicting the lamenting Cleina,[36] the book
reader may still become aware of a certain temporal illogicality in assigning to
the tombstone a description of events that have habitually taken place since its
erection (note ἐπὶ σάματι). In 4 the inscription upon the stone is paraphrased
within the poem itself, so that the primary narrating voice is easily identified with
a literary composer. In this the only epitaph for a young man, the epigrammatist
herself expresses concern for his parent's grief while assigning the customary

36. So Wilamowitz (1924) I 136, n. 6 and Gow-Page (1965) II 94.

consolation—that he died fighting for his country—to the song of the stone. The reader of 7 is perhaps again to imagine a relief, now depicting Erato in her father's embrace, but the vocalization of her final thoughts, poignantly expressing the pathos of death, is, within the collection, a natural extension of the narrator's own voice. In 8 where the inscriptional setting is clearly a maiden's statue, the narrating voice itself becomes dramatized as the narrator suggests her own participation in the grief by her direct address to the deceased Thersis. The speaker in 6 is that "anonymous first person mourner" once thought impossible in inscribed epigram, but known from two possibly early epigrams attributed to Simonides (36 *FGE* = *AP* 13.26, 75 *FGE* = *AP* 7.511) and now documented in certain sixth-century inscriptions (*CEG* 43, 51, *CEG*² 470 = 16a).[37] Within the collection the first person mourner merges of course with Anyte herself, whose sorrow for Antibia seems emblematic of the grief she feels for all the maidens lost to a premature death. This set of epigrams offers, then, a feminine perspective on death expressed through a chorus of female voices—grieving mothers, dying daughters, and the epigrammatist herself—a perspective that offers no comforting excuses (no equivalent of the *pro patria mori* offered for the deaths of young men) but sees in death only the senseless destruction of the goodness and beauty in life.

Since Greek literature was, in all times and places, overwhelmingly the province of men, those women who were provided an opportunity to compose literature had to find ways of expressing their female experience within the confines of genres created to define the male world. This entailed not simply a substitution of female for male within established forms, for the traditional usage of the forms was closely associated with the differing valuation society placed upon male and female modes of behavior. We have just observed how Anyte modified the centuries-old form of the solemn grave epitaph, not simply by substituting women for men as the more common objects of the form, but by expressing through the narrating and dramatized voices within the epitaphs a feminine perspective on the experience of death. So too, in her animal laments we may observe the modification of the epigram genre to express sensibilities more commonly permitted women than men.[38]

Greek men did from time to time commemorate dead animals. In the *Iliad* (23.171–74) Achilles sacrifices on Patroclus' funeral pyre four horses and two of the dead man's nine "table-fed" dogs, and in historical times a team of racehorses, three times victorious in the Olympic games, were buried opposite

37. See Hansen's notes on *CEG*² 470 = 16a. Day 26–27 argues that such anonymous speakers may echo threnodic elegy.

38. Herrlinger 57, who otherwise agrees with Wilamowitz's assessment of Anyte's "masculine" practice, observes that her animal epitaphs display "ein Gefühl für das Kleinleben der Tierwelt, wie es sich beim Mann nur selten finden wird." See now also Barnard.

the tomb of their owner Cimon (Hdt. 6.103).[39] The first surviving animal epitaphs that appear to have been inscribed at gravesites—those for the hound that saved Zenon from a wild boar (977 *SH*)—date to a half century or so after Anyte. In all these instances of a Greek male commemorating a dead animal, the animal was honored as a companion of the man's competitive and aggressive endeavors—war, athletic competition, or the hunt. Additional evidence suggests that remembrance of an animal for any other reason violated the code of behavior that defined manhood in Greek society. Theophrastus characterizes the man of "petty ambition" (μικροφιλοτιμία, *Char.* 21) as the type who sets up a miniature stone monument for his little Meletean lap dog, inscribed with an announcement of the deceased's breed.[40] Theophrastus never considers the possibility that this type of man feels genuine sorrow for the death of his pet; he interprets his actions as preference for ostentatious display rather than true accomplishment.[41] Aelian (*VH* 8.4) condemns another Athenian, an otherwise unknown Poliarchus, for erecting monuments inscribed with epigrams on the graves of his favorite hounds and gamecocks. Although hunting and cock fighting functioned as typical demonstrations of Greek manhood, Polyarchus has gone too far in his "extravagance" (τρυφή), a term suggesting both luxury and effeminacy. A later Greek epitaph for a dog attempts to deflect the passerby's natural response of laughter by pleading the master's genuine grief:

τὴν τρίβον ὃς παράγεις, ἄν πως τόδε σῆμα νοήσῃς,
   μή, δέομαι, γελάσῃς, εἰ κυνός ἐστι τάφος·
ἐκλαύσθην, χεῖρες δὲ κόνιν συνέθηκαν ἄνακτος,
   ὅς μου καὶ στήλῃ τόνδε ἐχάραξε λόγον.

(*GV* 1365)

If you should notice this tomb as you walk along the path,
   don't, I beg, laugh because it is a dog's grave.
I was lamented, and my master's hands piled up the dust.
   He also ingraved this verse on my tombstone.

---

39. Aelian, *NA* 12.40 reports that the Spartan Evagoras, another Olympic victor, also gave his horses an elaborate burial.

40. On the nature of Meletean dogs, see the references collected by R. C. Jebb, ed. *The Characters of Theophrastus* (London, 1909) *ad* 7.36 and the discussion by Otto Keller, *Die antike Tierwelt* I (Leipzig, 1909) 92–94. For Meletean dogs as the pets of children, see G. Van Hoorn, *Choes and Anthesteria* (Leiden, 1951) 47 with illustrations listed there; and Hilde Rühfel, *Kinderleben im Klassischen Athen* (Mainz am Rhein, 1984) 142 and *Das Kind in der griechischen Kunst* (Mainz am Rhein, 1984) 166. For a more general treatment, see Virginia T. Leitch, *The Maltese Dog: A History of the Breed*, 2nd ed., revised by Dennis Carno (New York, 1970).

41. A clearer example of motivation is found in Plutarch's story that Alcibiades lopped off the tail of an expensive and handsome dog in order to attract people's attention when he appeared with it in public (*Alcibiades* 9). The young cheetahs depicted on Greek vases, apparently as the pets of aristocratic youths, may reflect the same use of exotic animals as status symbols; see A. Ashmead, "Greek Cats," *Expedition* 20 (1978) 38–47.

Even, then, as late as the second or third century A.D., the open acknowledgment of grief for an animal potentially exposed a man to ridicule.

Of course, both men and women in Greek society must have felt affection for favorite pets, but social pressure discouraged men from the public display of that emotional attachment. Animals were to be treated by men as helpmates in their competitive endeavors, not as objects of sympathy and affection. But showing attachment to animals was surely more acceptable for women and children. Diodorus (13.82.6), in his account of fifth-century Acragas, refers to monuments set up for dead birds, "reared in the house by maidens and children." Although the activities that took place in the women's quarters seldom found expression in literature, certain artistic depictions give evidence that displays of affection for animals were common there. A fifth-century grave stele on which a girl tenderly holds two pigeons, one of them touching her lip with its beak, suggests a relationship between human and animal that is in no way utilitarian.[42] Another stele of classical date shows Mnesagora, apparently in her teens, holding out a pigeon to her little brother Nicochares, a child of only four or five.[43] In the Mnesagora stele the bird seems to symbolize the bond of affection that existed between the boy and his older sister, who may often have tended him. Sympathetic feeling for animals is entirely consistent with the nurturing and care-giving function that women performed in Greek society. Anyte manages to convey that sense of care, of empathy free of self-interest, through her adaptation of the highly conventional genre of grave epitaph to mourn dead animals.

We begin our discussion of Anyte's animal epitaphs with an atypical one, a memorial for a war horse killed in battle:

μνᾶμα τόδε φθιμένου μενεδαΐου εἵσατο Δᾶμις
    ἵππου ἐπεὶ στέρνον τοῦδε δαφοινὸν Ἄρης
τύψε, μέλαν δέ οἱ αἷμα ταλαυρίνου διὰ χρωτός
    ζέσσ᾽, ἐπὶ δ᾽ ἀργαλέαν βῶλον ἔδευσε φόνῳ.

(9 G-P = *AP* 7.208)

This memorial for a steed who perished unflinching
    Damis set up after Ares struck its tawny breast,
Dark blood erupted over its thick hide,
    and it stained the pain-giving soil with gore.

---

42. Gisela Richter, *Animals in Greek Sculpture* (Oxford, 1930) fig. 206. Clairmont 104 with n. 102 points out that such birds are suitable attributes for either unmarried women or mothers with children. He interprets men shown with dogs as references to hunting (31 on no. 8, pl. 4 and 110 on no. 33, pl. 17).

43. Clairmont no. 22 and pl. 11. A number of painted choes show clearly that birds were common playmates for small children; see Van Hoorn 48 with illustrations listed there.

Anyte honors Damis' battle companion by drawing upon epic terminology—
μενεδάϊος, "unflinching," describing in Homer the warrior or the warrior's
heart[44] and ταλαύρινος, in Homer an epithet of Ares meaning "enduring a bull's-
hide shield," and so "tough" or as here "thick." The stallion thus wears his own
protection into battle, as the war god bears a shield. To befit the manliness of
Damis who here commemorates his fallen companion, Anyte employs the cool
and solemn style of the earliest Greek epitaphs. She makes no direct reference to
the owner's grief at his loss, nor does she convey a sympathetic identification
with the dying animal.

In strong contrast to the Damis epigram is Anyte's lament for a young hound
killed by a viper:

ὤλεο δή ποτε καὶ σὺ πολύρριζον παρὰ θάμνον,
   Λόκρι, φιλοφθόγγων ὠκυτάτα σκυλάκων,
τοῖον ἐλαφρίζοντι τεῷ ἐγκάτθετο κώλῳ
   ἰὸν ἀμείλικτον ποικιλόδειρος ἔχις.

(10 G-P = Pollux 5.48)

You, too, once perished by a thickly-rooted bush,
   Locris, swiftest of puppies who love to bark.
Such pitiless poison was thrust into your nimble limb
   by a viper with iridescent neck.

The term Locris, which may here be partly name and partly description of
breed, indicates that we are dealing with a type of Locrian hound recommended
by Xenophon for boar-hunting.[45] But this Locris is a σκύλαξ, which usually
indicates a young animal, so perhaps here a puppy,[46] who barks not on the
bloodthirsty trail of the hunt but from the sheer joy of making the sound. From
a perspective that may even be characterized as maternal, the voice in the
epigram addresses the animal itself. The opening word, ὤλεο, "you perished,"
appears in the first line of Andromache's lament over the body of Hector in the
Iliad (24.725). As the sound of the word suggests, it may have been a conventional
feature of laments sung by women at funerals. Here it sets up a dialogue with the
lost hound, in which the speaker commiserates with the deceased by imagining
the event of death through the eyes of the dog itself. Locris has failed to spot
the viper camouflaged in the roots of the bush (πολύρριζον) where it sought its
quarry. The description of the snake's neck as ποικιλόδειρος, a term with epic

44. Appearing only at *Il.* 12.247 and 13.228; see Geoghegan *ad loc.* It has been suggested
that μενεδάϊος is the horse's name; for discussion, see Herrlinger *ad loc.* and Gow-Page (1965)
ad loc.

45. *Cyn.* 10.1; confirmed by Oppian *Cyn.* 1.375.

46. Anyte's fondness for Homeric terminology suggests that she is following the epic
connotation of σκύλαξ as "puppy" (*Od.* 12.86, 20.14) rather than the later usage to mean
simply "dog." Her use of the *hapax* φιλόφθογγος (2), which may be an allusion to *Od.* 12.86,
aids the suggestion.

and lyric pedigree, may connote both the sparkle of its scales and the speed of its movement.[47] It appropriately closes the poem since it suggests the dog's one startled glimpse of the snake that killed it.

Anyte practices another technique of identification with a dead animal in the following epigram, where a dolphin speaks its own epitaph:

οὐκέτι δὴ πλωτοῖσιν ἀγαλλόμενος πελάγεσσιν
   αὐχέν' ἀναρρίψω βυσσόθεν ὀρνύμενος,
οὐδὲ περὶ σκαρθμοῖσι νεὼς περικαλλέα χείλη
   ποιφύξω τἀμᾷ τερπόμενος προτομᾷ,
ἀλλά με πορφυρέα πόντου νοτὶς ὥς' ἐπὶ χέρσον
   κεῖμαι δὲ ῥαδινὰν τάνδε παρ' ἀιόνα.

(12 G-P = AP 7.215)

No longer shall I rejoice in the sailed sea
   as I toss up my head, lifting it from the depths.
Nor around the ship's gunwales lovely with their tholes
   shall I snort and blow, enjoying my image on the figurehead.
The purple swell of the sea has tossed me upon the land,
   and I lie on this narrow shore.

Though the poem at first seems conceived entirely from the animal's point of view, the reader may gradually recognize the voice of a human speaker sympathetically projecting into the persona of the dolphin. The picture of the living animal in the first two couplets—lifting its head out of the water and playfully sporting about the sides of a ship—represents the view of dolphins from shipboard. The formula in the last couplet, "I, So-and-So, lie here," is common on inscribed epitaphs as a convention for identifying the deceased. But the voice we hear in this poem is certainly not that of a stone, nor even that of the dead animal, but the voice of a passerby who sees the dolphin's body on the shore, feels pity for its loss, and re-creates in imagination, yet always from a human perspective, what it must have been like to be a dolphin gamboling in the waves. The speaker who impersonates the dolphin is no one in particular, and so any one of us. But the poet who conceived such a voice, full of compassion for all living creatures, was Anyte.

Another epigram again shows that for Anyte the concept of animals as servants of men, as objects of utility, has given way to a greater sense of the kinship between human and animal experience:

οὐκέτι μ' ὡς τὸ πάρος πυκιναῖς πτερύγεσσιν ἐρέσσων
   ὄρσεις ἐξ εὐνῆς ὄρθριος ἐγρόμενος,

---

47. Hesiod (*Op.* 203) uses the word of a nightingale and Alcaeus (345.2 *PLF*) of ducks. B. H. Fowler, "The Archaic Aesthetic," *AJP* 105 (1984) 148 points out that ποικίλος means "variegated, twisting, quick-moving, hence 'tricky,' 'wily.'" All of these may come into play in Anyte's poem.

ἦ γάρ σ' ὑπνώοντα σίνις λαθρηδὸν ἐπελθών
ἔκτεινεν λαιμῷ ῥίμφα καθεὶς ὄνυχα.

(11 G-P = AP 7.202)

No longer as before will you rouse me from bed,
  flapping your thick wings as you awake in the morning.
A marauder, coming stealthily upon you as you slept, swiftly
  placed his claw on your throat and killed you.

The pathetic nature of the speaker's grief, emphasized by the opening juxta-position of οὐκέτι μ' ("no longer me"), may seem excessive, disproportionate to the loss of a mere cock,[48] who awakened sleepers at dawn. So read, the poem seems too sentimental, perhaps even ironic.[49] But Snyder points out that the vigorous crowing of the wakened bird in the first couplet contrasts with the death of the sleeping bird in the second,[50] and it is a contrast that I think has point. The Greek word for the cock's attacker, σίνις, is elsewhere used for a variety of marauders—a lion, Paris, the mythical animal thief Autolycus, and as the proper name for a brigand killed by Theseus.[51] This use of a term that may designate either a human or animal marauder in place of the specific name of the cock's attacker (perhaps a fox or weasel) suggests the similarity between the cock's violent death and that which the human sleeper might experience at the hands of a nighttime robber. Escape from such dangers of the dark is precisely what the cock's crowing heralds. Its death not only means the loss of this comforting sound but also reminds us why it comforts.

In a final epitaph, Anyte identifies not with a dead animal but with a young girl who grieves:[52]

ἀκρίδι τᾷ κατ' ἄρουραν ἀηδόνι, καὶ δρυοκοίτᾳ
τέττιγι ξυνὸν τύμβον ἔτευξε Μυρώ

48. The Byzantine copyists disagreed whether the animal addressed is a cicada or a cock, the latter preferred by the corrector. Most later editors have chosen the cock, although the arguments of Maria Baale, *Studia in Anytes poetriae vitam et carminum reliquias* (Haarlem, 1903) 68 for an insect have been revived and extended by Geoghegan 111–15 and Barnard 169–70, and accepted by Diane J. Rayor, trans., *Sappho's Lyre: Archaic Lyric and Women Poets of Ancient Greece* (Berkeley, 1991) 190. But I read Nicias (4 G-P = *AP* 7.200), in which a boy kills an insect, as a humorous take on Anyte's animal epitaphs, combining features from both 11 and 20, and not as a simple imitation of 11.

49. G. Luck, "Die Dichterinnen der griechischen Anthologie," *MH* 11 (1954) 179 comments that the poem is "halb wehmütig, halb ironisch."

50. Snyder 72.

51. The word is used of a lion in Callim. *Ap.* 92, apparently imitating the manuscript reading in Aesch. *Ag.* 718; of Paris by Lycoph. 539; of Autolycus by Schol. L. to Soph. *OC* 378. The robber killed by Theseus is so named at Eur. *Hipp.* 977.

52. Although this poem bears a double ascription, to both Anyte and Leonidas, and Stadtmüller posited an ascription to Leonidas of Aleaxndria, other editors agree that there is little doubt of Anyte's authorship.

παρθένιον στάξασα κόρα δάκρυ, δισσὰ γὰρ αὐτᾶς
παίγνι' ὁ δυσπειθὴς ᾤχετ' ἔχων Ἀίδας.

(20 G-P = *AP* 7.190)

For her grasshopper, the nightingale of the fields, and her
    cicada, dweller in the oak, Myro made a common tomb,
A girl shedding a maiden's tear. For Hades,
    hard to dissuade, took away both her playthings.

Once again it is easy to read irony into the poem, now directed toward the
child who so extravagantly laments the ephemeral lives of two insects. But,
significantly, only here in Anyte's animal epitaphs does the compassionate voice
of the author identify with another human mourning a lost pet, and I suggest
that Myro may actually be a projection of Anyte herself. Pliny (*HN* 34.57) tells us
that in a poem by Erinna the sculptor Myron was said to have made a tomb
for a grasshopper and a cicada. Some scholars have assumed that, as Pliny
confuses Myron with the girl Myro, so he has likewise confused Erinna with
Anyte.[53] But misreading a proper noun is an easier mistake than confusing two
authors' names. Anyte's poem may well be a variation on a lost poem by Erinna,
a sign of homage to the premier female poet of the preceding generation. It
is also significant that Moero, another early Hellenistic female poet who was
linked with Anyte in the introduction to Meleager's *Garland*, is called Myro in
some ancient sources.[54] Certain readers of the *Garland* must have assumed that
Anyte's companion poet was the Myro of her epigram, and the reason for this
mistake is easy to surmise: the context of the epigram suggests that Myro is a
girl of poetic talent who would naturally grieve for the double loss of two such
pets. Grasshoppers and cicadas were highly valued in antiquity for the musical
sounds they made.[55] Myro's grasshopper is specifically called the "nightingale
of the field," nightingales being common metaphors for poets. The cicada's
corresponding designation δρυοκοίτης ("dweller in the oak") recalls Homer's
famous line describing cicadas that "sitting in a tree send forth lily voices"

53. This argument was made by Baale 158–60. But see U. W. Scholz, "Erinna," *A&A* 18
(1973) 29, who argues in favor of the ascription to Erinna. The literary significance of the Myro
poem, whether first by Erinna or Anyte, is indicated by Marcus Argentarius' close imitation
(21 G-P, *Garland* = *AP* 7.364), preserving both Myro's name and her loss of a cicada and a
grasshopper.

54. Gow-Page (1965) II 413–14 give a list of the passages that have either Moero or Myro
and point out that Myro is unmetrical in the Meleager line (1.5–6 G-P = *AP* 4.1.5–6). Moero
is also placed beside Anyte in a list of nine canonical female poets given by Antipater of
Thessalonica (*AP* 9.26), and Tatian, *Or. ad Graecos* 33 reports that Cephisodotus made statues
of both Anyte and "Myro." Baale 30–39, 158 argues that Myro was the poet's name, that
Anyte's epigram refers to her, and that the two were friends.

55. A series of epigrams in the *Anthology* is devoted to them: *AP* 7.189–90, 192–98, 200–201.
For other references, see Malcolm Davies and J. Kathirithamby, *Greek Insects* (Oxford, 1986)
113–49; Ian C. Beavis, *Insects and Other Invertebrates in Classical Antiquity* (Exeter, 1988) 62–78.

(*Il.* 3.152) and Hesiod's similar description of a cicada that "sitting in a tree pours forth a shrill song" (*Op.* 583). Anyte suggests, then, through literary allusion, that Myro grieves so intensely because the loss of her playthings means the loss of their music. The girl learns early in life that the harsh realities of death, "Hades hard to dissuade," parallel the limitations of art.

The Myro poem occupies a special place among Anyte's epigrams because it ties together the themes of female grief, children, animals, and landscape, the last three of which appear prominently in our remaining group of epigrams. In two of these, Anyte again displays her remarkable capacity to empathize with animals, but now as she describes figures depicted in works of art:

ἡνία δή τοι παῖδες ἐπί, τράγε, φοινικόεντα
    θέντες καὶ λασίῳ φιμὰ περὶ στόματι
ἵππια παιδεύουσι θεοῦ περὶ ναὸν ἄεθλα
    ὄφρ' αὐτοὺς φορέῃς ἤπια τερπομένους.[56]

(13 G-P = AP 6.312)

The children, placing purple reins upon you, goat,
    and a noseband about your shaggy mouth,
Train you in horse racing around the god's temple,
    to make you carry them gently for their pleasure.

θάεο τὸν Βρομίου κεραὸν τράγον, ὡς ἀγερώχως
    ὄμμα κατὰ λασιᾶν γαῦρον ἔχει γενύων
κυδιόων ὅτι οἱ θάμ' ἐν οὔρεσιν ἀμφὶ παρῇδα
    βόστρυχον εἰς ῥοδέαν Ναῒς ἔδεκτο χέρα.

(14 G-P = AP 9.745)

Look at Bromius' horned goat, how haughtily he casts
    his arrogant eye down over his shaggy face,
Proud because often in the mountains Nais took
    the tuft along his cheek into her rosy hand.

By addressing the goat in 13, the epigrammatist reveals her willingness to abandon, momentarily, adult seriousness and to enter a world of imagination and play where children (παῖδες) become the teachers (παιδεύουσι) and employ "purple reins" like those of Homeric heroes (cf. ἡνία φοινιχόεντα, *Il.* 8.116) to train a goat for "horse racing" like that celebrated in Pindaric encomium (cf. ἱππίων ἀέθλων, *Nem.* 9.9). While 13 apparently describes a painting or relief, the lemmatist to 14 suggests that the object described there is a bronze statue of a goat.[57] The invitation to observe in θάεο directs our attention first to the actual

56. In the last line I print the reading of PPl rather than the emendations ἐφορῇ νήπια preferred by Gow-Page.

57. The lemma reads εἰς τὸ αὐτό, referring to a bronze goat in the immediately preceding epigram by Leonidas. Gow-Page (1965) *ad loc.*, Geoghegan 137, and Barnard 174 all assume that the landscape details are part of the depiction and so posit a painting or relief.

representation of the animal, then to the saucy look in his eye, and finally in the second couplet to the poet's interpretation of that look: the goat's pride in a beard that has attracted the attention of a Naiad. As readers pretending to be observers, we are not to visualize the mountains and their nymph as part of the artwork, for they exist only in the mind's eye of the goat. Anyte presents for us, not an accurate description of an artwork, but an imaginative interpretation that arises from her own unique perspective on the represented figure. This epigrammatist capable of surmising the fanciful thoughts of a goat invites us to enter a playful bucolic world where we too can feel the caress of a rosy-handed Naiad.

The rustic setting in this poem links it to Anyte's pastoral epigrams, all containing descriptions of landscape scenes:

φριξοκόμᾳ τόδε Πανὶ καὶ αὐλιάσιν θέτο Νύμφαις
  δῶρον ὑπὸ σκοπιᾶς Θεύδοτος οἰονόμος
οὕνεχ' ὑπ' ἀζαλέου θέρεος μέγα κεκμηῶτα
  παῦσαν ὀρέξασαι χερσὶ μελιχρὸν ὕδωρ.

(3 G-P = *AP* 16.291)

The shepherd Theudotus placed this gift here under the peak
  for bristly Pan and the Nymphs of the grotto
Because they refreshed him, weary from the summer's heat,
  by offering him sweet water with their hands.

Κύπριδος οὗτος ὁ χῶρος ἐπεὶ φίλον ἔπλετο τήνᾳ
  αἰὲν ἀπ' ἠπείρου λαμπρὸν ὁρῆν πέλαγος
ὄφρα φίλον ναύτῃσι τελῇ πλόον· ἀμφὶ δὲ πόντος
  δειμαίνει λιπαρὸν δερκόμενος ξόανον.

(15 G-P = *AP* 9.144)

This is the precinct of the Cyprian, since it pleases her
  always from land to look upon a shining sea,
So that she may make sailing pleasant for sailors; and the water
  round about trembles, gazing at her gleaming image.

ἵζε' ἄπας ὑπὸ καλὰ δάφνας εὐθαλέα φύλλα
  ὡραίου τ' ἄρυσαι νάματος ἁδὺ πόμα
ὄφρα τοι ἀσθμαίνοντα πόνοις θέρεος φίλα γυῖα
  ἀμπαύσῃς πνοιᾷ τυπτόμενα Ζεφύρου.

(16 G-P = *AP* 9.313)

Sit, one and all, under the lovely luxuriant foliage of the laurel
  and draw a sweet draught from the flowing spring,
So that your limbs, exhausted from the labors of summer,
  may rest, struck by the breeze of Zephyr.

Ἑρμᾶς τᾷδ' ἔστακα παρ' ὄρχατον ἀνεμόεντα
  ἐν τριόδοις πολιᾶς ἐγγύθεν ἀιόνος
κεκμηῶσιν ἔχων ἄμπαυσιν ὁδοῖο,
  ψυχρὸν δ' ἀκραὲς κράνα ὑποιάχει.

(17 G-P = *AP* 9.314)

I, Hermes, stand here beside a breezy orchard
    by a crossroads near the white shore,
Bringing respite from the road to weary men,
    and a spring babbles, cool and pure.

ξεῖν’, ὑπὸ τὰν πέτραν τετρυμένα γυῖ’ ἀνάπαυσον—
    ἁδύ τοι ἐν χλωροῖς πνεῦμα θροεῖ πετάλοις—
πίδακά τ’ ἐκ παγᾶς ψυχρὸν πίε, δὴ γὰρ ὁδίταις
    ἄμπαυμ’ ἐν θερμῷ καύματι τοῦτο φίλον.

(18 G-P = AP 16.228)

Stranger, rest your weary limbs under this rock
    (sweetly sounds the breeze in the green foliage)
And drink cool water from the spring, for this respite
    from the summer's heat pleases travelers.

– τίπτε κατ’ οἰόβατον, Πὰν ἀγρότα, δάσκιον ὕλαν
    ἥμενος ἁδυβόᾳ τῷδε κρέκεις δόνακι;
– ὄφρα μοι ἑρσήεντα κατ’ οὔρεα ταῦτα νέμοιντο
    πόρτιες ἠυκόμων δρεπτόμεναι σταχύων.

(19 G-P = AP 16.231)

– Why, rustic Pan, do you sit in a lonesome, shady wood
    and play on this sweet-sounding reed?
– So that my calves may pasture on this dewy mountain,
    culling the fertile grasses.

These poems, lacking parallel in the earlier history of epigram, are all concerned with the lives of the humble. While the adjective οἰονόμος (3.2) may mean either "shepherd" or "solitary," the Theudotus who makes a dedication to Pan and the nymphs in 3 is clearly a countryman.[58] In 19 the piping Pan is explicitly a divine herdsman. Parallels elsewhere in Greek literature indicate that the customary inhabitants of groves like those described in 16 and 18 were flocks and their herders,[59] while πόνοις θέρεος in 16 suggests field laborers. The weary men who pass the statue of Hermes in 17, located between an orchard and a shore, would undoubtedly be farm workers or fishermen. If the temple to Aphrodite commemorated in 15 was anything like the one on the coast of Cyrene described in Plautus' *Rudens* (based on a play by Diphilus), it was a humble sort of shrine, a center of worship for fishermen.

In extending the subject matter of epigram to such lower-class persons, Anyte foregrounds the biographical reality of her life as a rural Peloponnesian. Her native district of Arcadia was a mountainous region, with few cities and a largely pastoral economy. By the third century Arcadia had already become a symbol

58. Detailed discussion of the word in Geoghegan 47–50.
59. Explicit in Pl. *Phdr.* 259a4–6: ἀνδράποδ’ ἄττα σφίσιν ἐλθόντα εἰς τὸ καταγώγιον ὥσπερ προβάτια μεσημβριάζοντα περὶ τὴν κρήνην εὕδειν. Cf. Leon. 86 G-P = *AP* 16.230 and 5 G-P = *AP* 9.326.

of the primitive life, free of the burdens of urban civilization.[60] Pan, mentioned in two of her epigrams (3, 19), was identified throughout Greece as a specifically Arcadian god (cf. Πᾶνα, τὸν Ἀρκάδα, "Simonides" 5 *FGE* = *AP* 16.232), and Hermes (17), while more pan-Hellenic, was believed to have been born on Mount Cyllene in Arcadia.   The references in Anyte to the sea suggest an occasional visit to the Peloponnesian coast, the likelihood of which is indicated by a biographical anecdote about her journey to Naupactus (Paus. 10.38.13). I am not suggesting that Anyte's epigrams should be read as an index to her biography, but rather that their contents were meant to be related to those "facts" about the author that would be evident, perhaps simply from its title, to any reader of her book—namely, that she was a woman from Arcadia.[61]

Although the arrangement of these epigrams within Anyte's collection is of course unknown, there is a remarkable degree of verbal and thematic repetition from poem to poem.   Four of the six epigrams are concerned with respite (παῦσαν, 3.4; ἀμπαύσῃς, 16.4; ἄμπαυσιν, 17.3; ἀνάπαυσον, 18.1; ἄμπαυμ', 18.4) from the heat (ὑπ' ἀζαλέου θέρεος, 3.3; πόνοις θέρεος, 16.3; ἐν θερμῷ καύματι, 18.4) provided weary workers or travelers (μέγα κεκμηῶτα, 3.3; ἀσθμαίνοντα, 16.3; ἀνδράσι κεκμηῶσιν, 17.3; τετρυμένα γυῖα, 18.1) by cool water (μελιχρὸν ὕδωρ, 3.4; ἁδὺ πόμα, 16.2; ψυχρόν, 17.4; πίδακα ... ψυχρόν, 18.3) and refreshing breezes (πνοιᾷ ... Ζεφύρου, 16.4; ἁδύ ... πνεῦμα, 18.2).   Pan's rest in a shady grove in 19 repeats the same theme on a divine level, while the suggestion in 15 of Aphrodite's ability to calm the sea makes that poem the nautical equivalent of the idyllic scenes in the other epigrams (cf. the parallelism of φίλον ναύτῃσι ... πλόον, 15.3, and ὁδίταις ἄμπαυμ' ... φίλον, 18.3–4). For the reading audience, these repeated themes may evoke literary associations as old as Hesiod, who identifies the poet with a herdsman (*Th.* 22–35) and proclaims "respite from cares" (ἄμπαυμά τε μερμηράων, *Th.* 55) a benefit of the Muses. Since I have elsewhere traced the analogical association of the poet and the herdsman in detail, it is sufficient here to point out that the pastoral quality so many readers have identified in Anyte's descriptions seems related to this long tradition and, most specifically, to Plato's revitalization of the analogy in the *Phaedrus*.[62]   As the Ilissus grove becomes in Plato's dialogue a metaphor for

60. On Arcadia as a political, social, and cultural entity, see Thomas G. Rosenmeyer, *The Green Cabinet: Theocritus and the European Pastoral Lyric* (Berkeley, 1969) 233–35 and Philippe Borgeaud, *The Cult of Pan in Ancient Greece*, trans. Kathleen Atlass and J. Redfield (Chicago, 1988) 3–22.

61. Snyder 68 suggests that the Naupactus anecdote, which concerns the healing of a blind man, may have derived from a lost dedicatory epigram. The suggestion now has support from a group of Posidippan epigrams on "cures" effected by Asclepius found on the new Milan papyrus.

62. Gutzwiller (1991) 23–79; see also Bruce D. MacQueen, *Myth, Rhetoric, and Fiction: A Reading of Longus's "Daphnis and Chloe"* (Lincoln, 1990) 168–74.

intellectual activity, so, on that model, Anyte's idyllic descriptions have at least the potential to reflect the very act of reading them.

Following this line of thinking, we may surmise that the two poems which address passersby, 16 and 18, played some programmatic role in Anyte's collection. These two epigrams differ from Anyte's other pastoral descriptions and similar epigrams of later authors by their lack of specificity concerning the identity of the speaker. While a rustic depiction of a deity can be assumed as the source of that voice,[63] all clues to the identity of the god are absent. An epigram by Nicias, partly imitative of Anyte 16, provides a more typical example:

ἵζευ, ὑπ' αἰγείροισιν, ἐπεὶ κάμες, ἐνθάδ', ὁδῖτα,
  καὶ πῖθ' ἆσσον ἰὼν πίδακος ἀμετέρας,
μνᾶσαι δὲ κράναν καὶ ἀπόπροθι ἂν ἐπὶ Γίλλῳ
  Σῖμος ἀποφθιμένῳ παιδὶ παριδρύεται.

(5 G-P = AP 9.315)

Sit here under the poplars since you're weary, traveler,
  and coming near drink from our water;
Even when you're far away, remember the spring, which
  Simus is constructing for his dead son, Gillus.

As Nicias names the dedicator and gives the reason for his dedication, so the adjective ἀμετέρας, "our," suggests an identity for the voice heard in the poem— perhaps, as Gow surmises, a relief of Naiads.[64] Similarly, Anyte in 3 names Theudotus as the dedicator and the aid of the local deities as the reason for his gift, while in 17 a statue of Hermes is identified as the speaker who offers aid to travelers. But 16 and 18 belong to a class by themselves because they fail, surprisingly, to provide any of the specific information that maintains the fiction of inscription. As a result, the reader more easily associates the voice speaking in these two poems with the poet herself.

In addition, 18 seems to have influenced other poetic openings of a programmatic nature. The second line—ἁδύ τοι ἐν χλωροῖς πνεῦμα θροεῖ πετάλοις ("sweetly sounds the breeze in the green foliage")—bears a clear resemblance to the beginning of *Idyll* 1:

ἁδύ τι τὸ ψιθύρισμα καὶ ἁ πίτυς, αἰπόλε, τήνα,
  ἁ ποτὶ ταῖς παγαῖσι, μελίσδεται.

(1.1–2)

Sweetly sings that whispering of the pine, goatherd,
  That one by the springs.

---

63. The lemma to 18 identifies the speaker as a statue of Pan. This is a natural assumption from the poem's context in Planudes' *Anthology*, where it occurs in a series of poems on Pan (though the lemmatist fails to notice that the immediately preceding poem is actually on Hermes), but it has no validity for Anyte's own collection.

64. Gow-Page (1965) *ad loc.*

While the structure and sense of Theocritus' lines seem influenced by Anyte, his use of the sequence ἁδύ (1) ... ἁδύ (2) ... ἅδιον (7) has a clear precedent in a poem that may have opened Asclepiades' collection:

> ἡδὺ θέρους διψῶντι χιὼν ποτόν, ἡδὺ δὲ ναύταις
>   ἐκ χειμῶνος ἰδεῖν εἰαρινὸν Στέφανον·
> ἥδιον δ' ὁπόταν κρύψῃ μία τοὺς φιλέοντας
>   χλαῖνα, καὶ αἰνῆται Κύπρις ὑπ' ἀμφοτέρων.

(1 G-P = AP 5.169)

Sweet for the thirsty an icy drink in summer and sweet
    for sailors to spot spring's Crown after a storm.
But sweeter still when one cloak covers two lovers,
    and the Cyprian is honored by both.

Although the contents of Asclepiades' priamel finds various parallels in earlier Greek literature,[65] the presumed context of his epigram suggests it was designed to differentiate his collection from Anyte's, where cool water was praised in several poems and calm sailing in 15. A dual reference to both Anyte 18 and Asclepiades 1 appears in a programmatic poem by Nossis, where the opening phrase ἅδιον οὐδὲν ἔρωτος ("nothing is sweeter than love," 1.1 G-P = AP 5.170.1) functions as a reminiscence both of Anyte, as an earlier composer of inscriptional epigrams, and of Asclepiades, as an innovative writer of erotic epigram. We may reasonably conjecture that these three poets—Theocritus, Asclepiades, and Nossis—all echoed Anyte 18 in making important statements about their art because Anyte's poem fulfilled a similar function within her own collection.

Confirmation that Anyte 16, as well as 18, was understood in antiquity to be a statement of the epigrammatist to the reader comes from its position within the *Garland*. In composing his anthology, Meleager formed a section, apparently a whole book, of descriptive epigrams, very largely pastoral in character. A block of twenty-five poems from that section survives in the *Anthology* (*AP* 9.313–338), and Anyte 16, followed by 17 on the statue of Hermes, stands at its head. Unfortunately, the position of Anyte 18 within Meleager's section is unknown since this poem was transmitted only in the *Planudean Anthology*, but it may well have stood together with 16 and 17 at the head of the descriptive section.[66] Why did Meleager choose to begin this section of his *Garland* with a sequence

---

65. On the rhetorical form called the priamel, see William H. Race, *The Classical Priamel from Homer to Boethius* (Leiden, 1982) and, for the priamel as an opening device, "How Greek Poems Begin" in *Beginnings in Classical Literature*, *YCS* 29, ed. Francis M. Dunn and Thomas Cole (Cambridge, 1992) 16–18. For Asclepiades' imitation of Aesch. *Ag.* 899–901, see Otto Knauer, *Die Epigramme des Asklepiades v. Samos* (Diss. Tübingen, 1935) 17–18 and Gow-Page (1965) *ad loc.*

66. Anyte may have found a model for the practice of placing more than one introductory poem at the opening of a collection in the series of four hymns that opens the *Theognidea* (1–18) or in similar sequences opening editions of other early poets; see West (1974) 42.

of at least two, and possibly three, epigrams by Anyte? Of course, Anyte did deserve pride of place as the initial exponent of the descriptive epigram, the primary model for a long tradition of pastoral epigrammatists.[67] But by placing 16 (possibly in combination with 18) at the opening of his descriptive section, Meleager also managed to expropriate the voice of Anyte for his own anthology, where the earlier epigrammatist's programmatic statement would subtly merge with the that of the editor himself.

Within her own collection, Anyte 16 and 18 seem to have functioned programmatically, by inviting the reader, figured as a weary traveler, to experience an epigram book, represented as a cool and enticing grove. The opening invitation in 16 to sit under the "lovely luxuriant foliage of the laurel" easily suggests the enjoyment of the verse that follows, since the laurel was sacred to Apollo as the patron of poetry. A parallel exists in the collection of Theocritus' epigrams, where the editor placed a dedication of roses and thyme to the Muses and of laurel to Apollo first in his collection, again with programmatic intent (1 Gow = *AP* 6.336). Anyte's further invitation, in 16.2 and 18.3, to drink refreshing water from a spring also finds parallels in programmatic contexts. It anticipates Callimachus' famous metaphor for the composition of his own brand of poetry in his *Hymn to Apollo* 110–12 (where Callimachus' πίδακος ἐξ ἱερῆς, 112, seems to echo Anyte's πίδακά τ' ἐκ παγᾶς, 18.3, both poets employing a Homeric *hapax* from *Il.* 16.825). But Propertius' later association of groves and springs, as sources of poetic inspiration, with both Callimachus and Philetas (3.1.1–4; cf. 3.3.51–52) suggests that Philetas, who was a contemporary of Anyte, had used a landscape setting, resembling that in Anyte 16 and 18, to make a programmatic statement about the nature of his poetry. While our information about the chronology of early Hellensitic poetry does not permit us to know whether Anyte borrowed from Philetas or vice versa, it should be observed that Anyte's programmatic image associates her poetry, not just with style, but with a specific place as well. Her invitation to the traveler/reader to find respite in a cool grove suggests not only the refreshing novelty of the epigram as poetic form but also the novel uniqueness of Arcadian rural values as a literary subject.

Although Anyte has long been recognized as an innovator for her animal epitaphs and pastoral descriptions, she has not been granted sufficient credit for her pivotal role in the history of epigram. The other composers of sepulchral, dedicatory, and descriptive epigrams in the first half of the third century all seem dependent, directly or indirectly, on Anyte, and therefore Asclepiades, as the earliest known composer of sympotic epigram, is the only rival claimant for the distinction of being the first epigrammatist to issue a book

67. For the pastoral theme in epigram, see C. E. Whitmore, "Pastoral Elements in the Greek Epigram," *CJ* 13 (1918) 616–20. For Anyte's importance in the pastoral tradition, see Snyder 74–76.

of verse. But his collection was quite possibly issued after hers, since in a programmatic priamel (1 G-P) he opposes his own interest in love to Anyte's programmatic images. To our knowledge, then, Anyte may well have been the first to act upon the poetic potential heralded by collections of earlier poetry, perhaps including collections of inscriptions attributed to Simonides, in which known poets acquired individualized personae through the readers' synthesis of the thematic, verbal, and structural similarities inherent in the poems.

Not only did Anyte set out to write more refined examples of the types of epigrams attributed to Simonides and Anacreon (1, 2, 4), but, more importantly, she developed for herself, as a woman and an Arcadian, a recognizable persona defined by its opposition to that of the traditional male epigrammatist. While the earlier epigrammatists celebrated, predominantly, men who died in battle or masculine successes worthy of dedicatory commemoration, Anyte offered the reader an alternative, like respite from the heat provided by soft breezes and cool water, in a world ruled by feminine sensibilities and rural values. In writing poetry to reflect her own feminine perspective on the world, Anyte shifted the focus of the genre from men to women, from adults to children, from humans to animals, and from upper to lower class. In doing so, she made it clear that epigram could now be free of its utilitarian function, its restriction to the inscriptional site—that is, that it had entered the realm of fully literary forms where imagination has free play.

NOSSIS

From the hand of Nossis, a native of Epizephyrian Locri in southern Italy, there survive eleven epigrams, eight dedicatory in form, seven of these concerning women.[68] Two of the other three were apparently the opening and closing poems of her collection, while the third is an epitaph for the phlyax writer Rhinthon. The date of her collection lies between the death of Rhinthon, whose *floruit* is placed by the *Suda* in the reign of Ptolemy Soter (d. 283/2), and the composition of Herondas' *Mimiambi*, where Nossis is twice mentioned in an uncomplimentary fashion (6.20–36, 7.57–58).[69] Since the poetry of Herondas belongs to the second quarter of the third century, Nossis' collection must be

---

68. A twelfth poem (12 G-P = *AP* 6.273), a call to Artemis for help in childbirth, is doubtfully ascribed to Nossis. Gow (1958a) 33 and Gow-Page (1965) II 443 argue that the manuscript heading ὡς Νοσσίδος descends from the *Garland* itself. If this is correct, then Meleager was uncertain about authorship and so could not have found the epigram in a collection of Nossis' poetry. This alone is sufficient reason to leave it out of account here.

69. For discussion of these references, see C. Neri, "Erinna in Eronda," *Eikasmos* 5 (1994) 221–32.

dated somewhat earlier, in the 280s or 270s.[70] She thus had the poetry books of Anyte and Asclepiades as models and perhaps knew some of the epigrams of Leonidas as well.

In contrast to Anyte who was labeled "unwomanly" and even considered masculine in her vigor, Nossis' feminine orientation has been discerned, but not often well understood. One theory, going back to Reitzenstein, makes her a *hetaira* because she celebrates dedications made in the temple of Aphrodite.[71] Another group of scholars, who argue for a noble birth, explain her dominant interest in women through a disputed ancient theory that the Locrian aristocracy was based on matrilineal descent.[72] Only recently have feminist scholars advanced the argument that Nossis' poetry is self-consciously woman-centered, probably homoerotic.[73] I here refocus this argument, by examining how Nossis conveys her appreciation for women, for the fineness and delicacy of female accomplishment and beauty, through gendered changes in the traditional dedicatory epigram. My special concern will be to show that Nossis produced her unique perspective, that of a woman looking at other women, by forging her epigrams into a collection.

Evidence that Nossis published a book of her poetry derives from two epigrams in which she names herself and makes programmatic statements. The first of these is now generally accepted as the prooemium of her collection:[74]

ἅδιον οὐδὲν ἔρωτος, ἆ δ' ὄλβια δεύτερα πάντα
  ἐστίν· ἀπὸ στόματος δ' ἔπτυσα καὶ τὸ μέλι.
τοῦτο λέγει Νοσσίς· τίνα δ' ἆ Κύπρις οὐκ ἐφίλασεν
  οὐκ οἶδεν χήνα τἄνθεα ποῖα ῥόδα.

(1 G-P = *AP* 5.170)

70. Confirmation for this general date comes from 2 G-P = *AP* 6.132 commemorating victory by Locri over the Bruttians, an epigram that seems related to a Leonidas dedication (35 G-P =*AP* 6.131) which can be dated before 272.

71. Reitzenstein (1893) 142. Gow-Page (1965) II 436 believe the theory may be true, although they note that it was unwelcome to Wilamowitz (1924) I 135.

72. The ancient source for this theory is Polybius 12.5.6, who is following Aristotle, although Timaeus disputed the claim. For evidence that Nossis' name is aristocratic, see I. Cazzaniga, "Nosside, nome aristocratico per la poetessa di Locri?," *ASNP* 2 (1972) 173–76 and, for a general analysis of Nossis' poetry taking account of what is known about historical Locri, see M. Gigante, "Nosside," *PP* 29 (1974) 22–39. Discussion of this trend is in O. Specchia, "Recenti studi su Nosside," *C&S* 23 (1984) 49–54.

73. Most important are the articles by M. B. Skinner: "Sapphic Nossis," *Arethusa* 22 (1989) 5–18; "Aphrodite Garlanded: Eros and Poetic Creativity in Sappho and Nossis," in *Rose di Pieria*, ed. Francesco de Martino (Bari, 1991) 90–96; and (1991b). See also Snyder 77–84, who suggests, however, that it may be "only a curious coincidence that the epigrams of Nossis . . . seem to reflect a distinctly female world" (77), and P. L. Furiani, "Intimità e socialità in Nosside di Locri," in de Martino 179–95.

74. Luck 183 was apparently the first to observe that the first epigram was a "Programmgedicht."

Nothing is sweeter than love. Everything desirable
   is second to it. I spit even honey from my mouth.
Nossis says this: The one who has never been loved by Aphrodite,
   that woman does not know what sort of flowers roses are.

Despite its apparent simplicity, this epigram offers a highly sophisticated and
allusive statement of Nossis' poetic creed. In both language and structure,
Nossis' quatrain evokes Hesiod's famous description of the poet's relationship
with the Muses:[75]

> ὃ δ' ὄλβιος, ὅντινα Μοῦσαι
> φίλωνται· γλυκερή οἱ ἀπὸ στόματος ῥέει αὐδή.

(Th. 96–97)

> Blest is the one whom the Muses
> love. Sweet song flows from his mouth.

Hesiod's "sweet song" becomes in a parallel passage "sweet dew upon the
tongue" (Th. 83), which, through the common association of dew with honey,[76]
stands as the direct antecedent of the "honey" that Nossis spits from her
mouth. In her introductory manifesto, then, Nossis rejects the inspiration of
Hesiodic epic, so proudly maintained by contemporary poets like Aratus and
Callimachus,[77] in favor of a tradition of more personal, erotic verse. Nossis'
substitution of Sappho for Hesiod as her primary archaic model is indicated
by the Sapphic character of the prooemium: the substitution of Aphrodite for
the Muse, the association of roses with poetic production (cf. βρόδων τὼν ἐκ
Πιερίας, "the roses from Pieria," 55.2–3 PLF), and the allusion in the first
phrase to the famous priamel that opens Sappho 16 (κάλλιστον, ... κῆν' ὄττω
τις ἔραται, "the most beautiful thing, ... whatever one loves," 16.3–4 PLF).
There seems little doubt that Nossis is here proclaiming Sapphic inspiration for
her woman-centered poetry.[78]

   Although other scholars have observed Nossis' gesture toward her archaic
models, it has been less noted that her quatrain alludes as well to her more
immediate predecessors. As we have seen, the phrase ἅδιον οὐδὲν ἔρωτος

75. See E. Cavallini, "Noss. A. P. V 170," Sileno 7 (1981) 179–83 and Skinner (1991a) 91–92.
76. See Jan H. Waszink, Biene und Honig als Symbol des Dichters und der Dichtung in der griechisch-
römischen Antike (Opladen, 1974) 6–9.
77. For the Hesiodic nature of Aratus' Phaenomena, see Callim. 56 G-P = AP 9.507 and, for
Callimachus' extended debt to Hesiod, H. Reinsch-Werner, Callimachus Hesiodicus: Die Rezeption
der hesiodischen Dichtung durch Kallimachos von Kyrene (Berlin, 1976).
78. Emphasized both by Gigante (1974) 25 and "Il manifesto poetico di Nosside," Letterature
comparate: Studi in onore di E. Paratore (Bologna, 1981) I 243–45 and by Skinner (1989) 7–11,
(1991a) 90–96, and (1991b) 32–33. But C. Riedweg, "Reflexe hellenistischer Dichtungstheorie
im griechischen Epigramm," ICS 19 (1994) 141–50 has now argued against any allusion to
Sappho and any intent to assert a poetic manifesto.

recalls Asclepiades' programmatic allusion to Anyte's collection and so defines Nossis' own position within the evolution of the genre as the first poet to combine erotic focus with inscriptional form. But the remainder of the epigram makes explicit allusion, I suggest, to another poet who provided Nossis with an even more important epigrammatic model. The metaphor of honey in the mouth, which occurs elsewhere in Hellenistic poetry (cf. Theoc. *Id.* 1.146, 7.80–85, 8.83), depends not only upon the punning identification of μέλι and μέλος but also upon the conventional representation of the poet as a bee (cf. Pl. *Ion* 534a–b). Yet Nossis' preference for ἔρως over μέλι cannot logically, in an introduction to a poetic collection, function as a simple rejection of poetry in favor of love. It rather seems likely that the contrast is that between the erotic poet and a nonerotic beelike poet, since already in Aristotle (*HA* 553a) we find mention of the chastity of bees.[79] This nonerotic honey represents, specifically, I suggest, the poetry of the maiden Erinna. In an admiring epigram Leonidas refers to her as a maiden bee (Παρθενικὴν νεάοιδον ἐν ὑμνοπόλοισι μέλισσαν Ἤρινναν Μουσέων ἄνθεα δρεπτομένην, 98.1–2 G-P = *AP* 7.13.1–2), and three later epigrams repeat the comparison of Erinna to a bee or of her poetry to honey (*AP* 2.110, 7.12.1, 9.190.1–2). This constellation of references to Erinna's beelike nature suggests that the symbol had a special aptness for the maiden poet, quite possibly because she had employed the image in her own *Distaff*.[80] Nossis' concern to define herself as an erotic poet in contradistinction to Erinna arises from the immediate and profound influence that Erinna's poetry had upon her own. Herondas recognizes the temporal relationship between the two when he refers to a character named Nossis as Erinna's daughter (6.20). Nossis follows in the footsteps of Erinna not only as a woman poet casting her gaze upon women but, more specifically, in composing four portrait poems that have as their direct model an epigram by Erinna celebrating the lifelike portrait of a certain Agatharchis:[81]

79. For further references, see Walter Robert-Tornow, *De apium mellisque apud veteres significatione et symbolica et mythologica* (Berlin, 1893) 12–19.

80. Other images descriptive of Erinna in the epigrams about her clearly derive from her own poetry. The age of nineteen, mentioned by both Asclepiades (28.2 G-P) and an anonymous epigrammatist (*AP* 9.190.4), corresponds to a number appearing in a fragmentary portion of the *Distaff* beside Erinna's own name (401.37 *SH*); Leonidas' βάσκανος ἔσσ', Ἀίδα (98.4 G-P), quoted as a statement of Erinna herself, reappears in one of the epigrams ascribed to her (2.3 G-P) and may have originated in a lost section of the *Distaff*; and references to her spinning with a distaff occur in three epigrams (*AP* 2.109, 7.12.4, 9.190.5–6).

81. The *AP* has also preserved two epitaphs for Baucis under the name of Erinna (7.710 and 712). While the second of these seems certainly a book epigram and so quite likely a later forgery, the first is just possibly a genuine inscription paralleled by *GV* 1415, a fifth-century epitaph set up by a woman for her friend. M. L. West, "Erinna," *ZPE* 25 (1977) 114–15 judges all three epigrams to be forgeries, but he also argues the untenable position that the *Distaff* itself had a male author; for a convincing refutation, see S. B. Pomeroy, "Supplementary Notes

ἐξ ἀταλᾶν χειρῶν τάδε γράμματα· λῷστε Προμαθεῦ,
  ἔντι καὶ ἄνθρωποι τὶν ὁμαλοὶ σοφίαν.
ταύταν γοῦν ἐτύμως τὰν παρθένον ὅστις ἔγραψεν
  αἰ καὐδὰν ποτέθηκ' ἧς κ' Ἀγαθαρχὶς ὅλα.

(3 G-P = AP 6.352)

This painting comes from delicate hands. My good Prometheus,
  there are even humans who equal you in wisdom.
If the one who so accurately painted this maiden had only
  added a voice, it would have been you, Agatharchis, yourself.

Nossis apparently felt her originality to lie in her adaptation of Erinna's po-
etry to a different stage in women's lives: while Erinna, who supposedly died
unmarried at nineteen, describes the portrait of the maiden Agatharchis and
mourns the marriage of her girlhood friend Baucis in her *Distaff,* all of Nossis'
female subjects, with the possible exception of Melinna in 8, are no longer
παρθένοι.

This interpretation of the honey image as a reference to Erinna's poetry
elucidates Nossis' proclamation in the much-misunderstood second couplet.
Although the transmitted κῆνα has often been emended to κῆνας or τῆνας,[82]
referring to either Aphrodite or Nossis herself, a series of parallel passages
extending from Hesiod (*Th.* 81–83, 96–97) through a variety of Hellenistic poets
show that the pronoun in the last line functions as the antecedent of τίνα.[83] The
one who is not loved (or "kissed") by Aphrodite is, then, a maiden poet, like
Erinna, and it is she who, though she culls flowers like a bee (Μουσέων ἄνθεα
δρεπτομένην, Leon. 98.2 G-P) does not know that roses are the best of blossoms.
Roses, with their sensual and erotic associations, are here symbols of Nossis'
own poetry or, what is much the same thing, symbols of the sensual, flowerlike

on Erinna," *ZPE* 32 (1978) 17–21. E. Cavallini, "Due poetesse greche" in de Martino 132–35
argues for the authenticity of all three epigrams.

82. Stadtmüller and Page print τῆνας τἄνθεα, with the genitive apparently referring to
Aphrodite. Gow-Page print κῆνα τ' in daggers because of the metrical difficulty but suggest
in the commentary (1965) *ad loc.* that κῆνας referring to Nossis rather than Aphrodite is the
correct reading. The argument of E. Degani, "Nosside," *GFF* 4 (1981) 52 in favor of this position
has found acceptance with Skinner (1989) 8 and (1991a) 92. While Heather White, *Essays in
Hellenistic Poetry* (Amsterdam, 1980) 17–20 has argued in favor of the manuscript reading, she
unnecessarily assumes that the roses provide an obscene reference. The reluctance to reading
κῆνα seems to have arisen because editors were hesitant to accept a unspecified referent that
was gendered female.

83. Callimachus in the Prologue to the *Aetia* (fr. 1.37–38) and again in the epigram that
probably concluded his collection (29.5–6 G-P = *AP* 7.525.5–6), the anonymous composer of a
poem that apparently ended an early collection of bucolic poetry ("Theoc." *Id.* 9.35–36), and
Bion in a programmatic piece (fr. 9.3–4). Each of these contains an expressed antecedent in
the main clause: ὃ δ' in Hesiod, πολιοὺς ... φίλους in Callimachus, τώς in "Theocritus,"
and τῆνον in Bion.

women who form the subject matter of that poetry (for a similar analogy of a beloved to flowers, cf. Rhianus 2 G-P = *AP* 12.58).

Although others have recently commented on the symbolism of Nossis' ἄνθεα,[84] it has apparently gone unnoticed that by identifying her epigrams with roses in an introductory poem Nossis makes the first known metaphorical association of a collection of poetry with flowers. Of course, the term *anthology* developed only later, with specific application to a selection of verse from a number of authors.[85] But Nossis deserves credit for first extending the metaphor of poetry as flowers to collected works. Both Sappho (55.2–3 *PLF*) and Pindar (*Ol.* 6.105; cf. 9.27) had used the metaphor of song as flower,[86] and the image of poet as bee had become explicit in Plato's *Ion* (534a–b). The extension of the metaphor to the collection came about when a woman poet sought to say what could not be said within the confines of conventional poetic language, that is, to state her place, as both follower and innovator, within the tradition of women's poetry. Although the dedicatory epigram had long been established as a concise, informational, unemotional form, Nossis could yet express her involvement with other women, the erotic excitement caused by their presence, by weaving a series of these short forms into a collection. The poet who was capable of composing poems that as a group delineate a woman's world was the one who understood "what sort of flowers roses are," the flowers beloved by Sappho and Aphrodite.

As Nossis identifies herself poetically in 1 as a faithful follower of Sappho, so she identifies herself biographically in 2 as a Locrian:

ἔντεα Βρέττιοι ἄνδρες ἀπ' αἰνομόρων βάλον ὤμων
 θεινόμενοι Λοκρῶν χερσὶν ὑπ' ὠκυμάχων,
ὧν ἀρετὰν ὑμνεῦντα θεῶν ὑπ' ἀνάκτορα κεῖνται
 οὐδὲ ποθεῦντι κακῶν πάχεας οὓς ἔλιπον.

(2 G-P = AP 6.132)

These weapons the Bruttians cast from their ill-fated arms,
 As they were struck by the battle-swift Locrians.
Singing of Locrian courage, they lie in the temple of the gods,
 Longing not at all for the forearms of the cowards they abandoned.

This epigram seems to vary by negation Leonidas 35 G-P = *AP* 6.131, in which arms taken from the Lucanians are said to long for (ποθέουσαι, 3) the enemy dead. But since Leonidas does not explicitly name his native Tarentum,

---

84. Degani 52 makes the important contribution of recognizing the metaphorical association of flowers with poetry in Nossis' prooemium, though he does so through a misinterpretation of the line; see also Skinner (1989) 8–9.

85. The first known epigram collection entitled Ἀνθολόγιον was that of Diogenianus, who lived in the second century A.D. (*Suda s. v.* Διογενειανός); see Waltz I xx–xxi.

86. For discussion of the image, see Deborah Steiner, *The Crown of Song: Metaphor in Pindar* (Oxford, 1986) 35–39.

that epigram could not have so easily served the function of biographical identification within his collection. Nossis seems to have learned such a use from Anyte's cauldron poem (2 G-P). And as Anyte shifts a father's consolation for his son's death to the song of the stone (4 G-P), so Nossis here chooses to praise the courage of the Locrian warriors, not in her own voice, but by ventriloquizing the sentiments of the enemies' weapons (ὑμνεῦντα). Both Anyte and Nossis thus find a way to express traditional masculine values within their collections without violating the construction of their own feminine personae.

In the prologue to his *Garland*, Meleager highlights the erotic nature of Nossis' collection by claiming that Eros melted wax on her tablets (δέλτοις κηρὸν ἔτηξεν Ἔρως, 1.10 G-P = *AP* 4.1.10). It is not necessary to assume, as some have, that Meleager here refers to lost homoerotic epigrams that were later expunged from the anthology tradition.[87] Meleager's description of Nossis' collection seems in fact to be based directly on her prooemium, where the image of poet as bee is modified to accommodate erotic inspiration. The apparent contradiction between her programmatic claim that "nothing is sweeter than love" and the nature of her surviving epigrams may result from a continuing misunderstanding of female eroticism. Like Sappho before her, Nossis celebrates the beauty of individual women, the sensual appeal of objects prized in their world. The erotic excitement she claims present in her collection arose not from any direct or indirect reference to sexual activity but merely from the casting of her gaze upon women as they go about the business of their private lives. There is no reason to assume, then, that the seven remarkably similar epigrams concerning dedications made by women or portraits painted of women were not to some degree exemplary of the whole collection:

> Ἥρα τιμάεσσα, Λακίνιον ἃ τὸ θυῶδες
> πολλάκις οὐρανόθεν νισομένα καθορῇς,
> δέξαι βύσσινον εἷμα τό τοι μετὰ παιδὸς ἀγαυᾶς
> Νοσσίδος ὕφανεν Θευφιλὶς ἁ Κλεόχας.

(3 G-P = *AP* 6.265)

> Esteemed Hera, you who often come from the sky
> to look upon your fragrant Lacinian temple,
> Receive a linen robe that Theuphilis, Cleocha's daughter,
> wove for you with her noble daughter Nossis.

> ἐλθοῖσαι ποτὶ ναὸν ἰδώμεθα τᾶς Ἀφροδίτας
> τὸ βρέτας ὡς χρυσῷ δαιδαλόεν τελέθει.
> εἵσατό μιν Πολυαρχὶς ἐπαυρομένα μάλα πολλάν
> κτῆσιν ἀπ' οἰκείου σώματος ἀγλαΐας.

(4 G-P = *AP* 9.332)

---

87. Gow-Page (1965) II 434; Skinner (1989) 14–15. But in (1991a) 93–94 with n. 31 Skinner concludes that the position I posit here is "equally plausible." Elsewhere Skinner (1991b) 35 points out that Meleager's image also refers to the process of encaustic painting.

Let us go to the temple and see Aphrodite's statue,
  how intricately it is adorned with gold.
Polyarchis set it up, enjoying the great wealth
  she has from the beauty of her own body.

χαίροισάν τοι ἔοικε κομᾶν ἄπο τὰν Ἀφροδίταν
  ἄνθεμα κεκρύφαλον τόνδε λαβεῖν Σαμύθας,
δαιδάλεός τε γάρ ἐστι καὶ ἁδύ τι νέκταρος ὄσδει·
  τούτῳ καὶ τήνα καλὸν Ἄδωνα χρίει.

(5 G-P = *AP* 6.275)

With joy, I think, Aphrodite has received this gift,
  a headband from the hair of Samytha.
For it is variegated and smells somewhat of sweet nectar;
  With this she, too, anoints lovely Adonis.

τὸν πίνακα ξανθᾶς Καλλὼ δόμον εἰς Ἀφροδίτας
  εἰκόνα γραψαμένα πάντ' ἀνέθηκεν ἴσαν.
ὡς ἀγανῶς ἕστακεν· ἴδ' ἁ χάρις ἁλίκον ἀνθεῖ.
  χαιρέτω, οὔ τινα γὰρ μέμψιν ἔχει βιοτᾶς.

(6 G-P = *AP* 9.605)

Her portrait Callo dedicated in the house of fair-haired Aphrodite,
  having had her image painted, a perfect likeness.
How gentle her stance! See how her charm blossoms!
  Let her rejoice, for her life incurs no blame.

Θαυμαρέτας μορφὰν ὁ πίναξ ἔχει· εὖγε τὸ γαῦρον
  τεῦξε τό θ' ὡραῖον τᾶς ἀγανοβλεφάρου.
σαίνοι κέν σ' ἐσιδοῖσα καὶ οἰκοφύλαξ σκυλάκαινα
  δέσποιναν μελάθρων οἰομένα ποθορῆν.

(7 ́ -P = *AP* 9.604)

This portrait shows Thaumareta's form. How well it depicts
  the lively youthfulness of the gentle-eyed girl.
Your house-guarding puppy, looking at you, would wag her tail,
  thinking she sees the mistress of the house.

αὐτομέλιννα τέτυκται· ἴδ' ὡς ἀγανὸν τὸ πρόσωπον.
  ἁμὲ ποτοπτάζειν μειλιχίως δοκέει.
ὡς ἐτύμως θυγάτηρ τᾷ ματέρι πάντα ποτῴκει·
  ἦ καλὸν ὅκκα πέλῃ τέκνα γονεῦσιν ἴσα.

(8 G-P = *AP* 6.353)

Melinna, her essence, is depicted. See how gentle her face.
  She seems to gaze at us tenderly.
How truly the daughter resembles her mother in all.
  How good when children are like their parents.

γνωτὰ καὶ τηλῶθε Σαβαιθίδος εἴδεται ἔμμεν
  ἅδ' εἰκὼν μορφᾷ καὶ μεγαλειοσύνᾳ.

θάεο· τὰν πινυτὰν τό τε μείλιχον αὐτόθι τήνας
ἔλπομ' ὁρῆν. χαίροις πολλά, μάκαιρα γύναι.

(9 G-P = *AP* 6.354)

For beauty and bearing this image is knowable
   even from afar as Sabaethis.
Observe! I think from here to see her wisdom and tenderness.
   Much joy to you, fortunate woman.

These seven poems bear an intriguing relationship one to another. Epigrams 4–6 are all dedications made in the temple of Aphrodite, linked by the repetition of the deity's name in the first line of each as they are differentiated by the variety of objects presented—a statue of the goddess, a headband, a portrait of the donor. Epigrams 7–9 also describe portraits of women. Although they are not specified as dedications, their resemblance to 6 suggests to the reader of the collection that these portraits, too, were presented to Aphrodite. Epigram 3, on a dedication to Hera made by Nossis and her mother, is the most distinctive of the poems. Skinner has argued that through the conventional association of weaving and poetry Nossis here pays "tribute to her mother as her earliest creative mentor."[88] While the epigram may indeed contain a personal statement of this sort, its emphasis on the mother-daughter relationship also links it to other poems. In 8 Melinna's portrait is praised because it shows forth her resemblance to her mother, while in the epilogue poem (11) Nossis identifies herself through reference to the "Locrian woman" who bore her. Such thematic links intertwining the poems suggest that the epigram book as a whole carries a meaning that could not be derived from any one poem read in isolation, either in inscribed form or in an anthology of works by various authors. Nossis' collection, it seems, delineated a society of Locrian women, bonded to one another through shared interests and values transmitted by women of the past.

   Among the thematic links between poems are the descriptive terms for the objects dedicated: βύσσινον (3.3) for Hera's robe, probably designating its linen fabric, more certainly its costliness;[89] χρυσῷ δαιδαλόεν (4.2) for Aphrodite's statue, referring perhaps to a patterned surface that is gilt; δαιδάλεος (5.3) for the headband, too, now perhaps indicating embroidery.[90] Delicacy of fabric, intricacy of design, sweetness of scent serve to define a feminine aesthetic,

88. Skinner (1991b) 23. In "Greek Women and the Metronymic," *AHB* 1 (1987) 39–42, Skinner argues that Nossis' reference to her mother as the daughter of Cleocha is not evidence for matrilineal descent at Locri but is "gender-specific," a speech trait of women addressing other women.

89. In Theoc. *Id*. 2.73 Simaetha dresses up in a χιτών made of βύσσος to attend a festival; the term may designate linen, cotton, or silk, or perhaps even a color; see Olck, "Byssos," *RE* 5 HB (1897) 1108–14.

90. Hesiod applies the adjective to Pandora's veil (*Th*. 574–75), where the "cunning" nature of the embroidered design is an appropriate sign of the wearer.

standards of beauty held by the women known to Nossis and reflected in both their possessions and persons. The sumptuousness of fine cloth is a proper gift for a noble family, proud to name three generations from grandmother to mother to daughter. The beauty of Aphrodite's golden statue mirrors the beauty of Polyarchis' own body from where came the means to purchase the gold. The multicolored headband has acquired its nectarous scent from the natural sweetness of Samytha herself, its former owner. The portraits all show forth a beauty that belongs both to the artistic object and to the woman it represents.

The females mentioned in the epigrams, both human and divine, are linked as well by a set of shared qualities, in both external appearance and its internal reflection. Three of the portraits convey a woman's gentleness (ἀγανῶς, 6.3; ἀγανοβλεφάρου, 7.2; ἀγανὸν τὸ πρόσωπον, 8.1), a quality visible in the face or eyes. Likewise, Sabaethis' shapeliness and bearing seem external manifestations of her internal wisdom and tenderness. Tenderness appears also as a quality of Melinna. In fact, the echo of her name in the adverb describing her (μειλιχίως, 8.2) may somehow explain why her very essence appears in the portrait from which she peers "tenderly." A similar kind of echo links Callo's visual "charm" (χάρις, 6.3) with the joy she is to feel in her portrait (χαιρέτω, 6.4), as Sabaethis is to rejoice (χαίροις, 9.4) in her portrait and Aphrodite feels joy (χαίροισαν, 5.1) in the dedication of a headband. Callo's blooming charm (χάρις ... ἀνθεῖ, 6.3) echoes as well in the epilogue poem where Nossis claims inspiration from the "bloom of Sappho's graces" (τὰν Σαπφοῦς χαρίτων ἄνθος, 11.2); this phrase, in turn, links Sappho's poetry with Nossis' own "blossoms" (τἄνθεα, 1.4) mentioned in the prooemium.[91] The qualities of the women described in the epigrams, their visual charm and internal joy, are, then, the qualities of Nossis' own poetry, transmitted to her by a process of Sapphic inspiration.

This brings us to one of the most surprising and innovative aspects of Nossis' collection, her use of a dramatic narrator. The voice heard in the epigrams once they have been gathered into a poetry book, far from being the anonymous voice of traditional dedicatory style, now seems to emanate from a single personality, who guides us, as it were, on a tour of an art gallery. When in 4 the narrating voice begins, "Let us go to the temple and see Aphrodite's statue," the participle ἐλθοῖσαι (4.1) shows that the speaker and addressees are all women. In the context of the collection it is natural to assume that the narrator is the epigrammatist herself. The "Nossis" who narrates thus assumes a double role, as an internal dramatic narrator speaking to her Locrian friends at the site of the dedications and, at the same time, as author and compiler

---

91. The connection is made even clearer when we remember that, as Nossis' blossoms are roses, so Sappho calls upon the "rosy-armed holy Graces" (βροδοπάχεες ἄγναι Χάριτες, 53 *PLF*).

speaking to us, her readers, from some uncertain literary or imaginative time and place.

It is in the context of this dramatic narrator that we must consider another theme linking the epigrams on portraits, the lifelike nature of the depictions. Since realism had been a major criterion for aesthetic worth from at least the early fourth century, Nossis' emphasis on verisimilitude is in part a compliment on the quality of the painting.[92]   But when the epigrams are considered as a group, this realism takes on significance as the narrator's subjective impression of the paintings.[93]   I suggest that Nossis emphasizes the lifelike nature of the portraits in order to invite us to enter *her* world, to see *her* women through *her* eyes—to view Callo's gentle stance and blossoming charm, to observe Sabaethis' wisdom and gentleness, to imagine as she does Thaumareta's puppy fawning at the sight of her mistress' likeness. Each woman is spotlighted for a moment and the reader asked to visualize her, physically and spiritually, as a type of woman worthy of adoration. But the true source of that adoration is the narrating voice, a projection of the epigrammatist, so that we come away from the collection, not just with a sense of the women who belonged to Nossis' world, but also with a knowledge of the poet herself, a woman with a Sapphic attachment to other women.

The personality generating this voice is further defined by two epigrams, epitaphic in form, concerning other literary figures—one local, male, and contemporary and the other foreign, female, and distantly past. The first of these is her epitaph for Rhinthon, a South Italian writer of phlyax plays:[94]

---

92. On realism in the art of the fourth century and later, see J. J. Pollitt, *Art in the Hellenistic Age* (Cambridge, 1986) 141–47. T. Gelzer, "Mimus und Kunsttheorie bei Herondas, Mimiambus 4," *Catalepton: Festschrift für B. Wyss* (Basel, 1985) 96–116 discusses the evidence for a critical theory promoting artistic realism. For the effects of pictorial realism upon the poetry of the age, see G. Zanker, *Realism in Alexandrian Poetry* (London, 1987).

93. The closest equivalent is found in two Hellenistic mimes, which are unlikely to be earlier than Nossis' collection. In Herondas' *Mimiambus* 4 two women visit a temple of Asclepius and exclaim upon the lifelike statues and paintings on display there, while in Theocritus' *Idyll* 15 two Alexandrian housewives attending a festival of Adonis marvel at the realistic depiction of figures woven on a tapestry (78–86). Both passages contain the same kind of exclamations and imperatives Nossis uses to describe her portraits. Yet in the poems by Herondas and Theocritus the women who comment so enthusiastically, and perhaps naively, on the realistic art objects they view are fictional characters of mime, from whom the male poet stands apart in a position of superior understanding. The narrator who takes us on a tour of dedications made by Locrian women conveys a more reliable message, because she is identified with the author herself.

94. A full study of Rhinthon may be found in Marcello Gigante, *Rintone e il teatro in Magna Grecia* (Naples, 1971). Oliver Taplin, *Comic Angels and Other Approaches to Greek Drama through Vase-Paintings* (Oxford, 1993), who argues that the so-called "phlyax vases" actually depict Athenian comedies produced in Magna Grecia, suggests that Rhinthon's contribution was

καὶ καπυρὸν γελάσας παραμείβεο καὶ φίλον εἰπώ
ῥῆμ᾽ ἐπ᾽ ἐμοί. ῾Ρίνθων εἰμ᾽ ὁ Συρακόσιος,
Μουσάων ὀλίγα τις ἀηδονίς, ἀλλὰ φλυάκων
ἐκ τραγικῶν ἴδιον κισσὸν ἐδρεψάμεθα.

(10 G-P = AP 7.414)

Laugh, and loudly; then as you pass by me, speak
a kind word. I am the Syracusan Rhinthon,
a lesser nightingale of the Muses, but from phlyax
tragedies I did pluck my own wreath of ivy.

The tragic burlesques of Rhinthon, who was a Syracusan, belong to the cultural sphere of Magna Grecia, and Nossis may even have known the playwright personally. This epigram serves, then, to situate Nossis' own poetic endeavor within an artistic culture that is local and contemporary. The posture granted to Rhinthon—his acknowledgment of his modest position in literary history and his simultaneous pride in his modification of an established genre—reflect the possibilities and limitations generally encountered by poets of the early Hellenistic age. We may be entitled to recognize a certain similarity between Rhinthon's achievement in turning the seriousness of tragedy to the comedy of burlesque and Nossis' accomplishment in adapting the dedicatory epigram that traditionally celebrated the successes of men to convey a woman's perception of the beauty and sensuousness of other women. Through its placement in the epigram collection (cf. the image of the ivy wreath with Nossis' roses), the Rhinthon epitaph may have served to suggest that Nossis' own poetry, though slight, was nonetheless innovative and worthy of praise.

As Wilamowitz pointed out long ago, certain epigrammatists—Leonidas, Callimachus, and Meleager—composed self-epitaphs that may have closed collections or portions of collections. Although no self-epitaph *per se* appears among Nossis' surviving poems, a poem of epitaphic from, concerning Nossis' poetic debt to Sappho, was viewed by both Reitzenstein and Wilamowitz as the epilogue of her collection:[95]

ὦ ξεῖν᾽, εἰ τύ γε πλεῖς ποτὶ καλλίχορον Μιτυλήναν
   τᾶν Σαπφοῦς χαρίτων ἄνθος ἐναυσόμενος
εἰπεῖν ὡς Μούσαισι φίλαν τήνᾳ τε Λόκρισσα
   τίκτεν· ἴσαις δ᾽ ὅτι μοι τοὔνομα Νοσσίς, ἴθι.[96]

(11 G-P = AP 7.718)

---

the subversion of Athenian tragedy and comedy under the influence of "Alexandrian" poetics (48–52).

95. Reitzenstein (1893) 139; Wilamowitz (1913) 298–99 and (1924) I 135.

96. Most editors have eliminated the reference to Nossis' Locrian mother by printing Brunck's Λοκρὶς γᾶ, but Λόκρισσα has been convincingly defended by C. Gallavotti, "L'epigramma biographico di Nosside" in *Studi filologici e storici in onore di V. de Falco* (Naples, 1971) 243, 245–46.

> If you, stranger, are sailing to Mitylene where dances are lovely
>   in order to borrow the flower of Sappho's graces,
> Announce that a Locrian woman bore one dear to the Muses
>   and to her. You should know that my name is Nossis. Now go.

Nossis' direct model for this poem was an epigram by Asclepiades in which a cenotaph asks the passerby to report to Euippus' father in Chios that his son has perished at sea so that only his name survives (31 G-P = *AP* 7.500).[97] By closing her collection as she had opened it, with an echo of Asclepiades, Nossis thus indirectly acknowledges her debt to the first composer of erotic epigram. But Nossis' epilogue is a remarkable modification of epitaphic form to serve as a proclamation of her poetic lineage. As Euippus sends a message of his death to his father, so Nossis sends a message of her birth across both temporal and spatial seas to her poetic mother Sappho. Despite the conventions of the form, the message is addressed to a stranger who is not literally a passerby but, like the ξεῖνε of Anyte 18, signifies the reader of the collection. Nossis delivers to this unknown reader, not just the "seal" of her name, but, through a rhetorical sleight of hand, a statement of her position within literary history. The type of reader who is summoned as Nossis' messenger is one who seeks inspiration from Sappho and is therefore an aspiring poet. By insisting that this new poet speak Nossis' name when she sails for Mitylene, Nossis claims for herself the right to be acknowledged as the inheritor of Sappho's graces, as an intermediary between the mother poet and any future Sapphic composers. Ultimately, then, Nossis' epilogue is a plea for poetic immortality, for a place within the tradition of women's poetry.

The personalized authorial voice that speaks directly to the reader in Nossis' epigram book owes much to the tradition of women's poetry in earlier Greek culture. Nossis acknowledges, most directly, the influence of Sappho's lyrical voice and, more obliquely, if my interpretation of the prooemium is correct, that her manner owed something to Erinna, who developed a personalized voice of grief in the *Distaff* and apparently composed an epigram that stands as a direct model for Nossis' portrait poems. I see in Nossis' assertion of independence from Erinna—her preference for *eros* over honey—not the "anxiety of influence" that is Harold Bloom's term for a poet's rejection of his literary precursors in the manner of an Oedipal boy's longing to replace his father, but rather the "anxiety of authorship" which is the alternative term coined by Sandra Gilbert and Susan Gubar to describe a woman author's "radical fear that she cannot create, that because she can never become a 'precursor' the act of writing will

---

97. For discussion of Asclepiades' epigram and the series of imitations it spawned, see Tarán (1979) 132–49.

isolate or destroy her."[98]   For Nossis, the problem with Erinna was perhaps not so much Erinna herself as what male poets had made of her. She had in fact become the darling of contemporary male epigrammatists: Asclepiades and Leonidas wrote epigrams celebrating her, and Antiphanes later cited her as a favorite of Callimachus' pedantic followers (9 G-P, *Garland* = *AP* 11.322). But in becoming the acknowledged "precursor" of important Hellenistic male poets, Erinna had in fact been isolated and destroyed—kept a child (ἁ παῖς, Leon. 98.4 G-P) confined to her loom until Hades snatched her away as bride (Leon. 98.3; Asclep. 28.3–4 G-P). Asclepiades makes it clear that the charm of her poetry was its slightness (οὐχὶ πολύς; cf. παυροεπὴς Ἤριννα καὶ οὐ πολύμυθος ἀοιδαῖς, "Erinna of few words and not lengthy in her songs," Antip. Sid., G-P 58.1 = *AP* 7.713.1), as befits a "nineteen-year-old maiden" (Asclep. 28.1–2). To become admired by male poets, Erinna had to die, and before knowing the kiss of Aphrodite. But Nossis rejects this role of sacrificial maiden, and offers as an alternative the Sapphic perspective of an adult woman speaking about women to a primary audience of women. As Skinner has pointed out, the historical result of Nossis' choice to define herself within a female subculture was denigration by some male authors and neglect by most others.[99]

Nossis was perhaps the first to synthesize what would come to be the two originating poles in the Hellenistic epigram tradition—the inscriptional as found in Anyte's collection and the elegiac originating in Asclepiades'. By combining the female persona of Anyte's external composer with Asclepiades' more subjective internal voice, Nossis reduced practically to the vanishing point, at least in her epigrams about women's dedications, the distance between the voice of the internal dramatic narrator and the voice of the external composer and organizer of the collection. The result was, perhaps, one of the most thematically coherent assemblages of Hellenistic epigrams. By repetition of theme and similarity of form, by the use of a dramatic narrator who speaks across the boundaries of individual poems, Nossis creates a sense of an author's persona that was by rule of genre absent from the earlier tradition of dedicatory epigram. It is precisely this sense of a creative presence who shapes and selects the poems we are reading that characterizes the poetry books of later Latin literature. It should be acknowledged as well that Nossis likely produced the first "anthology," in the sense that she troped her epigrams as a gathering of flowers. By adapting Sappho's metaphorical equation of roses with poetry, Nossis textualized her own "Sapphic circle" as a garland of blossoms. Even though Meleager's direct borrowing of the flower metaphor for his *Garland* lies behind the later tradition of "anthologies," both epigram collections and other

---

98. Bloom, *The Anxiety of Influence: A Theory of Poetry* (New York, 1973); Gilbert and Gubar, *The Madwoman in the Attic: The Woman Writer and the Nineteenth-Century Literary Imagination* (New Haven, 1979) 48–49.

99. Skinner (1991b) 35–37.

poetic types, Nossis' contribution to the process of literary development has been neither acknowledged by the ancients nor observed by modern scholars. This effacement of her accomplishment is directly related to the persona she created, that of a female poet speaking to other women about the beauties and joys of the world they inhabit.

LEONIDAS OF TARENTUM

As Anyte and Nossis adapted sepulchral and dedicatory epigram to a female perspective, so Leonidas of Tarentum modified the same epigram types to focus on the lives of the lower classes.[100] Although not all of Leonidas' extant epigrams commemorate fishermen, carpenters, farmers, weavers, and the like, many of his epigrams display an ideological perspective that is closely identified with the class values typical of such individuals.[101] Modern scholars have often found little to admire in Leonidas' poetry, largely because of a perceived contradiction between his rather ornate style and his principal subject matter. The ancient assessment was quite different, however. Leonidas' popularity with later composers of epigram variations is the probable reason that so many of his epigrams—about one hundred—are preserved in the *Anthology*. Leonidas was in fact the most influential of all Greek epigrammatists, finding a host of imitators down to the Byzantine era. The radical discontinuity between ancient and modern assessments of his work suggests that modern scholars have overlooked the significance of Leonidas' novel subject matter in its historical setting, which included publication in a collected format where the juxtaposition of individual epigrams with individual messages generated meanings of broader compass.

The most likely date for the publication of Leonidas' collection was the second quarter of the third century, although he may have been composing epigrams from shortly after 300 B.C. The dating proposed here follows the traditional chronology for Leonidas' life instead of the later chronology advanced by Gow,

100. The standard commentary on Leonidas is that of Gow-Page (1965). Among older works the most important is the study of Johannes Geffcken, *Leonidas von Tarent* in *Jahrbücher für classische Philologie*, Suppl. 23 (Leipzig, 1896). Largely derivative is the commentary by A. Olivieri, *Epigrammatisti Greci della Magna Grecia e della Sicilia* (Naples, 1949) 5–146; see also the discussion of select poems by Rocco Labellarte, *Leonida di Taranto: Antologia di Epigrammi* (Bari, 1969).

101. By my count close to half of Leonidas' epigrams deal with lower-class characters or rustic themes. In addition, his epigrams on more prosperous individuals and on philosophical topics tend to support an underlying perspective that finds value in simplicity and dignified poverty. Although some epigrams, such as those on literary or artistic works, do not seem to contribute to this theme, the majority of the extant epigrams evince a unifying philosophical perspective. It is important to keep in mind that we may have remnants of more than one epigram collection and that such poetry books, like many later Roman ones, were unlikely to be completely consistent in theme.

who sought to place Leonidas' *floruit* at the middle or in the second half of the century.[102] Gow wishes to discount the evidence provided by two epigrams on victories over the Lucanians (34 G-P = *AP* 6.129; 35 G-P = *AP* 6.131) because neither expressly names the victor. But it does seem very likely, if not certain, that the dedicating city was Tarentum, Leonidas' homeland and a traditional adversary of the Lucanians until 272 B.C. when both submitted to Rome. The imitation of one of these (35) by Nossis (2 G-P) strengthens the evidence that Leonidas was an established epigrammatist by the second quarter of the century. A Leonidean epigram on Aratus' *Phaenomena* (101 G-P = *AP* 9.25), which could not have been written before about 276 B.C., gives us a *terminus post quem* consistent with a *floruit* early in the second quarter of the century. And since Leonidas speaks of himself as an old man in an epigram that was apparently composed for his collection (37 G-P = *AP* 6.302), even the traditional dating of his birth to about 315 B.C. may not be far wrong. In questioning some of the more dubious biographical facts commonly drawn from Leonidean epigrams, Gow has also discounted other more persuasive evidence; his argument for a later dating is ultimately based only on a judgment of style.[103]

In the nineteenth century Leonidas was commonly viewed as a poor man's epigrammatist, a composer of epitaphs and dedications commissioned by members of the lower class.[104] At the end of that century, however, scholars began to

102. For the traditional chronology and the related biography constructed from the epigrams, see Geffcken (1896) 132 (where he claims to be able to order Leonidas' epigrams chronologically) and "Leonidas von Tarent," *RE* 24 HB (1925) 2023 (where he disavows his earlier attempt to order the poems); Bernhard Hansen, *De Leonida Tarentino* (Diss. Leipzig, 1914) 8–10; Luigia A. Stella, *Cinque poeti dell'Antologia Palatina* (Bologna, 1949) 77–79, 147–52 (who pushes the date of birth back to 340–45); Olivieri 5; Beckby I 24; Labellarte 7–8; L. Coco, "Leonida di Taranto," *C&S* 95 (1985) 61–62. Gow first set out his arguments against this chronology in "Leonidas of Tarentum," *CQ* 8 (1958) 113–23 and then more briefly in his commentary, Gow-Page (1965) II 308. Webster 218–20 accepts Gow's assessment on the grounds that Leonidas has borrowed from Callimachus and Apollonius and so places his poetic activity in the years 270–20. But Marcello Gigante, first in *L'epigramma in Magna Grecia* (Salerno, 1967) 25 and then in his important book on Leonidas, *L'edera di Leonida* (Naples, 1971) 17–19, has argued that Gow's conclusions are poorly founded.

103. Gow (1958b) 117 finds that Leonidas bears a closer resemblance to Dioscorides and Antipater of Sidon than to Callimachus and Asclepiades and concludes that "Leonidas' deplorable popularity with later and worse epigrammatists encourage[s] the suspicion that he is usually dated substantially—possibly as much as half a century—too early." Of course, the fallacy of this argument is to assume that Leonidas' popularity with epigrammatists of the second half of the third and of the second century suggests he belongs to that period. The underlying assumption is teleological, that Leonidas is an inferior stylist and so must belong to a period of decay.

104. See, for instance, Alfred and Maurice Croiset, *An Abridged History of Greek Literature*, trans. George Heffelbower (New York, 1904) 443. For discussion of the trend, see Geffcken (1925) 2023.

emphasize the literary character of Leonidas' work—its connection with other literature and philosophy and its obvious fictionality. But from this common approach developed diametrically opposed assessments, based on differing views about the proper role of epigram. On the one hand, Reitzenstein judged that no other early epigrammatist employed "such splendid, choice, or better-adorned language," which he connected with lyric and tragic precedent.[105] What Reitzenstein admired in Leonidas was his playful treatment of conventional epigram form, which he adduced as evidence that Leonidas' epigrams were not inscriptional, but "poetic παίγνια for the banquet" ("dichterische παίγνια beim Gelage").[106] Wilamowitz, on the other hand, judged Leonidas no poet at all, not even a "virtuoso of language" ("Künstler der Sprache"), because of a poetic style he labeled affected, careless in phrasing, and padded.[107] Believing only some few of Leonidas' epigrams to have been true inscriptions, Wilamowitz directed his criticism primarily against the poems deemed epideictic. While Reitzenstein's enthusiasm for Leonidas has found relatively few followers among twentieth-century critics, the counterview of Wilamowitz has been highly influential, based as it is on a commonly held assumption about epigram, namely, that epigram form derives its essential character from the limitations of space imposed by the stone and that any deviation from the inscriptional requirement of conciseness and simplicity is a deviation from the proper nature of the form.[108] Leonidas has received particularly harsh treatment as the one responsible for, the originator of, the rhetorical quality symptomatic of later Greek epigram.

Yet surely the apparent contradiction between Leonidas' style (an abundant use of neologisms, alliteration, and symmetry)[109] and his subject matter (the humble classes) signals a typically Hellenistic *literary* endeavor, the elevation of traditionally subliterary topics through the use of learned and allusive language. While Leonidas may well have recited individual epigrams at social gatherings and probably composed some genuine inscriptions, the shared themes displayed by many of the poems that have come down to us and the sometimes daunting language in which they are written indicate that they were intended to produce striking effects in a purely literary medium, namely, that

105. Reitzenstein (1893) 145.
106. Reitzenstein (1893) 149.
107. Wilamowitz (1924) I 143.
108. Gow (1958b) 113, for instance, calls Leonidas a "tedious writer" and in Gow-Page (1965) II 307 "a competent versifier" but "hardly ever more than that." For other examples of negative or guarded assessments, see O. Specchia, "Recenti studi su Leonida di Taranto," *C&S* 45–46 (1973) 125–26. Even so recent a critic as G. Zanker 162 finds that, because of Leonidas' artificial style and epideictic purpose, his "attitude to the realistic matter of his poems is . . . quite distant, for all his occasional success in evoking pathos."
109. For a detailed discussion of Leonidas' style, see B. Hansen 30–65. He concludes that Leonidas' stylistic artifice is better perceived by the ear than the eye, and of course we should remember that his poetry book was likely to be read aloud by its ancient readers.

of a poetry book. Leonidas modified the customary use of the inscriptional epigram—to celebrate and commemorate the well-to-do or at least the moderately well off—to present detailed portraits of lower-class individuals in their workaday world and to convey a philosophical position, heavily influenced by Cynic tenets, that valued the lives of such people. The epigram form, because of its characteristic ability to "sum up" an individual and to express succinctly the values of a certain societal group, was well suited, when organized in collective form, to represent a *class* of individuals in all their variety and connecting similarity. But since Leonidas' subjects included, in addition to poor laborers, individuals of higher class standing and even famous artists and literary figures, the fictive world encompassed by his epigrams seems to represent, not a part of society, but society as a whole. The unifying thread was not, then, subject matter, but perspective, the perspective of a creative artist who shared the lower-class values of his most sympathetically treated characters and who yet possessed the literary and philosophical expertise to produce a work of art appealing to the upper-class readers. The result was not just an anthology based on thematic commonality, but a poetry book expressing an ideology of class.

Of course, we should not assume that every epigram convincingly ascribed to Leonidas formed part of a single collection. Some few may have come to Meleager, or perhaps to an already syncretized text he was using, from a variety of sources—inscriptions,[110] privately produced anthologies of epigrams, or even other collections issued by Leonidas himself. But the great majority of the Leonidean epigrams display such consistency in topic, theme, and philosophical outlook that it seems likely Meleager's principal source was a carefully orchestrated epigram book, consisting of nearly one hundred poems, at a minimum, and perhaps considerably more. Remains of other Hellenistic epigram books—the new Posidippus collection, the Theocritus epigram book, and even reconstructed portions of Meleager's *Garland*—suggest that Leonidas may have employed sequencing of like poems and thematic linkage to provide coherency and structure. Consequently, it may not be entirely untrue to Leonidas' own arrangement to discuss his epigrams in thematic groups or categories. We will consider first those most closely mimicking genuine inscriptional types and then the more overtly "bookish" epigrams; in some of the latter

110. Weisshäupl (1889) 32–34 has argued persuasively that Meleager himself (like Philip and Agathias) did not copy epigrams from stone but only from poetic collections. We cannot rule out the possibility, however, that the editions used by Meleager were already contaminated with additions from a variety of sources, including, possibly, genuine inscriptions. An epigram commemorating Pyrrhus' victory over Antigonus in 273 B.C. (95 G-P = *AP* 6.130) is an example of a known inscription that was ascribed to Leonidas, though probably in a post-Meleagrian context; on the doubtful authenticity of the ascription, see Gow (1958b) 115–16 and Gow-Page (1965) I 392.

Leonidas speaks directly in his own poetic persona to provide moral instruction of a Cynic cast and to associate his own life with the lives of lower-class characters.

Among the most characteristic of Leonidean epigrams are dedications by working people who offer tools of their trade. A simple example is the offering made by the carpenter Theris:

Θῆρις ὁ δαιδαλόχειρ τᾷ Παλλάδι πῆχυν ἀκαμπῆ
    καὶ τετανὸν νώτῳ καμπτόμενον πρίονα
καὶ πέλεκυν ῥυκάναν τ᾽ εὐαγέα καὶ περιαγές
    τρύπανον ἐκ τέχνας ἄνθετο παυσάμενος.

(7 G-P = *AP* 6.204)

Theris the skillful-handed has offered to Pallas
    on the occasion of retirement from his craft
an uncurved ruler, a straight saw with bent handle,
    his axe and bright plane, and a rotating borer.

At the very beginning of the epigram, the splendid δαιδαλόχειρ, a Leonidean neologism, gives epic and mythical resonances to Theris' abilities as a carpenter. In other epigrams, too, an imaginative phrase sometimes challenges the assumption of banausic worthlessness, as another carpenter's axe is called "the chief magistrate of his craft" (8.6 G-P = *AP* 6.205.6), a fisherman's trident is labeled a "Posidonian spear" (52.5 G-P = *AP* 6.4.5), and a weaver's shuttle is called a "songstress of the loom" (41.5 G-P = *AP* 6.288.5) or "the guardian of Penelope's bed" (42.6 G-P = *AP* 6.289.6). In the Theris epigram the epithet so elevates the carpenter's skill that the reader is encouraged to reconceive his commonplace tools as instruments of high artistry. In the list of dedicated objects, the careful variation of noun-adjective word order enhanced by play with sound and meaning (note the pairing of ἀκαμπῆ with καμπτόμενον and εὐαγέα with περιαγές)[111] conveys not only the poet's own literary skill but also the carpenter's aesthetic appreciation of his tools—the tension of curved and straight lines, the flash of axe or plane, the whirling movement of the borer. While Leonidas' adjectives are largely prosaic, descriptive of the utilitarian, and so not evocative of traditional aesthetic categories, we may yet come to realize that in the world of such workmen beauty is a direct consequence of utility.

Unlike the offering of a carpenter's tools, the dedication of a woven garment finds precedent in the earlier history of epigram because such objects were sometimes offered by persons of aristocratic standing. In a couplet attributed

---

111. The reading εὐαγέα is commonly rejected, and Gow-Page (1965) *ad loc.* claim that "*bright* is plainly unsuitable." I cannot understand why this should be so, if we imagine the tools from the craftsman's perspective.

to Anacreon, one of the dedicators, Dyseris, may be correctly identified as the wife of the Thessalian prince Echecratidas:[112]

Πρηξιδίκη μὲν ἔρεξεν, ἐβούλευσεν δὲ Δύσηρις,
εἶμα τόδε· ξυνὴ δ' ἀμφοτέρων σοφίη.

("Anacreon" 7 FGE = AP 6.136)

This garment was made by Prexidice and designed
by Dyseris. The skill belongs to both of them.

In Hellenistic epigram as well, we find dedications by upper-class weavers, like the offering presented by Theuphilis and her "noble daughter" Nossis (3 G-P). A Leonidean epigram commemorating the dedication of a garment embroidered by three girls in competition (40 G-P = *AP* 6.286) may belong to the same class. But for many Hellenistic women weaving was a matter of hard work, a necessary trade through which a meager livelihood could be earned.[113] Such women appear in two other Leonidean epigrams, in which groups of three or four sisters, who have eked out a living by weaving, dedicate the tools of their trade to their patron goddess Athena (41 G-P = *AP* 6.288, 42 G-P = *AP* 6.289). In one of these the weaving instruments are presented as a tithe, a small offering (ἐξ ὀλίγων ὀλίγαν μοῖραν, 41.8) given in hopes of finding relief from hunger (θείης δ' εὐσιπύους ἐξ ὀλιγησιπύων, 41.10), while in the other three Cretan sisters have decided to give up their weaving equipment, lovingly described, in abandonment of their trade. Through the motif of retirement, for which Leonidas sometimes specifies old age as the cause (cf. 43 G-P = *AP* 5.206), a dedication comes to function like an epitaph by marking the closure of a person's professional, if not physical, lifetime.[114] The two points of stoppage are synchronized in Leonidas' epitaph for the old weaver Platthis, one of his most admired poems:

ἑσπέριον κἠῷον ἀπώσατο πολλάκις ὕπνον
  ἡ γρηῢς πενίην Πλατθὶς ἀμυνομένη,
καί τι πρὸς ἠλακάτην καὶ τὸν συνέριθον ἄτρακτον
  ἤεισεν πολιοῦ γήραος ἀγχίθυρος
καί τι παριστίδιος δινευμένη ἄχρις ἐπ' ἠούς
  κεῖνον Ἀθηναίης σὺν Χάρισιν δόλιχον,

112. See Page (1981) 139, who argues that "the fact that the recipient divinity is not named in the present epigram may be an indication of early date."

113. See Sarah B. Pomeroy, *Women in Hellenistic Egypt from Alexander to Cleopatra* (New York, 1984) 163–71.

114. The last line of the poem about the Cretan weavers (θῆκαν Ἀθαναίας παυσάμεναι καμάτων, 42.8) echoes the final words in Leonidas' two dedications by carpenters (ἐκ τέχνας ἄνθετο παυσάμενος, 7.4; ἐκ τέχνας θήκατο παυόμενος, 8.10). Such echoes promote the illusion of inscription by maintaining the conventional formulae typical of the form, while they also serve, within the collection, to reinforce thematic connectiveness.

ἢ ῥικνὴ ῥικνοῦ περὶ γούνατος ἄρκιον ἱστῷ
χειρὶ στρογγύλλουσ᾽ ἱμερόεσσα κρόκην·
ὀγδωκονταέτις δ᾽ Ἀχερούσιον ηὔγασεν ὕδωρ
ἡ καλὰ καὶ καλῶς Πλατθὶς ὑφηναμένη.

(72 G-P = AP 7.726)

Morning and evening the aged Platthis would fight
    against sleep in her struggle with poverty.
She would sing, though at the very door of grey old age,
    to her distaff and its assistant, the spindle,
And beside the loom until dawn's light she sang, traversing
    the long course of Athena with the Graces,
Or, wrinkled on wrinkled knee, laboriously twirling
    with her hand the thread needed for the loom.
At age eighty she gazed upon the water of Acheron,
    Platthis who wove beauty into beautiful cloth.

The epigram clearly offers a challenge to traditional assumptions about the praiseworthy by emphasizing Platthis' ability to take aesthetic pleasure in her weaving through her song and to produce high-quality work despite her extreme age and poverty. In a fragment from a third-century Cynic philosopher the virtue of contentment with little is illustrated by old women who hum as they chew coarse bread (γράδια φυστὴν φαγόντα τερετίζοντα, Stob. *Flor.* 3.1.98).[115] Although Leonidas is clearly not particularizing this exact sentiment, his Platthis epigram conveys much the same message.

The ornate literariness of Leonidas' epigrams about fishermen, who were among the most destitute individuals in Hellenistic society,[116] seems designed to create an acute dissonance between subject and style. Yet I would argue that the language of these poems should not be viewed as merely rhetorical, decoration without regard to content,[117] but rather as a means to shake the reader's complacent disregard for such marginal creatures by inculcating, against normative societal attitudes, an awareness of the skills required for their dangerous

---

115. Stobaeus' selection comes from a περὶ αὐταρκείας by Teles, who is quoting Bion of Borysthenes; cf. Geffcken (1896) 105.

116. The poverty of fishermen is evident from the emaciated appearance of the Vatican-Louvre Fisherman (Seneca type), a statue type which Brunilde S. Ridgway, *Hellenistic Sculpture I: The Styles of ca. 331–200 B.C.* (Madison, 1990) 335 (Pl. 173) associates with a third-century original; see also Pollitt 143 with Pl. 155; H. P. Laubscher, *Fischer und Landleute: Studien zur hellenistischen Genreplastik* (Mainz, 1982); and R. R. R. Smith, *Hellenistic Sculpture: A Handbook* (London, 1991) 138–39. The theme of the Theocritean *Idyll* 21, which is likely indebted to Leonidas 52 (see Gow-Page [1965] *ad* 52.7f.), is the poverty (πενία, 1) of the two fishermen who there engage in dialogue.

117. For such an attitude, cf. Geffcken (1896) 113 on 52 G-P, "ein ... inhaltsleeres und geschmackloses Gedicht"; but see now Gigante's sensitive discussion (1971) 62–63.

and unprofitable trade. As in the carpenter's dedication, the terms used to describe the items offered by Diophantus (52 G-P = *AP* 6.4) convey, through the high articulateness of poetic language, the fisherman's own perception of his gear: his hook becomes a worthy gift by virtue of being "easily swallowed" (εὐκαπές, 1),[118] the alliterative lengthened forms of δούνακα δουλιχόεντα (1) reinforce by the play of sound the semantically conveyed length of his "long rod," and his trap is celebrated as the "invention" of fishermen precisely because it saves these "sea-roaming net casters" (ἁλιπλάγκτων εὕρεμα δικτυβόλων, 4) from the hardships of seining in rough seas. In fact, the threefold repetition of τεχνασθέντα (3), τέχνας (7), and τεχνοσύνας (8) is designed to refigure the hard work of the fisherman as high craft.

A similar celebration of fishing skill appears in Leonidas' three epitaphs for fishermen, all of which gain their point by subverting the conventions of epigram form and the values it traditionally promoted. The demise of Theris at an advanced age, of natural causes, and in the shelter of his reed hut merits commemoration in verse because this perfectly uneventful death is so extraordinary for one who has lived his life as a diver:[119]

Θῆριν τὸν τριγέροντα, τὸν εὐάγρων ἀπὸ κύρτων
    ζῶντα, τὸν αἰθυίης πλείονα νηξάμενον,
ἰχθυσιληιστῆρα, σαγηνέα, χηραμοδύτην,
    οὐχὶ πολυσκάλμου πλώτορα ναυτιλίης,
ἔμπης οὔτ' Ἀρκτοῦρος ἀπώλεσεν οὔτε καταιγὶς
    ἤλασε τὰς πολλὰς τῶν ἐτέων δεκάδας,
ἀλλ' ἔθαν' ἐν καλύβῃ σχοινίτιδι λύχνος ὁποῖα
    τῷ μακρῷ σβεσθεὶς ἐν χρόνῳ αὐτόματος·
σῆμα δὲ τοῦτ' οὐ παῖδες ἐφήρμοσαν οὐδ' ὁμόλεκτρος
    ἀλλὰ συνεργατίνης ἰχθυβόλων θίασος.

(20 G-P = *AP* 7.295)

Theris the thrice-aged, who lived from fish-catching traps,
    was better at swimming than a gull.
A fish pirate, a seiner, a diver into caves,
    though not a sailor on a many-oared ship,
He did not meet his death from stormy Arcturus,
    nor did a squall end the many decades of his life,
But he died in his reed hut, like a lamp
    extinguishing itself in the course of time.
This tomb was set up not by children or a bedmate
    but by his fellow-working guild of fish-hunters.

118. Salmasius proposed εὐκαπές to replace the metrically difficult εὐκαμπές, which Geffcken (1896) 114 defended; see Gow-Page (1965) *ad loc.*

119. For a good discussion of this poem as a series of infractions of norms, see G. Guidorizzi, "Il mare e il vecchio (Leonida, *A. P.* VII 295)," *Acme* 30 (1977) 69–76.

Elsewhere in Greek epigram the sea commonly appears as a dangerous realm where humans are subject to forces beyond their control. But here Leonidas' initial description of Theris as an expert swimmer, diver, and net fisherman celebrates his ability to manipulate those dangerous forces. As Reitzenstein pointed out long ago, the third couplet subverts the common epitaphic *topos* of shipwreck in storm: despite his daily brush with a watery death, Theris dies not in a sea squall but in the comfort of his own bed.[120] So too, in the final couplet we find allusion, through rejection, to the epitaphic convention of naming the bereaved relatives: in the society that is the subject of Leonidas' poetry book, worker solidarity often takes the place of family love for those too poor to support an *oikos*. The dangers that Theris managed to escape can be surmised from two other epitaphs—that for Tharsys (65 G-P = *AP* 7.506), who was half-eaten by a sea creature, and for Parmis (66 G-P = *AP* 7.504), who died by choking on a raw fish. While both poems illustrate Leonidas' tendency to the baroque, I would resist the idea that he is simply enticed by bizarre happenstance. The careful structure given the poems suggests that Leonidas is attempting, through modification of traditional epigram form, to accommodate the previously unthinkable—praise of a fisherman. In 65 Leonidas builds his epigram around the conventions of the cenotaph, adapted to suit one who is partially buried on land and partially lost at sea. But beyond the macabre humor of the piece lies a genuine celebration of its subject, who in diving after an anchor, "a fixed weight in the sea" (ἔνοχον βάρος εἰς ἅλα, 3), was lifted out, half-eaten, himself a "cold weight from the sea" (ψυχρὸν βάρος ἐξ ἁλὸς, 9). For his fellow fishermen, Tharsys deserves remembrance as one who died heroically in the accomplishment of his task. The death of Parmis, who choked on his daily catch, is more mundane, and yet pathetic, precisely because the event was such an unexpected twist of fate. Parmis was a "consummate fisherman" (ἄκρος ... ἰχθυβολεύς, 66.2), normally the master of rock-dwelling perch and wrasses. But one day a freshly caught fish slipped into his gullet as he attempted to taste it, and he choked to death as he thrashed about among his lines and poles. While for us Parmis' death may seem more suitable to the tabloid than to serious literature, Gripon the fisherman (Γρίπων ὁ γριπεύς, 12), who erected his tomb, seems to have perceived a tragic irony in his fate.[121]

Most of the themes we have identified in Leonidas' epigrams about carpenters, weavers, and fishermen appear as well in his poems about hunters and herders. In these epigrams, too, the summing up of a lifetime devoted to a given occupation is conveyed by a detailed list of implements dedicated by retirees, by a herdsman in 47 G-P = *AP* 6.35 and by a man who combined the skills of a hunter and fowler in 50 G-P = *AP* 6.296. Later imitators were attracted by

120. Reitzenstein (1893) 147.
121. As suggested by the phrase νήματ' ἀναπλήσας ἐπιμοίρια (11), with its Leonidean adjective.

the clever symmetry of an epigram in which Leonidas commemorated a triple dedication of nets by three brothers who hunted, respectively, animals, fish, and birds (46 G-P = *AP* 6.13),[122] while another dedication by a hunter, known from a papyrus (51 G-P = P.Oxy. 662), seems likewise to strive for grace of structural symmetry.[123] Two dedications by herdsmen commemorating the killing of a wild beast that attacked their herds (48 G-P = *AP* 6.262, 49 G-P = *AP* 6.263) indicate that Leonidas was more interested in the dangers and hardships of herding life than in its idyllic qualities. The attack of a lion on a herd of animals is one of the most common subjects of Homeric simile, where the lion stands for the warrior and herdsmen are discounted as cowardly or ineffective.[124] By granting the herdsman the competences of the Homeric warrior, Leonidas suggests that heroic qualities are not the prerogative of the aristocratic. But one epigram is clearly idyllic in tone (19 G-P = *AP* 7.657), an epitaph in which the deceased Cleitagoras asks local herders to honor his grave with a garland of flowers, the piping of a syrinx to accompany the bleating of sheep, and a libation delivered directly from the udder of a ewe. Since names in Leonidas are often significant indicators of profession or class ranking, Labellarte may be right to suggest that Cleitagoras is a city dweller buried in the country.[125] If so, the poem's idyllic extravagance can be explained as the attitude toward the country maintained by an urbanized outsider.

Leonidas' extant oeuvre includes a number of other poems concerned with persons of higher social standing. If his name is any indication, the Aristocles who, like the weary travelers in Anyte, offers a gift to water nymphs (5 G-P = *AP* 9.326) is a member of the upper class (cf. ὁδοιπόρος, 5) rather than a countryman. Likewise, the prosperous (πολύαιγοι, 82.1 G-P = *AP* 9.744.1) pair who offer a bronze goat to Hermes are apparently the owners of goat flocks rather than hirelings or slaves who herd. The Neoptolemus who dedicates barley cakes and a cup of wine to rustic deities in 3 G-P (= *AP* 6.334) is identified by his patronymic as a member of the Epirot royal family. Leonidas' poems about the well-to-do are perhaps more likely than his epigrams for the poor to have been composed for truly inscriptional purposes; even the Neoptolemus dedication may reflect the reality of court life in Epirus, given that Plutarch (*Pyrrh.* 5.5) mentions the pastoral wealth of the regent murdered in 295 B.C. Yet even if

122. Geffcken (1896) 101 spoke of the poem as "ein wahres Meisterstück der Pointenepigrammatik" because of its later popularity. For discussion of the poem's appeal, see Gigante (1971) 63–65 and O. Longo, "Leonid. *AP* VI 13 e la sua fortuna," *MCr* 21–22 (1986–87) 277–302.

123. The names of the deities who receive the offering in the first line, Πανὶ καὶ ... Νύμφαις, repeat in the last couplet in a different case, Πὰν ὦ καὶ Νύμφαι, while the dedicator's name in 2, Γλῆνις, appears in the same line position in 6 as Γλῆνιν.

124. See Gutzwiller (1991) 26.

125. Labellarte 41. The more usual interpretation, as found in Gow-Page (1965) II 328 and Beckby (in his title), is that Cleitagoras is a herdsman.

composed for inscription, these epigrams could also have found an appropriate place in Leonidas' collection, since the individuals in them are celebrated for behavior or values they share with the poor.

Interesting in this respect are the two epitaphs for Aristocrates, whose name is clearly a signifier of class (cf. ἐσθλός, the first word of 10 G-P = *AP* 7.648 and repeated in 11.6 G-P = *AP* 7.440.6).[126] In the first, Aristocrates recommends with his dying words that even those beset by life-threatening poverty (δυσβίοτος πενίη, 10.4) obtain a wife and children. But though Aristocrates realizes that a man's property, his *oikos*, cannot be sustained without children to inherit, he himself, because of his misogynistic abhorrence of women, has chosen to avoid marriage and so comes in dying to mimic the condition of those too poor to maintain a household. Avoidance of marriage was advocated by the Cynics, who considered the truly self-sufficient man to be free of family obligations. Diogenes' definition of "marriage" was simply intercourse between a man who persuades and a woman who lets herself be persuaded (D.L. 6.72). He considered marriage and child rearing on the same order as sailing, engaging in politics, and courting a king—all activities to be avoided (D.L. 6.29). Aristocrates, though a man of refinement and some wealth, chooses, perhaps through philosophical persuasion, certain modes of living that are more commonly found, for practical reasons, among the poor. The resemblance he bears to a member of the lower class explains, I suggest, the praise heaped on him in the second epitaph, where he is celebrated not only for his kindness to foreigners and fellow countrymen and for his good humor at the symposium but also for his gentle manner of addressing the people (μείλιχα δημολογῆσαι, 11.5). These epitaphs give no hint of the person who commissioned them, traditionally of course a bereaved family member, of which Aristocrates had none; the perspective represented in them, if not that of the poet himself, seems to stem from a community of lower-class persons who admired the deceased because, despite his social standing, he embraced their own values and standards of behavior.

Other epitaphs and dedications depict individuals, primarily women and children, not in any professional capacity, but simply in certain stages of life. While these poems clearly reflect the kinds of epigrams actually inscribed in the Hellenistic era, they acquired in Leonidas' collection the literary function of defining, through their listing of unique particularities, universal qualities of human experience and then, through their juxtaposition one to another,

---

126. Both epigrams refer to the same man, since the repetition of the phrase ἤδει Ἀριστοκράτης (10.9, 11.5) removes any doubt. See the objection of Gow-Page (1965) II 321 to Geffcken's belief (1896) 79 in two persons of the same name. Although we cannot know whether the two poems stood together in Leonidas' collection, they may well have done so. If so, their placement would then be reminiscent of the pairs of epitaphs (called "Konkurrenzgedichten") known in inscription from the fourth century; on the poetic effect of such series, see Peek (1960) 33 and Lausberg 166–70.

the whole of human life. The universalizing tendency of these epigrams can be illustrated by pairing two dedications made at the point of transition from childhood to adulthood, one by a male and one by a female. In Philocles' dedication of toys to Hermes (45 G-P = *AP* 6.309), we can again see that Leonidas uses descriptive adjectives and phrases, not as mere literary affectation, but to produce a poetic effect, here to convey the boy's nostalgic longing for the items he has now outgrown—the ball that brought him fame as a player (reading εὔφημον, 1),[127] his noisy boxwood clapper, the dice that were his passion, and his whirling rhombus. Likewise, Aristodice (44 G-P = *AP* 6.281) expresses desires typical of adolescent girls when on the threshold of marriage she prays for delicate beauty in exchange for the many times she shook her maidenly hair in Cybele's precinct.[128] So too, a well-fringed sash and short frock dedicated to Artemis convey through their concrete particularity the relief and joy that Atthis feels after her successful delivery of a child (1 G-P = *AP* 6.202). In a contrary vein, two epitaphs deal with the tragic results of death in childbirth. One of them, an epitaph for four sisters who all died giving birth, announces in the final line that, after erecting the tomb, their father has perished as well (69 G-P = *AP* 7.463). While here we are shown directly the pain felt by parents who suffer the loss of their daughters (and the lines do seem to emanate from Aristodicus in anticipation of his own death),[129] an even more powerful pathos is conveyed by the other epitaph, in which a young mother calmly speaks from the grave with a passerby:

– τίς τίνος εὖσα, γύναι, Παρίην ὑπὸ κίονα κεῖσαι;
  – Πρηξὼ Καλλιτέλευς. – καὶ ποδαπή; – Σαμίη.
– τίς δέ σε καὶ κτερέιξε; – Θεόκριτος, ᾧ με γονῆες
  ἐξέδοσαν. – θνήσκεις δ' ἐκ τίνος; – ἐκ τοκετοῦ.
– εὖσα πόσων ἐτέων; – δύο κεῖκοσιν. – ἦ ῥά γ' ἄτεκνος;
  – οὔκ, ἀλλὰ τριετῆ Καλλιτέλην ἔλιπον.
– ζώοι σοι κεῖνός γε καὶ ἐς βαθὺ γῆρας ἵκοιτο.
  – καὶ σοί, ξεῖνε, πόροι πάντα Τύχη τὰ καλά.

(70 G-P = *AP* 7.163)

127. The manuscript reading εὔφημον has been variously emended because the adjective normally means "of good omen," "religiously silent." For the interpretation here given, see Waltz *ad loc.*

128. Geffcken (1896) 75 argues that the speaker of the epigram is the mother of Aristodice, rather than the girl herself, and Gow-Page ascribe the prayer to the mother Seilene in their heading, although in discussion (1965) *ad* 5f., they express uncertainty. But Geffcken's argument is based on his assumption that Aristodice is a small child and influenced by his acceptance of Meineke's emendation ἀδρύναις (4), which is clearly inferior to the manuscript reading ἀβρύναις, referring to the delicate beauty that from the time of Hesiod (fr. 339 M.-W.) and Sappho (e.g., 58.25 *PLF*) was the proper quality for maidens.

129. Geffcken (1896) 53, in his eagerness to deride the poem's epideictic quality, misses this fictionalized occasion, and so the pathos; but cf. Gow-Page (1965) II 374.

> – Who are you, lady, who lie under a Parian pillar?
> – Prexo, Calliteles' daughter. – From where? – Samos.
> – And who buried you? – Theocritus, to whom my parents
> married me. – How did you die? – From childbirth.
> – At what age? – Twenty-two. – Childless then?
> – No, I left behind Calliteles aged three.
> – I hope for you he lives and comes to a great old age.
> – And I, stranger, that Fortune be good to you.

In addition to the exquisite rhythm and sound pattern of the dialogue, the attraction of this poem for readers both ancient and modern lies in the transposition of the earlier tradition of address by deceased, monument, or passerby into an imaginative dialogue displaying a sympathetic bond between two human beings on opposite sides of death's divide.[130]

Poverty was clearly a prominent theme in the collection, and many of the poems in which Leonidas breaks with traditional epigram form do so in order to challenge conventional thinking about the poor or the rich. A mother who dedicates her son's portrait to Bacchus (39 G-P = *AP* 6.355) emphasizes, not the beauty or realism of the painting (cf. the portraits of Nossis' aristocratic friends), but its cheap or gaudy quality (ῥωπικὰ γραψαμένα, 2; δῶρον ῥωπικόν, 3–4), all that her poverty allows her to offer (οἷα πενιχρά, 1; ἀ λιτὰ ταῦτα φέρει πενία, 4). The suggestion, arising from the poem's context within the collection as a whole, is that the god values the intention of the dedicator more than the worth of the gift. In a more satiric vein, Leonidas plays with the indication of economic status normally provided by grave markers. The Attic kylix surmounting the grave of Maronis, whether sculpted in the round or carved in relief, is not here, as we might expect, a sign that her family was comfortably well-off, but rather a symbol of her incessant drinking (68 G-P = *AP* 7.455). Maronis herself groans not for the husband and children she left behind, but only that the cup is empty.

A series of other epitaphs shows more clearly that Leonidas' concern with poverty has its roots in Cynic thought. In one (75 G-P = *AP* 7.740) the stone itself speaks to boast that Crethon's vast wealth from herds and flocks made him the proverbial equivalent of Gyges. Then in the midst of listing the deceased's possessions, the monument breaks off in realization of the truth: "What is the point of a longer speech? Though judged fortunate by all, the poor fellow now has only this small portion of his vast estate" (5–6). While

---

130. Although addresses without replies are common, Peek (1960) 17–18 identifies only one pre-Hellenistic sepulchral dialogue, *GV* 1831 (= *CEG* 120) from the sixth or fifth century. But see the reservations expressed by M. L. del Barrio Vega, "Epigramas dialogados: orígenes y estructura," *CFC* 23 (1989) 194 on Peek's reconstruction. She argues (195–96) that all other inscribed sepulchral dialogues are later than the poems of this type composed by Leonidas and Callimachus.

the equality of all in death is a common sentiment in ancient epitaphs,[131] it is here used for particularly Leonidean purposes to underscore the vanity of prodigious acquisition. A counterpart to this poem may be Leonidas' epitaph for Diogenes the Cynic (59 G-P = *AP* 7.67). Asking Charon to receive him in his boat with his characteristic flask, wallet, and shabby cloak, the philosopher explains: "All that I possessed when alive I take with me to Hades, and I leave nothing beneath the sun" (7–8). A connection between these two poems, possibly even a juxtaposition within Leonidas' collection, is suggested by an anonymous epigram that combines the motifs of both: the deceased Diogenes laughs at Croesus because all the philosopher's worldly goods have come with him into Hades while the once wealthy king now has nothing (*AP* 9.145). Such contrasts between Cynic philosophers and wealthy kings were common in Cynic writings.[132] For instance, Diogenes' claim that Mausolus' tomb serves only to crush him with its weight (Lucian *Dial. Mort.* 29.2) provides the counterpart for another Leonidean epitaph, in which the deceased himself, apparently a poor man, speaks to reveal the folly of the attempt to deny death's nothingness through ostentatious adornment of the grave:

> ἀρκεῖ μοι γαίης μικρὴ κόνις, ἡ δὲ περισσὴ
>   ἄλλον ἐπιθλίβοι πλούσια κεκλιμένον
> στήλη, τὸ σκληρὸν νεκρῶν βάρος. εἴ με θανόντα
>   γνώσοντ' Ἀλκάνδρῳ τοῦτο τί Καλλιτέλευς;

(17 G-P = AP 7.655)

> I'm satisfied with a small bit of dust; let a costly
>   extravagant grave marker, a burdensome weight for corpses,
> crush some other man in his rest. What is it to Calliteles' son,
>   Alcander, whether they know me, now that I'm dead?

While this poem displays the formal conventions of inscribed epitaph, the message it conveys can only be expressed once the site of inscription has become a mere fiction: that is, only through its own absence can the monument deny the validity of the commemoration that is its reason for being. The irony of the Alcander epigram is especially choice, for there the deceased names himself in a poem that protests any need for the naming or for an inscribed context where the name may be read. Likewise, in 18 G-P (= *AP* 7.656) Alcimenes requests the passerby to deliver the ritual greeting at his humble tomb, even though it is entirely hidden by the brambles and thorns he battled when alive. So this poem,

---

131. See Richmond Lattimore, *Themes in Greek and Latin Epitaphs* (Urbana, 1962) 250–58. For sentiments similar to Leonidas' on the vanity of human ambition, see *AP* 7.325–27, 507a, 538, 727.

132. See Lucian *Dial. Mort.* 1–3, 20, 21.

too, by proclaiming the impossibility of being read as an inscription, assumes its own fictionality.

Epitaphs for the shipwrecked form a significant group of Leonidean poems, eight in number. Since these epigrams have precedents among the epitaphs attributed to Anacreon (3 *EG* = *AP* 7.263) and to Simonides (76 *EG* = *AP* 7.270), from which they scarcely differ in tone, we may ask how epitaphs for shipwrecked persons fit with the thematic concerns of Leonidas' collection. The sea travelers are clearly in some cases (15 G-P = *AP* 7.652, 16 G-P = *AP* 7.654) and probably in others to be understood as persons of some means, particularly merchants; yet these epitaphs are among the most pathetic of those surviving from Leonidas' hand. We are enticed to sympathize with the heart-rending sorrow of the relatives who mourn (14 G-P = *AP* 7.665, 15 G-P), or we are exposed to the imagined bitterness of the man whose body is lost at sea (16 G-P, 62 G-P = *AP* 7.273). The point of these poems, read in relation to other Leonidean epigrams, seems to be the contrast between the miserable end that can overtake the well-off in pursuit of their fortunes and the more peaceful and natural demise experienced by poor laborers, like the fisherman Theris and the weaver Platthis, who end their lives with dignity and receive respectful burial from their peers. The moral is made explicit in 60 G-P = *AP* 7.264 and 61 G-P = *AP* 7.266, where a drowned sailor castigates other sea adventurers who dare (τόλμαν, 60.3; τόλμης, 61.2) to set sail from within sight of his tomb. Although the danger of sea travel, undertaken only by the bold or greedy, is a commonplace from as early as Hesiod (*Op.* 618–94), the motif acquires a special resonance within the rich-poor thematics of Leonidas' collection.

The polyphony of voices speaking in Leonidas' epigram book included not only human voices but also those of deities, mostly in epigrams of the descriptive type. In a number of these the statue of a god speaks with or about the humble individuals who worship him. So Pan offers to join in the chase with hunter or fowler (29 G-P = *AP* 9.337), Hermes commends a woodcutter who has offered what he could from his meager resources (26 G-P = *AP* 9.335), and Priapus proclaims his protection of a garden, even if its vegetables are few (83 G-P = *AP* 16.236). As Leonidas' commonplace workers tend to assume a heroic cast, so his deities often display a particularly human dimension. Examples include Hermes' complaint that Heracles, who is attached to him in the form of a double herm, gulps down all the produce offered to them (27 G-P = *AP* 9.316) and Ares' description of his physical embarassment, in the form of blushing and sweating, when unbloodied weapons are presented him as a dedication (25 G-P = *AP* 9.322). Through these descriptive epigrams Leonidas rounds out his picture of society, by giving voice to the satisfied deities worshipped by the poor and by suggesting that, at least from the ideological perspective of this collection, there is no great distance between human and divine.

In turning from Leonidas' ostensibly inscriptional epigrams to his clearly epideictic ones, we more directly encounter the poetic persona governing

the collection.   Anyte and Nossis distinguished themselves from the tradi-
tional and anonymous epigrammatist by their gender and their residence in
the Greek periphery, Arcadia and Locri.   For Leonidas the corresponding
marks of distinction are his social position, expressed through his claims to
poverty, and his origin from Tarentum, another city on the margins of Greek
culture.[133]   Marcello Gigante has pointed out the importance of Tarentum's
democratic traditions for Leonidas' selection of epigrammatic subject matter:
he asserts that Leonidas rejects the Platonic and Aristotelian devaluation of the
banausic arts in favor of a philosophy, ultimately derived from the Tarentine
philosopher Archytas, in which the artisan, rather than the thinking man,
becomes the producer of civilization.[134]   While Leonidas' Tarentine origin may
have helped to develop his interest in the working classes, the portrait he paints
of himself in key epigrams—as a man deprived of a homeland, content with
little, sufficient unto himself—has broader philosophical connections to early
Hellenistic culture.

A growing admiration for the simple life can be traced throughout the fourth
century. Philosophically, the ideal of simplicity was rooted in an attempt to gain
happiness, as the τέλος of human existence, by reducing one's desires to the
barest necessities. After the death of Alexander, in a world where potentates
acquired enormous fortunes and caused continual disruption of civic existence
by their incessant warfare, an ideal that entailed freedom from desire for power,
status, and wealth had broad-based appeal as an oppositional strategy. The
philosophical home for the ideal of simplicity was Cynicism, and the model for
Cynic behavior was the life of Diogenes.[135] Among the well-known stories about
Diogenes' flaunting of convention are numerous references to the simplicity of
his diet and standard of living (τὸν εὐτελῆ βίον, D.L. 6.21). Observing a child
drinking with his hands, he threw away his cup and explained, "A child has
surpassed me in simplicity" (εὐτελείᾳ, D.L. 6.37). When invited to dine at a rich
man's house, he explained that he preferred "to lick salt at Athens" rather than to
enjoy his host's "sumptuous fare" (πολυτελοῦς τραπέζης, D.L. 6.57). According
to a foundational legend, Diogenes was sent from his native Sinope into exile
for adulterating the currency—a misunderstanding of Apollo's command to
adulterate the "political currency" (τὸ πολιτικὸν νόμισμα), meaning societal
convention (D.L. 6.20). In the third century Bion of Borysthenes rose from
boyhood enslavement to become an important Cynic philosopher and itinerant
preacher. For the Cynics, then, low social status and civic rootlessness were

133. For the history of this city, see George C. Brauer, Jr., *Taras: Its History and Coinage* (New
Rochelle, N.Y., 1986).

134. His thesis is developed primarily in (1971), but see also his "Reflessi epigrafici su Leonida
di Taranto," *PP* 42 (1987) 460–61.

135. On Cynicism, see Donald R. Dudley, *A History of Cynicism* (London, 1937) and H. D.
Rankin, *Sophists, Socratics and Cynics* (London, 1983).

matters of indifference, even an advantage for the acquisition of philosophical understanding.

If read against this ideological background, Leonidas' literary sophistication no longer appears in dissonance with his professed poverty and simplicity. We cannot now know, of course, to what extent his epigrams accurately reflect the historical realities of his own life or whether we are dealing with mere literary affectation, a poetic pose.[136] But according to Cynic precedent, a wandering life and contentment with plain living are in no way incommensurate with education, philosophical understanding, and literary production. I believe, then, that Cynic tenets are basic to the philosophical perspective of his collection, though Leonidas himself need not be viewed as a committed Cynic like Diogenes or Bion nor his epigram book as a Cynic manifesto.[137] In collected form, his epigrams offer, for the literary enjoyment of an educated audience, an alternative to traditional inscriptional epigram by focusing on the struggles, self-sufficiency, and indomitable spirit of those possessing the least material wealth in Greek society. To explain the source of such a focus, both within and across individual poems, Leonidas creates for himself a poetic ego who both shares the experiences of his lower-class characters and has the philosophical sophistication to reflect upon them. His epigram collection thus takes its place with works like Cercidas' *Meliambi* or the iambic poetry of Phoenix of Colophon in the category of literature evincing a Κυνικὸς τρόπος.

We begin our discussion of Leonidas' clearly epideictic poems with those in which the poet abandons the inscriptional format to offer moralizing advice directly to the reader. The longest of these, heavily influenced by Cynic tenets, is a meditation on the shortness of life, the corruption of the flesh, and the consequent futility of ambition:

μυρίος ἦν, ὤνθρωπε, χρόνος πρὸ τοῦ ἄχρι πρὸς ἠῶ
    ἦλθες, χὠ λοιπὸς μυρίος εἰν Ἀίδῃ.
τίς μοῖρα ζωῆς ὑπολείπεται ἢ ὅσον ὅσσον
    στιγμὴ καὶ στιγμῆς εἴ τι χαμηλότερον;
μικρή σευ ζωὴ τεθλιμμένη, οὐδὲ γὰρ αὐτή
    ἡδεῖ' ἀλλ' ἐχθροῦ στυγνοτέρη θανάτου.
ἐκ τοίης ὤνθρωποι ἀπηκριβωμένοι ὀστῶν
    ἁρμονίης ὑψοῦντ' ἠέρα καὶ νεφέλας.[138]

---

136. The latter is the position of G. Lombardo Radice, "Leonida Tarentino, poeta 'ricco,'" *Maia* 17 (1965) 141–57.

137. Geffcken (1896) 138 and *Kynika und Verwandtes* (Heidelberg, 1909) 4–18 proclaimed Leonidas an active adherent of Cynicism but later (1925) 2023 softened his stand; for criticism, see B. Hansen 20–24. Gigante (1971) 45–55 finds both Cynic and Pythagorean motifs in Leonidas but prefers to view him as basically nonphilosophical in his approach to life.

138. Hermann's suggested ὑψοῦντ' is accepted by Waltz, Beckby, and R. del Re, "Un epigramma di Leonida," *RFIC* 93 (1965) 430–37, but is oddly not mentioned by Gow-Page, who place in daggers the meaningless letters found in the manuscript. For a thorough defense

ὦνερ, ἴδ’ ὡς ἀχρεῖον, ἐπεὶ περὶ νήματος ἄκρον
    εὐλὴ ἀκέρκιστον λῶπος ἐφεζομένη
οἷον τὸ †ψαλὰ† θρῖον ἀπεψιλωμένον οἷον
    πολλῷ ἀραχναίου στυγνότερον σκελετοῦ.[139]
ἠοῦν ἐξ ἠοῦς ὅσσον σθένος, ὦνερ, ἐρευνῶν
    εἴης ἐν λιτῇ κεκλιμένος βιοτῇ
αἰὲν τοῦτο νόῳ μεμνημένος ἄχρις ὁμιλῇς
    ζωοῖς ἐξ οἴης ἡρμόνισαι καλάμης.

(77 G-P = AP 7.472)

Eternal was the time before you were born
    and eternal the time you'll be in Hades.
Is the portion of life left to you other than
    a jot and whatever is less than a jot?
Your life is short and difficult—not pleasant—
    but more bitter than hateful death.
Formed from such a conjuncture of bones, humans
    puff themselves up into the air and clouds.
How useless, when at the end of your life's thread
    a worm sits on your body's loosely woven fabric,
like a fig leaf that's been stripped bare or
    something more disgusting than a spider's corpse.
From day to day you should use your strength
    to seek contentment in your life of little,
Always remembering, while still among the living,
    from what sort of chaff you're formed.

Scholars have sought in various ways to make the poem more suitable for inscription—by breaking it into two or more shorter pieces,[140] by assuming it accompanied a depiction of a skeleton on a tomb,[141] or by attaching the epitaph for Pheidon (76 G-P = *AP* 7.472b) to part or to all of it.[142]   But though the poem conveys the ambiance of the graveyard, its length and generalized moral

---

of Hermann's suggestion, see A. Barigazzi, "Leonida, A. P. 7.472: l'uomo e la ragnetela," *Prometheus* 11 (1985) 197–202, who prefers to read ἠέρι καὶ νεφέλη.

139. A much troubled couplet. Since ψαλάθριον is unknown, I have printed Paton's text, which at least makes sense out of θρῖον.

140. Reitzenstein (1893) 154–56 separated 1–6 and 7–16 into distinct epigrams, while Gow-Page print the poem as a unit but incline to the view that 7–16 constitute a separate composition.

141. Weisshäupl (1889) 92; del Re 433.

142. In *Anthologia Graeca* (1794–1814) Friedrich Jacobs places 7.472b after lines 1–6 and omits the remaining lines, though in his later edition (1813–17), he treats it as an intrusive epigram; del Re 434–37 argues for the placement of 7.472b after line 16. But Barigazzi (1985) 195 has made a convincing case for the unity of the sixteen-line poem: 7–8 sum up the first half of the poem and make the transition to the second half. Notice that ἐκ τοίης ... ἀρμονίης (7–8) echoes in ἐξ οἴης ἡρμόνισαι (16) and that the vocative ὤνθρωπε in 1 is matched by the vocative ὦνερ in 9.

message indicate its connection to popular philosophical lectures such as those delivered by the Cynics.

Such short expositions on moral topics, conventionally called diatribes, were given polished literary form by Bion of Borysthenes, an itinerant Cynic preacher and philosopher at the court of Antigonus Gonatas.[143] Leonidas clearly knew the works of Bion since one of his epigrams (79 G-P), brief advice on passing to the underworld without fear, is a paraphrase of a saying by Bion (D.L. 4.49). Although Bion's speeches have perished, fragments, such as the extracts preserved by Teles, suggest kinship with Leonidas' philosophy and style. For example, Bion's lecture on self-sufficiency (Stob. *Flor.* 3.1.98), which places in the mouth of Poverty arguments against human striving for material wealth, employs the vocative ἄνθρωπε, found also in Leonidas' poem. Diatribe style and form influenced other Hellenistic compositions as well. The iambic poetry of Cercidas and Phoenix of Colophon, published by both as poetry books, can be interpreted as versified diatribe.[144] Among the fragments of Cercidas, a Cynic statesman from the second half of the third century, are complaints about the unequal distribution of wealth (fr. 4 *CA*) and advice on avoiding love affairs (fr. 5 *CA*). A poem from the first book of Phoenix, apparently a contemporary of Leonidas, is of particular interest. After an introductory discussion of the hedonistic life of the Assyrian monarch Ninus, the poet quotes an epitaph in which Ninus himself speaks from the grave to draw moral lessons for the passerby. He points out that after his death his enemies carried off his vast wealth: "And I came to Hades with neither gold nor horse nor silver wagon. I, who wore the Persian mitra, lie black ash" (fr. 1.22–24 *CA*). Phoenix's poem, which makes the same point about the uselessness of death found in Leonidas' Crethon epigram (75 G-P), shows how epitaph form could easily be used within moral exposition of the diatribe variety. But for placement within an epigram collection, where context raises the expectation of epitaph, Leonidas has composed a poem of more directly moralizing character. As a result, the voice speaking in the poem balances uncertainly between that of a poor man voicing his own epitaph and that of the poet revealing to us the bitter philosophy that undergirds his collection.[145]

Because such moralizing poems are so easily associated with the opinions of the epigrammatist, they serve as a way of personalizing the more objective

---

143. On Bion, see Dudley 62–69; Jan F. Kindstrand, *Bion of Borysthenes: A Collection of the Fragments* (Uppsala, 1976).

144. Cf. Machon's versified *Chreiai*, edited by A. F. S. Gow, *Machon: The Fragments* (Cambridge, 1965). There are two recent editions of Cercidas: Enrico Livrea, ed., *Studi Cercidei* (Bonn, 1986) and Liana Lomiento, ed., *Cercidas: Testimonia et Fragmenta* (Rome, 1993). For detailed discussion of Phoenix's text, see Gustav A. Gerhard, *Phoinix von Kolophon: Texte und Untersuchungen* (Leipzig, 1909).

145. For the view that the advice is given by the deceased, namely Pheidon, see del Re 435. For the view that Leonidas himself expresses tenets of Cynic philosophy, see Geffcken (1896) 128–31, (1909) 10–18; and M. Gigante, "Il filo del mantello," *PP* 24 (1969) 215–16 and (1971) 48.

voice heard in most of the other epigrams. Not surprisingly, then, 33 G-P = *AP* 7.736 has been read as a reflection of Leonidas' own life:[146]

μὴ φθείρευ, ὤνθρωπε, περιπλάνιον βίον ἕλκων
   ἄλλην ἐξ ἄλλης εἰς χθόν' ἀλινδόμενος·
μὴ φθείρευ· κενεή σε περιστέξαιτο καλιή
   ἣν θάλποι μιχκὸν πῦρ ἀνακαιόμενον,
εἰ καί σοι λιτή γε καὶ οὐκ εὐάλφιτος εἴη
   φυστὴ ἐνὶ γρώνῃ μασσομένη παλάμαις,
εἰ καί σοι γλήχων ἢ καὶ θύμον ἢ καὶ ὁ πικρὸς
   ἀδυμιγὴς εἴη χόνδρος ἐποψίδιος.

Don't wear yourself out, my man, leading a vagabond life
   roaming from one land to another.
Don't wear yourself out. May a bare hut and the warmth
   of a small fire provide you protection,
Even if you have only a meager bit of poor-quality bread,
   kneaded by your own hand in a stone's hollow,
Even if you have only pennyroyal or thyme or bitter
   but tasty salt to go with your bread.

Here, as if from personal experience, the poet advises abandonment of a wandering existence in favor of a settled life, even if it means extreme poverty. Within the collection the explicit moralizing message of this epigram would have been reinforced by the collective message garnered from the epitaphs and dedications. The vagabond life that Leonidas advises against is poignantly illustrated by his epitaphs for sea travelers, who all come to a miserable end, often without even the consolation of burial. The sparsely supplied hut, which is here Leonidas' symbol for the good life of contentment with little, is the likely dwelling for many of his poor laborers (cf. καλύβῃ σχοινίτιδι, 20.7). Leonidas' list of humble but sufficient foods seems based on the tenet that little can be a good thing when it accompanies a life free of desire and ambition; the same tenet underlies a number of dedications in which poor folk make meager but satisfactory offerings to a deity (26, 39, 41 G-P). The plainest foods—bread, vegetables, and salt—are common symbols of the simple life advocated by the Cynics.[147]

The moralizing poems, in which the epigrammatist appears to offer advice directly to the reader, lead us to three epigrams in which Leonidas names himself. While these three poems may indeed contain genuinely autobiographical material, we should recognize as well that their function within the collection was surely to construct the persona of an artist capable of composing such an array of epigrams about common people. All three probably occupied important

---

146. See Gow-Page (1965) II 343; Gigante (1971) 51, 131.
147. See the references listed by Kindstrand 215 on Bion F17.

positions in the epigram book; as Wilamowitz pointed out, Leonidas' self-epitaph was most likely the concluding poem:[148]

πολλὸν ἀπ' Ἰταλίης κεῖμαι χθονὸς ἔκ τε Τάραντος
  πάτρης, τοῦτο δέ μοι πικρότερον θανάτου.
τοιοῦτος πλανίων ἄβιος βίος, ἀλλά με Μοῦσαι
  ἔστερξαν, λυγρῶν δ' ἀντὶ μελιχρὸν ἔχω,
οὔνομα δ' οὐκ ἤμυσε Λεωνίδου· αὐτά με δῶρα
  κηρύσσει Μουσέων πάντας ἐπ' ἠελίους.

(93 G-P = *AP* 7.715)

I lie far from Italy and my native Tarentum,
  and this is more bitter to me than death.
Such a life of wandering is no life. But the Muses
  loved me, and I have sweet in exchange for bitter:
The name of Leonidas does not perish; the gifts
  of the Muses give me fame for all time.

We do not of course know the reason for Leonidas' separation from his home-land, whether forced exile or a willed desire to seek his fortune throughout the Greek world.[149] But this poem, when read in conjunction with the previously quoted one, 33 G-P, and another in which Leonidas pictures himself as an old man self-sufficiently (αὐτάρκης, 37.3 G-P) dwelling in the simplest of huts, cre-ate for the reader a portrait of an epigrammatist who has abandoned a life of wandering in favor of a poor but contented life governed by Cynic principles. As Diogenes proclaimed that his ability to philosophize was owed to the fact of his exile (D.L. 6.49), so Leonidas here finds consolation for his homelessness in gifts of the Muses. While a true Cynic philosopher would be unlikely to call the vagabond life "more bitter than death" (93.2) or to speak of "hateful poverty" (36.7–8 G-P), Leonidas represents himself as a more commonplace individual who finds Cynic moralizing a resource for dealing with the hardships of his existence.[150]

---

148. Wilamowitz (1924) I 140; so too Gabathuler 67–68. A tradition of denying the au-thenticity of this epigram goes back to Jacobs. Geffcken (1896) 12 rejected it on the grounds that Leonidas could lament the location of his burial place in a foreign land only in his dying hour. Gow-Page (1965) II 390, although rejecting Geffcken's argument as "absurd," nevertheless consider Leonidas' authorship "doubtful," apparently because the lemmatist has confused the Tarentine with Leonidas of Alexandria (a mistake that the Corrector attempted to remedy). But Gigante (1971) 20 has now vigorously defended the poem's authenticity ("un celebre componimento, della cui autenticità si dubitò solo per angustia di mente o carenza di forza critica"). Supposing an original book context for the poem eliminates any basis for suspicion about authorship.

149. On the prevalence of exile from the fourth century on, see Paul McKechnie, *Outsiders in the Greek Cities in the Fourth Century B.C.* (London, 1989).

150. Leonidas' resistance to extreme Cynic asceticism is indicated by 55 G-P = *AP* 6.298, a satirical epitaph for the Cynic Sochares, who perished from hunger.

Although the prologue to Leonidas' collection has not, to my knowledge, been previously identified, it is highly likely that Meleager included it in the *Garland*, since he anthologized the opening poems of other early Hellenistic collections (those of Anyte, Nossis, and Asclepiades). The best candidate among the surviving epigrams is 36 G-P = *AP* 6.300, a poem that later epigrammatists felt compelled to imitate even to the point of preserving the authenticating seal of Leonidas' name. In it Leonidas first identifies himself as a poor wanderer, foreshadowing his characterization of himself in 37 and the concluding epitaph. He then offers the goddess Lathria a selection of the fare available to a person of such means:

Λαθρίη, ἐκ †πλάνης† ταύτην χάριν ἔκ τε πενέστεω
   κἠξ ὀλιγησιπύου δέξο Λεωνίδεω
ψαιστά τε πιήεντα καὶ εὐθήσαυρον ἐλαίην
   καὶ τοῦτο χλωρὸν σῦκον ἀποκράδιον
κεὐοίνου σταφυλῆς ἔχ' ἀποσπάδα πεντάρρωγον,
   πότνια, καὶ σπονδὴν τήνδ' ὑποπυθμίδιον.
ἢν δέ με χὼς ἐκ νούσου ἀνειρύσω, ὧδε καὶ ἐχθρῆς
   ἐκ πενίης ῥύσῃ δέξο χιμαιροθύτην.

Lathria, accept this gift from a wanderer, a peasant,
   from Leonidas who has few resources.
Take some rich cakes, olive oil saved for the purpose,
   this fresh fig just cut from the branch,
five grapes pulled from a tasty bunch, mistress,
   and this libation poured from the bottom of the jar.
And as you saved me from disease, so if you save me
   from hateful poverty, you'll have a goat as sacrifice.

Encountering this poem at the head of the collection, the reader would easily recognize that the agricultural products symbolize Leonidas' epigrams, which in style exhibit qualities of richness, choiceness, and freshness but in subject matter mirror the humbleness of his poetic offerings. The symbolic use of such items at the opening of an epigram collection finds parallel in Nossis' roses (1.4 G-P), the assortment of grains suggested by the title of the *Soros*, and the plants that Meleager wove into his *Garland* (1 G-P). Leonidas' phrase ταύτην χάριν (1) is even repeated in Meleager's prooemium (1.4 G-P) with exactly the same meaning. But the closest parallel may be the introductory poem to Theocritus' collection (1 Gow = *AP* 6.336). Both dedicate vegetable matter to a deity or deities, and both close with a reference to a future sacrifice of a goat, a reference that has considerably more point in Leonidas' epigram than in the Theocritean poem. If the posthumous editor of the Theocritean collection composed the epigram to serve as prologue, it appears that he did so with the Leonidean prologue as a partial model.

Substantial evidence suggests, then, that 36 G-P stood as the prologue to Leonidas' collection. But who is the goddess, Lathria, to whom the dedication is made? Gaetulicus (*AP* 6.190) and Cornelius Longus (*AP* 6.191), who both reworked the epigram while preserving Leonidas' name, and Phanias, who produced a looser imitation (5 G-P = *AP* 6.299), clearly understood Aphrodite as the referent.[151] Following this interpretation, Geffcken suggested that the "disease" mentioned in 7 was a love affair,[152] a reading that is consistent with Leonidas' adherence to Cynic doctrine elsewhere in the collection. The Cynics believed that sexual needs should be relieved in the simpliest possible manner and that erotic entanglements were to be avoided. Leonidas' one explicitly erotic epigram accommodates such an approach to love. There (92 G-P = *AP* 5.188) Leonidas declares that he means Eros no harm and acknowledges his sweetness but, when the boy causes him pain, he, though a mortal, is entitled to escape the torment of love. The Cynic basis for this view of love is suggested by an epigram in which Leonidas satirizes an elderly Cynic caught by the snares of a lovely boy (54 G-P = *AP* 6.293). We have already observed that Aphrodite functioned as the patron deity of the epigram collections of Asclepiades and Nossis, and Eros may have served much the same purpose in Posidippus' poetry book (cf. 1 G-P = *AP* 5.134).[153] I propose that in his introductory poem Leonidas follows the tradition of naming Aphrodite as epigrammatic Muse but marks his attachment to her on grounds other than the erotic. For a parallel rejection of love in favor of philosophy, we may compare an epigram by the Epicurean Philodemus (17 G-P, *Garland* = *AP* 11.41), in which he asks the Muses to draw a *coronis* (the convoluted sign that marks the end of a book) upon his love madness since he has decided to devote himself to a life of wisdom.[154]

In one final poem, the poet expressly speaks of his self-sufficiency and proclaims that his appreciation for a life of simplicity is an inheritance "from his fathers":

φεύγεθ' ὑπὲκ καλύβης, σκότιοι μύες· οὔτι πενιχρή
 μῦς σιπύη βόσκειν οἶδε Λεωνίδεω.
αὐτάρκης ὁ πρέσβυς ἔχων ἅλα καὶ δύο κρίμνα·
 ἐκ πατέρων ταύτην ᾐνέσαμεν βιοτήν.

---

151. According to an interpretation of I. Cazzaniga, "Osservazioni critiche intorno allo hypomnema Antimacheo di Pap. Mil. Vogl. I 17, 33–36," *PP* 22 (1967) 63–74, the epithet refers to Artemis in Antimachus (182 Wyss) and so in Leonidas, but we should note as well that in Eubulus (67.8 *PCG*) the equivalent adjective λαθραία is applied to Aphrodite.

152. Geffcken (1896) 120.

153. Cf. as well Philip's invocation to Aphrodite that heads the epigram collection preserved as Book 13 of the *AP* (= 62 G-P, *Garland*).

154. For a different interpretation of this poem, namely, that Philodemus is announcing his intention to marry, see D. Sider, "The Love Poetry of Philodemus," *AJP* 108 (1987) 315–16 and (1997) 72–78.

τῷ τί μεταλλεύεις τοῦτον μυχόν, ὦ φιλόλιχνε,
    οὐδ' ἀποδειπνιδίου γευόμενος σκυβάλου;
σπεύδων εἰς ἄλλους οἴκους ἴθι—τἀμὰ δὲ λιτά—
    ὧν ἄπο πλειοτέρην οἴσεαι ἀρμαλιήν.

(37 G-P = *AP* 6.302)

Flee from my hut, furtive rodents. Leonidas'
    poor canister cannot support mice.
The old man can survive on salt and a couple of crumbs;
    from my fathers I learned to like this style of living.
So why do you burrow into this hovel, nibbler,
    since you won't find a taste of any leftovers?
Go run to some other house—my resources are few—
    where you'll get better rations.

A connection with the introductory poem in which the poet who labels himself ὀλιγησιπύου ("with sparsely filled canister") is suggested by the πενιχρὴ σιπύη, the "poor canister" from which he shoos away mice. The poem also contains a number of programmatic motifs that reappear in Leonidas' other epigrams: destitute weavers pray to become εὐσιπύους ἐξ ὀλιγησιπύων (41.10 G-P); the salt and bread crumbs recall the list of simple fare idealized in the moralizing 33; the hut reappears in that poem as in the Theris epitaph (20.7); and the words πενιχρός and λιτός occur often enough in the extant poems to be considered central to the thematic concerns of the collection as a whole.[155] The persona projected in this playful epigram—that of a poor but contented old poet—is designed, then, to connect Leonidas himself with the elderly poor who are the heroes of his epitaphs and dedications. Geffcken pointed out a connection as well to anecdotes about Diogenes, who was said to have learned the art of self-sufficiency (αὐτάρκεια; cf. αὐτάρκης, 37.3), of contentment with little, by observing the behavior of a mouse (D.L. 6.22).[156] In another anecdote the philosopher is said to have remarked, when mice climbed onto his table, "See, even Diogenes keeps parasites" (D.L. 6.40). Whether or not Leonidas' mouse poem is meant to recall this last story (its point is somewhat different), his choice of the motif suggests the Cynic ambience of the epigram book.

Since the other two poems in which Leonidas names himself probably functioned as the prologue and epilogue of the collection, it is reasonable to suppose that this poem, too, was set off by its position. Poem 37, although not a dedication, appears in a dedicatory sequence from the *Garland*—apparently placed there to follow (with one intervening epigram) Leonidas' dedication to Lathria. Since Meleager was likely preserving an original connection between the two, I suggest that Leonidas' mouse poem occupied the second position in his

155. The word πενιχρός occurs in 39.1 and 41.7 G-P, while λιτός is found in 33.5, 39.4, 73.4, 77.14, and 87.2.

156. Geffcken (1896) 126–27; cf. Gow-Page (1965) II 347.

epigram book, an arrangement paralleled by Catullus' placement of his sparrow poems (2, 3) immediately after his opening piece. If this supposition about placement is correct, the metaphorical meaning given the foodstuffs dedicated in the prologue—as symbols of Leonidas' epigrams on the humble—would then carry over to affect and enhance the meaning of the mouse poem. As a parallel to this imaging of poetry by property offered to a deity, we may note that in *Idyll* 22.221–23 Theocritus' poetic offerings are made synonymous with the resources of his *oikos*: "I bring you the gentle offerings of the Muses, such as they furnish and my house affords." More significantly, Ariston's imitation indicates that another Hellenistic epigrammatist understood Leonidas' foodstuffs to be symbols of his poetry book:

ὦ μύες, εἰ μὲν ἐπ' ἄρτον ἐληλύθατ', ἐς μυχὸν ἄλλον
   στείχετ'—ἐπεὶ λιτὴν οἰκέομεν καλύβην—
οὗ καὶ πίονα τυρὸν ἀποδρέψεσθε καὶ αὔην
   ἰσχάδα καὶ δεῖπνον συχνὸν ἀπὸ σκυβάλων·
εἰ δ' ἐν ἐμαῖς βύβλοισι πάλιν καταθήξετ' ὀδόντα
   κλαύσεσθ', οὐκ ἀγαθὸν κῶμον ἐπερχόμενοι.

(3 G-P = AP 6.303)

If you've come for bread, go to another hovel,
   mice,—since I live in a barren hut—
where you'll nibble on rich cheese and dry figs
   and a great feast from the leftovers.
If you sharpen your teeth on my books again,
   you'll find you've come to no good banquet.

Here Ariston's resources are so meager that the mice are driven by hunger to sample his books, a variation of the Leonidean poem that concretizes the metaphorical underpinnings of its model. Since Leonidas constructed his mouse epigram with formulae from popular exorcisms,[157] the humorous function of the poem within the collection was perhaps to act as an apotropaic charm against the physical destruction of the poetry book itself. For this purpose, a position near the beginning, perhaps immediately following the dedication, would have been well suited.

Two other Leonidean epigrams seem also to carry symbolic meaning, although there is no basis for conjecturing their position within the collection. Both look back to Anyte, the only Hellenistic epigrammatist who clearly influenced Leonidas.[158] One of these, 86 G-P (= *AP* 16.230), is an invitation to a

---

157. See Gigante (1971) 50.

158. For Anyte's influence on Leonidas, see A. Izzo D'Accinni, "Leonida di Taranto e i suoi contemporanei," *GIF* 11 (1958) 310–13. Practically all commentators have agreed that Leonidas 21 G-P = *AP* 7.198, an epitaph for a grasshopper, derives from Anyte's Myro poem (20 G-P), and Geffcken (1896) 9 argues that the double ascription of 20 G-P to Anyte or Leonidas had its foundation in the Tarentine's imitation.

traveler to quaff cool water from a bubbling spring instead of the warm water provided by a muddy stream. Lacking any indication of the specific source of its voice, the epigram was probably intended, like Anyte 16 and 18, to mimic rustic inscriptions while actually sending a message about poetry directly from the poet to the reader.[159] The contrast between the muddy stream and the pure spring mirrors, of course, the imagery found in Callimachus' *Hymn to Apollo* (108–12; cf. too Callim. 2 G-P = *AP* 12.43), where different types of poetry are symbolized by the contrast between the filthy Euphrates and clear droplets of spring water. Employing similar imagery, Leonidas' epigram apparently functions as an invitation to the reader to abandon the polluted production of more traditional poets in favor of his own refreshingly original epigrams on less common topics.

In the other epigram a cicada claims, not only to sit singing in lofty trees, but also to perch upon the spear of Athena. The concluding explanation for this surprising posture is as follows:[160]

> ὅσσον γὰρ Μούσαις ἐστέργμεθα τόσσον Ἀθήνη
> ἐξ ἡμέων, ἡ γὰρ παρθένος αὐλοθετεῖ.

(91.7–8 G-P = AP 6.120.7–8)

For as much as the Muses love me, so much I love
Athena. For the maiden invented the flute.

I have already argued that in Anyte's Myro poem (20 G-P; cf. Leonidas' imitation, 21 G-P) the grasshopper and the cicada represent sources of poetic inspiration for the poet, and Anyte's lament inspired a number of later epigrams on cicadas or grasshoppers, in several of which the insect, as intermediary between the poet and the Muses, sings to the poet himself (Simias 2 G-P = *AP* 7.193, Mnasalces 12 G-P = *AP* 7.192, Meleager 12 G-P = *AP* 7.195 and 13 G-P = *AP* 7.196). In his epigram Leonidas maintains the cicada's established function (with Μούσαις ἐστέργμεθα, cf. Μοῦσαι ἔστερξαν in the epilogue, 93.3–4) but broadens the basis for the insect's inspiration. By perching on the spear of Athena, the cicada validates Leonidas' choice to write poetry devoted to lower-class workers, who often labor under the tutelage of that goddess. The poem's final image, Athena's invention of the flute, unites with epigrammatic succinctness the realms of poetry and handicrafts.

Leonidas' epigram book was probably the most sophisticated collection of inscriptional poetry issued in the Hellenistic era; it certainly represents a culmination in the development of the type during the first half of the third century. Anyte was perhaps the first to show how an epigram book could be given coherency by the author's persona, defined by its distinctness from

159. Radice 153 reads the poem as an "autoesortazione" to inner peace.

160. Gow-Page (1965) II 389 are uncertain whether the epigram "is prompted by the occurrence of such an incident or by a representation of Athena so attended." Geffcken (1896) 86 thinks of the latter explanation.

the anonymous male epigrammatist of traditional epigram. Nossis advanced the construction of a female persona even further by overtly asserting, in prologue and epilogue, her poetic program and by situating her own voice not only outside the world of the collection as creating epigrammatist but also inside as an internal narrator. Leonidas, like Nossis, provided the reader with essential "facts" about his persona in a self-naming prologue and epilogue and then reinforced the conclusions to be drawn from these programmatic poems in epigrams offering moralizing advice to the reader. But in his case he distinguished himself from the impersonal epigrammatist of inscribed verse, not on the basis of gender, but on the basis of class, a condition perhaps resulting from his loss of inherited community but also fostered by philosophical proclivities. While Nossis projected herself as one of the aristocratic women of Locri and a spokesperson for its standards of beauty, Leonidas represented himself as an active participant in the poverty-stricken existence of the lower classes and as an advocate for a lived philosophy characteristic of the poor. His achievement was to weld a variety of poignant individual epigrams—on men and women, rich and poor, gods and humans—into a coherent statement of class ideology, founded on Cynic principles, that stands as a counterpart and a challenge to the whole tradition of archaic and classical inscribed epigram. It was likely the appeal of the message derived from the book as a whole, not simply the artistry of single epigrams, that induced so many later epigrammatists to follow Leonidean models.

CHAPTER FOUR

The Third Century:
Erotic and Sympotic Epigram

In the prooemium to his *Garland* Meleager groups together in one couplet the
trio of Asclepiades (under his pseudonym Sicelidas), Posidippus, and Hedylus:

ἐν δὲ Ποσείδιππόν τε καὶ Ἡδύλον, ἄγρι' ἀρούρης,
Σικελίδεώ τ' ἀνέμοις ἄνθεα φυόμενα.

(1.45–46 G-P = *AP* 4.1.45–46)

In it he placed wild flowers, Posidippus and Hedylus,
    And the wind-born anemones of Sicelidas.

Although each of these three epigrammatists composed a number of votive or
sepulchral epigrams, their poetry is distinguished by the dominating presence
of erotic, sympotic, and satiric types, that is, by epigrams that imitate oral
rather than written speech. Reitzenstein was led by this literary circumstance to
suppose that all the epigrams of Asclepiades and his followers were composed for
oral performance in a banquet setting, as the Hellenistic equivalent of archaic
elegy and Attic scolia.[1] While some more cautious scholars have abandoned
altogether attempts to define the historic context for this poetry, others still
assume, on the basis of Reitzenstein's assertions, that Asclepiades, Posidippus,
and Hedylus must in some time and place have belonged to a circle of literary
acquaintances who dined and composed together. But, of course, the imitation
of oral speech no more guarantees that a sympotic epigram was recited than
the imitation of written speech guarantees that an inscriptional epigram was
inscribed. Reitzenstein's fundamental mistake was to confuse the representation

1. See, for instance, Reitzenstein (1893) 86: "an Stelle der Elegie tritt schon im vierten
Jahrhundert das Epigramm." Although Wilamowitz resisted the extension of Reitzenstein's
theory to the inscriptional forms of epigram, he was inclined to accept the ideal of symposium
performance as the primary, or originally intended, purpose of erotic-sympotic epigram; see,
for instance, Wilamowitz (1924) I 120.

of a speech act with the speech act itself. While third-century epigrammatists probably did recite some of their epigrams for friends at banquets, certain poems betray clear evidence of composition for a book setting.

The combination of oral performance with collection in written form is not surprising when we consider the literary background to the origin of erotic-sympotic epigram. Toward the end of the fifth century the types of verse that had traditionally been performed at symposia—scolia, elegy, and lyric song—were supplemented by other forms of amateur entertainment, including recitation of dramatic passages and intellectual discussion.[2] Epigrams of the inscriptional type, whether genuine inscriptions or imaginary ones, may also, on occasion, have been recited at banquets.[3] Sometime between the last decades of the fifth century and the end of the fourth many of the elegiac couplets that had formed part of the earlier oral repertoire were gathered, for purposes of preservation, into collections. The diverse elegiac corpus from which were later selected anthologies ascribed to Theognis was apparently assembled at this time,[4] as the body of Mimnermus' verse may have acquired the title of *Nanno* during the same time period.[5] The sequence of twenty-five Attic scolia preserved by Athenaeus (15.694c–695f = 884–908 *PMG*) is another collection of symposium

2. Some of our best evidence for this change comes from Aristophanes' *Clouds* 1353–76, where Strepsiades asks his son to sing a song by Simonides, which Pheidippides scorns as old-fashioned. When the father then proposes a passage from Aeschylus, Pheidippides prefers something from Euripides, the content of which so shocks his father that they. fall to blows. See also Eupolis, *PCG* V 377, fr. 148. For the substitution of intellectual discourse for old-fashioned song, Plato's *Symposium* provides obvious evidence. On this change in symposium entertainment, see M. Vetta, "Introduzione: Poesia simposiale nella Grecia arcaica e classica," in *Poesia e simposio nella Grecia antica*, ed. Massimo Vetta (Bari, 1983) lvii–lix.

3. The epitaph for Midas quoted by Plato (*Phdr.* 264d) was particularly suitable for oral circulation because the order of its four lines was a matter of indifference. The mock epitaph composed by Theocritus of Chios (1 *EG*, pp. 56–57) to criticize Aristotle's construction of a cenotaph for Hermias of Atarneus (1 *EG*, p. 56) was clearly never inscribed, and likely provided symposium entertainment for enemies of the Academy.

4. For the history of the Theognidean sylloge, see West (1974) 40–59. Theognis' poetry was known, apparently in a written text, to various fourth-century authors: Xenophon (*Symp.* 2.4), Plato (*Meno* 95d, *Leg.* 630a), and Isocrates (*Ad Nicoclem* 43). The passage from "Xenophon" quoted by Stobaeus *Flor.* 88.14 *may* refer to a text that began with our lines 183–90; for the controversy, see T. Hudson-Williams, *The Elegies of Theognis* (London, 1910) 86–89 and West (1974) 56. These and other authors (Pl. *Leg.* 811a; Xen. *Mem.* 1.6.14; Aeschin. *In Ctes.* 135; Isoc. *Ad Nicoclem* 44) provide evidence that the process of composing anthologies of select passages or gnomic maxims was common in the fourth century; see Hudson-Williams 16–19 and Barns (1951) 1–19.

5. Mimnermus' elegies had been collected under the title of *Nanno* before the beginning of the Hellenistic age, as evidenced by knowledge of the collection on the part of third-century poets (Hermesianax, 7.35–40 *CA*; Posid., 9.1–2 G-P). West (1974) 75–76 has suggested that Antimachus, a Colophonian poet of the late fifth century, emphasized the importance of Nanno in Mimnermus' collection in order to create a Colophonian precedent for his *Lyde*.

song that may have been edited in the pre-Hellenistic period.[6] As we have already seen, the beginning of the third century witnessed the formation of epigram sylloges—Anyte's author-edited collection and probably assemblages attributed to Simonides and Anacreon as well. In collected form, the genres of elegy and epigram lost much of their original distinctness, which had largely derived from the symposium setting for the one and the inscriptional setting for the other. The remaining differences in content and length were insufficient to maintain separate generic status.

Early in the Hellenistic age a new type of epigram with erotic and sympotic, rather than dedicatory and sepulchral, themes came into existence as heir to this dual, now coalesced tradition. Its character was formed by adapting the language and themes of old elegy to the rhythm and structures of inscriptional verse. This innovative type of epigram, whose earliest known practitioner was Asclepiades of Samos, was not simply the next stage in the evolution of Greek symposium song, as Reitzenstein maintained. Its origin precisely coincides with the period in which epigram was conceptualized as a literary form; erotic-sympotic epigram, a composite derived from two originally distinct genres that had become similar through collection, existed from the start as a form with aesthetic pretensions. A careful reading of these epigrams will reveal that, although some were likely performed orally, they passed into the *Anthology* from a context in which they coexisted with other epigrams in collected form.

As preliminary analysis, we may consider some of the ways in which old elegy differs from Hellenistic erotic-sympotic epigram. The needs of amateur symposium performers determined that the length of archaic elegiac song was expandable or contractable at will. It is too simplistic to assume that lines in our Theognis assemblage which duplicate parts of songs elsewhere attributed to Solon, Tyrtaeus, and Mimnermus are merely extracts from longer elegies of fixed shape, since the oral culture of the symposium must have originally provided the building stones for the set pieces of the famous elegists.[7] We should think not of direct borrowing one from the other but of complicated patterns of interaction between longer and shorter versions circulating in the repertoires of oral singers with varying levels of skill. The erotic-sympotic epigram of the Hellenistic era is, however, of definitive length. Inheriting brevity as an essential characteristic from inscriptional verse, epigram developed a rhythmical shape based on the finality of the concluding pentameter. While the reader of the

6. For the arrangement of the collection, see Ulrich von Wilamowitz-Moellendorff, *Aristoteles und Athen* (Berlin, 1893) II 316–22; C. M. Bowra, *Greek Lyric Poetry*, 2nd ed. (Oxford, 1961) 373–97; M. van der Valk, "On the Composition of the Attic Skolia," *Hermes* 102 (1974) 1–20.

7. For the *Theognidea* as an oral assemblage whose doublets and varying ascriptions are a result of recomposition in performance, see G. Nagy, "Theognis and Megara: A Poet's Vision of his City," in *Theognis of Megara: Poetry and the Polis*, ed. Thomas Figueira and G. Nagy (Baltimore, 1985) 48–50.

Theognis collection may experience a sense of flow, or continuity, from one selection to the next, the reader of an epigram collection must mentally pause after each individual poem to savor the poignancy or wit conveyed by its final words.[8] The differing experience in reading a collection of archaic elegy and a Hellenistic epigram book is not, then, based on the length of individual selections (since, though most epigrams are short, some could be of considerable length)[9] but on the difference between the sense of continuity linking the elegiac extracts and the isolated individuality of the finite epigrams.

Despite such devices as the "seal" of the poet's name near the beginning of the Theognidean collection (19–30), the discourse of old elegy has a generalizing character. The poet's amatory object may be consistently named, like Theognis' Cyrnus or Mimnermus' Nanno, but the erotic relationship presented in the poetry is ever mutable, reflecting all the customary and commonplace moments in any such love affair. Archaic elegy could survive, through repetition or reperformance (see Theog. 237–54), only if it represented circumstances common to other symposium singers. In Hellenistic epigram, on the other hand, the love objects are continually varied, by name and nature as well as by sex, but the condition depicted in each epigram is specific to the individual lover in a given time and place. Although erotic epigram did sometimes adapt the imagery and motifs of earlier lyric (which displayed a greater variety of love objects than elegy), the listlike sequences of lovers in epigram are most reminiscent of the parades of individuals found in collections of inscriptional verse. Yet the speaker of erotic epigram—far different from the disengaged epigrammatist of traditional inscription—is a lover whose speech act is dramatized as monologue (speech directed to himself) or as dialogue (speech directed to another or divided between two speakers). The task that falls to the reader is to comprehend in its brief fullness the lover's particular and momentary emotional state, whether it be delight or despair or delusion. While the reader of collected elegy experiences systematically the various moments that occur in each and any love affair, the reader of such epigram sequences has the experience of penetrating, time and again, the emotional core of a lover through fragmentary but intense glimpses into an individual psyche.

8. Laurens 56 characterizes the difference between elegy and epigram as that between "une forme ouverte" and "une forme fermée."

9. E.g., 705 ("Seal of Posidippus"), 961 ("Epithalamium of Arsinoe"), and 978 *SH*; Callim. 14 and 54 G-P; Mel. 1 and 122 G-P. Cameron (1993) 12–13 suggests that the concept of extreme brevity as a generic marker for epigram derives from Meleagrian practice. But though Meleager seems to have anthologized mostly shorter epigrams, the reason may have been that the longer epigrams tended to be somehow unsuitable for his anthology. He seems himself to have followed earlier practice in opening his collection with an epigram of fifty-eight lines and by including longer epigrams of his own within his collection (e.g., 122 G-P at twenty lines).

The intended setting for archaic elegy at the time of composition was the site of performance, normally the symposium itself.[10] But at least some erotic epigrams were composed for a book setting, and others, perhaps first read at a banquet, were later given place by their authors in a designed poetry book. Although many of the epigrams found in books invite the reader to imagine a symposium as the dramatic site for the speech act, the author who composes for the book is free to dramatize other settings as well. Consequently, we find the epigrams of Asclepiades and Posidippus set in such locations as the street where the lover begs entrance to his darling's house or the bedroom where lovers meet or the lonely weep. The poet's placement of a dramatized setting within a book context has yet another important effect: as both poet and editor, he assumes a double position equivalent to that of internal and external narrator. By the use of the first person and a consistently characterized persona, the poet situates himself as an internal narrator speaking from within the dramatized setting of various poems. The person or persons explicitly or implicitly addressed by this narrator within the dramatized framework of the poem constitute the internal audience. But as the organizer of the collection and as the creator of the various voices that may speak within it, the epigrammatist exists also as an external narrator. In this capacity he addresses an external audience, which for our purposes consists of both the implied audience (those readers presupposed by the language and structure of the collection) and the real audience (that is, historical readers). While the internal narrator provides the reader with the primary clues for constructing the poetic persona projected by the author himself, there are also times when the external narrator stands apart from his internal equivalent, to cast an ironic or distanced gaze upon his dramatized speech act. We will find that this distancing maneuver is particularly characteristic of Asclepiades and contributes considerably to the appeal that his poetry has had for readers.

Old elegy and erotic-sympotic epigram may also be compared on the basis of the social background to which they refer. The erotic themes of archaic elegy form an integral part of the larger social, political, and civic concerns of the poetry.[11] The symposium of the late archaic and classical ages was a cultural institution through which adult males of a certain aristocratic group reinforced

10. West (1974) 10–13 lists eight different circumstances under which archaic elegy may have been performed. But E. L. Bowie, "Early Greek Elegy, Symposium and Public Festival," *JHS* 106 (1986) 13–35 has argued that these can be collapsed to two—symposium as the site for shorter and more personal elegies and public festival as the site for longer elegies on historical and political topics.

11. See Massimo Vetta, *Theognis elegiarum liber secundus* (Rome, 1980) xxxiv–xxxvii; J. M. Lewis, "Eros and the *Polis* in Theognis Book II," in Figueira and Nagy 197–222. There has been much recent work on the symposium; see, prominently, Oswyn Murray, ed., *Sympotica: A Symposium on the Symposion* (Oxford, 1990); William J. Slater, ed., *Dining in a Classical Context* (Ann Arbor, 1991); Oswyn Murray and M. Tecusan, eds., *In Vino Veritas* (London, 1995).

and inculcated an allegiance to their values and beliefs. The adolescent boys who attended the symposium were instructed in the behavioral expectations of the group partly by sharing an erotic relationship with an older male. Although the symposium survives into the Hellenistic period with many of its external trappings intact, the social function of the gathering has clearly changed dramatically. No longer are the guests bound together by family connections and shared civic and political aspirations but by looser and more shifting bonds based on personally chosen social and intellectual interests. Instead of the communal sharing of emotional experience presupposed by old elegy, epigram depicts the particular and unique emotions that set apart and define individual selves. The lover of Hellenistic epigram seems younger than the lover of old elegy, and he chooses the sex and social status of his desired through personal preference alone. His feelings of joy or sorrow are not a communal experience that the other symposiasts share from time to time, but an emotional circumstance that hinders his participation in the conviviality of the moment and marks his alienation from group experience. Consequently, erotic epigram makes no attempt to instruct with lessons valuable beyond the immediate moment, but rather strives to illustrate the lover's interior emotional condition at a given point in time. Although in this respect the poetry has become aestheticized, it is yet illustrative of the social realities of the poet's life. In a world lacking a civic and political center, the poetic ego who speaks in erotic epigram illustrates, through his constantly frustrated search for reciprocated affection, the perpetual estrangement of Hellenistic man.

Asclepiades, as the undisputed founder of the erotic-sympotic epigram, will be studied together with Posidippus and Hedylus, to whom he is linked by a number of bonds. From external evidence it appears likely that they were acquainted with one another. Asclepiades and Posidippus are both named in a Delphic decree,[12] while Asclepiades and Hedylus share the homeland of Samos. Posidippus and Hedylus were clearly present in Alexandria in the 270s;[13] although direct proof of Asclepiades' residence in Egypt is lacking, he may also have enjoyed the patronage of the Ptolemies, who were at this period in control of Samos. Other evidence clearly points to associations among the poetry of the three epigrammatists.[14] As we have seen, Meleager groups the trio together in the prooemium to his *Garland* (1.45–46 G-P), and the *Garland* sequence in Book 5 of the *AP* consists primarily of epigrams by Asclepiades, Posidippus, and Hedylus interspersed with Meleagrian variations. While Posidippus and Hedylus were clearly imitators of Asclepiades, the nature of their relationship is complicated by the presence in the *AP* of six attributions shared by Asclepiades

---

12. *Fouilles de Delphes* III.3, no. 192.

13. Both write poetry celebrating the Ptolemaic monuments of that period: Posid. 11, 12, 13 G-P; Hed. 4 G-P.

14. For a more detailed treatment of the evidence, see Cameron (1993) 369–72.

and Posidippus and one shared by Asclepiades and Hedylus. Gow has argued that some of these alternative attributions, those denoted by ἤ rather than οἱ δέ, descend from Meleager himself.[15] Because of the evident imitations by the two younger epigrammatists and on the basis of the shared attributions, Reitzenstein posited that Meleager had used an anthology combining the poetry of the three but lacking authorial ascriptions. His theory included the assumption that this anthology, which he identified with the *Soros*, preserved in written form the oral interaction between these poets as they performed their epigrams at banquets.[16]

Although Reitzenstein's view has seldom been accepted unreservedly, his general thesis has been extremely influential throughout the century. Some scholars still speak of an Ionic-Alexandrian school or assume that the epigrams of Asclepiades, Posidippus, and Hedylus originated as oral compositions formed as they dined together.[17] Yet other scholars have recently offered modifications of Reitzenstein's thesis. Tarditi has proposed that the *Soros* was a mixed collection by our three epigrammatists, but with authorial ascriptions added. Meleager's uncertainty about authorship in several cases stems, he suggests, from discrepancies that developed between later copies of this anthology and the separate editions of the three poets.[18] Cameron has now made a similar suggestion, with the further supposition that Hedylus was the editor of this collection, who added a selection of his own work to that of his predecessors.[19] An anthology of epigram variations, serving as the model for the later collections of Meleager, Philip, and Agathias, is certainly possible within the first half of the third century. But it is incautious to assume that the alternative ascriptions in Meleager are conclusive evidence for it or that Aristarchus' reference to the *Soros* refers to a such a "heap" of poetry. It is important to remember that, as soon as an epigram was issued by its author, it began to acquire new and multiple contexts, most of which are now irretrievably lost to our view. In addition to reviewing the remaining evidence for the different collections in which the poetry of Asclepiades, Posidippus, and Hedylus may have appeared, I will particularly focus upon the internal evidence provided by the surviving epigrams themselves, evidence that each of these poets published a thematically coherent single-authored epigram book. The symposium played a significant part in

15. Gow (1958) 32–33; Gow-Page (1965) I xxx, II 117.

16. Reitzenstein (1893) 101–2. See also W. and M. Wallace, "Meleager and the *Soros*," *TAPA* 70 (1939) 191–202, who, following a suggestion of Reitzenstein (101, n. 1), argued that six poems from the Meleagrian sequence at *AP* 5.134–215 headed ἄδηλον are also works of Asclepiades, Posidippus, or Hedylus and were copied by Meleager from the *Soros*. But Gow-Page (1965) II 116 with n. 6 have shown that Reitzenstein's assumption of an anthology without authorial ascription could not be correct, since Aristarchus learned from the *Soros* that the Berisus epigram was written by Posidippus.

17. For the characteristics of this "school," see Beckby I 29–33.

18. Tarditi 25–26.

19. Cameron (1993) 374–75.

each of these three collections—as an imaginary, or metaphorical, context for their production.

ASCLEPIADES

Asclepiades of Samos was the earliest of the erotic epigrammatists. His birth should be placed about 340–30 B.C. on the basis of 44 G-P = *AP* 9.752, an epigram on an amethyst ring belonging to a Cleopatra who is undoubtedly the sister of Alexander, murdered about 308 B.C.[20] This chronology fits with Theocritus' reference to Asclepiades in the seventh *Idyll*, likely written in the 270s, where the Samian is associated with Philetas as a master poet whose talents are not to be challenged (7.39–41). Ascribed to Asclepiades are thirty-five epigrams of relatively certain authorship (1–33, 41–42 G-P), among which a dominant group of twenty-seven erotic poems exhibit traces of pairing and other forms of thematic linkage that suggest an author-edited poetry book.[21] One epigram

20. For this view, see Otto Knauer, *Die Epigramme des Asklepiades v. Samos* (Diss. Tübingen, 1935) 76; William Wallace and Mary Wallace, *Asklepiades of Samos* (Oxford, 1941) ix–x, 91; Stella 73–74; and Fraser I 557. Wilamowitz (1924) I 144 dates Asclepiades' productive period to 320–290. But Gow-Page (1965) II 114–15, though they assert that Asclepiades has a strong claim to authorship (II 148), omit the Cleopatra epigram from their discussion of Asclepiades' life and opt for a birth date of about 320. Alan Cameron, "Two Mistresses of Ptolemy Philadelphus," *GRBS* 31 (1990) 291–94, (1995) 237, has now argued that the Cleopatra epigram was much more likely written by Antipater of Thessalonica, to whom it is also ascribed, and that it refers to Cleopatra Selena, the daughter of Antony and Cleopatra. Yet stylistic parallels with Asclep. 32 G-P and close parallels in subject matter among Posidippus' epigrams on stones (20 G-P as well as epigrams known only from the Milan papyrus) are clear indications of the Asclepiadean authorship of 44 G-P; see Gutzwiller (1995), where I argue that the figure of Methe ("Drunkenness") engraved on the amethyst is a symbol of Argead connection with Dionysus. The appearance of the name Asclepiades on Samian coins issued about 300 B.C. also points to a birth date before 320; see John P. Barron, *The Silver Coins of Samos* (London, 1966) 137–40.

21. Of the forty-seven epigrams printed in the edition of Gow-Page, fourteen are of disputed authorship. The six poems ascribed also to Posidippus (34 G-P = *AP* 5.194, 35 G-P = *AP* 5.202, 36 G-P = *AP* 5.209, 37 G-P = *AP* 12.17, 38 G-P = *AP* 12.77, 39 G-P = *AP* 16.68) and one ascribed also to Hedylus (40 G-P = *AP* 5.161) are probably in some cases, possibly in others, imitations of Asclepiades by the alternative epigrammatist. Of the remaining dubious epigrams I accept as almost certainly Asclepiadean 41 G-P = *AP* 7.217, which is clearly sepulchral and so not an erotic epigram by Plato; 42 G-P = *AP* 5.189, which is more in the style of Asclepiades than Meleager; and 44 G-P = *AP* 9.752, the poem on Cleopatra's ring. In his *Epigrammata Graeca* Page eliminated, without comment, most of the epigrams that I consider doubtful. Of my thirty-six genuine poems, he omits 44 G-P and prints in addition 46 G-P = *AP* 12.36, ascribed to Asclepiades of Adramyttium (which seems thematically to belong with the Philippan epigram that precedes it in the *AP*) and 47 G-P, a fragment from P.Tebt. 1.3 headed]ιαδου. I. G. Galli Calderini, "Su alcuni epigrammi dell'*Antologia Palatina* corredati di lemmi alternativi," *AAP* 31 (1982) 239–80 has discussed in detail ten poems for which there are alternative lemmata

with prooemial characteristics and another bearing the "seal" of the poet's name offer further indications that Asclepiades published his erotic epigrams in the form of a collection. Given the early date of this assemblage (and in one epigram Asclepiades claims he is not yet twenty-two), it is possible that the epigrams were interspersed with poems in other meters, such as the lyric meters known as the greater and lesser Asclepiads.[22] It is also possible that the collection contained a number of nonerotic epigrams, either intermingled with the love poetry in the manner of Catullus' *libellus*, or placed in separate sections such as we find in the new Posidippus papyrus; in addition to the erotic epigrams, there survive epitaphs, dedications, poems on literary figures, and poems on works of art. But whatever the extent of the collection's variety (and we may of course be dealing with remnants from more than one collection), the evidence offered by the surviving epigrams indicates that a persona with a discernible identity gave coherency to Asclepiades' collected verse. The poet chose to define his authorial presence not, as in the inscriptional epigrammatists, by place of origin or by a perspective that is gender or class conscious, nor even, like the earlier Greek elegists and the later Roman love poets, by a consistently named beloved. The identifying characteristic of this youthful Asclepiades is his entrapment within an endless cycle of love, a cycle of desire and betrayal, symbolized by the dice game of the Erotes.[23]

Since Asclepiades speaks with the voice of the traditional male aristocrat who, because of his favored position in society, needs no explicit identifying characteristics, scholars have had little basis to decide whether his epigrams should be associated with Samos or Alexandria. Some have assumed that he belonged to a Samian intellectual circle headed by Duris, who was not only tyrant

---

in the *Anthology*; in five cases she decides in favor of the authorship of Asclepiades. But for purposes of reconstructing a poetry book it is best to err on the side of caution, and so I have excluded from my discussion all poems about which there remains any serious doubt, though some of these may well have been written by the Samian.

22. Reitzenstein, "Asklepiades von Samos," *RE* 4 HB (1896) 1625 has suggested, perhaps correctly, that Theocritus' *Idylls* in lyric meters (28–30) are similar to Asclepiades' lyric compositions; see Richard Hunter, *Theocritus and the Archaeology of Greek Poetry* (Cambridge, 1996) 19, 172–74. If Theocritus' *Idylls* are an accurate guide, these lyric poems were also predominantly erotic in theme. By chance, the one epigram that survives in a nonelegiac meter, 33 G-P = *AP* 13.23, in iambic lines of alternating length, is an epitaph. Asclepiades also composed hymns (218 *SH*), perhaps in hexameters, and choliambic verses (216, 217 *SH*).

23. The fact that Asclepiades is unwilling to devote more than one epigram to any beloved does not, in the ancient view, count against the seriousness of his emotions, as some modern scholars suggest. See, for instance, Peter Green, *Alexander to Actium: The Historical Evolution of the Hellenistic Age* (Berkeley, 1990) 175: "Asclepiades' attitude to passion is on the whole lighthearted, bisexual, and cheerfully inconstant: the act, the moment of ecstasy, achieved or in prospect, is paramount." The same view can be found in Fraser I 563: "We notice at once the absence of deep emotion, while lighter feelings are not lacking. The passion of single and exclusive love . . . is quite missing in Asclepiades."

of Samos but also an important historian, and by his brother Lynceus, a comic poet and friend of Menander.[24] The two brothers, whose family was deeply involved in the heady project of rebuilding Samian citizen life after the return of its exiled population, were among the best educated men of their generation. They had trained at Athens with the Peripatetics where they likely knew the Samian-born Epicurus.[25] While Duris wrote history with a tragic cast, Lynceus' fragments are filled with chatter about drinking parties and luxurious living.[26] To my mind, it is highly likely that Asclepiades' epigrams reflect Samian aristocratic life in the first two decades of the third century. But other scholars have wished to claim Alexandria as the site of his acquaintance with Posidippus and Hedylus (the latter a Samian by birth or ancestry).[27] Although direct evidence for an Egyptian sojourn is lacking, it is certainly possible that a famous poet working in Samos, which came under Ptolemaic protection in 281 B.C., would eventually be attracted to the court in Alexandria. But even if we accept the various threads of circumstantial evidence pointing to the simultaneous presence of Asclepiades, Posidippus, and Hedylus at the court of Ptolemy Philadelphus, that does not lead to the conclusion that the three of them produced poetry in any kind of joint enterprise. Since the most influential of Asclepiades' epigrams seem to have been composed in his youth, and so likely in Samos, the similarities between his poetry and that of the other two should be construed as allusive rather than collaborative.

To begin, we will consider how Asclepiades constructed erotic epigram by combining the themes of old elegy with epigrammatic form.[28] A good example is the poem in which the poet attempts to seduce a maiden by a conventional appeal to the brevity of youth:

φείδῃ παρθενίης· καὶ τί πλέον; οὐ γὰρ ἐς Ἅιδην
    ἐλθοῦσ᾽ εὑρήσεις τὸν φιλέοντα, κόρη.

<hr>

24. Augusto Rostagni, *Poeti alessandrini* (Turin, 1916) 204–11; Wallace and Wallace (1941) x–xi; Calderini (1982) 240.

25. For the history of Samos during this period, see Graham Shipley, *A History of Samos, 800–188 B.C.* (Oxford, 1987). On Duris as a historian and intellectual, see Robert B. Kebric, *In the Shadow of Macedon: Duris of Samos*, Historia Einzelschriften, Heft 29 (Wiesbaden, 1977). On Lynceus, see A. Körte, "Lynkeus von Samos," *RE* 26 HB (1927) 2472–73. For the possible influence of Duris on Hellenistic literary theory, see L. Ferrero, "Tra poetica ed istorica: Duride di Samo," in *Miscellanea di studi alessandrini* (Turin, 1963) 68–100.

26. In one fragment (*apud* Ath. 11.499c), for instance, Lynceus chats about banquets that took place at his house in Samos.

27. Fraser I 558–59; Cameron (1990) 287–95, (1993) 371–72, (1995) 237–39.

28. Various echoes of elegy in epigram have been catalogued by Paul Kägi, *Nachwirkungen der älteren griechischen Elegie in den Epigrammen der Anthologie* (Diss. Zurich, 1917). An important study of sympotic motifs in Hellenistic epigram can be found in G. Giangrande, "Sympotic Literature and Epigram," in *L'épigramme grecque*, Entretiens sur l'antiquité classique, 14 (Geneva, 1968) 119–72.

ἐν ζωοῖσι τὰ τερπνὰ τὰ Κύπριδος, ἐν δ' Ἀχέροντι
ὀστέα καὶ σποδιή, παρθένε, κεισόμεθα.

(2 G-P = AP 5.85)

Shun maidenhood. What good is it? You won't find
    anyone to love you, girl, when you come to Hades.
The pleasures of the Cyprian are for the living. In Acheron
    we will lie, maiden, bones and ash.

Both the *carpe diem* theme in the first couplet and the *memento mori* theme of the second find parallels in the *Theognidea* (with the first couplet, cf. οὐκέτι δηρὸν ἕξεις Κυπρογενοῦς δῶρον ἰοστεφάνου, "not for long will you have the gift of the violet-crowned Cyprian-born goddess," Theog. 1303–4; and with the second, cf. ἐγὼ δὲ θανὼν γαῖα μέλαιν' ἔσομαι, "in death I will become black earth," Theog. 878). But Asclepiades combines them in such a way as to create a poem of epigrammatic shape and rhythm. That the two couplets constitute a complete poem with a defined beginning and end is suggested, formally, by the balanced placement of παρθενίης (1) and παρθένε (4). In terms of content, the final κεισόμεθα, cut off and emphasized by the vocative before it, creates a simultaneous end to the poem and to life. The result is an epigram that stifles the flow characteristic of elegiac collections and imitates instead the end-stopped completeness of sepulchral inscription.

In another epigram as well Asclepiades personalizes the generalizing *topoi* of symposium speech:

οἶνος ἔρωτος ἔλεγχος· ἐρᾶν ἀρνεύμενον ἡμῖν
    ἤτασαν αἱ πολλαὶ Νικαγόρην προπόσεις·
καὶ γὰρ ἐδάκρυσεν καὶ ἐνύστασε καί τι κατηφές
    ἔβλεπε, χὠ σφιγχθεὶς οὐκ ἔμενε στέφανος.

(18 G-P = AP 12.135)

Wine tests for love. As Nicagoras was denying his love
    to us, a series of many toasts betrayed him.
He wept and hung his head and looked downcast,
    and his garland did not stay bound.

The poem is offered, in epigrammatic fashion, as proof of the opening gnome that "wine tests for love," a proof accomplished not by the generalizing truths typical of elegy (cf. Theog. 499–502) but by the report of the specific occasion on which wine betrayed Nicagoras' condition as a lover. While the Theognidean version of the *in vino veritas* commonplace (ἀνδρὸς δ' οἶνος ἔδειξε νόον, "Wine reveals the mind of a man," Theog. 500) was composed to be performed at symposia, the epigram does not dramatize symposium speech at all but rather presents the speaker recalling, at some indefinite time and place, the events of a certain gathering: Nicagoras denied to his friends that he was in love until his tears and demeanor betrayed his true condition. With the pronoun "we" (ἡμῖν) the poet need not be addressing his companions who were present at the symposium, because these fellow symposiasts would have no reason to be told what they had witnessed themselves, and yet the use of the unexplained ἡμῖν suggests an auditor who is familiar with the banqueters, and so not necessarily synonymous with the implied reader. Just as the poem assumes epigrammatic character by its reference to a specific individual and event and by its assumption of an internal auditor, it also displays a cohesion and completeness that associates it with the fixity of epigram rather than the fluidity of elegy. In the last line the garland slipping from the brow of the drunken lover provides the reader, imagistically, with a final and finalizing proof for the truth of the opening gnome.[29]

In a similar way, Asclepiades adapts the form of inscriptional epigram to the oral discourse of the lover. Epigram 6 G-P is the most overtly epigrammatic of the erotic poems:

Λυσιδίκη σοί, Κύπρι, τὸν ἱππαστῆρα μύωπα
    χρύσεον εὐκνήμου κέντρον ἔθηκε ποδός,
ᾧ πολὺν ὕπτιον ἵππον ἐγύμνασεν, οὐδέ ποτ' αὐτῆς
    μηρὸς ἐφοινίχθη κοῦφα τινασσομένης.
ἦν γὰρ ἀκέντητος τελεοδρόμος, οὕνεκεν ὅπλον
    σοὶ κατὰ μεσσοπύλης χρύσεον ἐκρέμασεν.

(6 G-P = *AP* 5.203)

Lysidice has dedicated to you, Cyprian, the riding spur,
    the golden goad of her shapely foot,
With which she exercised many a supine horse, though
    her thigh did not ever grow red, she bounced so lightly.
She finished the race without applying the spur and has therefore
    hung her golden tool on your entry way.

The epigram resembles, in formal terms, those Leonidean dedications in which tools no longer needed are presented to a deity. But here Lysidice is only metaphorically a horsewoman, in actuality a hetaira who sits bestride her man,[30] and the spur is dedicated, not upon her retirement, but because she is so skillful at love making that she has no need of a goad.

29. L. Landolfi, "Silentium Amoris," *Orpheus* 5 (1984) 169 notes the poem's "tecnica anulare."

30. The sexual imagery in the poem has been commonly misunderstood. Gow–Page (1965) *ad loc.* claim that in 4f. Asclepiades is thinking of Lysidice "not as κελητίζουσα but in the more normal σχῆμα in which the rider is the man, and the spur seems to have been transferred to him"; in other words, in the course of the poem she somehow changes position. But for the interpretation that Lysidice remains on top in the position of "rider," cf. Alan Cameron, "Asclepiades' Girl Friends," *Reflections of Women in Antiquity*, ed. Helene P. Foley (New York, 1981) 295, reprinted in (1995) 516; and G. Zanker 216, n. 22. For other references to this sexual position, see J. R. Heath, "The Supine Hero in Catullus 32," *CJ* 82 (1986) 28–36.

In formal terms, Asclepiades gives his poem the structural elements of traditional dedicatory epigram—name of dedicator, deity addressed, object dedicated, and reason for the gift. But the poem is almost certainly a fictive inscription, a purely book epigram. If Lysidice had in fact employed a golden spur in her love making, it was not as a sadistic stimulant, but as a prop, part of her costume. And so, even if the spur were not needed to bring the lover to orgasm on the model of actual horse racing, it would remain useful in her trade and would not likely be dedicated to the goddess for the reason given. Of course, we may understand that the expressed reason is pretextual and that Lysidice makes the offering as a public celebration of her skill. But I argue that this reading of the poem is also to be understood as fictive, because the perspective of the speaking voice in the poem is ultimately not that of the dedicating hetaira but that of the erotic poet. How, then, are we to understand the vocative Κυπρί, through which the voice speaking in the poem is most clearly revealed? If the poem were a simple transference of inscriptional verse to a book context, the reader would hear in the vocative the voice of the anonymous epigrammatist of traditional epigram expressing the wishes of the dedicator to the goddess. But because of the play with form and motif, the reader may hear instead the ironizing voice of a clever poet imitating an inscriptional epigrammatist in order to entertain a literary audience with an erotic double entendre.

While the reader who encounters the poem in isolation or in an anthology may prefer to hear the vocative in the first way, the second is a more likely choice if the epigram is encountered in the vicinity of other Asclepiadean addresses to Aphrodite or the Erotes. Aphrodite, who is invoked as "dear Cypris" (3.4 G-P), "Paphian" (4.2 G-P), and "mistress Cypris" (7.3 G-P), and her sons the Erotes, who are also invoked in three poems, (8, 15, 17 G-P), are clearly the inspiratory deities of the collection.[31] In each of these epigrams Asclepiades' address to the goddess or her sons signals his own emotional involvement in the matter at hand. In his condemnation of the female lovers Bitto and Nannion, for instance, the vocative δεσπότι Κύπρι subtly suggests that the poet's hostility may somehow be motivated by personal, erotic loss:

αἱ Σάμιαι Βιττὼ καὶ Νάννιον εἰς Ἀφροδίτης
   φοιτᾶν τοῖς αὐτῆς οὐκ ἐθέλουσι νόμοις,
εἰς δ᾽ ἕτερ᾽ αὐτομολοῦσιν ἃ μὴ καλά. δεσπότι Κύπρι,
   μίσει τὰς κοίτης τῆς παρὰ σοὶ φυγάδας.

(7 G-P = *AP* 5.207)

The Samians Bitto and Nannion refuse to approach
   Aphrodite's temple as her rules command,

---

31. L. Defreyne, "Erotes and Eros in the Epigrams of Asclepiades," *Aevum Antiquum* 6 (1993) 199–236 has studied the references to the god of love in Asclepiades, but without considering the effect they would have in a collection.

But they follow their own unlovely course. Mistress Cypris,
  despise those fugitives from your bed.

So, too, 6 G-P illustrates how the address to Aphrodite changes its function as the reader's gaze slips from the poem in isolation to the poem in its book context. Within the confines of a poetry book, in association with Asclepiades' other addresses to Aphrodite and the Erotes, the vocative seems to emanate not from the featureless composer of a dedicatory epigram, but from an involved author who calls upon his patron deity, the Muse of his collection, to join in his amusement at Lysidice's dedication.

An example of a poem that combines the precedents of both inscriptional epigram and old elegy is provided by the epigram that apparently opened Asclepiades' collection:

ἡδὺ θέρους διψῶντι χιὼν ποτόν, ἡδὺ δὲ ναύταις
  ἐκ χειμῶνος ἰδεῖν εἰαρινὸν Στέφανον·
ἥδιον δ' ὁπόταν κρύψῃ μία τοὺς φιλέοντας
  χλαῖνα, καὶ αἰνῆται Κύπρις ὑπ' ἀμφοτέρων.

(1 G-P = AP 5.169)

Sweet for the thirsty an icy drink in summer, and sweet
  for sailors to spot spring's Crown after a storm.
But sweeter still when one cloak covers two lovers,
  and the Cyprian is honored by both.

Asclepiades' priamel on sweetness stands in a tradition of generalizing priamels illustrated by an epigram that, according to Aristotle (*Eth. Eud.* 1214a5–6), was inscribed on the propylaea of the Letöon at Delos:

κάλλιστὸν τὸ δικαιότατον, λῷστον δ' ὑγιαίνειν·
  πάντων ἥδιστον δ' οὗ τις ἐρᾷ τὸ τυχεῖν.

Justice is the noblest thing. Health is the best.
  But sweetest of all is to obtain what one desires.

The couplet inscribed at Delos appears again, with a small change in the pentameter, in our Theognidean collection (255–56)[32] at the head of a long section that Martin West calls the Florilegium Magnum (255–1230), and which he argues was formed, like the shorter section that he calls the Florilegium Purum (1–254), in the early third century B.C.[33] It is highly likely, then, that Asclepiades knew a collection of extracts from archaic elegy that was headed

---

32. Aristotle quotes the same epigram again in *Eth. Nic.* 1099a25–28 where the pentameter reads ἥδιστον δὲ πέφυχ' οὗ τις ἐρᾷ τὸ τυχεῖν. The text of the pentameter in Theognis is πρᾶγμα δὲ τερπνότατον, τοῦ τις ἐρᾷ, τὸ τυχεῖν.

33. West (1974) 45, 58–59. The Florilegium Purum was a carefully edited collection, headed by a series of four invocations to deities and ending with a coda. For a detailed study of its arrangement, see Friedrich S. Hasler, *Untersuchungen zu Theognis* (Winterthur, 1959). Partial

by the couplet known as the Delian epigram. I have already argued, on the basis of parallels with Nossis and Theocritus, that Asclepiades' epigram functioned as an allusion to the introductory epigram in Anyte's collection of inscriptional verse. By choosing to begin his collection with this deceptively simple priamel, Asclepiades was employing a technique of multiple allusion: his epigram not only recalls Anyte's path-breaking collection of inscriptional verse (by echoing her ἁδύ, 18.2 G-P) but also points to the importance of the codification of old elegy as a precedent for his own innovative collection. To model his opening on the Delian epigram signaled the dual roots of his poetry in oral and written discourse, in both elegy and epigram.

His opening epigram also foreshadows, programmatically, the thematic concerns of his collection and sets these concerns within the context of the philosophical thought of the day. The Delian epigram distinguishes justice, health, and the attainment of one's desires on the basis of three different qualities—nobleness, goodness, and sweetness. By limiting his three actions to only one quality (ἡδονή), Asclepiades recalls the teachings of the contemporary philosopher Epicurus. Epicurus taught that pleasure, defined as the absence of pain, was the highest good.[34] To support this basic tenet, he proclaimed that pleasure is obtained through a process of fulfilling desire, that is, of removing pain. He set out two categories of pleasure—physical pleasures, examples of which are satisfying hunger and thirst and avoiding cold (τὸ μὴ πεινῆν, τὸ μὴ διψῆν, τὸ μὴ ῥιγοῦν, *Sent. Vat.* 33), and a superior category of mental pleasures, which were defined as release from disturbances of the mind. These mental disturbances were often imaged as a storm of the soul (ὁ τῆς ψυχῆς χειμὼν, *Ep. Men.* 128; cf. χειμάζειν, D.L. 10.137). Epicurus' category of physical pleasures seems to underlie Asclepiades' initial statement about the sweetness of a cool drink for the thirsty, while Asclepiades may give an example of Epicurus' second category of mental pleasure in his description of sailors who emerge safely from a storm. My reading of the epigram as making reference to two Epicurean categories of pleasure is supported by Lucretius' echo in the priamel that opens his second book (cf. *suave . . . suave . . . dulcius*, 2.1–7 with Asclepiades' ἡδὺ . . . ἡδὺ . . . ἥδιον),

---

confirmation for West's thesis comes from a papyrus fragment (P.Oxy. 2380) which shows that as late as the second or third century A.D. line 255 was still being marked as the beginning of a new section of the collection. P.Oxy. 2380 contains portions of lines 254–78, and line 255 begins substantially to the right of the other lines. The papyrus does not, however, reveal what preceded the beginning of 255, whether a blank space or a heading or something other. See M. Gronewald, "Theognis 255 und Pap. Oxy. 2380," *ZPE* 19 (1975) 178–79.

34. For pleasure in Epicurean philosophy, see J. C. B. Gosling and C. C. W. Taylor, *The Greeks on Pleasure* (Oxford, 1982) 345–413. On the relationship of Epicurus' views of pleasure to Aristotle's, see Philip Merlan, *Studies in Epicurus and Aristotle* (Wiesbaden, 1960) 1–37 and J. M. Rist, "Pleasure: 360–300 B.C.," *Phoenix* 28 (1974) 167–79. Daniel H. Garrison, *Mild Frenzy: A Reading of the Hellenistic Love Epigram*, Hermes Einzelschriften, Heft 41 (Wiesbaden, 1978) 60–61 has also noted a connection between Asclepiades' and Epicurus' views of pleasure.

where the first segment concerns the pleasure of watching ships in storm from the safety of shore. This sequence of adjectives may even have functioned as a signpost for Epicurean influence in a poetic text.

In the third colon of his epigram Asclepiades seems to veer away from Epicurean teachings. He clearly reworks the third segment of the Delian epigram ("sweetest of all is to obtain what one desires"), interpreting it in sexual terms. For Epicurus sex was permissible as a form of pleasure, but not actively encouraged because fraught with the possibility of turning to pain. Asclepiades may seek to bring sexual passion under his Epicurean umbrella by alluding to the lovers with a term (τοὺς φιλέοντας) that suggests the condition of friendship (φιλία) Epicurus recommended as a source of pleasure. He also bolsters his attempt to remodel erotic desire as a higher pleasure by replacing the archaic goal of sexual conquest, as expressed in the Delian epigram, with a different goal of mutual affection—one cloak but a dual honoring of the Cyprian. He seems, then, to be modifying Epicurean tenets to give a quasi-philosophical basis to a new ideal of reciprocity in romance. But, as we will find, the forms of erotic experience depicted throughout the poetry book tend to validate the genuine Epicurean view that erotic desire produces pain and so to undercut the alluring picture that Asclepiades presents in this probably introductory epigram.

In the aftermath of Foucault's influential analysis of ancient sexuality, some classical scholars have pointed to a movement, beginning in the Hellenistic period and intensifying throughout later antiquity, toward greater symmetry between the sexes in erotic relationships.[35] Recently, other scholars have argued that this shift is not the radical change envisioned by Foucault but involved more subtle modifications to old paradigms of power and dominance.[36] The persona of the epigrammatic lover in Asclepiades' collection, defined by the constancy of his desire and the inevitability of pain, needs to be understood as a reflection of a young man's attempt to come to terms with changing social realities of the erotic relationships between men and women in the early Hellenistic period.

Male-composed erotic poetry of the pre-Hellenistic period was largely concerned with persuasion. The lover was usually an older man who sought to win over a person of lesser status, either an adolescent male or a female who was typically of a different social standing. The love object was often represented as childlike, compared to flowers or young animals, all images suggesting vulnerability. So Ibycus' Euryalus was reared among roses by gentle-eyed Peitho

35. Michel Foucault, *The Use of Pleasure: The History of Sexuality* II, trans. Robert Hurley (New York, 1985) and *The Care of the Self: The History of Sexuality* III, trans. Robert Hurley (New York, 1986). Among a number of classical studies stimulated by Foucault, we may cite the comprehensive study by David Konstan, *Sexual Symmetry: Love in the Ancient Novel and Related Genres* (Princeton, 1994).

36. See, for example, Simon Goldhill, *Foucault's Virginity: Ancient Erotic Fiction and the History of Sexuality* (Cambridge, 1995).

(288 *PMG*). Theognis' lover is a lion who refrains from drinking the blood of a fawn taken from its mother (949–50 = 1278c–d W). Anacreon plans to tame a Thracian filly who now prances through the meadow (417 *PMG*). In all these instances the beloved is to be plucked or tamed or attacked. The lover may represent himself as enthralled or compelled by the love object, but the beloved is typically unconscious of the power he or she holds, like the boy with the maiden's glance who does not know that he is the charioteer of Anacreon's soul (360 *PMG*). Love in archaic and classical Greece was not normally represented as a sharing of mutual affection, but rather as a game of pursuit, which an adult male might either win or lose but in which his role as pursuer was never altered.

Although much of Asclepiades' approach to sexual experience descends directly from earlier male-dominated aristocratic culture, the particular quality of his desire and pain, its innovative feel, is related to new modes of behavior for women. While men in Hellenistic society continued to occupy positions of greater power and control, opportunities had increased for women to express their own desire or to respond more actively to the desire of others. The prominent example of Apollonius' Medea shows the interest of male poets in creating literary portraits of such women. Cameron has argued that most of the women in Asclepiades' epigrams were not hetairas, as traditionally assumed, but women with the freedom to choose their own sexual partners.[37] While I prefer to assume a less rigid division between hetairas and respectable women so that hetairas may sometimes express a personal preference and other women sometimes take a lover outside of marriage, it is undoubtably true that the women in Asclepiades' epigrams tend to play a more active role in their erotic relationships than their counterparts in earlier Greek poetry. Concomitantly, apart from the epigram in which the poet attempts to seduce a maiden (2 G-P), we generally find Asclepiades' lover reacting to the behavior of his love object rather than seeking to control through direct persuasion.

Before turning to the epigrams representing Asclepiades' own erotic involvement, it is useful to glance at a series of poems that depict women as desiring subjects or as beings in control of their own sexuality. The Nicarete epigram, for instance, focuses on the girl's desire for Cleophon:

Νικαρέτης τὸ πόθοισι βεβλημένον ἡδὺ πρόσωπον
    πυκνὰ δι᾽ ὑψηλῶν φαινόμενον θυρίδων
αἱ χαροπαὶ Κλεοφῶντος ἐπὶ προθύροισι μάραναν,
    Κύπρι φίλη, γλυκεροῦ βλέμματος ἀστεροπαί.[38]

(3 G-P = *AP* 5.153)

---

37. Cameron (1981), reprinted in revised form (1995) 494–519.

38. Instead of Wilamowitz's βεβαμμένον printed by Gow-Page, I have accepted the βεβλημένον of the codex. The idea of Nicarete's being "struck" with desire anticipates the image of Cleophon's lightning glance.

Nicarete's sweet face, struck with desire,
   appearing often at the high windows,
Has been drained by the lightning flashing, dear Cypris,
   from the tender glance of Cleophon on her porch.

It is not commonly recognized that the scenario envisened in this poem is
that of the *komos*, or revel made to the beloved's domicile.[39] Yet the phrase
ἐπὶ προθύροισι, "on her porch," echoing other Asclepiadean paraclausithyra
(13.4, 14.4, 42.2 G-P), reveals that the purpose of Cleophon's frequent visits to
Nicarete's domicile is courtship. In addition, the image of lightning flashing from
his eyes recalls the storm motif found elsewhere in Asclepiades' paraclausithyra
(11, 12, 14, 42 G-P). Scholars have generally failed to recognize the dramatic
background for the poem because the poet does not present, as usual in *komos*
poetry, the lover's pleas for admission or his emotional response to exclusion.
Here the poet, acting as external narrator, focuses upon Nicarete's mounting
desire rather than the pain of the lover she has not yet admitted to her company.
Whatever her reason for merely watching Cleophon from her window, the
appearance of her face, drained by desire, conveys to the observer the intensity
of her longing.

Other women in Asclepiades' epigrams are more actively in control of their
sexuality. In 20 G-P = *AP* 12.161 Dorcion, who is either a hetaira or at least
promiscuous in her favors, dresses like a "tender boy" to hurl the "swift arrow
of Aphrodite *pandemos*" and "flashes the lightning of desire from her eyes": she
wears a man's petasus on her head and a chlamys that reveals her naked thigh. It
is unclear whether Dorcion intends to deceive the ephebes to whom she is dear
(φιλέφηβος, 20.1) about her sex or whether she merely uses cross-dressing as
a means of sexual provocation. But her play with gender ambiguity nevertheless
gives her a degree of control over her erotic encounters. As Anacreon may
have been attracted to the boy with a maiden's glance because of his feminine
vulnerability (360 *PMG*), contrariwise, Dorcion's adoption of male clothing
provides her with the masculine trait of command over her own eroticism.
The poet attributes to her knowledge (ἐπίσταται, 20.1) of how to attract young
men, and it is she who casts the lightning glances of desire. Elsewhere as well
Asclepiades refers to nonconventional sexual behavior on the part of women,
as in the epigram on the Samian pair, Bitto and Nannion (7 G-P). The poet
objects bitterly to their mode of sexuality and asks "mistress Cypris" to "hate
those fugitives from her bed." But the more usual response of Greek males to
Lesbian love was simply to ignore it altogether, and the remarkable thing about
Asclepiades' epigram is that he felt any need to acknowledge this form of female
desire at all.

---

39. An exception is Webster 50, who finds the whole epigram "a very compressed account
of a serenade."

Perhaps the most memorable Asclepiadean portrait of a woman in an active sexual role is his pseudo-dedicatory epigram on Lysidice (6 G-P). The poem throughout displays a series of inversions in normal meanings, transferring to Lysidice the usually masculine role of command and accomplishment. It is she, not her male partner, who possesses the "goad," or "prick," κέντρον being used for the male member by the contemporary poet Sotades in a line satirical of the Ptolemies (1 *CA*; cf. D.L. 2.81). When the poet claims that her thigh is not reddened she bounces so lightly, it is unclear whether he is thinking of flesh bloodied by the application of the spur or the flush that comes from hard exercise. In either case, we may be tempted to contrast Lysidice's love making, accomplished without any "reddening" (ἐφοινίχθη, 6.4), with the blushing cheeks commonly descriptive of maidens in love in Hellenistic poetry (e.g., Callim. fr. 80.10, αἰδοῖ δ᾽ ὡς φοί[νικι] τεὰς ἐρύθουσα παρειάς, "reddening your cheeks with blushing modesty"; cf. Erinna 401.34 *SH*, [φοι]νίκεος αἰδώς, "blushing modesty"). Scholars have long recognized that Asclepiades' collocation of ἀκέντητος τελεοδρόμος recalls Pindar's first *Olympian*, where Hiero's horse Pherenicus rushes forth δέμας ἀκέντητον ἐν δρόμοισι παρέχων, "offering his body ungoaded in the race" (20–21). Since Lysidice is not horse but rider, the meaning of ἀκέντητος changes in Asclepiades from "ungoaded" to "without goading." There is no reason to assume, then, that τελεοδρόμος, "finishing the race," refers only to the completion of the race by the horse, that is, her male partner, since it may suggest as well the sexual satisfaction of Lysidice as rider or mistress.

Support for my argument that Asclepiades' persona as lover acquires its innovative nature in response to the sexual independence of the women he desires is provided by Theocritus' *Idyll* 14.[40] In this poem a young man named Aeschinas relates to a friend the events of a dinner party attended by himself and three other young men—one an Argive, one a Thessalian, and the other of unstated nationality like Aeschinas himself. The narrator's girlfriend Cynisca is present, and the other men probably have female companions as well (cf. Posid. 10.1 G-P = *AP* 5.183.1). After the meal, the guests drink toasts in the name of the person loved by each. When Cynisca refuses to call out a name and is teased, she reveals that she has taken a fancy to a young neighbor named Lycus. Aeschinas confesses that in anger he struck Cynisca and she dashed from the party in tears. During the two months that have since elapsed, Aeschinas has been longing for Cynisca, and she has adopted Lycus as her lover. Although it is unclear whether Cynisca is to be understood as a hetaira, she is treated at the symposium as a guest, and she makes choices for herself about her sexual partners on the basis of her own preferences and desires. Aeschinas, on the

---

40. The *Idyll* has been studied as an example of the changed nature of the symposium in the Hellenistic period by Joan Burton, "The Function of the Symposium Theme in Theocritus' *Idyll* 14," *GRBS* 33 (1992) 227–45, and (1995) 24–28.

other hand, finds himself trying to cope with the pain engendered by longing for one who is free to choose another. The solution offered by his friend at the end of the dialogue is to become a mercenary soldier for Ptolemy Philadelphus.

In contrast to the dialogue-framed narrative of *Idyll* 14, Asclepiades' epigram collection reduces each love affair to a single, brief speech act whose dramatic setting may or may not be discernible. Yet his erotic epigrams do seem to presuppose the type of symposium culture described in Aeschinas' account, as Cynisca's reluctance to toast her beloved parallels Nicagoras' silence in 18 G-P and the singing of a song called "my Lycus" (τὸν ἐμὸν Λύκον, *Id.* 14.30) by one of Aeschinas' friends recalls a group of five Asclepiadean epigrams with named beloveds. In fact, Aeschinas' introductory explanation for his haggard appearance—ἐμὲ δ' ἁ χαρίεσσα Κυνίσκα ὑβρίσδει, "the charming Cynisca wrongs me," (*Id.* 14.8–9)—parallels a sentence structure common to all five epigrams, consisting of a first person pronoun, the name of a girlfriend with a descriptive adjective or phrase, and a verb defining the relationship of the two. Without any intent to suggest these poems appeared as a series in Asclepiades' collection, I group them for purposes of analysis:

τῷ θαλλῷ Διδύμη με συνήρπασεν, ὤμοι ἐγὼ δέ
  τήκομαι ὡς κηρὸς πὰρ πυρὶ κάλλος ὁρῶν.
εἰ δὲ μέλαινα, τί τοῦτο; καὶ ἄνθρακες· ἀλλ' ὅτε κείνους
  θάλψωμεν, λάμπουσ' ὡς ῥόδεαι κάλυκες.

(5 G-P = AP 5.210)

Didyme has caught me with her budding youth, alas, and I
  melt like wax by the fire when I see her beauty.
If she's black, what of that? So are coals. But when we
  kindle them, they glow like rosebuds.

Ἑρμιόνη πιθανῇ ποτ' ἐγὼ συνέπαιζον ἐχούσῃ
  ζώνιον ἐξ ἀνθέων ποικίλον, ὦ Παφίη,
χρύσεα γράμματ' ἔχον· "διόλου" δ' ἐγέγραπτο "φίλει με,
  καὶ μὴ λυπηθῇς ἤν τις ἔχῃ μ' ἕτερος."

(4 G-P = AP 5.158)

I used to play with persuasive Hermione, who had a sash
  embroidered with the colors of many flowers, Paphian.
And on it was written in golden letters, "Go ahead and love me,
  but don't be hurt if another holds me, too."

ἡ λαμπρή μ' ἔτρωσε Φιλαίνιον, εἰ δὲ τὸ τραῦμα
  μὴ σαφές, ἀλλ' ὁ πόνος δύεται εἰς ὄνυχα.
οἴχομ', Ἔρωτες, ὄλωλα, διοίχομαι, εἰς γὰρ ἑταίραν
  νυστάζων ἐπέβην τήνδ', ἔθιγόν τ' ἀΐδα.[41]

(8 G-P = AP 5.162)

41. Gow-Page print Waltz's ἔχιδναν in 3 where I have retained the corrector's ἑταίραν. In the last line, which is clearly corrupt, I have accepted Meineke's emendation.

Wanton Philaenion has wounded me, and even if the wound
  is not obvious, the pain sinks to the core.
I'm lost, Erotes, I'm done for, I'm gone, for I carelessly
  trod upon this whore, and I've touched death.

Νύξ, σὲ γάρ, οὐκ ἄλλην, μαρτύρομαι, οἷά μ' ὑβρίζει
  Πυθιὰς ἡ Νικοῦς οὖσα φιλεξαπάτις.
κληθείς, οὐκ ἄκλητος, ἐλήλυθα· ταῦτα παθοῦσα
  σοὶ μέμψαιτ' ἔτ' ἐμοῖς στᾶσα παρὰ προθύροις.

(13 G-P = AP 5.164)

Night, I call you, and no other, to witness how Pythias,
  Nico's daughter, that cheater at love, wrongs me.
I came invited, not uninvited. Let her someday suffer as I do,
  complaining to you as she stands on my threshold.

ὡμολόγησ' ἥξειν εἰς νύκτα μοι ἡ 'πιβόητος
  Νικὼ καὶ σεμνὴν ὤμοσε Θεσμοφόρον,
κοὐχ ἥκει, φυλακὴ δὲ παροίχεται. ἆρ' ἐπιορκεῖν
  ἤθελε; τὸν λύχνον, παῖδες, ἀποσβέσατε.

(10 G-P = AP 5.150)

That popular Nico promised to visit me tonight,
  even swore it by holy Thesmophorus.
But she hasn't come and it's past midnight. Did she intend
  to perjure herself? Slaves, extinguish the light.

It may not be accidental that Theocritus' Aeschinas employs not only the same sentence structure found in Asclepiades' five epigrams but even the very verb ὑβρίζει that appears in 13 G-P. Since we know that Theocritus admired Asclepiades as a master poet, it seems likely that Aeschinas' narrative account of his unhappy affair with Cynisca is a kind of fleshing out of the type of situation that we find in Asclepiades' briefer epigrams.

But if the narrative of Aeschinas and the epigrams of Asclepiades reflect the same culture of erotic relationships, the difference in genre produces a very different effect for the reader. While the reader of Theocritus' mime stands with the poet at an objective distance with the suffering lover, the isolated, unframed first-person speech acts that constitute Asclepiades' erotic epigrams so distill and intensify the lover's emotion that the reader sympathetically engages with his situation. The effect of viewing the lover's numerous affairs in this crystalized form is to acquire knowledge of the lover's condition qua lover, if not the specific facts of his life. In this sense, Asclepiades' catalogue of love objects is more effective than a fuller narrative account at conveying the essence of erotic experience, just as a catalogue of sepulchral or dedicatory epigrams can distill the essence of individual lives.

The trick of reading an Asclepiadean erotic epigram is to comprehend the precise nature of the lover's feelings at the moment of the speech act.

Asclepiades' particular talent was to convey this emotional content through the conversational tone of his poetry. In 5 G-P the position of ὤμοι is crucial, for it gives emotional resonance to the poet's simple statement that Didyme has captured him with her youthful beauty. Both the presence of the interjection and the poem's structural similarity to four other epigrams about Asclepiades' girlfriends speak against Cameron's theory that 5 is not a love poem at all, but a poetic compliment to the Didyme who was a mistress of Ptolemy Philadelphus.[42] The speech act being represented here is a justification of the poet's choice of love object, and this is accomplished by a clever, if not quite logical, intertwining of the metaphors of fire and vegetation. Didyme's blackness is excused by the comparison with coals, which when lit, that is, when Didyme becomes warm with the fire that melts the poet, glow like rosebuds. The last phrase (ῥόδεαι κάλυκες) rounds off the epigram by echoing the vegetable motif with which the poem begins (τῷ θαλλῷ).[43] The tone of the epigram conveys the first blush of love when the poet's indifference to others' perception of Didyme coexists with his expectation of reciprocal desire.

While in archaic poetry the verb ἁρπάζω is often used to describe the abduction of a young girl, typically from a flowery field that symbolizes her ripeness, or readiness for plucking, in 5 it is Didyme who has "seized" the poet with her "youthful bloom." Likewise, in 4 Asclepiades teases us with the image of the ζώνιον, "sash," which figures so heavily in earlier scenes of seduction, but here becomes Hermione's means of claiming sexual independence, of announcing her right to choose multiple lovers. The word ποτε in the first line conveys, at the outset, the poet's emotional distance from his affair with Hermione, and the rest of the poem explains the reason for his lack of involvement. When the girl was undressing, the poet discovered imprinted on her undergarment a notice of the casualness of the affair. Since Asclepiades discovered early on that Hermione made no pretense to fidelity, his poem is a distanced and relatively uninvolved account of their affair. Other epigrams indicate that the sexual independence of

---

42. Cameron (1990) 291, who argues that the poem "would be a perfectly acceptable compliment to the mistress of another man—even a king." But since the phrase κείνους θάλψωμεν (5.3–4) suggests that Didyme is sexually aroused by the poet, I suspect that the king would not be amused. F. M. Snowden, Jr., "Asclepiades' Didyme," *GRBS* 32 (1991) 239–53, who supports Cameron's suggestion that Didyme is a black woman, is more reluctant to accept her as Ptolemy's mistress (240). I remain unconvinced that Didyme, though dark-skinned, is connected with Egypt at all: the only other Didyme mentioned in the *Anthology* (Callim. 43 G-P = *AP* 7.521) is a prominent citizen of Cyzicus.

43. Gow-Page (1965) *ad* 1 rejects the ms. reading τῷ θαλλῷ on the grounds that "the words seem indefensible" and have driven out some other dative to be construed with ὁρῶν. If an emendation is to be made, τῷφθαλμῷ seems best; see W. Ludwig, Review of Gow-Page, *Hellenistic Epigrams, Gnomon* 38 (1966) 23. But the ms. reading is defended by Knauer 17. We may also note the use of θάλος with reference to the girl Eirenion in 34.3 G-P = *AP* 5.194.3, attributed to Posidippus or Asclepiades.

the women Asclepiades desires is more commonly a source of emotional pain. It has been argued that Philaenion's wounding of the poet in 8 concerns his discovery that she is a hetaira. But charges of "whore" were a traditional reaction to betrayal, a mode of renunciation. The Philaenion in 8, who is directly called a hetaira, may be no more or less professional than Hermione, since the charged word is an indicator of the poet's emotional state rather than Philaenion's social circumstance. The poem built on the subtle metaphor of the viper's sting is about the pain of loving one who is untrue, a pain like even to death.[44] The difference between the objective, playful account of his affair with Hermione and his tormented description of his relationship with Philaenion has little to do with the social status of the desired woman and everything to do with the degree of the poet's involvement.

In other cases a discernible dramatic setting helps to define the precise emotional condition of the lover who speaks. 13 G-P, the Pythias poem, is yet another example of an epigram that reworks elegiac precedent, such as this Theognidean couplet:

εἴ τι παθὼν ἀπ' ἐμεῦ ἀγαθὸν μέγα μὴ χάριν οἶδας,
    χρῄζων ἡμετέρους αὖθις ἵκοιο δόμους.

(Theog. 957–58)

I pray that, if you fail to respond to my desire for you,
    you may someday come to my house—desiring me.

In adapting Theognis to epigram form, Asclepiades again abandons the generalized nature of the sentiment: the setting is now fixed as a nighttime vigil before Pythias' door and the circumstances motivating the speech are revealed to be the poet's disappointment that the girl who invited him now refuses admittance. The conversion of the Theognidean couplet into a true paraclausithyron gives more emotional force to the final wish for revenge because it reflects the pain of a given individual at a given time and place.[45] Part of our pleasure in the poem is our ability to know more about the lover than he himself expresses in words: since the paraclausithyron was properly a speech act of the wooer to the wooed and, in heterosexual terms, of male to female, the poet's wish for a reversal of their roles is a form of delusion that marks the depth of his torment.

Epigram 10, another poem that defines its dramatic setting, also involves a discontinuity between the internal narrator's perception of events and the

---

44. E. K. Borthwick, "A 'femme fatale' in Asclepiades," *CR* 17 (1967) 250–54, has shown how the viper image runs through the whole poem. See also Cameron (1981) 293 and (1995) 513–14, who argues convincingly that the viper image is more effective if implicit rather than expressed.

45. On the characteristics of the paraclausithyron, see Frank O. Copley, *Exclusus Amator: A Study in Latin Love Poetry* (Baltimore, 1956) 1–6 and, for Asclepiades' influence on the later tradition of epigrammatic paraclausithyra, see Tarán (1979) 52–114.

understanding gained by a sensitive reader.[46] Nico had sworn by "holy Thes-mophorus" to pay the poet a nocturnal visit, and he has been waiting for her in vain. The final address to the slaves to extinguish the lamp fixes the time of the speech act as the final moment of despair when the lover gives up hope for Nico's arrival. He wonders aloud if she could have willingly perjured herself. But the ancient reader would recognize that an oath by the Thesmophoran Demeter to visit a lover was an oath that cancelled itself out, that was meant to have no force. The Thesmophoria was a women's festival from which men were excluded and so a time of sexual abstinence. Swearing to keep a tryst by Thesmophoran Demeter was like swearing peace by Ares or sobriety by Dionysus. A parallel use of an ineffectual oath to deceive a man is found in Aristophanes' *Lysistrata* 949 where Myrrhine swears by Artemis that she will finally recline beside her husband Cinesias—just before she abandons him. The choice of the virgin goddess invalidates the oath and allows Myrrhine to avoid perjury. Like the desperate Cinesias, the lover of 10 G-P has missed the obvious insincerity of Nico's oath. But the reader's perception of it is the key to appreciating fully the poignancy of the poem as an illustration of love's delusion.

The delusion that is an essential part of the lover's condition plays a key role in 9 as well, a problematic epigram that forms a pair with 10. Ludwig has suggested that the similarities linking 9 and 10—the lamp motif and the repetition of χοὺχ ἥχει in each—indicate that the two poems were paired in Asclepiades' collection:[47]

λύχνε, σὲ γὰρ παρεοῦσα τρὶς ὤμοσεν Ἡράκλεια
   ἥξειν, χοὺχ ἥχει· λύχνε, σὺ δ' εἰ θεὸς εἶ
τὴν δολίην ἀπάμυνον· ὅταν φίλον ἔνδον ἔχουσα
   παίζῃ, ἀποσβεσθεὶς μηκέτι φῶς πάρεχε.

(9 G-P = AP 5.7)

> Lamp, Heracleia swore three times in your presence that she
>   would come, and she hasn't come. Lamp, if you are a god,
> Punish her deceit. Whenever she's playing, having a lover
>   within, extinguish yourself and give them no more light.

---

46. Cameron (1981) 285 and (1995) 505 presupposes a poetry book by finding an allusion to 10 in 13: "the reader is meant to recall the faithless Niko and reflect 'like mother like daughter.' " But given the separativeness inherent in the poems within an epigram book, the reader is likely to find the linkage provided by the name Nico more ambiguous, suggestive alone. This removes the rather messy and biographically specific situation created by the picture of Asclepiades as lover of both mother and daughter.

47. W. Ludwig, "Ein Epigrammpaar des Asklepiades (A. P. V 7/150)," *MH* 19 (1962) 160–61. For discussion of such pairing in the Theognis collection, e.g., 1337–40 and 1341–44, see Vetta (1980) xxviii–xxxi. Similar pairs are found in the collection of Attic scolia (884–908 *PMG*), which, like the Theognis collection, may have served as an organizational model for Asclepiades. On thematically linked pairs of poems in Roman elegy, see John T. Davis, *Dramatic Pairings in the Elegies of Propertius and Ovid*, Noctes Romanae 15 (Bern, 1977).

Scholars have disagreed extensively about the dramatic setting of the poem, the location of the lover and his lamp. But the lover clearly awaits Heracleia in his own residence, and Marcovich has offered the most convincing explanation for the lamp, that as a deity it is conceived as ubiquitously present, both in the lover's apartment and in Heracleia's.[48] It is, again, a mark of the lover's condition that he exalts such an ordinary object to divine status. The more difficult problem, as Cameron has pointed out, is why the lover asks the lamp to extinguish itself when Heracleia is entertaining another lover. Darkness surely would not prevent love making. Cameron concludes that the lover's final wish enacts a deviously apt revenge—for Heracleia is only teasing (παίζῃ) her male friend, who will take the opportunity provided by the extinguished lamp to pounce upon her.[49] Yet surely παίζῃ refers here, not to teasing, but to sexual play, like συνέπαιζον in the Hermione epigram (4.1 G-P): the lover who is the projection of Asclepiades' own persona is never devious, always gullible, tormented, and helpless. The point of the poem, its final poignancy, is the utter ineffectiveness of the revenge he requests from the lamp: despite the lover's exaltation of his bedroom ally to divine status, the most the lamp can do is to produce darkness, which will offer no hindrance at all to Heracleia's infidelity.[50] The poem is yet another example, then, of the lover's tormented helplessness in the face of a woman's sexual independence.

We can see now that unlike the poetry books of Anyte, Nossis, and Leonidas, where the unity of the collection depended upon a strict correspondence between the authorial voice that occasionally spoke within an epigram and the projected qualities of the author who organized the collection, the epigram book of Asclepiades projected an organizing authorial presence that sometimes stood at an ironic distance from the persona of the twenty-two-year-old lover whose voice served as the collection's most cohesive device. In that respect, Asclepiades the

---

48. M. Marcovich, "Der Gott Lychnos," *RhM* 114 (1971) 333–39, reprinted in *Studies in Graeco-Roman Religions and Gnosticism* (Leiden, 1988) 1–7. Other scholars have suggested that the lamp is in Heracleia's room but that the poet awaits her in his own residence (I. G. Galli [Calderini], "Su un epigramma di Asclepiade [Anth. Pal. V 7 = 9 Gow-Page]," *Vichiana* 5 [1976] 192–205) or that the lamp is in a room that Heracleia uses as an accommodation address (Gow-Page [1965] II 123, hesitantly; G. Giangrande, "Asclépiade, Héracleia, et la lampe," *REG* 86 [1973] 319–22, with more confidence).

49. Cameron (1981) 283–84 and (1995) 503.

50. Of course, darkness might encourage sleep for a less-than-enthusiastic lover, and this seems to be the suggestion of Meleager 51.5–6 G-P = *AP* 5.165.5–6 (κοιμάσθω μὲν λύχνος, ὁ δ' ἐν κόλποισιν ἐκείνης ῥιπτασθεὶς κείσθω δεύτερος Ἐνδυμίων); see D. De Venuto, "Alcuni aspetti della tecnica letteraria di Meleagro," *RCCM* 10 (1968) 296 for the argument that the sleeping Endymion here represents an effeminate, a *semivir*. Meleager's companion epigram (ἢ νέος ἄλλος ἔρως, νέα παίγνια; μήποτε, λύχνε, ταῦτ' ἐσίδῃς, εἴης δ' ὧν παρέδωκα φύλαξ, 52.5–6 G-P = *AP* 5.166.5–6) is a better guide to the ineffectiveness of the abandoned lover's threat.

lover stands to Asclepiades the poet-editor as the various nonauthorial speakers in Leonidas' inscriptional epigrams stand to Leonidas the poet-editor. But by giving the internal speaker an "I"–persona, Asclepiades fosters a considerable degree of slippage between internal and external narrators and so creates the appearance of providing a biographical account. The effect of this slippage is also to obscure the dynamics of power and control that are at work in the collection. The external narrator, the "real" Asclepiades, has the power to choose the persona he projects: the lover's helpless passivity is in that sense a pose disguising the cultural dominance that belongs to the one who possesses the right to speak, the opportunity to express his pain and so to criticize, expressly or implicitly, those causing him anguish.

Some of the most effective expressions of the lover's pain occur in Asclepiades' paraclausithyra or songs sung before a beloved's door, a group of poems that appear to have provided cohesiveness to the collection through their consistency of tone and verbal linkages. Like the lamp poems (9 and 10 G-P), 14 and 42 G-P were perhaps paired in the collection:

> ὑετὸς ἦν καὶ νὺξ καί, τὸ τρίτον ἄλγος ἔρωτι,
> οἶνος· καὶ Βορέης ψυχρός, ἐγὼ δὲ μόνος.
> ἀλλ' ὁ καλὸς Μόσχος πλέον ἴσχυεν· καὶ σὺ γὰρ οὕτως
> ἤλυθες οὐδὲ θύρην πρὸς μίαν ἡσυχάσας.
> τῇδε τοσοῦτ' ἐβόησα βεβρεγμένος. ἄχρι τίνος, Ζεῦ;
> Ζεῦ φίλε, σίγησον· καὐτὸς ἐρᾶν ἔμαθες.[51]

(14 G-P = *AP* 5.167)

There was rain and darkness and that third burden for lovers,
    wine. There was also a cold north wind, and I was alone.
But lovely Moschus was stronger yet: you too would have
    gone forth, not pausing in even one doorway.
Standing there drenched, I shouted this: "How long, Zeus?
    Silence please, Zeus; you too learned to love."

> νὺξ μακρὴ καὶ χεῖμα μέσον, Πλειὰς δὲ δέδυκεν,
> κἀγὼ πὰρ προθύροις νίσομαι ὑόμενος,

---

51. The epigram is generally considered corrupt and obscure. I have kept the reading of P except in 1 where τό, found in an apographon, must be added to make the line metrical. A summary of the various interpretations of the second and third couplet can be found in Tarán (1979) 56–62 and will not be repeated here. I accept the explanation of Knauer 9 that the σύ in 3 is a friend or "Zechgenosse," i.e., the internal audience for the collection, an explanation that allows the second couplet to form a coherent and comprehensible unit. The address to Zeus in 5–6 then becomes a quotation from the narrated event. I also accept the ms. reading σίγησον rather than Hermann's σιγήσω, printed by Gow-Page and others. As a result, the movement becomes much more dramatic: the poet reproves Zeus for the weather with a typical lover's complaint (cf. Theog. 1299), and the god answers with thunder. In response the poet, assuming a familiar tone, asks for greater sympathy on the grounds that they are both lovers.

τρωθεὶς τῆς δολίης κείνης πόθῳ· οὐ γὰρ ἔρωτα
Κύπρις ἀνιηρὸν δ' ἐκ πυρὸς ἧκε βέλος.[52]

(42 G-P = *AP* 5.189)

Night is long, it's the midst of winter, the Pleiades have set,
  and I pace in the rain before her door,
Wounded by desire for that deceitful girl. For it wasn't love
  that Cypris hurled at me, but a painful shaft of fire.

Each opens in a similar fashion (ὑετὸς ἦν καὶ νὺξ ... ἐγὼ δὲ, 14.1–2; νὺξ μακρὴ καὶ χεῖμα ... κἀγὼ, 42.1–2), while their contrasting contents also suggest their association. Moschus, the male love object in 14, invites an address to Zeus, as the unnamed female love object in 42 prompts a reference to Aphrodite. Despite the formal similarities between 14 and 42, Tarán believes that 13, the Pythias poem, is the actual "companion piece" for 42 because she finds in both a tone of "vindictiveness."[53]   The situation is in fact more complicated than this, given that 13, 14, and 42 are connected as well, through an intricate pattern of interrelationships, with two other Asclepiadean epigrams on the *komos* motif:

νεῖφε, χαλαζοβόλει, ποίει σκότος, αἶθε, κεραύνου,
  πάντα τὰ πορφύροντ' ἐν χθονὶ σεῖε νέφη·
ἢν γάρ με κτείνῃς τότε παύσομαι, ἢν δέ μ' ἀφῇς ζῆν
  καὶ διαθῇς τούτων χείρονα κωμάσομαι·
ἕλκει γάρ μ' ὁ κρατῶν καὶ σοῦ θεός, ᾧ ποτε πεισθείς,
  Ζεῦ, διὰ χαλκείων χρυσὸς ἔδυς θαλάμων.

(11 G-P = *AP* 5.64)

Cast snow and hail, bring on darkness, singe me with lightning,
  Drench the earth with all your leaden storm clouds.
If you kill me, then I'll stop, but if you let me live
  and do even worse than this to me, I'll still go on a revel.
For that god stronger even than you compels me, the one who once
  persuaded you, Zeus, to penetrate bronze chambers as gold.

αὐτοῦ μοι στέφανοι παρὰ δικλίσι ταῖσδε κρεμαστοί
  μίμνετε μὴ προπετῶς φύλλα τινασσόμενοι
οὓς δακρύοις κατέβρεξα—κάτομβρα γὰρ ὄμματ' ἐρώντων—
  ἀλλ' ὅταν οἰγομένης αὐτὸν ἴδητε θύρης

---

52. I have printed, without any confidence in its correctness, the rather drastic emendation for the second part of line 1 offered by Ludwig (1966) 23, since no plausible explanation of the ms. reading, μέσην δ' ἐπὶ Πλειάδα δύνει, has been offered. On the various attempts to make sense of it, see Gow-Page (1965) *ad loc.*

53. Tarán (1979) 82–83.

στάξαθ᾽ ὑπὲρ κεφαλῆς ἐμὸν ὑετὸν ὡς ἂν ἐκείνου
ἡ ξανθή γε κόμη τἀμὰ πίῃ δάκρυα.[54]

(12 G-P = *AP* 5.145)

Remain here hanging on these double doors, and don't drop
   your petals on the ground, garlands soaked
with my tears. For lover's eyes drip with rain.
   But when the door opens and you see him,
Drop my rain shower onto his head so that his foliage—
   that boy's golden curls—may drink in my tears.

We may point to a number of superficial resemblances linking this series of poems—references to night (νύξ, 13.1; νύξ, 14.1; νύξ, 42.1), to rain (ὑετόν, 12.5; ὑετός, 14.1; ὑόμενος, 42.2), to doors (παρὰ διχλίσι, 12.1; παρὰ προθύροις, 13.4; θύρην πρὸς μίαν, 14.4; πὰρ προθύροις, 42.2), to Zeus (Ζεῦ, 11.6; Ζεῦ, Ζεῦ φίλε, 14.5–6). But more interesting is a pattern of imagery that emerges when the poems are viewed in relation one to the other. Hutchinson has observed that "Asclepiades very commonly gives force to his poems by exploiting the boundary between people and things, and between things of different kinds."[55] The *komos* poems, when read as a group, exploit a crossing of the boundaries that separate the realms of stormy weather and of love. For instance, 11 and 14 present essentially the same conceit, that the poet's desire is stronger than even the worst of storms because Eros is stronger than Zeus. Elsewhere the shafts of love merge with shafts of lightning, as in 42 where Aphrodite hurls a weapon of fire, or in 17 (quoted below) where the lover begs the Erotes to end his suffering with a thunderblast. Finally, in 12 the lover himself becomes the source of storm when his tears are transformed into "my rain shower" to wet the foliage/hair of his coy beloved. These images of course convey "the extravagance of the lover's feeling,"[56] but they also suggest that the world of the lover's desire has become, in his obsessive view, synonymous with the universe itself. While the reader may feel that the authorial presence authorizes an ironic view of the lover by the repetitive depiction of an obsessive behavior directed to a series of love objects, the first-person identification of poet and lover works as well to evoke a sympathetic response to the intensity of his pain.

Epigrams in which Asclepiades shifts his angle of view to a lover who is not identified with his own "I" persona provide us with a more rounded portrait of the poet's cultural situation, often making clear the importance of the symposium as the institution around which erotic activities were organized. Among these poems are two epigrams that are modeled not on inscription nor on old elegy

---

54. P.Oxy. 3724 confirms Schneidewin's emendation ἐκείνου for the ἄμεινον transmitted by the ms. in 5; Gow-Page, although admitting that ἄμεινον is corrupt, reject ἐκείνου in the belief that the corruption conceals a proper name.

55. Hutchinson 266.

56. Hutchinson 268.

but on prototypes in comedy or mime. Both consist of a master's instruction to his slave to purchase the necessary supplies for a dinner party, and in that respect both find a parallel in Aeschinas' narrative account of his gathering (*Id.* 14.14–17). Both end with a reference to a girl with whom the master is in some way romantically involved, and in both cases it is clearly this reference to a girl that is the real point of interest in the poem, its epigrammatic conclusion. Aeschra the perfume-seller, with whom the speaker of 25 G-P = *AP* 5.181 has had a sexual encounter, is probably typical of the women known to the poet-lover of the collection—not a professional hetaira nor a protected maiden, but an independent woman who may sometimes confuse business and love. The social position of Tryphera in 26 G-P = *AP* 5.185 is harder to assess. Cameron has suggested that Demetrius' master is organizing his dinner party merely as an excuse to spend an evening with her.[57] But I prefer to see the invitation to Tryphera, who is perhaps a flute girl (cf. Leonidas 43 G-P = *AP* 5.206), as simply the last in the list of party preparations, so that her presence, and whatever entertainment she may provide, become devoid of emotional content. Both poems present, then, a more formal or distanced picture of the relationship between lover and mistress, one decidedly in contrast to other depictions of the poet's own anguished desire.

As we have now seen, most of Asclepiades' erotic epigrams take the form of speech acts that reveal the poet's momentary emotional reaction to a love object, while a smaller number of poems deal with the romantic relationships of others and so provide a more rounded and objective portrait of the social setting in which Asclepiades' affairs take place. In yet another small group of poems the poet speaks as if to himself about his condition as lover, without indication of dramatic setting, so that the reader has the sense of eavesdropping on the poet's private thoughts. It is in these epigrams that Asclepiades comes closest, both through specific biographical information and through comments that seem to stem from his emotional core, to identifying the "I" persona of the lover with the poet who is the author-editor of the collection.

Intensity of desire is a characteristic of youth, and belonging to this group of epigrams is the poem in which Asclepiades reveals himself as quite a young man, who yet sees death as his only escape from erotic torment:

οὐκ εἴμ' οὐδ' ἐτέων δύο κείκοσι καὶ κοπιῶ ζῶν·
  ὥρωτες, τί κακὸν τοῦτο; τί με φλέγετε;
ἢν γὰρ ἐγώ τι πάθω τί ποιήσετε; δῆλον, Ἔρωτες,
  ὡς τὸ πάρος παίζεσθ' ἄφρονες ἀστραγάλοις.

(15 G-P = *AP* 12.46)

I'm not yet twenty-two and I'm sick of living.
  Erotes, why this mistreatment? Why do you burn me?

57. Cameron (1981) 289 and (1995) 508.

For if I die, what then will you do? Clearly, Erotes,
    you'll go on heedlessly playing dice as before.

Anacreon had earlier referred to the dice of Eros as "madness and battle din" (ἀστραγάλαι δ' Ἔρωτός εἰσιν μανίαι τε καὶ κυδοιμοί, 398 *PMG*). Campbell comments that the mock-heroic tone in κυδοιμοί "shows how far Anacreon was from taking love's anguish seriously."[58] But the revision of the dice image in Asclepiades' epigram is considerably less playful. We may assume that Asclepiades here follows the Hellenistic preference for depicting Eros as a child, and his portrait is reminiscent of the beginning of Apollonius' Book 3 where the boy Eros is playing dice with Ganymede—and cheating. The paradoxical effect of making Eros a child is that he acquires both the child's uninhibited sensuality and the child's perverse indifference to the pain of others. Armed with bows and arrows, the Erotes shoot from the sheer joy of hitting their target. While Sappho expects Aphrodite to appear as her ally to relieve her pain (1 *PLF*), Asclepiades knows that the Erotes as his tormenters will remain insensitive (ἄφρονες, 15.4) to his plight, distracted not at all by consequence from their childish play with dice. Their game is of course the dice game of love, and the stakes, as Meleager later tells us (15 G-P = *AP* 12.47), are the lover's own soul. While Aphrodite comforts Sappho with the promise that the one who now flees soon will pursue, the ceaseless gambling of the Erotes suggests the more sinister version of this motif, in which love always and only consists of flight and pursuit, of desire and rejection.

Among the epigrams securely ascribed to Asclepiades, a reciprocal arrangement of loving and being loved (φιλέων τε καὶ ... φιληθείς, 22.3; cf. τοὺς φιλέοντας, 1.3) appears only in four poems, all on male homosexual relationships:

εἰ πτερά σοι προσέκειτο καὶ ἐν χερὶ τόξα καὶ ἰοί,
    οὐκ ἂν Ἔρως ἐγράφη Κύπριδος ἀλλὰ σὺ παῖς.

(21 G-P = AP 12.75)

If you had wings on your back, a bow and arrows in your hand,
    Not Eros, but you, would be registered as Cypris' son.

μικρὸς Ἔρως ἐκ μητρὸς ἔτ' εὐθήρατος ἀποπτὰς
    ἐξ οἴκων ὑψοῦ Δάμιδος οὐ πέτομαι,
ἀλλ' αὐτοῦ φιλέων τε καὶ ἀζήλωτα φιληθείς,
    οὐ πολλοῖς εὐχρὰς δ' εἰς ἑνὶ συμφέρομαι.

(22 G-P = AP 12.105)

I, a small Eros, easily caught, flew away from my mother,
    but I don't fly on high from the house of Damis.
Here loving and being loving without jealousy, I associate
    not with many, indiscriminately, but one with one.

58. David A. Campbell, *Greek Lyric Poetry* (London, 1967) 327.

οὔπω τοξοφορῶν οὐδ' ἄγριος ἀλλὰ νεογνός
   οὑμὸς ˝Ερως παρὰ τὴν Κύπριν ὑποστρέφεται
δέλτον ἔχων χρυσέην, τὰ Φιλοκράτεος δὲ Διαύλου
   τραυλίζει ψυχῇ φίλτρα κατ' Ἀντιγένους.

(23 G-P = AP 12.162)

My Eros does not carry a bow nor is he cruel, but he's
   a young child who goes about by Cypris' side
with a golden tablet, and he lisps Philocrates' love poetry
   for Antigenes into the soul of Diaulus.

εὗρεν ˝Ερως τι καλῷ μῖξαι καλόν, οὐχὶ μάραγδον
   χρυσῷ, ὃ μήτ' ἀνθεῖ μήτε γένοιτ' ἐν ἴσῳ,
οὐδ' ἐλέφαντ' ἐβένῳ, λευκῷ μέλαν, ἀλλὰ Κλέανδρον
   Εὐβιότῳ, πειθοῦς ἄνθεα καὶ φιλίης.

(24 G-P = AP 12.163)

Eros found how to mix fair with fair, not emerald with gold,
   whose color is not the same nor would it be of equal worth,
Nor ivory with ebony, black with white, but Cleandrus with
   Eubiotus, whose trust and friendship blossom equally.[59]

While these poems offer various difficulties of interpretation, it is nevertheless clear that Asclepiades is here presenting a concept of Eros and of the relationships he governs that differs from that presented in the other poems we have examined. Eros is scarcely more than a baby, manageable, still tied to his mother, not yet the cruel wielder of a bow. As such he functions as an emblem of the youths whose romantic relationships he directs. In 21 a boy is more like Eros than Eros himself, in 22 Eros dwells with Damis as his faithful friend an   lover, in 23 and 24 he fosters the erotic friendships of Philocrates and Antigen s, of Cleandrus and Eubiotus. In 23 as well (if rightly interpreted)[60] Eros is an emblem of Asclepiades' own love for Diaulus, the love of a poet who is not yet confident enough to express his emotions in his own words, but rather inscribes the verses of Philocrates. Asclepiades seems, then, to recall in these poems a period of his adolescence when homoerotic friendships could be maintained without the painful intensity that characterizes his adult love affairs. The somewhat older

59. Gow-Page (1965) II 132 seem to have the correct understanding of the poem: "A. is apparently saying that green and gold, black and white, are combinations of καλά which depend for their effect on contrast, whereas the alliance of his two friends is a harmony." Even so, the first pentameter may be corrupt, and I have been able to translate it o ly by construing ἐν ἴσῳ with both verbs.

60. The translation given here follows the interpretation of Wilamowitz (1924) II 115. In defense of the rather complicated analogy of Philocrates and Antigenes to Asclepiades and Diaulus, we may compare the equally complicated analogy in 24 of emeralds and gold or ivory and ebony to Cleandrus and Eubiotus.

Erotes who play dice are indifferent to his suffering; the love they inspire is
"bitter" (πικρὸς Ἔρως, 16.4 G-P), not "sweet."

If this is the reality of love, always to desire the one who flees and to flee the
one who desires, what escape can there be for the adult lover from his constant
torment? Later epigrammatists will propose to put an end to the cycle of love
by turning to intellectual pursuits (Posidippus 6 G-P) or even by establishing a
faithful relationship with a wife (Philodemus 15 G-P, *Garland* = *AP* 10.21, 17 G-P,
Garland = *AP* 11.41, 21 G-P, *Garland* = *AP* 11.34).[61] But the almost twenty-two-
year-old lover of Asclepiades' collection exists at that moment of youth when
love is all, and he can conceive of an end to love only in the oblivion of death:

τοῦθ' ὅτι μοι λοιπὸν ψυχῆς ὅτι δήποτ', Ἔρωτες,
 τοῦτό γ' ἔχειν πρὸς θεῶν ἡσυχίην ἄφετε.
ἢ μὴ δὴ τόξοις ἔτι βάλλετέ μ' ἀλλὰ κεραυνοῖς
 καὶ πάντως τέφρην θέσθε με κἀνθρακιήν.
ναὶ ναὶ βάλλετ', Ἔρωτες, ἐνεσκληκὼς γὰρ ἀνίαις
 ἐξ ὑμέων τοῦτ' οὖν, εἴ γέ τι, βούλομ' ἔχειν.[62]

(17 G-P = AP 12.166)

Whatever remains of my soul, whatever it be, Erotes,
 at least let that have peace in the name of the gods.
Or else don't strike with your bow, but with thunderbolts,
 reducing me completely to ash and cinder.
Yes, yes, strike me, Erotes, because dried up with suffering
 I want to have this from you if anything.

Yet death itself is described as if it were an erotic experience, an extension of the
Erotes' torment. The thunderbolt that is to end the lover's pain is already in
archaic poetry an image for passion (Ibycus 286 *PMG*), and Asclepiades himself
elsewhere boasts that he will brave the storms and thunder of Zeus to go on a
komos under the compulsion of love (11 G-P). The reduction to ash and coals that
the lover prays for suggests not so much the oblivion of death as a yet more
intense form of desire. We will remember that black Didyme becomes even
more desirable when she glows like coals (5 G-P), and in 16 G-P = *AP* 12.50 the
arrows of Eros reduce Asclepiades to a living ash (ἐν σποδιῇ, 16.4). In 36 G-P
= *AP* 5.209, ascribed alternately to Asclepiades or Posidippus, the fire of love
reduces Cleandrus to "dry coals" (ἄνθρακας . . . ξηρούς, 3–4). The effectiveness
of 17 as a lover's *cri de coeur* lies, then, in the poet's paradoxical identification

---

61. See Sider (1987), who argues that Xanthippe, named in at least four of Philodemus'
epigrams, is the wife for whom he gives up his earlier promiscuous relationships.

62. In 3 Gow-Page print in daggers the corrupt reading of P, but assert in their commentary
that "Hermann's ἢ μὴ δὴ τόξοις ἔτι is satisfactory in sense." While Gow-Page also print the
corrupt reading of P in line 6, I offer the text now presented in the Budé, which combines
Boissonade's τοῦτ' οὖν with εἴ γέ τι, proposed by Jacobs (1813–17).

of love and death, in the suggestion that his only escape from love through death is no escape at all, but merely an intensification of desire.

But if Asclepiades' young lover suffers so intensely, more intensely even than archaic love poets, we may ask what is the source of this erotic pain, what has changed about the experience of love? I have already suggested that it has to do with a new and different reaction by women, as Asclepiades' preferred love objects, to the lover's pursuit. We may see this more clearly by examining an epigram in which the speaker is not the lover, but a woman of the type he is likely to desire:

πρόσθε μοι Ἀρχεάδης ἐθλίβετο, νῦν δέ, τάλαινα,
    οὐδ' ὅσσον παίζων εἰς ἔμ' ἐπιστρέφεται.
οὐδ' ὁ μελιχρὸς Ἔρως αἰεὶ γλυκύς, ἀλλ' ἀνιήσας
    πολλάκις ἡδίων γίνετ' ἐρῶσι θεός.

(19 G-P = AP 12.153)

Archeades used to fret over me, but now, poor me,
    he doesn't care even enough to tease me.
Honeyed Eros is not always pleasant, but when he causes pain
    the god often becomes sweeter for lovers.

The epigrammatic point of the poem lies in the final line, where we fail to get the expected conclusion—"Eros is not always sweet, but sometimes painful." Instead the poet provides a delightful twist—"Eros is not always sweet, but as a source of pain he becomes even sweeter." By seeing here the woman's side of such relationships, we get a better sense of the behavior that is causing the relentless cycle of desire and pain. Because both men and women now function as desiring subjects and as objects of desire, the game has changed from a simple one of flight and pursuit to a one of jockeying for dominance and control. Since resistance increases desire, the trick is to resist even when longing is mutual. As a result, that ideal scenario laid out in Asclepiades' opening poem, of one cloak covering two lovers who are equally worshippers of Aphrodite, is never realized in the specific situations covered by the epigrams of the collection. The paradox set out by Archeades' female lover becomes, then, a revision of Asclepiades' programmatic opening: what is really "sweeter," ἡδίων, is not fulfilled mutual desire, but desire intensified by the pain of rejection. The generalizations provided by the opening priamel thus undergo questioning and revision in the course of the collection, with the repeated demonstration that *pace Epicuri* pleasure and pain are inextricably bound.[63]

If this is so, is there any possible relief for the painful cycle caused by the dice game of the Erotes? We do find a resolution of sorts in 16 G-P, where an

---

63. I disagree with Garrison's thesis that Hellenistic epigrams, including Asclepiades', offer "a uniform view of a world in which men may love without being hurt" (34).

unidentified person, a symposium companion, responds with soothing advice to the poet's complaints of erotic torment:[64]

πῖν', Ἀσκληπιάδη· τί τὰ δάκρυα ταῦτα; τί πάσχεις;
  οὐ σὲ μόνον χαλεπὴ Κύπρις ἐληίσατο,
οὐδ' ἐπὶ σοὶ μούνῳ κατεθήκατο τόξα καὶ ἰούς
  πικρὸς Ἔρως· τί ζῶν ἐν σποδιῇ τίθεσαι;
πίνωμεν Βάκχου ζωρὸν πόμα· δάκτυλος ἀώς·
  ἦ πάλι κοιμιστὰν λύχνον ἰδεῖν μένομεν;
πίνωμεν, δύσερως· μετά τοι χρόνον οὐκέτι πουλύν,
  σχέτλιε, τὴν μακρὰν νύκτ' ἀναπαυσόμεθα.

(16 G-P = *AP* 12.50)

Drink, Asclepiades. Why these tears? What's wrong with you?
  You're not the only one difficult Cypris has taken captive,
Nor against you alone has bitter Eros directed his bow and arrows.
  Why do you turn yourself into living ash?
Let us drink the strong drink of Bacchus. Dawn comes apace.
  Or should we again wait for the bedtime lamp to bring rest?
Let us drink, unhappy lover. The time approaches,
  poor fellow, when we'll rest during that long night.

The poem likely occupied an important position in the collection, perhaps near the end, since it acts as Asclepiades' signature piece, his *sphragis*. If this conjecture is correct, the epigram would function, not like the introductory "seal" in Theognis' collection (19–23), but more like the traditional *sphragis* of the nome, which, as in Timotheus' *Persae*, appears near the end of the poem, just before the epilogue (791.229 *PMG*).[65] We may imagine, then, that in the collection as ordered by the author himself the reader would encounter this poem after a long series of epigrams in which the poet recounts his various love affairs and laments his lover's condition. In such a context the poem's effect

64. Gow-Page (1965) II 127 state: "It is not quite plain whether A. is addressing himself or is addressed by comrades at a symposium." Since then, most scholars have assumed the latter; see Beckby IV 514, Garrison 23, Hutchinson 275–76. E. W. Handley, "Two Epigrams by Asclepiades (XXV, XVI G.-P.)," *MH* 53 (1996) 145–47 now argues that Asclepiades here speaks to himself in the manner of lovers in New Comedy; his thesis is based, however, on an unlikely interpretation of the apparently corrupt reading πίνομεν οὐ γὰρ ἔρως in the last couplet (taking Ἔρως as a vocative). In line 7 I have printed, without great confidence, Kaibel's suggestion (πίνωμεν, δύσερως), but an adverb, such as Jacobs's χαλερῶς or Page's γεραρῶς, may be the correct solution. Also worthy of consideration is Aubreton's οὐ γὰρ ἔδος, "there is no time to waste," a Homeric expression. Gow-Page print the emendation κατεθήξατο "sharpened" in line 3, but see Giangrande (1968) 129 for an explanation of how the ms. reading κατεθήκατο is here used *contraria significatione*.

65. See W. Kranz, "Sphragis: Ichform und Namensiegel als Eingangs- und Schlussmotiv antiker Dichtung," *RhM* 104 (1961) 3–46, 97–124, especially 24–25 on Theognis and 27–28 on Timotheus.

would be quite dramatic. As we have already seen, 18, the Nicagoras poem, presupposes an internal auditor; so too in 14, the Moschus poem, the address in the second couplet (σύ) is best understood as a comment to the person to whom the epigram is spoken. But it would only be near the end of the collection, where we imagine 16 to have been placed, that the reader would discover the true significance of that σύ, because only there would the internal auditor speak in turn. If the reader had grown accustomed to the idea of overhearing the poet as he speaks to himself or others in the many moments of his life, it would certainly be disconcerting, even revisionary, to find that all the poems of the collection had a previously disguised internal setting, namely, a symposium that served as the fictionalized site of their recitation.

The unnamed symposiast's advice to Asclepiades may present, then, the internal auditor's response to the content of the collection. He offers the consolation that Asclepiades is not alone in suffering the torments of passion. In language that recalls a famous drinking song by Alcaeus (πίνωμεν· τί τὰ λύχν' ὀμμένομεν; δάκτυλος ἀμέρα, "Let us drink. Why do we await the lamp? Dawn is but a finger's breath away," 346.1 *PLF*) and echoes symposium talk in the *Theognidea* (πίνωμεν, "let us drink," 763; πῖν' οἶνον, "drink wine," 879), the symposiast proposes that Asclepiades find comfort in the pleasures of drink. His call to drink away cares is premised on the observation that little time is left in the night, which by metonymic transfer becomes the long night of death. The advice of the symposiast turns out to be related to the message delivered by the poet to a maiden he attempts to seduce in 2 G-P—that the pleasures of Aphrodite exist only for the living and death comes only too soon. If in Hades we are to lie as bones and ash (2.4), why, the companion asks, do you make yourself into a living ash? The resolution he offers to love's pain is the intoxicating effect of drink, which, according to the Alcaean model, brings forgetfulness of care (λαθικάδεον, 346.3 *PLF*). While in the fictionalized setting of the symposium the companion's advice seems directed to a single instance of love longing, in the context of the epigram book as a whole the advice assumes a more generalized significance. To the extent that the book itself is troped as a symposium, the entire cycle of desire and rejection—the dice game of the Erotes—becomes the subject of the symposium talk conducted by Asclepiades and his drinking companions. The call to drink, as a call to the symposium, urges the solace of song, so that Asclepiades' collection is offered as both a statement of the lover's condition and a source of escape from it. The collection thus delivers its message, not through any one poem or any one voice, that of the poet or another, but through the interrelated variety of introductory priamel, poems with a suggested dramatic setting, and response of an interlocutor.

The epigram collection issued by Asclepiades early in the third century B.C., when he was still apparently quite a young man, inaugurated the erotic-sympotic type of epigram. Asclepiades created an innovative literary form that homogenized the characteristics of epigram and elegy by combining the formal features of inscription—brevity, particularity, completeness—with motifs drawn from the symposium songs that constituted old elegy. Although we cannot know whether all the surviving epigrams ascribed to Asclepiades came from a single poetry book, strong indications signal the existence of an author-edited collection that included epigrams in which Asclepiades, posing as a young lover, complains about his various erotic misfortunes as well as erotic poems about other lovers spoken either by the narrator or by another. Throughout this set of epigrams, whatever their arrangement may have been, runs a unifying thematic, informed by the tension between the sweet ideal of mutuality in love and the bitter reality of flight and pursuit, of desire and rejection, symbolized as the dice game of the Erotes.

The only resolution for the incommensurability of erotic idealism and the reality of sexual behavior comes in Asclepiades' signature poem (16), where a friend and symposium companion advises the lover to seek relief for his persistent torments in the temporary pleasures of wine. While we may complain that the advice is not truly helpful because it has no long-term efficacy for the young lover, it does provide a kind of poetic closure for the collection, the only world in which the lover's persona has actual existence. The placement of this epigram near the end of the collection, as conjectured, would also suggest to the reader that the various poetic utterances of the lover—his series of epigrams on female types, his paraclausithyra (both dramatized and recalled), his vignettes of other lovers, the monologues seemingly addressed to himself—are all framed by a collective dramatic setting (independent of whatever individualized dramatic settings the poems themselves have), which takes the form of a symposium attended by Asclepiades and his friends. The epigrams within the collection do, then, represent performances of symposium song, like the elegiac extracts in the *Theognidea*, though they are not simply songs that have been collected into a book (as Reitzenstein thought), but rather pseudo-performances composed as book poetry and only fictionalized as song. In the next two sections of the chapter, we will examine how Asclepiades' dramatization of a symposium as the setting for his collection was adapted and extended in the collections of Posidippus and Hedylus.

POSIDIPPUS

Among the twenty-two epigrams in the *Greek Anthology* ascribed to Posidippus, solely or with an alternate ascription, is a dominant group of sixteen on erotic-sympotic themes.[66] The important discovery of the Milan Papyrus now helps us to understand how Posidippus' other epigrams—consisting of inscriptions,

---

66. The sixteen erotic-sympotic epigrams preserved in the *Anthology* are Posid. 1–10, 23 G-P; [Asclep.] 34–38 G-P. Of these 23 G-P = Mel. 54 G-P = *AP* 5.215, which concerns Heliodora, was almost certainly composed by Meleager.

some clearly not genuine, and ecphrastic types—were organized in poetry books. But the third-century context for Posidippus' erotic poetry, his most compelling work, remains uncertain. The situation is complicated by the fact that several of the Posidippan epigrams preserved in the *Anthology* imitate epigrams by Asclepiades,[67] while six of them, five on erotic themes, bear an alternate ascription to the Samian. Reitzenstein's supposition that Meleager was extracting from an anthology containing epigrams by both Asclepiades and Posidippus may offer the best explanation for his uncertainty about authorship. But I will argue, from the evidence of the poetry itself, that before the construction of any such anthology there likely existed a single-authored epigram book in which the poetic persona of the Posidippan lover stood in contrast to the young lover of Asclepiades' collection, as Stoicism did to Epicureanism.

The recognition that accrued to Posidippus, a native of Macedonian Pella, demonstrates the surprisingly high status obtained by the poetic form of epigram in the Hellenistic world.[68] Awards of *proxenia* are recorded by a Delphic inscription of ca. 276/75 and, again, by an inscription from Thermon of 264/63, which names Posidippus' profession and place of origin (Ποσειδίππῳ τῷ ἐπιγραμματοποιῷ Πελλαίῳ).[69] While these decrees indicate literary activity celebrating the Aetolians,[70] other epigrams (11–13 G-P and 702 *SH*), reveal that Posidippus was writing for the Ptolemies from the late 280s through the 270s. As a Macedonian, Posidippus was likely associated as well with the literary circle around Antigonus Gonatas, who was educated in Athens as a Stoic and had strong ties to Zeno.[71] An epigram mentioning the Stoics Zeno and Cleanthes (1 G-P) adds further evidence that Posidippus was poetically active in the 270s and 260s B.C., since these two philosophers were working together between about 280 and Zeno's death in 262. Posidippus was born, then, no later than about 305 and may have lived on into the 250s or 240s. Evidence for a long life comes from an elegy that names its own author, found on writing tablets of the first century A.D. (705 *SH*).[72] In this poem written in a Thebes that is uncertainly

67. For an enumeration of Posidippus' borrowings from Asclepiades, see Fraser I 569–70, II 813, n. 145.

68. On Posidippus' life, see Gow-Page (1965) II 481–84 and the commentary by Emilio Fernández-Galiano, *Posidipo de Pela* (Madrid, 1987) 9–15, who prints the testimonia.

69. *Fouilles de Delphes* III.3, no. 192; *IG* 9².I.17.24. O. Weinreich, "Die Heimat des Epigrammatikers Poseidippos," *Hermes* 53 (1918) 434–39 first identified Posidippus' place of origin from the second inscription, which he wrongly dated to 280. That Pella was his homeland is now confirmed by 705.16 *SH*.

70. See Peek (1953) 429.

71. See William W. Tarn, *Antigonos Gonatas* (Oxford, 1913) 223–56.

72. Scholars held the poem to be an inferior work of the first century A.D. until C. A. Trypanis, "Posidippus and Delphi," *CR* 2 (1952) 67–68 and then, independently, Peek (1953) 440–41 pointed out the precise fit with known facts about Posidippus the epigrammatist. Scholars now accept its authenticity: see H. Lloyd-Jones, "The Seal of Posidippus," *JHS*

Boeotian or Egyptian, the elderly Posidippus names Macedonia, the islands, and the Asian coast as areas in which he wishes to receive recognition. In addition, he hopes that his fellow Pellans will erect a statue of him, scroll in hand, in their agora, and he declares himself successful enough at his profession to leave a comfortable home and fortune to his children.[73] Despite Posidippus' rather distasteful self-flattery, the poem offers confirming evidence for the high status that could be afforded a Hellenistic epigrammatist.[74]

From ancient references and papyrological discoveries can be pieced together a good bit of information about Posidippus' collected works. Careful analysis indicates a variety of epigram books assembled at different times for different purposes. The collection of the Milan papyrus, consisting of over one hundred epigrams divided into nine or more sections, has already been discussed. Dating to the second half of the third century, this papyrus quite possibly contains a posthumous collection; it does not appear to be a comprehensive edition of Posidippus' epigrams, since the section concerning shipwrecks lacks an epigram on this topic preserved in the *Anthology* (15 G-P = *AP* 7.267). But importantly, the papyrus does teach us that the smattering of nonerotic epigrams known from manuscripts and papyri are not at all untypical of Posidippus' work.

A comment by Aristarchus (schol. A *ad Il.* 11.101), previously quoted, gives evidence for two collections, an earlier one called the *Soros* and a later one known simply as the *Epigrammata*. The *Epigrammata* is the easier to assess: it was, in all likelihood, a comprehensive and authoritative edition assembled by the poet himself toward the end of his life. The deletion of the Berisus epigram under the influence of Zenodotus' scholarship indicates Posidippus' desire to control the final form of the poetic oeuvre he would leave to posterity. Athenaeus is quite possibly referring to this collection when he cites two poems "in the epigrams" of Posidippus—a pseudo-inscription for a statue of a famous fifth-century athlete (14 G-P = Ath. 10.412d–e) and a parodic epitaph for a parasite (16 G-P = Ath. 10.414d–e)—and refers to a third, an epigram on a certain Aglais who blew the trumpet in the great Ptolemaic Pompe (702 *SH* = Ath. 10.415a–b). Since Athenaeus discusses these poems in his section on gluttony, they likely formed part of a thematic sequence on that topic within

---

83 (1963) 75–99, reprinted in *Greek Comedy, Hellenistic Literature, Greek Religion, and Miscellanea* (Oxford, 1990) 158–95; A. Barigazzi, "Il testamento di Posidippo di Pella," *Hermes* 96 (1968) 190–216; and the annotation in Lloyd-Jones and Parsons 340–43.

73. M. W. Dickie, "Which Posidippus?" *GRBS* 35 (1994) 372–83 has argued that the statue of a seated Posidippus in the Vatican, usually interpreted as the Athenian comic poet, may rather be a copy of the bronze statue the epigrammatist hoped would be erected in the Pellan agora.

74. While Posidippus seems to have been known primarily as an epigrammatist, he wrote other works as well. He composed an *Asopia* in elegiacs or hexameters (698 *SH*), an *Aethiopia* (699 *SH*), elegies of various sorts (700, 705, and probably 961 *SH*), and perhaps a prose work called *On Cnidos* (706 *SH*).

Posidippus' *Epigrammata*. The collection probably contained epigram types like those known from the Milan papyrus, as well as as erotic-sympotic epigrams, descriptive epigrams on monuments and art works, and epitaphs for historical figures. Posidippus' elegy on old age was, quite possibly, either the introductory or the concluding poem of this collection:

εἴ τι καλόν, Μοῦσαι πολιήτιδες, ἢ παρὰ Φοίβου
    χρυσολύρεω καθαροῖς οὔασιν ἐκλύετε
Παρνησοῦ νιφόεντος ἀνὰ πτύχας ἢ παρ' Ὀλύμπου
    Βάκχῳ τὰς τριετεῖς ἀρχόμεναι θυμέλας,
νῦν δὲ Ποσειδίππῳ στυγερὸν συναείσατε γῆρας
    γραψάμεναι δέλτων ἐν χρυσέαις σελίσιν.
λιμπάνετε σκοπιάς, Ἑλικωνίδες, εἰς δὲ τὰ Θήβης
    τείχεα Πιπ[ ] . . . ς βαίνετε . . . αλαδες
χεῖ σὺ Ποσείδιππόν ποτ' ἐφίλαο, Κύνθιε, Λητοῦς
    υ . . . .
[. .] . [. . . . .] . . . . . [. .] . . . .
    †φημητινιφιεντοιχειατ† τοῦ Παρίου.
τοίην ἐκχρήσαις τε καὶ ἐξ ἀδύτων καναχήσαις
    φωνὴν ἀθανάτην, ὦ ἄνα, καὶ κατ' ἐμοῦ,
ὄφρα με τιμήσωσι Μακηδόνες οἵ τ' ἐπὶ νήσων
    οἵ τ' Ἀσίης πάσης γείτονες ἠϊόνος.
Πελλαῖον γένος ἁμόν· ἔοιμι δὲ βίβλον ἑλίσσων
    †ἀμφωτ† λαοφόρῳ κείμενος εἰν ἀγορῇ.
ἀλλ' ἐπὶ μὲν Παρίῃ δὸς ἀηδόνι λυγρὸν ἐφ.[
    νᾶμα κατὰ γληνέων δάκρυα κεινὰ χέω[ν
καὶ στενάχων, δι' ἐμὸν δὲ φίλον στόμα [
    . . . [. . .] . . . .]
[. .] . . . .
    μηδέ τις οὖν χεύαι δάκρυον. αὐτὰρ ἐγὼ
γήρᾳ μυστικὸν οἶμον ἐπὶ Ῥαδάμανθυν ἱκοίμην
    δήμῳ καὶ λαῷ παντὶ ποθεινὸς ἐών,
ἀσκίπων ἐν ποσσὶ καὶ ὀρθοεπὴς ἀν' ὅμιλον
    καὶ λείπων τέκνοις δῶμα καὶ ὄλβον ἐμόν.

                                                        (705 *SH*)

If, Muses of my city, you have heard anything beautiful
    in your pure ears from Phoebus of the golden lyre
in the glens of snowy Parnassus or when celebrating
    in Olympus the triennial festivals for Bacchus,
now help Posidippus to sing of his hateful old age,
    inscribing the golden leaves of his tablet.
Leave your peaks, Heliconian maids, and come to the walls
    of . . . . . . Thebes . . . .
And if ever you loved Posidippus, Cynthian god, ...
    of Leto, ...

. . . .

> . . . . of the Parian.
> May you send forth and sound out from your holy shrine,
>   oh lord, such an immortal report, even in my ears,
> so that the Macedonians will honor me, and the islanders,
>   and the neighbors of all the Asian shore.
> I am Pellaean by birth. May I stand unrolling a book,
>   . . . set up in the crowded market place.
> Give sad lament for the Parian nightingale . . . ,
>   casting streams of tears from your eyes
> And groaning, but from my dear mouth . . . .
>   . . . .
>   . . . .
> So may no one shed a tear. But in old age
> may I travel the mystic path to Rhadamanthus,
>   adored by the city and all its people,
> Steady without a staff, sure of speech among the crowd,
>   leaving to my children both home and wealth.

Lloyd-Jones has demonstrated that this elegy of twenty-five lines displays several features of the poetic *sphragis*.[75] While he thinks of an introductory poem, Barigazzi has argued for the concluding position.[76] Since a *sphragis* could stand at either end of a poem or collection, the matter remains debatable. The lengthy invocation to the Muses followed by an address to Apollo suggests the initial position (cf. Theog. 1–24), and we need only look at the epithalamium for Arsinoe that introduced a collection of mixed epigrams (961 *SH*) or the first poem of Meleager's *Garland* for the placement of an elegiac poem longer than the normal epigram at the head of a collection. But the concluding references to Posidippus' heroization after death argue instead for the final place (cf. Theog. 237–54 where Cyrnus is promised poetic immortality), and there are other examples in Hellenistic poetry of invocations in later positions.[77] In either case, the emphasis on old age and impending death in Posidippus' elegy shows that he intended this collection to be a final one, and so, we may assume, the comprehensive *Epigrammata*. When at the end of a long and productive life, Posidippus gathers his epigrammatic œuvre for presentation to posterity, he emphasizes in either his preamble or conclusion not any one thematic concern

---

75. Lloyd-Jones 96 lists the following *sphragis* features: an appeal to the Muses (and, we may add, to Apollo) bound up with the poet's introduction of himself, reference to the poet's homeland (Πελλαῖον γένος ἀμόν, 16) and to his individual manner (which Lloyd-Jones finds in a contrast between Posidippus and Archilochus, 18–19), and a final sentence beginning αὐτὰρ ἐγώ (21) with a concluding prayer.

76. Barigazzi (1968) 201–2.

77. See Ap. Rhod. 3.1–5, 4.1–5; Callim. *Aetia* fr. 86 (beginning of Book 4), *Iamb.* 13.1 = fr. 203.

or debts owed to any patrons, but the fame and fortune that have accrued to him from the body of poetry he presents.

The *Soros*, the other Posidippan collection mentioned by Aristarchus, is more difficult to judge. Even if Reitzenstein was correct to assume an anthology of epigrams by Asclepiades, Posidippus, and perhaps Hedylus, there is no reason to identify that collection with the *Soros*. Given the fact that Aristarchus mentions only epigrams by Posidippus, it is more reasonable to surmise that the *Soros* was limited to his poetry. We still, however, have no way to know if it consisted of mixed epigrams or a single epigram type. The adoption of the name Berisus from the *Iliad* tells us little, and we certainly cannot extrapolate from it a collection of epigrams on Homeric heroes in the manner of the Aristotelian *Peplos*.[78] The principal evidence we have is the title of the collection. The word σωρός means a "heap," especially a heap of grain, and it has been suggested that the title refers to verse that is polished or choice, as a result of the winnowing process.[79] But examination of other contemporary parallels for the heaping metaphor suggests a somewhat different connotation. In Demetrius' *On Style*, possibly an early third-century work and certainly a work reflecting Peripatetic critical thought,[80] the paratactic style of Hecataeus or Herodotus is described as follows: "Here the phrases seem thrown upon one another in a heap (σεσωρευμένοις) without connection or support, and without aiding one another, as we find in periods" (1.12). In Demetrius the σωρός metaphor suggests not the polishing of literary language but the discreteness or disconnectedness of literary expression that yet forms a whole. It may also be relevant to mention the σωρίτης λόγος, a method of logical argument used by the Academics against the Stoics. In the *sorites* argument certainty of knowledge was challenged by exploiting through small progressive steps the absence of a sharp boundary between contradictory predicates.[81] Again, we find the metaphorical connection between accumulated

78. As did Theodor Bergk, *Poetae Lyrici Graeci*, 4th ed. (Leipzig, 1882) II 342, who identifies this collection with the *Soros*. Cf. also Franz Susemihl, *Geschichte der griechischen Litteratur* (Leipzig, 1892) II 531. The *Peplos* was a lost work of antiquarian research attributed to Aristotle, basically in prose but including a series of epigrams on Homeric heroes which were later extrapolated and circulated separately. For fragments, see Valentin Rose, *Aristotelis qui ferebantur librorum fragmenta* (Leipzig, 1886) 394–407.

79. Webster 45, citing Theoc. *Id.* 7.155; Santirocco 8–9. For the connection of σωρός with grain, see Cic. *Acad.* 2.92.

80. G. M. A. Grube, *A Greek Critic: Demetrius on Style* (Toronto, 1961) 39–56 places the date of the work in the first half of the third century. For a later dating, see Dirk Marie Schenkeveld, *Studies in Demetrius "On Style"* (Amsterdam, 1964) 135–48 and G. Morpurgo-Taliabue, *Demetrio: dello stile* (Rome, 1980) 141–49. For connections between Demetrius' literary terminology and that of Callimachean poetic theory, see D. L. Clayman, "The Origins of Greek Literary Criticism and the *Aitia* Prologue," *WS* 11 (1977) 27–34.

81. See M. F. Burnyeat, "Gods and Heaps," in *Language and Logos: Studies in Ancient Greek Philosophy Presented to G. E. L. Owen*, ed. Malcolm Schofield and M. Nussbaum (Cambridge,

language and heaped up grain that must underlie the use of the title *Soros* for an assemblage of short and distinct epigrammatic poems. A parallel is found in one of Theocritus' epigrams, where he refers to the collection of Epicharmus' *Maxims* as a σωρὸν ῥημάτων, a "heap of words" (17.7 G-P = *AP* 9.600.7, according to the reading in P).[82] Whatever the precise connotation of Posidippus' *Heap* of epigrams, we may assume that he offered some explanation for his metaphorical title at the opening of his collection, as Meleager later explained his *Garland* in his introductory poem.

Yet a third collection of epigrams, labeled simply σύμμεικτα ἐπιγράμματα, began with an epithalamium for Arsinoe (961 *SH*). This collection was clearly not the *Soros*, not only because of the absence of this title but also because the expected reference to the grain metaphor is missing in the introductory poem. It was also not the comprehensive *Epigrammata*, because a collection with this epithalamium as introductory poem should have been produced not much later than the time of Ptolemy Philadelphus' marriage to the first or second Arsinoe, that is, between 280 and 274. A parallel is provided by the third and fourth books of the *Aetia*, which are surrounded by the *Victoria Berenices* and the *Lock of Berenice* poems celebrating, respectively, the Nemean victory of the queen and her recent marriage to Euergetes at a time not much later than the events themselves. As pointed out earlier, the way in which Posidippus' name follows the heading in the *Miscellaneous Epigrams* leaves open the possibility that we are dealing with a multi-authored anthology. As a result, it remains uncertain whether the heading refers to Posidippan epigrams of mixed types or epigrams by various authors. If speculation on content is not too bold, we may easily imagine Posidippus' poems on Ptolemaic monuments appearing here, as well as certain of his amatory poems. A poem celebrating the marriage of Ptolemy II and his second wife would make an excellent introduction for a collection of epigrams written in the 270s under Ptolemaic support and emphasizing, in part, Ptolemaic themes.

Up to this point we have developed evidence for four separate epigram books: the one on the Milan Papyrus; the comprehensive *Epigrammata*, perhaps with the elegy on old age at its opening or conclusion; the *Soros*, which contained the Berisus epigram and probably began with some reference to the heap-of-grain metaphor; the collection of *Miscellaneous Epigrams* that began with the epithalamium for Arsinoe and likely contained poems on Ptolemaic themes. There was overlap between at least some of these collections, since Aristarchus expected to find a poem from the *Soros* in the *Epigrammata*; Posidippan epigrams

1982) 315–38; A. A. Long and D. N. Sedley, *The Hellenistic Philosophers* (Cambridge, 1987) I 221–25, 229–30.

82. A collection of Pseudo-Epicharmea was circulating in the third century, perhaps composed by a certain Axiopistus who lived about 300 B.C. (Ath. 14.648d); see Powell 219–22 and Page (1942) 439–44.

from the *Miscellaneous Epigrams* probably flowed there as well. I will now argue, on the basis of evidence from the surviving epigrams themselves, for the existence of one other epigram book by Posidippus. This collection, which apparently included most or all of the Posidippan epigrams preserved by Meleager, was perhaps written as a pendant to Asclepiades' book of erotic-sympotic epigrams. The fictionalized setting is again the symposium and the themes are again primarily erotic, but Posidippus varies the epigram book he imitates by shifting the philosophical background from Epicurean to Stoic and by adjusting the lover's persona accordingly. If some of the epigrams from this collection were later anthologized with the Asclepiadean epigrams they varied, and if Meleager later extracted from that anthology in constructing his *Garland*, then we may understand why so many Posidippan epigrams that seem to look back to Asclepiadean models have survived in the *Anthology*.

In all likelihood, the following epigram was placed at or near the beginning of this collection:

Κεκροπί, ῥαῖνε, λάγυνε, πολύδροσον ἰκμάδα Βάκχου,
    ῥαῖνε· δροσιζέσθω συμβολικὴ πρόποσις·
σιγάσθω Ζήνων, ὁ σοφὸς κύκνος, ἅ τε Κλεάνθους
    Μοῦσα, μέλοι δ' ἡμῖν ὁ γλυκύπικρος Ἔρως.

(1 G-P = AP 5.134)

Sprinkle, Cecropian jug, the dewy moisture of Bacchus,
    sprinkle it. Let the toast that I contribute bedew us.
Let Zeno, the wise swan, be silent, and Cleanthes' Muse,
    and let bittersweet Eros be my topic.

Under the influence of Schott's belief that Posidippus was a student of Stoicism in Athens, commentators have read the epigram as a simple convivial song.[83] Giangrande even claimed that Posidippus' epigram "was only meant for private circulation amongst his fellow students."[84] But the ornate character of the language indicates the "bookish" nature of the piece, and several features signal its introductory function within Posidippus' collection. The device of beginning a book with a divine invocation is too common to need illustration; by playfully substituting the Cecropian jug for Bacchus himself, Posidippus may here invent the practice of composing a hymnlike poem addressed to a wine

---

83. Paul Schott, *Posidippi epigrammata collecta et illustrata* (Diss. Berlin, 1905) 44–46. Gow-Page (1965) II 484 call the poem "an exhortation to drink and love," and Fernández-Galiano 67 an "epigrama simpótico en que se exhorta a beber y a contar al amor olvidando la filosofía." But in questioning Schott's biographical approach, Peek (1953) 430 hints at a further use for the poem: "Ist das Symposion die geeignete Gelegenheit zur Abgabe einer programmatischen Erklärung im Sinne der 'Lebenswahl'? Und ist μέλοι δ' ἡμῖν ὁ γλυκύπικρος Ἔρως überhaupt eine Entscheidung, die über Ort and Zeit dieses Sympotikon hinaus Gültigkeit haben könnte?"

84. Giangrande (1968) 167, n. 2.

jar.[85] The rejection of Stoicism in favor of "bittersweet Eros" as the preferred topic for Posidippus' "symposium" fits the pattern of the *recusatio*, a device for defining a poetic program negatively that often appears at the beginning of a poetry book.[86] Perhaps the most striking parallel for our purposes is *AP* 12.2, almost certainly the second poem in Strato's *Mousa Paidike*,[87] where the poet rejects trite mythological themes in favor of "sweet Eros, mingled with the jolly Graces, and Bacchus." As an introduction for a collection of erotic epigrams, this poem lies in a direct line of descent from Posidippus. Yet another pointer to the original function of Posidippus' epigram is Meleager's reuse of it. It stands at the head of the long *Garland* sequence in Book 5 of the *AP* (134–215), indicating that, just as Meleager expropriated Anyte's introductory poem to begin his sequence of descriptive epigrams (*AP* 9.313), so too he expropriated the initial poem of a Posidippan epigram book to head his amatory section.

Posidippus' introductory epigram was written to allude specifically to what was apparently the first poem in Asclepiades' epigram book (1 G-P). The silencing of Zeno and Cleanthes in favor of Eros provides a clear parallel to Asclepiades' preference for the pleasure of erotic reciprocity over the forms of *hedone* advocated by Epicurus. In each case a philosophical standard is rejected or modified to accommodate the poet's erotic interest, but Posidippus varies and thus personalizes the motif by substituting Stoicism for Epicureanism. In addition, Posidippus' epithet for Eros, "bittersweet," seems to acknowledge that Asclepiades' initial emphasis on the sweetness of love (ἥδιον) gives way in the course of the collection to the recognition that Eros is "bitter" (πικρός, 16.4). And while Asclepiades eventually reveals, mostly through 16 G-P, that the symposium is the fictionalized setting for the recitation of his collection, Posidippus, assuming the reader's knowledge of the earlier poetry book, begins with a reference to the symbolic nature of the symposium setting. The sprinkling of wine from an Attic jug is a clear allusion to the poetic inspiration that had traditionally been thought to derive from the drinking of wine.[88] Here the sprinkling takes the form of a

85. Cf. the following examples: anon. 57 G-P = *AP* 5.135; Marc. Argent. 23 G-P, *Garland* = *AP* 6.248, 24 G-P, *Garland* = *AP* 9.229, 25 G-P, *Garland* = *AP* 9.246; Hor. *Carm.* 3.21.

86. E.g., Callim. *Aetia*, fr. 1 Pf.; Verg. *G.* 3.3–9; *Priapea* 1.3–6. For full discussion of the *recusatio*, see Walter Wimmel, *Kallimachos in Rom* (Wiesbaden, 1960).

87. *AP* 12.1, where the Muses are rejected in favor of the inspiration of the male god Zeus, is clearly the original opening of the collection, as 12.258, excusing Strato's theme, seems the original conclusion. Cf. Cameron (1993) 79; Aubreton, Buffière, and Irigoin xxxiv.

88. The motif apparently goes back to the fifth century, since an epigram attributed to a variety of authors (including Nicaenetus) quotes the following verse of Cratinus: οἶνός τοι χαρίεντι πέλει ταχὺς ἵππος ἀοιδῷ, ὕδωρ δὲ πίνων οὐδὲν ἂν τέκοις σοφόν (Nicaenetus 5 G-P = *AP* 13.29). See S. Commager, "The Function of Wine in Horace's Odes," *TAPA* 88 (1957) 75–80; N. B. Crowther, "Water and Wine as Symbols of Inspiration," *Mnemosyne* 32 (1979) 1–11, especially 5, n. 20.

συμβολικὴ πρόποσις. A πρόποσις was a toast drunk near the beginning of the symposium (cf. *Id.* 14.18–19), and the adjective συμβολική refers, at least in its literal sense, to the practice of each guest bringing a contribution, or σύμβολον, to the dinner party.[89] But by the third century the word σύμβολον had also acquired the meaning of "sign" or "allegory,"[90] so that there arises the possibility for συμβολικὴ πρόποσις to be understood not only as "contributed toast" but also as "symbolic toast" or "symbolic first-drinking." Through this secondary meaning Posidippus suggests that the drinking of wine at the symposium has become simply a symbol for the recitation or reading of his collection.

Posidippus' epigram provides a valuable indication of the relationship between philosophical thought and literary criticism that existed in the Hellenistic period. His call to bedew the symposium with wine makes direct allusion to certain Stoic practices and tenets of belief. Zeno, who was known for his austere personality, was satirized in Philemon's play entitled *Philosophers* because he preferred to eat simple foods and to drink water (ἐπιπιεῖν ὕδωρ, *PCG* VII 273, fr. 88), and Diogenes Laertius (7.27) tells us that the saying "more temperate than the philosoher Zeno" became all but proverbial. That Posidippus is thinking of Stoic prescription against drunkenness is indicated by the rare verb δροσιζέσθω, "bedew" (2), reinforced by the adjective πολύδροσον, "dewy" (1). The same verb appears in a passage from Epictetus, which surely repeats an earlier Stoic *topos* contrasting cicadas and snails:

> Cicadas are musical (μουσικοί), snails mute (ἄφωνοι). Snails are happy when moist, and cicadas when warm. Dew summons snails and they sink down into it, while the midday sun arouses cicadas and they sing in its light. Therefore, the man who wants to become musical and harmonious does not let his soul, when bedewed with wine in drinking bouts (ἐν τοῖς πότοις ὑπὸ τοῦ οἴνου δροσισθῆ), continue to be defiled. But he bids his soul, when enflamed by reason (ὑπὸ τοῦ λόγου) during discussions, to prophesy and to sing the oracles of justice. (*Gnom.* 26 = Stob. 3.1.150)

The cicada, likened to a man warmed by the fire of reason, is here praised for avoiding the moisture of dew, which is then compared to wine that besots a man's soul. In his programmatic epigram where he rejects the inspiration of Zeno and Cleanthes, Posidippus modifies this Stoic tenet by presenting himself as a poet who benefits from the dew of wine. Posidippus' point here seems to be that wine is the proper accompaniment for song about Eros, which he prefers to the more serious topics found in the philosophical writings of the Stoics.

---

89. This was a common practice in Athens, honored at the Lyceum (Antig. Car. *apud* Ath. 12.547d–f). Individual contributions to a party were apparently known in Alexandria, but there each guest drank his own wine (Eratosthenes *apud* Ath. 7.276b).

90. See Callim. frs. 59.7, 384.36; Chrysippus 2.908 *SVF*; Demetr. *Eloc.* 5.243.

As Asclepiades 1 set out a certain tension between the Epicurean concept of pleasure and the poet's desire for erotic satisfaction as the theme to be examined in the following collection, so Posidippus 1 thematizes for his collection a conflict between Stoic principles of seriousness, symbolized by the drinking of water rather than wine, and the power of Eros, associated with the abandonment of reason characteristic of the symposium. In an epigram that seems introductory, Posidippus suggests that he is deserting philosophy for love, but in other poems this picture is modified when the poet's erotic adventures are shown to be controlled by his rational faculties and scholarly experiences.

The identification of Posidippus with a cicada implicit in 1 G-P is made explicit in another epigram:

τῶν Μουσῶν τέττιγα Πόθος δήσας ἐπ' ἀκάνθαις
  κοιμίζειν ἐθέλει πῦρ ὑπὸ πλευρὰ βαλών·
ἡ δὲ πρὶν ἐν βύβλοις πεπονημένη ἄλλα θερίζει
  ψυχὴ ἀνιηρῷ δαίμονι μεμφομένη.[91]

(6 G-P = *AP* 12.98)

Desire, having bound the Muse's cicada on a bed of thorns,
  wishes to silence it by tossing a torch into its side.
But the soul that previously labored among books now gathers
  other harvests by reproving painful misfortune.

This poem appears in the *AP* at the head of a short sequence of epigrams that all concern love's ability to distract the scholar or philosopher from his intellectual labors (*AP* 12.98–101). Posidippus' epigram provides a particularly complex version of the *topos*. Desire, which has succeeded in binding the poet on thorns, that is, making him fall in love, now wishes to "put him to sleep," or silence his song, by torturing him with fire. With a pun on "thorns" (ἐπ' ἀκάνθαις) Posidippus here makes reference to proverbial lore about the Acanthian cicada (Ἀκάνθιος τέττιξ), which stood for the "mute or unmusical" (ἄφωνος καὶ ἄμουσος, Zenob. 1.51) person because, according to Simonides (610 *PMG*), the cicadas of Acanthus do not sing.[92] The Acanthian or "thorny" cicada is thus the opposite of the normal one, and so like the mute snails of the Epictetus passage. But Desire has overlooked the fact that cicadas thrive in heat; according to Epictetus, they are "aroused" (διεγείρει) by the sun's flame rather than put to sleep (κοιμίζειν, 6.2 G-P). Consequently, the torture of love becomes for the Muses' cicada a stimulus to song. The second couplet

91. The ms. reading in 3, ἄλλαθερίζει, was interpreted as ἄλλ' ἀθερίζει by Brunck and Jacobs (1813–17), and so printed by Gow-Page. But I prefer the division ἄλλα θερίζει, now printed by Aubreton in the Budé. Whether the cicada actually resists Desire is disputed. Gow-Page (1965) II 486–87 assume that he does, but Fraser I 570 with II 813, no. 146 interprets the same reading to mean that the poet is vanquished by love.

92. Cf. Paus. 6.6.4. For additional references, see Fernández-Galiano 79–80.

works out this thought through a careful parallelism with the first. The soul that is now "bound on thorns" (δήσας ἐπ' ἀκάνθαις) previously "labored in books" (ἐν βύβλοις πεπονημένη). In later Greek epigram pedantic scholars who concentrate on "thorny" passages are labeled "thorn-gatherers" or "bookworms who feed on thorns."[93] The convoluted arguments of philosophers were also labeled "thorny" (Lucian *Dial. Mort.* 10.8), and Lucian characterizes the Stoics as especially "spiny" fish (ἀκανθώδεις, *Pisc.* 51), hard to grasp or swallow. The imagery almost certainly goes back to the literary and philosophical debates of the early third century, and Posidippus seems to suggest here that his intellectual labors with books, his previous experience with "thorns," has inured him to the tortures of Desire. And so, although Desire wishes to put him to sleep (κοιμίζειν ἐθέλει), he "gathers other harvests" (ἄλλα θερίζει), namely the literary harvest of erotic verse. For the symbolic use of this verb, we may compare Philip, who refers to the making of an anthology as "harvesting the grain of a new page" (σελίδος νεαρῆς θερίσας στάχυν, 1.3 G-P, *Garland* = *AP* 4.2.3; cf. ἀπέθρισε, Mel. 1.17 G-P = *AP* 4.1.17.). Here Posidippus uses the reaping metaphor to indicate that, though Desire may turn him from his previous scholarly or philosophical endeavors, it yet acts as a stimulus for a different type of literary production. In a final parallelism Posidippus responds to Desire's torture by fire (πῦρ ὑπὸ πλευρὰ βαλών) with verbal recrimination against painful misfortune (ἀνιηρῷ δαίμονι μεμφομένη). The poem thus becomes the proof of its own premise, that despite Desire's attempt to silence the poet, the learned Posidippus has the means to resist by voicing condemnation of his torment. We may surmise that 2 G-P served a programmatic function in Posidippus' collection, quite possibly as part of an opening sequence, where it would expand upon the latent cicada imagery of the introductory epigram and explain the poet's turn from philosophy to erotic song as a response to the tortures of desire.

In another epigram Posidippus employs a military image to convey his ability to resist Eros:

> εὐόπλῳ καὶ πρὸς σὲ μαχήσομαι οὐδ' ἀπεροῦμαι
>   θνητὸς ἐών, σὺ δ', Ἔρως, μηκέτι μοι πρόσαγε.
> ἢν με λάβῃς μεθύοντ' ἄπαγ' ἔκδοτον, ἄχρι δὲ νήφω
>   τὸν παραταξάμενον πρὸς σὲ λογισμὸν ἔχω.
>
>   (7 G-P = *AP* 12.120)

> I am well-armed and, though mortal, I will fight you
>   and not despair; so, Eros, attack me no more.
> If you catch me drunk, take me as your captive,
>   but sober I marshal reason against you.

93. Antip. Thess. 20.2 G-P, *Garland* = *AP* 11.20.2 (ποιητῶν φῦλον ἀκανθολόγων); Philip 60.1 G-P, *Garland* = *AP* 11.321.1 (σῆτες ἀκανθῶν); Philip 61.2 G-P, *Garland* = *AP* 11.347.2 (σῆτες ἀκανθολόγοι); cf. Antiph. 9.2 G-P, *Garland* = *AP* 11.322.2 (σῆτες ἀκανθοβάται).

The contrast here drawn between sobriety, which fights desire, and drunkenness, which does not, again looks back to the conflict in G-P 1 between Stoic philosophy, banished from the symposium, and erotic song, inspired by drink. Sobriety is now directly connected with reason (λογισμός), which in Stoic thought is opposed to passion, including erotic desire. Desire was defined by the Stoics as an "irrational appetite" (ἄλογος ὄρεξις), and erotic passion was rejected by strict Stoics as a desire for affection based solely on beauty (D.L. 7.113). In 7 G-P Posidippus offers a poetic statement of the Stoic doctrine that the man trained in reason is equipped with the power to overcome passion. He thus sets in contrast to Asclepiades' lover, who is hopelessly vulnerable to the shafts of love, his own persona as an epigrammatic poet employing reason to combat desire.

The alternatives of drunkenness and sobriety are resolved, in Theognidean elegy (cf. 467–96), by the advice to drink in moderation. This old symposium motif was modified to form the basis of another Posidippan epigram, one which must have functioned programmatically within the collection:

Νανnοῦς καὶ Λύδης ἐπίχει δύο καὶ φιλεράστου
 Μιμνέρμου καὶ τοῦ σώφρονος Ἀντιμάχου·
συγκέρασον τὸν πέμπτον ἐμοῦ τὸν δ' ἕκτον ἑκάστου,
 Ἡλιόδωρ', εἶπας ὅστις ἐρῶν ἔτυχεν·
ἕβδομον Ἡσιόδου τὸν δ' ὄγδοον εἶπον Ὁμήρου
 τὸν δ' ἔνατον Μουσῶν, Μνημοσύνης δέκατον.
μεστὸν ὑπὲρ χείλους πίομαι, Κύπρι· τἆλλα δ', Ἔρωτες,
 νήφοντ' οἰνωθέντ' οὐχὶ λίην ἄχαριν.[94]

(9 G-P = AP 12.168)

Pour two ladles of Nanno and Lyde, two of Mimnermus,
 dear to lovers, and of sober Antimachus.
Mix in the fifth of me and the sixth, saying,
 Heliodorus, of whomever has chanced to love.
Say the seventh is of Hesiod and the eighth of Homer,
 the ninth of the Muses and the tenth of Mnemosyne.
I will drink the cup full to the brim, Cypris. And what's more, Erotes,
 whether of water or wine, it's not at all unpleasant.

The poem's strikingly complex imagery is founded on the metaphorical identification of poetry and wine that was introduced to the reader in Posidippus' introductory epigram. The initial phrase seems to refer to the lover's toast that was common at symposia (cf. Callim. 5.1 G-P). But as we read through the poem, we discover that the cup is not to be filled with the unmixed wine

---

94. In 1 φιλεράστου is the emendation of Jacobs in his later edition (1813–17) for φερεκαστου in P (retained and daggered by Gow-Page). The last line of the text has been much emended, but I follow the interpretation of the ms. reading given by Giangrande in two articles, "Konjekturen zur Anthologia Palatina," *RhM* 106 (1963) 260–63 and "Interpretationen Hellenistischer Dichter," *Hermes* 97 (1969) 440–48.

used for the lover's toast (cf. Mel. 42.2, 43.4 G-P), but with a series of pairs—Mimnermus and Nanno, Antimachus and Lyde, Posidippus and any lover, Hesiod and the Muses, Homer and Mnemosyne—pairs who represent the literary components of Posidippus' poetic cup. Giangrande has argued that the Muses and Mnemosyne are here the love objects of Hesiod and Homer, as Nanno and Lyde are the mistresses of Mimnermus and Antimachus,[95] but it is hard to see how this pairing of lover and beloved extends to ὅστις ἐρῶν ἔτυχεν, "whoever has chanced to love" (4), who can scarcely represent Posidippus' love object. It is better to perceive a looser or more fluid association between each poet and his partner, who is variously, or simultaneously, beloved, subject, and source of inspiration. When the ladling has been done, the full cup that the poet consumes contains a mixture of the literary ingredients from which his epigram collection has been fashioned.

He begins, appropriately, with the elegists—Mimnermus, "dear to lovers," who was for Hellenistic poets considered the father of elegy, and "sober" Antimachus, admired by Asclepiades (32 G-P, *Garland* = *AP* 9.63) but rejected by Callimachus as no true follower of Mimnermus (fr. 398 with fr. 1.11–12 Pf.). The mention of Antimachus' sobriety, referring to his labored style, indicates that Posidippus' cup will contain, not just the unmixed wine that symbolizes the lover's unrestrained passion, but a more temperate brew. In the second couplet Posidippus cites his own contribution as on a par with that of his epic and elegiac predecessors (Heliodorus may be both cupbearer and love object, cf. Antip. Thess. 3 G-P, *Garland* = *AP* 11.24); in fact, any lover (ὅστις ἐρῶν ἔτυχεν) may contribute to the cup of erotic poetry. The third couplet, like the first, likely refers to a moderate mixture of wine and water. Antipater of Thessalonica, an epigrammatist of the first century B.C., pours a libation of wine to "virile Homer" (20 G-P, *Garland* = *AP* 11.20), while he rejects the "sweet-speaking water" from the Heliconian spring that inspired Hesiod (3 G-P, *Garland*). In these passages Antipater associates the rivalry between those who preferred either Homer or Hesiod as poetic models with the drinking of wine or water, and it seems likely that this association was already present in Posidippus' couplet. By including portions of both Homer and Hesiod with their female companions, Mnemosyne and the Muses, Posidippus again chooses a middle course between polarities, a mixture of opposites. The cup that the poet quaffs at the end of the poem contains, then, a temperate mixture of wine and water, and the poetry it produces or symbolizes is characterized as νήφοντ᾿ οἰνωθέντ᾿, alternately drunk or sober, as Posidippus' passion is moderated by reason.[96]

95. Giangrande (1969) 443–48.

96. On the significance of "sober drunkenness" as a metaphor for styles of literary composition, see Hans Lewy, *Sobria ebrietas: Untersuchungen zur Geschichte der antiken Mystik* (Giessen, 1929) 45–54.

This epigram clearly performed an important programmatic function in Posidippus' collection. Just possibly, it came near the beginning as part of an opening sequence, since it carries on the motif of the toast introduced in 1 G-P. But we may imagine its complex imagery becoming more effective later in the collection after the reader has acquired some familiarity with Posidippus' style and themes. Catullus 27 offers a close parallel:

> Minister vetuli puer Falerni
> inger mi calices amariores

(Catullus 27.1–2)

> You, steward of the good old Falernian,
> fill my cups with a more pungent mixture.

The argument made by some scholars that Catullus' "more bitter cups" refer to the following sequence of poems on satirical themes[97] gains support when it is recognized that Catullus likely had a model for such a usage in Posidippus' cup metaphor. While Catullus 27 functions as a transitional piece introducing a new sequence, it will later be shown that Meleager employed Posidippus' cup poem as the final epigram in his amatory collection. He thus begins and ends the erotic section of his *Garland* with symbolic poems from Posidippus' epigram book, very possibly preserving the positions they held in the earlier collection. The cup poem seems thus to have functioned in Posidippus' book much as 16 G-P may have done in Asclepiades' collection, as a summarizing and concluding piece. Just as Asclepiades 16 revealed the symposium as the site for the recitation of the other epigrams and called upon the poet-lover to drown his sorrows in drink, so Posidippus here overtly acknowledges his use of the symposium as a metaphor for his collection and drinks down (cf. πίομαι, 7) the cup of his own poetry.

At this point we have seen that in his programmatic poems Posidippus carefully constructs for us the persona of a lover whose passions can be moderated by reason. We will now consider how this poetic ego appears in his more straightforwardly erotic epigrams. One of the most striking features of Posidippus' amatory poetry is his frequent imitation and variation of Asclepiades. While the reader of Asclepiades is asked to identify not only the dramatic setting of the lover's speech act but also the particular emotional condition that produced it, the reader of Posidippus is called upon to recognize, in addition to the dramatic setting of the poem, certain literary allusions to one or more poems by Asclepiades. The result of this intrusion of the literary, this shadow cast upon the text by poetic models, is an awareness that the emotion of the lover projected from the poem is mediated by the rationality of the poet who holds up to us his adaptation of

97. The programmatic nature of Catullus 27 was first suggested by Wiseman 7–8, and developed by Marilyn B. Skinner, *Catullus' "Passer": The Arrangement of the Book of Polymetric Poems* (Salem, N.H., 1981) 27–28.

an epigrammatic progenitor. In Posidippus, then, we have the beginning of that striving after stylistic variation, at the cost of the appearance of emotional sincerity, that many scholars have found destructive, in the course of its development, to the spontaneity and sparkle of early Hellenistic epigram. But Posidippus in fact found something of a solution to the problem of sterile duplication. Any attempt to imitate on like terms Asclepiades' successful projection of a young lover's agonized voice was bound to suffer by comparison. Posidippus chose instead to follow in the path of Asclepiades by creating a unique poetic persona protected by the shield of reason.

It speaks against the theory that Posidippus' epigrams were composed for an anthology, for each to stand beside its Asclepiadean model, that his epigrams tend to combine motifs from more than one poem. The following epigram, for instance, draws the name Philaenis from Asclepiades' Philaenion in 8 G-P but the adjective πιθανός, "persuasive," and the general motif of incessant infidelity from his Hermione poem (4 G-P):[98]

Μή με δόκει πιθανοῖς ἀπατᾶν δακρύοισι, Φιλαινί·
    οἶδα· φιλεῖς γὰρ ὅλως οὐδένα μεῖζον ἐμοῦ
τοῦτον ὅσον παρ' ἐμοὶ κέκλισαι χρόνον· εἰ δ' ἕτερός σε
    εἶχε φιλεῖν ἂν ἔφης μεῖζον ἐκεῖνον ἐμοῦ.

(2 G-P = *AP* 5.186)

Don't think you're fooling me with persuasive words, Philaenis.
    I know. For you love no one more than me—
As long as you're lying beside me. But if another holds you,
    you would say you love him more than me.

Posidippus' models reflect two different moments for the lover: in 8 G-P Asclepiades conveys through the viper image the torment of the initial recognition that his love is untrue, while in 4 G-P he reflects with objective amusement on a former girlfriend who had a clever way of revealing her unwillingness to commit to a single lover. An attempt to pinpoint the emotional moment in Posidippus' epigram produces a quite different result. The setting is highly charged: the lover lies in bed with Philaenis, who is professing her faithfulness with "persuasive tears," and rejects her declaration of love with a clever variation of the message written on Hermione's undergarment. As in Asclepiades, the perspective in the poem is that of the lover who speaks, and yet the emotional content of his speech is considerably subdued. He speaks with self-assurance, with the superiority of one convinced he is right: unlike Asclepiades' lover, who was apparently fooled by Hermione at least in the early stages of their affair,

98. πιθανοῖς is Reiske's emendation for πιθανῶς found in P and App. B.–V. The correctness of the change has little effect on my argument. The name Philaenis is also given to a prostitute who competes with another prostitute in a "horse race" in [Asclep.] 35 G-P = *AP* 5.202, probably by Posidippus.

he scarcely seems "persuaded" by Philaenis at all. We are offered no evidence that she is indeed untrue, so that we may wonder if he actually "knows" (οἶδα, 2) or only suspects. It is Philaenis who weeps and, perhaps, loves; the emotional moment is in fact hers.

There are, again, two Asclepiadean models for the following epigram:

Πυθιὰς εἰ μὲν ἔχει τιν' ἀπέρχομαι· εἰ δὲ καθεύδει
    ὧδε μόνη μικρὸν πρὸς Διὸς εἰσκαλέσαι.
εἰπὲ δὲ σημεῖον, μεθύων ὅτι καὶ διὰ κλωπῶν
    ἦλθον Ἔρωτι θρασεῖ χρώμενος ἡγεμόνι.

(4 G-P = AP 5.213)

If Pythias has another, I'll go away. But if she's sleeping alone,
    invite me in, by Zeus, for a little while.
Give her this sign, that drunk and threatened by thieves
    I've come with bold Eros as my guide.

The name Pythias and the paraclausithyron setting come from Asclepiades 13 G-P, while the phrase εἰπὲ δὲ σημεῖον (3) is lifted from one of his mimelike epigrams:

εἰπὲ δὲ σημεῖον Βάκχων ὅτι πέντ' ἐφίλησεν
    ἑξῆς, ὧν κλίνη μάρτυς ἐπεγράφετο.

(25.11–12 G-P = AP 5.181.11–12)

Give her as sign the fact that Bacchon loved her five times
in a row, and her bed acts as witness of it.

Again, Posidippus has altered the emotional content of the poem to reflect the persona of his rational lover. While in 13 Asclepiades calls piteously on Night to witness Pythias' abuse of him and ends with a hopeless cry for revenge, Posidippus states matter-of-factly that if Pythias is occupied, he will go away. The speech act represented in his epigram is not a lover's cry of despair but a calculated plea designed to obtain information and, if possible, to effect entry. As Bacchon in Asclepiades 25 gave a "sign" for his slave to carry to Aeschra—a description of their sexual encounter—so here the lover gives the shadowy doorkeeper a "sign" of his love in order to persuade Pythias to admit him.[99] We may object that the σημεῖον he gives, that he has come drunk through thieves with Eros as his leader, could scarcely differentiate him from any other komast.[100] That, however, is precisely the point: he is a generic lover because he is no lover at all. His σημεῖον is designed to persuade Pythias by declaring his love, not

99. A σημεῖον is found in some Hellenistic documents as proof of the author's identity, as explained by H. C. Youtie, "Σημεῖον in the Papyri and its Significance for Plato, Epistle 13," *ZPE* 6 (1970) 105–16. For the meaning of the device in these poems, see R. Merkelbach, "Σημεῖον im Liebesepigramm," *ZPE* 6 (1970) 245–46.

100. Cf. Gow-Page (1965) *ad* 3.

to distinguish his passion as stronger than that of another. We as readers know from the opening line (ἀπέρχομαι, "I'll go away") that the statement is pure ploy.

Two other epigrams, without dramatic settings, pose as the interior monologue of an anguished lover:

Δάκρυα καὶ κῶμοι τί μ' ἐγείρετε πρὶν πόδας ἆραι
    ἐκ πυρὸς εἰς ἑτέρην Κύπριδος ἀνθρακιήν,
λήγω δ' οὔποτ' ἔρωτος, ἀεὶ δέ μοι ἐξ Ἀφροδίτης
    ἄλγος ὁ μὴ κρίνων καινὸν ἄγει τι Πόθος.[101]

(3 G-P = AP 5.211)

Tears and revels, why do you spur me on, before my feet
    are out of the fire, into other coals lit by the Cyprian?
I never cease to love, but always indiscriminate Desire
    brings me some new pain from Aphrodite.

Ναὶ ναὶ βάλλετ', Ἔρωτες· ἐγὼ σκοπὸς εἷς ἅμα πολλοῖς
    κεῖμαι. μὴ φείσησθ', ἄφρονες· ἢν γὰρ ἐμέ
νικήσητ' ὀνομαστοὶ ἐν ἀθανάτοισιν ἔσεσθε
    τοξόται ὡς μεγάλης δεσπόται ἰοδόκης.

(5 G-P = AP 12.45)

Strike me, Erotes, yes do. I lie here a single target for you,
    the many. Don't spare me, fools. For if you defeat me,
You'll make a name for yourselves among the immortals
    as bowmen, masters of a huge quiver.

The first poem owes much to Asclepiades 15, which likewise concerns the poet's inability to escape the cycle of love. As Asclepiades asks the Erotes, "Why do you burn me?" Posidippus asks, "Why do you spur me on?" But Posidippus addresses "tears and revels," not the Erotes, and scholars have pointed out that these are the result of love, not its cause.[102] Consequently, we may wonder about cause and effect, whether in fact Posidippus himself is not in control of his emotions and behavior. While Asclepiades' poem gains much of its power from the final image of the thoughtless, dice-playing Erotes, Posidippus' last line is more like a joke, because the tiny putti depicted in Hellenistic art will require a large quiver filled with many arrows in order to defeat him.[103] The second Posidippan poem begins with a direct quotation from Asclepiades 17, ναὶ

---

101. Gow-Page (1965) *ad* 3f. state that the second pentameter "is beyond certain repair," and all but the first and last words are daggered in their edition. But the participle can be defended and Bosch's correction for κοινὸν ἄγοντι is perfectly reasonable. For parallels supporting the reading here offered, see Fernández-Galiano 73.

102. Schott 51, who despairs of finding the correct reading; Fernández-Galiano 72, who accepts the transmitted text and cites as parallel Mel. 64 G-P = *AP* 5.190. For various proposed emendations, see Stadtmüller.

103. For this explanation of the line, see G. Giangrande, "Théocrite, Simichidas et les *Thalysies*," *AC* 37 (1968) 496.

ναὶ βάλλετ᾽, Ἔρωτες ("Yes, yes, strike me, Erotes"), and borrows as well the adjective ἄφρονες from 15. But Posidippus has modified Asclepiades' images of love's hopelessness and torment to present a picture of himself as a worthy adversary of the Erotes. As Gow points out, ἄφρονες, which means "heedless" in Asclepiades, carries the meaning "foolish" in Posidippus.[104] Asclepiades' thoughtless, destructive children become in Posidippus fools to pass up so great a challenge. His cry, "Strike me, Erotes, yes do," is not Asclepiades' wish for death as the only end to love but a throwing down of the gauntlet, a provocation. Though Posidippus bears the trappings of a lover, he is yet resistant to the pain of love. Because of his capacity for sober reason, he is the Erotes' most difficult target and so, if conquered, their greatest triumph. But among the epigrams we have from the hand of Posidippus we never find the poet so vanquished. Desire may bind him on thorns and torture him with fire, but the poet's soul, hardened by the labors of his studies, can still hurl insults at the demons of love.

Later Greek epigrammatists distinguished between water drinkers, who wrote or studied poetry adorned with obscure words and a convoluted style, and wine drinkers, whose poetic intoxication was associated with emotional intensity such as the sheer madness of love.[105] Though this imagery was employed in a polemic directed against the pedantic followers of Callimachus, whom Antipater of Thessalonica calls both "tribe of thorn-gathering poets" and "water drinkers" (20 G-P, *Garland* = *AP* 11.20), the quarrel itself seems to have had its roots in the third century. As Asclepiades in 16 G-P sets himself up to be viewed as a wine drinker, so Callimachus draws his inspiration from the dew of the air (fr. 1.34 Pf.) or the pure spray from a holy fountain (καθαρή ... πίδακος ἐξ ἱερῆς ὀλίγη λιβάς, *Ap.* 111–12), language echoed by Antipater in condemning water-drinking poets (κρήνης ἐξ ἱερῆς πίνετε λιτὸν ὕδωρ, 20.4 G-P, *Garland*). Posidippus plots a middle course: like Callimachus (fr. 1.29–34 Pf.), he is the Muses' cicada, but one who consumes not natural dew but the dew of wine.[106] Though chronologies are uncertain for this period, Callimachus seems in the *Aetia* prologue to be responding to Posidippus rather than vice versa; the Florentine scholia place both Asclepiades and Posidippus among the Telchines against whom Callimachus grumbles. If this is correct, we may view Posidippus' imagery as an attempt to vary Asclepiades' important poetic achievement. The Samian had produced an innovative epigram collection in which a key poem (16 G-P) suggested a symposium setting and presented drink as solace for the love madness experienced by the epigrammatist's poetic ego. Posidippus, in forming a collection that was strongly imitative of Asclepiades and yet was distinguished

104. Gow-Page (1965) *ad* 5.2.

105. See Antip. Thess. 20 G-P, *Garland* = *AP* 11.20, 36 G-P, *Garland* = *AP* 9.305, and 37 G-P, *Garland* = *AP* 11.31.

106. The image of the cicada drunk on dew appears in later epigrammatists (Mel. 13.1 G-P = *AP* 7.196.1, Antip. Thess. 2.1–2 G-P, *Garland* = *AP* 9.92.1–2).

by the different character given the poet's persona, presents his erotic epigrams in the setting of a symposium that is not so much fictionalized as metaphorical. As he drinks a cup filled with various influences, he is inspired by this temperate mixture of water and wine to sing his own brand of sympotic song. The persona Posidippus projects, then, is characterized by mediation between polarities—his passion being tempered by reason, his drunkenness moderated by sobriety, his erotic song controlled by literary indebtedness. While Asclepiades asserted the ideal of a sweet Eros but experienced the reality of a bitter one, the gulf between the two being the source of his torment, Posidippus proclaims from the beginning that his topic is "bittersweet Eros" (1.4 G-P). Although Sappho, from whom the term descends (130 *PLF*), may have had in mind an experience of love like that of Asclepiades, Posidippus' use of the term in the context of his collection suggests, not an inseparable simultaneity of bitterness and sweetness, but a mediation between the two—the bitterness of erotic pain mediated by the sweetness of reason.

In examining the surviving epigrams by Posidippus, we have identified a series of poems displaying an internal cohesion and an adherence to a programmatic position set out by two epigrams on sympotic themes (1 and 9 G-P). We may conclude, then, that we are dealing with the remnants of a poetry book, which was apparently constructed as a complement to the earlier book of erotic epigrams by Asclepiades. While Asclepiades' collection shows a man who hopes for Epicurean contentment coming to terms with the reality of his relentless desires, Posidippus' collection shows how a man whose soul is tempered by Stoic rationality manages erotic experience through objective resistance to emotional torment. Given their evident interconnections, it is scarcely surprising if these two epigram books were later combined in an anthology or transmitted in tandem.

In closing, we may ask how Posidippus' book of erotic epigrams relates to the other Posidippan collections we have identified. In all likelihood, the great majority, if not all, of the epigrams in this collection eventually found their way into the comprehensive assemblage known as the *Epigrammata*, and we cannot be certain that the Milan Papyrus, as a gathering of diverse epigrams, did not also contain erotic-sympotic epigrams in sections now lost. What we need to ask, then, is whether the original source for the erotic epigrams could have been either of the other two collections known to us. It seems unlikely that *Miscellaneous Epigrams* would be deemed an appropriate title for an epigram collection emphasizing Posidippus' own erotic experiences or that he would begin such a collection with the epithalamium for Arsinoe. The *Soros*, on the other hand, is a much more likely candidate. The collection known by this title surely included some indication of the metaphorical identification of its poetic contents with a heap of grain, and we have already seen that in 6 G-P, a poem that seems to form a complementary pair with the introductory epigram (1 G-P), Posidippus speaks of composing erotic verse as "harvesting grain" (θερίζει). A likely connection between the title and the σωρίτης argument fits as well with the strong Stoic influence evident throughout Posidippus' erotic epigrams. Although the collection doubtless included a more explicit explanation of its metaphorical title, it is not an improbable hypothesis that Posidippus' ten to fifteen surviving epigrams of the erotic-sympotic type belonged to the poetry book known to Aristarchus as the *Soros*.

What else can be surmised about this collection? We know, of course, that the *Soros* contained an epigram making reference to a Trojan hero called Berisus, and scholars have suggested that this epigram was composed under the influence of Asclepiades' epitaph for Ajax (29 G-P = *AP* 7.145). If imitation of Asclepiades were a unifying feature of the collection, then a number of Posidippan epigrams not here discussed in detail would meet the criterion of inclusion. Posidippus wrote a mimelike epigram in which a master gives his slave instructions for the preparation of a symposium (10 G-P = *AP* 5.183) as a variation of Asclepiades' two dramatic sketches (25, 26 G-P). His epitaph for a sailor who wishes to avoid burial near the sea (15 G-P = *AP* 7.267) repeats the theme of Asclepiades 30 G-P = *AP* 7.284, and his epitaph for Doricha, made famous by Sappho as her brother's lover (17 G-P), is, like Asclepiades' Archeanassa poem (41 G-P = *AP* 7.217), a celebration of a famous hetaira of the past. Posidippus' epigram on Lysippus' statue of Alexander (18 G-P = *AP* 16.119) may have been suggested by an epigram on the same theme (43 G-P = *AP* 16.120), if by Asclepiades rather than Archelaus. If the five epigrams ascribed alternately to both poets could be assigned to Posidippus, we would then have additional imitations. The most commonly accepted of these is [Asclep.] 35 G-P = *AP* 5.202, a dedication made by the hetaira Plangon upon defeating a rival in a "horse race," which is probably Posidippus' imitation of Asclepiades' Lysidice epigram (6 G-P). By positing on the basis of the internal evidence of the epigrams themselves that Posidippus published an epigram collection entitled *Soros* that imitated and responded to a famous poetry book by Asclepiades, we answer the much-debated question concerning the purpose of Posidippus' numerous variations of Asclepiadean epigrams.

HEDYLUS

Athenaeus (7.297a–b) reports that Hedylus was a Samian or Athenian, the son of Hedyle, who wrote an elegy about Glaucus' love for Scylla (456 *SH*), and the grandson of Moschine, an Attic iambic poet (559 *SH*).[107] He came, then, from a literary family, and Athenaeus knew of a poem, now lost, in which

107. For the life of Hedylus, see Gow-Page (1965) II 289; Fraser I 558; I. G. Galli Calderini, "Edilo epigrammista," *AAP* 32 (1983) 365–71. The only extensive commentary on Hedylus is also by Calderini, "Gli epigrammi di Edilo: interpretazione ed esegesi," *AAP* 33 (1984) 79–118.

Hedylus continued his mother's interest in Glaucus by discussing his love for Melicertes (457 *SH*).[108] His uncertain origin suggests that his family was among the Athenian cleruchs at Samos who were forced out of the island about 321 B.C. Hedylus clearly knew the work of both Asclepiades and Posidippus. But it remains unclear whether he was personally acquainted with Asclepiades, since the reference to the Samian in one of Hedylus' epigrams (6.4 G-P) could indicate only literary indebtedness. An epigram on a dedication made in Arsinoe's temple at Zephyrium (4 G-P) connects him with Egypt, where he presumably knew both Posidippus and Callimachus. Epigrams by Posidippus on gluttons (14 and 16 G-P, 702 *SH*) offer parallels to Hedylus' satirical epigrams, and our epigrammatist is very likely the same Hedylus who wrote a commentary on Callimachus' epigrams (458 *SH*). If this is a correct assumption, he was probably somewhat younger than Posidippus, and so likely influenced by the Pellan as well as by Asclepiades.

Meleager seems to have anthologized relatively few of Hedylus' epigrams, since only five survive for us in the *AP*: two erotic dedications (1 G-P = *AP* 6.292, 2 G-P = *AP* 5.199); a warning about three rapacious and elderly whores, ascribed alternatively to Asclepiades ([Asclep.] 40 G-P = *AP* 5.161); and two satirical epigrams, one on a doctor and one on gout (11 G-P = *AP* 11.123, 12 G-P = *AP* 11.414), the authorship of which is often denied to Hedylus.[109] But in all likelihood, a collection of Hedylus' epigrams circulated in antiquity: Athenaeus has preserved, in whole or in part, eight additional epigrams, some of which apparently formed a unit within his *Epigrammata*. If this small body of poetry is sufficient evidence, we may conclude that Hedylus followed the lead of Asclepiades and Posidippus in centering his collection around the symposium while creating a distinctive flavor through his largely satirical tone.

Satirical epigram is generally considered a later phenomenon, a characteristic of the poetry of the imperial period.[110] Its best-known practitioners, Lucillius

108. We also have three couplets from an epigram or elegy on deer that swam from Cilicia to Cyprus, which Strabo (14.6.3) cites as the work of "either Hedylus or someone." While Calderini (1983) 370 asserts that this poem must have been an elegy, Lloyd-Jones and Parsons *ad* 459 *SH* suggest that we have an entire epigram on an artistic depiction of deer dedicated in a temple.

109. Following earlier editors, Gow-Page (1965) II 289 claim that these two last epigrams are "plainly spurious." They do appear in *AP* 11, which has no Meleagrian sequences, and in character they could easily belong with satirical epigrams of the imperial period. Even so, Calderini (1984) 102–6 argues in favor of the attribution to Hedylus. Because of decided doubt about their authenticity, I pass over discussion of them here.

110. On satirical Greek epigrams, see Franz J. Brecht, *Motiv- und Typengeschichte des griechischen Spottepigramms*, Philologus Supplementband 22, Heft 2 (Leipzig, 1930); Laurens 140–55; Vincenzo Longo, *L'epigramma scoptico greco* (Genoa, 1967); and L. Robert, "Les épigrammes satiriques de Lucillius sur les athlètes," *L'épigramme grecque* (Geneva, 1968) 179–295.

and Nicarchus, belong to the first or early second centuries A.D. But insults and mockery had long been an established part of the symposium exchange, and Catullus' invective epigrams probably had Hellenistic models. An early Hellenistic elegy found on the Elephantine papyrus includes in its list of appropriate behavior for symposiasts, ἐς ἀλλήλους τε φλυαρεῖν καὶ σκώπτειν τοιαῦθ' οἷα γέλωτα φέρειν, "to poke fun at each other and to mock, just enough to produce laughter" (5–6).[111] The final qualifier was an essential reminder, for the teasing that took place at a symposium had the potential to spill over into anger and violence (cf. Theog. 493–94, ὑμεῖς δ' εὖ μυθεῖσθε παρὰ κρητῆρι μένοντες, ἀλλήλων ἔριδας δὴν ἀπερυκόμενοι, "we enjoy good conversation by the wine bowl as long as we refrain from quarrels"). Examples of this type of controlled abuse may be found in Philokleon's twisted replies to the scolia begun by his son in Aristophanes' *Wasps* 1224–48 and in the riddling, sometimes obscene, scolia quoted by Athenaeus (903, 904, 905 *PMG*). In all likelihood, poems like the parodic epitaph for Hermias of Atarneus composed by Theocritus of Chios to make fun of Aristotle (1 *EG*, p. 56) circulated in a symposium setting. In writing satirical epigram for a collection with sympotic themes, Hedylus was, like Asclépiades and Posidippus before him, practicing the conversion of oral performance to a written context.

Several of Hedylus' epigrams concern excessive fondness for food on the part of symposiasts. The topic of ὀψοφαγία, or deeds of famous food lovers, derives from fourth-century comedy.[112] Ascribed to Lynceus, a brother of Duris of Samos who was both a scholar and a comic poet, was a work or works entitled *Reminiscences* ('Απομνημονεύματα) or *Witty Sayings* ('Αποφθέγματα), which consisted of anecdotes about parasites, hetairas, and lovers of food.[113] Lynceus mentioned the ὀψοφάγος Phyromachus (Ath. 6.245e), who appeared in comedy and about whom we have a satirical epitaph by Posidippus (16 G-P; cf. 14 G-P on the gluttony of a famous athlete). It seems, then, that Lynceus may have been a source for the satirical themes that were introduced into epigram by Posidippus and, perhaps more extensively, by Hedylus. We will find evidence that certain of the characters appearing in Hedylus' epigrams may have been historical personages of the recent past. A collection of such epigrams could be viewed as the poetic equivalent of Lynceus' prose collection; in it the wit of sympotic anecdotes would be translated into the point of epigrammatic form.

111. P.Berol. 270.2. For the text and discussion of the elegy, see E. Iscra and N. Marincic, "Poesia conviviale in un papiro di Elefantina," *QFC* 4 (1983) 18–21. On mockery at symposia, see E. Pellizer, "Della zuffa simpotica," in *Poesia e simposio nella Grecia antica*, ed. Massimo Vetta (Bari, 1983) 29–41.

112. See Brecht 72.

113. Ath. 6.245a,d; 6.248d; 10.434d; 13.583f. See Körte 2472–73.

Athenaeus reports that lovers of food were "catalogued" by Hedylus in his *Epigrammata* (ἐν ἐπιγράμμασιν ὀψοφάγους καταλέγων, 8.344f), a statement indicating that Athenaeus knew a text of fixed order.[114] The three epigrams he quotes may, therefore, retain their original sequential arrangement. The first is a fragment of an epigram about a certain harp player named Phaedon:

Φαίδων δὲ φυκί᾿ ἐνείκαι
χορδάς θ᾿, ὁ ψάλτης ἐστὶ γὰρ ὀψοφάγος.[115]

(7 G-P = Ath. 8.344f)

Let Phaedon endure bass and tripe (or strings),
for the harp player is a glutton.

The joke here is the pun on χορδή, which means both tripe and the string of a musical instrument. The second epigram is more nearly complete, a warning about admitting to the banquet a certain Agis (perhaps the author of a cookbook mentioned by Athenaeus, 12.516c),[116] whose attempts to get at food are of mythical proportions:

ἑφθὸς ὁ κάλλιχθυς· νῦν ἔμβαλε τὴν βαλανάγραν
    ἔλθῃ μὴ Πρωτεὺς Ἆγις ὁ τῶν λοπάδων.
γίνεθ᾿ ὕδωρ καὶ πῦρ καὶ ὃ βούλεται· ἀλλ᾿ ἀπόκλειε
    . . . .
ἥξει γὰρ τοιαῦτα μεταπλασθεὶς τυχὸν ὡς Ζεύς
    χρυσορόης ἐπὶ τήνδ᾿ Ἀκρισίου λοπάδα.

(8 G-P = Ath. 8.344f–345a)

The beauty fish is served. Now throw the bolt to keep
    Agis, that Proteus of dishes, from getting in.
He can change into water, fire, anything at all. But lock him out
    . . . .
For maybe he'll come changed into a stream of gold
    like Zeus to get at Acrisius' dish.

Here the joke depends on the cleverness of the mythical allusions. Agis is first compared to the shape-shifter Proteus, who was a proverbial trickster, and the meaning seems to be simply that Agis' "ingenuity in getting at food is inexhaustible."[117] But the Proteus image just lays the groundwork for the

114. So interpreted by Fraser I 608, II 816, n. 159.
115. I print the optative ἐνείκαι, which was Jacobs' emendation, rather than the infinitive form preferred by Gow-Page. The joke seems to be that because Phaedon is a harp player, he can digest tripe/strings but because he is an ὀψοφάγος, a term that often suggests a love of fish (e.g., Archippus, *PCG* II 548, fr. 28), he likes to eat bass.
116. So noted by Gow-Page (1965) II 294. Calderini (1984) 107, n. 164 points out, however, that the name Agis recurs in 11 G-P, where it refers to a doctor, and in [Asclep.] 40 G-P, where Agis is a discarded lover; she concludes that Agis is simply "un nome convenzionale."
117. Gow-Page (1965) *ad* 2 f.

second mythical allusion, the story of Danae and Zeus. The "beauty fish" of the first line is now assimilated to a beautiful girl, namely Danae, who is locked away from her suitors, and Agis is compared to an excluded lover, who will, like Zeus, assume any form to get at this "dish."[118] This is the joke that rounds off the poem and gives it its epigrammatic point. The third epigram of the series combines the techniques of pun and mythical parallel:

> ὀψοφάγει, Κλειώ· καταμύομεν. ἢν δὲ θελήσῃς
> ἔσθε μόνη. δραχμῆς ἐστιν ὁ γόγγρος ἅπας.
> θὲς μόνον ἢ ζώνην ἢ ἐνώτιον ἤ τι τοιοῦτον
> σύσσημον· τὸ δ᾽ ὁρᾶν, ναὶ μὰ τόν, οὐκ ἔχομεν.
> ἡμετέρη σὺ Μέδουσα· λιθούμεθα πάντες ἀπλάτου
> οὐ Γοργοῦς, γόγγρου δ᾽ οἱ μέλεοι λοπάδι.[119]

(9 G-P = Ath. 8.345a–b)

Be gluttonous, Cleio. We're closing our eyes. If you want,
  eat it all yourself. The whole conger eel costs a drachma.
Just give us your sash or an earring or some such deposit.
  But by god, we're not able to watch.
You're our Medusa. Poor us, we're all turned to stone,
  not by a horrible Gorgon, but by a plate of *gongros*.

Mockery of hetairas was a common practice at symposia, as evidenced, for instance, by one of the Attic scolia (905 *PMG*). This Cleio is apparently a historical personage, identical with the Cleo who is said to outdrink men in an epigram by Phalaecus (1 G-P = Ath. 10.440d) and in Aelian (*VH* 2.41). In Hedylus' epigram Cleio is eating more than her share of a conger eel.[120] Her fellow diners agree to let her have it all, if she agrees to cover the expense with some pledge of payment, such as an article of her attire. But her gluttony is so disgusting that they cannot bear to watch, a circumstance producing the Medusa image with the pun on Gorgon and γόγγρος ("conger eel"). The three poems

118. M. Henry, "The Edible Woman," in *Pornography and Representation in Greece and Rome*, ed. Amy Richlin (Oxford, 1992) 250–68 has studied the identification of women, especially hetairas, with food in Athenaeus' *Deipnosophistae*. The analogy goes back to comic literature of the fifth and fourth centuries, as shown by J. Davidson, "Fish, Sex, and Revolution," *CQ* 43 (1993) 63–64.

119. The manuscript of Athenaeus presents corrupt readings in lines 4 and 5, which Gow-Page retain in daggers. In 4 I have printed ναὶ μὰ τόν suggested by Jacobs (1794–1814) V 830 with οὐκ ἔχομεν in place of the οὐ λέγομεν found in the ms., while in 5 I print Kaibel's πάντες ἀπλάτου, which Gow-Page (1965) *ad loc.* find ingenious and Calderini (1984) 111, n. 178 deems persuasive.

120. Since Alexis, *PCG* II 50, fr. 50 uses the phrase τοὖψον λαβοῦσαι of feasting women, probably hetairas, with a secondary reference to performing fellatio, the beginning of Hedylus' epigram, ὀψοφάγει, Κλειώ· καταμύομεν, may tease the reader by initially suggesting a similar sexual reference. On the Alexis passage, see Jeffrey Henderson, *The Maculate Muse: Obscene Language in Attic Comedy*, 2nd ed. (New York, 1991) 167–68.

that Athenaeus cites from Hedylus' "catalogue" of gluttons seem, then, to have not only a similarity of theme, excessive love of food, but also a similarity of satirical technique through play on language and myth.

In these three epigrams the dramatic setting is the symposium and the narrator presents himself as one of the banqueters. Other epigrams continue to display sympotic themes but assume more traditionally epigrammatic forms, imitating written rather than oral discourse. Three take the form of dedications made by women to commemorate a symposium experience. In the first of these a girl who has lost her virginity during a dinner party dedicates to Aphrodite the clothing she wore as a sign of the goddess's victory:

οἶνος καὶ προπόσεις κατεκοίμισαν Ἀγλαονίκην
  αἱ δόλιαι, καὶ ἔρως ἡδὺς ὁ Νικαγόρεω,
ἧς πάρα Κύπριδι ταῦτα μύροις ἔτι πάντα μυδῶντα
  κεῖνται, παρθενίων ὑγρὰ λάφυρα πόθων,
σάνδαλα καὶ μαλακαὶ μαστῶν ἐκδύματα μίτραι,
  ὕπνου καὶ σκυλμῶν τῶν τότε μαρτύρια.

(2 G-P = AP 5.199)

Wine and deceitful toasts put to sleep Aglaonice,
  as did the sweet love of Nicagoras.
And so all these items, still moist with perfume, lie dedicated
  to the Cyprian—the damp spoils of her maiden's desire—
Her sandals and the soft sashes stripped from her breasts,
  witnesses of her sleep and of love's struggles.

As Posidippus' amatory epigrams are meant to be read against the background of Asclepiades' collection, so this poem, Hedylus' most erotic epigram, is clearly a pendant to Asclepiades 18 G-P, where the unmixed wine of the love toasts betrays Nicagoras' erotic longing to his dinner partners.[121] Hedylus finds it amusing that the wine used for such toasts at another symposium should, in his epigram, become the lover's means of seducing Aglaonice.

Another dedicatory epigram, which has been unnecessarily emended by most editors, is best interpreted as a kind of companion piece to the Aglaonice poem:

αἱ μίτραι τό θ' ἁλουργὲς ὑπένδυμα τοί τε Λάκωνες
  πέπλοι καὶ ληρῶν οἱ χρύσεοι κάλαμοι
πάνθ' ἅμα Νικονόη συνέκπιεν· ἦν γὰρ Ἐρώτων
  καὶ Χαρίτων ἡ παῖς ἀμβρόσιόν τι θάλος.

121. Noted by Reitzenstein (1893) 91–92. Against the suggestion of Wilamowitz (1924) I 145, n. 3 that the epigrams reflect two different stages in an actual love affair, Ludwig (1968) 308 has argued that Hedylus' epigram is "ein παίγνιον, ein fiktives Weihepigramm, Erfüllung der Aufgabe, zu einem bekannten Epigramm des grossen Sikelidas ein Gegenstück zu dichten."

τοιγὰρ τῷ κρίναντι τὰ καλλιστεῖα Πριάπῳ
νεβρίδα καὶ χρυσέην τήνδ᾽ ἔθετο προχοήν.

(1 G-P = AP 6.292)

Her sashes, her purple slip, her fine Laconian dress,
  and the gilded ornaments on her tunic,
All these together Niconoe drank away. For the girl
  was a heavenly shoot of the Erotes and the Graces.
Therefore to Priapus who judges the fairest offering
  she dedicated a fawn skin and this golden pitcher.

As Aglaonice was seduced by the effects of wine, so Niconoe has been persuaded by large amounts of drink to remove her clothing (perhaps as pledges, as in 9 G-P) and to reveal her youthful beauty to those who desire her. And as Aglaonice dedicated the spoils of her first love making to Aphrodite, so Niconoe has dedicated to Priapus, the god of lust and as such a judge of the fairest, items which suggest that she has behaved like a wanton Bacchant. Most editors reject the manuscript reading with its reference to drink in line 3 and view Niconoe as the winner of a beauty contest among hetairas.[122] But the reading given here is preferable not only because it preserves the transmitted text but also because it explains the position of the poem within its Meleagrian sequence in the *AP*. There it is sandwiched between a poem on a woman too fond of wine (*AP* 6.291)[123] and a dedication of love spoils to Aphrodite made by an old Cynic's young lover (Leon. 54 G-P = *AP* 6.293). Apparently, then, Meleager found in his reading of Hedylus' poem a reference to excessive drinking and to a dedication made as a memorial for an erotic encounter. On this reading, the poem finds a close parallel in an anonymous epigram preserved in Meleager's *Garland* (36 G-P = *AP* 5.200), in which a girl named Alexo dedicates perfume, sashes, and

122. Gow-Page, Paton, and Pontani print the dative Νικινόῃ while placing the transmitted σὺν ἔκπιε (P; συνεπέκπιεν in Pl and *Sud.*) in daggers; Waltz and Beckby print Stadtmüller's emendation, Νικονόη συνεπήιεν. See Stadtmüller's apparatus for other suggestions. Editors are of course influenced by the desire to remove the anacoluthon created if Niconoe is the subject of a verb of drinking in 3. But both Jacobs (1794–1814) V 333 and Wilamowitz (1924) I 145, n. 2 found the reading in Planudes comprehensible. For the history of scholarship on the problem, see Calderini (1984) 84–86, who decides in favor of emendation.

123. The Meleagrian context guarantees that the Antipater to whom this poem is ascribed is the Sidonian rather than his later namesake from Thessalonica, although Gow-Page classify it with the poems assigned to the latter (101 G-P, *Garland*). The epigram is repeated after *AP* 9.164 with the heading ἀδέσποτον, where it precedes a long series by Pallades. Gow-Page (1968) II 100 decide that it "perhaps better be regarded as anonymous," largely because they find its position puzzling in both sequences. But surely the position in *AP* 6 reflects Meleager's original ordering and that in *AP* 9 a careless reordering by Cephalas. If the Niconoe epigram is properly understood, the function of 6.291 within its Meleagrian sequence becomes clear, and the Antipater to whom it is ascribed is shown to be the earlier epigrammatist by that name.

garlands to Priapus as gifts in exchange for a "holy pannychis," that is, a night of love making.[124] Niconoe, like Aglaonice in 2 G-P, is probably not an experienced hetaira, but still a girl (ἡ παῖς, 4) commemorating her first experience of love.

Though the Niconoe epigram remains a somewhat difficult poem, we should remember that Hedylus anticipated the reader would puzzle out its dramatic circumstance in the context of his other epigrams, such as the Aglaonice piece and the following poem, the third in our series of dedications by women:

ἡ διαπινομένη Καλλίστιον ἀνδράσι, θαῦμα
    κοὐ ψευδές, νῆστις τρεῖς χόας ἐξέπιεν
ἧς τόδε σοί, Παφίη, ζωροῖς ἀμέτροισι θυωθέν·
    κεῖται πορφυρέης Λέσβιον ἐξ ὑέλου.
ἣν σὺ σάου πάντως, ὡς καὶ πάντων ἀπ' ἐκείνης
    σοὶ τοῖχοι γλυκερῶν σῦλα φέρωσι πότων.[125]

(3 G-P = Ath. 11.486b)

Kallistion in competition with men—it's amazing but true—
    drank down two gallons on an empty stomach.
Her Lesbian cup of purple glass, still redolent of all that
    unmixed wine, lies here dedicated to you, Paphian.
Keep her always safe, so that your walls may have from her
    the spoils of all her sweet drinking bouts.

While this epigram takes the form of a dedication like the Niconoe and Aglaonice poems, it also bears similarity to the Cleio epigram (9 G-P), in that it concerns a hetaira with a prodigious capacity for consumption. Within Hedylus' collection the poems on Kallistion and Cleio would have provided an interesting contrast: the first, written from the hetaira's point of view, celebrates her pride in her enormous drinking capacity, while the second, written from the viewpoint of male symposiasts, participates in the criticism often directed at hetairas for their gluttony and greed. As the Cleio epigram ended with a pun on Gorgon and *gongros*, so too the Kallistion dedication ends with a play on words. The correct reading in the last line is surely σῦλα ... πότων rather than the σῦλα ... πόθων found in the text of Athenaeus. But the phrase παρθενίων ... λάφυρα πόθων in 2.4, which was apparently imitated by Callimachus in the *Lock of Berenice* (as evidenced by *de virgineis ... exuviis*, Catull. 66.14), indicates that "spoils of desire" was the more commonplace phrase, here modified to describe the drinking

124. The poem, together with its companion piece, another anonymous epigram in which a Leontis dedicates her lyre to Aphrodite to commemorate her "pannychis" with a lover (37 G-P = *AP* 5.201), appeared in Meleager's *Garland* as a variation of Hedylus' Agla nice epigram.

125. In 3 I have printed the ζωροῖς ἀμέτροισι (*sc.* ποτοῖς) suggested by Gow-Page (1965) *ad loc.* for the incomprehensible ms. reading. For other emendations, see Calderini (1984) 92–94. In 5 I print Musurus' ἀπ' for the ἐπ' of the ms. in a phrase that Gow-Page describe as "plainly corrupt." On the substitution of πότων for the πόθων in the ms. of Athenaeus, see Gow-Page *ad loc.* and Calderini 95.

habits of one who had long since given up her maiden spoils.[126] This word play, reminiscent of the three epigrams from Athenaeus' "catalogue," suggests that Hedylus' tone may not have wandered for long from the satiric.

Hedylus' remaining poems in epigrammatic form might also fit well in a collection based on sympotic themes. His celebration of a rhyton in the shape of the god Bes made by Ctesibias for Arsinoe's temple at Zephyrium is addressed to ζωροπόται, "drinkers of unmixed wine" (4.1 G-P = Ath. 11.497d), who are later identified as young men (νέοι, 4.10) called to the temple for a party. The only epitaph attributed to Hedylus commemorates a certain piper named Theon, whose songs included the "drunken trifles of Glauce's Muses" and the compositions of Battalus, "a sweet drinker of unmixed wine" (10.7–8 G-P = Ath. 4.176d).[127] An epigram on three aging whores is much more in the manner of Hedylus than Asclepiades, to whom it is also ascribed:[128]

Εὐφρὼ καὶ Θαῒς καὶ Βοίδιον, αἱ Διομήδους
  γραῖαι, ναυκλήρων ὁλκάδες εἰκόσοροι,
Ἄγιν καὶ Κλεοφῶντα καὶ Ἀνταγόρην ἕν' ἑκάστη
  γυμνούς, ναυηγῶν ἥσσονας, ἐξέβαλον.
ἀλλὰ σὺν αὐταῖς νηυσὶ τὰ ληστρικὰ τῆς Ἀφροδίτης
  φεύγετε, Σειρήνων αἵδε γὰρ ἐχθρότεραι.

           ([Asclep.] 40 G-P = *AP* 5.161)

Euphro, Thais, and Boedion, the aged daughters
  of Diomedes, twenty-oared vessels for merchants,
each cast ashore one of these, naked, worse off
  than the shipwrecked—Agis, Cleophon, and Antagoras.
Avoid the piracy of Aphrodite by avoiding her ships,
  creatures more hateful than the Sirens.

The extended comparison of women to ships and the mythical allusions to the daughters (= man-eating mares) of Diomedes and to the Sirens find parallels in Hedylus' other satiric epigrams.[129] Even if the symposium does not explicitly

---

126. For the parallel with Callimachus, see K. Gutzwiller, "Callimachus and Hedylus: A Note on Catullus 66.13–14," *Mnemosyne* 46 (1993) 530–32. Gow-Page (1965) *ad* 3.5f. suggest that ὑγρὰ λάφυρα πόθων in 2.4 G-P may "at some stage have contributed to the error."

127. Fraser I 573 points out that Theon's epitaph "gives some idea of the popular and sentimental musical pieces of the Alexandrian stage in the early third century." Glauce is known as a popular singer also from Theoc. *Id.* 4.31; see the note of Gow (1952) *ad loc.* for additional references.

128. So most scholars: Wilamowitz (1924) I 146, n. 1; Gow-Page (1965) II 144; Beckby I 656; Fraser I 574. But Calderini (1982) 249–53 argues for the authorship of Asclepiades. The epigram appears a second time after *AP* 11.9, where it is attributed to Simonides (cf. *AP* 5.159).

129. Gow-Page (1965) *ad* 1f. quote the scholium to Ar. *Eccl.* 1021, where the mythical mares of Diomedes are explained as Diomedes' daughters, who were prostitutes and wore men out with love making.

appear in this poem, we have already seen that it was a typical setting for the expression of animosity toward hetairas.

In 8 and 9 G-P (perhaps in the fragmentary 7 as well) the poet appears as an internal narrator, in the guise of a satiric symposiast. This dramatic persona reappears in two other epigrams, which function together as authentications of Hedylus' authorship and as statements of his poetic program. The first of these, the only known poem in which Hedylus names himself and thus (we may assume) the *sphragis* of the collection, employs contemporary literary terminology to define Hedylus' relationship to other erotic-sympotic epigrammatists and to stake out for his collection a place within the poetic debates of the day:

πίνωμεν, καὶ γάρ τι νέον, καὶ γάρ τι παρ' οἶνον
    εὕροιμ' ἂν λεπτὸν καί τι μελιχρὸν ἔπος.
ἀλλὰ κάδοις Χίου με κατάβρεχε καὶ λέγε "παῖζε
    Ἡδύλε"· μισῶ ζῆν ἐς κενὸν οὐ μεθύων.

(5 G-P = Ath. 11.473a)

Let us drink, and so over wine I hope to invent
    something new, some sweet and refined song.
Drench me with amphoras of Chian wine and say, "Play,
    Hedylus." I hate to live pointlessly, unintoxicated.

Hedylus' opening πίνωμεν is clearly an echo of the πίνωμεν in Asclepiades' *sphragis* poem (16.5 G-P).[130] But wine in Asclepiades was presented as solace for the pain of love, while here it functions as a source of poetic inspiration. As in Posidippus, drink for Hedylus has become an overarching metaphor for the process of composition. Yet the metaphorical torrent that Hedylus calls for ("drench me with amphoras of Chian wine") seems deliberately chosen to contrast with the milder bedewing that Posidippus summons in 1 G-P.[131] This impression is confirmed by the final phrase in which Hedylus declares the only life worth living to be a drunken one. Hedylus seems, then, to have adopted Posidippus' use of the symposium as metaphor for the epigram collection, while distinguishing himself by rejecting Posidippus' middle position between drunkenness and sobriety, symbolizing the production of learned yet inspired poetry that comes from the consumption of watered wine. His own poetic ego is that of an uninhibited imbiber, and the few epigrams that survive for us do suggest that lack of restraint, whether in drink, food, or sex, was thematized

---

130. Not recognizing the conventional nature of Hedylus' self-idenfication here, Calderini (1984) 96 states: "restio ad esternare le sensazioni del proprio vivere intimo, in questo solo epigramma il poeta parla in prima persona." Reading the poem in purely biographical terms, Calderini then concludes that Hedylus here gives evidence for the bohemian nature of his artistic existence.

131. Gow-Page (1965) II 293 explain that the κάδος was a vessel "for storing . . . or carrying liquids, not, except in comic exaggeration. . ., of drinking-vessels" and that, as the equivalent of an amphora, it held about nine gallons.

in the collection. This programmatic poem also declares Hedylus' originality by proclaiming that the poetry he will compose under the influence of wine will be a new discovery (τι νέον ... εὕροιμ'), "some sweet and refined song" (λεπτὸν καί τι μελιχρὸν ἔπος). The terminology used here obviously recalls Callimachus' poetic program, as stated, for instance, in his description of Aratus' *Phaenomena* (μελιχρότατον and λεπταὶ ῥήσιες, 56 G-P). While it would be necessary to know the relative chronology of the two poems in order to understand the full significance of Hedylus' statement for the poetic debates of the day, it does seem clear that Hedylus and Callimachus share similar stylistic preferences, even though one writes as a water drinker and the other as a lover of wine.

Hedylus 6 G-P is linked to 5 by a number of linguistic echoes (πίνωμεν, πίνει; παρ' οἶνον, παρ' οἶνον; κάδοις, κάδοις; παῖζε, παίζει; μεθύων, μέθυε) so that Athenaeus' quotation of the two in the same context may provide an indication that they were found close together in the *Epigrammata*:

> ἐξ ἠοῦς εἰς νύκτα καὶ ἐκ νυκτὸς πάλι Σωκλῆς
>   εἰς ἠοῦν πίνει τετραχόοισι κάδοις,
> εἶτ' ἐξαίφνης που τυχὸν οἴχεται· ἀλλὰ παρ' οἶνον
>   Σικελίδεω παίζει πουλὺ μελιχρότερον,
> ἐστὶ δὲ δὴ πουλὺ στιβαρώτερος· ὡς δ' ἐπιλάμπει
>   ἡ χάρις, ὥστε, φίλος, καὶ γράφε καὶ μέθυε.[132]

(6 G-P = Ath. 11.473a)

From dawn to night and again from night to dawn
  Socles drinks from three-gallon jugs,
and then suddenly he may go away. But over the wine
  his trifles are sweeter than those of Sicelidas,
and he's also more vigorous. His poetry has such charm,
  friend, that you too should get drunk and write.

Reitzenstein's citation of the epigram as evidence that such pieces were performed at symposia continues to have influence on critical thinking about the poem.[133] Gow declares that it "was no doubt intended for, and perhaps composed impromptu on, some convivial occasion," and Calderini claims that it documents a poetic contest between Asclepiades and Socles.[134] Far from being a true drinking song, the epigram in fact provides evidence that epigram composition now took written form (γράφε, 6). As a poem composed for the book, it reflects upon Socles' habitual behavior at symposia and fails to provide any dramatic setting at all for the speech act it represents. The friend to whom

---

132. Gow-Page retain the πολύ of the ms. in their text, although in their commentary, (1965) *ad* 5, they defend πουλύ.

133. Reitzenstein (1893) 89.

134. Gow-Page (1965) II 293, citing Wilamowitz (1924) I 144; Calderini (1984) 101.

Hedylus offers advice on poetic composition in the final line could as well be the reader of the collection as a dramatized internal auditor.

The poem has presented other difficulties of interpretation as well. Scholars have been puzzled by the reason for Socles' sudden disappearance from the drinking party, and Giangrande has offered the explanation that he leaves on a *komos*. According to this interpretation, Socles surpasses Asclepiades not only in the sweetness of his verse but also in the strength (στιβαρώτερος, 6.5) of his ability to withstand the enervating effect of wine on sexual performance.[135] But though στιβαρός originally connoted physical strength, it developed within the Hellenistic period a secondary application to literary style. Dionysius of Hali-carnassus uses the term for the diction of both Thucydides and Pindar (*Thuc.* 24, *Comp.* 22), and it appears in an epigram by Antipater of Thessalonica (13.2 G-P, *Garland* = *AP* 7.39.2) to describe the majestic eloquence of Aeschylus. As the comparative στιβαρώτερος comes just after the comparative μελιχρότερον, which clearly refers to Socles' poetry, it is hard to deny it any reference to style, but the change to the nominative would seem to support as well Giangrande's claim that in the context of Socles' prodigious consumption of wine the adjective may connote physical endurance. The answer to this interpretive dilemma is to recognize that here, once again, the drinking of wine at a symposium is symbolic for the composition of poetry, so that writing in a manly style and drinking manly amounts of wine coalesce into the same realm of activity. Under this reading of the poem, Socles suddenly leaves the party, not for some sexual rendevous (of which there is no hint in the text), but to commit to writing the poetry that his drinking has inspired. Hedylus' concluding advice, καὶ γράφε καὶ μέθυε, follows naturally only if there is some allusion in the earlier lines to written, rather than oral, composition.

Although we have relatively few epigrams from the hand of Hedylus, the evidence they provide indicates that the *Epigrammata* known to Athenaeus (or at least some section within such a comprehensive edition) was unified by the-matic consistency and an identifiable poetic ego. Preserving the fictionalized symposium setting from the collections of Asclepiades and Posidippus, Hedylus varied the developing tradition of erotic-sympotic epigram by casting his own poetic persona, not as a lover, but as satirical symposiast. Love appears in Hedy-lus' epigrams, not as the subjective experience of the poet, but, together with eating and drinking, as one of the unrestrained behaviors that typically occur at symposia. While the epigrammatist sometimes takes a critical perspective on those excessively indulging in the sympotic pleasures of wine, food, and sex, the licentiousness invited by unrestrained drinking is also used figuratively to set out the poetics governing the collection. In 5 G-P, Hedylus' signature piece recalling in various ways programmatic poems in the collections of Asclepiades

---

135. Giangrande (1968) 160–63.

and Posidippus (Asclep. 16; Posid. 1, 9), Hedylus attributes the novelty of his own "refined and sweet" verse to the inspiration gained from huge quantities of wine. As lack of restraint characterizes the often satirized subjects of the epigram collection, so too it gives character to the epigrammatic poet.

Reitzenstein's thesis concerning a joint edition by Asclepiades, Posidippus, and Hedylus has undergone a revival of interest in recent years. But our examination of the poetry of these three epigrammatists has shown that at least one of the bases for Reitzenstein's theory—the large number of imitations of Asclepiades by Posidippus and Hedylus—can be explained by the likelihood that Posidippus and Hedylus composed erotic-sympotic epigram books that looked back and alluded to the seminal collection of Asclepiades. The alternative ascriptions cannot be explained this way, however, and it does seems possible that Meleager used an edition that combined the poetry of these three, perhaps by grouping the variations on a given theme. Scribal discrepancies that crept in over time would then account for the uncertain attributions, which always involve only two of the poets rather than all three. Even so, there is no reason to suppose that the three epigrammatists collaborated on this edition, or that Hedylus was its editor (as Cameron has suggested). Its genesis could well belong to the second half of the third century or to sometime in the second. Even though we cannot prove the existence of multi-authored anthologies before Meleager, it would in no way be surprising if small anthologies of thematically related poems were produced in the period between the first flowering of Hellenistic literary epigram and the Meleagrian crystalization of it.

CHAPTER FIVE

The Book and the Scholar:
Callimachus' *Epigrammata*

Callimachus' *Epigrammata* formed the most famous and admired of Greek epigram collections. Athenaeus informs us that it belonged to the canon of works read by boys in school (15.669c), and Martial, who was undoubtedly a connoisseur, awards Callimachus the palm of victory among earlier Greek epigrammatists (4.23). Pliny praises Callimachus' epigrams (obliquely, through comparison with a Latin epigrammatist) for their charm and human feeling, their sweetness, expressiveness, and wit (*Epist.* 4.3.3–4).[1] We may also mention numerous echoes in the Roman elegists, whose claim to Callimachus as a model for love elegy was surely based, very largely, on his erotic epigrams.[2]

There is no plausible reason to deny that the *Epigrammata* was issued as a poetry book by Callimachus himself.[3] The various references to the *Epigrammata* of Callimachus in ancient authors precisely parallel references made to the *Iambi*, a copy of which has been found on papyrus with the heading Ἴαμβοι (P.Oxy. 1011).[4] Also indicative of the author's own editorship are the ancient

---

1. In praising the Greek epigrams and mimiambi of Arrius Antoninus: "quantum ibi humanitatis venustatis, quam dulcia illa quam amantia quam arguta quam recta! Callimachum me vel Heroden, vel si quid his melius, tenere credebam."

2. For the claim of Callimachus as model, see Prop. 2.1.39–42, 2.34.31–32, 3.1.1–2, 3.9.43, 4.1.64; Ov. *Ars Am.* 3.329, *Rem. Am.* 381–82, 759–60.

3. For the argument that Meleager did not collect scattered epigrams of Callimachus but worked from an author-edited collection, see Amédée Hauvette, *Les épigrammes de Callimaque: étude critique et littéraire* (Paris, 1907) 8–10, printed also in *REG* 20 (1907) 302–305; Émile Cahen, *Callimaque et son oeuvre poétique* (Paris, 1929) 206–8. See also Pfeiffer II xcii, who accepts without question the existence of an epigram book before the time of Meleager but leaves open the possibility of editing by a scholar other than the author.

4. Ath. 7.327a (ἐν Ἐπιγράμμασιν), 15.669c (τὰ Καλλιμάχου ... ἐπιγράμματα); D.L. 1.79 (ἐν τοῖς Ἐπιγράμμασι), 2.111 (ἐν Ἐπιγράμμασιν); Achilles Tatius *Vita Arati* 4 (ἐν τοῖς Ἐπιγράμμασιν); Eustratius in Arist. *Eth. Nic.* 6.7.2 in *Commentaria in Aristotelem Graeca*, ed. G. Heylbut (Berlin, 1892) XX 320–21 (ἐν τῷ ἐπιγράμματι); Steph. Byz. *s. v.* Δύμη

commentaries on the *Epigrammata*. While the commentary by Archibius cannot be dated earlier than the first century B.C., it seems excessively cautious to deny the work referred to as εἰς τὰ ἐπιγράμματα Καλλιμάχου (*Et. Gen. s. v.* ἀλυτάρχης) to Hedylus the satirical epigrammatist, who must have been an Alexandrian scholar-poet in the mode of Callimachus himself. While it was once thought that Hellenistic poetry did not receive scholarly attention so early, notes on a late third-century papyrus of the *Aetia* have now shown commentary on Callimachus to have begun by a quarter century or so after his death.[5] At a time when other epigrammatists, like Posidippus, were issuing authoritative editions of their own poetry, it is incredible that Callimachus, who spent so much of his life bringing order to the haphazard remains of earlier Greek literature, would not have provided that his own epigrams be read in an artistic arrangement.

It is in fact likely that in the late 240s Callimachus issued a final edition of his complete poetic oeuvre, reediting some earlier works and even placing his poetry books and individual poems in the order in which he wished them preserved for posterity. At that time he apparently put the *Aetia* in final form by adding the so-called "Victoria Berenices" as the first episode of the third book of the *Aetia* and the "Lock of Berenice" as the concluding episode of that work and by composing the prologue and epilogue as well. In the last line of the epilogue he declares that he now passes to the "pedestrian pasture of the Muses" (fr. 112.9), a reference to the *Iambi* that follow in our papyrus (P.Oxy. 1011). The Diegeseis indicate that the *Iambi* were followed by four melic poems (not apparently arranged as a poetry book unless they were in fact a continuation of the *Iambi*)[6] and that these in turn were succeeded by the *Hecale*, Callimachus' short epic poem. Since Callimachus' six hymns display a logical arrangement in the manuscript tradition in which they descend, they too were likely organized

---

(ἐν Ἐπιγράμμασιν); Schol. γένος Dionys. Per. in *Geographi Graeci minores*, ed. K. Müller (Paris, 1882) II 427 (ἐν τοῖς Ἐπιγράμμασι); Schol. Ov. *Ib.* 591 (a Callimacho epigramma); Caesius Bassus in *Grammatici Latini*, ed. H. Keil (Leipzig, 1874) VI 255, VI 261 (in epigrammatibus); *Suda s. v.* Ἀρχίβιος (τῶν Καλλιμάχου ἐπιγραμμάτων); *s.v.* Μαριανός (Καλλιμάχου ... ἐπιγραμμάτων); *Et. Gen. s. v.* ἀλυτάρχης (τὰ ἐπιγράμματα Καλλιμάχου). Similar references to the *Iambi* occur, for which see Dawson 133. About the beginning of the sixth century A.D., Marianus produced paraphrases in iambic verse of several Callimachean books—the *Hecale, Hymns, Aetia,* and *Epigrammata* (*Suda, s. v.* Μαριανός = test. 24 Pf.).

5. Gow-Page (1965) II 289 find the existence of a Hedylus commentary surprising "unless it was by some other Hedylus." But in addition*SH*) to the papyrus commentary on the *Aetia* (255, 258, 261 *SH*), we now have from the second century B.C. a commentary on a riddle poem about an oyster (983–84 *SH*); see P. J. Parsons, "Callimachus: Victoria Berenices," *ZPE* 25 (1977) 4–5.

6. For the scholarship on the number of *Iambi*, see Clayman (1980) 4–7, who follows Dawson 132–33 in the belief that the book of *Iambi* consisted of only thirteen poems, not seventeen. Horace's book of seventeen *Epodes* may, however, have been based on his knowledge of an edition of Callimachus that included the *Iambi* followed by four melic poems to fill out the roll.

by the author, although we do not know what their position may have been in the final reediting.[7] Like these other works, then, the collection known in antiquity as Callimachus' *Epigrammata* was, in all likelihood, an author-edited poetry book given authoritative form in the late 240s B.C. If Callimachus, like Posidippus, had issued earlier epigram collections, limited by type or theme, these have vanished from the record without a trace. I therefore treat all of Callimachus' surviving epigrams as part of a comprehensive edition known as the *Epigrammata*.

Before turning to Callimachus' epigram collection itself, it is useful to consider what the remains of his other poetry books reveal about principles of arrangement used in his collections. My discussion will be limited to the two books most certainly edited by Callimachus himself, the *Aetia* and the *Iambi*. While the *Iambi* consists of a series of thirteen discrete poems, the *Aetia*, though not a continuous poem (ἓν ἄεισμα διηνεκές, fr. 1.3 Pf.), is divided into four books of *aitia* that are connected by various narratorial devices. Since the beginnings and endings of these episodes were marked off in the papyri by *paragraphoi* and *coronides*, they were clearly perceived as forming a poetry book.

Although we still have only a small portion of the poetry from the *Aetia*, we do know from the Florentine scholia and the Diegeseis the sequence of episodes for the first part of Book 1 and for most of Books 3 and 4.[8] As a result, certain principles of ordering become evident. Beginnings and endings are connected through ring composition: the prologue, including the dream of meeting the Muses on Helicon (frs. 1–2), is echoed in the reference to Hesiod in the epilogue (fr. 112); and the epinician for Berenice that opens Book 3 (254–268c *SH*) is balanced by the "Lock of Berenice" that closes Book 4 (fr. 110). It has been posited that a fragment dealing with the poet's poverty and mentioning a dream (253 *SH*) may have served as the conclusion of Book 2, thus echoing the Heliconian dream scene that follows the prologue (fr. 2 Pf.).[9] If this is correct, a

7. For discussion of the hymns as a poetry book, see D. L. Clayman, "Hellenistic Poetry at Alexandria," in *Ancient Writers: Greece and Rome*, ed. T. James Luce (New York, 1982) I 465 and Neil Hopkinson, ed., *Callimachus: Hymn to Demeter* (Cambridge, 1984) 13; M. W. Haslam, "Callimachus' Hymns," in *Callimachus*, ed. M. A. Harder, R. F. Regtuit, and G. C. Wakker (Groningen, 1993) 115.

8. The most comprehensive study of the structure of the *Aetia* is Nita Krevans, *The Poet as Editor: Callimachus, Virgil, Horace, Propertius and the Development of the Poetic Book* (Diss. Princeton, 1984) 230–300. See also A. Swiderek, "La structure des *Aitia* de Callimaque à la lumière des nouvelles découvertes papyrologiques," *JJP* 5 (1951) 229–35; A. Harder, "Aspects of the Structure of Callimachus' *Aetia*," in *Callimachus*, ed. Harder *et al.* (1993) 99–110.

9. Krevans (1984) 236–37; A. Harder, "Some Thoughts about Callimachus *SH* 239 and 253," *ZPE* 67 (1987) 29–30; Cameron (1995) 137–40. Another candidate for the opening of Book 2, fr. 178 Pf. on Callimachus' symposium conversation with a merchant named Theugenes, is discussed by J. E. G. Zetzel, "On the Opening of Callimachus, *Aetia* II," *ZPE* 42 (1981) 31–33.

neatly symmetrical pattern of ring composition emerges. Books 1 and 2 and Books 3 and 4 are both framed by balancing episodes, while the *Aetia* as a whole is framed by a prologue and epilogue.

Within the *Aetia* books themselves there seems to be no rigid plan or exact symmetry, but the poet does tend to group related stories in clusters. Examples include three *aitia* for insulting rituals (frs. 3–25), two *aitia* for unusual marriage customs (frs. 67–77), and dual poems on statues of Hera (frs. 100–101) and on statues of Apollo (fr. 114).[10] It has also been pointed out that the opening sequence in Book 1—on the Muses, Charites, and Apollo Aegletes (frs. 2–21)—concern deities connected with poetry and may therefore have a programmatic force.[11] The pattern may descend from the songs that open the *Theognidea* (two to Apollo, one to Artemis, and one to the Muses and Charites), and those that begin the book of Attic scolia (Athena, Demeter and Persephone, Leto, and Pan).

In addition to the devices of ring composition and grouping by theme, the *aitia* of Books 1–2 are also linked by the narrative device of dialogue with the Muses. Recalling his dream of meeting the Muses on Helicon (fr. 2), Callimachus begins each episode by posing a question to one of the goddesses and then narrating her reply. Some of the stories seem, however, to be told by Callimachus himself as digressions from or complements to the episodes narrated by the Muses. It has been argued, for instance, that the story of Thiodamas, in which Heracles kills an ox (frs. 24–25), is Callimachus' reply to the Muses' similar narrative explaining a sacrifice at Lindus (frs. 22–23).[12] In Books 3 and 4 the dialogue with the Muses disappears in favor of discrete episodes not linked by any narrative device. In most of these *aitia*, the poet speaks in his own voice and often addresses the subject of the narrative. In a smaller number of poems the subject of the *aition* is itself enlivened to speak, as in the cases of Simonides' tomb (fr. 64), a Pelasgian wall (fr. 97), and Berenice's catasterized lock (fr. 110). We may also mention an unplaced poem in which the poet holds a conversation with a statue of Apollo at Delos (fr. 114.4–17). As this last example makes clear, the source for Callimachus' animation of inanimate objects is the epigrammatic tradition, the giving of voice to stone. While Books 1 and 2 present a form of catalogue poetry that probably found a precedent in Antimachus' *Lyde*, Books 3 and 4 seem to show the influence of Hellenistic epigram books. Even though these structural differences distinguish the first two books from the second two, the *Aetia* as a whole is given cohesion by the persistent interaction between narrator and narratorial audience. As a consequence of the reader's continuing involvement

10. Krevans (1984) 242–43 posits that fr. 114.1–3 concludes an *aition* involving the Milesian statue of Apollo, while fr. 114.4–17 preserves a separate dialogue between the poet and a statue of Delian Apollo; Giulio Massimilla, ed., *Aitia: libri primo e secondo* (Pisa, 1996) 375 concurs.

11. Harder (1993) 100–103.

12. A. S. Hollis, "Teuthis and Callimachus, *Aetia* Book 1," *CQ* 32 (1982) 118.

in the question of who speaks to whom, the focus of interest is shifted from the subject matter itself to the manner of narration.

Only relatively small portions of the *Iambi* survive for us, but the Diegeseis provide as well the sequence of the poems, their first lines, and summaries of their contents. While the *Iambi* display a controlled *poikilia* through differences in generic form, meter, and dialect, scholars have identified several cohesive principles operating within this variety.[13] *Iambi* 1–5 and 13 are written in the Ionic dialect and choliambic meter, apparently as a generic signal of Callimachus' affinity with archaic iambography. *Iambi* 6–12, on the other hand, display a variety of iambic meters, and some are written in the Doric dialect. Organization by purely formal features, such as meter and dialect, gestures toward techniques of scholarly editing; yet in a poet like Callimachus formal arrangement seems effortlessly combined with artistic design. The arrangement of poems within the collection is anything but mechanical.

The opening poem, in which Hipponax returns from the dead to chastise quarrelsome scholars (fr. 191), and the concluding piece, in which Callimachus defends his use of poetic variety, or *polyeideia* (fr. 203), concern Callimachus' generic models and his innovative relation to them. While poetics are appropriate topics for points of opening and closing, I hesitate to speak of ring composition. The very number of the *Iambi*—thirteen—poses an obstacle to the type of balanced symmetry found in the *Aetia*. The reincarnation of Hipponax as Callimachus' surrogate Muse leads naturally to a sequence of three poems concerning speech, poetry, and rivalry (*Ia.* 2–4). Likewise, *Iambus* 12, in which the poet laments the current preference for money over poetry, prepares for the final poem defending Callimachus' literary choices. The *Iambi* thus display groupings of poems on similar themes, as do the *Aetia*. While some scholars have proposed that the iambic book was structured through concentric circles in a manner familiar from Roman poetry books,[14] I am not inclined to accept such an elaborate architectonic scheme as an intentional ordering principle for the book. The separation of paired poems by one intervening poem (2 and 4 as fables, 3 and 5 as erotica, 7 and 9 on statues of Hermes) does seem, however, a more clearly discernible device. We can thus posit two primary structuring devices in the *Iambi*—grouping in sequence (e.g., 1–4, 12–13) and placement of paired poems in noncontiguous positions (2 and 4, 3 and 5, 7 and 9), devices that by operating together create a desired tension between variety and cohesion.

As in the *Aetia*, Callimachus' manipulation of the voices speaking in the *Iambi*, those of himself and others, becomes the element that controls the collection's fragmented heterogeneity, its unbalancing of inchoate symmetries. The angry

13. See Dawson 142–44; Clayman (1980) 48–49.

14. Dawson 142–43 asserts that no "Roman *Gedichtbuch* was more carefully organized than the *Iambi*," while Clayman (1980) 49 elaborates his scheme of concentric circles.

Hipponax in *Iambus* 1 sets the critical tone that carries over to the poet's voice in 2–5 and again in 12–13. In the middle section the voice of a less satirical Callimachus alternates with a series of other voices—a statue of Hermes (7), a dialogue between the lover of a boy and an ithyphallic Hermes (9), and a deceased brothel keeper who addresses those passing his tomb (11). As in the *Aetia*, Callimachus here juxtaposes poems in his own voice with others presenting voices drawn from the epigrammatic tradition. It is not surprising, then, that the alternation of speakers observable in *Iambi* 6–11 finds some parallel in Hellenistic epigram books; we have already observed a similar kind of alternation, that of gender and epigram type, in both the Mnasalces fragment and the middle section of the Theocritean collection.

Since the *Aetia* and the *Iambi* were given final form no earlier than 245 B.C., I would suggest that both were significantly influenced by the several single-authored epigram collections produced in the earlier decades of the third century. The observable connection between the epigram genre and Callimachus' other poetry books makes it all the more reasonable to posit that his epigram book shared some of the features found in the *Aetia* and the *Iambi*. In attempting to discover what is knowable about the *Epigrammata*, then, we may justifiably look for evidence of opening and closing statements concerning poetics, organization by thematic grouping or by pairing (with or without intervening poems) and by tensions created through sequences of speaking voices within the epigrams. But above all, we may expect to find in Callimachus' epigram collection the same kind of structural aesthetic found in his other poetry books, one that eschews unity for variety, symmetry for imbalance, and singularity of voice or view for a manipulated heteroglossia. And even if such an aesthetic is typical of Callimachean or Hellenistic poetry books in general, it can be argued that Callimachus' *Epigrammata*, with its numerous brief poems and its mixture of epigram types, was perhaps the purest example.

THE *EPIGRAMMATA*

Callimachus' *Epigrammata* was a collection of more (probably considerably more) than sixty epigrams primarily in elegiac couplets with an admixture of poems in other meters.[15] Included were erotic, dedicatory, and sepulchral epigrams as well as a number of epigrams, largely on literary topics, that do not fit into these three main divisions. Quite possibly the collection was sectioned by epigram type or theme, in the manner of the Posidippus collection on the Milan Papyrus. As in that collection, the categories employed by Callimachus were likely more

---

15. A scholarly commentary on Callimachus' epigrams remains a desideratum. Pfeiffer and Gow-Page (1965) are now supplemented by Luigi Coco, *Callimaco: epigrammi* (Manduria, 1988), who offers a good summary of scholarship on individual poems but includes little original material.

various than those we now construct on the basis of Meleager's divisions. Since the epigrams in the Posidippus collection are all elegiac, the new papyrus gives us no clue as to whether Callimachus' nonelegiac epigrams were separated by meter or interspersed with elegiac poems on the basis of theme.[16] The material itself, which was likely composed over a great many years, perhaps sometimes for inscription, but more often for a fictive setting, whether written or oral,[17] had an innate heterogeneity that could easily be translated into a pleasing variety. More difficult to determine, given only the scattered remnants that survive of the book, are the means by which Callimachus provided cohesion to his miscellaneous epigrams.

Once again, I suggest that the reader tends to associate the artistic integrity of the epigram book with the projected persona of the poet. Although Callimachus was much indebted to other epigrammatists (especially to Asclepiades, Posidippus, and Leonidas), he did not identify his artistic presence, as they did, by gender or age, by class or philosophical ideology, or by a limited emotional and chronological perspective. The Callimachean persona is based on a more elusive quality that readers have often interpreted as personality.[18] I here argue that his creative presence within the collection is detectible through his constant self-reflection, in both theory and practice, upon his own literary, intellectual, and emotional position. All of Callimachus' literary works are informed by a reliance on art (τέχνῃ κρίνετε, μὴ σχοίνῳ Περσίδι τὴν σοφίην, "judge my wisdom by art, not the Persian chain," fr. 1.17–18 Pf.), which is not to be understood simply as technical skill, but as an acute awareness of the cultural and literary sources that contribute to the composition at hand. For epigram this means, in part, attention to the history of the genre, transference from its functional existence on stone or in the symposium to a more purely aesthetic form within the confines of the book. While Callimachus' epigrams run the gamut from what appear to be simple inscriptions to overt statements of poetic creed, it is largely through arrangement, the juxtaposition of poem with poem, that Callimachus melds theory with practice and brings to bear the force of his

16. That Callimachus' short nonelegiac poems were considered epigrams is clear from Caesius Bassus, *Grammatici Latini* VI 255, 261 = frs. 402, 401 Pf. Separation by meter occurs in *AP* 13, which has an ancient origin, and in the Theocritean collection. But both of these formations were post-Meleagrian and perhaps influenced by his limitation of epigram to poems in elegiac meter.

17. A. Köhnken, "Gattungstypik in kallimacheischen Weihepigrammen," *Religio Graeco-Romana: Festschrift für Walter Pötscher*, ed. Joachim Dalfen, G. Petersmann, and F. Schwarz (Horn, 1993) 119–30 has attempted to define the essentially literary character of Callimachus' dedicatory epigrams.

18. Cf., for instance, Fraser I 594: "Callimachus, in his epigrams as elsewhere, is very aware of his audience, and in all his various moods conscious of his own personality and of his significance as poet. He strikes ... a note of intellectual and (still more) emotional self-criticism."

personality, his self-reflection on himself and his art, to the epigram book as a whole.

Dedicatory Epigrams

In an earlier chapter I argued that five of Callimachus' fifteen surviving dedications occur in the *AP* in a sequence that, in all likelihood, descends from the *Epigrammata* (*AP* 6.146–50). We will now examine this sequence in more detail:

καὶ πάλιν, Εἰλείθυια, Λυκαινίδος ἐλθὲ καλεύσης
   εὔλοχος ὠδίνων ὧδε σὺν εὐτοκίη,
ὡς τόδε νῦν μέν, ἄνασσα, κόρης ὕπερ, ἀντὶ δὲ παιδός
   ὕστερον εὐώδης ἄλλο τι νηὸς ἔχοι.

                  (23 G-P = 53 Pf. = *AP* 6.146)

And come here again, Eileithyia, when Lycaenis calls,
   bringing successful birth with easy delivery from pain
So that, as now you have this gift for a girl, mistress,
   your fragrant temple may have another for a boy.

τὸ χρέος ὡς ἀπέχεις, Ἀσκληπιέ, τὸ πρὸ γυναικός
   Δημοδίκης Ἀκέσων ὤφελεν εὐξάμενος,
γιγνώσκειν· ἢν δ᾽ ἄρα λάθῃ καὶ δίς μιν ἀπαιτῇς,
   φησὶ παρέξεσθαι μαρτυρίην ὁ πίναξ.[19]

                  (24 G-P = 54 Pf. = *AP* 6.147)

Know, Asclepius, that you have received payment for the debt
   Aceson owed because of his vow on behalf of his wife
Demodice. If you forget and demand payment a second time,
   the tablet says that it will bear witness for him.

τῷ με Κανωπίτᾳ Καλλίστιον εἴκοσι μύξαις
   πλούσιον ἡ Κριτίου λύχνον ἔθηκε θεῷ
εὐξαμένα περὶ παιδὸς Ἀπελλίδος· ἐς δ᾽ ἐμὰ φέγγη
   ἀθρήσας φήσεις, "Ἕσπερε, πῶς ἔπεσες;"

                  (16 G-P = 55 Pf. = *AP* 6.148)

Calliston, the wife of Critias, dedicated me, a lamp rich
   with twenty wicks, to the Canopian god, in payment of a vow
made for her daughter Apellis. When you look into my lights,
   you will say, "Hesperus, how did you fall?"

φησὶν ὅ με στήσας Εὐαίνετος—οὐ γὰρ ἔγωγε
   γιγνώσκω—νίκης ἀντί με τῆς ἰδίης
ἀγκεῖσθαι χάλκειον ἀλέκτορα Τυνδαρίδῃσι.
   πιστεύω Φαίδρου παιδὶ Φιλοξενίδεω.

                  (25 G-P = 56 Pf. = *AP* 6.149)

---

19. In line 3 I have printed Stadtmüller's addition of δίς to an obviously corrupt text. Pfeiffer claims that μιν must refer to Aceson and assumes a missing accusative before καί, but Gow-Page *ad loc.* point out that after χρέος an *acc. rei* is not required.

Euaenetus who placed me here declares—for I myself have
  no knowledge—that I, a bronze cock, am dedicated
to the Tyndaridae because of a victory I won.
  I trust the son of Phaedrus, son of Philoxenus.

Ἰναχίης ἕστηκεν ἐν Ἴσιδος ἡ Θάλεω παῖς
  Αἰσχυλὶς Εἰρήνης μητρὸς ὑποσχεσίη.

(18 G-P = 57 Pf. = AP 6.150)

In the temple of Inachian Isis stands Aeschylis, Thales'
  daughter, because of a promise made by her mother Eirene.

Certain formal principles of ordering are immediately evident. Epigrams 23
and 24 are both dedications addressed to deities (cf. Εἰλείθυια and Ἀσκληπιέ,
each in the first line), one of whom has aided a woman in childbirth and one
of whom has cured a woman of disease. The speaker in both is that impersonal
epigrammatist who traditionally acts as a voiceless surrogate for the dedicator, a
woman in one epigram and a man in the other. Epigrams 16 and 25 are likewise
paired, as poems in which the speakers are the dedicated objects themselves,
a lamp for Sarapis and a bronze cock for the Tyndaridae; both dedications
are made on behalf of children or adolescents, Callistion's daughter Apellis
and Phaedrus' son Euaenetus.[20] The fifth epigram in the series, a single couplet
commemorating a statue of the girl Aeschylis, continues the theme of dedications
made on behalf of young people but probably also acted as a transitional
poem (to something now lost) through its changed mode of presentation—
its old-fashioned simplicity. In formal terms, then, Callimachus' dedicatory
sequence is somewhat reminiscent of the papyrus fragment containing epigrams
by Mnasalces (though that included both dedications and epitaphs), in that it
provides linkage by juxtaposing poems displaying similar themes or voices and
at the same time creates variety by alternating other features such as gender.

Callimachus' sequence becomes even more interesting when we pass beyond
formal elements of design to those features that may be construed as evidence
for the presence of the epigrammatist's own personality. Both 23 and 24 are
ostensibly thank offerings presented to a deity, but both deviate seriously in
tone from the more traditional exemplars of the form. As an example of the
conventional type, we may look to 18 where the spare dignity of the distich
with its simple verb (ἕστηκεν) and series of names suggests the statue's elegance;
the very simplicity of the poem thus enhances the glory of the three parties

---

20. While I have analyzed the sequence of 6.146–49 as a set of two pairs, an observant
reader may find a more complicated structural connection. The presence of the key words
γιγνώσκειν and γιγνώσκω (on which, see the discussion below) in the second and fourth
poems of the sequence (24 and 25 G-P) suggests a linkage of these two, thus creating an
intertwining of the two pairs.

involved—the goddess, the dedicating mother, and the represented maiden.[21] But 23, despite the complimentary reference to Eileithyia's "fragrant temple," does not quite manage to convey a genuine feeling of gratitude; what the reader senses instead is Lycaenis' disappointment that the goddess has brought her a girl in place of the desired male child.[22] Epigram 24 scarcely makes any pretense at all that the relationship between deity and worshiper is other than a business transaction. Instead of the customary imperative "receive" (δέξαι; cf. 21.2 G-P = *AP* 6.347.2), politely requesting that the deity find the offering acceptable, Asclepius is told to "know" (γιγνώσκειν) that Aceson's "debt" has been paid. Worse yet, the epigram insinuates that Asclepius engages in sloppy bookkeeping, if not sleazy business tactics, and offers itself, in the form of the plaque on which it is inscribed, as a witness in case the god again demands payment.[23] The juxtaposition of these two poems within the collection encourages the reader to construe their particular deviations from convention as indicative of the poet's own religious attitudes. The "deconstruction" of the traditional relationship of god and worshiper, of the epigrammatic pretense that the exchange of gift and payment is always mutually satisfying, reflects the same fracturing of religious sensibility that Bulloch has identified in Callimachus' *Hymns*.[24] As the hymns often remind the reader of their distance from actual ritual by dramatizing their own cult settings, so here 24 calls attention to its fictiveness, to its necessary existence only in a book, by expressly stating what an inscribed epigram need never state, that its "voice" emanates from a written tablet (φησὶ ... ὁ πίναξ).

The second pair of 16 and 25, in which the speakers are the dedicated objects themselves, also calls into question the traditional rhetoric of such epigrams. Dedications spoken by a devoted object are among the earliest of Greek epigrams, like the well-known bronze statuette that reads, "Manticlus dedicated me to the Far-Darter" (326 *CEG*). Svenbro, in disputing the animist explanation of these first-person dedications, has pointed out that the ego of such inscriptions lacks "any psychological depth." He asserts that the first-person grammar reveals the presence or "hereness" of the inscribed object in contrast to the absence or "thereness" of the writer.[25] I suggest that Callimachus,

21. Cf. the comment of J. Ferguson, "The Epigrams of Callimachus," *G&R* 17 (1970) 69: "It is no ordinary skill which has woven a pattern to all intents and purposes out of five proper names and four other simple words."

22. Cf. E. A. Schmidt, "Interpretationen kallimacheischer Epigramme," *Hermes* 104 (1976) 149.

23. Hutchinson 72, in an interesting discussion of Callimachus' play with dedicatory voices, says of this epigram, "The tablet ... shows a dogged concern for its owner's interests, and a correspondingly suspicious attitude towards the god it addresses." See also the comments of D. Meyer, "Die Einbeziehung des Lesers in den Epigrammen des Kallimachos," in *Callimachus*, ed. Harder *et al.* 168–72, who provides an interesting treatment of Callimachus' fictive reader.

24. A. W. Bulloch, "The Future of a Hellensitic Illusion," *MH* 41 (1984) 209–30.

25. Svenbro 41–43.

by transferring these dedications from stone to book and by personalizing his objects with individualized character, essentially reverses the situation, making evident to the book reader the absence, or fictive existence, of the object that speaks and bringing to the reader's attention the presence (in absence) of the epigrammatist through his self-conscious manipulation of the written word. The lamp dedicated by Callistion in 16 does manage to convey the essential information about dedicator and deity, but its exaggerated pride in its own light, comparing its twenty wicks to a fallen Hesperus, undercuts the munificence of Callistion's gift by a hubristic assertion of its own self-worth. This undermining of the dedicatory setting reminds us that the object itself is only imaginary, the product of the poet's inventive mind. As Callistion's lamp is proud, so Euaenetus' cock is self-effacing. As a bronze cock, an object devoid of life, it cannot possibly know the circumstances of its own dedication (οὐ γὰρ ἔγωγε γιγνώσκω) and so attributes the information it gives us entirely to the young man who dedicates it (φησὶν ὅ με στήσας Εὐαίνετος).[26] But we as readers know that it is not Euaenetus, but Callimachus himself, who here reveals the great lie in the convention of the speaking object.

Other Callimachean dedications, whose position within the epigram book cannot now be known, also give overt indications of their fictiveness. A tragic mask of Dionysus, dedicated to the Muses by a boy in exchange for progress in his studies, speaks of itself, depreciatingly, as a "small" gift offered for a great benefaction (26 G-P = *AP* 6.310). Another mask, a comic one paired with the Dionysiac mask in the *AP* and just possibly in Callimachus' collection as well, reveals its imaginary status by pointing out to the reader what the viewer would already know, that the Pamphilus it represents is not the young lover but a dark-complected old man (27 G-P = *AP* 6.311). The dedication of a salt cellar to the Samothracian gods is not a meditation on an unusual offering, but an elaborate literary conceit based on the ambiguity of ἅλς, meaning both salt and sea (28 G-P = *AP* 6.301): Eudemus offers his salt cellar to the gods of seafaring because by eating cheap salt as his only condiment he has escaped "great storms of debt." The most complex and lovely of Callimachus' dedications is his poem on a nautilus shell dedicated by Selenaia to Aphrodite-Arsinoe in her shrine at Zephyrium (14 G-P = 5 Pf.). I have shown elsewhere that the epigram conveys much of its meaning by suggesting complex parallels between the nautilus and the girl who dedicated it: as a sailor the shell symbolizes Selenaia's successful crossing of the seas controlled by the marine Aphrodite and as an incubator for halcyon eggs it represents the potential fertility of the girl who apparently

---

26. Cf. Köhnken 129: "Damit wird die eigentliche Aufgabe eines Weihgegenstandes auf den Kopf gestellt, denn die Weihgabe z. B. für einen Sportsieg soll ja eigentlich für das Faktum des Sieges Zeugnis ablegen Gerade von dieser Aufgabe distanziert sich der kallimacheische Hahn." On the cock's acknowledgment of its own fictionality, see Meyer 166–67.

makes this dedication to the goddess of sexuality in anticipation of marriage.[27] Much of the poem's referentiality clearly relates to the occasional nature of its composition. But there is no reason to suppose that the poem did not also find a place in Callimachus' *Epigrammata* (probably the source from which Athenaeus cites it) where its references would assume a more indeterminate character. In that context, in conjunction with Callimachus' other dedicatory epigrams, the reader may feel even more strongly that behind the voice of the empty shell, which expressly mentions its own lifelessness (εἰμὶ γὰρ ἄπνους, 14.9), lies the vivid imagination of Callimachus himself.

Several other Callimachean dedications show no trace of self-irony and display the spare simplicity more typical of genuine inscriptions. Commentators have pointed to the high artistic merit of these poems but have otherwise had little to say about their purpose or function. I suggest that, whether or not they were actually composed for inscription, within Callimachus' epigram book they likely contributed to the project of enhancing meaning through arrangement. As an example of how this may have worked, we will examine two single distichs, which when juxtaposed, form a complementary and contrasting pair:

Ἄρτεμι, τὶν τόδ' ἄγαλμα Φιληρατὶς εἴσατο τῇδε·
ἀλλὰ σὺ μὲν δέξαι, πότνια, τὴν δὲ σάου.

(21 G-P = 33 Pf. = AP 6.347)

For you, Artemis, Phileratis set up here this statue.
You in turn, mistress, accept it and protect her.

τίν με, λεοντάγχ' ὦνα συοκτόνε, φήγινον ὄζον
θῆκε – τίς; – Ἀρχῖνος. – ποῖος; – ὁ Κρής. – δέχομαι.

(22 G-P = 34 Pf. = AP 6.351)

For you, lion-strangling, boar-slaying lord, I, an oak club, was dedicated ...
– By whom? – Archinus. – From where? – He's a Cretan. – I accept.

The dedication to Artemis displays an archaic elegance that helps Callimachus avoid any charge of excessive artificiality in style. But it also provides a prototype for the epigram formula that the reader must have in mind in order to appreciate fully Callimachus' deviation in 22. Here just as the dedicated club is about to mention the name and ethnic of its dedicator, the god impatiently interrupts, "Who? From where?" When the answers prove satisfactory, perhaps because of the manly reputation of Cretans, the god accepts (δέχομαι), turning the imperative conventionally spoken by the dedicator (δέξαι in 21.2 G-P) to a first-person verb. But the joke is not just a formally literary one, since Heracles' curt, impatient questions charmingly convey his known personality. The unexpected insertion of the god's voice with his abrupt, no-nonsense style to convert the

27. K. J. Gutzwiller, "The Nautilus, the Halcyon, and Selenaia: Callimachus's *Epigram* 5 Pf. = 14 G.–P.," *CA* 11 (1992) 194–209.

straightforward dedication into a dialogue is all the more effective because of the contrast with the flattering vocatives in the first line.

A final dedication is aesthetically interesting because of its complicated internal structure:

Δήμητρι τῇ Πυλαίῃ,
τῇ τοῦτον οὐκ Πελασγῶν
Ἀκρίσιος τὸν νηὸν ἐδείματο, ταῦθ' ὁ Ναυκρατίτης
καὶ τῇ κάτω θυγατρί
τὰ δῶρα Τιμόδημος
εἵσατο τῶν κερδέων δεκατεύματα· καὶ γὰρ εὔξαθ' οὕτως.

(19 G-P = 39 Pf. = AP 13.25)

> For Pylaean Demeter,
> For whom Acrisius of the Pelasgians
> Built this temple, and for her daughter below,
> Timodemus of Naucratis
> Set up these gifts
> As tithings from his profits. For so he had vowed.

The underlying pattern of the poem is one of the most common for dedicatory epigrams: τῷ θεῷ ὁ δεῖνα ταῦτα δῶρα εἵσατο (cf. 21 G-P).[28] But through the use of unusual meters, creating two matching metrical sequences (AABAAB), Callimachus has managed to postpone the revelation of the poem's underlying structure until the reader reaches the last line. The relative clause naming Acrisius as the mythical founder of Demeter's temple replicates by its insertion of οὐκ Πελασγῶν Ἀκρίσιος within the phrase τοῦτον ... τὸν νηόν the larger pattern of the poem as a whole, in which nouns and their modifiers (ταῦθ' ... τὰ δῶρα, ὁ Ναυκρατίτης ... Τιμόδημος) or correlated nouns (Δήμητρι ... θυγατρί) are everywhere separated, so that the reader is forced to hold in abeyance closure of any grammatical construction until the end of the epigram. This mentally taxing structure creates parallelisms between metrically equivalent positions and so enhances meaning: as Δήμητρι τῇ Πυλαίῃ rightly matches καὶ τῇ κάτω θυγατρί, so Acrisius' foundation gift (Ἀκρίσιος τὸν νηὸν ἐδείματο) becomes a parallel, and a precedent, for Timotheus' tithing (εἵσατο τῶν κερδέων δεκατεύματα). In all likelihood, the epigram was a commissioned piece, written by the Alexandrian poet for an Egyptian merchant to have inscribed in the sacred precinct at Thermopylae.[29] This suggests that Callimachus, like Posidippus and Asclepiades, had a reputation for epigram that extended to even north-central Greece. Yet the poem almost certainly came into the thirteenth book of the *AP* from Callimachus' *Epigrammata*. Whether in the original collection it appeared

28. See Lazzarini 58, 111–15.

29. Gow-Page (1965) II 176–77 suggest that "the failure to name the object dedicated is natural enough if the inscription is on or close by it."

in a separate section of metrically diverse poems (cf. Theoc. *Ep.* 17–22 Gow) or was included in a dedicatory section, we cannot now know. But the complicated internal structure through which Timotheus' gift gains its measure of glory reflects on the level of the individual poem the practice of using arrangement to generate meaningful connections within the collection as a whole.

Sepulchral Epigrams

In an important article on the "rhetoric of epitaph," George Walsh has argued that the primary function of sepulchral epigram is "to win a reading," to arrest the movement of the passerby in order for the dead to receive a fleeting moment of recognition.[30] Walsh's article contains important insights into Callimachean poetic effect, especially in the analysis of how Callimachus' epigrams capture "thought in motion, often unfolding the elements of mental life one by one in a dramatic progression."[31] Curiously, though, his emphasis upon epitaph as an inscribed form results in a failure to distinguish between the fictive reader (the imaginary reader of the stone) and the implied reader (a construct based upon the author's evident assumptions about the circumstances of reading), who, for Callimachus' epigrams in their collected form, was clearly a book reader. He states, for instance, that "Callimachus' achievement does *not* [my italics] depend upon" the early third-century conversion of epitaph from public record into a vehicle for personal sentiment but that, rather, "his epigrams derive their essential quality from the conventional functions of actual grave markers."[32] While it is true that Callimachus' innovations were based on traditional epitaphic forms and came eventually to influence actual inscriptions, the majority of Callimachus' epigrams do assume a reading context in which both the stone and its reader belong to the fictive realm of literature. In fact, Callimachus' creation of "thought in motion," or of dramatized speech, depends upon the nonreality of the setting projected.

My own analysis of Callimachus' epitaphs will focus on their character as book poetry. Like the dedications, the sepulchral epigrams range from brief, objectively styled poems in which the poet's persona is almost entirely effaced to poems, characterized by wit or pathos, in which an identifiably Callimachean tone is evident through the poet's manipulation of convention and voice. This combination of possibly genuine inscriptions with clearly fictive epigrams contributes, once again, to the fracturing of poetic unity typical of Hellenistic poetics in general and epigram books in particular. Once again, I

---

30. Walsh (1991) 78.

31. Walsh (1991) 77. Walsh's study of "thought in motion" in Callimachus' epitaphs was partially anticipated by L. Braun, "L'arte di Callimaco negli epigrammi funerari," *SCO* 35 (1985) 57–70.

32. Walsh (1991) 78.

am concerned to discover how Callimachus uses arrangement to suggest his own poetic presence within the heterogeneity of the collection. Through the polyphony of voices sounding in the epitaphs—voices of the casual observer, the mourner, the gravestone, the many dead, as well as the poet himself—Callimachus manages to convey his own views on death, immortality, and art.

We begin with Callimachus' two epitaphs for Timon, the legendary Athenian misanthrope who was known to fifth-century comedians (Ar. *Av.* 1549, *Lys.* 805–20; Phryn. *PCG* VII 404, fr. 19) and was brought on stage as a character in fourth-century drama (Antiphanes *Timon*, *PCG* II 431, fr. 204):[33]

Τίμων, οὐ γὰρ ἔτ' ἐσσί, τί τοι, σκότος ἢ φάος, ἐχθρόν;
– τὸ σκότος, ὑμέων γὰρ πλείονες εἰν Ἀίδῃ.

(51 G-P = 4 Pf. = AP 7.317)

Timon, since you no longer exist, what do you hate, darkness or light?
– Darkness, for there are more of you in Hades.

μὴ χαίρειν εἴπῃς με, κακὸν κέαρ, ἀλλὰ πάρελθε·
ἶσον ἐμοὶ χαίρειν ἐστὶ τὸ μή σε πελᾶν.

(52 G-P = 3 Pf. = AP 7.318)

Don't wish me well, hateful fellow, but pass on by.
Not coming near me is the same as wishing me well.

These two poems, which are quite possibly the earliest of the series of eight epigrams on Timon in the *AP* (7.313–20),[34] surely stood together in the *Epigrammata*, as they do in the *AP*, because the identity of the speaker in the second is supplied by the first. As Walsh points out, the second epigram is an excellent example of Callimachus' reversal of epitaphic convention: while epitaph normally attempts through its rhetoric to entice the moving passerby to offer the dead the ritual

---

33. According to legend, Timon became a misanthrope when deserted by his friends because he had been reduced to poverty through his naive generosity. As an almost inconceivable type—a totally "nonpolitical animal" who rejected all human association—Timon was an obvious target for humor. But Lucian's dialogue (*Timon*), in which the misanthrope is treated more sympathetically, suggests that the Cynics may have used the figure of Timon to show the advantages of self-sufficient poverty over troublesome wealth. The epigrammatists' source of interest in Timon was the rhetorical possibility for complete reversal of convention that accompanies rejection of all fellow humanity. Ancient references are discussed in Franz Bertram, *Die Timonlegende: eine Entwicklungsgeschichte des Misanthropentypus in der antiken Literatur* (Diss. Heidelberg, 1906); P. Photiadès, "Le type du Misanthrope dans la littérature grecque," *CE* 68 (1959) 305–26; A. M. Armstrong, "Timon of Athens—A Legendary Figure?" *G&R* 34 (1987) 7–11.

34. There is no good reason to identify the Zenodotus of 7.315 (alternately ascribed to Rhianus) with the early third-century scholar or the Ptolemaeus of 7.314 with the Egyptian monarch. Both Leonidas' version (7.316, alternately ascribed to Antipater) and Hegesippus' epigram (7.320) apparently take Callimachus 52 G-P as a model; cf. Geffcken (1896) 76 and Gow-Page (1965) II 304.

greeting that consists of a mere reading, Timon's epitaph redefines that greeting in oppositional terms as the absence of stoppage and reading.[35] But of course the irony for the reader, who assumes the role of the fictive passerby, is that the very act of reading Timon's prohibition is, in itself, a offering of the prohibited greeting. The ironic manipulation of the implied reader into this impossible fictive position underscores the nonreality of the pretended reading situation and so provokes an awareness of the author's intrigue in creating the reader's predicament. The presence of the Callimachean persona is more directly revealed by the first Timon poem, which belongs to the category of epitaphs in dialogue form. While stone epitaphs of this type conventionally present customary queries of the passerby to the tomb about the identity of the deceased, the Callimachean questioner initially addresses Timon by name and so needs to offer the reader some other signal that the addressee is a deceased person and the poem is an epitaph: οὐ γὰρ ἔτ' ἐσσί, "since you no longer exist" (cf. οὐκ ἐπὶ πουλὺ ἦσθα, 42.1–2 G-P = *AP* 7.725.1–2).[36] As a result, the reader is likely to construe the person curious about Timon's preference for life or death, not as a visitor to the grave, but as the clever poet who contrives Timon's response. The wit of the poem works by a double reversal. The reader naturally expects the misanthrope to prefer death to life, so that his reply that he finds darkness more hateful than light comes as a surprise. But confirming the reader's initial expectation after all, Timon gives as his reason for hating death the presence in Hades of "more of you" (with a play on "the majority" as a euphemism for the dead).[37] Because Callimachus so clearly breaks the illusion of an imaginary setting, the reader may choose to hear the poem as a conversation between author and subject rather than passerby and tombstone; as a result, the boundary is blurred between the fictionalized world of the epitaph and the world in which author and reader share knowledge of that fiction.

Another Callimachean epitaph that betrays its own fictiveness takes the form of an epigram within an epigram,[38] that is, a literary epigram that quotes the inscribed *alter ego* it is pretending to be:

σύντομος ἦν ὁ ξεῖνος, ὃ καὶ στίχος οὐ μακρὰ λέξων
"Θῆρις Ἀρισταίου Κρής" ἐπ' ἐμοὶ δολιχός.

(35 G-P = 11 Pf. = *AP* 7.447)

The stranger was reticent, so that the line which says briefly
"Theris, son of Aristaeus, a Cretan" is too long upon me.

---

35. Walsh (1991) 81.

36. Cf. Hutchinson 72: "The choice of expression jauntily stresses the impossibility of the conversation before it begins."

37. Cf. Leon. 78.6 G-P = *AP* 7.731.6; Crinagoras 35.6 G-P, *Garland* = *AP* 11.42.6 with Gow-Page (1968) *ad loc.* for additional references.

38. For discussion of "l'inscription dans l'inscription," see Laurens 107–10.

The poem has sometimes been misunderstood because of a desire to comprehend it as a genuine inscription. Although σύντομος elsewhere means "concise in language" when it refers to persons, Gow-Page suggest that it here means "short" and assume that the quoted inscription was too lengthy because it was engraved on a statue of Theris that replicated his lack of height.[39] But we now have a parallel from the Milan papyrus in Posidippus' epigram for the Cretan Menoetius, who calls himself ὀλιγορρήμων, "brief in speech," in reporting to passersby his name, patronymic, and place of origin:

τί πρὸς ἐμ' ὧδ' ἔστητε; τί μ' οὐκ ἥασατ' ἰαύειν,
  εἰρόμενοι τίς ἐγὼ καὶ πόθεν ἢ ποδαπός;
στείχε(τέ) μου παρὰ σῆμα· Μενοίτιός εἰμι Φιλάρχω
  Κρής, ὀλιγορρήμων ὡς ἂν ἐπὶ ξενίης.

(25 Bastianini-Gallazzi)

Why do you stand here beside me? Why do you prevent my sleep
  by asking who I am and from where or what country?
Go on past my tomb. I am Menoetius, the son of Philarchus,
  a Cretan, brief in speech as proper in a foreign land.

It is surely significant that both are Cretans, who, like Laconians, had a reputation for conciseness,[40] and Demetrius (*Eloc.* 5.242) attributes to the Spartans the quality of βραχυλογία, "brevity," which, as the opposite of μακρολογία, "verbosity," is directly implied by the phrase οὐ μακρὰ λέξων.[41] By limiting his epitaph to a single distich, Callimachus manages to relate Theris' brevity not only to his ethnic character but also to the art form through which he speaks. Although the reticent Theris wanted only the essential phrase Θῆρις Ἀρισταίου Κρής, giving name, lineage, and place of origin, inscribed on his tomb, the fact that Callimachus is writing a book epitaph requires that the poem reach at least one distich in length. It is for that reason that the στίχος (meaning verse as well

39. Gow-Page (1965) II 192, following Wilamowitz, *Callimachi Hymni et Epigrammata*, 3rd ed. (Berlin, 1907) 57. But Wilamowitz later (1924) II 121 argued that the epigram referred to brevity in speech, citing Aeschin. *De Falsa Legatione* 51; cf. Poll. *Onom.* 4.20, 6.149.

40. Cf. as well 22 G-P = 34 Pf. = *AP* 6.351, where Heracles' curt dialogue with a Cretan dedicator is complete in the space of only one couplet.

41. Posidippus' ill-tempered Menoetius, who is almost as hostile to passersby as was Timon, explains that brevity of speech is appropriate for those buried in a foreign land. M. Gronewald, "Der neue Poseidippos und Kallimachos Epigramm 35," *ZPE* 99 (1993) 28–29, citing the proverb συστομώτερον σκάφης that refers to lack of free speech for metics in Athens (Theophr., fr. 103 Wimmer), suggests that Menoetius is laconic because as a foreigner he possessed no freedom of speech, or παρρησία. But see the refutation by E. Voutiras, "Wortkarge Söldner? Ein Interpretationsvorschlag zum neuen Poseidippos," *ZPE* 104 (1994) 28–30, who argues that Menoetius displays a reticence typical of soldiers. Menoetius' peevish tone and Theris' curtness indicate that both were reticent by temperament as much as by circumstance (note the inclusion of the Menoetius epigram in the τρόποι section of the Posidippus collection).

as line of writing), though it speaks οὐ μακρά, is too long on Theris' tomb. Once again, there is a blurring of the boundary between the fictive world in which the epitaph is inscribed on a grave marker and the literary world of the book for which it was actually composed. This breaking of fictive illusion encourages the reader to identify the message of the poem with the epigrammatist's own self-interest, so that Theris' preference for a concise epitaph suggests by transference the poet's preference for the literary form—epigram—that is principally characterized by brevity.[42]

We turn now to the evidence for the poetic ordering of Callimachus' sepulchral epigrams. As I have shown in an earlier chapter, nine of Callimachus' twenty-five, or perhaps twenty-six, epitaphs[43] appear in a sequence in the *AP* (7.517–25) that I believe represents, with omissions, a section from the *Epigrammata*:

ἠῷοι Μελάνιππον ἐθάπτομεν, ἠελίου δέ
  δυομένου Βασιλὼ κάτθανε παρθενική
αὐτοχερί, ζώειν γὰρ ἀδελφεὸν ἐν πυρὶ θεῖσα
  οὐκ ἔτλη· δίδυμον δ' οἶκος ἐσεῖδε κακόν
πατρὸς Ἀριστίπποιο, κατήφησεν δὲ Κυρήνη
  πᾶσα τὸν εὔτεκνον χῆρον ἰδοῦσα δόμον.

(32 G-P = 20 Pf. = AP 7.517)

At dawn we were burying Melanippus, but at the setting
  of the sun the maiden Basilo died by her own hand,
For she couldn't bear to live when she had placed
  her brother on the pyre. A double misfortune the house
Of their father Aristippus saw, and all Cyrene was downcast
  to see a family with noble children bereft.

Ἀσταχίδην τὸν Κρῆτα τὸν αἰπόλον ἥρπασε Νύμφη
  ἐξ ὄρεος, καὶ νῦν ἱερὸς Ἀσταχίδης.

---

42. Other scholars as well have found allusion to poetics in the epigram; see Hauvette 22; Meyer 173–75; Gronewald (1993) 29.

43. The uncertain epitaph is 62 G-P = 36 Pf. = *AP* 7.454, which is quoted without author's name in Athenaeus (10.436d–e) but said in the *AP* to have the same author as the preceding epigram (46 G-P = 19 Pf.). Wilamowitz, "Die Thukydideslegende," *Hermes* 12 (1877) 346, n. 29 and (1924) I 133, n. 3 denied Callimachus' authorship on the belief that Athenaeus had found the poem in Polemon, and Pfeiffer rejected it because he considered the elision at the diaeresis unworthy of Callimachus. But E. Livrea, "Due epigrammi Callimachei," *Prometheus* 15 (1989) 199–202 has now argued for the authenticity of the *Anthology* ascription, and I believe there to be insufficient reason for rejecting the Callimachean authorship of a poem that occurs in a Meleagrian sequence. Given the thematic concerns of Asclepiades, Posidippus, and Hedylus with drinking and composing poetry, a satirical epitaph for a "heavy wine-drinker" could easily have served as a Callimachean contribution to this ongoing conversation about poetic theory.

οὐκέτι Δικταίῃσιν ὑπὸ δρυσίν, οὐκέτι Δάφνιν,
ποιμένες, Ἀστακίδην δ' αἰὲν ἀεισόμεθα.

(36 G-P = 22 Pf. = *AP* 7.518)

Astacides the Cretan goatherd a Nymph snatched
from the mountain, and now Astacides is holy.
No longer under the Dictaean oaks, no longer will we shepherds
sing of Daphnis, but always of Astacides.

δαίμονα τίς δ' εὖ οἶδε τὸν αὔριον ἁνίκα καὶ σέ,
Χάρμι, τὸν ὀφθαλμοῖς χθιζὸν ἐν ἁμετέροις,
τᾷ ἑτέρᾳ κλαύσαντες ἐθάπτομεν; οὐδὲν ἐκείνου
εἶδε πατὴρ Διοφῶν χρῆμ' ἀνιαρότερον.

(44 G-P = 14 Pf. = *AP* 7.519)

Who can know tomorrow's fortune, when even you,
Charmis, present yesterday in our sight,
We mourned and buried the next day? Your father
Diophon saw nothing more painful than that.

ἢν δίζῃ Τίμαρχον ἐν Ἅιδος ὄφρα πύθηαι
ἤ τι περὶ ψυχῆς ἢ πάλι πῶς ἔσεαι,
δίζεσθαι φυλῆς Πτολεμαΐδος υἱέα πατρός
Παυσανίου· δήεις δ' αὐτὸν ἐν εὐσεβέων.

(33 G-P = 10 Pf. = *AP* 7.520)

If you seek Timarchus in Hades so that you may learn
either about the soul or about your fate after death,
Seek the son of Pausanias of the tribe Ptolemais.
You will find him among the blessed.

Κύζικον ἢν ἔλθῃς ὀλίγος πόνος Ἱππακὸν εὑρεῖν
καὶ Διδύμην, ἀφανὴς οὔτι γὰρ ἡ γενεή·
καί σφιν ἀνιηρὸν μὲν ἐρεῖς ἔπος, ἔμπα δὲ λέξαι
τοῦθ' ὅτι τὸν κείνων ὧδ' ἐπέχω Κριτίην.

(43 G-P = 12 Pf. = *AP* 7.521)

If you come to Cyzicus, it is slight effort to find Hippacus
and Didyme, since their family is well known.
You will speak a bitter word to them, but nevertheless
say this, that I hold here their son Critias.

Τιμονόη. – τίς δ' ἐσσί; μὰ δαίμονας οὔ σ' ἂν ἐπέγνων
εἰ μὴ Τιμοθέου πατρὸς ἐπῆν ὄνομα
στήλῃ καὶ Μήθυμνα, τεή πόλις. ἦ μέγα φημί
χῆρον ἀνιᾶσθαι σὸν πόσιν Εὐθυμένη.

(40 G-P = 15 Pf. = *AP* 7.522)

"Timonoe." Who are you? By god, I wouldn't have known you
if your father's name, Timotheus, and your city, Methymna,
Hadn't been on your tomb. I say, your husband, Euthymenes,
bereft of you, must be in great grief.

οἵτινες Ἀλείοιο παρέρπετε σᾶμα Κίμωνος
ἴστε τὸν Ἱππαίου παῖδα παρερχόμενοι.

(39 G-P = 60 Pf. = *AP* 7.523)

Whoever walks past the tomb of Elian Cimon,
know you pass by the son of Hippaeus.

– ἦ ῥ' ὑπὸ σοὶ Χαρίδας ἀναπαύεται; – Χ. εἰ τὸν Ἀρίμμα
τοῦ Κυρηναίου παῖδα λέγεις, ὑπ' ἐμοί.
– ὦ Χαρίδα, τί τὰ νέρθε; Χ. πολὺ σκότος. – αἱ δ' ἄνοδοι τί;
Χ. ψεῦδος. – ὁ δὲ Πλούτων; Χ. μῦθος. – ἀπωλόμεθα.
Χ. οὗτος ἐμὸς λόγος ὔμμιν ἀληθινός, εἰ δὲ τὸν ἡδύν
βούλει, Πελλαίου βοῦς μέγας εἰν Ἀίδῃ.

(31 G-P = 13 Pf. = *AP* 7.524)

– Does Charidas rest under you? – If you mean
the son of Cyrenaean Arimmas, he does.
– Charidas, what's below? Ch. Much darkness. – And what about return?
Ch. A lie. – And Pluto? Ch. A myth. – We're lost!
Ch. I'm telling you the truth. But if you prefer a pleasant lie,
a large ox can be had for only a Pellaean in Hades.

ὅστις ἐμὸν παρὰ σῆμα φέρεις πόδα Καλλιμάχου με
ἴσθι Κυρηναίου παῖδά τε καὶ γενέτην.
εἰδείης δ' ἄμφω κεν· ὁ μέν ποτε πατρίδος ὅπλων
ἦρξεν, ὁ δ' ἤεισεν κρέσσονα βασκανίης.
οὐ νέμεσις, Μοῦσαι γὰρ ὅσους ἴδον ὄμματι παῖδας
μὴ λοξῷ πολιοὺς οὐκ ἀπέθεντο φίλους.

(29 G-P = 21 Pf. = *AP* 7.525)

You who carry yourself past my tomb, know that
I am son and father of Cyrenaean Callimachus.
You should know both. One commanded his country's
arms, whereas the other sang beyond envy.
No wonder, for those children whom the Muses look upon with eyes not aslant
they do not abandon as friends even when aged.

Though we assume this sequence is lacunose, it nevertheless indicates that Callimachus organized his sepulchral section, at least in part, in accordance with the voices speaking in the poems, a principle of arrangement found also in the *Aetia* and the *Iambi*. We are fortunate, too, because the sequence seems to preserve the conclusion of Callimachus' *Epigrammata*.

The first three poems are linked by the unusual feature of first-person plural verbs (ἐθάπτομεν, ἀεισόμεθα, ἐθάπτομεν).[44] The overt placement of the author

44. One other Callimachean epitaph displays a first-person plural speaker, a poem commemorating the death of the shipwrecked Sopolis (45 G-P = 17 Pf. = *AP* 7.271), whom "we mourned" (ἐστένομεν) and whose empty tomb "we pass by" (παρερχόμεθα). Whether this poem originally stood with *AP* 7.517–19, or in a separate section on shipwrecked persons, or

within the community of mourners dramatically alters the traditional objectivity of sepulchral epigram. One of the usual pathetic effects of epitaph is the feeling of finality conveyed by the reporting of irrecoverable death. But in 32 G-P, where the burial of Melanippus at dawn is succeeded by the suicide of his sister Basilo at dusk, the deaths unfold before our eyes in a narrative told by an internal narrator, an observer of the events. Likewise, in 44 G-P we are asked to share the narrator's surprise that Charmis, hale and hearty one day, is mourned and buried the next. This inclusion of the epigrammatist within the pathetic events removes them from the realm of timeless truth and places them within the localized and the particular. If the dirgelike quality of 32 and 44 argue against their genuineness as inscriptions, it is still possible that both were composed by Callimachus to commemorate actual Cyrenaean deaths.[45] Yet within the collection they serve the purpose of naming the poet's community and providing him with a circle of friends. The author of these poems is not just any epigrammatist, but the particular Cyrenaean poet who composed all the pieces within the collection (cf. Καλλιμάχου ... Κυρηναίου, 29.1–2 G-P). Even so, these two epigrams for seemingly historical persons are separated by 36 G-P, an epitaph for the Cretan goatherd Astacides who acquires a mythical status like that of Daphnis. Whether or not any credence should be given to the old interpretation of the poem as an example of the bucolic masquerade and of Astacides as a disguised poet, the quatrain has the effect of providing the epigrammatist with a purely fictive presence among the herdsmen of Crete. The epigrammatic persona that the reader may construct from 32 and 44 is thus unsettled by the placement of this intervening poem with its imaginary setting. We may recall that the separation of similar poems by a different intervening poem is a principle of arrangement known also from Callimachus' *Iambi*.

The next two poems in Callimachus' epitaphic sequence (33 and 43 G-P) address the reader or passerby, a parallelism enhanced by the similarity of ἢν δίζῃ and ἢν ἔλθῃς in the opening clauses. Callimachus again creates variety by play with the source of the voice heard in each poem. In the Critias epigram the voice who addresses the passerby is named, in conventional fashion, as the stone, though Callimachus remakes it as something distinctly his own by adding a psychological element. To see this more clearly, it is useful to look at the epigrammatic precedents for the poem. The famous Simonides epitaph for the

---

elsewhere, we cannot now know. But it shares with *AP* 7.517–19 the effect of including the epigrammatist within a community of mourners.

45. Aristippus in 32 is likely the Cyrenaean magistrate whose name appears on coinage struck about 300 B.C. His son Melanippus was probably named for his grandfather Melanippus, who is named on coinage of about 325 B.C. See Pfeiffer *ad loc.*; Gow-Page (1965) II 190; Fraser I 579, II 824, n. 203; and Claude Meillier, *Callimaque et son temps* (Lille, 1979) 116. Meillier 117 argues as well for a Cyrenaean connection for 44, although he admits that no epigraphic evidence can be adduced.

Spartan dead at Thermopylae ("Stranger, report to the Lacedaemonians that we lie here, obedient to their commands," 22b *FGE*) was the ultimate model for an epitaph by Asclepiades for the shipwrecked Euippus ("Traveler, when you come to Chios, say to my father Melesagoras that the evil East wind destroyed me with ship and cargo," 31 G-P = *AP* 7.500). Asclepiades' poem in turn seems to have inspired Callimachus' epitaph for Critias. While both Asclepiades' and Callimachus' poems encode the essential epitaphic information of name, family, and origin partly in the message and partly in the directions about where to deliver it, upon closer inspection it becomes evident that Callimachus' speaker is given a psychological characterization absent from the more objective style of Asclepiades' epitaph. In the Critias epitaph the speaker induces the passerby to seek out Hippacus and Didyme with the argument that delivering a message to a family so "well known" will be "slight effort." By labeling the message a "bitter word," the speaker also attempts to engage the sympathies of the passerby. While Asclepiades' model makes clear from the initial phrase that the deceased is addressing a passerby (ὦ παρ' ἐμὸν στείχων κενὸν ἠρίον, "You who pass my empty tomb"), Callimachus' poem, despite all its pathos, acquires an ironic touch by revealing only in the penultimate word (ἐπέχω) that the subtly manipulative speaker is a lifeless stone.

The companion piece to 43, the epitaph for Timarchus, gives no sure indication of the identity of the speaker, who may be either the stone, as in 43, or the poet. If we construe the speaker as the grave marker, we are likely to read the poem, with Gow-Page, simply as a "laudatory epitaph":[46] his father's name and *phyle* provide Timarchus' "address" in Hades where he has earned a place among the righteous. But recent interpreters have tended to hear the voice of Callimachus himself as the speaker so that the epitaph gains in complexity. Meillier has argued that Timarchus is almost certainly the Cynic philosopher from Alexandria mentioned by Diogenes Laertius (6.95). He further points out the play on Ἄιδος / Πτολεμ-αΐδος, emphasized by line position, and suggests that the "address" given is in fact a reference to the local records of Alexandrian citizens.[47] Expanding upon this interpretation, Livrea has now argued that Timarchus' Cynic writings on the soul and existence after death must have refuted traditional or mythical beliefs in immortality and the underworld. In this reading, Callimachus' satire is directed, not against Timarchus himself, but against the foolish believer who seeks him in Hades. The philosopher exists after death only in the records of his *phyle* and has earned a place among the blessed only in terms of his reputation among the living.[48] Although Livrea

---

46. Gow-Page (1965) II 190.

47. Meillier 197–99.

48. E. Livrea, "Tre epigrammi funerari Callimachei," *Hermes* 118 (1990) 314–18. Livrea 316 points to the saying of Antisthenes cited by Diogenes Laertius 6.5: τοὺς βουλομένους ἀθανάτους εἶναι ἔφη δεῖν εὐσεβῶς καὶ δικαίως ζῆν.

has made an important contribution to our understanding of the poem, I believe that he has missed one crucial point. The reference to Timarchus as son of Pausanias from the Ptolemais tribe suggests, not just local citizenship records, but also the biographies attached to Callimachus' own literary inventories, which apparently began with name of father and place of origin.[49] It is pointed out to the interlocutor of the epigram that Timarchus' philosophical views on death and the soul are not to be found by a visit to Hades, since the afterlife was a figment of the imagination in the view of the Cynic philosopher (and apparently in Callimachus' view as well), but are to be gleaned from a perusal of his writings (note the resemblance of περὶ ψυχῆς to book titles). It is only in the literary sense that Timarchus has gained immortality, a home among the "blessed," who are here redefined as those whose books have found inclusion in literary catalogues such as the *pinakes* of the epigrammatist himself.

This reading of the Timarchus epigram brings into focus its connection with another epitaph for a philosopher, one that also satirizes belief in immortality:[50]

εἶπας, Ἥλιε χαῖρε, Κλεόμβροτος ὡμβρακιώτης
  ἥλατ᾽ ἀφ᾽ ὑψηλοῦ τείχεος εἰς Ἀίδην,
ἄξιον οὐδὲν ἰδὼν θανάτου κακὸν ἀλλὰ Πλάτωνος
  ἕν τὸ περὶ ψυχῆς γράμμ᾽ ἀναλεξάμενος.

                                        (53 G-P = 23 Pf. = *AP* 7.471)

Saying "Farewell, Sun," Cleombrotus the Ambracian
  leapt from a high wall into Hades,
Not because of some misfortune provoking death, but because
  he read one book by Plato on the soul.

In all likelihood, Callimachus intended the reader to associate the Cleombrotus who here commits suicide with the person of that name, a companion of the hedonistic philosopher Aristippus, who is mentioned in the *Phaedo* (59c) as absent in Aegina at the time of Socrates' death. Callimachus' interest in Cleombrotus' suicide, mentioned in a variety of later sources,[51] may have been stimulated by the continuing concern of philosophers attached to the Cyrenaic school with the topic of suicide. The Cyrenaic Hegesias, known as

49. Parallel examples can be found in the openings to the biographies of Diogenes Laertius, e.g., Ἀρχύτας Μνησαγόρου Ταραντῖνος (8.79); see Blum 156.

50. The repetition of περὶ ψυχῆς in the same line position and the echo of ἐν Ἅιδος in εἰς Ἀίδην suggests that the two poems may have stood beside or near each other in the original sequence.

51. On these sources, see T. Sinko, "De Callimachi epigr. XXIII W.," *Eos* 11 (1905) 1–10; L. Spina, "Cleombroto, la fortuna di un suicidio," *Vichiana* 18 (1989) 12–39; S. A. White, "Callimachus on Plato and Cleombrotus," *TAPA* 124 (1994) 136–42; G. D. Williams, "Cleombrotus of Ambracia: Interpretations of a Suicide from Callimachus to Agathias," *CQ* 45 (1995) 154–69.

the "persuader of death" (πεισιθάνατος, D.L. 2.86), was banned from lecturing on the subject by Ptolemy (either Soter or Philadelphus) because of his ability to convince people that life was not worth living (Cic. *Tusc.* 1.83–84). In the Cleombrotus epigram Callimachus may be tracing contemporary philosophical fascination with suicide back to Plato's influence on a companion of the founder of the Cyrenaic school. The parallel with the Timarchus epitaph suggests that Callimachus is satirizing Cleombrotus' naive acceptance of Plato's views on the immortality of the soul; since the *Phaedo* forbids suicide, Cleombrotus is guilty as well of misreading the text. Suicide as a result of tremendous grief is comprehensible, as shown by the example of Basilo, who is perhaps meaningfully named the daughter of a certain Aristippus of Cyrene (32 G-P). But the tragic ambiance of Cleombrotus' melodramatic address to the landscape as he prepares to hurl himself from a great height is undercut when the poet reveals in the second couplet that Cleombrotus had met with no true misfortune: he had merely read Plato's book on the soul, the *Phaedo* itself. Cleombrotus thus makes the very mistake that Callimachus warns against in the Timarchus epigram: those who peruse Timarchus' skeptical views on the soul's survival will avoid the headlong rush to death that might be inspired by Plato's belief in a sentient afterlife. Within the confines of his collection, then, Callimachus projects an individualized persona for his narratorial voice not only to express his personal involvement in the grief he commemorates but also to suggest, when poem is compared with poem, his personal philosophical views on such topics as the survival of the soul.

These views come into even clearer focus when the Timarchus and Cleombrotus poems are compared with another epigram of sepulchral character:

εἶπέ τις, Ἡράκλειτε, τεὸν μόρον ἐς δέ με δάκρυ
    ἤγαγεν ἐμνήσθην δ' ὁσσάκις ἀμφότεροι
ἠέλιον λέσχῃ κατεδύσαμεν. ἀλλὰ σὺ μέν που,
    ξεῖν' Ἁλικαρνησεῦ, τετράπαλαι σποδιή,
αἱ δὲ τεαὶ ζώουσιν ἀηδόνες, ᾗσιν ὁ πάντων
    ἁρπακτὴς Ἀΐδης οὐκ ἐπὶ χεῖρα βαλεῖ.

                                                  (34 G-P = 2 Pf. = *AP* 7.80)

Someone told me of your fate, Heraclitus, and it brought
    a tear to my eye. I remembered how often the two of us
sank the sun with our talk. But you, Halicarnassian friend,
    have perhaps been ash for a long, long time.
Yet your nightingales live on, untouched by the hand
    of Hades, the snatcher of all.

This remarkable poem, much discussed in the past, has recently provoked stimulating readings by several scholars. Walsh has analyzed the poem as an example of "audible thought," as Callimachus' *reflection* upon his reaction to the news of his old friend's death.[52] Richard Hunter has shown how the absence of conventional epitaphic features marks the poem as a new, or perhaps final, stage in the journey from inscriptional epitaph to literary form: "now there is no tombstone and no corpse, merely memory."[53] J. G. MacQueen has observed that Callimachus' reminiscence about Heraclitus—how the two often sank the sun with conversation—can be read metaphorically as an indication that "words live on after the darkness of death."[54] I would add that the unique format of this epitaph, a speech act directed to the deceased himself, acts as a metapoetic example of a conversation surviving the onset of darkness, or death: for the brief moment of the poem Callimachus does converse with Heraclitus even across the barrier of death. Yet he has no illusions about death's finality, for he recognizes that his friend became perhaps long ago nothing but ash. Even so, the poem ends with an affirmation of the only kind of immortality Callimachus accepts, the deathlessness of art. While Anyte had suggested the fragility of art by lamenting that Hades, "hard to dissuade," carried off Myro's pet insects (20 G-P), Callimachus boldly asserts that Heraclitus' "nightingales" yet live, untouched by the hand of Hades "the snatcher of all." Whether the term *nightingales* preserves the title of a collection by Heraclitus or is simply a metaphor for his poetry, the epigram offers confirmation for my interpretation of the Timarchus and Cleombrotus epigrams, that Callimachus believed death to be irrevocable and survival possible only through the literary preservation of the written word. Although the position of the Heraclitus epigram within the collection remains uncertain (and it could have belonged to an ecphrastic section on literary themes rather than to the sepulchral section), it nonetheless served to reinforce important themes within the poetry book, and to link Callimachus' reflections on death with his own artistic persona.

After this digression to thematically related epigrams, we return to examining the sequence of Callimachus' sepulchral section, as outlined by the lacunose series preserved in the *AP*. While in 33 and 43 the stone speaks, or the poet speaks usurping the role of the stone, the next epitaph in the sequence, the Timonoe poem (40 G-P), is placed in the mouth of a visitor to a tomb. In an admirable exposition of this poem, Walsh has argued that "the internalization of epitaph rhetoric . . . carries the genre as far as it can go."[55] He shows how the basic epitaphic information of name, patronymic, and birthplace is modified to accommodate a brief psychological drama, a speech act that represents the emotional reaction of a specific visitor to a specific tomb. The poem begins with

---

52. G. B. Walsh, "Surprised by Self: Audible Thought in Hellenistic Poetry," *CP* 85 (1990) 1–4.

53. R. Hunter, "Callimachus and Heraclitus," *MD* 28 (1992) 123.

54. J. G. MacQueen, "Death and Immortality: A Study of the Heraclitus Epigram of Callimachus," *Ramus* 11 (1982) 50.

55. Walsh (1991) 97.

the name of the deceased, which the reader is free to interpret as the "voice" of the stone, that is, the name written on the tomb, or, what is much the same thing, the passerby's vocalization of a name read from the inscription. The name of Timonoe is then followed by the question that in inscribed dialogues should rightly precede, as illustrated by this epitaph from the third or second century B.C.:

άφθιτος, ού θνητή. – θαυμάζω, τίς δ'; – Ἰσιδώρα. –
τίς πόλις; – αἱ μεγάλαι Θῆβαι. – τίς ἀνήρ; – Θεόδωρος.

(GV 1845.1–2)

I'm immortal, not mortal. – I'm amazed. Who are you? – Isidora. –
What's your city? – Great Thebes. – Your husband? – Theodorus.

Callimachus has modified the usual form to dramatize the reaction of a passerby whose casual reading of a name on a tombstone leads him to discover that this Timonoe is someone he knows. The name of her father Timotheus and her native city, Methymna, are reported to us, not in their inscriptional format, but through the passerby's reaction to reading them. Likewise, the name of her husband Euthymenes, which should more properly appear as the answer to a question as does the name of Isidora's husband in the dialogue above, is conveyed to us by the passerby who knows the man and so can give personal testimony to the grief he must feel.

As the Timonoe epitaph dramatizes the act of reading an inscription, a related poem (which perhaps accompanied it in the *Epigrammata*) dramatizes the act of composing an inscription:

τίς, ξένος ὦ ναυηγέ; Λεόντιχος ἐνθάδε νεκρόν
  εὗρεν ἐπ' αἰγιαλοῦ χῶσε δὲ τῷδε τάφῳ
δακρύσας ἐπίκηρον ἐὸν βίον· οὐδὲ γὰρ αὐτός
  ἥσυχον, αἰθυίῃ δ' ἴσα θαλασσοπορεῖ.

(50 G-P = 58 Pf. = AP 7.277)

Who are you, shipwrecked stranger? Leontichus found a body
  here on the shore and covered it with this tomb
As he wept for his own perishable life. For he is never
  at rest, but travels the sea like a gull.

The opening question ("Who are you ... ?") mimics the questions typically asked by the passerby who stops before a tomb.[56] But as the name "Timonoe" turns out to be the fictive reader's vocalization of the inscription, so the reader

56. Some scholars (Waltz, Gow-Page, and Beckby) have construed the remainder of the poem as the deceased's answer to just such a question by introducing a μ' in the second line ("Leontichus found me . . ."). Stadtmüller, Émile Cahen (in the Budé edition, *Callimaque* [Paris, 1922]), Pfeiffer, and Coco, however, retain the ms. reading as I do, and in fact the poem, as transmitted in the manuscript, represents a much more interesting hermeneutical puzzle, one

of 50 gradually recognizes that the opening query about the identity of the deceased represents Leontichus' own dialogue with himself as he muses on the identity of the shipwrecked corpse he has just buried. Having finished the task of covering the body, he now contemplates how he can mark the grave of one whose name he does not know. His only knowledge concerns his own actions and feelings, which therefore become the substance of the epigram. Reading this poem in juxtaposition with Callimachus' Sopolis epitaph (45 G-P = *AP* 7.271) reveals the two sides of the pathos connected with death at sea: the deceased's family and friends can erect only a cenotaph lacking the body, while the stranger who buries the corpse lacks means to name the dead. The two parts of a proper burial, body and name, σῶμα and σῆμα, are thus forever separate for a victim of shipwreck. The Leontichus epigram exposes by unraveling the conventions of sepulchral epigrams in another way as well. Epitaphs for those who died at sea are numerous in the *Anthology*, and part of the pathetic effect of such poems stems from the reader's sympathy with the shipwrecked person, the realization that such misfortune could befall any one of us at any time. It is this selfish empathy that produces our compassion. But in the second couplet of 50 Leontichus overtly states that he weeps in anticipation of his own similar misfortune. By denying ἡσυχία to himself, he seems to contrast unfavorably his own restless sea travel, more fit for gulls than humans, with the dead sailor's peaceful repose. Like 40, then, the Leontichus epigram offers an example of Callimachus' self-conscious dramatization of epigrammatic convention to reflect the psychological movement of speech or thought.

Next in the *AP* sequence we come to a simple epitaph in a single distich (39 G-P). I have argued in the dedicatory section that such objectively styled epigrams may function as models, as examples of the traditioral epigrammatic formats from which most of Callimachus' poems deviate. The position of 39, just before a concluding sequence of epigrams, suggests that such simple poems may also have served, through their arrangement within the collection, to clean the palate, to prepare the reader for more complicated or meatier epigrams to follow. But even so, we should not discount the potential of Callimachus' editing skills for polyvalent effect. The attentive reader may note that the initial uncertainty of the speaker in 40 (" 'Timonoe.' Who are you?") is neatly answered by the determination of the stone in 39 that passersby should have definitive knowledge (ἴστε τὸν Ἱππαίου παῖδα παρερχόμενοι, "know you pass by the son of Hippaeus"), a turn of phrase that will echo in the last poem in the sequence (ἴσθι Κυρηναίου παῖδά τε καὶ γενέτην, "know the son and father of Cyrenaean [Callimachus]," 29.2 G-P). In addition, the combination of speaking voices in 40 and 39—first passerby and then stone—prepares for the important

---

best solved by examining the poem in conjunction with the Timonoe poem. See now the reading of Bing (1995) 124–26.

conversation between passerby and stone that takes place in the penultimate poem in the sequence (31 G-P).

While I earlier suggested that the Charidas epitaph seems to reflect Callimachus' own views on death, we are now in a better position to comprehend its summary character. In a collection that mocked anyone foolish enough to seek the Cynic philosopher Timarchus in Hades and included a satire on Cleombrotus' suicide as a result of a belief in immortality, we should scarcely be surprised by a statement of Cynic or Sceptic nihilism. And the prominent place given the poem—in the final sequence just before an epitaph for Callimachus' father—indicates that its message had meaning for the sepulchral section as a whole. The Charidas poem illustrates, yet again, how Callimachus exposes the conventionality of grave epigram by pushing epitaph rhetoric beyond its sustainable limits. The reading of the deceased's name, patronym, and countryland on the tombstone is here entirely replaced by an impossible conversation in which an acquaintance of Charidas seeks communication with his dead friend through the medium of the stone. The stone's reply, confirming that it marks the grave of the Charidas being sought, somehow opens up a direct channel through which the passerby may speak to the soul of the deceased in Hades. It is clear from the second couplet that Charidas denies popular beliefs about the underworld, but understanding the poem's movement as a whole is complicated by uncertainties in interpreting the final couplet. Scholars generally agree that Charidas here asserts the truth of his description of Hades as nothingness but offers his interlocutor the choice of an agreeable lie. The difficulty lies in knowing just what is meant by the "large ox in Hades."

Two primary approaches have developed, each supported by a significant literary parallel. At the beginning of the first *Iambus* Hipponax describes Hades as the place where an ox can be bought for a penny (βοῦν κολλύβου πιπρήσκουσιν, fr. 191.2). If we follow this parallel, Charidas, who speaks from the grave just as Hipponax does, is offering the proverbial cheapness of things in Hades as his agreeable lie.[57] This interpretation not only grants the epigram a witty point on which to end, but if we should suppose that Callimachus' sepulchral section closed his epigram book, then 31 G-P as part of the concluding sequence would provide a link back to the opening of another Callimachean poetry book, the *Iambi*. It seems to me not incredible that, as Callimachus used ring composition to link points of opening and closing in the *Aetia*, so too he may have used ring composition to link his various poetic books published as a sequence in the final editing of his oeuvre. This sequence could easily have been

---

57. For the proverb, cf. Pherecrates *PCG* VII 144, fr. 86. This interpretation was advanced by G. Kaibel, "Zu den Epigrammen des Kallimachos," *Hermes* 31 (1896) 265–66, who supplies βοός with Πελλαίου and assumes a Pellan coin marked with an ox. Most editors have accepted the interpretation; see Cahen (1922) 108, Waltz *ad loc.*, Gow-Page *ad* 6, Beckby II 592, and Coco (1988) 86–87.

marked by numbered tags attached to scrolls. A second interpretation, however, is supported by a proverb quoted in Aeschylus' *Agamemnon*, where a large ox on the tongue (βοῦς ἐπὶ γλώσσῃ μέγας, 36) refers to the speaker's silence. If this parallel is followed, then Charidas is refusing to tell any lies and offers his silence instead.[58] Livrea has suggested that the two interpretations might be combined if the Pellaean coin, which may have been stamped with a representation of an ox or made of leather, is taken as a reference to the obol normally placed on the tongue of the dead: Charidas thus suggests that the "great ox" obtainable in Hades for an obol, itself the "ox on the tongue," produces the eternal silence of the dead.[59] This attractive interpretation not only brings a suitable closure to the epigram but is particularly effective in the concluding sequence to the book. After the various voices of the dead and of those speaking to or for the dead have sounded in Callimachus' sepulchral section, last of all (or nearly so) comes Charidas to proclaim the truth—the falsity of all consciousness after death and so the falsity of all communication with those perished. Having demonstrated that his own conversation is impossible as well as most of the conversations that have preceded it in Callimachus' book, he announces, in the final words of the poem, silence both for himself and for all others no longer living. Callimachus' sepulchral section thus ends by revealing the fictionality of all its voices, and the only voice that remains to sound in the following epitaphs is that of the poet himself.

Gabathuler confidently asserted that Callimachus' epitaph for his father (29 G-P) served as the concluding poem for his epigram collection,[60] and its final position in the *AP* sequence can now be adduced as confirming evidence for that assumption. Callimachus' father bases his claim to renown upon the accomplishments of his father and his son, one for his military leadership in Cyrene and the other because his poetry triumphed over envy. The poem was surely not composed as a genuine epitaph, since the deceased is unnamed, his own accomplishments are ignored, and his son is given an unusual prominence. But even so, in an attempt to save its epitaphic form, important scholars such as Pfeiffer and Gow have wished to excise the final couplet, which repeats (apparently with slightly different wording) in the prologue to the *Aetia* (fr. 1.37–38 Pf.). Gow-Page assert that the reference to Callimachus' old age is irrelevant

58. Stadtmüller *ad loc.* first offered this interpretation. In adapting it, G. Giangrande, "Callimaque et le ΒΟΥΣ ΜΕΓΑΣ aux enfers," *REG* 82 (1969) 380–89, has tried to explain why an ox should be found in Hades: he emends Πελλαίου to Πελλανίου, which he interprets as an epithet of the Cyrenaean Poseidon, who as a chthonic deity received the sacrifice of an ox. For objections to Giangrande's emendation, see M. Markovich, "Callimachus' Epigram XIII Again," *REG* 83 (1970) 351–55 and Meillier 131–33.

59. Livrea (1990) 318–24. Livrea's reading is supported by explanations of the proverb found in Pollux 9.61 and Hesychius *s. v.* βοῦς ἐπὶ γλώσσῃ, both of whom connect the "bull upon the tongue" with the purchasing of silence with currency.

60. Gabathuler 56.

in the epigram, whereas it follows naturally in the *Aetia* passage.[61] It could also be noted that an epitaph, purportedly composed at the time of his father's death, would not logically refer to the old age of Callimachus himself. But these arguments against the last couplet, as well as other readings of the epigram through epitaphic convention, fail to take account of the poem's probable function as a closure piece for an epigram collection. Because of the fracturing of the epitaphic form and the poem's sequential position, the reader is likely to hear the authorial voice of Callimachus strongly superimposed upon the fictive voice of the father. The poem is clearly Callimachus' signature piece, the only extant epigram in which he names himself expressly, and the fiction of the father's voice is obviously designed to deflect the distastefulness of direct self-praise: the true subject of the poem is Callimachus, not his father. As a result, the phrase ὁ δ' ἤεισεν κρέσσονα βασκανίης, "the other sang beyond envy," which offers the main point of the poem, lifts the veil covering Callimachus' covert presence and encourages the reader to hear the final self-quotation in the poet's own voice. The reference to his old age is still perhaps inadequately prepared for unless we assume, with good reason, that the version of the *Epigrammata* to which this epigram was appended formed part of the final editing of Callimachus' entire poetic oeuvre that took place after 246 B.C. The reader of Callimachus' collected poetry books, arranged in sequential order (marked on the scrolls), would have advance knowledge from the *Aetia* prologue of his old age and of his struggle against envy (cf. ἔλλετε Βασκανίης ὀλοὸν γένος, fr. 1.17). It appears, then, that as the Charidas epigram may allude to the opening of the *Iambi*, the second book in Callimachus' sequence of poetry books, so the epitaph for Battus alludes to the opening of the first book in the sequence. This pattern of concentric rings between ordered poetry books suggests that the *Epigrammata* was the concluding book in the final edition.

Scholars have argued that 30 G-P, Callimachus' self-epitaph, was composed as a companion to 29 because neither is complete without the other: only from the patronym in 30 do we learn the name of Callimachus' father Battus and only in 29 do we read Callimachus' own name:[62]

61. Gow-Page (1965) *ad* 5 f.

62. Wilamowitz (1924) I 175, n. 2; Gabathuler 5; Fraser I 576; Bing (1995) 126–28, who argues that the cross-referencing of the two epigrams in a book context mimics the interplay between epitaphs in family grave plots; but in opposition, see Cameron (1995) 78–79. The absence of 30 from the *AP* sequence is no obstacle to this thesis, because we know that it had been anthologized earlier by Meleager. It appears in the *Garland* among epitaphs for famous persons, mostly poets, the series that introduced Meleager's epitymbia; there it was given a place of honor preceding a series of epitaphs for Meleager himself (*AP* 7.416–19, 7.421). This position suggests that in composing self-epitaphs to conclude a recognizable sequence within the *Garland* Meleager was following a Callimachean precedent.

Βαττιάδεω παρὰ σῆμα φέρεις πόδας εὖ μὲν ἀοιδήν
εἰδότος, εὖ δ' οἴνῳ καίρια συγγελάσαι.

(30 G-P = *AP* 7.415)

You carry yourself past the tomb of Battiades, who knew well
how to sing and how to tell jokes properly over wine.

Although there is currently no way to know whether 30 G-P preceded or followed
the epitaph for Battus (if that was his name rather than a reference to descent
from the mythical founder of Cyrene),[63] I like to think of it as the last poem in
the collection (and so perhaps in the oeuvre), a coda summing up Callimachus'
career through the epigrammatic brevity of a single couplet. The poem is most
easily comprehended if it refers to Callimachus' entire body of poetry, not just
his epigrams. Since the εὖ μὲν / εὖ δ' clauses contrast serious poetry with light-
hearted sympotic banter, ἀοιδή apparently refers to longer poetry like the *Hecale*,
perhaps the *Hymns* and *Aetia*. The epigrams, then, fall under the second rubric,
playful poetry composed under the influence of wine. Given the likely position
of this poem in the *Epigrammata* and the importance of wine as a symbol of
poetry in the collections of Asclepiades, Posidippus, and Hedylus, it seems clear
that Callimachus here alludes to the position occupied by his epigram book in
the developing tradition of such collections. In this context καίρια becomes an
important qualifier. While Asclepiades is ruled by his emotions and so finds in
drink both solace and inspiration, wine plays only a small role in Callimachus'
erotica. In two epitaphs he satirizes men who died from too much drink (42 G-P
= *AP* 7.725; 62 G-P = *AP* 7.454): Callimachus, a man of knowledge (εἰδότος),
understands the proper limits for the consumption of wine. Here, then, at the
conclusion of the epigram book, and perhaps the oeuvre, we find a succinct
statement of its underlying thematic, that the restraint which is both the result
and producer of knowledge, of self-reflection, informs all Callimachus' epigrams
in terms of both theory and practice. If in fact the epigram book was placed last
in the set of collected works, then the suggestion prevails that the epigrammatic
aesthetic, a taste for brevity and reserve, was exemplary of Callimachus' entire
poetic endeavor.

Erotic Epigrams

It is unfortunate that no evidence remains for the sequential ordering of Cal-
limachus' erotic epigrams, of which thirteen, or possibly fourteen, survive. But
apart from the uncertainly attributed Conopion epigram (63 G-P = 63 Pf. =
AP 5.23),[64] the erotic poems do form a coherent group in which Callimachus

63. Cameron (1995) 8 points out that "Battos is not otherwise found at this period" and that
Strabo (837) takes the patronym Battiades as merely a "claim to descent from the ancient royal
house."

64. The poem, addressed by an *exclusus amator* to a female lover, is attributed to Rufinus
by Planudes, but to Callimachus in the *AP*. Pfeiffer has condemned the poem for reasons of

represents himself as a lover of boys. In doing so, he inscribes himself within the Theognidean tradition of erotic elegy. While the elegiac poet authenticates his claim to authorship by attributing his generic verse to a lover called "Theognis" and addressing it to an *eromenos* named "Cyrnus," Callimachus' erotic epigrams, addressed to an ever-changing series of boys, are marked by the individualized voice of a distinct poetic ego. Our task is to identify the features that give these poems their characteristically Callimachean tone.

As Callimachus reveals himself in his dedicatory and sepulchral epigrams by self-awareness of the epigrammatic tradition in which he works, so in his erotic epigrams he conveys the experience of love through constant reflection on his own condition. The principal precedent for Callimachus' amatory verse was clearly Asclepiades, whose epigrams he varied and reacted against. Because Asclepiades' young lover is so immersed in the dramatic present of his erotic experience, the reader is encouraged to distinguish the lover's persona from the author who ordered the collection. But in Callimachus' epigrams this distinction is much harder to draw: the voice heard in the poems represents the poet's objective, rational self, who speaks not in the throes of passion but in reflection upon passion. The characteristic movement of the poems, the impression they give of being "audible thought," results from the interaction of the two, of reason upon passion and of passion upon reason. As a result, the speaker's reflection about his erotic experience works to associate Callimachus the lover with Callimachus the scholar-poet, and so, once again, to integrate the collection as a whole.

We begin with a poem that concretizes the rational-erotic division in the Callimachean persona:

ἥμισύ μευ ψυχῆς ἔτι τὸ πνέον, ἥμισυ δ' οὐκ οἶδ'
    εἴτ' Ἔρος εἴτ' Ἀίδης ἥρπασε, πλὴν ἀφανές.
ἦ ῥά τιν' ἐς παίδων πάλιν ᾤχετο; καὶ μὲν ἀπεῖπον
    πολλάκι "τὴν δρῆστιν μή νυ δέχεσθε, νέοι."
Θεύτιμον δίφησον· ἐκεῖσε γὰρ ἡ λιθόλευστος
    κείνη καὶ δύσερως οἶδ' ὅτι που στρέφεται.[65]

(4 G-P = 41 Pf. = *AP* 12.73)

---

style, content, and metrics, but Denys Page, ed., *The Epigrams of Rufinus* (Cambridge, 1978) 15 argues that Planudes carelessly carried over τοῦ αὐτοῦ from the two preceding epigrams attributed to Rufinus. For the scholarship for and against the Callimachean attribution, see Coco (1988) 183–84.

65. Gow-Page place daggers before ὑπέχεσθε, the ms. reading in 4, because it "seems incapable of the meaning *take in, receive*" and because Callimachus nowhere else employs μή in hiatus (*ad loc.*). Page suggests the emendation printed here. Without great confidence I print in 5 Schneider's Θεύτιμον and the δίφησον suggested by Jacobs (1813–17) IV 747, in place of the corrupt letters found in the ms.; the name is derived from a translation, or adaptation, by Q. Lutatius Catulus (fr. 1 Courtney, p. 70).

Only half of my soul still breathes; the other half I don't know
   whether Eros or Hades has taken it, just that it's gone.
Has it escaped again to some boy love? I often warned them,
   "Boys, don't take in that runaway slave."
Go, look for Theutimus. For I know that passionate creature,
   who ought to be stoned, is loitering there.

The halved soul derives from Asclepiades 17 G-P, where the poet, with typical irrationality, begs the Erotes either to leave in peace "the part of my soul that remains" (τοῦθ' ὅτι μοι λοιπὸν ψυχῆς) or to destroy it utterly. Callimachus, significantly, rephrases Asclepiades' opening clause to make reference to the breath (τὸ πνέον) that in Stoic thought imparts intelligence to the soul it occupies. If but half of his soul still breathes, that is, thinks rationally, then we can better understand how the other half, rendered irrational by passion, can slip away unseen.[66] Yet Callimachus' epigram is not at all a static and stilted picture of a divided self but rather illustrates, through the image of the runaway slave, the thought processes of a lover weighing resistance versus surrender. The breathing half of his soul, which claims not to know (οὐκ οἶδ') where the other half has gone, quickly surmises its destination. At this point we may begin to suspect that the lover's soul is not so divided after all. While the runaway slave should technically refer to only half of Callimachus' soul (ἥμισυ), the choice of a feminine noun (τὴν δρῆστιν, κείνη) suggests an identification of the impassioned entity with the soul as a whole (ψυχή): in the end, Callimachus does know (οἶδ') where to look for the runaway. As a result, his castigation of his soul's lost half as a uncontrollable slave of passion in need of punishment (λιθόλευστος ... καὶ δύσερως) seems spoken with some self-irony. The reader recognizes that the divided soul is only a pretense, a conceit, that Callimachus' longing for the boy is felt as present even when it is analyzed as absent.

Knowledge of the erotic condition is one of the principal themes in the amatory section of the *Epigrammata*. It is expressed positively through the verbs οἶδα (1.6, 4.1, 4.6, 7.1), ἐπίσταμαι (5.4), γιγνώσκω (12.2, 12.5), and μανθάνω (13.6) and negatively through forms of λανθάνω (9.3, 13.1). Through this theme of knowledge about lovers, himself and others, Callimachus represents himself reflecting on his emotions and yet feeling even in the act of reflecting. A good example of knowledge failing to block emotion is found in the lovely Menippus epigram:

οἶδ' ὅτι μευ πλούτου κενεαὶ χέρες, ἀλλά, Μένιππε,
   μὴ λέγε πρὸς Χαρίτων τοὐμὸν ὄνειρον ἐμοί.
ἀλγέω τὴν διὰ παντὸς ἔπος τόδε πικρὸν ἀκούων·
   ναί, φίλε, τῶν παρὰ σεῦ τοῦτ' ἀνεραστότατον.

(7 G-P = 32 Pf. = *AP* 12.148)

---

66. See Arist. *Eth. Nic.* 1.13 for a discussion of how the two parts of the soul, the rational and the irrational, interact.

> I know that my hands are empty of wealth, Menippus, but don't,
>> in the name of the Graces, speak what is evident.
> A pain passes through all of me when I hear this bitter word.
>> Yes, friend, of all you've done this is the most unloverlike.

While the motif of the corrupt *eromenos* is familiar from Theognis, it acquires a changed significance in Alexandria where boys like Menippus were unlikely to share the social standing of their lovers. Callimachus was descended from the Cyrenaean aristocracy, although his removal to Alexandria may have brought with it a period of economic deprivation;[67] Menippus likely belonged to a lower social class. In 3 G-P = 46 Pf. = *AP* 12.150 Callimachus finds utility in his poverty by claiming that hunger and the Muses have the common effect of arresting the "disease of boy love" (φιλόπαιδα νόσον, 3.6). But 7, as poetry attempting to ease an erotic wound, shows the painful reality behind Callimachus' bravado. When the poet admits that he "knows" his hands are empty, he suggests that he knows as well the necessity of Menippus' infidelity, his economic need for a wealthy lover. What Callimachus finds painful is Menippus' unwillingness to pretend that money is irrelevant to their relationship. The most "unloverlike" of the boy's actions is not his infidelity, but his failure to conceal it.[68] The poem begins, then, in knowledge, in the acknowledgment that Menippus speaks truly about Callimachus' poverty, but ends in pain as knowledge of Menippus' economic position fails to alleviate the suffering caused by his behavior.

In two other epigrams (12 G-P = 30 Pf. = *AP* 12.71; 13 G-P = 43 Pf. = *AP* 12.134) Callimachus' condition as lover is revealed, obliquely, through his ability to detect the plight of others in love. The two poems seem connected, not only through theme, but also through similarity of dramatic movement, from ignorance to knowledge. Epigram 12 expresses the poet's shock at the appearance of the Thessalian Cleonicus. Poor thing, I didn't recognize (οὔ σ' ἔγνων) you, he says; you're nothing but bones and hair. This enunciation of Cleonicus' physical condition, a common symptom of love (cf. Theoc. *Id*. 2.89–90), leads the speaker to suspect the cause of his plight, that he is subject to Callimachus' own fate (δαίμων οὑμός). In the last couplet comes full awareness—"I know (ἔγνων). Euxitheus has captured you"—as the speaker remembers an earlier occasion when Cleonicus looked squarely at the beautiful boy with both his eyes. We

---

67. Cameron (1995) 3–11 has argued that all Callimachus' claims to poverty are mere pose and that, born into the Cyrenaean aristocracy, he came to Alexandria as a royal page of the Ptolemies.

68. Giangrande (1968) 137–39 makes the interesting point that Menippus is a homonym for the famous Menippus of Gadara, who was usurious despite his praise of the simple life. I find the point insufficient reason, however, for giving ἀνεραστότατον a passive translation, "most unbecoming."

need not assume that Callimachus is also madly in love with Euxitheus,[69] just that both men are lovers of the same stamp, unable to resist full exposure to such compelling beauty. In 13 Callimachus speaks to a symposium companion to point out his failure to notice (ἐλάνθανεν) that one of the guests, a stranger, is wounded by love. The symptoms are, again, unmistakable—he sighs deeply and, when the wine begins to take effect, the rose petals fall from his garland (a kind of sympathetic magic). As in 12, the beginning of the third couplet is reserved for the poet's proclamation of the truth detected from these physical clues—the stranger is thoroughly roasted by love (ὤπτηται μέγα δή τι). And yet, again, Callimachus' posture of superiority through knowledge is undermined by the relevation of how he achieved this insight—it takes a thief to catch a thief, or, as the Greeks said, to know (ἔμαθον) the tracks of a thief. Nowhere in the extant epigrams does Callimachus overtly grant to himself the sorts of symptoms attributed to Cleonicus and the unnamed stranger, but he does acknowledge (9 G-P = 44 Pf. = *AP* 12.139) fire hidden under the ash, a river quietly undermining a wall. For Callimachus knowledge of love betrays experience of love.

In another epigram Callimachus illustrates, more directly, the personal reserve that characterizes his erotic practice:

εἰ μὲν ἑκών, Ἀρχῖν', ἐπεκώμασα μυρία μέμφου,
   εἰ δ' ἄκων ἥκω τὴν προπέτειαν ἔα.
ἄκρητος καὶ ἔρως μ' ἠνάγκασαν, ὧν ὁ μὲν αὐτῶν
   εἷλκεν, ὁ δ' οὐκ εἴα τὴν προπέτειαν ἐᾶν·
ἐλθὼν δ' οὐκ ἐβόησα τίς ἢ τίνος ἀλλ' ἐφίλησα
   τὴν φλιήν. εἰ τοῦτ' ἔστ' ἀδίκημ' ἀδικέω.

                            (8 G-P = 42 Pf. = *AP* 12.118)

If my *komos* was made willingly, Archinus, censure me at length,
   but if unwillingly I came, forgive my rashness.
Unmixed wine and love compelled me, one of which dragged me
   there and the other forbade me to let go my rashness.
On arrival I didn't call out my name and lineage but merely
   kissed the doorpost. If that is sin, then I have sinned.

Ancient poets were fond of replicating the komast's discourse in their poetry because his pleas to be admitted to the beloved's house represented the moment of greatest emotional torment, of least intellectual control. Here the poet admits that he was under the influence of both unmixed wine and *eros*, two forces that compel a lover to irrational, and sometimes violent, behavior. Yet Callimachus, unlike Asclepiades, chooses to dramatize, not the speech delivered before the beloved's door, but a later discussion with Archinus exculpating his nighttime activities. He does so with terminology that was commonplace in the contemporary discourse of lovers and analyzed in the ethical philosophy

69. As does Walsh (1991) 100.

of the day. In Menander's *Aspis* Chaereas points out that, in seeking the girl he loves through marriage rather than violence, he has done nothing "rash or unworthy or unjust" (οὐθὲν ποήσας προπετὲς οὐδ' ἀνάξιον οὐδ' ἄδικον, 290–91; cf. προπετῇ, 324), while in the *Dyscolus* Sostratus excuses falling in love with a beautiful girl at first sight by saying that "if you say this is a sin, then perhaps I have sinned" (εἰ τοῦτ' ἀδίκημ' εἴρηκας, ἠδίκηκ' ἴσως, 303). For the Stoics προπέτεια was a hastiness, caused by lack of cognition, and resulting in a yielding to passion.[70] Callimachus employs this term as explanation for his actions before Archinus' house, but even as he admits to the effects of passion, he denies that he engaged in the more extreme aspects of *komos* behavior—shouting his name and patronymic (οὐκ ἐβόησα; cf. Asclep. 14.5, ἐβόησα), assaulting the door, delaying till dawn. Merely kissing the doorpost signals Callimachus' restraint as a lover, and is yet also a sign of his tenderness and sincerity. By not calling out to Archinus, he denied himself any possibility of entrance on the night of the *komos*, but through his later reflection upon the event he presents himself as a truer lover than those who express their passion more vehemently. Callimachus' form of erotic persuasion is thus founded upon restraint, the rational presentation of desire.

The reserve that defines Callimachus as lover is also characteristic of Callimachean poetics, and it is this unity of Callimachus' artistic and erotic selves that helps to integrate the amatory section with the other portions of the *Epigrammata*. The connection between poetics and erotics is made explicit in 2 G-P, which has a programmatic character and was perhaps an introductory poem in the erotic section:

ἐχθαίρω τὸ ποίημα τὸ κυκλικὸν οὐδὲ κελεύθῳ
 χαίρω τὶς πολλοὺς ὧδε καὶ ὧδε φέρει·
μισέω καὶ περίφοιτον ἐρώμενον, οὐδ' ἀπὸ κρήνης
 πίνω· σικχαίνω πάντα τὰ δημόσια.
Λυσανίη, σὺ δὲ ναίχι καλὸς καλός· ἀλλὰ πρὶν εἰπεῖν
 τοῦτο σαφῶς ἠχώ φησί τις "ἄλλος ἔχει."

(2 G-P = 28 Pf. = *AP* 12.43)

I hate the cyclic poem, nor do I like the road
 that carries many here and there.
I also hate the wandering lover, nor do I drink from
 the public fountain. I loathe all things common.
Lysanias, you are beautiful, beautiful. But before I say
 this, an echo clearly says, "He's another's."

70. The parallels with Stoic discourse were noted by Kaibel (1896) 267. On προπέτεια and its opposite ἀπροπτωσία, see D.L. 7.48; 2.131 *SVF*. Kaibel points out that Callimachus' εἷλκεν (8.4) also reflects Stoic usage; cf. δεῖ γὰρ τὸν ἀπρόπτωτον ἀνέλκυστόν τε εἶναι, 2.131 *SVF*. For προπέτεια in Peripatetic ethics, see Arist. *Eth. Nic.* 7.7.8.

Reitzenstein pointed to a precedent for this poem in Theognis (579–84),[71] a passage in which the first two couplets begin with the word ἐχθαίρω. But 2 G-P has another important precedent as well. Scholars have recently emphasized the resemblance of the poem to the priamel form,[72] and I suggest that Callimachus is alluding to one particular priamel, namely, Asclepiades' introductory epigram (1 G-P). We have already observed that Theocritus in his first *Idyll* and Nossis in the opening poem of her epigram collection directly echo the language of Asclepiades 1; I have also argued that Posidippus' programmatic epigram (1 G-P) enunciated a rejection of Stoicism in favor of love as a corollary to the Epicurean ambiance of Asclepiades' initial poem. It is in no way surprising, then, that Callimachus should include in his amatory section a poem that alludes to Asclepiades' influential priamel. But Callimachus, who is always independent of thought, indicates his indebtedness to the Samian only by asserting his difference. Consequently, Asclepiades' sequence of ἡδύ ... ἡδύ ... ἥδιον, listing what is pleasant, suffers reversal in Callimachus' sequence of ἐχθαίρω, ... οὐδὲ ... χαίρω, ... μισέω, ... σιχχαίνω, listing what the poet detests. This reversal is not just a modification of Asclepiades through Theognidean precedent but goes to the heart of the distinction that Callimachus would draw between his own approach to both love and art, and the approach of the Samian. While Asclepiades' young lover is characterized by his wholehearted embrace of life's pleasures, with the consequences be damned, the Callimachean persona is defined, here and elsewhere, by personal reserve, by striving after the refined and the exclusive.

My argument that Callimachus 2 alludes directly to Asclepiades 1 is strengthened by evidence that elsewhere in his collection he echoed an Asclepiadean epigram to make a statement about his poetic preferences. A fragment of a lost epigram, which was known in antiquity as part of the *Epigrammata*, echoes "in derision" (as Gow-Page put it)[73] the opening of Asclepiades' epigram praising Antimachus:

71. Reitzenstein (1893) 69. The precedent is complicated by the fact that it is not at all certain how to divide the six Theognidean lines into distinct poetic units. The first two couplets can be read as connected songs, a form of dialogue by which a man and a woman engage in the exchange of abuse; the third couplet can then stand on its own. But through his imitation Callimachus seems to interpret the six lines as a single unit, with the last couplet as a loose and conciliatory comment on the opinions expressed in the previous two. As a result, 2 G-P comes to illustrate how a reader, who must divide sequences of letters into words, must also divide sequences of lines in a poetry book into units of thought that form coherent poems.

72. A. Henrichs, "Callimachus *Epigram* 28: A Fastidious Priamel," *HSCP* 83 (1979) 207–12; E.-R. Schwinge, "Poetik als praktizierte Poetik: Kallimachos' Echo-Epigramm (28 Pf.)," *WJA* 6 (1980) 101–105.

73. Gow-Page (1965) II 217. According to Schol. γένος Dionys. Per. (*GGM* II 427), this reference to the *Lyde* was found "in the epigrams" of Callimachus.

Λυδὴ καὶ γένος εἰμὶ καὶ οὔνομα, τῶν δ' ἀπὸ Κόδρου
σεμνοτέρη πασῶν εἰμι δι' Ἀντίμαχον·
τίς γὰρ ἔμ' οὐκ ἤεισε; τίς οὐκ ἀνελέξατο Λυδήν,
τὸ ξυνὸν Μουσῶν γράμμα καὶ Ἀντιμάχου;

(Asclep. 32 G-P = AP 9.63)

I am Lyde in both origin and name, and of all women from Codrus
I am the most exalted because of Antimachus.
Who has not sung of me? Who has not read the *Lyde*,
the joint composition of the Muses and Antimachus?

Λύδη καὶ παχὺ γράμμα καὶ οὐ τορόν.

(Callim. 67 G-P = fr. 398 Pf.)

The *Lyde* is a fat work and imprecise.

The parodic repetition of Λύδη καὶ ... καὶ οὐ, with the humorous separation
of the οὐ in οὔνομα to become the negative particle, shows that Callimachus'
interest in echoes extended beyond the Lysanias epigram. As Asclepiades' com-
plimentary book label for the *Lyde* suggests that his epigrammatic poetry was
indebted to Antimachus' mythological elegy, so Callimachus in his criticism of
the *Lyde* indicates he follows this literary tradition by modifying its stylistic stan-
dards. The opposite of Antimachus' "fat work" (παχὺ γράμμα) is Callimachus'
"refined Muse" (τὸ μὲν θύος ὅττι πάχιστον θρέψαι, τὴν Μοῦσαν δ' ὠγαθὲ
λεπταλέην, *Aet*. fr. 1.23–24), and the word τορόν, which can mean "lucid" and
is probably an allusion to Antimachus' famed opaqueness, suggests by etymol-
ogy something finely worked, as if by a craftsman.[74] Callimachus, through his
criticism of Asclepiades' praise of Antimachus, thus touts his own striving for
refinement and craftsmanship.

We return, then, to 2 G-P as an example, in both theme and practice, of
Callimachus' fastidious taste. Structurally, the poem is extraordinarily complex,
an intricately designed work of art. It appears, in priamel fashion, to list
four objects of dislike and to conclude with a summary phrase—"I loathe all
things common." But this reading of the poem leaves the third couplet as a
kind of unnecessary appendage. It is better, then, to understand the first two
couplets as parallel constructions, listing two main objects of dislike—the cyclic
poem and the wandering *eromenos*—and two subsidiary and symbolic objects of
dislike—the much traveled road and the common fountain.[75] The connection
between roads and poetry found elsewhere in Callimachus (fr. 1.25–28 Pf.)

74. N. Krevans, "Fighting against Antimachus: The *Lyde* and the *Aetia* Reconsidered," in
Callimachus, ed. M. A. Harder, R. F. Regtuit, and G. C. Wakker (Groningen, 1993) 149–60
has argued that Callimachus is criticizing Antimachus for both florid language and metrical
roughness.
75. For this interpretation of the lines, see A. Barigazzi, "Amore e poetica in Callimaco
(ep. 28 e 6)," *RFIC* 101 (1973) 188; K. J. McKay, "Bird-Watching in Theognis and a Calli-
machean Echo," *GB* 2 (1974) 114; Schwinge 102.

and Callimachus' imitation of a Theognidean phrase in which the fountain is undoubtedly metaphorical (ἔπινον ἀπὸ κρήνης, 959) make it all the easier to take the second item in each couplet as an explanatory complement to the first.[76] This reading sets up a strict parallelism between the cyclic poem, which lacks unity and conciseness, and the promiscuous lover, who lacks selectivity—a parallelism between the poetic and erotic realms.[77] Now if I am correct in positing that the Lysanias epigram was somehow introductory to Callimachus' amatory section, the function of the parallelism becomes clearer, for the analogy between cyclic poem and unfaithful *eromenos* helps to situate Callimachus' erotic poems within the broader aesthetic context of the collection as a whole. The final couplet also becomes more functional within its book context, which includes not just the preceding two couplets but also the group of erotic epigrams that follows. It serves as an example of Callimachus' fastidious taste, specifically his erotic taste, and so acts as transitional material between the generalizing couplets that precede and the poems on individual lovers that are to come.

The nature of the echo in the final couplet has received what is surely an excessive amount of scholarly attention.[78] Questions arise because ναίχι καλὸς καλός and ἄλλος ἔχει do not match perfectly in vowel sounds or syllable length and because ἄλλος ἔχει seems to reverse the order of the phrase it echoes. While it is now generally agreed that the vowels in ναίχι and ἔχει may have sounded alike in the colloquial speech of Callimachus' day,[79] this leaves the problem of

76. For the metaphorical use of the fountain, see L. P. Wilkinson, "Callimachus, *A. P.* xii. 43," *CR* 81 (1967) 5–6; for the metaphors of both the road and fountain, see Barigazzi (1973) 187–88.

77. R. F. Thomas, "New Comedy, Callimachus, and Roman Poetry," *HSCP* 83 (1979) 180–87 has argued that περίφοιτον ἐρώμενον in 3 refers to the peripatetic lover of Menandrian comedy, rather than a promiscuous boy love, and that the second couplet has a specifically literary reference—the rejection of contemporary drama—to parallel the rejection of cyclic epic in the first couplet. But his interpretation of the phrase is highly unlikely, on which see Cameron (1995) 388–89.

78. Not only have scholars attempted to alter the final couplet with a number of different emendations, but the scholarly discussion concerning the best reading has been marred by an unfortunate quarrel carried on in print between Giangrande and a number of other European scholars. The origins of this quarrel lie in an emendation suggested for line 5 (σὺ δὲ καλὸς νήχ' εἴ) by Q. Cataudella, "Tre epigrammi di Callimaco," *Maia* 19 (1967) 356–58, to which Giangrande, "Callimachus, Poetry and Love," *Eranos* 67 (1969) 33–42 objected vehemently (proposing that line 6 be emended to φησι τί; κάλλος). For the further history of the quarrel, see P. Krafft, "Zu Kallimachos' Echo-Epigramm (28 Pf.)," *RhM* 120 (1977) 1–16 and Coco (1988) 121–22. Yet another emendation (ἄλλον ἔχει, partially anticipated by Schneider) has recently been proposed by Cameron (1995) 393.

79. Although doubts have been expressed by Gow-Page (1965) *ad* 5f. and Q. Cataudella, "Iterum de epigrammate Callimachi xii, 43, in quo de echo luditur," *Eranos* 69 (1971) 5–7, see now B. M. Palumbo Stracca, "L'eco di Callimaco (Ep. 28 Pf.) e la tradizione dei versi 'echoici,'" *SIFC* 6 (1988) 217; Aubreton (1994) 100; and Cameron (1995) 391.

syllable length and order, as well as the matter of the disappearance of the ν and the κ in the echoing phrase. Scholars have offered various emendations to remove these difficulties. But I believe that the poem's witty point lies precisely in the imperfection of the echo. Callimachus, who has just explained the extraordinary refinement of his tastes, addresses to Lysanias an aesthetic judgment of the boy's beauty. But for a man so focused on exclusivity the very acknowledgment of beauty immediately raises the question of fidelity. How can he be sure that one so handsome is his alone, unshared? His doubts, motivated by his refined taste, come to him in the form of an echo of his own words, transformed into a statement of commonness. The imperfection of the echo reflects its unreality, its quality as imagined thought, or suspicion. Callimachus moves, then, from an objective statement of his own taste to a concrete example of how his fastidiousness plays out in the erotic realm, how it affects his relationships with lovers. The characteristically Callimachean tone of the poem lies in the self-irony of the final couplet, where Callimachus undercuts his stance as arbiter of the refined with an illustration of how refinement can inhibit fulfillment of desire.

Other epigrams contribute to Callimachus' project of defining his erotic desire in terms of the aesthetics of refinement. In 1 G-P (= 31 Pf. = *AP* 12.102) Callimachus begins with the image of the hunter who suffers the hardships of frost and snow in order to pursue his prey but refuses to accept the body of a wounded animal found ready at hand. "My desire is like this," he says. "It knows how to pursue what flees but passes by what lies to hand." Here lack of availability is cited as the criterion for desire, seemingly because it arouses a need for Callimachus' knowledge (οἶδε, 1.6) of the game of love. We may think, by analogy, of the πόνος, or labor, that a refined poet employs in the creation of a carefully wrought work of art. Callimachus provides us with a specific example of erotic pursuit and its pleasures in his Menecrates epigram:

"ληφθήσει· περίφευγε, Μενέκρατες" εἶπα Πανήμου
  εἰκάδι, καὶ Λῴου τῇ—τίνι; τῇ δεκάτῃ
ἦλθεν ὁ βοῦς ὑπ' ἄροτρον ἑκούσιος. εὖ γ', ἐμὸς Ἑρμῆς,
  εὖ γ', ἐμός· οὐ παρὰ τὰς εἴκοσι μεμφόμεθα.

(10 G-P = 45 Pf. = *AP* 12.149)

"You will be caught. Just try to escape, Menecrates," I said
  on the twentieth of Panemus, and on—what day of Loius?
On the tenth the bull came willingly under the yoke. Well done,
  the luck was mine alone, mine. I don't regret those twenty days.

Here, as often in the erotic epigrams, the conversational tone gives access to the lover's emotional response. Callimachus' reckoning of the exact number of days between the conversation that initiated his pursuit of Menecrates and the boy's yielding to the yoke of love conveys his evident satisfaction with the outcome of the game. If the poem is read in isolation, the final clause can be understood to mean that the success of the chase was worth the twenty days of waiting. But if read in conjunction with Callimachus' other epigrams touting the lover's restraint as the mark of his desire and exclusivity of possession as the criterion of that desire,[80] the twenty days become necessary, the delay that brings pleasure to the winning of the boy.

In one final erotic epigram Callimachus establishes his personal knowledge with its fastidious taste as a standard for measuring beauty:

ἔγχει καὶ πάλιν εἰπὲ "Διοκλέος"· οὐδ' Ἀχελῷος
κείνου τῶν ἱερῶν αἰσθάνεται κυάθων.
καλὸς ὁ παῖς, Ἀχελῷε, λίην καλός, εἰ δέ τις οὐχί
φησίν, ἐπισταίμην μοῦνος ἐγὼ τὰ καλά.

(5 G-P = 29 Pf. = *AP* 12.51)

Pour a toast and say again, "For Diocles." Acheloos has
nothing to do with the holy cups dedicated to him.
The boy is beautiful, Acheloos, too beautiful. If anyone
denies it, I am content to be beauty's only connoisseur.

Gow-Page may be correct to suggest that Acheloos is here "the name not of the river but of a member of the party, and that Callimachus jokes on its equivalence to ὕδωρ."[81] If we follow this reading, Callimachus, as he calls for a toast in the name of Diocles, notices that Acheloos is paying no heed to the gesture and mentions the fact in a line that puns on the absence of water in the toasting cup. He then reaffirms to Acheloos the boy's beauty and asserts his intention to hold to this judgment even in the face of dissent. The poem stands as a kind of corollary to the echo epigram. There Lysanias' beauty arouses Callimachus' suspicion, the belief that the boy favors others too. Despite his beauty, then, he falls into the category of πάντα τὰ δημόσια, that which Callimachus detests. But Diocles, perhaps because Acheloos fails to find him appealing, stands among τὰ καλά, a category defined for Callimachus by the exclusivity of its appeal.[82]

If I am correct to argue that Callimachus' *Epigrammata* took the form of a carefully orchestrated collection, then we would expect to find within it an artistically designed opening and closing. In all probability, the epigrams occupying key positions would survive, because they were surely memorable to readers of the

80. Gow-Page (1965) *ad* 3 explain the phrase ἐμὸς Ἑρμῆς as a nominative that modifies the proverbial expression κοινὸς Ἑρμῆς, which refers to a sharing of good fortune: "'Ἐμός will mean on the contrary that the ἕρμαιον is exclusively C.'s."

81. Gow-Page (1965) *ad* 1f.

82. Cf. Hauvette 53: "A la petite scène de comédie, esquissée en quelques traits, succède une pensée chère à Callimaque, l'expression du raffinement exquis de l'artiste qui se plaît dans la contemplation solitaire d'un idéal interdit aux profanes." Giangrande (1968) 149 points out that Callimachus is here reversing a Theognidean expression, τῶν δὲ καλῶν οὔ τι σὺ μοῦνος ἐρᾷς (696).

collection and so likely to be quoted, if not anthologized. I have already shown that the concluding section of the collection can likely be identified in a series of epigrams that provide Callimachus' own view of death as utter nothingness and offer direct statements about his poetic achievement (*AP* 7.517–25). But what about the opening of the epigram book? Among epigrams already discussed only the echo poem (2 G-P) has an introductory character. Playing its part in the battle of books, it functions as a counterpart to Asclepiades' opening epigram, analogizing poetry to love in an expression of Callimachus' own taste (or distaste), his loathing of "all things common." Yet the final address to Lysanias links the poem so closely to other epigrams on individual *eromenoi* that it unlikely served as the main introduction for the collection.

My candidate for the first poem in Callimachus' *Epigrammata* is an anecdotal epigram on the sage Pittacus, which Schneider ordered first in his edition but which Gow-Page treat as an embarrassing misfit, with "no claim to be called an epigram at all":[83]

ξεῖνος Ἀταρνείτης τις ἀνείρετο Πιττακὸν οὕτω
    τὸν Μιτυληναῖον, παῖδα τὸν Ὑρράδιον·
"ἄττα γέρον, δοιός με καλεῖ γάμος· ἡ μία μὲν δή
    νύμφη καὶ πλούτῳ καὶ γενεῇ κατ' ἐμέ,
ἡ δ' ἑτέρη προβέβηκε. τί λώιον; εἰ δ' ἄγε σύμ μοι
    βούλευσον ποτέρην εἰς ὑμέναιον ἄγω."
εἶπεν· ὁ δὲ σκίπωνα γεροντικὸν ὅπλον ἀείρας·
    "ἠνίδε κεῖνοί σοι πᾶν ἐρέουσιν ἔπος."
(οἱ δ' ἄρ' ὑπὸ πληγῇσι θοὰς βέμβικας ἔχοντες
    ἔστρεφον εὐρείῃ παῖδες ἐνὶ τριόδῳ.)
"κείνων ἔρχεο," φησί, "μετ' ἴχνια." χὠ μὲν ἐπέστη
    πλησίον, οἱ δ' ἔλεγον "τὴν κατὰ σαυτὸν ἔλα."
ταῦτ' ἀίων ὁ ξεῖνος ἐφείσατο μείζονος οἴκου
    δράξασθαι, παίδων κληδόνα συνθέμενος·
τὴν δ' ὀλίγην ὡς κεῖνος ἐς οἰκίον ἤγετο νύμφην,
    οὕτω καὶ σύ γ' ἰὼν τὴν κατὰ σαυτὸν ἔλα.

(54 G-P = 1 Pf. = *AP* 7.89)

A stranger from Atarneus questioned Pittacus
    the sage of Mitylene and son of Hyrras:
"Honored sir, I have the choice of two marriages,
    with a bride who is my equal in wealth and rank
Or with a superior bride. What is better? Please
    advise me which marriage I should pursue."
Lifting his staff, an old man's weapon, he replied,
    "Those boys there will tell you all you need to know."
(Using whips to turn their tops swiftly, the boys

---

83. Gow-Page (1965) II 205. There can be no doubt, however, that the poem appeared in the *Epigrammata*, for Diogenes Laertius (1.79) cites it from the "epigrams" of Callimachus.

were spinning them in the wide crossroads.)
"Follow their example." The stranger stood near them
    as they repeated, "Follow your own course."
Hearing this, he avoided grasping the more prestigious
    marriage, since he understood the boys' message.
And just as that man led the poor bride to his home,
    so you, too, go now and follow your own course.

Several features of the poem suggest that it occupied the initial position. At sixteen lines it is the longest of Callimachus' epigrams, and we know from the *Miscellaneous Epigrams*, which began with a twenty-five-line epithalamium for Arsinoe, and from the *Garlands* of Meleager and Philip with their proems of fifty-eight and fourteen lines, respectively, that ancient epigram books did sometimes commence with longer elegiac poems. The second-person address in the final line is also an indication that this poem had a unique function within the collection. A large number of Callimachus' epigrams are addressed to a named individual, but only here do we find a generic σύ, which provides a direct address by the poet to the reader.[84] A parallel for such a generic second-person address in a programmatic context is offered by the concluding epigram in Nossis' collection (ἴθι, 11.4 G-P). In addition, the poem consists of an anecdote about Pittacus that is reminiscent of a tale concerning the Seven Sages in the first *Iambus*.[85] Of course, in *Iambus* 1 a Hipponax *redivivus* relates the story to a audience of quarreling poets and here the poet himself speaks to the reader, but these are mere generic differences between the fuller iambus and the shorter epigrammatic form. The parallel with the first *Iambus* shows clearly that the Pittacus anecdote is just the sort of introduction that Callimachus was likely to have given his *Epigrammata*.

But how did the poem function as the opening piece for a collection of epigrams? Since Callimachus' poetry book included epigrams of both the erotic-sympotic and the inscriptional types, he needed to avoid an introductory poem that could be classified in either of these categories or that seemed to announce a specific theme, like Posidippus' "bittersweet Eros" (1.4 G-P). Instead, he versifies a proverbial piece of wisdom and leaves it to the reader to find the applicability of this advice for the context. It is important to note that the key phrase in which the advice is encoded, τὴν κατὰ σαυτὸν ἔλα ("follow your own course"), has an ambiguous reference that shifts as the words are repeated: the boys apparently

84. The manuscript of Diogenes Laertius (1.80) contains the proper name Δίων (printed by Gow-Page), but the reading γ' ἰών (printed by Jacobs, Stadtmüller, Cahen, Waltz, Beckby, and Paton) is transmitted both by the *Palatine Anthology* and by Planudes. Schneider I 407, assuming the need for a proper name, suggested γ' Ἴων. But for a comparable use of ἰών, see Asclep. 25.10 G-P = *AP* 5.181.10.

85. In fact, the advice here delivered by Pittacus was elsewhere ascribed to other members of that group; for references, see Gow-Page (1965) *ad* 12.

refer to their tops, while Pittacus intends the stranger to understand a reference to brides. When the poet utters the phrase at the end of the epigram, the reader is to understand yet another application, and if the poem was indeed the first in the collection, this was surely to the epigrams that follow.

What Pittacus advises the Atarnean stranger is restraint, to forgo the opportunity for high status that others would seize, to choose the poor wife (τὴν ὀλίγην νύμφην, 15) who belongs to his own social class. The concept that less is more is basic to Callimachus' poetic program, as in the *Aetia* prologue he accepts the charge that he rolls forth a short tale like a child and he is advised to keep his Muse thin, to travel the narrow path. Such statements of poetic philosophy were found in the epigram collection as well, in a number of poems directly concerned with literary topics.[86] Callimachus praises the "pure road" followed by Theaetetus in composing his dramas, a road that denies him the laurels awarded by popular taste (57 G-P = 7 Pf. = *AP* 9.565). In his own dramatic competitions Callimachus hopes for the two-syllable word (νικῶ, "I won"), brief but best (58 G-P = 8 Pf. = *AP* 9.566). Aratus, whose "refined words" (λεπταὶ ῥήσιες) are a sign of his sleepless labor, is praised for his restraint in imitating only the "sweetest" part of Hesiod (56 G-P = 27 Pf. = *AP* 9.507). It is reasonable to conclude that the Pittacus anecdote was to be understood as but another imagistic illustration of Callimachus' philosophy of life and poetics.[87] As the introduction to an epigram collection, it surely suggested Callimachus' choice to compose in the briefest of poetic forms, the "poor bride" (ὀλίγην νύμφην) representing the genre that Philip would later call τὴν ὀλιγοστιχίην (1.6 G-P, *Garland*). In the *Aetia* prologue Callimachus, or perhaps another, is named ὀλιγόστιχος (fr. 1.9). He begins his epigram collection, then, not with the announcement of any one theme, but with the suggestion that his philosophy of restraint, of refined choice, will be the glue that holds together the many and diverse poems that constitute the *Epigrammata*.

86. For Callimachus' epigrams on literary themes, see Gabathuler 54–65, Riedweg 126–41.

87. A reference to Callimachean poetics has been suggested by Goffredo Coppola, *Cirene e il nuovo Callimaco* (Bologna, 1935) 167–68 and E. Livrea, "From Pittacus to Byzantium: The History of a Callimachean Epigram," *CQ* 45 (1995) 480, but neither scholar comments on the epigram's position within Callimachus' collection.

CHAPTER SIX

The Art of Variation:
From Book to Anthology

This book throughout has stressed the importance of context, both literary and historical, for the interpretation of Hellenistic epigram. While the brevity of the epigram form produces a susceptibility to change of context and so of meaning, I have privileged interpretations that look to the historical settings in which the epigrams were written and to the literary contexts, namely poetry books, in which the authors themselves sited their compositions. In turning to the topic of epigram variation, we explore a phenomenon by which the epigrams themselves, through overt intertextuality, reveal or incorporate the literary context in which they are to be read, a context that was perhaps originally meant to be physically absent but in the case of anthologies became physically present. The development of variation as an aesthetically pleasing phenomenon signals the canonization of epigram as an established literary form and is directly connected with the advent of anthologizing, the primary medium through which Hellenistic epigrams were preserved and the genre itself obtained its longevity. In terms of historical context, the argument will be made that the flowering of the art of variation in the late second century B.C. was connected with anxiety about the endangered status of Greek culture in the face of increasing Roman hegemony. One response to this perceived threat was preservation through repetition, the remaking of the past for present consumption.

The commonness of variation and of stock themes is often cited as one of the reasons for the minor status attaching to epigram as an art form. Such a view is based on a hierarchizing of genres, authors, and perceived historical periods that is allied to ideas of creativity and originality, of the direct expression of emotion, ideas that are themselves products of now outmoded aesthetic judgments. In a return to the critical assessments of antiquity, some recent scholars have given a more positive valuation to imitation as the fundamental condition of all discourse. Such scholars reject the evaluative dichotomizing of original and derivative, because, as Aristotle (*Poet.* 1448b) points out, imitation is a natural human activity, and so the basis for literature itself. In the words of Joel Weinsheimer, imitation "consists in a relation to something else which . . . both is and is not the same as itself" and so "is doubly ambiguous, for it is neither a copy nor an original."[1] Each original is in fact a copy of something that went before, just as each copy can in its turn become the original when it is imitated. If imitation is applied to textual matter in a broad sense, it can also become a means of linking the activities of poet and scholar. As a form of imitation, poetry serves to comment on earlier literature, just as scholarly explication performs a creative function in its rewriting of a literary text.

Even early Greek literature is highly imitative, in the sense that authors worked with a limited range of topics, generic forms, and modes of expression. But the close rewriting of specifically acknowledged texts, such as we find in sequences of epigram variations, is primarily a phenomenon of the late Hellenistic age when the Greek literary tradition was perceived as both distant or inaccessible and dominating or inescapable. As an aesthetically valued practice, variation is predicated upon an overarching awareness of a fixed tradition consisting of other written texts. The earliest literary epigrams, those written in the first decades of the third century, soon became subject to variation by other epigrammatists. Anyte's animal epitaphs were widely imitated by later third-century poets, such as Nicias and Mnasalces, while Posidippus' erotic epigrams vary motifs developed by Asclepiades. Callimachus endeavored to put his personal stamp on the major types of literary epigram that had developed in the early third century by exposing through imitation their fictiveness as inscribed or oral speech. Other examples could of course be cited as well. These variations were usually a reworking of a motif, rather than a reproduction of a whole epigram. They serve to mark a poet's allegiance to a certain variety of epigram or a theme or often to highlight, though their points of alteration, a poet's difference from his predecessor, the quality of his uniqueness within a tradition. In this sense third-century variation was often agonistic, and so led to development within the genre. For reasons that remain unclear Meleager included in his *Garland* less material from poets writing in the second half of the third century and the first half of the second, although he did make some selections from collections by Mnasalces, Dioscorides, Alcaeus of Messene, Rhianus, and Theodoridas. But the epigrams he chose from newer poets, those writing within a generation of his anthology, show a marked increase in the frequency of variation as well as the closeness of the imitation. It is not uncommon for a poet to imitate an epigram so closely as to repeat names, basic information, and even poetic structure—a trend that continues throughout later antiquity. Different motivating principles for variation were now at work. Foremost among Meleager's immediate prececessors was another poet from the

---

1. Weinsheimer, *Imitation* (London, 1984) 2.

Levant, Antipater of Sidon, who composed mostly dedications and epitaphs and who was particularly fond of imitating Leonidas. Meleager, a great admirer of Antipater, adopted his mode of variation to the erotic type of epigram. He also developed a sophisticated literary context for variation by using connections between earlier and later epigrammatists as the organizing principle of his anthology.

Once epigram had become accepted as a legitimate literary genre, professing its master practitioners and its favored texts, variation emerged as a form of supplementation by which an author might insert himself within the tradition without subverting it. An essentially conservative strategy, variation allows movement without fundamental change. The poet both conceals his own individuality by adopting the topic of another and reveals it by the alterations that are necessary in paraphrase. While third-century epigram advertised its status as disembodied writing, as literary text, the variation of an epigram presents itself as an act of reading as well as writing. In this age of intense scholarship, variation became valued as a form of criticism and interpretation; the practitioner of epigram variation accepts secondary status as imitator but in compensation gains the right to articulate the meaning of the original. We will find that for Antipater of Sidon the process of reading becomes thematized as a connective among his epigrams, while for the anthologizer Meleager the interconnectiveness between original and variation functions as a global theme linking the disparate contents of his *Garland*.

Variation, which is often treated as an effete literary process, is in fact derived from the nonbook contexts, written and oral, in which epigram originally functioned. Even a cursory reading of Hansen's collection of archaic inscriptions (*CEG*) shows that the language used for commonplace epitaphs and dedications was highly repetitive, bordering on the formulaic. Similarity of expression, rather than uniqueness in wording, was thus endemic to epigram from its inscriptional beginnings. In the fourth century there began to appear multiple epigrams on the same theme inscribed on a single monument. Peek argues that such a series creates an almost lyric effect, directed to the expression of emotion rather than the simple conveyance of information.[2] A more practical motivation was likely ostentatious display, on the part of those who could afford to commission more than one epigram. An example of serial epigrams composed to celebrate wealth are the parallel poems found on a statue base at Delos, one by Antipater of Sidon and one by Antisthenes of Paphos (*Inscr. Dél.* 2549). Both celebrate the same set of dedications made by a Palestinian banker named Philostratus. Antipater's poem (42 G-P) reads very much like a versified temple inventory, while Antisthenes', apparently composed for second place, supplements the list of dedications with information about the benefactions of the

2. Peek (1960) 33.

dedicator.[3] So Meleager's grouping of epigrams that vary a single theme parallels the inscriptional practices of the day. The richness of the book context, in which an epigram gains its literary effect by being read in conjunction with the poem it varies, provides a literary counterpart to the richness of the inscriptional site, derived from its combination of plastic and verbal representation.

The parallel between an epigram series in a book and an inscribed series has another aspect as well; epigrams composed for the book sometimes moved to an inscriptional site, where they could be matched with other poems varying a given theme. An example of such a series has been found in the House of the Epigrams in the Via Stabiana at Pompeii. Leonidas' epigram on three brothers who dedicate nets to Pan (46 G-P = *AP* 6.13) was there inscribed beneath a fresco depicting that very scene.[4] Adjacent and thematically related frescoes also bear inscriptions: Eros wrestling with Pan in the presence of Aphrodite is accompanied by a quatrain describing the scene; the presence of Homer before fishermen is explained by a line from the *Contest of Homer and Hesiod* stating the fishermen's riddle that Homer was unable to solve; a scene depicting a goat nibbling a vine gains interest when the vine is given voice (in the inscription) and vows to gain revenge through the goat's sacrifice. This last inscription appears in the *Anthology* as a couplet ascribed to Evenus of Ascalon (3 G-P, *Garland* = *AP* 9.75) and its pentameter occurs at the end of a six-line Leonidean epigram (32 G-P = *AP* 9.99).[5] The House of the Epigrams was thus decorated with a series of frescoes, connected through the common theme of rustic worship and inscribed with verses known from such sources as epigram books.[6] A similar phenomenon

3. For an attempt to reconstruct the text as well as comments on the literary aspects of the poems, see W. Peek, "Antipater von Sidon und Antisthenes von Paphos," *Philologus* 101 (1957) 101–13. Antisthenes is otherwise known only as the author of another honorific inscription at Delos, celebrating a certain Simalus for his hospitality (*Inscr. Dél.* 1533); see W. Peek, "Delische Weihepigramme," *Hermes* 76 (1941) 412–13.

4. Published by C. Dilthey, "Dipinti Pompeiani accompagnati d'epigrammi Greci," *Annali dell'Instituto di Corrispondenza archeologica* 48 (1876) 294–314; see Kaibel (1878) 1103. For the possibility that the painted scenes derive from illustrated books which included the inscriptions, see Karl Schefold, *Vergessenes Pompeji* (Bern, 1962) 45–46, 47.

5. Since the story of the vine and the goat appears in Aesop (404 Halm), Gow-Page (1968) II 291, argues that the couplet ascribed to Evenus was probably known to Leonidas, who built his epigram around it. Lausberg 211 argues, however, that as an epigrammatist called Evenus (probably the same poet) shortened another of Leonidas' epigrams on a work of art (23 G-P = *AP* 16.182) to a single couplet (10 G-P, *Garland* = *AP* 16.165), Leonidas may have been the first to turn the fable to epigrammatic form. It favors Lausberg's suggestion that Evenus' couplet on the goat and vine was apparently composed to accompany an illustration, since the speaker of the lines cannot be identified without a literary or artistic context. The lines were also known to Ovid (*Fasti* 1.357–58) and Suetonius (*Dom.* 14).

6. A fifth painting, placed on the right wall to balance the painting of Pan and Eros, contains a representation of Dionysus and was undoubtedly also accompanied by an epigram, now lost. For the arrangement of the frescoes to create an interweaving of motifs, see B.

occurred with one of Antipater's epigrams, an epitaph for Homer (9 G-P = *AP* 7.6), which was inscribed with modifications on a headless double herm of Homer and Menander found at Rome. There Antipater's poem begins a series continuing with two additional epigrams on Homer (*IG* 14.1188); a second series of three epigrams on Menander was inscribed on the other side of the herm (*IG* 14.1183). It is believed that the sophist Aelian set up the herm and composed at least some of the poetry celebrating these two masters of Greek literature.[7] Meleager's poetic and editorial technique of completing an epigram series with his own variation acquired, then, a parallel in the artistic realm when book epigrams were inscribed together with variations composed by the person constructing the monument.

Epigram variation was practiced in oral contexts as well, and the roots of the phenomenon again extend back into the archaic age. The oral circulation of elegy among symposiasts necessarily produced a certain fluidity in the texts, while variation was an inherent characteristic of scolia, which were often performed as responsive pairs. Improvisation was a valued skill among symposiasts, and Simonides in particular had a reputation for clever repartee, often in verse. Callistratus in his *Symmikta* quotes a six-line epigram that Simonides supposedly improvised (ἀπεσχεδίασε) at a dinner party (Ath. 3.125c–d). While epigrams may have sometimes been performed orally before the Hellenistic era, the improvising of epigrams became a highly valued skill in the second century B.C. Antipater of Sidon was apparently the first epigrammatist to acquire a reputation for epigram variations produced extemporaneously. In the *De Oratore*, whose dramatic date is 91 B.C., Cicero reports that Antipater was known as an improviser to Q. Lutatius Catulus (consul 102 B.C.) and other Romans of his generation: *solitus est versus hexametros aliosque variis modis atque numeris fundere ex tempore tantumque hominis ingeniosi ac memoris valuit exercitatio, ut, cum se mente ac voluntate coniecisset in versum, verba sequerentur* ("He made a habit of expounding hexameters and other verses in various forms and meters extempore, and since he was a witty man with a good memory, practice brought him to the point that when he deliberately decided to cast his ideas into verse, words followed automatically," 3.194). In Cicero's own generation Licinius Archias of Antioch was admired for his skill at extemporaneous composition, which often involved variation of a topic: *quotiens ego hunc vidi, cum litteram scripsisset nullam, magnum numerum optimorum versuum de iis ipsis rebus, quae tum agerentur, dicere ex tempore! quotiens revocatum eandem rem dicere commutatis verbis atque sententiis!* ("How often I have seen

Neutsch, "Das Epigrammenzimmer in der 'Casa degli Epigrammi' zu Pompeji," *JDAI* 70 (1955) 160.

7. The person who commissioned the inscriptions, apparently Aelian, had to change the last line of Antipater's epitaph, Ὅμηρον ... ἁλιρροθία, ξεῖνε, κέκευθε κόνις, to fit the context of a portrait herm: Ὅμηρον ... ὁρᾷς τοῦτον δαίδαλον ἀρχέτυπον. See Skiadas 71.

him deliver impromptu, without any written notes, a large number of excellent verses about whatever matter was under discussion! How often I have seen him give an encore performance on the same subject with changed phraseology and expression!" *Arch.* 8.18). Quintilian (10.7.19) later links Antipater and Archias as skilled improvisers in verse. It is even possible that Archias was personally acquainted with Antipater in Rome during the decade following his arrival in 102 B.C., since the Catulus who "remembered" Antipater's improvisations in 91 B.C. was also a patron of Archias during that time period. It is thus extremely tempting to identify Cicero's client with the Archias who composed several close variations of Antipater and other Meleagrian epigrammatists preserved in the *Anthology*. But the identification with Licinius Archias of Antioch, even if likely, remains based on circumstantial evidence. More than one Archias, perhaps as many as five, contributed to the *AP*, and none of the variations of Antipater by Archias can be securely assigned to one of the longer Meleagrian sequences.[8] Even so, it is clear that Antipater played the key role in establishing variation as a new trend in epigram and that he was followed in this practice by Meleager and Licinius Archias, both of whom shared with him a home in the Levant. A third follower of Antipater was Amyntas, who was probably composing in the late second or early first century B.C.[9] Amyntas is known only from a papyrus of the Augustan age (P.Oxy. 662), which contains (with other epigrams) Leonidas' epitaph for Prexo (70 G-P = *AP* 7.163), followed by Antipater's imitation (21 G-P = *AP* 7.164), followed in turn by Amyntas' version (1 *FGE*). It is interesting that Archias also composed a variation of the same epigram (13 G-P, *Garland* = *AP* 7.165), though it does not appear on the papyrus.

In the latter half of the second century B.C., then, serial epigrams written for inscription and variations produced extemporaneously provide precedent and even raw material for the collection of epigrams that vary other epigrams into poetry books. The practice of composing epigram variations for poetry books, a practice that grants these texts a claim of high literary quality, is thoroughly consistent with the critical concerns of the age. Major literary critics of the late Hellenistic period, Greek and Roman, discuss the imitation of one's

8. Both Helen Law, "The Poems of Archias in the *Greek Anthology*," *CP* 31 (1936) 225–43 and Gow-Page (1968) II 432–35 have attempted, with similar results, to group the various epigrams ascribed to Archias by distinguishing characteristics. A group that varies Meleagrian authors, especially Leonidas and Antipater (4–14 G-P, *Garland*), was likely composed by Archias of Antioch, although one of these poems (12 G-P, *Garland*) is ascribed by the corrector of the Palatine Codex to an Archias of Byzantium. It may be that this poem is by a later homonymous author or that its ascription in the Palatine is false; Planudes has simply Ἀρχίου. Both Law 236–37, who assigns the group to the Byzantine, and Gow-Page (1968) II 434–35, who assume Cicero's Archias, believe that this series of variations was in Meleager's *Garland*. None of the poems appear, however, in sequences that are certainly from either Meleager or Philip, since they have been excerpted by Cephalas to thematic sequences.

9. For discussion of Amyntas and his date, see Page (1981) 5–6.

predecessors.[10]   Although imitation could be badly done, Greek μίμησις, or Latin *imitatio*, did not have the connotation of derivative inferiority that the term has acquired in modern times. Seneca even claims that the position of the last writer is best, for he finds the language for the topic already prepared and need only give it a new arrangement (*Ep.* 79.6) One of the most enthusiastic advocates of imitation is "Longinus," who asserts that sublimity in composition is obtained by imitation of and rivalry with great authors of the past. He describes imitation as a form of mystic inspiration, which produces a flow of effluences from the mouth of the sublime writer into the soul of the imitator (13.2). For "Longinus" both imitation and rivalry (μίμησίς τε καὶ ζήλωσις) are necessary to obtain the effect of sublimity. Another ancient critic, Dionysius of Halicarnassus, defines imitation as the activity of making an impression of a model and rivalry as the competitive spirit that moves the imitator to attempt to outdo his predecessor.[11] Even if failure to improve on the masters is the likely outcome, "Longinus" urges ambitious writers to engage agonistically with their models, as Plato entered the ranks in competition with Homer (13.4). Although "Longinus" distinguishes imitative borrowing from plagiarism, or κλοπή (13.4),[12] he does not explain how to determine the difference between the two. From other sources it is clear that one of the distinguishing marks (in addition to the more subjectively judged success of the imitation) is the imitator's acknowledgment of his model.[13] Certainly in the case of the epigram variations practiced by Antipater and Meleager, the reader's awareness of the exact poem being imitated was all important to the intended effect.

The more practical aspects of imitation are discussed by rhetorical theorists in their accounts of how good orators are to be trained. For Cicero and Quintilian imitation was conceived as paraphrase, which for Roman writers took one of two forms—translation from the Greek or paraphrase of other Latin authors. Cicero (*De Or.* 1.154–55) recommends only the former alternative on the grounds that the reworking of admirable Latin passages, prose or poetry, produced either tautology or inferior presentation. Quintilian, on the other hand, valued paraphrase from the Latin because, as a practice of interpretation (*interpretationem*), it developed the faculty of understanding and, as a form of rivalrous emulation (*certamen atque aemulationem*), it honed the literary skills of the imitator (10.5.5). Much of his description of Latin paraphrase recalls the

10. For a thorough discussion, see Kroll 139–78; D. A. Russell, "De imitatione" in *Creative Imitation and Latin Literature*, ed. David West and T. Woodman (Cambridge, 1979) 1–16.

11. περὶ μιμήσεως, fr. 3 in *Opuscula* II, ed. Hermann Usener and L. Radermacher (Leipzig, 1904–29) 200.

12. One of the activities of Hellenistic scholars (the ancient version of *Quellenforschung*) was to compile the κλοπαί of various authors. On plagiarism, see Eduard Stemplinger, *Das Plagiat in der griechischen Literatur* (Leipzig, 1912); Russell (1979) 11–12.

13. See, for instance, Cic. *Brut.* 76, Sen. *Suas.* 3.7.

techniques used in epigram variation. He recommends that the aspiring orator choose the simplest subjects for paraphrase, because "true merit consists in expanding what is naturally contracted, amplifying the small, lending variety to sameness and charm to the commonplace, and speaking at length about circumscribed subjects" (10.5.11). We may observe that, in general, epigram variations tend to expand their models and to add linguistic decoration. Self-variation, or the production by one author of more than one epigram on a single theme, is also paralleled by Quintilian's comments on the human tendency to speak twice or more on the same topic, so that we commonly enter into rivalry with ourselves as well as others (10.5.7).

The extemporaneous variation of epigram, as practiced by Antipater and Archias, has a decided similarity to declamation, the art of delivering speeches for rhetorical display. Declamation can be documented as early as the third century B.C. and had come to dominate the educational system of both the Greeks and the Romans by the first century B.C.[14] The most skilled declaimers would give public performances in which they spoke in elaborate style on a theme chosen by the audience. It was possible to do this because the topics were drawn from set themes, best illustrated by the *suasoriae* and *controversiae* of Seneca the Elder. The topics were always hypothetical, debates about imaginary court cases or past historical events. The parallel with epigrams of the late second century B.C. is striking, for as variations of earlier epigrams they deal with known themes; they are concerned with subjects whose status as historical or fictive is irrelevant or with the common currency of Greek culture—famous persons and events of the past, major art objects, canonized literary figures. We can better understand the Romans' admiration for poets like Antipater and Archias if we recognize their similarity to orators, for whom Quintilian claims the ultimate skill was extemporaneous speaking (10.7.1).[15] As Alexander Peloplaton was much admired for delivering a speech twice on the same day, expressing identical arguments in completely different words (Philostr. *VS* 571–74), so Cicero commends Archias for saying the same thing *commutatis verbis atque sententiis* ("with changed phraseology and expression," *Arch.* 8.18). Declaimers were not concerned to discover new topics but to preserve the heritage of past speech through some novelty of expression. Parallels exist in the matter of publication as well. Just as Cicero published in reworked and polished form speeches he had delivered or intended to deliver, so we may assume that Antipater reworked for a

---

14. On papyrological evidence for Greek declamation in the third century B.C., see D. A. Russell, *Greek Declamation* (Cambridge, 1983) 4. For general discussion of Latin declamation with bibliography, see George Kennedy, *The Art of Rhetoric in the Roman World, 300 B.C.–A.D. 300* (Princeton, 1972) 312–22.

15. See, in general, Hazel L. Brown, *Extemporary Speech in Antiquity* (Menasha, Wis., 1914); Russell (1983) 79–86. For discussion of the connection between improvisation in prose and poetry, see Alex Hardie, *Statius and the "Silvae"* (Liverpool, 1983) 74–85.

collection epigrams he had composed extemporaneously. Seneca's *controversiae* in fact constitute an anthology of passages from his favorite orators arranged by topics; as variations on a theme, these sets of rhetorical extracts resemble the groups of epigram variations that we find in Meleager's *Garland*.

Both Quintilian (10.5.9) and "Longinus" (13.4) compare literary imitation to the copying of an original art object. The comparison is apt, for the copying of Greek art works for Roman patrons, like the recitation of epigram variations at Roman gatherings, stems from a desire to assimilate through reproduction a culture that was conceived as a fixed product of the past.[16] And as imitation, properly done, was not considered plagiarism, so the ancients did not make sharp distinctions between copy and original, or artisan and artist.[17] Late Hellenistic copiers of statues often signed their products with their own names rather than that of the sculptor whose work they copied. Because of the techniques used each art work was in some sense an original creation. As literary variations reproduce the words and sentiments of earlier poems to a greater or lesser extent, so too copies of art works display a broad latitude in similarity to the original. Some, as free-hand variants, exhibit considerable change in form, while it was also possible to produce nearly exact replicas through the pointing system. And as late Hellenistic imitators, like Antipater, became themselves models for other poets to vary, so too Greek sculptors of the first century B.C. began to produce models of their art works that could be used for mass production.[18] Also related to the series of epigram variations are the replica series, in which a popular type of statuary, often based on a famous Greek original, was reproduced countless times with changes in "material, scale, quality, and iconographic detail."[19] In art as in literature, Greek patriotism for a culture whose independence and dominance was fading worked together with a Roman desire to assimilate the symbols of that culture to produce an interest, not in innovation and change, but in replication with variation. Artistic talent was thus conceived as the ability to create the most striking reproductions.

Epigram variation should not be viewed, then, as an effete product of degenerate Hellenic culture, but as as aesthetically satisfying response to historical circumstance with ties to other forms of poetry, to rhetoric, and to art. My reading of the epigrams composed by Antipater of Sidon and Meleager will thus focus on their intertextuality, in the double sense of their relationship to other literary texts and of their relationship to the textual codes of the social system

16. On the nostalgic aspects of the art of this period, see Green (1990) 566–85.

17. As argued by Brunilde S. Ridgway, *Roman Copies of Greek Sculpture* (Ann Arbor, 1984). See also, on the neoclassical impulse behind Roman sculptural practice, M. Marvin, "Copying in Roman Sculpture: The Replica Series," in *Roman Art in Context: An Anthology*, ed. Eve d'Ambra (Englewood Cliffs, N. J., 1993) 161–88.

18. See Pollitt 163.

19. Marvin 169.

within which the poets worked. As a native of a Greek colony in a period when Greece itself was being colonized by Rome, Antipater carved an intellectual niche for himself with his Roman patrons through his facility in reproducing, without substantive change but with novelty of expression, various textual *topoi* of Greek culture. The connecting theme in Antipater's epigrams, which must have come together at some point in a collection, is the process of reading as interpretation, with the reading of epigram functioning as a symbol for the interpretive reading of the cultural past. Taking Antipater's achievement in variation one step further, Meleager employed the dual roles of editor and composer to create a textual context for the intertextuality of epigram. In an anthology that was partially organized through sequences of variations, Meleager juxtaposed original and copy to bring the whole tradition of the past into the presence of contemporary compositions. The interweaving of a garland as the image for his anthology aptly symbolizes the intertextual process of variation and, as I will argue, reappears within the *Garland* as a theme connecting Meleager's skills as editor and as composer. In this reading of Antipater and Meleager, the lack of originality and the exuberance of style for which they have commonly been criticized become marks of a successful intellectual response to their historical situation.

ANTIPATER OF SIDON

Antipater, whose long life encompassed a good portion of the second century B.C., was a Greek from the Phoenician city of Sidon.[20] He wrote primarily epitaphs and dedications, a substantial number of which vary earlier epigrammatists, most particularly Leonidas. Certain difficulties exist in dividing the surviving epigrams between the Sidonian and his namesake from Thessalonica, who wrote in the Augustan age and figured prominently in Philip's *Garland*. Some few of the forty-six epigrams ascribed to the Sidonian and the thirty-five ascribed to the Thessalonican seem incorrectly assigned, while the ninety-six epigrams ascribed

---

20. Antipater's birth should be placed no later than 170 B.C., since the most likely subject for 25 G-P = *AP* 7.241 is the death of Ptolemy Philometor's son Eupator about 150 B.C. That Antipater lived to an old age is attested by Pliny *HN* 7.172 and Val. Max. 1.8.16; cf. Cic. *Fat.* 5. The supposition of Gow-Page (1965) II 32 that he died about 125 is, in all likelihood, too early, since Philostratus, the Delian banker for whom he composed an epigram (42 G-P), erected other inscriptions toward the end of the second century. We know only that his death preceded the dramatic date of Cicero's *De Oratore*—91 B.C.—and the publication of Meleager's *Garland*, which was likely as late as the decade of the 90s. Antipater was said by Meleager to be a native of Tyre (122.13–14 G-P = *AP* 7.428.13–14) but was called a Sidonian elsewhere—such as in the *Anthology*, by Cicero (*De Or.* 3.194), and in a Delian inscription (*Inscr. Dél.* 2549). Meleager's claim, made in the context of a *Garland* epigram, may have been an attempt to suggest a literary link with his predecessor by ascribing to him a homeland in the city in which Meleager himself grew to manhood.

simply to Antipater must be distributed between the two homonymous poets on the basis of style or environment in the *Anthology*.[21] It is nonetheless clear that the Antipater from Sidon was a key figure in establishing variation, especially close variation, as the future trend in epigram composition. His approach to third-century inscriptional epigram clearly influenced Meleager, who applied his talents to erotic epigram, while Antipater's own variations became the models for later epigrammatists.

Although Antipater was obviously a prominent poet in his own day and became an influential figure in the history of epigram, modern scholars have found little to admire in his surviving poetry. Gow-Page call him "a rhetorician, fond of long sentences, too fond of adjectives and especially of long compounds" and asserts that "he had few ideas of his own."[22] Setti, who even more severely criticizes Antipater for lack of originality and a rhetorical style, blames his "fervid and exuberant oriental nature."[23] Given our current more sympathetic approach to the multicultural society of the Hellenistic world, we recognize the inappropriateness of explaining a poet's intertextual relationships and stylistic proclivities in terms of supposedly inferior ethnic characteristics.[24] It is more useful, and interesting, to view variation and the complicated style that accompanies it as a

21. My numbers are derived from Gow-Page (1965) II 31, who are relying on Giovanni Setti, *Studi sulla Antologia Greca: gli epigrammi degli Antipatri* (Turin, 1890) 13–15. The thirty-five epigrams assigned to the Thessalonican include five ascribed to Antipater of Macedon, who is apparently the same person, and six ascribed to the Sidonian but clearly derived from Philip's *Garland*; see Gow–Page (1968) II 21. While Setti assigned all ninety-six epigrams ascribed to Antipater without an ethnic to one poet or the other on the basis of style and position in the *Anthology*, Gow-Page (1965) II 31–34 take a much more conservative approach, assigning to the Sidonian only those poems in whose ascription they have a high degree of confidence. All the others were then edited in the *The Garland of Philip* with those certainly composed by Antipater of Thessalonica. As a result, Gow-Page themselves admit (1968) II 20 that the latter collection surely includes a good number of poems actually composed by the Sidonian. Since my discussion must be limited to only a selection of Antipater's epigrams, I have chosen from Gow-Page's collection in the *Hellenistic Epigrams* except in a few cases discussed in the notes below.

22. Gow-Page (1965) II 32.

23. Setti 38. We may compare, however, the somewhat more complimentary assessment of Reitzenstein, *RE* 2 HB (1894) 2513–14: "In der Metrik sorgfältig, in der Sprache kühn und prunkvoll, öfters in die ältere Lyrik erinnerd, vor allem stets rhetorisch." Antipater has received more than his share of the neglect literary scholars have allotted so many of the epigrammatists. In addition to Setti's discussion of his style in the interests of establishing authenticity, the reader may consult Webster's analysis (1964) 204–8 of his epigrams by type.

24. For stereotypic views of the orient, see, generally, Edward W. Said, *Orientalism* (New York, 1978); and, for classicists, M. Katz, "Ideology and 'the Status of Women' in Ancient Greece" in *History and Theory* 31 (1992) 86–95. As examples of recent multicultural approaches to Hellenistic studies, see S. M. Burstein, "The Hellenistic Fringe: The Case of Meroë" in *Hellenistic History and Culture*, ed. Peter Green (Berkeley, 1993) 38–54 and the response there by Frank Holt 54–64; L. Koenen, "The Ptolemaic King as a Religious Figure," in *Images and*

product of Antipater's position at the crossroads of culture.[25]   As an educated Greek from a Phoenician city in the late second century, Antipater existed as a marginal citizen within a Hellenistic culture that was itself in the process of being marginalized by the dominating power of Rome.[26]   His response to this historical circumstance was a neoclassical one, to adopt the Greek cultural tradition as the subject matter of his poetry and to express his contemporary concerns through selectivity, approach, and stylistic innovation.

In an epigram inscribed at Delos, Antipater commemorates a double portico set up by a wealthy banker for the two defenders of the island—Athens and Rome (42 G-P).[27] It is at the intersection of these two—the intellectual heritage of Athens and the political might of Rome—that Antipater produced his poetry. His epigrams as a group demonstrate his concern with preserving the Greek culture of the past, with negotiating the fragmented diversity of contemporary Hellenistic intellectual experience, and with adapting to the demands of the Romans who function as both masters and patrons.   Not only do many of his poems extend the Greek epigrammatic tradition through variation, but a number of them concern the great poets and thinkers of the past.   His acquaintance with various Hellenistic intellectual centers is suggested both by the Delos inscription and by his lament for a Ptolemaic prince (25 G-P = *AP* 7.241).   The shadow of Roman dominance appears behind an epigram commemorating a dedication by a certain Lycortas, apparently a relative of Polybius, perhaps his nephew (46 G-P = *AP* 6.111).[28]   As more direct evidence for the influence of Rome, we know that Antipater displayed his talents as an improviser to appreciative Roman audiences (Cic. *De Or.* 3.194). From the hand of Q. Lutatius Catulus, who heard Antipater's improvisations and became an intimate friend of Archias (Cic. *Arch.* 6), survive two erotic epigrams in Latin that are essentially variations of compositions found in the *Garland*, including epigrams by Callimachus and Meleager.[29]   It seems, then, that Antipater's

---

Ideologies: Self-Definition in the Hellenistic World, ed. Anthony Bulloch, E. S. Gruen, A. A. Long, and A. Stewart (Berkeley, 1993) 25–115.

25. Scholars have begun to treat variation as itself a creative process; see, for instance, the studies of Ludwig (1968); Tarán (1979); and Laurens 65–96.

26. For the relationship between Greece and Phoenicia in this period, see F. Millar, "The Phoenician Cities: A Case-Study of Hellenisation," *PCPS* 29 (1983) 55–71; John D. Grainger, *Hellenistic Phoenicia* (Oxford, 1991).

27. Illuminating comments on the wealthy self-indulgence of the leading Delian citizens during this period are found in Green (1990) 571–74.

28. Lycortas is Gow's plausible correction of the manuscript reading Lycormas. For the possible bearers of this name, all members of the family of Philopoemen and Polybius, see Gow-Page (1965) II 70–71.

29. Fr. 1 Courtney, p. 70 varies Callimachus 4 G-P = *AP* 12.73, and fr. 2 Courtney, p. 77 seems related to Meleager 79 G-P = *AP* 12.127.   On Catulus and his connection with two contemporary writers of Latin epigrams, Porcius Licinus and Valerius Aedituus, see Henry

influential role in disseminating the technique of epigram variation extended both to his Greek imitators and to Roman philhellenes. But even though he likely benefited from Roman patronage and may have been resident at Rome, Antipater's attitude to the Romans was highly ambivalent. He composed two epigrams (59 G-P = *AP* 9.151, 68 G-P = *AP* 7.493) lamenting the destruction of Corinth in 146 B.C., the finalizing act of Roman mastery over Greece, while a subversive approach to Roman dominance is suggested by an epigram (61 G-P = *AP* 9.567) concerning a Greek theatrical performer who will tame Roman aggression with her "soft charms." For a poet like Antipater who had moved from the outskirts to the center of the Greek world, Hellenic civilization was not a lived reality inherited as a birthright but a body of cultural symbols or icons to be assimilated as the gateway for entrance into the contemporary intellectual sphere.[30] This set body of knowledge, including literary texts, art works, and historical events, was worn as a badge of achievement—not to be surpassed in agonistic and individualizing rivalry but to be preserved by repetition, at best to be enhanced by decoration. The Romans served both as a threat to this culture, reinforcing Greek patriotism among those marginally Greek, and as an audience for whom Hellenic tradition had to be repackaged and disseminated.[31]

Antiquity has left us no direct information about Antipater's publication of his epigrams. Yet Meleager was unlikely to have known the seventy or so epigrams composed by the Sidonian from any source other than an epigram collection. The Delos dedication shows that Antipater did write genuine inscriptions, but, as Gow points out, practically none of the poems transmitted in the *Anthology* seem to have been inscribed. Many in fact may have originated as "impromptu compositions,"[32] later polished and reworked for publication. The large number of variations among the surviving epigrams suggests the possibility that Antipater anticipated Meleager in issuing an anthology of epigrams by

---

Bardon, "Q. Lutatius Catulus et son 'cercle littéraire,' " *LEC* 18 (1950) 145–64 and *La littérature latine inconnue* (Paris, 1952) I 115–32. For the variation of epigrams in Meleager's *Garland* by these Latin epigrammatists, see Laurens 159–81.

30. For the preservation of Greek identity through the cultivation of such institutions as the gymnasium and the theater, see A. Giovannini, "Greek Cities and Greek Commonwealth" in Bulloch *et al.* (1993) 268–74.

31. The love affair with the Hellenic past that we find already in Antipater only intensifies throughout the Empire period; see G. Anderson (1993) 101–32. For the attitude of Greek intellectuals to Rome, see Arnaldo Momigliano, *Alien Wisdom: The Limits of Hellenization* (Cambridge, 1975) 1–49 and M. H. Crawford, "Greek Intellectuals and the Roman Aristocracy in the First Century B.C." in *Imperialism in the Ancient World*, ed. P. D. A. Garnsey and C. R. Whittaker (Cambridge, 1978) 193–207. J. P. V. D. Balsdon, *Romans and Aliens* (Chapel Hill, 1979) 54–58 provides a list of Roman patrons and the Greek scholars attached to them up to the time of Augustus.

32. Gow-Page (1965) II 33.

himself and others.[33]   We have as yet, however, no papyrological evidence for anthologies of this sort before the time of Meleager; a papyrus preserving Amyntas' variation of Antipater's variation of a Leonidean epigram (P.Oxy. 662) is no earlier than the Augustan age. It is equally possible, then, that the Antipater collection was arranged by epigram type, like the earlier Posidippan collection on the Milan papyrus.

Previous epigrammatists developed their authorial personae through their choice of themes, key biographical information, and significant arrangement. But from Antipater we have no *sphragis* poems, self-epitaphs, or programmatic poems of introduction and conclusion. Nor do his epigrams as a body emphasize themes that identify the author in terms of class, gender, or regional background. Meleager later provided essential information about him—his place of origin and poetic interests—in a parodic epitaph that imitates his own poetic technique (122 G-P = *AP* 7.428), perhaps because this information was missing from Antipater's own poetry. Yet I will argue, on the basis of the surviving epigrams, that a collection of Antipater's poetry likely had a unifying focus in its projection of the author as an interpreter of earlier Greek texts and culture. A comprehensive edition of Antipater's epigrams would have included—and prominently, if Meleager's selection is in any way an accurate guide—variations of earlier epigrams, epitaphs for poets and famous personages of past ages, and enigmatic epitaphs that draw the reader into the process of decipherment and interpretation. The faceless, nonagonistic stance adopted by the creative presence behind such a collection would both conceal the author and leave traces of him throughout the intertextual web.

Antipater's variations may be divided into three general categories: (1) epigrams that repeat the subject, poetic structure, and sentiment of an earlier epigram with only a change of wording, (2) epigrams that repeat the subject of an earlier epigram while changing the poetic structure or sentiment, and (3) epigrams that repeat a motif with a change in the specific subject matter. Antipater's self-variations are not so much a fourth category as a subcategory of one and two. I have already suggested a general reason for Antipater's interest in variation, a desire to demonstrate his belonging to a culture that had become a product of the past, iconic in the present. So his preference for Leonidas was probably influenced by the previous canonization of that poet as the greatest third-century composer of inscriptional epigrams, although Antipater's numerous variations may have furthered Leonidas' reputation as an epigrammatist worthy of admiration and imitation. There is no sign that Antipater was attracted by the philosophical or class themes of the Leonidean collection itself.

---

33. Luck (1967) 36–39, 50–51 advances the hypothesis that Meleager used an earlier anthology compiled by Antipater, but his speculation that Meleager borrowed certain sequences from such an anthology remains without sufficient manuscript support.

More specific reasons may be adduced for the selection of epigrams within the three categories outlined above.

The first category, that of close variation, is perhaps the most difficult to appreciate for those embued with modern ideas of originality. The rewriting of an earlier poem with only minor changes in expression seems a mere act of virtuosity, a meaningless challenge of doing what has been done before. But a different point of view on the part of the ancients is suggested by the number of poems chosen for variation that contain within themselves examples of variation on a theme. Their appeal may lie in their own internal illustration of the variety that the imitator mimics externally through comparison with the original.

One of the most popular epigrams with later imitators was a dedication by Leonidas in which three brothers—a hunter, a fisherman, and a fowler—offer nets to Pan:[34]

οἱ τρισσοί τοι ταῦτα τὰ δίκτυα θῆκαν ὅμαιμοι,
    ἀγρότα Πάν, ἄλλης ἄλλος ἀπ’ ἀγρεσίης,
ὧν ἀπὸ μὲν πτανῶν Πίγρης τάδε, ταῦτα δὲ Δᾶμις
    τετραπόδων, Κλείτωρ δ’ ὁ τρίτος εἰναλίων.
ἀνθ’ ὧν τῷ μὲν πέμπε δι’ ἠέρος εὔστοχον ἄγρην,
    τῷ δὲ διὰ δρυμῶν, τῷ δὲ δι’ ἠιόνων.

(46 G-P = *AP* 6.13)

Three brothers have dedicated to you, huntsman Pan,
    these nets, each from a different chase:
Pigres these from fowl, Damis these from beasts,
    and Cleitor the third from creatures of the sea.
In exchange give successful hunting to one in the air,
    to the other in the woods, and to the third on the shore.

The popularity of the poem is shown also by its inscription bene⌐ h a fresco in the House of the Epigrams in Pompeii, which itself functions as a variation in a visual medium. The poem is a nearly perfect example of internal variation, an epigram in three couplets on three brothers who are generally alike in their occupation of hunting but specifically different in terms of the type of animal hunted. The first couplet, which begins with the key word τρισσοί, stresses in the initial line the likeness of the dedicators and the objects dedicated through the generic term δίκτυα and the choice of the word ὅμαιμοι to indicate their common bloodline, turning then in the pentameter to an expression of the difference between them, ἄλλης ἄλλος. The second couplet specifies the nature of this difference not only by providing the names of the brothers and the types of animals they hunt but also by the structure of the lines. The second member of the couplet varies the first by reversing the position of genitive and accusative (πτανῶν Πίγρης τάδε,

34. For a list of later variants, see Gow-Page (1965) II 34–35. For a discussion of the whole series of epigrams on the theme, see Laurens 80–83.

ταῦτα δὲ Δᾶμις τετραπόδων) and by use of the synonymous ταῦτα for τάδε. The third member provides further variation by replacing the accusative (now understood) with ὁ τρίτος, an adjective that reinforces verbally the play with the number three. The third couplet suggests a balance between the likeness and difference of these three brothers by the highly symmetrical structure of dative pronoun and prepositional phrase (τῷ μὲν ... δι᾽ ἠέρος ..., τῷ δὲ διὰ δρυμῶν, τῷ δὲ δι᾽ ἠιόνων), the perfect balance in the pentameter effecting closure by conveying a sense of order and completion.

The clever internal variation in this poem was likely one of the reasons that Antipater, and others after him, chose to imitate it:

Πανὶ τάδ᾽ αὔθαιμοι τρισσοὶ θέσαν ἄρμενα τέχνας·
    Δᾶμις μὲν θηρῶν ἄρκυν ὀρειονόμων,
Κλείτωρ δὲ πλωτῶν τάδε δίκτυα, τῶν δὲ πετηνῶν
    ἄρρηκτον Πίγρης τάνδε δεραιοπέδην.
τὸν μὲν γὰρ ξυλόχων, τὸν δ᾽ ἠέρος, ὃν δ᾽ ἀπὸ λίμνης
    οὔποτε σὺν κενεοῖς οἶκος ἔδεκτο λίνοις.

(Antip. 1 G-P = *AP* 6.14)

To Pan three brothers have dedicated this equipment:
    Damis a purse net for beasts that roam the mountains,
Cleitor these nets for fish, and Pigres this unbreakable
    neck chain for the feathered birds of the air.
For never did they return home with empty nets, one
    from the woods, one from the air, one from the sea.

Because it varied an earlier epigrammatist, the interest generated by Antipater's poem lies not only in the play with sameness and difference between the three brothers but additionally in the play of sameness and difference between his epigram and Leonidas'. A striking similarity in wording in the first line (τρισσοί ... θῆκαν ὅμαιμοι; αὔθαιμοι τρισσοὶ θέσαν) signals Antipater's dependence on Leonidas. But while Leonidas designates the objects offered by all three brothers with the word δίκτυα, which refers in Homer (*Od.* 22.386) to the nets of fishermen but came also to be used for any kind of large net,[35] Antipater is concerned to avoid this lack of dictional precision. Consequently, he opens with the generic circumlocution ἄρμενα τέχνας before specifying that the hunter Damis offers a purse net (ἄρκυς), Cleitor the large δίκτυα used for fishing, and Pigres no net at all but a collar for snaring birds. He also adorns Leonidas' rather spare second couplet with poetic or recherché vocabulary. He describes the wild

---

35. On the different types of hunting nets, see Xen. *Cyn.* 2.4–9, Oppian *Cyn.* 1.150–57, Pollux 5.26–35. A purse net (ἄρκυς) was constructed like a bag, while the long net (δίκτυον) was much larger and designed to be stretched out over a space of ground. Explanatory discussion can be found in Denison B. Hull, *Hounds and Hunting in Ancient Greece* (Chicago, 1964) 10–18.

beasts as "mountain-dwelling," a rare compound adjective;[36] he designates the fish as the "swimming ones" using an adjective as a noun; and he employs the unusual and self-explanatory noun δεραιοπέδη, qualified by the adjective "unbroken," for the instrument that snares the birds.[37] The third couplet with its threefold repetition of the article and its three genitives appears at first a close approximation of Leonidas' final couplet. But Antipater makes the reader work harder by postponing the single appearance of the preposition ἀπό to the third colon and by replacing Leonidas' εὔστοχον ἄγρην with the litotes of οὔποτε ... κενεοῖς ... λίνοις. Finally, we may note that Leonidas' closing symmetry is replaced by a triple assonance in οι, so placing a final acoustic emphasis on the flax fibers (λίνοις) that are the common element in all three dedications.

The next known poet to treat the three-brothers theme is Archias, in all likelihood to be identified with Licinius Archias of Antioch. From his hand we have, not one variation of the theme, but four:

σοὶ τάδε, Πὰν σκοπιῆτα, παναίολα δῶρα σύναιμοι
   τρίζυγες ἐκ τρισσῆς θέντο λινοστασίης,
δίκτυα μὲν Δᾶμις θηρῶν, Πίγρης δὲ πετηνῶν
   λαιμοπέδας, Κλείτωρ δ' εἰναλίφοιτα λίνα.
ὧν τὸν μὲν καὶ ἐσαῦθις ἐν ἠέρι, τὸν δ' ἔτι θείης
   εὔστοχον ἐν πόντῳ, τὸν δὲ κατὰ δρυόχους.

                      (4 G-P, *Garland* = *AP* 6.16)

To you, Pan of the heights, three brothers gave
   splendid gifts from three kinds of net hunting:
Damis nets for beasts, Pigres neck collars for birds,
   and Cleitor nets that drift in the sea.
May you yet again grant the one good hunting in the air,
   the other in the sea, and the third among the thickets.

ἀγραύλῳ τάδε Πανὶ βιαρκέος ἄλλος ἀπ' ἄλλης
   αὔθαιμοι τρισσοὶ δῶρα λινοστασίης,
Πίγρης μὲν δειραγχὲς ἐΰβροχον ἄμμα πετηνῶν,
   Δᾶμις δ' ὑλονόμων δίκτυα τετραπόδων,
ἄρκυν δ' εἰναλίων Κλείτωρ πόρεν· οἷς σὺ δι' αἴθρας
   καὶ πελάγευς καὶ γᾶς εὔστοχα πέμπε λίνα.[38]

                  (5 G-P, *Garland* = *AP* 6.179)

To rustic Pan these gifts from three brothers, each
   from a different kind of life-sustaining hunt:
Pigres a well-knit noose to choke the necks of birds,

36. The variant ὀρεινόμος describes a goat in Theophrastus (*Hist. Pl.* 9.18.3) and Centaurs in Euripides (*HF* 364).

37. According to Gow-Page (1965) *ad loc.* it occurs elsewhere only in Antip. Thess. 80.4 G-P, *Garland* = *AP* 9.76.4.

38. In line 3 I print Brunck's emendation δειραγχές for δειραχθές.

Damis nets for beasts that roam the woods,
Cleitor gave a purse net for fish. Send success
  to their nets in the air and sea and land.

ταῦτά σοι ἔκ τ' ὀρέων ἔκ τ' αἰθέρος ἔκ τε θαλάσσας
  τρεῖς γνωτοὶ τέχνας σύμβολα, Πάν, ἔθεσαν·
ταῦτα μὲν εἰναλίων Κλείτωρ λίνα, κεῖνα δὲ Πίγρης
  οἰωνῶν, Δᾶμις τὰ τρίτα τετραπόδων.
οἷς ἅμα χερσαίῃσιν, ἅμ' ἠερίῃσιν ἐν ἄγραις,
  Ἀγρεῦ, ἅμ' ἐν πλωταῖς ὡς πρὶν ἀρωγός ἴθι.

(6 G-P, Garland = AP 6.180)

Three brothers, Pan, gave you these symbols
  of their craft from the mountains, air, and sea:
Cleitor these nets for fish, Pigres those nets
  for birds, and Damis a third set for beasts.
Be their helper as before, hunter god,
  in pursuits on land, air, and water.

τρίζυγες, οὐρεσίοικε, κασίγνητοι τάδε τέχνας
  ἄλλος ἀπ' ἀλλοίας σοὶ †τάδε†, Πάν, ἔθεσαν·
καὶ τὰ μὲν ὀρνίθων Πίγρης, τὰ δὲ δίκτυα θηρῶν
  Δᾶμις, ὁ δὲ Κλείτωρ εἰναλίων ἔπορεν.
τῶν ὁ μὲν ἐν ξυλόχοισιν, ὁ δ' ἠερίῃσιν ἐν ἄγραις
  αἰέν, ὁ δ' ἐν πελάγεσσ' εὔστοχον ἄρκυν ἔχοι.

(7 G-P, Garland = AP 6.181)

Pan who dwells on the mountains, three brothers gave you
  these gifts, each from a different craft:
Pigres gave his fowling nets, Damis his nets
  for beasts, and Cleitor his for catching fish.
May the one have good aim with his snare in the thickets,
  the other in the air, and the third on the sea.

These poems not only present internal variation of phrase (as in Leonidas'
original) and variation of a model (as in Antipater's imitation), but they also
add Archias' own self-variation to the complexity of the intertextual matrix.
In writing the same poem four times over, Archias did not completely avoid
repetition of his own language and structure (note τρίζυγες in 4.2 and 7.1). But
key examples suggest that achieving variety while staying within the limits set by
Leonidas' original was one of his goals. For instance, Archias uses four different
words for brother: αὔθαιμοι (Antipater's word, varying Leonidas' ὅμαιμοι),
σύναιμοι (from the same noun base), γνωτοί, and κασίγνητοι. He also alters
the order of the brothers' names in three of the four instances, repeating only the
order found in Leonidas:

Damis – Pigres – Cleitor (4)
Pigres – Damis – Cleitor (5)

Cleitor – Pigres – Damis (6)
Pigres – Damis – Cleitor (7).

But Archias was primarily concerned to demonstrate his simultaneous reliance
upon both Leonidas and Antipater, since dual models made the art of variation
more difficult and interesting. As we have seen, one of the primary differences
between Leonidas and Antipater was Antipater's specification of the type of
hunting equipment dedicated by each brother. Two of Archias' epigrams (6
and 7) follow Leonidas in using pronouns only, while two (4 and 5) follow
Antipater in naming the nets. But none of Archias' four epigrams are modeled
on either Leonidas or Antipater exclusively, and he marks a new stage in the art of
variation by combining words and phrases from both predecessors in deliberate
collocations. Epigram 5 offers several examples of this technique. There ἄλλος
ἀπ' ἄλλης (5.1) echoes Leonidas' ἄλλης ἄλλος (46.2), while αὔθαιμοι τρισσοί
(5.2) is taken directly from Antipater; the phrase ὑλονόμων ... τετραπόδων
(5.4) combines Leonidas' noun with a modification of Antipater's adjective
ὀρειονόμων (1.2); finally, the phrase εὔστοχα ... λίνα (5.6) unites Leonidas'
εὔστοχον (46.5) with Antipater's λίνοις (1.6), which, like Archias' λίνα, brings
the poem to a close. The same approach to combining his predecessors can be
demonstrated in 4 as well. There εἰναλίφοιτα λίνα (4.4) recalls both Leonidas'
εἰναλίων (46.4) and Antipater's λίνοις (1.6), while δρυόχους (4.6) combines in
its etymological formation Leonidas' δρυμῶν (46.6) and Antipater's synonym
ξυλόχων (1.5). We can see, then, that Archias found a dual method of extending
the art of variation, not only by varying two predecessors simultaneously but
also by doing so in multiple self-variations.

The epigrams on the three brothers have been examined in some detail
because they provide a particularly good illustration of the complicated ways
in which variation was applied as an aesthetic principle. Even if Antipater's
followers were the first to exploit the possibilities of combining both originals
and previous variations, Antipater's epigrams set the standards for what the
imitator's art should be, that is, they were the "original" variations. But at
the same time, Antipater is the first known epigrammatist to interpret a model
through a series of (self-)variations on the same theme.

The most popular artistic topic in the *Anthology* was Myron's *Cow*, on which
survive thirty-six epigrams all concerned with the lifelike quality of the famous
statue.[39] Myron of Eleutherae was one of the most important sculptors of the

___

39. *AP* 9.713–42, 9.793–98. Ausonius translated several of the epigrams into Latin
(*Epigr.* 63–71; cf. fragmenta dubia, *Epigr.* 6–8), now edited by R. P. H. Green, *The Works
of Ausonius* (Oxford, 1991), and four additional Latin epigrams are found in the *Epigrammata
Bobiensia* (10–13), edited by Wolfgang Speyer (Leipzig, 1963). For analysis of the themes de-
veloped in the whole series, see O. Fuà, "L'idea dell'opera d'arte 'vivente' e la *bucula* di Mirone
nell'epigramma Greco e Latino," *RCCM* 15 (1973) 52–55; W. Speyer, "Myrons Kuh in der
antiken Literatur und bei Goethe," *Arcadia* 10 (1975) 171–79; Lausberg 223–37; and Laurens

first half of the fifth century, and his *Cow* was originally placed as a dedication on the Acropolis at Athens. It was later moved to Rome, but not until after the lifetime of Antipater.[40] Scholars have often scoffed at the seemingly endless repetition of the theme, and Gow-Page speak of the tediousness of the series, ending only with Julian of Egypt.[41] But as Myron's *Cow* evoked so many epigrams because of its status as a cultural commonplace, known even to those who knew nothing of art, so in turn the serial repetition of the epigrams contributed to the continuing fame of the statue. Pliny the Elder's comment is instructive: *Myronem ... bucula maxime nobilitavit, celebratis versibus laudata quando alieno plerique ingenio magis quam suo commendantur* ("Myron's heifer made him extremely famous by being praised in a large number of poems—inasmuch as many find praise from another's talent rather than their own," *HN* 34.57). This remark suggests that the fame of the statue continued to increase just because of its fame, not through genuine appreciation of its merits. We may also note how Pliny treats the cow, rather sarcastically, as a living entity in the manner of the epigrams he comments upon. Just as Myron's *Discobolus* was reproduced in countless imitations for a Roman market that desired the recognition value of the original piece, so Greek epigrammatists produced in verse a "replica series" on Myron's *Cow*, which conveyed in numerous variations, not the visual appearance of the statue, but the essential artistic quality for which it had become a cultural icon—the realism with which the animal was depicted.

While Leonidas' epigram on the *Cow* is the earliest known treatment of the topic,[42] Antipater's sequence of five certainly, more probably six, couplets was surely responsible for setting in force the long variation series on the subject.

83–85. For the evidence provided by the epigrams for the appearance of the statue, see Schwarz 24–27.

40. Tzetzes *Chil.* 8.194 preserves the information that the *Cow* originally stood on the Acropolis. It was still in Athens in Cicero's day (*Verr.* 4.60), but Pausanias does not mention it in his survey of the city. Procopius *Goth.* 4.21 reports its presence in the Forum Pacis at Rome.

41. Gow-Page (1965) II 64: "The whole series is a somewhat tedious competition in thinking of a new way to say that it was a very lifelike representation of a cow."

42. The sequence *AP* 9.713–42 (followed by 9.793–98 all by Julian, the prefect of Egypt, on which, see Hendrich Schulte, *Julian von Ägypten* [Trier, 1990] 101–9) attempts to present the poems in chronological order. It begins with two anonymous couplets, then two couplets ascribed to Anacreon, and two more by Evenus, followed by Leonidas and the Antipater variations. But Anacreon died about the time that Myron was born, and, though Lausberg 223–24 suggests that the two couplets attributed to him may yet be early even if clearly not Anacreontic, the lines seem to me to presuppose knowledge of the epigrammatic *topos* in a way that Leonidas' contribution does not. The same is true of the couplets bearing the name of Evenus, who was perhaps equated by the compiler with the Evenus of Paros to whom lines are ascribed in the *Theognidea*, rather than the homonymous poet included in Philip's *Garland*. The two anonymous epigrams head the sequence because they provide the essential information about Myron and his sculpture. It is unlikely, then, that 9.715–18, whoever the composers, predate the Leonidean poem, and the anonymous poems are probably later as well.

Leonidas' couplet invites the reader to imagine an inscriptional setting in which an admirer of the statue looks to the accompanying epigram to learn basic information about the dedication, perhaps even the name of the artist himself. But to the surprise and delight of the viewer, what is found are words spoken by this very lifelike creature:

οὐκ ἔπλασέν με Μύρων· ἐψεύσατο, βοσκομέναν δέ
ἐξ ἀγέλας ἐλάσας δῆσε βάσει λιθίνῳ.

(Leon. 88 GP = AP 9.719)

Not did Myron sculpt me. He lied. But he drove me pasturing
from the herd and bound me to a stone base.

Inscriptions of the archaic and classical period sometimes name the artist in order to compliment him, and Leonidas' epigram at first appears just a playful Hellenistic reversal of that motif—denial of Myron's artistry. But the poem is in fact much more interesting. Leonidas grants to Myron's sculpted heifer a resentful peevishness that confirms her appearance of vitality over her true nature as stone. The poem does, then, function as praise of Myron's sculpting despite its initial disclaimer (οὐκ ἔπλασεν).

Antipater's series of couplets on the *Cow* may be read, in the order transmitted by the *Anthology*, as an extended working out of the possibilities set up by Leonidas' clever poem:

εἰ μή μου ποτὶ τᾷδε Μύρων πόδας ἥρμοσε πέτρᾳ
ἄλλαις ἂν νεμόμαν βουσὶν ὁμοῦ δάμαλις.

(Antip. 36 G-P = AP 9.720)

If Myron had not fixed my feet to this stone,
I would be pasturing, a heifer with the other cows.

μόσχε, τί μοι λαγόνεσσι προσέρχεαι; ἐς τί δὲ μυχᾷ;
ἁ τέχνα μαζοῖς οὐκ ἐνέθηκε γάλα.

(Antip. 37 G-P = AP 9.721)

Calf, why do you approach my flanks? Why do you low?
Art placed no milk in my udders.

τὰν δάμαλιν, βουφορβέ, παρέρχεο μηδ' ἀπάνευθε
συρίξῃς· μαστῷ πόρτιν ὑπεκδέχεται.[43]

(Antip. 38 G-P = AP 9.722)

---

43. I print ὑπεκδέχεται from Pl instead of ἀπεκδέχεται from P, a verb that means "is waiting for, expecting." Gow-Page (1965) *ad* 2 state that "ὑπεκ- . . . would mean that the cow was suckling a calf, and it is reasonably plain that Myron made only the one animal." But this is to read each epigram as an isolated unit referring directly to a known art object, whereas in fact Antipater's purpose in composing the poem is to make an amusing variation of a theme within an epigram series, not to accurately describe the *Cow*.

Pass by the heifer, cowherd, and don't pipe to her
  from afar. She has a calf at her udder.

ἀ μόλιβος κατέχει με καὶ ἀ λίθος, εἵνεκα δ' ἂν σεῦ,
  πλάστα Μύρων, λωτὸν καὶ θρύον ἐδρεπόμαν.

(Antip. 39 G-P = AP 9.723)

The lead and stone bind me fast; but thanks to you, sculptor Myron
  I would otherwise be feeding on clover and rush.

ἀ δάμαλις, δοκέω, μυκήσεται· ἦ ῥ' ὁ Προμηθεύς
  οὐχὶ μόνος, πλάττεις ἔμπνοα καὶ σύ, Μύρων.

(Antip. 40 G-P = AP 9.724)

The heifer, I think, will low. It is not Prometheus alone
  who sculpts living creatures, but you too Myron.

ἀ δάμαλις, δοκέω, μυκήσεται· ἢν δὲ βραδύνη
  χαλκὸς ὁ μὴ νοέων αἴτιος, οὐχὶ Μύρων.

(Antip. [Thess.] 84 G-P, Garland = AP 9.728)

The heifer, I think, will low. But if she delays,
  the unthinking bronze is at fault, not Myron.

This set of six couplets falls into two groups of three. The first poem is a paraphrase of Leonidas, and its purpose is to orient the reader to Antipater's model. But the next two epigrams are much freer variations, both working out the thought of the pentameter in 36—that the heifer ought to be pasturing with her herd. Epigram 37 develops the hints of personality Leonidas had given the cow, as she shoos away a calf with the regretful acknowledgment that art has placed no milk in her udders.[44] Epigram 38 was clearly designed to occupy the third position in the series, for here an unidentified observer, whom the book reader naturally equates with the poet, remarks to a cowherd upon the very scene rejected as impossible in 37. The cowherd is asked to pass by without summoning his cow—not (as the reader expects) because she is bronze but because she is nursing her calf. Even Myron's own statue has underestimated

---

44. *AP* 9.734 is similar, addressed to a bull rather than a calf, and we might assume Antipater's epigram was the imitation if an ascription to Dioscorides were verifiable. But the heading in P and Pl reads Διόκριδο and the epigram has been excluded both from Gow-Page's edition and from Page's *Epigrammata Graeca*. Against the ascription Lausberg 560, n. 25 makes the additional argument that from Dioscorides we have no other couplets or descriptions of art works. It should be noted, however, that a couplet by Demetrius of Bithynia (1 *FGE* = *AP* 9.730), referring to calf, bull, and herdsman, is a combined imitation of "Anacreon" 9.715, Antipater 37 G-P = *AP* 9.721, and the Dioscorides epigram. If Page (1981) 37 is correct to date Demetrius to the era between Antipater and Philip of Thessalonica, the probability is very high that he encountered the three epigrams he varied in Meleager's *Garland*; we may assume, then, that the author of 9.734 was Meleagrian, although the ascription to Dioscorides must remain uncertain.

his ability to grant life to stone! While Leonidas' couplet gains point if the reader imagines the dedicatory site, whether the Acropolis or some place more generic, Antipater's first three poems conjure up an entirely imaginary setting derived from the fictive landscape of Leonidas' poem. In this landscape of the mind, existing only within the epigram book, not only do we find a bronze cow with her calf and cowherd, but even the poet speaks from within the setting itself.

The next epigram, 39, beginning the second half of the sequence, initially appears to provide another paraphrase of Leonidas. The point has, however, been subtly altered, so that the sculptor is not now the cause of the cow's immobility but the source of its liveliness—"it's thanks to you, sculptor Myron, I would be feeding on clover and rush."[45] The original sequence likely continued not just with epigram 40 but also with *AP* 9.728 = Antip. [Thess.] 84 G-P, *Garland* as well, which is ascribed in the *Anthology* to Antipater without an ethnic and is separated from the rest of the Antipater sequence by three anonymous epigrams, probably late intruders into the original series.[46] There is every reason to believe that *AP* 9.728, like 40 G-P, is by the Sidonian, so that the two poems, beginning with the same sequence of words, form a complementary pair paralleling 37 and 38.[47] In both epigrams the poet interprets for the reader his fictive reaction to a viewing of the cow—his expectation that she is about to moo. In the first this expectation leads to a rather conventional compliment to the sculptor, comparison with Prometheus (cf. Erinna 3 G-P = *AP* 6.352). But the other poem, sequentially and so temporally second in the reading of the epigram series, can be interpreted as representing the situation a brief space of time later when no sound has emerged from the mouth of the heifer. The viewer's expectation of sound remains (ἁ δάμαλις, δοκέω, μυκήσεται, "the heifer, I think, will low"), but the delay is blamed upon the inanimate bronze. So just as the epigrammatic point of the third epigram in the sequence depends upon the reader's encountering it in the position immediately following the second epigram, so too in the second half of the six-epigram sequence the humorous

45. Gow-Page (1965) II 64 assert that 39 "makes the same point as" 36, but Lausberg 227 recognizes the change in meaning: "Nicht der Künstler Myron ist schuld, dass sie es nicht kann, denn der hat sie als voll lebendige gebildet, sondern nur Blei und Stein, die sie festhalten."

46. Cf. A. S. F. Gow, "Antipater of Sidon: Notes and Queries," *CR* 4 (1954) 4.

47. It is extremely unlikely that the epigram was composed by the Thessalonican, since we have no other poems by him on the *Cow* theme and he does not elsewhere present such close variations of his namesake. Gow-Page (1965) II 64 admit the capriciousness of their choice to print the epigram with those of the Thessalonican: "It is possible that *A. P.* 9.728 should be added to the following five exercises [by the Sidonian];" cf. Gow, "Antipater of Thessalonica: Notes and Queries," *CR* 16 (1966) 6, n. 1. It is assigned to the Sidonian by Setti 109, Beckby, and Waltz. Gow (1954) 4–5 and Gow-Page (1968) II 86 argue that the first four words of the epigram were accidently transcribed from 9.724, but no such supposition is necessary if the poem is interpreted within its original sequence.

point of the last epigram is dependent upon the presence of 40 G-P immediately preceding it.

A reading of Antipater's Myron epigrams in linear sequence shows, then, that the series is not a haphazard assortment of impromptu variations, but a designed meditation on the implications of Leonidas' couplet. Antipater's series is transmitted in the *Anthology* within a much longer sequence of epigrams on the *Cow* compiled by a Byzantine editor. But the arrangement outlined above, in which the epigrams fall into two groups of three each consisting of a paraphrase of Leonidas followed by a complementary pair, indicates that the sequence displays neither a careless arrangement nor the design of an editor, whether Meleager or another. The most logical explanation for the arrangement is that the *Anthology* has preserved the basic sequence taken over by Meleager from Antipater's poetry book. The delightful wit that emerges when Antipater's Myron epigrams are read in the sequence originally intended suggests just how much our appreciation of his epigrammatic art is hampered by the overall loss of the poetic arrangement that the poet provided his epigram collection.

As an example of the second category of Antipater's variations, epigrams that repeat the subject of an earlier poem while changing the poetic structure or sentiment, we will examine his reworking of the only surviving epigram by Heraclitus, the Halicarnassian poet whose death Callimachus lamented (34 G-P = *AP* 7.80):

ἁ κόνις ἀρτίσκαπτος, ἐπὶ στάλας δὲ μετώπων
  σείονται φύλλων ἡμιθαλεῖς στέφανοι.
γράμμα διακρίναντες, ὁδοιπόρε, πέτρον ἴδωμεν,
  λευρὰ περιστέλλειν ὀστέα φατὶ τίνος.
"ξεῖν', Ἀρετημιὰς εἰμι· πάτρα Κνίδος· Εὔφρονος ἦλθον
  εἰς λέχος· ὠδίνων οὐκ ἄμορος γενόμαν,
δισσὰ δ' ὁμοῦ τίκτουσα τὸ μὲν λίπον ἀνδρὶ ποδηγόν
  γήρως, ἓν δ' ἀπάγω μναμόσυνον πόσιος."

                                    (Heraclitus 1 G-P = *AP* 7.465)

The earth is recently dug, and on the faces of the stele
    quiver garlands of half-wilted flowers.
Deciphering the letters, traveler, let us look to see
    whose smooth bones the stone claims to cover.
"Stranger, I am Aretemias, my country Cnidos. I came to the bed
    of Euphron not without the experience of childbirth.
In giving birth to twins, I left one to comfort my husband's
    old age, and one I take as a remembrance of him."

The appeal of Heraclitus' epigram derives both from the complicated inter-pretive demands it places on the reader and from the moving characterization given Aretemias. In composing a variation Antipater made no attempt to repro-duce the experience of reading Heraclitus' epigram but rather wrote what is essentially a commentary on the earlier epigram and the memorable effect it had upon readers.

In the first quatrain of Heraclitus' poem an unidentified speaker stands before a freshly dug grave, its garlands only partially wilted, and invites a passerby to join in the process of deciphering the engraved epitaph. We have already noted that Callimachus sometimes transcended the conventions of inscribed epitaph by substituting a dramatization of the experience of reading an inscription (as in the Timonoe epitaph). Heraclitus takes this process one step further: his speaker cannot be the passerby whose words or thoughts we encounter in Callimachean poems, since the narrating voice addresses that conventional figure. Hunter has recently argued that in a collection of Heraclitus' verse (perhaps entitled *Nightingales*, as suggested by Callimachus 34 G-P) the speaker can be taken as no one other than the poet, who addresses the reader as ὁδοιπόρε, a traveler engaged in a poetic journey past the tombstones of Heraclitus' collection.[48] In support of Hunter's suggestion, we may note that Heraclitus likely had a precedent for his metaphorical journey in Anyte's epigram book, where, I have argued, the reader was figured as a traveler invited to take repose in her poetic grove. To push speculation a bit further, it seems not unlikely that Heraclitus' Aretemias epitaph was chosen by Antipater for imitation and by Meleager for anthologizing not just because of its high poetic quality but also because, like Anyte 16 and 18 G-P, it occupied a programmatic position in an epigram collection. What better introduction to a poetic assemblage than an invitation from the poet to the reader to join in the very act of reading (γράμμα διακρίναντες)?

The second quatrain adds to the interplay between speaker and addressee—or poet and reader—the complication of the ventriloquized voice of the literary subject, the deceased Aretemias herself. We recognize of course that these two lines transcribe the epitaph engraved on the tomb. But within the dramatic setting of the poem, the words are also those spoken by the narrator, or the narrator in conjunction with the passerby, as the inscription is deciphered and read aloud. And to the extent that we identify the narrator with the poet and the traveler with the implied reader, the epitaph constitutes a text in the process of composition; composition itself thus becomes a joint project of writer and reader. But because the Aretemias epitaph is delivered in first person, a third personality appears to triangulate the relationship of composing and reading. In conventional fashion, Aretemias addresses a ξεῖνος, who is generically any passerby but in the dramatic context set up by the first quatrain the ὁδοιπόρος as reader or even the narrator as poet. By entering into a dialogue with reader and composer, Aretemias stakes a claim for her independence as fictive character. It

---

48. Hunter 115–16. Both Wilamowitz (1924) II 122 and Neil Hopkinson, ed., *A Hellenistic Anthology* (Cambridge, 1988) 247 had earlier recognized the unusual quality of this unidentified speaker, but even so Gow-Page (1965) II *ad* 1 argued for the possibility that the poem was actually cut on a tombstone.

is partly for this reason that we are left with such a strong sense of her personality, particularly of her devotion to her husband Euphron. The division of the twins is presented as a deliberate act on her part, linking husband and wife despite the separation of death. Though epitaphs are normally a memorialization of the dead by the living, Aretemias takes with her to Hades one of the twins to act as a remembrance of her husband (μναμόσυνον πόσιος).[49] The lack of a return to the dramatic setting at the poem's close enhances Aretemias' apparent independence as character. Though various third-century epigrammatists were concerned to explore the underpinnings of literariness by manipulating the one poetic genre whose essential nature had always been its writtenness, none succeeded more fully than Heraclitus in suggesting within the brief compass of a single epigram the possibilities of textual interplay between reader, writer, and character.

Since epigram variation is concerned with the relationship between reading and composition, it is hardly surprising that Antipater would choose this particular epigram for imitation. But though the deceased Aretemias is the subject of both poems, the changes in structure and sentiment in Antipater's epigram are designed to reveal his temporal relationship to Heraclitus, his epigonal status. After all, Antipater could hardly pretend to stand before the freshly dug grave of a woman whose epitaph was composed over a hundred years before:

ἦ πού σε χθονίας, Ἀρετημιάς, ἐξ ἀκάτοιο
    Κωκυτοῦ θεμέναν ἴχνος ἐπ' ἀιόνι,
οἰχόμενον βρέφος ἄρτι νέον φορέουσαν ἀγοστῷ
    ᾤκτειραν θαλεραὶ Δωρίδες εἰν Ἀίδᾳ
πευθόμεναι τέο κῆρα· σὺ δὲ ξαίνουσα παρειάς
    δάκρυσιν ἄγγειλας κεῖν' ἀνιαρὸν ἔπος·
"διπλόον ὠδίνασα, φίλαι, τέκος ἄλλο μὲν ἀνδρὶ
    Εὔφρονι καλλιπόμαν ἄλλο δ' ἄγω φθιμένοις."

(53 G-P = *AP* 7.464)

It's true, Aretemias, that when you stepped out
    of death's boat onto the shore of Cocytus
Carrying your newborn child deceased in your arms,
    the young Dorian women in Hades mourned
As they learned your fate. And you tore your cheeks
    when with tears you gave that piteous report:
"Of the two children I bore, friends, one I left for Euphron,
    my husband, and one I bring to the dead."

In Antipater's imitation there is no longer any ambiguity about the status of the speaker. The voice heard in the poem is that of the poet himself who addresses Aretemias, not as the deceased questioned by a passerby, but as a character

---

49. Gow-Page (1965) II *ad* 8 comment: "a novel turn, for the memories are usually left to the survivors by the dead."

made famous, heroized, by an earlier epigrammatist. As a result, there is no longer any pretense of an inscription or a dramatized reading of an inscription. Antipater offers a narrated vignette of Aretemias' arrival in the underworld, an event set in the past (ᾤχτειραν, ἄγγειλας) and given an aura of the heroic past through the interaction between Euphron's wife and the Doric women in Hades.

Antipater's paraphrase of Heraclitus' final couplet, the one part of the poem that is a close variation, is expressly marked as a version of a famous passage (χεῖν' ἀνιαρὸν ἔπος), converted from epitaph to Aretemias' explanation of her fate in the underworld. Heraclitus' epigram effectively evokes pathos by emphasizing the recentness of Aretemias' death, and so the freshness of Euphron's grief, and by demonstrating the deceased's virtue through her lack of self-pity and devotion to her husband. Antipater, however, makes no attempt to reproduce these effects for the reader, but rather seeks merely to describe them by narrating the sorrow felt by the Dorian women when they learn of Aretemias' fate. Even Aretemias, who speaks so unemotionally in Heraclitus' epitaph,[50] tears her cheeks in mourning as she reiterates her earlier couplet, demonstrating that Heraclitus' poem has its pathetic effect even upon its own subject. Antipater does not, then, attempt to surpass Heraclitus or to enter into agonistic rivalry with him.[51] In imitating the Aretemias epitaph he rather celebrates a significant poem in the history of epigram by granting its famous character the stature of a heroine and by dramatizing the poem's moving effect upon readers. In so doing, Antipater sets himself up as an admirer of Heraclitus, a reader as well as a writer of epigrams.

For the third category of variations—epigrams that repeat a motif with a change in the specific subject—we will examine Antipater's epitaph for the courtesan Lais, which is a loose and much expanded variation of Asclepiades' epigram on Archeanassa:

Ἀρχεάνασσαν ἔχω τὰν ἐκ Κολοφῶνος ἑταίραν,
    ἇς καὶ ἐπὶ ῥυτίδων ὁ γλυκὺς ἕζετ' Ἔρως.
ἇς νέον ἥβης ἄνθος ἀποδρέψαντες ἐρασταὶ
    πρωτόβολοι, δι' ὅσης ἤλθετε πυρκαϊῆς.[52]

(Asclep. 41 G-P = *AP* 7.217)

---

50. Cf. Wilamowitz (1924) II 122–23: "Was folgt, muss die Inschrift sein, in der die Tote das Wort führt und ganz sachlich ohne ein Wort der Stimmung das Tatsächliche gibt. Das ist rührend genug, und die Liebe zu dem Gatten kommt durch die Retizenz nur stärker heraus. Ethos ist mehr wert als Pathos."

51. Setti 83, in complaining that the subject of the poem is "molto frigido ed insulso," typically misjudges the purpose of Antipater's epigonal composition.

52. The ἁ printed by most editors, including Gow-Page, as the first word in 3 was introduced from the Platonic versions of the epigram, whereas the second ἇς in P seems confirmed by the repetition of ἧς in Antipater's variation; see R. Reitzenstein, "Platos Epigramme," *NGG* (1921)

I hold Archeanassa, the hetaira from Colophon;
    Sweet Eros perched even upon her wrinkles.
You lovers who plucked the fresh bloom of her youth,
    first-struck lovers, with what fire you burned.

Scholars have debated whether Asclepiades' poem was composed as an epitaph or an erotic poem. Wilamowitz's judgment that it was "ein unverkennbares Erotikon" held the day until Ludwig presented a detailed argument for its sepulchral character, accepted by Gow and Page.[53] Antipater's imitative epitaph for Lais and the juxtaposition of the two poems among the *epitymbia* in Book 7 of the *AP* show clearly that it was conceived as sepulchral in the epigrammatic tradition. But both Diogenes Laertius (3.31) and Athenaeus (13.589c–d) transmit reworked versions of the poem, which they attribute to Plato as declarations of his love for the Colophonian hetaira.[54] It appears that the Platonic version of the Archeanassa poem formed part of a collection of epigrams, partly erotic, composed perhaps as early as the third century and falsely ascribed to Plato.[55] Meleager accepted this sylloge as genuinely Platonic and included some of its epigrams in the *Garland* (Mel. 1.47–48 G-P = *AP* 4.1.47–48). In the context of the Platonic collection, which included a number of love poems for various persons, the first-person speaker who holds Archeanassa would naturally be assumed to be the epigrammatist rather the tomb of the deceased hetaira. The Archeanassa epigram offers, then, one of our best examples of how context determines meaning.

But the debate over the correct categorization of Asclepiades' epigram has obscured its inherent ambiguity. While it is true that the verb ἔχω occasionally appears in genuine inscriptions representing the voice of the tomb (e.g., *GV*

54 and W. Ludwig, "Plato's Love Epigrams," *GRBS* 4 (1963) 63, n. 9. I have also accepted Ludwig's argument (63, n. 10) for the form and meaning of πρωτόβολοι.

53. Following Wilamowitz (1924) II 116 are Knauer 20 and Beckby II 579 (if his reference to *AP* 5.13 is an indicator). The remarks of Ludwig (1963) 63–68 are favorably received by Gow-Page (1965) II 144–45 and Page (1981) 167–68.

54. In Diogenes the first pentameter is modified to read ἕζετο δριμὺς ἔρως, while Athenaeus transmits πικρὸς ἔπεστιν ἔρως. The latter is clearly an attempt to remake the poem into an erotic epigram. For other more minor changes, see Gow-Page's apparatus.

55. Ludwig (1963) has shown convincingly that the epigrams transmitted under the name of Plato are falsely ascribed. For discussion of the presumed sylloge and its date, see Page (1981) 125–27; he argues that the "Platonic" epigram collection used by Meleager was circulating "at a date not far removed from 250 B.C." (126). But he points out that not all the extant epigrams ascribed to Plato were in this sylloge; some of the amatory epigrams in Diogenes (though not necessarily the Archeanassa poem) came from a book by Aristippus (probably a pseudonym for a forger posing as the Cyrenaean) called περὶ παλαιᾶς τρυφῆς, an ancient scandal sheet that claimed to reveal the sexual indiscretions of famous persons (D.L. 3.29).

591, 593), it also has specifically erotic connotations.[56] Diogenes, in cataloguing Plato's love objects, introduces the Platonic version of the epigram with the phrase ἔχειν τε Ἀρχεάνασσαν [φασί], "and [they say] he held Archeanassa" (3.31), and Asclepiades himself uses the verb in one of his unambivalently erotic epigrams (ἤν τις ἔχῃ μ' ἕτερος, "if another holds me," 4.4 G-P = *AP* 5.158.4). In referring to possession of a hetaira the verb was particularly apt: Aristippus remarks on his liaison with Lais, ἔχω, ἀλλ' οὐκ ἔχομαι, "I hold her but I am not held" (D.L. 2.75),[57] suggesting that he is master, not slave, to his passion. In the first line of Asclepiades' poem, where there is no direct reference to death, the erotic overtones of the verb are inescapable. In fact, the epigrammatic bite of Asclepiades' poem is his suggestion that the grave is Archeanassa's final lover: enclosing her in the embrace of death, the tomb comments upon the desirability of the aged hetaira even at the time of her demise. And to the extent that the reader may perceive ἔζετ' as present rather than imperfect tense, the suggestion becomes even more macabre—that the wrinkled flesh of the deceased beauty yet endures in the grave to arouse the lover who holds her forever. Such a reading of the epigram grants psychological coherency to the second couplet, for the address to Archeanassa's early lovers, more than simple praise of her youthful beauty, conveys the tomb's identification with others who have felt desire for her.

In his imitation Antipater transfers Asclepiades' metaphor of the tomb as lover to the Corinthian courtesan Lais:

τὴν καὶ ἅμα χρυσῷ καὶ ἁλουργίδι καὶ σὺν ἔρωτι
  θρυπτομένην, ἁπαλῆς Κύπριδος ἁβροτέρην,
Λαΐδ' ἔχω, πολιῆτιν ἁλιζώνοιο Κορίνθου,
  Πειρήνης λευκῶν φαιδροτέρην λιβάδων,
τὴν θνητὴν Κυθέρειαν, ἐφ' ᾗ μνηστῆρες ἀγαυοί
  πλείονες ἢ νύμφης εἵνεκα Τυνδαρίδος
δρεπτόμενοι χάριτάς τε καὶ ὠνητὴν ἀφροδίτην,
  ἧς καὶ ὑπ' εὐώδει τύμβος ὄδωδε κρόκῳ,
ἧς ἔτι κηώεντι μύρῳ τὸ διάβροχον ὀστεῦν
  καὶ λιπαραὶ θυόεν ἆσθμα πνέουσι κόμαι,
ἧς ἔπι καλὸν ἄμυξε κάτα ῥέθος Ἀφρογένεια
  καὶ γοερὸν λύζων ἐστονάχησεν Ἔρως.
εἰ δ' οὐ πάγκοινον δούλην θέτο κέρδεος εὐνήν,
  Ἑλλὰς ἂν ὡς Ἑλένης τῆσδ' ὕπερ ἔσχε πόνον.[58]

(Antip. 23 G-P = *AP* 7.218)

---

56. Waltz IV 149, n. 2 notes that, though the poem takes the form of an epitaph, the poet "reprend ici le thème classique de la 'belle vieille,' si souvent traité dans les épigrammes amoureuses."

57. Cf. Ath. 12.544d, Cic. *Fam.* 9.26, Lactant. *Div. Inst.* 3.15.

58. For a defense of the mss. reading ἀγαυοί in 5, which Gow-Page emend to ἄγερθεν, see Heather White, *New Essays in Hellenistic Poetry* (Amsterdam, 1985) 77–79.

The one who exalted in gold and purple with Love's company,
   the one more delicate than tender Aphrodite,
Lais I hold, a citizen of sea-girt Corinth,
   brighter than the clear drops of Peirene,
The mortal Cytherean, who had more noble suitors
   than sought the daughter of Tyndareus as bride,
To pluck her charms and her mercenary love making.
   Her tomb has the odor of sweet-scented saffron,
Her skull is still soaked with the fragrance of incense,
   and her anointed hair has a perfumed scent.
For her the Foam-born one tore her lovely face,
   and Eros groaned and wailed mournfully.
If she had not made her bed the common slave of gain,
   Hellas would have struggled as it did for Helen.

Antipater reveals himself as a reader of Asclepiades by echoing Ἀρχεάνασσαν
ἔχω with Λαΐδ᾽ ἔχω, by recalling ἄνθος ἀποδρέψαντες with δρεπτόμενοι
χάριτας, and by imitating Asclepiades' anaphora of relative pronouns (ἃς ...
ἃς) in his repetitions of ἧς. But above all, he continues to eroticize death's
embrace by his long series of appositional phrases describing Lais' charms and
by dwelling upon the sensual odor of the hetaira's body as it molders in the
grave.

   By changing the subject and expanding the epitaph, however, Antipater
modifies Asclepiades' original concept of a courtesan's epitaph to speak to the
concerns of his own historical period. While Archeanassa was in later times
unknown apart from her supposed connection with Plato, Lais had by the second
century B.C. become part of the cultural heritage passed on from classical Greece
to the various ethnic groups comprising the Hellenistic world. In comedy and
biography the Corinthian courtesan was associated with a number of well-
known men of the late fifth or fourth century, such as Euripides, Demosthenes,
Diogenes the Cynic, and Aristippus the Cyrenaean; she was treated as a cultural
commonplace by later Greek and Roman writers.[59] Celebrating the iconic status
of one dead but not gone, Antipater suggests that Lais' tomb and her not-yet-
decayed body are still redolent of the saffron perfume and myrrh she used in her
love making. Through a fictive presence at her grave, that is, the reading of
the epigram, we may yet have some experience of this mortal Aphrodite. In

59. The legends about Lais were spawned by at least two, possibly three hetairas with the
same name; see Geyer, "Lais," *RE* 23 HB (1924) 513–16. Her conversation with Euripides
was reported by Machon (fr. 18 Gow = Ath. 13.582c–d), and her liaison with Demosthenes
by Athenaeus (13.588c). She supposedly consorted with Diogenes the Cynic without pay, but
Aristippus reportedly paid a large amount to spend two months with her yearly (Ath. 13.588e);
additional references to Aristippus in Ath. 12.544b; 13.588c, f; 13.599b; D.L. 2.74–75; Plut.
Amat. 4. Lais is mentioned not only in various comedies but also by Hermesianax (7.95–98 *CA*,
apud Ath. 599b) and Propertius 2.6.1.

the decades following the destruction of Corinth, an epitaph celebrating one of that city's most famous citizens (πολιῆτιν ἁλιζώνοιο Κορίνθου) must have had a particular poignancy. A quotation from comedy reported by Athenaeus (4.137d)—οὐ Κόρινθος οὐδὲ Λαΐς, "neither Corinth nor Lais"—suggests that Lais had come to function as a symbol for all the past glory of her native city. Antipater certainly provides what some might consider an excess of praise in heroizing Lais, who is mourned by both Aphrodite and Eros and favorably compared with Helen. The exalting of a historical courtesan to the ranks of legendary heroines and the company of deities is accomplished through deliberate modifications of the anecdotal tradition. While other sources report that in her youth Lais charged exorbitantly for her favors and lowered her standards only when old age was upon her (Ath. 13.570b–d, 585d), Antipater touts her as a savior of Greece because she averted civil strife by making her indiscriminate bed the slave of gain—prostitution as self-sacrifice.

In 146 B.C., following a crushing military defeat of the Achaean League, Lucius Mummius decided to make an example of Corinth in a manner that would leave an indelible impression upon the Greek world. The city's inhabitants were either killed or sold into slavery. Corinth itself was plundered and then burned with the effect that it was rendered uninhabitable until Julius Caesar repopulated it with Roman freedmen over a century later.[60] The destruction of Corinth unmistakably marked the end of Greek autonomy, and the inclusion of a lament for it among Antipater's poetry provides a historical context for the sense of irrecoverable loss, of nostalgia for an unattainable past, that permeates his surviving epigrams:

ποῦ τὸ περίβλεπτον κάλλος σέο, Δωρὶ Κόρινθε;
    ποῦ στεφάναι πύργων; ποῦ τὰ πάλαι κτέανα;
ποῦ νηοὶ μακάρων; ποῦ δώματα; ποῦ δὲ δάμαρτες
    Σισύφιαι λαῶν θ' αἵ ποτε μυριάδες;
οὐδὲ γὰρ οὐδ' ἴχνος, πολυκάμμορε, σεῖο λέλειπται,
    πάντα δὲ συμμάρψας ἐξέφαγεν πόλεμος.
μοῦναι ἀπόρθητοι Νηρηίδες Ὠκεανοῖο
    κοῦραι σῶν ἀχέων μίμνομεν ἀλκυόνες.

(59 G-P = AP 9.151)

Where is your much-admired beauty, Dorian Corinth?
    Where is the crown of your towers? Your wealth of old?
Where the temples of your gods? Your houses? Where the ladies

60. Crinagoras, an epigrammatist of the Augustan age who wrote flattering poems for members of the imperial household, composed a lament for Corinth on the occasion of its repopulation, expressing the sentiment that the city should better remain deserted than receive slaves to replace the Bacchiads (37 G-P, *Garland* = *AP* 9.284). The issue of Corinth clearly raised high levels of resentment even among Greeks who otherwise made successful accommodation to Roman mastery.

descended from Sisyphus and your once numerous citizenry?
Not even a trace is left of you, lamentable city;
  war has snatched and devoured all.
Only we the Nereid daughters of Ocean remain unplundered
  to sing halcyon laments for your sorrows.

The tone of high pathos—conveyed by the anaphora of ποῦ, the near person-
ification of Corinth as a beautiful woman, the pitiable direct address to the
city, and the image of war as a devouring monster—is legitimized, rendered
stylistically unobjectionable, by the revelation in the last line that the singers
of this halcyon lament are the Nereids, who, alone unplundered, search the
desolate horizon of the Isthmus for some remnant of Corinth's once magnificant
structures and teeming populace. Another epigram on the destruction of the
city, an epitaph for two Corinthian maidens murdered by their mother before
committing suicide herself, ends with the justification that "death in freedom was
better for us than slavery" (68.8 G-P = *AP* 7.493.8). Although Rome is not men-
tioned directly in either of these poems, it is named as the target of Antipater's
subversive thoughts in a unique and fascinating epigram on Antiodemis, a mime
in a type of licentious performance known as λυσιῳδία. Whether performed by
women or men impersonating women, these songs—named for the Lysis who
first composed them—were clearly appropriate only for a feminine persona:[61]

ἡ καὶ ἔτ᾽ ἐκ βρέφεος κοιμωμένη Ἀντιοδημὶς
  πορφυρέων Παφίης νοσσὶς ἐπὶ κροκύδων,
ἡ τακεραῖς λεύσσουσα κόραις μαλακώτερον ὕπνου,
  Λύσιδος ἀλκυονίς, τερπνὸν ἄθυρμα Μέθης,
ὑδατίνους φορέουσα βραχίονας, ἢ μόνη ὀστοῦν
  οὐ λάχεν, ἣν γὰρ ὅλη τοὐν ταλάροισι γάλα,
Ἰταλίην ἤμειψεν ἵνα πτολέμοιο καὶ αἰχμῆς
  ἀμπαύσῃ Ῥώμην μαλθακίνῃ χάριτι.

                                                    (61 G-P = *AP* 9.567)

Antiodemis, a nursling of the Paphian, cuddled
  from her babyhood in purple coverlets,
whose melting eyes glance softer than sleep,
  Lysis' halcyon, a pleasant toy of Drunkenness,
whose arms are like water, who alone has no bones
  in her body but is all milk set in baskets,

61. Strabo 14.1.41 reports that Lysis, who perhaps lived in the early third century B.C.,
was the first to imitate the talk of *cinaedi* in song. Athenaeus 14.620e preserves information
from Aristoxenus that the lysiode sang women's parts in male dress, and a male lysiode
named Metrobius is reported as the lover of Sulla (Plut. *Sulla* 36.1). Yet in addition to
Antiodemis, we hear of a female lysiode who associated with the Epicurean philosopher
Diogenes (Ath. 5.211b–c). For additional references, see Maas, "Σιμῳδοί,'" *RE* 2nd ser. 5 HB
(1927) 159–60.

has gone over to Italy so that she might put a stop
   to Rome's warmongering with her delicate charms.

Antipater's description of Antiodemis—her luxurious habits, her seductiveness, the pleasure she offers from song and drink, the supple sensuousness of her acrobatic form—feeds into the Roman stereotype of a decadent Greece that is corrupt, enervated, and feminized.[62] But by embracing the stereotype of the oppressor, Antipater suggests the one subversive response left to Greece, to pacify Roman militancy with Hellenic culture.

It is within this historical climate that we should understand Antipater's series of epitaphs on famous poets of the past. Other scholars have argued that the large number of such fictitious epitaphs from the Hellenistic period reflect both a sense of mourning for the past greatness of Greek culture and an ardent desire to bridge the gulf between then and now.[63] Simias of Rhodes composed two epitaphs for Sophocles (4 G-P = *AP* 7.21, 5 G-P = *AP* 7.22) and another for Plato (6 G-P = *AP* 7.60). Leonidas produced epitaphs for Alcman (57 G-P = *AP* 7.19), Hipponax (58 G-P = *AP* 7.408), and Pindar (99 G-P = *AP* 7.35), and the ascription of an epitaph for Hipponax to Theocritus (13 G-P = *AP* 13.3) can likely be trusted. Antipater seems, however, more directly influenced by the epitaphs for long-dead poets written in the period covering the end of the third century and the beginning of the second by such epigrammatists as Damagetus, Mnasalces, Alcaeus of Messene, and Dioscorides.[64] This last poet is particularly worthy of attention. From his hand come a series of poems on writers of tragedy and comedy, which were evidently published together as a chronological sequence. An inscription for a statue or tomb of Thespis, celebrating that shadowy figure as the inventor of tragic song (20 G-P = *AP* 7.410), makes a pair in the *Anthology* with an epigram that distinguishes Aeschylus' contribution to the genre invented by Thespis (21 G-P = *AP* 7.411).[65] Two other epigrams, now separated in the *AP* (22 G-P = *AP* 7.37, 23 G-P = *AP* 7.707) but "evidently meant to be read together,"[66] are spoken by Satyrs mounted on the tombs of Sophocles and Sositheus, the Hellenistic

---

62. For a summary statement of this stereotype, see E. Rawson, "The Romans" in *Perceptions of the Ancient Greeks*, ed. K. J. Dover (Oxford, 1992) 4–5.

63. See especially P. Bing, "Theocritus' Epigrams on the Statues of Ancient Poets," *A&A* 34 (1988a) 117–23 and (1988b) 50–90.

64. Damagetus 2 G-P = *AP* 7.9 (Orpheus); Mnasalces 18 G-P = *AP* 7.54 (Hesiod); Alcaeus 11 G-P = *AP* 7.1 (Homer), 12 G-P = *AP* 7.55 (Hesiod, though perhaps not technically an epitaph), 13 G-P = *AP* 7.536 (Hipponax); and, in addition to those discussed below, Dioscorides 19 G-P = *AP* 7.31 (Anacreon).

65. Gow-Page (1965) *ad* 21.1 comment that the opening words of the Aeschylus epigram— Θέσπιδος εὕρεμα τοῦτο, "this was the invention of Thespis"—look like a reference to the preceding poem; cf. as well Gabathuler 83.

66. Gow-Page (1965) II 254. Cf. Gabathuler 86; Bing (1988b) 40: "Their sequential connection . . . is that between neighboring texts *on the page* [author's italics]."

reviver of satyr plays. The second of these compares himself to his companion
Satyr (κἠγώ, 23.1) as if physically present but speaks of Sophocles' tomb as
located in the city of Athens (ἐν ἄστει, 23.1). The Satyr surmounting Sositheus'
tomb thus breaks the dramatic illusion of the inscriptional site, since he claims
no location for himself other than the page of Dioscorides' epigram book. A
probably related epitaph on the comic writer Machon, who died sometime in
the second half of the third century, makes explicit the transference of Greek
literary innovation from Athens to the banks of the Nile (24 G-P = *AP* 7.708).[67]
We have from Dioscorides, then, a series of five connected epigrams, reflecting a
contemporary appreciation of preclassical drama and its archaizing revival in
the third century.[68]

But the sheer number of epitaphs for famous poets written by Antipater—
covering a long chronological period from Orpheus through Homer and the
lyricists to the postclassical favorites Antimachus and Erinna—suggests this
poet's particular anxiety about his seemingly endangered connection to the
Greek cultural past. Since most of these poems were transmitted in the ar-
rangement made by Cephalas at the beginning of *AP* 7, we have lost manuscript
evidence for their original ordering, although the series of no less than five poems
on Anacreon does show internal signs of thematic linkage and pairing. Even
so, the significant arrangement of Dioscorides' poems on dramatists provides
a precedent for the grouping of these poems within one section of Antipater's
collection, and such a sequencing fits as well with our understanding of third-
century collections that were arranged by epigram type. It may be permitted,
then, to read the epitaphs one against the other (though no evidence remains for
Antipater's own order) and so to reconstruct from them the poet's sense of his
fragile and threatened connection to the distant and not so distant literary past.

The sorrow evoked by the loss of the once magical power of poetry is
illustrated by Antipater's pathetic lament for Orpheus (10 G-P = *AP* 7.8, modeled
on an epigram by Damagetus, 2 G-P = *AP* 7.9), whose song, since it existed
only as oral performance, perished utterly with its singer. Antipater's other
epitaphs emphasize the tenuous link that the written page provides with the
great composers of the past. Sappho, a "mortal Muse" (θνατὰν Μοῦσαν) who
sang with the "immortal Muses" (Μούσαις ἀθανάταις), plaited for posterity
an "ever-living garland of the Pierides" (ἀείζωον Πιερίδων στέφανον), to be a
source of "pleasure for Hellas" (Ἑλλάδι . . . τέρψιν) and a "glory" (κλέος) for her
homeland (11 G-P = *AP* 7.14). The great Homer, when he expired on the tiny
island of Ios, left behind the "holy breath" (ἱερὸν . . . πνεῦμα) with which he had
enunciated the themes of his epic poetry (8 G-P = *AP* 7.2). And Homer continued

67. Though Athenaeus 6.241f reports that the epigram was inscribed on Machon's tomb,
Gow-Page (1965) II 254 point out that "it need not necessarily have been written originally
for that purpose."

68. Cf. Gabathuler 88–89.

to live in other ways as well, for Antipater reports that Stesichorus, in accordance with Pythagorean doctrine, was a reincarnation of Homer, a second receptacle for his soul (Antip. [Thess.] 74 G-P, *Garland = AP* 7.75).[69] Though Pindar lies covered with dust, we may still hear his poetry, copied from songs sung by the Muses at the marriage of Cadmus (18 G-P = *AP* 7.34); so too, the dying shouts of Ibycus, though heard only by passing cranes, were yet effective in avenging his murder (19 G-P = *AP* 7.745). The period when poets trafficked with divinity and left behind inspired verse as a memorial to the greatness of their performances ended, in Antipater's view, during the fifth century; as a result, his epitaphs for later poets reflect concern with emulation of the past and the difficulties of acquiring fame. He requests praise for Antimachus, who, though yoked behind Homer in the chariot race of the Muses (ὑπέζευκται),[70] was yet undeserving of the criticism directed at him by Callimachus (66 G-P = *AP* 7.409).[71] Recognition for Erinna, who succeeded in gaining remembrance despite the small quantity of her poetic production, comes from a host of inferior and forgotten poets, who speak, as if from their own graves, to celebrate her accomplishments (58 G-P = *AP* 7.713).

Antipater's extreme concern with his epigonal status may be shown by a more detailed look at one of his epitaphs for Homer, itself a variation of an epitaph by Alcaeus of Messene:

τὰν μερόπων Πειθώ, τὸ μέγα στόμα, τὰν ἴσα Μούσαις
　φθεγξαμέναν κεφαλάν, ὦ ξένε, Μαιονίδεω,
ἅδ' ἔλαχον νασῖτις Ἴου σπιλάς, οὐ γὰρ ἐν ἄλλα
　ἱερὸν ἀλλ' ἐν ἐμοὶ πνεῦμα θανὼν ἔλιπεν,
ᾧ νεῦμα Κρονίδαο τὸ παγκρατές, ᾧ καὶ Ὄλυμπον
　καὶ τὰν Αἴαντος ναυμάχον εἶπε βίαν
καὶ τὸν Ἀχιλλείοις Φαρσαλίσιν Ἕκτορα πώλοις

69. Attributed to the Sidonian by Setti 75–76, Paton, Waltz, Beckby, and Gabathuler 35, though Gow-Page (1968) II 77 are basically noncommittal and so print the poem among those of the Thessalonican. C. O. Brink, "Ennius and the Hellenistic Worship of Homer," *AJP* 93 (1972) 558–60 discusses the parallel with Ennius' notion that he himself was the reincarnation of Homer and argues for the likelihood of a common Hellenistic source: "This particular metempsychosis was a Hellenistic invention expressing . . . the dependence of later writers on Homer" (559).

70. The image of the chariot race had been employed in connection with epigonal status as early as the fifth century by Choerilus of Samos, who claimed to be left behind in the poetic race, looking for a place to direct his "newly yoked chariot" (317 *SH*).

71. His statement that Antimachus' poetry (apparently the *Thebaid*) is forged on the anvil of Muses "if you happen to have a well-tuned ear" (εἰ τορὸν οὖας ἔλλαχες, 66.3–4) expresses disagreement with Callimachus' judgment that the *Lyde* was "fat" and "not well-tuned" (οὐ τορόν, fr. 398 Pf.), while his further comment about "the path untrodden and not traversed by others" (τὰν ἄτριπτον καὶ ἀνέμβατον ἀτραπὸν ἄλλοις, 66.5) expropriates Callimachus' own poetic principles as stated in the *Aetia* prologue (fr. 1.25–28 Pf.).

ὀστέα Δαρδανικῷ δρυπτόμενον πεδίῳ.
εἰ δ' ὀλίγα κρύπτω τὸν ταλίκον ἴσθ' ὅτι κεύθει
καὶ Θέτιδος γαμέταν ἀ βραχύβωλος Ἴκος.

(Antip. 8 G-P = AP 7.2)

Stranger, it has fallen to me, the island rock of Ios, to hold
    Maionides, the persuader of men, the loud-sounding voice,
Who sang like the Muses. For in no other place but in me
    did he leave his holy breath when he died,
The breath with which he told of Zeus' all-powerful nod,
    of Olympus and Ajax's strength in fighting from ships,
and of Hector's bones torn by the Pharsalian horses
    of Achilles on the Dardanian plain.
If, small as I am, I cover one so great, know that even Icos
    of few clods hides the husband of Thetis.

The island of Ios displayed the tomb of Homer until at least the time of Pausanias (10.24.2), and the epigram inscribed upon it was been preserved in the *Anthology*, as also elsewhere:[72]

ἐνθάδε τὴν ἱερὴν κεφαλὴν κατὰ γαῖα καλύπτει,
ἀνδρῶν ἡρώων κοσμήτορα, θεῖον Ὅμηρον.

(AP 7.3)

Here the earth covers that sacred bard,
divine Homer, the marshaller of heroes.

Antipater did not imitate this simple inscription directly, but through the intermediary of an epitaph by Alcaeus of Messene (11 G-P = *AP* 7.1). Alcaeus had expanded the inscribed epitaph from Ios with the background story about the circumstances of Homer's death—that he died from frustration when unable to solve a riddle posed by children—and with a report that his body was embalmed and buried by the Nereids because he had glorified Thetis and her son. Though most of this sounds like publicity put out by the inhabitants of Ios to tout their famous burial, the epigrammatic point of Alcaeus' poem is something that they perhaps did not emphasize—the ironic contrast between the smallness of the island and the greatness of the poet buried there.[73] Yet it is precisely this point that Antipater develops in his variation, through the mechanism of transferring the epitaph to the mouth of the tiny island. The bombast of the first couplet (note how κεφαλάν echoes the inscription) is not just an example of Antipater's "fervid and exuberant" style; it is rather designed to reflect the excessive pride of

72. For its transmission in the biographies of Homer, see Skiadas 7 with n. 3, who also demonstrates (8–10) its close connection with known inscriptional forms.

73. Skiadas 56–61 has shown how Alcaeus and then Antipater in imitation have modified the commonplace contrast between greatness of the deceased and the smallness of the grave to accommodate the motif of the smallness of the island.

the undeserving island, which, as any cultivated reader would know, received the body of Homer through no merit of its own (note ἔλαχον, 8.3), but because of the vexing riddle of the children. Antipater's interest in this motif may stem, I suggest, from a sense of identification with the tiny island, which received the dying breath (πνεῦμα, 8.4) of the great Homer, much as a contemporary poet is heir to Homer's literary estate.[74] Like Ios, Antipater feels himself small in comparison with the monumental literary figures of the past, who lie deeply buried under the only memorial he can make to them, not rivalrous imitations, but the smaller commemoration of fictitious epitaph.

As Ios claims to have received Homer's dying breath, the source of his epic poetry, so in his series of poems on Anacreon Antipater suggests that the disappearance of the great lyricist may not yet be final, that the desire or gesture of the living may reanimate the dead.[75] One epigram (16 G-P = *AP* 7.29) begins with a soothing anaphora of εὕδεις ... εὕδει ... εὕδει—"You sleep among the dead, Anacreon, ... and your sweet night-prattling lyre sleeps, and Smerdis, the springtime of desire, also sleeps." Anacreon's slumber among the dead is not simply a synonym for death, for the phrasing implies a mere suspension of consciousness that may yet be reversed into wakefulness. So in a poem that seems a companion piece (15 G-P = *AP* 7.27; cf. the parallelism of the opening words, εὕδεις ἐν φθιμένοισιν, "you sleep among the dead," and εἴης ἐν μακάρεσσιν, "may you be among the blessed"), Antipater prays that Anacreon obtain a position among the blessed, where he may still pursue the activities celebrated in his poetry—singing with flowers in his hair, glancing at the boys he loves, drinking in wine-soaked garments. This revivification of the poet has its counterpart even in the world above. In another epigram (13 G-P = *AP* 7.23) the poet calls for extraordinary phenomena, even Dionysiac miracles, at Anacreon's tomb—ivy and purple flowers encircling it, fountains of milk and wine bubbling up over it—and all to connect the world above with the world below, to provide pleasure to Anacreon's bones and ash. In yet another epitaph the commerce between upper and lower is more clearly figured as a gesture made by the living to the dead because of the connecting link that Anacreon's poetry provides past and present :

ξεῖνε, τάφον πάρα λιτὸν Ἀνακρείοντος ἀμείβων,
  εἴ τί τοι ἐκ βίβλων ἦλθεν ἐμῶν ὄφελος,
σπεῖσον ἐμῇ σποδιῇ, σπεῖσον γάνος, ὄφρα κεν οἴνῳ
  ὀστέα γηθήσῃ τἀμὰ νοτιζόμενα,

74. M. L. Chirico, "*Topoi* ed imitazione in alcuni epigrammi di Antipatro Sidonio," *AFLN* 21 (1978–79) 11–21 has demonstrated that Homer's influence upon Antipater's diction and style is greater than that of any of his other models.

75. For an analysis of how Antipater recalls Anacreon's poetry in his epitaphs, see M. L. Chirico, "Antipatro Sidonio interprete di Anacreonte," *AFLN* 23 (1980–81) 43–57; cf. Barbantani 55–60.

ὡς ὁ Διωνύσου μεμελημένος εὐάσι κώμοις,
    ὡς ὁ φιλακρήτου σύντροφος Ἁρμονίης,
μηδὲ καταφθίμενος Βάκχου δίχα τοῦτον ὑποίσω
    τὸν γενεῇ μερόπων χῶρον ὀφειλόμενον.

(14 G-P = AP 7.26)

Stranger, you who pass the simple tomb of Anacreon,
    if any benefit has accrued to you from my books,
Pour a libation on my ash, a libation of sparkling wine,
    so that my bones may rejoice moistened by drink,
So that I who partook in the sounding revels of Dionysus,
    I who was reared in the company of wine-loving song,
May not in death submit without Bacchus to this place
    that is due all those endowed with speech.

Our pleasure in this poem comes from the opportunity of experiencing directly the personality of Anacreon, who even in Hades pleads with a passerby for the favor of one last drink and offers as enticement the benefits that endure from his poetry books. So the stranger pausing at Anacreon's tomb is expressly characterized as a reader of lyric and is easily identified with the implied reader of Antipater, traversing this series of epitaphs.[76] His libation (σπεῖσον), even before it is poured, has earned converse with Anacreon, as in 15 G-P Antipater prays for the reanimation of the Tean poet because all his life was offered as a libation to the trio of Muses, Dionysus, and Eros (κατεσπείσθη, 15.10). A final epitaph synthesizes what has been uncovered through a reading of the other four:

τύμβος Ἀνακρείοντος· ὁ Τήιος ἐνθάδε κύκνος
    εὕδει χἠ παίδων ζωροτάτη μανίη.
ἀκμὴν οἱ λυρόεν τι μελίζεται ἀμφὶ Βαθύλλῳ
    ἵμερα καὶ κισσοῦ λευκὸς ὄδωδε λίθος,
οὐδ' Ἀίδης σοι ἔρωτας ἀπέσβεσεν, ἐν δ' Ἀχέροντος
    ὢν ὅλος ὠδίνεις Κύπριδι θερμοτέρῃ.[77]

(17 G-P = AP 7.30)

The tomb of Anacreon. The Tean swan sleeps here
    as does his untempered passion for boys.
Some lyre song for Bathyllus still sounds with desire,

---

76. Cf. Bing (1988b) 63.

77. In place of Gow's rather radical emendation of the third line (οἶν' ἐρόεντι ... ἥμερα), I have printed the reading of PPl supplemented by Huet's addition of τι, accepted also by Waltz, Beckby, and Paton. The objection of Gow (1954) 3–4 and Gow-Page (1965) II 47 to οἱ, namely, that the transition from third to second person in the last couplet is intolerably rough, seems to me fallacious: it is the speaker's recognition of Anacreon's continued existence from the sounds and odors surrounding the tomb that prompts his address to the deceased in 5–6. Cf. White (1985) 65.

and the white marble exudes the perfume of ivy.
Not even Hades has extinguished your passions, and living still
in Acheron you suffer the birth pangs of the goddess's heat.

In two Greek words we are told the essential—τύμβος Ἀνακρείοντος, "the tomb of Anacreon." But all else goes to contradict the finality of that statement. The bard and his desire only slumber; his song can still be heard; the tombstone exudes the scent of ivy. The dichotomy found elsewhere between immortal poetry and mortal poet (e.g., 11.1–2 G-P = *AP* 7.14.1–2, τὰν μετὰ Μούσαις ἀθανάταις θνατάν) is dissolved here, transcended by the final image of Anacreon giving birth (ὠδίνεις) even in Hades through the warmth of his desire. This rebirth of poetry even in the midst of death can simply be read as mere wishful thinking, like the poet's prayers in 13 and 15, but the reader may also get the sense that Anacreon is kept alive, or even transformed into a new life, by the poetry that Antipater composes about him. The loss of the literary past is thus, paradoxically, the very basis for its preservation: it is through his reading of Anacreon that Antipater finds his own poetic voice.

Throughout the corpus of his epigrams Antipater presents himself as an interpreter of the past, especially of Greek literature and its traditions. In examining one last group of epigrams, his enigmatic grave epitaphs, I will show that through the fictional dramatization of viewing and decoding symbols engraved on tombstones, Antipater demonstrates the basis of the imitator's art— that all composition is a form of interpretation and that the writer must also be a reader.[78]

Although most of these riddling epitaphs were clearly composed to be read in books, they were based on the actual grave practices of the period, at least as they are found in the eastern part of the Hellenistic world. On East Greek stelae dating from the second century B.C. to the first century A.D., human representations are often accompanied by symbolic attributes, which convey through a commonly known visual language the specific praiseworthy qualities of the deceased.[79] Although the great majority of these stelae have only brief inscriptions identifying the dead, an important exception is the Menophila relief

78. For recent discussion of these largely neglected poems, see the stimulating essay by Simon Goldhill, "The Naive and Knowing Eye: Ecphrasis and the Culture of Viewing in the Hellenistic World" in *Art and Text in Ancient Greek Culture*, ed. Simon Goldhill and R. Osborne (Cambridge, 1994) 197–223.

79. Published in Ernst Pfuhl and H. Möbius, *Die ostgriechischen Grabreliefs*, 2 vols. (Mainz, 1977–79). For discussion of the attributes, see E. Pfuhl, "Das Beiwerk auf den ostgriechischen Grabreliefs," *JDAI* 20 (1905) 47–96 and 123–55. H. von Hesberg, "Bildsyntax und Erzählweise in der hellenistischen Flächenkunst," *JDAI* 103 (1988) 309–65 has studied the associative syntax of the symbols on the reliefs. For the iconography of the reliefs as reflections of self-image, see P. Zanker, "The Hellenistic Grave Stelai from Smyrna: Identity and Self-Image in the Polis," in Bulloch *et al.* (1993) 212–30.

from Sardis, which belongs to the late second or early first century B.C. The draped figure of Menophila stands facing forward, while she is accompanied on either side by the miniature figure of a servant. On her head is a crown, in a separate register behind her head appear a basket, a bundle of scrolls, and a lily, and beside her is inscribed the letter alpha. This relief, uniquely, is accompanied by an epigram that names the deceased and then deciphers the pictorial message of the attributes:

κομψὰν καὶ χαρίεσσα(ν) πέτρος δείκνυσι. τίς ἐντί; –
    Μουσῶν μανύει γράμματα· Μηνοφίλαν. –
τεῦ δ' ἔνεκ' ἐν στάλᾳ γλυπτὸν κρίνον ἠδὲ καὶ ἄλφα,
    βύβλος καὶ τάλαρος, τοῖς δ' ἔπι καὶ στέφανος; –
ἢ σοφία(μ) μὲν βίβλος, ὁ δ' αὖ περὶ κρατὶ φορηθείς
    ἀρχὰν μανύει, μουνογόναν δὲ τὸ ἕν,
εὐτάκτου δ' ἀρετᾶς τάλαρος μάνυμα, τὸ δ' ἄνθος
    τὰν ἀκμάν, δαίμων ἄντιν' ἐληίσατο. –
κούφα τοι κόνις ἀμφιπέλοι τοιῇδε θανούσῃ.
    αἴ, ἄγονοι δὲ γονεῖς, τοῖς ἔλιπες δάκρυα.

                                                    (GV 1881)

The stone displays a cultured and graceful woman. Who is she? –
    The writings of the Muses tell us. Menophila. –
Why is there carved on the stele a lily and an alpha,
    a book, a basket, and a crown as well? –
The book indicates her education, the crown on her head
    her office, and the number one that she was an only-born.
The basket is a sign of her orderly virtue, and the flower
    shows her youth, which fate has taken from her.
So then may the earth rest lightly on such a woman as this.
    Ah, to your childless parents you have left only tears.

Menophila was clearly an unusual person. In young adulthood she had already held public office and was recognized for her intellectual achievements.[80] As a result, the normal brief inscription, the "writings of the Muses" (Μουσῶν ... γράμματα), was considered an inadequate accompaniment to the "stone" (πέτρος), the visual representation that reveals the essence of Menophila's self-image. The basket, scroll, and crown belong to the common pictorial vocabulary of funereal praise and would probably require no interpretaton for the viewer. But the lily, which stands for the bloom of youth, and the alpha, which in its numerical value indicates that Menophila was an only child, would not be so

80. P. Zanker 218, discussing the book rolls found on the reliefs for men, states that the scroll "indicates education and literary and philosophical interests. Its great popularity reflects the increased importance attached to a man's intellectual training and pursuits in the course of the Hellenistic age." For interpretation of the symbols on Menophila's stele, see Josef Pircher, *Das Lob der Frau im vorchristlichen Grabepigramm der Griechen* (Innsbruck, 1979) 54–55.

easily decoded.[81] To explain them, we have this unusual example of an inscribed epigram that parallels the enigmatic epitaphs of the literary epigrammatists.

The interest that epigrams like the Menophila inscription held for Antipater and other Hellenistic poets lay in the parallel between the process of interpreting the visual symbols carved on grave reliefs and the process of interpreting the components of a literary text. The epitaph for Menophila consists of a dialogue between a viewer of the relief, who recognizes only that the deceased presents herself as a cultured and refined person, and the inscription itself, that is, the epigram within the epigram, which gives her name and interprets the symbols on her tomb. While Antipater's enigmatic epitaphs include dialogue poems that are quite similar to the Menophila inscription (20, 29, and 31 G-P), his culminating poem—related to an important series of epigrams by Leonidas, Alcaeus of Messene, and finally Meleager—dramatizes the process of decoding puzzling emblems found on a grave relief. But, in this imaginary world of fictitious inscriptions, clues to the decipherment of the symbols come not from the visual context nor from knowledge of a common pictorial vocabulary, but from the interpreter's intellectual play with the language of other literary texts.

We begin, then, with the poems that served as "pre-texts" for Antipater's series of enigmatic epitaphs. The first known riddle poem of this type was composed by Leonidas:

τί στοχασώμεθά σου, Πεισίστρατε, χῖον ὁρῶντες
    γλυπτὸν ὑπὲρ τύμβου κείμενον ἀστράγαλον;
ἦ ῥα γενὴν ὅτι Χῖος, ἔοικε γάρ; ἦ ῥ' ὅτι παίκτας
    ἦσθά τις, οὐ λίην δ', ὠγαθέ, πλειστοβόλος;
ἦ τὰ μὲν οὐδὲ σύνεγγυς, ἐν ἀκρήτῳ δὲ κατέσβης
    Χίῳ; ναί, δοκέω, τῷδε προσηγγίσαμεν.

(Leon. 22 G-P = AP 7.422)

What are we to infer about you, Peisistratus, seeing this die,
    lying in the Chian position, carved on your tomb?
That you were Chian by birth? It's likely. Or that a gamester
    you were, my good man, but not too lucky?
Or is that not it, and did you die from untempered wine
    from Chios? Yes, I think, we're close to it now.

The reader is to envision a tombstone bearing the name of the deceased and an engraved knucklebone thrown in the position known as the Chian. In a manner familiar from Callimachus' epigrams, Leonidas' poem presents the dramatized thought of an unidentified passerby, who tries to decipher the meaning of the single die. Dice do occasionally appear on the East Greek stelae, as toys with

81. The unique status of these symbols is pointed out by D. M. Robinson, "Two New Epitaphs from Sardis" in *Anatolian Studies Presented to Sir William Mitchell Ramsay*, ed. W. H. Buckler and W. M. Calder (London, 1923) 350.

children and sometimes also with adults.[82] In their latter usage they may refer to the alternation of good and bad luck that falls to every person in the course of a lifetime (cf. Agathias, *AP* 9.768). The puzzlement for the speaker in Leonidas' epigram stems not from the presence of the die itself but from the particular throw rendered on the relief. The knucklebone was in the Chian position when it rested on one of its two narrow sides; numerically, it counted as a one and was the lowest, or unluckiest, throw.[83] The first two interpretations of the die hazarded by the viewer—that the deceased was from Chios or had been an unlucky gamester—are obvious possibilities but quickly rejected in favor of a third, less obvious, choice—that Peisistratus perished from an excess of Chian wine. Since the speaker makes it clear from the outset that the meaning of Peisistratus' single attribute is to be guessed, not known, it is uncertain on what basis the third interpretation is to be preferred.[84] Was the speaker acquainted with Peisistratus and so knowledgeable about his personal habits? Or is the third alternative more attractive because less obvious, appealing to the Hellenistic preference for esoteric allusion? Whatever motivation we as readers may choose to fill in, the speaker states unequivocally that the third interpretation, like all readings, is mere opinion (δοκέω), the best approximation (προσηγγίσαμεν) of authorial intention. But in the end because the poet dramatizes himself as speaker, because the composer who intends presents himself as the viewer who deciphers, we as readers may in turn interpret the last interpretation as the "correct" one, the one validated for us by the poet dramatized as viewer.

A second riddle poem of this sort was written by Alcaeus of Messene, who flourished about the time of the turn from the third to the second century B.C.:

δίζημαι κατὰ θυμὸν ὅτου χάριν ἁ παροδῖτις
  δισσάκι φεῖ μοῦνον γράμμα λέλογχε λίθος
λαοτύποις σμίλαις κεκολαμμένον. ἦ ῥα γυναικί
  τᾷ χθονὶ κευθομένᾳ Χιλιὰς ἦν ὄνομα;
τοῦτο γὰρ ἀγγέλλει κορυφούμενος εἰς ἓν ἀριθμός.
  ἦ τὸ μὲν εἰς ὀρθὰν ἀτραπὸν οὐκ ἔμολεν,
ἁ δ' οἰκτρὸν ναίουσα τόδ' ἠρίον ἔπλετο Φειδίς;
  νῦν Σφιγγὸς γρίφους Οἰδίπος ἐφρασάμαν.

82. With children, Pfuhl-Möbius I 206, Nr. 777, Taf. 114; I 211, Nr. 804, Taf. 117; I 219, Nr. 841, Taf. 122; II 476, Nr. 1987, Taf. 286; II 522, Nr. 2182, Taf. 312. With adults, I 135, Nr. 400, Taf. 65; I 209, Nr. 793, Taf. 116.

83. For the various throws in knucklebone play, see Mau, "Ἀστράγαλος," *RE* 4 HB (1896) 1793–95; Gow-Page (1965) *ad* 22.1f.

84. For the connotation of στοχασώμεθα, cf. Pl. *Grg.* 464c, οὐ γνοῦσα ... ἀλλὰ στοχ-ασαμένη. Cf. Goldhill (1994) 202 on this epigram: "The process of interpretation is strongly stressed by the framing phrases ... : the ecphrasis does not merely dramatise a moment of seeing meaning but also of seeing oneself seeing."

αἰνετὸς οὐκ δισσοῖο καμὼν αἴνιγμα τύποιο,
    φέγγος μὲν ξυνετοῖς ἀξυνέτοις δ' ἔρεβος.

(16 G-P = AP 7.429)

I wonder to myself why this roadside marble
    has acquired two phis as its only inscription,
engraved by stone-carving chisels. Was Chilias the name
    of the woman buried in the earth here?
For this the letters summed up into one number announce.
    Or have we not traveled a straight path at all,
And was the one who piteously inhabits this tomb called Pheidis?
    Now I Oedipus have pondered the riddles of the Sphinx.
Praise to the one who invented the enigma of this double carving,
    a light to the intelligent but darkness to the unintelligent.

The poem again dramatizes the thoughts of a passerby before a tomb, this one displaying no name at all but only two phis (and apparently a representation of the deceased woman). In a conversation with his θυμός, or organ of intellect, the speaker first assumes that the letters are to be interpreted, like the alphas on Menophila's relief, as having numerical value. If the two phis, eaching standing for 500, are added together, they give 1,000 and so the deceased's name is perhaps Chilias (from χιλιάς, "a thousand"). But this supposition is quickly rejected in favor of one in which the speaker now expresses great confidence—the dead woman's name is Pheidis (φ δίς, "phi twice"). He is so proud of his achievement in solving the riddle that he calls himself a second Oedipus, the conqueror of the Sphinx. Again, we may wonder why the second interpretation is preferred to the first. Is it just the more difficult solution, since letters on gravestones seem commonly to represent numbers? Or, as Gow-Page suggest,[85] is Pheidis (cf. φειδώ, "thrift") an appropriate name for a woman whose thriftiness is exemplified by the brevity of her tomb inscription? Alcaeus' fictitious epitaph actually tells us more about the viewer of the tomb than the deceased, as his persistence in solving the puzzle before him gives way to pride of achievement. Even his play on words at the end—the person who constructs such an αἴνιγμα ("riddle") is αἰνετός ("praiseworthy")—suggests that his own facility with words and syllables parallels that of the riddle maker: because this tombstone has carved upon it no words at all, the person who views and interprets the visual symbols becomes in fact the composer of Pheidis' epitaph.

The most complicated of Antipater's enigmatic epitaphs is built upon the example provided by both Leonidas 22 and Alcaeus 16. Once again the thoughts of a person trying to decipher the emblems on a stele are dramatized, and once again an initial interpretation is rejected in favor of the "correct" one:

85. Gow-Page (1965) *ad* 16.7.

ἁ στάλα φέρ' ἴδω τίν' ἐρεῖ νέκυν. ἀλλὰ δέδορκα
    γράμμα μὲν οὐδέν που τμαθὲν ὕπερθε λίθου,
ἐννέα δ' ἀστραγάλους πεπτηότας, ὧν πίσυρες μέν
    πρᾶτοι Ἀλεξάνδρου μαρτυρέουσι βόλον,
οἱ δὲ τὸ τᾶς νεότατος ἐφάλικος ἄνθος ἔφηβον,
    εἷς δ' ὄγε μανύει Χῖος ἀφαυρότερον.
ἦ ῥα τόδ' ἀγγέλλοντι, "καὶ ὁ σκάπτροισι μεγαυχής
    χὼ θάλλων ἥβᾳ τέρμα τὸ μηδὲν ἔχει";
ἦ τὸ μὲν οὔ, δοκέω δὲ ποτὶ σκοπὸν ἰθὺν ἐλάσσειν
    ἰὸν Κρηταιεὺς ὥς τις ὀιστοβόλος.
ἧς ὁ θανὼν Χῖος μέν, Ἀλεξάνδρου δὲ λελογχώς
    οὔνομ', ἐφηβείη δ' ὤλετ' ἐν ἁλικίᾳ.
ὡς εὖ τὸν φθίμενον νέον ἄκριτα καὶ τὸ κυβευθέν
    πνεῦμα δι' ἀφθέγκτων εἶπέ τις ἀστραγάλων.

(32 G-P = *AP* 7.427)

Let me see whose death this stele reports. But I see
    no writing engraved anywhere on the stone,
Just nine dice, tossed, of which the first four
    bear witness to the throw called Alexander,
The next four the ephebe throw, the bloom of youthful maturity,
    and this one shows the lowest throw, the Chian.
Do they announce: "A man who proudly ruled with the scepter
    and was in the bloom of youth came to naught"?
No, that's not it, but I think that now I shoot my arrow
    straight at the target, like a Cretan bowman.
The dead man was a Chian, he had acquired the name
    of Alexander, and he died in ephebic youth.
How well someone has said with voiceless dice that the young man
    died through recklessness, his life staked and lost.

The dice point back to Leonidas' epigram, while the need to discover even
the name of the deceased derives from Alcaeus' Pheidis poem. The nine dice,
divided into two groups of four and a single die, represent the three throws known
as Alexander, ephebe, and Chian. The speaker's first attempt at interpretation
seems, surprisingly, the more original of the two: Alexander indicates that the
deceased was a king, ephebe that he was young, and the Chian throw—the
lowest—that all came to naught. Again, we are not told why the speaker
rejects this interpretation, although Meleager in his variation (122.7–8 G-P = *AP*
7.428.7–8) seems to suggest as a possible explanation that the modesty of the
tomb may be unfitting for one of so high a rank. But Antipater's dual imitation
of Leonidas and Alcaeus in his transitional couplet (with δοκέω in 32.9 cf.
Leon. 22.6 and with ποτὶ σκοπὸν ἰθὺν ἐλάσσειν ἰόν in 32.9–10 cf. Alcaeus 16.6)
indicates that he initially fails to hit the mark because he has paid insufficient
attention to literary precedent. His second, correct interpretation follows the
first suggestion made in Leonidas' epigram that the single die indicates place

of origin: the deceased is a Chian named Alexander, who died in ephebic youth. Reading the dice so seems disappointingly simple, but in the final couplet we find the interpretation supplemented with the suggestion that Alexander died from reckless behavior, having staked his life and lost.[86] This surprising conclusion derives, I believe, from Leonidas' second interpretation, that the deceased was a poor gamesman (οὐ λίην ... πλειστοβόλος, Leon. 22.4); in Antipater he becomes a gamesman of his own life. So Antipater's epigram, like the other two, produces a somewhat arbitrary and idiosyncratic interpretation of the tomb symbols. As a dramatization it is far-fetched. But within a book setting it reveals Antipater as a careful reader of other riddle poems and so suggests an analogy between composing an interpretation of a grave stele and composing an epigram variation. As the viewer of emblems engraved on tombstones constructs the meaning of the relief by weighing the conventional significance of such emblems against the visible syntactic context, so Antipater composes his epigrams by fitting components taken from earlier literature into his own syntactic pattern of meaning. Leonidas and Alcaeus had composed riddling epitaphs in which the viewer of a tombstone essentially composes an epigram through the process of interpretively reading symbols; Antipater "advances" in his variation beyond his predecessors by explicitly calling attention, through his intertextual references, to the analogy between the viewer of the tombstone and the composer/reader of a literary epigram.

Before concluding our discussion of enigmatic epitaphs and so of Antipater, we will take a look at the Meleagrian sequence in which these poems were embedded in order to gain some insight into Antipater's importance as a model for Meleager in combining the skills of editor and composer. The riddle poems occur within a long Meleagrian sequence of sepulchral epigrams (*AP* 7.406–507a) and directly follow an initial section of epitaphs for famous figures of the past. The transitional poem that concludes these initial epitaphs and introduces the enigmatic pieces is a self-epitaph by Meleager (5 G-P = *AP* 7.421), itself both an epitaph for a famous personage and a riddle poem in which the deceased's identity is to be guessed from an emblem of the mythological Meleager. The sequence of enigmatic epitaphs then proceeds as follows:

7.422 = Leonidas 22 G-P	(on Peisistratus)
7.423 = Antipater 28 G-P	(on Bittis)
7.424 = Antipater 29 G-P	(on Lysidice)
7.425 = Antipater 30 G-P	(on Myro)
7.426 = Antipater 31 G-P	(on Teleutias)
7.427 = Antipater 32 G-P	(on Alexander)
7.428 = Meleager 122 G-P	(on Antipater of Sidon)
7.429 = Alcaeus 16 G-P	(on Pheidis)

86. On the meaning of the conclusion, see Goldhill (1994) 200–201.

It is highly unusual for Meleager to group several poems by a single author without intervening poems by other epigrammatists. But he presents two such groupings for Antipater, these riddle poems and the series on Myron's *Cow*. It is not unreasonable to suppose that in both instances Meleager, who owed so much to Antipater's technique of variation, incorporated into his *Garland* a sequence that originally appeared in Antipater's own poetry book. Such a sequence, followed directly by Meleager's laudatory epitaph for Antipater, constitutes an open acknowledgment of the younger poet's debt to his famous compatriot. If in fact he did preserve a section of Antipater's own poetic arrangement, Meleager may thereby suggest that part of what he derived from the Sidonian was a technique of enhancing meaning through editorial design.

The five Antipater poems are obviously grouped by sex, the three on women preceding the two on men. Within Antipater's own epigram book they were likely supplemented by two other surviving poems (and perhaps other, now lost poems as well). One of these, Antipater's variation (27 G-P = *AP* 7.353) of Leonidas' epitaph for Maronis (68 G-P = *AP* 7.455), explains the reason for a carved (γλυπτήν, 27.2; cf. γλυπτόν, *GV* 1881.3; γλυπτόν, Leon. 22.2; γλυπτόν, Antip. 29.2) drinking cup upon the old woman's tomb. It makes an obvious companion piece with the epitaph on Bittis (28 G-P), who, like Maronis, is talkative (ἀείλαλος, 27.3; ἀεὶ πολύμυθον, ἀεὶ λάλον, 28.1), elderly (πολιῆς, 27.1; πολιοκρόταφον, 28.4) and a lover of wine (κύλικα, 27.2; κύλιξ, 28.2).[87] But because Bittis, unlike Maronis, speaks her own epitaph, she adds to these negative qualities neutral or positive ones, her Cretan origin and fondness for weaving. In the next epitaph in the series, that for Lysidice, attributes that normally designate male achievement are interpreted as emblems of a wife's virtue, especially, in contrast to the two preceding poems, her propensity for silence (οὐ πολύμυθον, οὐ λάλον, 29.9–10). The following epitaph, for Myro, comes last in the set on women because it contains the most difficult, and seemingly arbitrary, interpretations. Who would have suspected that a bow emblemized Myro's good housekeeping or that a whip indicated her just treatment of her servants? The series shows a progression, then, from parodic to complimentary epitaphs and from relatively simple interpretations to more difficult ones. In the original epigram collection the two epitaphs for men were possibly accompanied by Antipater's epitaph for Aristomenes (20 G-P = *AP* 7.161), which is structurally a twin to the Teleutias poem (31 G-P).[88] In each a

87. In the *AP* it occurs within a long thematically arranged sequence (7.1–363) which includes both Meleagrian and non-Meleagrian authors and which probably reflects the design of Cephalas. The poem has clearly been excerpted from its original position within the order created by Meleager, who likely grouped it either with Antipater's other riddle epitaphs or with the Leonidas poem it varies.

88. Like the Maronis epitaph, Antipater's poem for Aristomenes has been removed from its original position in Meleager's *Garland* to the Cephalan sequence (7.1–363).

passerby questions an animal surmounting a tomb, an eagle in one and a lion in the other, and the animal then explains how it symbolizes the ἀρετή of the deceased warrior. The Alexander epigram is reserved for the end of the sequence because it is the longest and most complicated of Antipater's enigmatic epitaphs, the poem that links his whole series to the exemplars composed by Leonidas and Alcaeus.

It is my suggestion that Meleager took over from Antipater, with little or no modification, this series of epitaphs already structured through pairing and thematic linkage and added to it the two poems that paved the way for Antipater's riddling epitaphs and his own contributions to the epigram type. By setting the Leonidas poem before the group by Antipater and placing his own variation at the end, he follows the general technique found elsewhere in the *Garland* of grouping models with copies. We might suppose, then, that the Alcaeus epigram, which served as a model for Antipater as well as for Meleager 122, has been misplaced. If it were moved forward to precede the Antipater poems, the whole sequence would be surrounded by Meleagrian interpretations of the form, that is, his self-epitaph (5 G-P = *AP* 7.421) and his epitaph for Antipater. But Meleager, as we shall see in greater detail, was more interested in the aesthetics of design than in chronological accuracy. Against the chaos of editorial disruption remains the reasonable possibility that Meleager chose to end the sequence with Alcaeus' reference to Oedipus, the mythological interpreter of riddles.

As Antipater's Alexander epitaph acts as a culmination for his series of riddle poems by echoing the introductory piece by Leonidas, so Meleager's Antipater epitaph appropriately closes the entire sequence by providing an intertextual commentary on Antipater's own method of variation and interpretive reading:

ἁ στάλα, σύνθημα τί σοι γοργωπὸς ἀλέκτωρ
   ἕστα καλλαΐνα σκαπτροφόρος πτέρυγι
ποσσὶν ὑφαρπάζων νίκας κλάδον, ἄκρα δ' ἐπ' αὐτᾶς
   βαθμῖδος προπεσὼν κέκλιται ἀστράγαλος;
ἦ ῥά γε νικάεντα μάχᾳ σκαπτοῦχον ἄνακτα
   κρύπτεις; ἀλλὰ τί σοι παίγνιον ἀστράγαλος;
πρὸς δ' ἔτι λιτὸς ὁ τύμβος· ἐπιπρέπει ἀνδρὶ πενιχρῷ
   ὄρνιθος κλαγγαῖς νυκτὸς ἀνεγρομένῳ.
οὐ δοκέω, σκᾶπτρον γὰρ ἀναίνεται· ἀλλὰ σὺ κεύθεις
   ἀθλοφόρον νίκαν ποσσὶν ἀειράμενον;
οὐ ψαύω καὶ τᾷδε· τί γὰρ ταχὺς εἴκελος ἀνὴρ
   ἀστραγάλῳ; νῦν δὴ τὠτρεκὲς ἐφρασάμαν·
φοῖνιξ οὐ νίκαν ἐνέπει, πάτραν δὲ μεγαυχῆ
   ματέρα Φοινίκων τὰν πολύπαιδα Τύρον·
ὄρνις δ' ὅττι γεγωνὸς ἀνὴρ καί που περὶ Κύπριν
   πρᾶτος κἠν Μούσαις ποικίλος ὑμνοθέτας·
σκᾶπτρα δ' ἔχει σύνθημα λόγου, θνάσκειν δὲ πεσόντα
   οἰνοβρεχῆ προπετὴς ἐννέπει ἀστράγαλος.

καὶ δὴ σύμβολα ταῦτα· τὸ δ᾽ οὔνομα πέτρος ἀείδει,
   Ἀντίπατρον προγόνων φύντ᾽ ἀπ᾽ ἐρισθενέων.

(122 G-P = *AP* 7.428)

Stele, why does the emblem of a fierce-eyed cock stand
   upon you, holding a scepter in his scarlet wing
and clutching with his talons a victory branch, and why
   does a tossed die lie at the edge of your base?
Do you conceal a scepter-bearing king, victor in battle?
   But why then the gaming instrument of the die?
Also the tomb is a simple one, befitting a poor man
   wakened before morning by the cock's crow.
No, the scepter's against it. Or do you conceal an athlete
   who carried off victory in a footrace?
I haven't got it there either. For how is a swift man
   like a knucklebone? *Now* I've found the right answer.
The palm doesn't speak of victory, but his proud fatherland,
   Tyre, the mother of the Phoenicians, home to many boys.
The cock shows that he was a much-heard man, concerned with
   Aphrodite, and a subtle interpreter of the Muses.
The scepters are a sign of eloquence, and the thrown die indicates
   that he died thrown down when sotted with drink.
So these are the symbols. The stone sings out his name,
   Antipater, descended from illustrious ancestors.

The first word in Meleager's poem (ἁ στάλα) is copied from the opening of Antipater 32 (ἁ στάλα), which stands immediately before in the *AP* and is Meleager's principal model. But it is typical of Meleager to combine more than one original in producing a variation,[89] and so here he echoes several of the riddle poems in the sequence. The cock, which is the main σύνθημα or emblematic "password" for the poet Antipater, derives from the Lysidice epitaph (29.3–4), while the phrase γοργωπὸς ἀλέκτωρ, "fierce-eyed cock" (122.1), recalls as well the "fierce" (γοργός, Antip. 20.2) eagle on Aristomenes' tomb. At the same time, the scepter held by the cock was suggested by the false guess in the Alexander riddle (σκάπτροισι μεγαυχής, Antip. 32.7), and the single die looks back to Leonidas 22 as well as to the intermediate variation in Antipater 32.[90] Meleager also provides himself greater opportunity to echo and vary his predecessors by increasing the number of rejected interpretations from one to

---

89. Cf. Tarán (1979) 167: "He was brilliant . . . in combining different motifs by crossing themes and conceits borrowed from different models, but perhaps his most striking originality lay in his blending the language and conceits appropriate to two non-erotic types of epigrams into a whole which was none the less oriented towards the erotic theme."

90. Other vocabulary from the earlier riddle poems is echoed by Meleager as well: cf. δοκέω in 122.9 with Leon. 22.6 and Antip. 32.9; ἐφρασάμαν in 122.12 with Alc. 16.8; μεγαυχῆ in 122.13 with Antip. 32.7.

three. Through this series of guesses, Meleager seems to suggest that the act of reading, or correct interpretation, is both dependent upon an understanding of other texts and equally independent of them, in that the components of any given text must be synthesized into meaning on the terms of that text alone. So even the poet's own initial interpretation of the palm as a symbol of victory (νίκας κλάδον, 122.3) turns out to be misleading, as he discovers that the palm (φοῖνιξ)—read as a rebus—symbolizes Phoenician Tyre. Nor is the scepter a sign of kingship, as in Antipater 32.7, but of eloquence, and the cock does not emblemize wakefulness, as in Antipater 29.7, but a sonorous poet and perhaps a lover.[91] The single die is the most interesting of all, for in Meleager's three rejected guesses it acts as the stumbling block that invalidates the suggestion. But the final solution of the riddle, in which the die tossed forward (προπεσών, 122.4; προπετής, 122.18) indicates that Antipater died by falling (πεσόντα, 122.17) when drunk, can be worked out only if Meleager (and the reader as well) assumes from Leonidas' poem that the die is represented in the Chian position and so stands for the dangers of overindulging in Chian wine.[92] Meleager reveals that a combination of intertextual knowledge and independent thinking is crucial in deciphering the σύμβολα of the tomb to discover that the stone sings out the name of Antipater.[93] But the reader may feel that, in the final analysis, the literary context of Meleager's epitaph offers the best clue to the identity of the deceased. For who would be designated by such a complicated series of σύμβολα other than the poet Meleager varies, the epigrammatist whose technique of composing enigmatic epitaphs by varying his predecessors is demonstrated in the immediately preceding poems? We may assume that Meleager chose to celebrate Antipater in the form of a riddling epitaph precisely because this type of epigram had most clearly demonstrated

91. The "birds of the Muses" who vie with Homer in Theocritus *Id.* 7.47 are apparently cocks; see Gow (1952) *ad loc.* The connection of Antipater with Aphrodite is surprising, given the nature of his surviving poetry. But as one overtly erotic epigram survives from the hand of Leonidas (92 G-P = *AP* 5.188), so too Antipater may have produced a body of erotic material not transmitted by later anthologies. There does survive one pederastic epigram in a satirical vein (65 G-P = *AP* 12.97).

92. Pointed out by both Gow-Page (1965) *ad* 17f. and Goldhill (1994) 204. Another tradition about his death, that he died at an advanced age from a fever that beset him annually on his birthday, was known to Roman writers (see Pliny *HN* 7.172, Val. Max. 1.8.16). Though neither story carries great credibility, the existence of a rival report increases the likelihood that Meleager's description of his death was intended only as a literary echo of Leon. 22 and Antip. 32.

93. The word σύμβολα is particularly resonant in this context: as tallies, originally in the form of divided knucklebones, σύμβολα were used for personal identification (Hdt. 6.86; Eur. *Med.* 613; cf. Pl. *Symp.* 191d), while etymologically, as something "thrown together," they recall the various "throws" (βόλα) of the dice that play in this poem and its models (cf. πλειστοβόλος, Leon. 22.4; βόλον, Antip. 32.4; όιστοβόλος, Antip. 32.10).

Antipater's interest in the interaction between reading and composition, in creativity through interpretation.

Antipater's main contribution to the history of epigram was his technique of variation, which provided later epigrammatists with a procedure for extending the genre through continual remaking of the great "originals" of the past. As a consequence, we may attribute to him the impetus for the earliest epigram anthologies, which were based, as Meleager's *Garland* and the Amyntas papyrus show, on grouping poems in sets of variations. While it is just possible that Antipater anticipated Meleager in combining models and variations in an anthologizing poetry book, the two sequences of Antipater epigrams that have been preserved, on Myron's *Cow* and the riddling epitaphs, offer evidence that the epigrammatist created his effects not just through literary allusion but also through the contextual setting he gave his compositions. We may come closer to the truth in speculating that he combined his variations of earlier epigrammatists with poems on literary greats, enigmatic epitaphs, and various other pieces to produce a poetry book thematized by the interpretive process itself. Antipater's methods of reading the Greek cultural past provided a basis for the continuance and renewal of literature in a period when Hellenic heritage seemed endangered, a fragile survival to be tended, analyzed, and reworked in addressing new concerns raised by the overlordship of Rome.

MELEAGER

Our biographical information about Meleager comes primarily from his four self-epitaphs.[94] He was a native of Gadara in Palestine, spent his youth in Tyre, and settled in later life on the island of Cos, where he composed his *Garland*.[95] From the fringes of Syro-Phoenician culture, he thus moved progressively closer to the center of the Hellenic world. In addition to about one hundred thirty known epigrams, predominantly erotic, he wrote Menippean satire, now lost, under the influence of the Cynic Menippus, also a native of Gadara.[96] According to the lemmatist's notes on the introduction to the *Garland*, Meleager flourished in the time of the last Seleucus, that is, Seleucus VI Epiphanes Nicator, who ruled in 96–95 B.C. Although it is unclear what source the lemmatist could have

---

94. 2–5 G-P = *AP* 7.417–19, 7.421; cf. also anon. 7.416. For discussion of Meleager's life, see Henri Ouvré, *Méléagre de Gadara* (Paris, 1894) 19–58; Gow-Page (1965) I xiv–xv, II 606–7.

95. For Tyre in this period, see Grainger, and for Hellenistic Cos, see Susan M. Sherwin-White, *Ancient Cos* (Göttingen, 1978). On Meleager's trilingual epitaph (4 G-P = *AP* 7.419) as an expression of the Syro-Phoenician community on Cos, see M. Luz, "Salam, Meleager!" *SIFC* 6 (1988) 222–31.

96. For Meleager's prose works, see Ath. 4.157b, 11.502c.

had for this information,[97] he may have correctly indicated the approximate date of Meleager's anthology. A date in the 90s would fit a collection that included Antipater of Sidon and conceivably Archias of Antioch, but contained none of the epigrams of his fellow Gadaran Philodemus, who was born about 110 B.C. Since Meleager's epigrams seem to have been written over the course of a lifetime, he no doubt issued one or more smaller collections consisting entirely of his own epigrams before the publication of the *Garland*. As pointed out in Chapter 2, P.Oxy. 3324, containing four epigrams by Meleager, is probably a fragment of a Meleager sylloge rather than a selection made from the *Garland* and suggests that Meleager's techniques of arrangement were first worked out in single-authored editions. But, although his epigram on a garland of boy loves (78 G-P = *AP* 12.256) has sometimes been interpreted as the introduction to a book of pederastic poems, it lacks a definitively prooemial character and so cannot be offered as additional evidence for a sylloge of Meleagrian poems.[98] Given the paucity of evidence about earlier editions, our focus will here be on the *Garland* itself, an anthology that was clearly a literary masterpiece and the primary vehicle through which Hellenistic epigrams were transmitted to the modern world.

Knowledge of the arrangement of the *Garland* has increased dramatically in the last century. Nineteenth-century scholars had identified in the *Palatine Anthology* long sequences of epigrams composed by authors known to have been included in the anthologies of Meleager, Philip, and Agathias.[99] But a statement of the lemmatist that Meleager's *Garland* was ordered alphabetically hampered evaluation of these sequences.[100] While the poems in the Philippan sequences displayed sustained alphabetical ordering, those in the Meleagrian sequences did not and so appeared to have suffered massive rearrangement. In 1895 Carl Radinger conclusively proved the falseness of the lemmatist's claim by showing

97. It occurs together with a comment that Meleager was a native of Gadara, which is clearly derived from the poetry itself; see Gow-Page (1965) I xiv. For various scholarly opinions on the date of the *Garland*, see Chapter 2, note 1.

98. See Radinger 110–12 and Wifstrand 72–75.

99. The groupings of short and long sequences made by Weisshäupl (1889) 2–25 and by Stadtmüller in his margins and at the head of pages (both based on the work of earlier scholars) are conveniently correlated and discussed by Gow-Page (1965) I xxiv–vi. The first systematic discussion of the longer sequences and their importance in reconstructing the sources of Cephalas was presented by Lenzinger, whose summary chart (Tafel I) is conveniently reproduced by Cameron (1993) as his Table; cf. my Table I.

100. *Anthologia Palatina: Codex Palatinus et Codex Parisinus*, a phototype facsimile edited by Karl Preisendanz (Lugduni Batavorum, 1911) 81: συνέταξεν δὲ αὐτὰ κατὰ στοιχεῖον, ἀλλὰ Κωνσταντῖνος ὁ ἐπονομαζόμενος Κεφαλᾶς συνέχεεν αὐτὰ ἀφορίσας εἰς κεφάλαια διάφορα, ἤγουν ἐρωτικὰ ἰδίως καὶ ἀναθεματικὰ καὶ ἐπιτύμβια καὶ ἐπιδεικτικά. For discussion of the reasons for rejecting the lemmatist's statement, see Gow-Page (1965) I xvii–xviii and Cameron (1993) 19–24.

that the Meleagrian sequences were organized on entirely different principles.[101] They are characterized by a rhythmic alternation of major authors and by the placement of copy after original, by epigram pairs, and by thematic grouping of poems. Shortly afterwards, Weisshaüpl analyzed the three long Meleagrian sections in *AP* 7 to show that they displayed a similarity in sequence of topic and so must represent three different selections from the funereal section of the *Garland*.[102] It has since become clear that the three Meleagrian sections in *AP* 6, in parallel fashion, represent separate but sequential selections from the dedicatory section of the *Garland*. Another advance was made in 1926 when Wifstrand, in analyzing the arrangement of erotic epigrams, demonstrated that the heterosexual poems in *AP* 5 and the homosexual poems in *AP* 12 were originally integrated in a single section of Meleager's anthology.[103] Since then, in 1965, Lenzinger (see his Tafel I) systematically demonstrated that Cephalas tended to follow the same pattern for constructing each book of his anthology in combining his own thematically ordered sections with sequences drawn from Philip, Meleager, and Agathias. More recently, Cameron has drawn the logical conclusion from the work of these earlier scholars, that Meleager's *Garland* was published on four papyrus rolls, each consisting of a single book corresponding to Cephalas' categories of erotica (*AP* 5 and 12), anathematica (*AP* 6), epitymbia (*AP* 7), and epideictica (*AP* 9).[104]

As a result of these incremental advances in knowledge, we are now in a position to describe the *Garland* and, despite losses and disruptions, to present literary analysis of its structure. If we count in Gow-Page the number of Hellenistic epigrams preserved in the *AP* excluding the Theocritean poems, which entered the *Anthology* from another source, we find that Meleager's *Garland* consisted of some 750 epigrams in about 4,500 verses. This number is certainly too low, since some of the anonymous epigrams now in sections arranged by Cephalas must have come from Meleager and Gow omits most of the epigrams in the *Anthology* by pre-Hellenistic poets, though certainly some of these were included in the *Garland*. We must also recognize the loss of an entirely unknown number of poems in the course of transmission. Given these uncertainties, we can ascertain only the minimum number of epigrams included in each of Meleager's books: 245 erotica, 147 anathematica, 282 epitymbia, and 70 epideictica (to be supplemented with others from *AP* 16).[105] In addition, a

---

101. Radinger 100–107.

102. R. Weisshäupl, "Zu den Quellen der Anthologia Palatina," *Serta Harteliana* (Vienna, 1896) 184–88.

103. Wifstrand 8–22.

104. Cameron (1968) 324–31, (1993) 24–33.

105. Martial, who limits his epigram books to about one hundred poems, criticizes collections as large as three hundred epigrams (2.1); Meleager was likely one of the offenders he had in mind.

prooemium and an epilogue stood outside of the structure of the four books proper. Our analysis of the *Garland*'s structure will reveal a set of four uniquely designed poetry books, in each of which the practice of editing becomes an aesthetic endeavor rivaling poetic composition itself.

Meleager's long introductory poem (1 G-P = *AP* 4.1), spoken by a Muse, sets out the metaphorical identification of his collection with a garland, while the epilogue (129 G-P = *AP* 12.257) gives voice to the *coronis*, the convoluted mark that signaled the end of a manuscript text. Both were placed outside of the structure of the four epigram books because they concern Meleager's role as editor rather than poet. The prooemium replaces the title and author's name that stood at the beginning of a roll or on the back of the papyrus, and the concluding poem, whether it substituted for or accompanied the *coronis*, repeats the name of author and work at the end of the papyrus roll. In other words, Meleager here expands the margins of his own text by converting front and back matter into poetry.

The reader may be surprised to find his or her curiosity about authorship converted into text in the very first line on the scroll:

Μοῦσα φίλα, τίνι τάνδε φέρεις πάγκαρπον ἀοιδάν,
  ἢ τίς ὁ καὶ τεύξας ὑμνοθετᾶν στέφανον;

(1.1–2 G-P = AP 4.1.1–2)

Dear Muse, to whom do you bring this song of fruits and flowers,
  or rather, who constructed this garland of poets?

Here we have not two questions, but a single one stated in two different forms (note ἤ, not καί): the person to whom the Muse brings the crown of all-blossoming song—text, inspiration, and recognition all in one—is the composer. Bornmann, who has explicated this point, cites depictions in earlier Greek art of the Muses crowning a poet;[106] we may also note Lucretius' claim to novelty through the metaphor of a crown of flowers plucked in that place where the Muses had previously veiled no poet's head (*iuvatque novos decerpere flores insignemque meo capiti petere inde coronam, unde prius nulli velarint tempora Musae*, 1.928–30). To be compared as well is the conclusion of the third book of Horace's *Odes*: "Consent to encircle my hair, Melpomene, with Delphic laurel" (*mihi Delphica lauro cinge volens, Melpomene, comam*, 3.30.15–16). Accordingly, the Muse answers the reader's question by naming Meleager as composer and Diocles as dedicatee:

---

106. F. Bornmann, "Meleagro e la corona delle Muse," *SIFC* 45 (1973) 230. P. Claes, "Notes sur quelques passages de Méléagre de Gadara," *AC* 39 (1970) 468–71 had anticipated Bornmann in pointing out that the Muse speaks all the lines in the prooemium, including the final couplet, which editors have usually allotted to Meleager.

ἄνυσε μὲν Μελέαγρος, ἀριζάλῳ δὲ Διοκλεῖ
μναμόσυνον ταύταν ἐξεπόνησε χάριν.

(1.3–4 G-P)

The accomplishment was Meleager's, and he labored over this gift
so that illustrious Diocles would be remembered.

The Muse then proceeds with the table of contents for the *Garland*, listing
the plant identifications for forty-seven epigrammatists, as well as the "newly
written sprouts" (1.55) of anonymous others and the "early white violets" (1.56)
of Meleager himself. Within the *Garland* Meleager will assume his own poetic
voice, but here on the poeticized margins of the text, the Muse speaks for him,
naming him as an editor whose task is merely to pluck and plait. At the end
of the list of epigrammatists, the Muse, in ring fashion, reiterates and expands
her answer to the question (τίνι . . . φέρεις, 1; φίλοις . . . φέρω, 57):

ἀλλὰ φίλοις μὲν ἐμοῖσι φέρω χάριν· ἔστι δὲ μύσταις
κοινὸς ὁ τῶν Μουσέων ἡδυεπὴς στέφανος.

(1.57–58 G-P)

It is for my friends I bring this gift, and my initiates have as well
common possession of the Muses's sweet-sounding garland.

It is evident from numerous parallel passages that those designated as friends
of the Muses are poets[107]—here meaning Meleager, certainly, but, as the plural
suggests, others as well, apparently the other poets of the *Garland*. As the
poets are priests of the Muses, interpreters of their song, so the μύσται, or
"initiates," are devotees of literature, such as the reader to whom the Muse is
speaking.[108] Structurally, then, the prooemium has come full circle, from reader's
question to Muse's inclusion of the reader in her answer. The "commonality"
of the Muse's garland (κοινὸς . . . στέφανος) suggests the collaborative nature
of epigram production, the difficulty of containing epigram creativity within
fixed borders.

The coronis poem was clearly composed as a counterpart to the prooemium.
It is richly metaphorical, linking the completion of Meleager's anthology with
athletic endeavor, religious experience, and the initial garland motif:

ἁ πύματον καμπτῆρα καταγγέλλουσα κορωνίς,
    οἰκουρὸς γραπταῖς πιστοτάτα σελίσιν,
φαμὶ τὸν ἐκ πάντων ἠθροισμένον εἰς ἕνα μόχθον
    ὑμνοθετᾶν βύβλῳ τᾷδ' ἐνελιξάμενον
ἐκτελέσαι Μελέαγρον, ἀείμνηστον δὲ Διοκλεῖ
    ἄνθεσι συμπλέξαι μουσοπόλον στέφανον.

107. See, for instance, Hes. *Th.* 96–97; Theoc. 1.141, 11.6; Callim. fr. 1.37–38 repeated in
29.5–6 G-P; Hor. *Carm.* 1.26.1.
108. For this interpretation of the μύσται, see Gow-Page (1965) *ad* 57 with passages cited.

οὖλα δ' ἐγὼ καμφθεῖσα δρακοντείοις ἴσα νώτοις
σύνθρονος ἵδρυμαι τέρμασιν εὐμαθίας.

(129 G-P = AP 12.257)

I, the *coronis*, who announce the final turn,
  a most trustworthy guardian of the written page,
I say that Meleager has finished, having enrolled in this book
  the labor of all poets gathered into one
And that he plaited from flowers a Muse-tended garland
  so that Diocles would be always remembered.
I, curled up tightly like the coils of a snake's back,
  sit enthroned at the end of his wisdom.

The *coronis* announces the final turn (καμπτῆρα), which is the last lap of the race (cf. τέρμασιν, 8) and the last turn of the scroll (cf. ἐνελιξάμενον, 4), with its own twisted form upon the page (οὖλα ... καμφθεῖσα, 7). Gigante's simple emendation οἰκουρός in 2 lends point to the *coronis*'s comparison of its convoluted form to snaky coils.[109] As οἰκουρός was a traditional epithet for the snake who guarded Athena's house on the Acropolis (Ar. *Lys.* 759), so here the snakelike *coronis* sits enthroned at the end of the anthology to watch over the garland, the *sacra* the Muse presents to her holy worshipers. Bing has pointed out a further metaphorical subtlety in this complex poem, based on a fragment of Simonides (187 *PMG*) in which the word κορωνίς designates a garland of violets.[110] Here too the twisted snakelike mark of punctuation at the end of the anthology is a garland, the *Garland*'s garland (cf. στεφάνου στέφανος, Mel. 45 G-P = *AP* 5.143), the wreath crowning the victor at the end of a race.

Since we are no longer able to determine the order of Meleager's four poetry books (although they were probably labeled α', β', γ', δ'), we do not know which section was headed by the prooemium and which ended with the *coronis* epigram. Cephalas placed the prooemium first in what is now *AP* 4, a book that also contained the prooemia of Philip and Agathias, and the *coronis* epigram in *AP* 12 just before the last poem, which was the concluding epigram in Strato's Μοῦσα Παιδική. These positions were chosen to mark the beginning and end of material taken from Meleager in Cephalas' anthology and may have nothing to do with their original positions in the *Garland*. In analyzing the arrangement of Meleager's four books, I will follow the order in the *AP*—erotic poems (*AP* 5 and 12), dedications (*AP* 6), sepulchral epigrams (*AP* 7), and epideictic poems (*AP* 9). But, as we will see, thematic linkage to other poems with garland references suggests that the prooemium may have preceded the erotic epigrams and the *coronis* poem may have followed the dedicatory epigrams.

109. "Meleagro, *A.P.* XII 257,2," *PP* 33 (1978) 58–59.
110. Bing (1988b) 34.

The amatory book was the one in which Meleager had the most personal stake because it contained the bulk of his own epigram production. Not surprisingly, then, its structure was the most elaborate among the four poetry books in the *Garland*. Amatory epigrams from the *Garland* occur in two long sequences of Meleagrian authors, one from *AP* 5 (134–215) on heterosexual themes and one from *AP* 12 (37–168) on homosexual themes. But it has been conclusively shown that Meleager did not separate his erotic epigrams by the sex of the beloved and that these two sequences were originally combined as a single book within the *Garland*. It was apparently Cephalas who culled what he perceived as homosexual epigrams from the *Garland* and placed them in a separate book surrounded by poems taken primarily from Strato's Μοῦσα Παιδική (12.1–11, 175–229, 231, 234–55, 258).[111] Only a late compiler would have made the kind of careless mistakes found in the current distribution. Not only do some homosexual poems (e.g., 5.142, 145) remain in *AP* 5, but a greater number of heterosexual epigrams have been removed to *AP* 12. Cephalas evidently did not understand that names, or nicknames, ending in -ιον were given to women.

Supporting evidence for the unity of Meleager's amatory book comes from two ancient papyri. Wifstrand pointed out the importance of *BKT* 5.1.75, which dates from the first century A.D.[112] The sequence of poems it contains— 12.76, 12.77, 12.78, 9.15, 12.106, 5.152, 12.19—represents, almost certainly, a selection from the *Garland*. Not only do 12.76–78 occur in the same order as in the *AP*, but Cameron has now pointed out that 9.15 has the same subject matter (the contagion of love's fire) as 12.79, a poem that does not appear on the papyrus.[113] Although Cephalas later moved the anonymous 9.15 to the epideictic book, it must have originally stood close after 12.78 in the vicinity of 12.79. More important, the presence of 5.152 on Meleager's girlfriend Zenophila in this selection of poems indicates clearly that the separation of homosexual and heterosexual epigrams occurred some time after the date of the papyrus. P.Oxy. 3324, of the late first century B.C. or early first century A.D., points in the same direction. It contains, following an unidentified epigram, 9.16, 5.190, 12.157, 5.152, all by Meleager. Cameron has argued that this papyrus is also a

---

111. So Wifstrand 8, Gow (1958a) 24, Lenzinger 25–26, Cameron (1993) 239–42. But for the argument that Cephalas knew only Strato's Μοῦσα Παιδική and that a later redactor inserted poems from Meleager's *Garland*, see R. Aubreton, "Le livre XII de l'Anthologie Palatine: la Muse de Straton," *Byzantion* 39 (1969) 35–52; W. M. Clarke, "The Manuscript of Straton's *Musa puerilis*," *GRBS* 17 (1976) 371–84; and Aubreton (1994) xxxv–xxxviii. The date of Strato is uncertain. Cameron, "Strato and Rufinus," *CQ* 32 (1982) 168–71 and (1993) 65–69 argues he is Hadrianic on the basis of an identification of the doctor Capito in *AP* 11.117 with a medical scholar favored by Hadrian, while Page (1978) 23–27 is more cautious, assigning his upper limit to the middle of the third century.

112. Wifstrand 10–13 identified the fourth poem on the papyrus as 9.15 and the fragment at the end of the papyrus as a remnant of 12.19.

113. Cameron (1993) 27.

selection from the *Garland*,[114] and it certainly seems *related* to Meleager's amatory section. 5.190 and 12.157, which both display the sea-of-love theme, probably stood close together in the *Garland*, and 9.16, which I would group with 12.88–95 as epigrams on multiple loves,[115] likely preceded them at some interval. But Cameron ignores the fact that 5.152 is out of order, following rather than preceding 5.190, whereas in the *AP* sequence it seems rightly placed next to its companion piece, 5.151. P.Oxy. 3324 cannot, then, be a sequential selection from the *Garland*, as *BKT* 5.1.75 apparently is. Either the compiler of the papyrus did some reordering, or, alternatively, this fragmentary text may preserve, not the *Garland* at all, but an otherwise unknown edition of Meleager's epigrams that shared some of the same ordering techniques. I will argue below that Meleager borrowed key elements of his structure from earlier epigram books; so too he likely reused the elements of design from a book of his own amatory epigrams.

In order to reconstruct Meleager's book of erotic epigrams, we must fit together the long sequence from *AP* 5 with that from *AP* 12, that is, to reverse as much as possible the activity of Cephalas. Wifstrand has provided the groundwork for this project. He was able to match a good number of poems in *AP* 12 to those in *AP* 5 (in order) on the basis of thematic similarity, and he also recognized one larger grouping in which Meleager continually linked a series of short sequences.[116] But Wifstrand displayed very little appreciation for the broader dynamics of poetry books. As a result, he missed the significance of opening and closing sequences and of transitional poems, and he failed to recognize the more general organizational principles on which Meleager constructed his anthology. It is my belief that, despite the loss of some epigrams and the displacement of others, we can identify a sophisticated artistic design in which smaller rhythmic units based on alternation of authors and similarity of theme are combined to form larger segments organized by gender and by generalizing motifs (see Tables II and III). In fact, enough remains of the amatory book to indicate a pattern of interlocking parallelism, which descends from archaic ring composition and reappears in some of the most sophisticated Roman poetry books, such as Vergil's *Eclogues*, Propertius' Monobiblos, and Horace's *Carmina* 1–3.[117]

114. Cameron (1993) 27–28.

115. Rather than with 12.106, as Cameron (1993) 27 suggests in his attempt to prove that both papyri are direct excerpts from the *Garland*.

116. Wifstrand 14–22.

117. On the *Eclogues*, see Brooks Otis, *Virgil: A Study in Civilized Poetry* (Oxford, 1964) 128–43 and John Van Sickle, *The Design of Virgil's "Bucolics"* (Rome, 1978); on the Monobiblos, see O. Skutsch, "The Structure of the Propertian *Monobiblos*," *CP* 58 (1963) 238–39 and B. Otis, "Propertius' Single Book," *HSCP* 70 (1965) 1–44. For various Augustan poetry books with an emphasis on Horace's *Carmina*, see Helena Dettmer, *Horace: A Study in Structure* (Hildesheim, 1983).

The opening sequence as preserved in *AP* 5 (134–49) consists of sixteen poems divided into three shorter sequences (134–37, 138–41, 142–49). The general theme of the section is the symposium and the themes of the three subordinate sequences are wine, song, and garlands/*charis*. Meleager opens with Posidippus' address to an Attic wine jug (Κεκροπί, ῥαῖνε, λάγυνε, πολύδροσον ἰκμάδα Βάκχου, "sprinkle, Cecropian jug, the dewy moisture of Bacchus," 1.1 G-P), followed by an anonymous imitation. Agathias, who copied Meleager's method of grouping epigrams by alternation of authors and thematic association,[118] would later imitate Meleager's programmatic opening for the beginning of his epideictic book (σπείσατέ μοι, Μοῦσαι, ... ἡδὺν ἀπὸ στομάτων Ἑλικωνίδος ὄμβρον ἀοιδῆς, "pour out for me, Muses, the sweet moisture of Heliconian song from your mouths," 9.364.1–2). Since 5.134 was probably an introductory poem for one of Posidippus' collections, Meleager himself here recalls and expropriates the thematics of an earlier epigram book even as he ventriloquizes Posidippus' call for Bacchic inspiration. The Meleagrian pair that follows (ἔγχει ... Ἡλιοδώρας, 5.136.1; ἔγχει ... Ἡλιοδώρας, 5.137.1) links the drinking theme directly to a named beloved, even as 5.136, possibly the first poem by Meleager himself, calls for the crowning of the poet (with ἀμφιτίθει στέφανον, 5.136.4, cf. ἀμφιτίθει ... στεφάνους, 6.313.4, on which more later). In a context where wine clearly stands for poetry, the call to mingle "again, again, and again" (πάλιν ..., πάλιν πάλιν, 136.1) the sweet name of Heliodora with unmixed wine foreshadows the importance of Heliodora as subject in the epigrams to follow. In addition, the reference to a στέφανος, in conjunction with the garland theme in the third short sequence, provides a typically Meleagrian associative link with the prooemium and so suggests that the introductory poem for the *Garland* may have stood directly before the amatory book.

As Wifstrand noted, 12.49–51 cohere with the initial sequence on wine in 5.134–37. 12.50, Asclepiades' *sphragis* poem (πῖν', Ἀσκληπιάδη; ζωρὸν πόμα; κοιμιστάν), and 12.49, Meleager's variation (ζωροπότει; κοιμάσει), together associate the initial call to drink with release from erotic pain;[119] they therefore probably followed 5.135. 12.51 by Callimachus (ἔγχει καὶ πάλιν εἰπὲ 'Διοκλέος') was clearly the model for Meleager's 5.136 (ἔγχει καὶ πάλιν εἰπέ ... Ἡλιοδώρας) and most likely either preceded or followed it in the usual manner of pairing original and copy. The poem also provides a male counterpart to Meleager's Heliodora and suggests that the opening sequence originally contained a rhythmic cadence of male/female love objects to supplement its alternation of authors.

118. See Mattsson 1–16.

119. The motif of putting to sleep passion in 12.49 (φλόγα τὰν φιλόπαιδα κοιμάσει) will echo in 5.215 (τὸν ἄγρυπνον ... πόθον Ἡλιοδώρας κοίμισον), a key poem in the closing sequence of the amatory book; on which, see below. For a more detailed reading of the opening and closing poems in Meleager's amatory book, see my "The Poetics of Editing in Meleager's *Garland*," *TAPA* 127 (1997): 169–200.

Yet this hypothesis leaves the initial series of Meleagrian poems in *AP* 12 (37–48) without a position in the opening sequence; I believe, however, they have been displaced from their original location within the body of the amatory book. While 12.1–11 are all from Strato's Μοῦσα Παιδική, 12.12–36 display a thematic arrangement like that made by Cephalas in other books of his anthology (e.g., 6.1–53, 6.179–226, 7.1–363, 9.1–214, 9.584–827; see Table I). The final theme of this Cephalan section—the growth of hair as nemesis for a boy's erotic resistance[120]—carries over into the Meleagrian sequence without a discernible break (12.39–41). In fact, a short Meleagrian sequence (12.29–33) is included toward the end of the Cephalan section.[121] It appears, then, that Cephalas has removed 12.37–48 from its *Garland* position, just as he did 12.29–33, and that the original Meleagrian section began with 12.49.

In the second short segment of the opening sequence (5.138–41), thematized by song, an epigram describing how Athenion's song on the fiery destruction of Troy set the poet ablaze (ἐν πυρὶ ... ἐφλεγόμαν) prepares for two related epigrams by Meleager on the charm of Zenophila's sweet music (ἁδὺ μέλος, χάρις, πυρὶ φλέγομαι, 5.139; ἡδυμελεῖς, χάριτες, χάριτας, 5.140). The sweetly singing Zenophila here plays the role of inspiring Muse, as she holds the poet captive (ποῖ σε φύγω, 5.139.3), casting upon him with her beauty, song, and grace a form of desire (βάλλει πόθον, 139.5) that is both erotic passion and poetic impulse. The fourth poem, in which Meleager swears that he prefers Heliodora's whisper to the lyre of Apollo, furthers the suggestion that the theme of the beloved's song here substitutes for more traditional references to inspiratory deities. We may also note at this point Meleager's pattern of linking poems within sequences and sometimes across shorter sequences by the repetition of key words, which generally point up his theme. This pattern is most consistently discernible in the amatory section where Meleager's own variations provide a persistent cadence at the end of sequences, and we may even surmise that some of Meleager's epigrams were composed for their *Garland* position.

The third segment in the opening sequence (5.142–49) begins with paired couplets that contrast male and female beauty through a conceit that involves a garland. Dionysius is not the garland's rose, but the garland the rose of Dionysius (5.142); while Heliodora's garland fades, she herself crowns the wreath (στεφάνου στέφανος, 5.143). The στέφανος theme of this segment extends itself to include a paraclausithyron (5.145), in which wreaths are abandoned on a boy's door, and

120. On the development of this motif in epigram, see S. L. Tarán, "ΕΙΣΙ ΤΡΙΧΕΣ: An Erotic Motif in the *Greek Anthology*," *JHS* 105 (1985) 90–107.

121. It is just possible that [Asclep.] 46 G-P = *AP* 12.36 should be added to the beginning of the long Meleagrian series. It is ascribed to an otherwise unknown Asclepiades of Adramyttium, and so it is conceivably a composition by the famous Asclepiades; for discussion, see Gow-Page (1965) II 150. Against the authorship of the Samian is that fact that it differs in tone from his other pederastic poems.

eventually gives way to the balancing theme of the beloved's grace surpassing the Graces themselves (Χάριτας χάρισιν, 5.148; Χάριν ἐν χάριτι, 5.149), a theme anticipated already in 5.140 (χάριτες, χάριτας). Meleager's emphasis on χάρις, the quality of grace or charm, assumes a greater significance when we remember that his own prose works in the style of Menippus were entitled the *Charites* (Ath. 4.157b), a title with which he plays in his self-epitaphs (7.417.4, 7.418.6, 7.419.4, 7.421.13–14);[122] to say that the graceful Heliodora conquers the Graces suggests, programmatically, that Meleager's erotic epigrams, of which she is a subject, outshine his own earlier works. Central to this section are two poems in which Meleager plaits garlands for his two principal girlfriends, one for Zenophila and one for Heliodora (5.144, 147). The poems are linked by opening references to white violets (ἤδη λευκόϊον θάλλει, 144.1; πλέξω λευκόϊον, 147.1), the very flowers with which Meleager identifies his own epigrams in the proem (4.1.56). In the tradition of Nossis, Zenophila herself becomes a rose in Meleager's garland; for Heliodora he plaits a crown that will cast its blossoms down over her lovely tresses—as a work adorns its own subject. A related third poem, on a garland of Meleager's boy loves at Tyre (12.256), has been displaced by Cephalas to immediately precede the *coronis* poem as part of a concluding sequence to his own pederastic book. There is some likelihood that this epigram originally appeared in the opening sequence of Meleager's amatory book to provide homosexual contrast to the Heliodora and Zenophila poems, although its present position preserves the possibility that it functioned as a balancing garland piece in Meleager's own closing sequence. However that may be, it is easy to assume that all three epigrams on weaving garlands for or about love objects were early works that planted the seed from which grew Meleager's concept of the anthology as a garland of poetic blossoms; their creative use in the *Garland* sequence testifies to Meleager's skill at editing.

My own analysis indicates that Meleager's amatory book falls into seven distinct sections (Table III). Between the opening sequence and a long section devoted to pederastic love occurs a short transitional section consisting, in its present condition, of only two epigrams (12.52–53). The first is a propempticon for Andragathus who has sailed away from Rhodes leaving the poet to long for him, and the second carries a message to Phanion on the Coan shore that the poet returns to her, not by sea, but overland. The poems are linked as a contrasting pair by a series of oppositions: a male love object versus a female one, the South Wind that carries away Andragathus versus the North Wind that brings Phanion a message, traveling beloved versus traveling lover. This mirror-image quality is reinforced by the verbal repetition of language at the beginning of one (οὔριος ἐμπνεύσας, 52.1) and at the conclusion of the other (οὔριος ... πνεύσεται, 53.8). Since the Phanion poem was clearly composed during

---

122. On χάρις as a literary quality, see Demetrius' *On Style* 128–89.

Meleager's Coan period and its companion piece, set in Rhodes, probably stems from the same time frame, Meleager may have constructed the pair with their *Garland* position in mind. To anticipate our structural analysis, the suggestion of reciprocal affection in both homosexual and heterosexual relationships in this short transitional group correlates with a like theme in a parallel transitional group that leads to the closing sequence (5.209–10, 12.162–65). In fact, what may be the opening poem in that section (5.209) contains a clear echo of the Phanion epigram (with 12.53.3–4, ἐπ᾽ ἠϊόνων ... ἴδητε Φανίον εἰς χαροπὸν δερκομέναν πέλαγος, cf. 5.209.1–2, πάρ᾽ ἠϊόν᾽ εἶδε ... Νικοῦν ἐν χαροποῖς κύμασι νηχομένην). The verbal echo signals the correspondence between the two transitional sections.

Wifstrand identified 12.54–70 and 12.71–97 as two coherent groupings that reveal Meleager's organizational technique at its best.[123] He also posited that 12.108, which mentions a mosquito (κώνωψ), once stood in the vicinity of 5.151–52, Meleager's well-known pair on mosquitoes and Zenophila, and that 12.109 (φλόγα βάλλων; though a better choice is its companion piece, 12.110, ἤστραψε γλυκύ) is related to 5.153 (γλυκεροῦ βλέμματος ἀστεροπαί).[124] Various connections between the epigrams in *AP* 5 and those in *AP* 12 proceed apace after that. But Wifstrand failed to express the evident conclusion to be drawn from his observations, namely, that Meleager created a lengthy and carefully arranged section devoted exclusively to pederastic love (12.54–97) followed by a section that mixed love poems for women and boys (5.150–91, 12.98–160). As a result, the implications of his correlations for the overall structure of the book remain unrecognized. Most important, Wifstrand missed the section devoted exclusively to women (5.192–208, 12.161), which follows the mixed section and provides a balancing counterpart to the sequence on boys. Once this essential correspondence is noted, the structure of the book falls easily into place. The long section of mixed male-female epigrams constitutes the central core of the collection, framed by interlocking parallel sections—those on boys and women, the short transitional sections, and the opening and closing sequences. The amatory book forms, then, a classic example of ring composition, adorned within its longer sections by multiple short sequences thematically linked.

We turn now to the pederastic section, which displays a clear structural arrangement through 12.95 but has suffered some disruption at the end. In contrast to the two groupings made by Wifstrand, I divide 12.54–95 into five short sequences, each united by a single theme and often linked by verbal repetitions. At the same time, the section displays an overall movement from poems devoted to single boys to those concerned with multiple boys or with generalizing themes. It is to be borne in mind that the division into short sequences, while helpful

123. Wifstrand 15–17.

124. Wifstrand 20. The reader is cautioned that Wifstrand used Stadtmüller's numbering for *AP* 5 so that his 5.150 = 5.151 in the traditional system.

for analysis, is overly schematic, since Meleager was principally interested in linear progression from poem to poem and often connected through theme or vocabulary an epigram in one sequence to an epigram in the next. For example, the first poem, 12.54, in which Antiochus is praised as an "Eros stronger than Eros," clearly forms a pair with 12.55, in which Echedemus is named a "second Phoebus," and yet 12.55, but not 12.54, must be classified as part of the first short sequence (12.55–62), in which boys are celebrated in association with their native cities—Athens (Echedemus' city), Cos, Troezen, Tyre, and Cnidus. Within the sequence there are further connections between poems: 12.57, on a boy who is the namesake of the sculptor Praxiteles, is Meleager's self-variation on 12.56; 12.60, which does not mention a city at all, gains depth of meaning by its juxtaposition with 12.59 (Meleager sees only Theron because, like Myiscus, he outshines the stars); 12.61–62 form an anonymous pair on the fair Aribazus. 12.63 is again transitional: Heraclitus ignites the thunderbolts of Zeus, a motif that introduces the next section on the king of the gods, while Diodorus melts stone, a motif that looks back to the stone-melting boy in 12.61. All the epigrams in the second sequence, 12.63–70, concern Zeus, usually as a potential rival of the poet, who fears his boy love will become a second Ganymede. The sequence begins with a poem by Alcaeus of Messene and continues with alternating epigrams by Meleager and the anonymous poet whose book of erotic epigrams contributed so heavily to Meleager's amatory section.[125] It ends cleverly (12.70) when Zeus himself finally speaks to reassure Meleager, who nevertheless fears that a "lying Zeus" may appear in disguise and so trembles at the buzzing of every fly. The third sequence, 12.71–78, is structured, not as a unified sequence, but as sets of pairs. Callimachus' compassion for Cleonicus, who was ruined by one glimpse of Euxitheus, is matched by Meleager's concern for Damis, undone by the sight of Heraclitus (12.71–72); Meleager then varies Callimachus' motif of love like to death (Ἔρος ... Ἀΐδης, 12.73) in 12.74 (Ἔρως Ἀΐδη); in 12.75–78 Meleager twice reworks Asclepiades (or once, alternatively, Posidippus) on the theme of boys who look like Eros. The epigrams found in 12.64–78, which seem largely undisturbed by losses or disruptions in order, provide an excellent illustration of the rhythm of the amatory book, in which Meleager's variations, and to some extent those of the anonymous poet, produce a persistent commentary on the erotic epigrams of earlier composers.

The next sequence, 12.79–87, to which 9.15 is to be added on the evidence of *BKT* 5.1.75, is unified by the theme of love's flame and includes seven sequential poems by Meleager himself. The initial epigram, on Antipater's kiss, brings to an end, with 12.81, the long preceding series of poems on single boys; with its warning to the passionate (δυσέρωτες) to avoid contact with the poet's twice-kindled flame, it also sets the course for poems about love as an inescapable

---

125. For the supposition that Meleager knew an edition of pederastic epigrams by an anonymous author, see Gow (1958a) 25, Gow-Page (1965) II 560.

abstract force. The sequence is bound together by various thematic and verbal links: for instance, the pair 12.84–85 both contain the phrase ἕλκει τῇδ' ὁ βίαιος Ἔρως and concern the theme of escape from the sea only to fall into the dangers of boy love on dry land. The exclusively pederastic nature of the longer section seems broken here by 12.82–83, which are usually taken to refer to Phanion, one of Meleager's girlfriends. But φανίον means "little torch," playing on the theme of love's flame, and editors commonly choose to capitalize as a proper name only one of the three occurrences of the word in these two epigrams (12.82.6). Even there, however, Meleager may simply be addressing the "torch" that lights a fire in his heart rather than an actual girl. Through this ambiguity, Meleager is perhaps teasing the reader with the (apparent) intrusion of the heterosexual into a homosexual context, and I suspect that the last of his seven sequential epigrams comments on this possibility:

> ἁ Κύπρις θήλεια γυναικομανῆ φλόγα βάλλει,
>   ἄρσενα δ' αὐτὸς Ἔρως ἵμερον ἀνιοχεῖ.
> ποῖ ῥέψω; ποτὶ παῖδ' ἢ ματέρα; φαμὶ δὲ καὐτάν
>   Κύπριν ἐρεῖν, "νικᾷ τὸ θρασὺ παιδάριον".

> (Mel. 18 G-P = *AP* 12.86)

The Cyprian, being female, throws flames of woman madness.
    Eros is the charioteer of desire for males.
On which side should I come down? The son or the mother? I think
    even the Cyprian will say, "The bold brat wins."

Homosexual poems then proceed. The increasing length of the epigrams in 12.79–85, as well as the intensity of feeling evoked by Meleager's persistent, sequential attempts to escape the reoccurrence of love's flame produce a crescendo effect that carries over into the next sequence. 12.88–95, which likely included 9.16,[126] build their momentum on the theme of multiple loves. The anonymous 12.87, linked by theme to Meleager's 12.86, is transitional, rejecting the love of women because boys are forever catching the poet's roving eye in their nets. The speakers in 12.88 and 12.91 have two loves, those of 12.89–90 and 9.16 have three. In 12.92 Meleager declares his own eyes to be "boy-hunting hounds," while in 12.93 boys become an inescapable labyrinth. 12.93–95 take the multiplicity of love objects to a peak of intensity by naming three, then six, and then eight boys, each with different attributes or charms. At the end of the last poem (12.95), where Meleager predicts various explicitly sexual favors for Philocles if he is loved by the "flower-gathering Graces" (ἀνθολόγοι Χάριτες), the poet grants the lover a veritable "Roman platter" of boys (Ῥωμαϊκὴν λοπάδα, translating

---

126. The position of 9.16 in the *AP*, directly after 9.15, which does not share the same subject, suggests that this epigram stood not far from, though not right beside, 9.15 in Meleager's arrangement.

lanx satura). With this extravagance of phrase (and of love objects), the reader naturally feels that a turning point, if not a conclusion, has been reached.

But 12.95 does not mark the end of the pederastic section, since 12.96–97 concern boys with physical deformities and correlations with *AP* 5 do not begin until 12.108. Wifstrand despaired of finding the same kind of coherent structures in the remainder of the Meleagrian sequence in *AP* 12 and suggested that Meleager was not able to sustain his associative method of arrangement. But I believe that the end of the pederastic section and the beginning of the mixed male-female group has been disrupted by the removal of a block of epigrams to conclude the section of poems by various authors (some Meleagrian and Philippan and some unknown) that immediately precedes the sequence from Meleager's *Garland*. The two poems on physical deformities (12.96-97), the second of which involves sexual double entendres,[127] fit well with 12.29–33 and 12.37–40, epigrams by Meleagrian authors primarily concerning the charm of boys' buttocks and the ruin produced by the growth of pubic hair. The sexually explicit couplet at 12.95.5–6, surprising in the context, prepares for this shift in tone. The last poem in the sequence on buttocks, in which Meleager rejects both Theron and Apollodorus as too old to be attractive, looks to the approaching conclusion of the pederastic section:

στέργω θῆλυν ἔρωτα· δασυτρώγλων δὲ πίεσμα
    λασταύρων μελέτω ποιμέσιν αἰγοβάταις.

(94.3–4 G-P = AP 12.41.3–4)

I adore female love. Let goat-mounting herdsmen
    enjoy squeezing hairy-assed fags.

The promised turn to love of women is delayed by three more pederastic epigrams—now on greedy and promiscuous boys (12.42–44). Dioscorides' poem on the "boy vulture" Hermogenes, who lacks either shame or pity, and Callimachus' well-known epigram analogizing the cyclic poem, the common road, and the public fountain to the promiscuous Lysanias precede the concluding poem of the section, by Glaucus:

ἦν ὅτε παῖδας ἔπειθε πάλαι ποτὲ δῶρα φιλεῦντας
    ὄρτυξ καὶ ῥαπτὴ σφαῖρα καὶ ἀστράγαλοι,
νῦν δὲ λοπὰς καὶ κέρμα, τὰ παίγνια δ᾽ οὐδὲν ἐκεῖνα
    ἰσχύει. ζητεῖτ᾽ ἄλλο τι, παιδοφίλαι.

(1 G-P = AP 12.44)

There was a time when boys who like gifts were persuaded
    by a quail, a stitched ball, and dice.

127. See P. G. Maxwell-Stuart, "Antipater's Eupalamus: A Comment on *Anth. Graec.* 12.97," *AJP* 96 (1975) 13–15; E. Livrea, "Il piede di Eupalamo (Antip. *A.P.* XII 97)," *GIF* 31 (1979) 325–29.

But now it takes pricey dinners and cash, not toys.
Time to change your habits, boy lovers.

The claim that times have changed, that boys care only for good meals (λοπάς) and money, evoking and undermining the "Roman platter" (λοπάδα) of 12.95, leads to Glaucus' finalizing call for the rejection of boy love. In the Meleagrian context the addressed παιδοφίλαι, "boy lovers," meld effortlessly with the implied readers of the collection, who are thus invited to turn their attention from exclusively pederastic epigrams to epigrams that concern female love objects as well.

The advantages of my suggestion that 12.29–33 and 37–44 originally concluded the pederastic section are evident: it not only explains the break in sequencing after 12.95 but also provides a strikingly coherent structure for the section on boys. The effect of epigrams celebrating individual boys building to a crescendo of poems on multiple boys—touching, kissing, enticing, arousing as in 12.95—is undercut and finally negated by a series that begins with physical deformities and proceeds to moral depravity. In Meleager's pederastic cycle, desire is first ignited and then defused. To lend support to this analysis, we will find that the parallel section on women displays the same rhythmic structure, proceeding from epigrams on individual women as love objects through poems on multiple women as love objects to a section on undesirables. Meleager's complicated patterns of arrangement indicate not only that he had a considerable range of epigrams from which to select but also that his aesthetic interest in the *Garland* extended to the process of editing in its own right.

The next section, a mixture of homosexual and heterosexual epigrams, is harder to analyze. This is largely because almost every short sequence has been divided between *AP* 5 and 12, so that the precise arrangement within each sequence has been lost. But I do not believe that Meleager here abandoned the careful interweaving of blossom with blossom so evident in the pederastic cycle. This long mixed section constituted the center of Meleager's amatory book, forming the linchpin in his pattern of interlocking segments. Meleager could here most effectively show how the bittersweet experience of love transcends the boundary of gender attraction and permeates all the diverse possibilities for the lover.

The beginning of the heterogeneous section has been rendered uncertain by Cephalas' transposition. It appears, however, that 12.98–101 with 12.45–48 formed an introductory sequence which included poems on love's power by Posidippus, Asclepiades, and the anonymous epigrammatist, as well as the usual imitative contributions by Meleager himself (with the anonymous 12.99, ἠγρεύθην ὑπ' Ἔρωτος, cf. the displaced Meleager 12.23, ἠγρεύθην . . . Μυΐσκε). But the respective order of the two groups of poems, 12.45–48 and 12.98–101, is unclear. References to dice in 12.46–47 suggest 12.45–48 followed, as now, directly on 12.44 where dice are also mentioned; this would mean that Posidippus' defiant challenge to the Erotes to use him as target practice

(12.45) opened the heterogeneous section. But a number of intervening poems sometimes separate Meleager's verbal repetitions, and it would be equally effective, in my opinion, to open the section with 12.98, where Posidippus declares his ability as a scholar, or the Muse's cicada, to resist the debilitating effects of desire. In either case, a short group of poems about poets and Eros appeared as the opening sequence of Meleager's long middle section, and Posidippus was given pride of place as epigrammatic progenitor. The poet's desire to escape through his studies and the inevitability of his capture by Eros offer an effective introduction to a section that is necessarily various in its topics.

The section 12.102–120 can be fitted closely together with 5.150–168 as a series of short sequences flowing easily one from the other. Callimachus' poem comparing the lover to a hunter who pursues fleeing game but passes by what lies at hand (12.102, with the first word ὡγρευτής cf. the opening of 12.99, ἠγρεύθην— prey now becomes predator) heads up a series of poems (12.103–6) that counter this view with a preference for fidelity (e.g., μισῶ κοινὸν ἔρωτα, 12.104). The theme of longing for exclusivity and of betrayal by a beloved dominates the various short sequences in this section. Since 12.107–8 form a pair and 12.108 seems related to 5.151–52, this leaves 5.150, Asclepiades' Nico poem, isolated within the Meleagrian series. But the references to Nico's false oath (ὡμολόγησ', ὤμοσε) and the poet's call to extinguish the lamp (λύχνον) are strong indications that the poem once belonged to the short sequence on lover's oaths now found at 5.6–8 (ὤμοσε, ὤμοσεν; λύχνε, ὤμοσεν, λύχνε; λύχνε, ὠμόσαμεν). These three epigrams by Callimachus, Asclepiades, and Meleager have been removed from their Meleagrian context and yet retain their Meleagrian arrangement.[128] While Cephalas apparently constructed the first portion of his book of erotic epigrams from an anthology dominated by the poems of Rufinus (5.2–103), it remains unclear whether 5.6–8 were Cephalas' addition to this so-called *sylloge Rufiniana* or whether an ancient editor was responsible for the selection.[129] I have generally resisted the temptation to reintegrate into the longer Meleagrian

128. See the lengthy analysis by Scevola Mariotti, *Il V libro dell'Antologia Palatina* (Rome, 1965) 84–113.

129. The Rufinian material ends with a poem by Rufinus (5.103), but, though 5.1 is clearly Cephalas' own heading, the beginning point of the earlier sylloge is less certain. M. Boas, "Die Sylloge Rufiniana," *Philologus* 73 (1914) 6–7 points out a verbal link between 5.2 (γουνάσομαι, κλαύσομαι), an anonymous poem that he attributed to Rufinus on stylistic grounds, and 5.103 (παρακλαύσομαι, γουνάσομαι). But Cameron (1993) 79 has recently noted that 5.9 is a *sphragis* poem beginning with Rufinus name and suggests that 5.9 "was meant (though not necessarily by Rufinus himself) to mark the beginning of the Rufinian series." As a further indication that 5.2–8 may be Cephalas' own arrangement, Page (1978) 11 points out that apart from 5.3–8 "there are very few places [in this Sylloge Rufiniana] where more than two epigrams similar in theme are juxtaposed." Rufinus' date is disputed: Page (1978) 49 prefers the fourth century, but Cameron (1982) and (1993) 80 argues that he belongs to the first century. Both agree that the Rufinian sylloge is no earlier than the fourth, but Cameron (1993)

sequences short groups of epigrams removed by Cephalas to segments of his own organization, in order to avoid as much as possible more subjective forms of conjecture in reconstructing Meleager's poetry books. Since Meleager's method of associative linking was aesthetically oriented rather than pedantically geared toward categorization, a poem with a given theme might find any number of homes in his *Garland*. Conjecture beyond the guidelines provided by the ordering within the long sequences is therefore particularly dangerous. But in the case of the false-swearing epigrams, the verbal links at the beginning of the poems are so compelling and the lacuna in the long sequence so blatantly obvious that I present my conjecture with some degree of confidence. The series of four poems that results offers an excellent illustration of how Meleager's organizational technique produces a multifaceted look at a recurring erotic experience. Callimachus' distanced report of Callignotus' false oath to his girlfriend Ionis is supplemented by two epigrams in which Asclepiades makes a personal complaint that a girlfriend has failed to keep a promised tryst. There follows Meleager's epigram in which an abandoned woman laments her lover's deceitful oath; varying both his predecessors, Meleager combines the erotic situation of Callimachus' epigram with the personal perspective of Asclepiades' to produce the novelty of the woman's voice.

The sequence of oaths was apparently followed (allowing, as always, for the possibility of lost or displaced epigrams) by 12.107–8, companion pieces linked structurally and verbally (εἰ δ' ἕτερον στέρξειε; στέρξεις, εἰ δ' ἕτερον); in both a lover threatens to punish a boy's infidelity in metaphorical language taken from the world of nature. The reference at the end of 12.108 to a mosquito attack suggests that this epigram was followed by 5.151–52. In the first of these— both examples of Meleager's talent for conveying deeply felt passion through humorous motifs—the poet begs the mosquitoes buzzing around his bed to attack him rather than the sleeping Zenophila (a reversal of the sentiment in 12.108), while in the second he sends a mosquito to summon Zenophila from a rival's bed. The next sequence consists of three poems concerned with lightning flashing from the eyes of a beloved (5.153, 12.109–10). Again, variety is achieved by a change in the gender of the lover and beloved and in the speaker's perspective. Nicarete is withered by Cleophon's lightning glance and Diodorus by Timarion's fiery eyes, while Meleager himself suffers the effect of lightning from Myiscus' eyes. Meleager next grouped a series of eight couplets on individual love objects, six female and two male (5.154–57, 12.111–14; note the typical Cephalan mistake in distribution). This set of couplets, six by Meleager himself, presents a rather positive view of love, to be offset by the following sequence (5.158–63), on the pain caused by loving a hetaira. Variety is here created by interspacing poems on single hetairas with meaner-spirited epigrams on groups of two or three hetairas

89–90 assumes that the fourth-century redactor knew Rufinus only through the intermediate *Anthologion* by Diogenian of Heraclea.

(5.159 and its imitation 5.161). The final poem, on a bee that signifies Heliodora's sting (5.163), forms a pair with 5.162, in which Asclepiades compares Philaenion to a viper.

The next short sequence consists of eleven epigrams on *komoi* (5.164–68, 12.115–20), in which verbal linkage was easy to sustain (e.g., addresses to Night in 5.164–67, κωμάσομαι in 12.115–17). The concluding poem was more likely 12.120 (Posidippus) than 5.168 (anonymous), and there is significance in ending with a major poet rather than, as usual, with Meleager himself. Posidippus' vow to battle Eros with the force of reason (λογισμός), provided only that he can remain sober, looks back to 12.98, the Posidippan poem about the scholar's resistance to love, which may have begun the long heterogeneous section; its. drinking theme also echoes the Posidippan opening of the amatory book and anticipates, as I will argue below, another Posidippan poem on love and wine that likely closed this book of Meleager's anthology (12.168). It becomes clear, then, that Posidippan epigrams were placed at key junctions in the amatory book, and 12.120 must have stood at or near its center, just before a major break in the long heterogeneous section.

The blocks of poems that follow in both *AP* 5 (169–87) and *AP* 12 (121–54) do not fit together quite so well to form the sorts of tightly knit sequences we observed in 5.150–68 and 12.102–20, perhaps because of the loss of certain transitional epigrams. For instance, it is difficult to say just how 5.169–71 relates to 12.121–35. 5.169–71 form a coherent and structurally important trio consisting of Asclepiades' introductory priamel (ἡδὺ θέρους διψῶντι χιὼν ποτόν), Nossis' introductory imitation (ἅδιον οὐδὲν ἔρωτος, ἃ δ' ὄλβια), and a further variant by Meleager (ἡδύ, ὄλβιον) that reduces the generalized sweetness praised by his predecessors to a wine cup's pleasure in Zenophila's kiss. In all likelihood, these three epigrams, following directly on 12.120, introduced the "second half" of Meleager's amatory book. Since the next correspondence across Cephalan books is between 5.172 and 12.136, my belief that 5.169–71 form a close sequence indicates that 12.121–35 then followed, perhaps originally supplemented with now lost poems, but not with the intrusion of any of the epigrams now in *AP* 5. The pair 12.121–22, on boys embraced by the Graces, lacks a verbal link with 5.169–71 but fits with the general mood, a celebration of love's sweetness. Although Wifstrand associated 5.169 (ἡδύ, χλαῖνα) with 12.125 (ἡδύ, χλαῖναν) and 5.171 (ψυχὰν τὰν ἐν ἐμοὶ προπίοι) with 12.133 (ψυχῆς ἡδὺ πέπωκα μέλι), it is difficult, despite the verbal linkage, to work out sequences in which these poems would have stood side by side. It appears that Meleager changed somewhat his associative method in this section to disperse thematic echoes over a longer series of epigrams. So Asclepiades' idealized picture of two lovers covered by one blanket in 5.169 is converted in 12.125 into a sweet dream of an eighteen-year-old boy brought by Eros under Meleager's blanket. The meeting between the Graces and Cleonicus in 12.121 is echoed in Meleager's chance meeting of Alexis in 12.127. There are also verbal resonances from the introductory priamels. For instance, the thirst mentioned by Asclepiades in 5.169 reappears toward the end of the series (διψῶσῃ, 12.132a.6; διψῶν, 12.133.1) and Nossis' honey from 5.170 repeats as well (μελιχρότερον, 12.123.4; μέλιτι, 12.132b.8; μέλι, 12.133.6).

5.172–75 fit with 12.136–38 more neatly. Meleager's contrasting pair addressed to the Morning Star (ὄρθρε, ταχὺς ἐπέστης, 5.172; ὄρθρε, ὠκὺς ἐπέστης, 5.173), in which the star comes quickly when he sleeps with Demo and slowly when another holds her, must have stood beside two poems addressed to birds that awake the lover at dawn (12.136; ὀρθροβόας, 12.137). It is natural, then, to link 5.174, in which Meleager envies Sleep his visit to Zenophila, and 12.138 about the sleep of Antileon under a vine. Meleager's 5.175, in which a girl's infidelity is betrayed by her lack of sleep, completes the set of three. We may suppose, without great confidence, that 12.139–54 continued unbroken by any poems now in *AP* 5; the group is nevertheless "mixed," as is evident from the heterosexual topics in 12.147 and 12.153. 125.139–44, which begin with Callimachus' epigram about fire under the ash, concern the awakening of desire for a specific boy; Meleager's 12.141 is a close imitation of 12.140 and 12.143–44 concern gods, Hermes and Eros, themselves caught by love for a boy. While 12.145 is isolated in its present context, 12.146–47 are a clever pairing on the theme of having one's love—first male, then female—snatched away (ἀγρεύσας, 146.1; ἄρπασται, 147.1). A group of three poems by Callimachus (12.148–50) is loosely tied to the preceding poems by the reintroduction of the "catching" motif (ληφθήσει, 149.1). A reference to a stone (λίθος; πέτρῳ) joins 12.151 to 12.152, while Asclepiades' impersonation of a woman in love in 12.153 is matched through contrast by Meleager's meditation on his love for Myiscus in 12.154. These last two appropriately close the sequence by returning us to the motifs of sweetness and honey (μελιχρός, ἥδιον; ἡδὺς ὁ παῖς, μέλιτι). Although the loss of certain epigrams has perhaps obscured the broader structure of this section, Meleager may also have allowed himself, toward the middle of his large amatory book, the freedom to group poems two at a time without constructing the more complicated sequences that we have found in the earlier portions of the book.

Wifstrand classed 5.175–87 with 12.155 as a unit dominated by poems with a mimelike character. But I prefer to associate 5.175 with the preceding poems on sleep and to treat as another group the next five (5.176–80), all epigrams by Meleager on the personified Eros, only two of which (5.177–78) are at all mimelike. The opening of the first (δεινὸς Ἔρως, δεινός, 5.176) contrasts with the ἡδύ theme of the previous group and prepares the reader for Meleager's vivid descriptions of Eros as runaway child, auctioned slave, or haughty archer. The set becomes a kind of virtuoso demonstration of Meleager's ability to produce a powerful and consistent portrait of love's effect through clever manipulation of mythology's metaphors. The mime sequence (5.181–87, 12.155) continues the now familiar pattern of epigrams by Asclepiades and Posidippus interspersed with variants by the anonymous poet and Meleager. The poems predominantly concern relationships between young men and hetairas—their parties, trysts, and accusations of betrayal—perhaps reflecting an origin in comedy. But one rather obscure epigram, in which a slave summons a boy to meet with his master (12.155), preserves the mixed heterosexual-homosexual nature of the sequence.

We come at last to the concluding epigrams (5.188–91, 12.156–60) in Meleager's long heterogeneous section. P.Oxy. 3324 provides external evidence that 5.190 was here followed (though perhaps not directly) by 12.157.[130] It appears, then, that the storm tormenting the lover in Asclepiades' paraclausithyron (χεῖμα, 5.189) was converted into a stormy sea of love in Meleager's 5.190 (κώμων χειμέριον πέλαγος), a theme that continues in 12.156 (χειμῶνι, νηχόμεθα), 12.157 (χειμαίνει, νήχομαι), and 12.159 (πρυμνήσι’, χεῖμα).[131] The other poems in the group are more loosely connected. The theme of vengeance for the wounds of love links 5.188 (τίσομαι) at the beginning of the group with 12.160 (τῖσαι) toward the end. My own preference for the final epigram in Meleager's long mixed section of his amatory book is 5.191, a *komos* poem in which Meleager threatens to leave tear-soaked "suppliant garlands" (τοὺς ἱκέτας στεφάνους) on his girlfriend's doorstep; they are to be inscribed with the following epigram (ἓν τόδ’ ἐπιγράψας):

> "Κύπρι, σοὶ Μελέαγρος, ὁ μύστης
> σῶν κώμων στοργᾶς σκῦλα τάδ’ ἐκρέμασεν".
>
> (73.7–8 G-P = *AP* 5.191.7–8)
>
> "For you, Cyprian, Meleager, the initiate
> of your revels, has suspended these spoils of love."

This epigram within an epigram finds an unmistakable parallel in another Meleagrian poem no longer in its *Garland* sequence:

> ἠγρεύθην ὁ πρόσθεν ἐγώ ποτε τοῖς δυσέρωσι
>   κώμοις ἠϊθέων πολλάκις ἐγγελάσας·
> καί μ’ ἐπὶ σοῖς ὁ πτανὸς Ἔρως προθύροισι, Μυΐσκε,
>   στῆσεν ἐπιγράψας, "σκῦλ’ ἀπὸ Σωφροσύνης."
>
> (99 G-P = *AP* 12.23)
>
> I have been caught, I who once laughed often
>   at the passionate revels of young men.
> But winged Eros stood me on your doorstep, Myiscus,
>   inscribed with the words, "Spoils from Restraint."

I have already hinted that this poem may have stood close to 12.99, which also begins ἠγρεύθην, and so near the opening of the mixed section. Its reference to

---

130. Wifstrand 21 noted a thematic correspondence between the two poems before the discovery of the papyrus.

131. For the development of this theme in Greek poetry, including epigram, see Gutzwiller (1992) 199–202 and P. Murgatroyd, "The Sea of Love," *CQ* 45 (1995) 9–25.

love's beginning suits this context.[132] If my conjecture is correct, the opening and closing of the mixed section was, then, tied together by these matching epigrams, in each of which an inscription referring to the spoils of love is left on the doorstep of the poet's beloved.[133] But even leaving aside speculation about the position of 12.23, it is evident that 5.191, a poem "sealed" with Meleager's name, functions metaphorically to dedicate a major section of the erotic collection to the Cyprian goddess.

The following section on women as love objects (5.192–208, 12.161), a counterpart to the section on boys, is again tightly structured in short sequences. Meleager opens the section with a series of epigrams on individual women (12.192–96). The one poem displaced to *AP* 12, Asclepiades' epigram on the cross-dressing Dorcion (12.161), must belong to this sequence, which is brought to a typical close by Meleager's two epigrams on Zenophila (5.195–96). There follow a pair of epigrams (5.197–98), in which Meleager swears to Eros in the name of a series of girlfriends, three in the first poem and five in the second. The remainder of the heterosexual section is dominated by dedications made by women, first after love making (5.199–201) and then by prostitutes compared to horse riders (5.202–3). These last two poems, satirical in tone, are capped by Meleager's distasteful comparison of an old prostitute to a ship (5.204). Likewise, the next two dedications, of a love charm offered by a witch and of musical instruments presented by retiring flute girls, are capped by Asclepiades' condemnation of two Samians who practice lesbian love (5.205–7). This rejection of love between women forms a pair, then, with Meleager's own statement of his preference for heterosexual activity, which concludes, programmatically, the female section:

οὔ μοι παιδομανὴς κραδία· τί δὲ τερπνόν, Ἔρωτες,
    ἀνδροβατεῖν εἰ μὴ δούς τι λαβεῖν ἐθέλοι;
ἁ χεὶρ γὰρ τὰν χεῖρα. καλά με μένει παράκοιτις·
    ἔρροι πᾶς ἄρσην ἀρσενικαῖς λαβίσιν.[134]

(9 G-P = AP 5.208)

My heart is not boy-mad. What pleasure, Erotes, in mounting a male,
    if the giver doesn't want to receive?
One hand should wash the other. A lovely woman awaits me in bed.
    To hell with male lovers and male embraces.

---

132. Gow-Page (1965) II 660, apparently without thinking of the epigram's original *Garland* position, comment that its "motif, 'First Love,' recalls anon. V and IX, Meleager CIII," which appear in the *AP* as 12.99–101.

133. As parallels to the dedication of the spoils of love, cf. Hor. *Carm.* 1.5.13–16, 3.26, Prop. 2.14.27–28.

134. The text of the second couplet is uncertain, and Gow-Page despair. But με μένει could reasonably have been corrupted into μεν ειν, though ἔρροι is pure rewriting. The general sense is in any case not in doubt.

Although considerably shorter, the section on women is structured to form a parallel with the section on boys. In both, epigrams naming individual love objects precede epigrams listing multiple loves; in both, satirical or critical poems occur near the end; and, if my reconstruction of the homosexual sequence is correct, both reserve poems comparing male and female love for the conclusion (12.41, 12.44, 5.208). In addition, the same cyclical pattern of desire mounting and desire diffused appears in both. The internal correspondences between these two sections are particularly strong evidence that Meleager intended to structure his amatory book in a symmetrical pattern of arrangement.

Corresponding to the short transitional section (12.52–53) between the opening sequence and the section on boys is another short transitional section (5.209–210, 12.162–65) between the section on girls and the concluding sequence. The verbal echo linking these two transitional sections (in 12.53 and 5.209) has already been noted. The dominating theme of the second transitional section is mutual love. The heterosexual love of Clearchus and Nico (ἴσος ἀμφοτέροις φιλίης πόθος, 5.209.7) finds its homosexual counterpart in the matched beauty of Cleandrus and Eubiotus (12.163) and the sweet reciprocal affection of Cleobulus and Alexis (ἡδὺ δὲ παιδοφιλεῖν καὐτὸν ἐόντα καλόν, 12.164.2). The blackness of lovely Didyme in 5.210 links that poem to 12.165, where the "white-flowered" Cleobulus (λευκανθής) and the "honey-tinted" Sopolis (μελίχρους)—both "flower-bearers" (ἀνθοφόροι) of Aphrodite—equally attract Meleager, who puns on his own name (μέλας = "black," ἄργος = "white") to present himself as the weaver of a erotic garland made of black and white (῎Ερωτες πλέξειν ἐκ λευκοῦ φασί με καὶ μέλανος, "the Erotes say that I will weave from black and white"). Meleager has again placed a *sphragis* poem, again linked to the garland theme (cf. 5.191), to signal that a major segment of his amatory book concludes.

While Meleager frames his three longer sections with these brief transitional segments depicting idealized mutual love, he returns in his closing sequence to the experience more commonly addressed by the erotic epigrammatist—the pain caused by a ceaseless cycle of desire and loss. 5.211, 12.166, and 5.212 form a short sequence on this very topic by the three major epigrammatists of the amatory book. Posidippus asserts that tears and reveling compel him to rush from one love to another, Asclepiades expects peace only when the Erotes have utterly destroyed him, and Meleager asks the same mischievous deities why, when they ever fly to him, they have no strength to fly away. 5.211 and 12.166 are also linked by the motif of coals (ἀνθρακιήν, ἀνθρακιήν), which has carried over to provide verbal linkage from the transitional section (ἄνθρακας, 5.209.3; ἄνθρακες, 5.210.3). There follows another sequence of three poems, in each of which a poet asks a specific beloved for fulfillment of his desire (εἰσκαλέσαι, 5.213.2; μ' ἐς ὅρμον δέξαι, 12.167.3–4; δέξαι Πόθον, 5.214.3)—final specific examples of the lover's pain sketched in the preceding short sequence. 5.214, a charming poem in which Meleager asks Heliodora to play with the ball Eros tosses her—Meleager's own heart—and warns her against "unsportsmanlike hubris,"[135] sets up the final epigram in the long Meleagrian sequence from *AP* 5:

λίσσομ', Ἔρως, τὸν ἄγρυπνον ἐμοὶ πόθον Ἡλιοδώρας
    κοίμισον αἰδεσθεὶς μοῦσαν ἐμὰν ἱκέτιν.
ναὶ γὰρ δὴ τὰ σὰ τόξα, τὰ μὴ δεδιδαγμένα βάλλειν
    ἄλλον, ἀεὶ δ' ἐπ' ἐμοὶ πτανὰ χέοντα βέλη,
εἰ καί με κτείναις, λείψω φωνὴν προΐεντα
    γράμματ', "Ἔρωτος ὅρα, ξεῖνε, μιαιφονίαν."[136]

(54 G-P = *AP* 5.215)

I beg you, Eros, put to sleep my sleepless passion for Heliodora,
    out of respect for my suppliant Muse.
Or else, by your bow that has learned to strike no other,
    that always casts its winged missiles against me,
Even if you kill me, I'll leave behind writings that project
    my voice: "Observe, stranger, the murderous act of Eros."

To my knowledge, scholars have, amazingly, not recognized the conclusory nature of this poem. Here Meleager prays to Eros for release from his passion for Heliodora in exchange for "my suppliant Muse," that is, the gift of the epigram book that now ends. To add a note of finality, he concludes, in the tradition of earlier epigram books, with a self-epitaph, but one suitable to close a collection of erotic verse—for in it he names Eros his murderer.[137]

I have already speculated that 12.256, on a garland of boy loves plaited by Eros for Aphrodite, formed part of Meleager's opening or closing sequence. In either position it would not only loop back to the proem (πάγκαρπον,

---

135. For Meleager's use of an Anacreontic motif in this epigram (358 *PMG*), see R. Pretagostini, "Le metafore di Eros che gioca," *AION(filol)* 12 (1990) 225–38. I hazard to speculate that 11 G-P = *AP* 6.162, now displaced to a Cephalan sequence in the dedicatory book, may have originally been part of the final sequence in Meleager's amatory section. In this poem Meleager dedicates to Aphrodite a lamp, his previous "playmate" (συμπαίστορα) and "an initiate of [the goddess's] all-night revels" (μύστην σῶν ... παννυχίδων; cf. 5.191.7–8). Not only does the word συμπαίστορα echo the image of Desire as a "playmate" (συμπαίκταν) in 5.214.3, but the theme of dedication of "professional" equipment suits well the closing sequence of an erotic book. As Meleager requests in 5.215 that Eros "put to sleep" (κοίμισον) his "wakeful passion" (ἄγρυπνον ... πόθον), so in this dedication he renders to the goddess his lamp, elsewhere called "fond of wakefulness" (φιλάγρυπνον, 5.197.3).

136. This epigram appeared a second time in the *AP*, after 12.19, with a different reading in the fifth line, φωνεῦντ' ἐπὶ τύμβῳ, preferred by Gow-Page. The text printed here is found both at 5.215 in the hand of the Corrector and in Planudes. It seems to me that ἐπὶ τύμβῳ is just the sort of gloss a scribe would add to elucidate the obvious but implicit fact that Meleager intends the final phrase to be his epitaph.

137. Meleager was likely the model for the epitaph in Prop. 2.1.78: "huic misero fatum dura puella fuit." For other such inscriptions worked into Propertian elegy, see 1.7.24, 2.11.6, 2.13.35–36, 4.7.85–86.

4.1.1; πάγκαρπον, 12.256.1) but would also reinforce the garland poems in the opening sequence (5.144, 5.147), as well as the garland references at the end of the mixed male-female section (5.191) and the second transitional section (12.165). The explanation Meleager gives in 12.165 for his pederastic passions, that as one named "Meleager" he plaits from black and white and so longs for both light and dark "flower bearers of Cypris," neatly echoes this garland of boys woven by Eros from "Cypris' flower-bearing grove" at Tyre. But either the last or next to last poem in the amatory book was, in all likelihood, *AP* 12.168, the epigram in which Posidippus describes his poetry as a heady cup of wine combining inspiration from Mimnermus, Antimachus, Hesiod, and Homer.[138]   Scholars have previously believed that the Meleagrian sequence continued on to 12.171, 172, or even 174. But Evenus (12.172) and Philodemus (12.173) are Philippan authors and Fronto (12.174) is later still.[139]   That leaves 12.169–71, all by Dioscorides, a Meleagrian author. But nowhere else in the long sequences from his amatory book does Meleager place together even two poems by Dioscorides, and this particular set of three shows no sign of thematic linkage. Given the programmatic nature of 12.168, it is logical to assume that 12.169–71 were added to the end of the Meleagrian selection by Cephalas or by an ancient supplementer of the *Garland*, and so do not reflect Meleager's arrangement at all. As the poem placed first in Meleager's amatory collection (5.134) may have headed an erotic collection by Posidippus, so too it is likely that his concluding poem was lifted from the end of that same collection. But, leaving aside speculation about the exact nature of Meleager's source, it is clear that he signaled the importance of Posidippus for the development of erotic epigram by recycling these programmatic poems at the beginning and end of his amatory book. In doing so, he expropriated for his own use Posidippus' list of literary progenitors, as well as the metaphor of the collection as a symposium.

Meleager's amatory book was a complex literary work with claims to poetic originality, both from the addition of his own compositions and from the meaningful arrangement he gave to his selection of epigrams. By constructing short sequences on a single theme, often beginning with an epigram by Posidippus, Asclepiades, or the anonymous poet of pederastic verse and commonly ending with one or more of his own poems, Meleager created a rhythmic cadence that

138. The recognition that 5.215 and 12.168 stood together in the original *Garland* sequence may explain a puzzling textual variant. 5.215 also appears in P after 12.19 where Ἡλιοδώρου takes the place of the feminine form of the name. If 5.215 stood with 12.168 before Cephalas transferred it to the pederastic section, the masculine could be a variant that developed because some scribe assumed Posidippus' addressee in 12.168, Heliodorus, was referred to in the other poem as well. This mistake may be connected to an alternate ascription (in Planudes) of 5.215 to Posidippus.

139. On possible identifications of Fronto, to whom is ascribed also 12.233, see Page (1981) 115, Aubreton *et al.* (1994) 127, n. 5. He may be either M. Cornelius Fronto, the tutor of Marcus Aurelius, or the uncle of Longinus from Phoenician Emisa, mentioned by the *Suda*.

suggests the exchange of song or speech among symposiasts. The anthologist thus enters into direct dialogue with his own models—weaving the intertextuality of epigram variation into the fabric of a single context. The effect of this polyphony of voices was to present a variety of points of view, which yet together suggest the uniformity or universality of erotic experience. The longer sequences of the book give the impression of movement, not the chronological movement of narrative as much as the emotional movement of longer lyric, not the history of a single romantic relationship but the course of multiple relationships each moving toward a similar denouement. The pervasive presence of Meleager's poetry, combining and modifying his predecessors, encourages the reader to view the book as a product of the editor's own erotic sensibilities. But the other three books as well, where the epigrams composed by Meleager are considerably fewer, acquire meaning beyond that conveyed in individual poems through the organizing hand of the anthologist.

Among the dedicatory epigrams in *AP* 6 are found two longer sequences of Meleagrian authors (6.110–32 and 6.262–313) and one minor series (6.351–58). The sepulchral book, *AP* 7, also contains two longer Meleagrian sequences, both following, as in *AP* 6, alphabetically arranged sequences from Philip's *Garland*. It is clear that Cephalas employed the same method of constructing his anthology in both books and that he made two major selections from the *Garlands* of Philip and Meleager in each case (see Table I). Lenzinger and Cameron have included 6.133–57 in the first Meleagrian sequence, but this is certainly erroneous. As explained in Chapter 2, this section—consisting of an alphabetical grouping from Archilochus and Anacreon, a group by Callimachus, and then a miscellaneous group of Hellenistic poets—corresponds to 7.507b–29—consisting of an alphabetical grouping by Simonides, a group by Callimachus, and then a miscellaneous group of Hellenistic poets; in addition, 7.507b–29, like 6.133–57, appears directly after the first Meleagrian sequence within the Cephalan book. Whatever Cephalas' source for 6.133–57 and 7.507b–29, whether a separate collection or an appendage to Meleager's anthology, it is clear that these two series of dedications and epitaphs did not originally form part of the *Garland*. The grouping by author rather than theme and the partial use of alphabetization are contrary to Meleager's methods of organization. In addition, we may note the repetition in the Palatine Codex of Callimachus' 6.146 after 6.274 where it is thematically suited.[140] The epigram's position in a series of other Callimachean poems in 6.146–50 must stem from a non-Meleagrian source, since we have

---

140. For the duplication of epigrams in P, some of which result from Cephalas forgetting that he had already removed an epigram to his own thematic arrangement and some of which were the Corrector's attempt to group poems on a given theme, see Wifstrand 26–27, Gow (1958a) 59–62. It is only the first group, those resulting from Cephalas' carelessness, that are significant for reconstructing the *Garland*.

within the second long Meleagrian sequence in *AP* 6 the position Meleager gave it, grouped thematically with other poems on childbirth. Cephalas, in his careless manner, failed to notice that he had twice copied out the poem, each time from a different source.

Wifstrand found it difficult to follow Meleager's organizational technique in *AP* 6.[141] It is true that verbal linkage within and across sequences is much reduced and that a rhythmic alternation of authors is less discernible because no poets serve as truly dominating models for the dedications and no poet is as persistently imitative as Meleager was in the erotic field. But other principles of arrangement are clearly in evidence. The dedicatory epigrams are often paired by model and imitation, and short sequences grouped by type of dedication are organized into longer segments based on the gender, age, or social status of the dedicators. Nor, despite some removals, has *AP* 6 been as seriously disrupted as Wifstrand claims by Cephalan transferences to the epideictic section, *AP* 9. All the examples cited by Wifstrand are in fact instances in which Cephalas removed epigrams from Meleager's epideictic book to his own thematically organized section in *AP* 6.[142]

Of the longer sequences, 6.110–32 preceded 6.262–313 with only 6.262–64 providing the overlap (see Table IV). The shorter sequence, 6.351–58, which apparently also retains its Meleagrian order, overlapped both longer sequences, 6.351 finding its counterparts in the first sequence and 6.352–58 fitting better with the themes of the second. In terms of overall design, the dedicatory book falls into three segments differentiated by the gender and status of the dedicators—first men, then women and adolescents, and third lower-class men and children. There is thus a progressive movement throughout the book from persons of higher social standing to those of lower status, the primary means by which the two sections on men are distinguished.

The first of the three major sections in Meleager's dedicatory book (6.110–32, 6.262–64, 6.351) consists of dedications by men, many of whom celebrate their accomplishments in hunting and war. Of the three shorter groups in this section, the first (6.110–16, 6.262–63) concerns animals slain in a heroic manner. Several of the dedicators here and in the third group can be identified as historical persons of prominent status—Philip V of Macedon (6.114–16), Pyrrhus (6.130), and Lycortas (6.111)—and others have names suggesting aristocratic breeding—Cleolaus (6.110), Leontiades (6.112), Nicomachus (6.113), Alexander (6.128, 6.264), and Hagnon (6.129). The second group (6.117–20) is more miscellaneous, probably because severely excerpted, and contains dedications by less prominent individuals as well as a short sequence of poems that link

---

141. Wifstrand 27–28.

142. *AP* 6.162 which belongs with 9.322–23, 6.334 which repeats after 9.328 where it belongs, and 6.189 which probably also belongs with 9.327–29.

masculine endeavor with poetry. A triple dedication by a lyre player, an archer, and a hunter (6.118) is followed by a dedication of Dionysian grapes to Aphrodite (6.119) and then Leonidas' epigram on a cicada, the emblem of song, perched on the spear of a helmeted Athena (6.120). The third group of epigrams in the first section (6.121–32, 6.264, 6.351) consists of dedications of spears and shields to commemorate military victory, thus returning us to the realm of praise for the noble deeds of men.

The second section of the book (6.265–92, 6.352–58) consists of dedications primarily to goddesses and made primarily by women. Meleager was clearly not concerned with absolute gender consistency within his major sections, nor are these sections in their present condition marked off by the kinds of transitional poems we observed in the amatory book. But the second section does appear to begin with Nossis' *sphragis* poem commemorating the gift of a linen robe to Hera (6.265), and Nossis was probably viewed as the primary model for the writing of women's dedicatory epigrams. In addition to two other poems in this section attributed to Nossis (6.273, 6.275), it is likely that the two Nossis epigrams at 6.353–54 and, perhaps, the Nossis epigrams misplaced to 9.604–5 were originally situated in this section of the dedicatory book. The first sequence of four dedications to Artemis (6.266–69) consists of two poems on young women, one on a man who was apparently a legal scholar, and another on a male hunter. The transition from the Artemis dedications to the next sequence on childbirth (6.270–74, 6.146), consisting of offerings to either Artemis or Eileithyia, is a natural one; the subject matter here shifts the focus more directly to women. The sequence 6.275–82 deserves examination in some detail because here Meleager's method of thematic linkage is again in evidence. Dedications of a veil and snood, items that grace the hair, are followed by dedications of hair itself, two by girls who prepare to marry and two by adolescent males. In the next poem a bride dedicates a series of items, including a veil for her hair, and in the succeeding epigram the Great Mother's favor is asked for a girl of marriageable age who tosses her "maiden hair" in dance (6.281). One additional poem (6.282), in which Calliteles offers Hermes souvenirs of his youth, rounds out this series on adolescent dedications with a gender alternation but drops the linking reference to hair. The three poems at 6.283–85 show an interesting variety of approaches to the topic of weaving and sex: a hetaira turns to the loom in her old age, a girl earns a dress by sleeping with a youth, and yet another woman chooses the gaiety and profit of prostitution in place of the hard work and poverty of weaving. A close-knit series of four dedications by groups of female weavers (6.286–89) extends the subject in another direction. Three dedications by women of low reputation—a hetaira, a drunkard, and a winner of a beauty contest judged by Priapus—bring the section to its conclusion. Clearly, then, the method of associative linking so prominent in the amatory book continued at least in some portions of the dedicatory book as well.

The third section (6.293–312) returns us to dedications by men, but now men who are poor or of low social status. Meleager's grouping suggests that in Greek culture adult males who demonstrated their manhood by achievement stood at the top of the social order while those who failed to establish themselves through poverty, foolish behavior, or the ineffectiveness of age fell to the lowest rank, beneath women and youths. Grouped with them, or below them, in Meleager's social microcosm we find only children. A sequence surrounded by Leonidas' two epigrams on the Cynic Sochares (6.293, 298) contains dedications by old men retiring from various professions—a schoolmaster, a scribe, a hunter and fowler, and a farmer. The poverty that normally beset men of such occupations becomes the theme of the succeeding group of poems (6.299–303), which includes two statements by Leonidas on his own penury (6.300, 302). The hunger theme that runs through this sequence leads into a short run of miscellaneous poems dealing with food, gluttony, or poverty. Several of the epigrams on food or poverty, like Leonidas' address to mice (6.302) and Phanias' address to a fisherman (6.304), are not dedications at all. But Meleager was often inconsistent about formal type, since he was more interested in the literary effect produced by his juxtapositions than by cataloguing epigrams in typological niches. A final sequence dominated by dedications relating to children (6.308–12) includes three dedications of masks celebrating a literary or dramatic triumph (6.308, 310–11). Since we know Meleager sometimes admitted epigrams that are not formal dedications, we may speculate that 9.565–66, two Callimachean poems on the success or failure of poets, were also originally part of this short sequence, later removed by Cephalas to the epideictic book. The emphasis here on poetic victory (νικήσας, 6.308.1; νίκης, 6.311.2; and perhaps νικῶ, 9.566.2) forms a sequence leading to a poem that clearly brought closure to Meleager's selection of dedications, Bacchylides' address to Nike.

6.313, the last poem in the second sequence, was surely the concluding epigram in Meleager's dedicatory book, despite its lack of recognition as such by earlier scholars:

κούρα Πάλλαντος πολυώνυμε, πότνια Νίκα,
    πρόφρων †Κρανναίων† ἱμερόεντα χορόν
αἰὲν ἐποπτεύοις, πολέας δ' ἐν ἀθύρμασι Μουσᾶν
    Κηΐῳ ἀμφιτίθει Βακχυλίδῃ στεφάνους.

("Bacchylides" 2 *FGE* = *AP* 6.313)

Much-famed daughter of Pallas, reverent Victory,
    may you always look on the lovely dances of the . . . . . .
with good favor, and in the sport of the Muses place
    many crowns on the head of Cean Bacchylides.

For such prayers to Nike at the conclusion of a literary work, we may compare the preserved endings of Menandrian plays, the *Dyscolus* (968–69), the *Samia*

(736–37), and the *Sicyonius* (422–23).[143] Here Bacchylides' prayer for victory in musical competition serves metonymically as Meleager's own prayer for poetic success. In fact, the phrase ἀμφιτίθει στεφάνους repeats in an early epigram by Meleager in the amatory book (5.136.4)—that is, a poem that may have appeared near the beginning of the anthology proper. The reference to garlands at the end of the Bacchylides epigram suggests that, as the amatory book possibly stood first in the anthology, so the dedicatory book may have stood last. The Bacchylides epigram would then fall just before the *coronis* poem, with the result that the *coronis* itself, as crown, would provide the victory wreath requested in 6.313.

Despite the existence of an identifiable closing poem, no suitable opening epigram appears in any of the three Meleagrian sequences in *AP* 6. But analogy to the amatory book, which opens and closes with programmatic epigrams by Posidippus, suggests that the Bacchylides poem had a counterpart at the beginning of the dedicatory book—if not an epigram by the Cean himself, then one by another pre-Hellenistic poet. Only one another poem attributed to Bacchylides survives in the *AP*, a dedication by a farmer to Zephyr for aid with the winnowing of grain (6.53). Although I would not rule out a programmatic function for this poem given the symbolic connection of grain with poetry in Posidippus' *Soros*, a survey of epigrams displaced to sections arranged by Cephalas reveals two poems that are, to my mind, more likely candidates for the initial position, both attributed to Simonides:[144]

> εὐχεό τοι δώροισι, Κύτων, θεὸν ὧδε χαρῆναι
>   Λητοΐδην, ἀγορῆς καλλιχόρου πρύτανιν,
> ὥσπερ ὑπὸ ξείνων τε καὶ οἳ ναίουσι Κόρινθον
>   αἶνον ἔχεις χαρίτων, δέσποτα, τοῖς στεφάνοις.
>
> (62 FGE = AP 6.212)

Pray, Cyton, that the divine son of Leto, guardian of the square
    where lovely dances are performed, rejoices in your gifts,
Just as you, lord, receive from both foreigners and Corinthians
    praise for your victory's delight in the form of crowns.

> ἓξ ἐπὶ πεντήκοντα, Σιμωνίδη, ἤραο ταύρους
>   καὶ τρίποδας πρὶν τόνδ' ἀνθέμεναι πίνακα,
> τοσσάκι δ' ἱμερόεντα διδαξάμενος χορὸν ἀνδρῶν
>   εὐδόξου Νίκας ἀγλαὸν ἅρμ' ἐπέβης.
>
> (27 FGE = AP 6.213)

143. Cf. too Theocritus' prayer to Heracles for victory known from a marginal note in the Antinoe Papyrus on the lost ending of *Idyll* 24. In Menander, of course, and perhaps in Theocritus as well, such prayers made reference to an actual contest.

144. 6.210–26 are all by Meleagrian authors, but, as Lenzinger 7–8 has shown, they belong to a larger section thematically organized by Cephalas (6.179–226). 6.212–13 head a series of six epigrams attributed to Simonides, in violation of Meleager's usual method of intermingling authors.

Fifty-six bulls and as many tripods you won,
  Simonides, before setting up this tablet,
And as often as you directed the lovely chorus of men
  you mounted the glorious chariot of famed Victory.

In the first of these, a Hellenistic composition rather than a true inscription by Simonides, the poet speaks in his own voice to bid Cyton to pray for Apollo's favorable response to his dedication. Although we are not told the assumed occasion for Cyton's dedication, perhaps athletic victory, the placement of the poem at the opening of an epigram book would produce a natural transference in meaning so that the reader would understand Apollo as the patron of song and the gifts offered as the many poetic dedications to follow. Specific links to the Bacchylides poem are provided by the motif of the prayer and the key word στέφανος, which ends both poems. In the second of the epigrams, also a Hellenistic composition, the poet addresses Simonides himself to comment on, or elucidate, an inscribed plaque commemorating his fifty-six choral victories. At the head of Meleager's epigram book, not only would the reference to Simonides' *pinax* anticipate the many inscriptional dedications in the collection[145] but Simonides' achievement of poetic victory, the mounting of Nike's chariot, would provide an anticipatory parallel to the invocation of Nike at the end. These various similarities with 6.313, as well as the analogy of Meleager's practice in the amatory book, strongly suggest that one or both of the Simonidean epigrams appeared at the opening of the dedicatory book. By beginning and closing his dedicatory book with poems by Simonides and Bacchylides, Meleager gestures toward the pre-Hellenistic origin of dedicatory epigram as an art form, in contrast with the advent of amatory epigram in the early third century. Since none of these three epigrams are truly inscriptional nor composed by the poets to whom they are attributed, it is all the more likely that Meleager found them in a Hellenistic collection of pseudoinscriptional verse, a book that he in turn recalls by his significant reuse.

In organizational method, Meleager's dedicatory book may not have differed greatly from earlier Hellenistic epigram books. Arrangement by type of dedication and by gender or age of dedicator was logical and so probably typical. But Meleager's collection must have been distinguished by its comprehensiveness. Third-century composers of dedicatory epigrams seem to have concentrated, though not exclusively, on certain types of individuals or on certain themes— Nossis on women, Leonidas on the lower classes, Posidippus on the upper strata of society. Meleager's dedicatory book, however, as an anthology, embraces all

---

145. Boas (1905) 177–78 proposed that another dedicatory epigram (28 *FGE*) in which Simonides commemorates a victory in a dithyrambic contest in 477/6 likely followed *AP* 6.213 as the text inscribed on the *pinax*. Even though the poem is not now in the *Anthology*, the supposition has some merit. Page (1981) 242 argues convincingly that 28 *FGE* is not a genuine Simonidean inscription, but a Hellenistic forgery like *AP* 6.212–13.

segments of humanity—young and old, male and female, rich and poor. In this presentation of society's heterogeneity there results a dissolution of ideological centrality and so a tendency for the reader to seek the controlling focus in the editor's design rather than in the subject matter of the poetry.

Meleager's book of sepulchral epigrams was a longer and more ambitious anthology. Structured through a progressive ordering of human types similar to that found in the dedications, Meleager's collection of epitymbia attempts to convey through suggestive arrangement a philosophical perspective on death and the human condition. An initial analysis of *AP* 7 was offered by Weisshäupl, who demonstrated that the three longer Meleagrian sequences (7.406–507a [506 according to Weisshäupl], 7.646–56, 7.707–40) show an unmistakable similarity in sequencing of topics.[146] The manuscript repetition of 7.462 before 7.729, both poems dealing with women and childbirth, offers confirming evidence that the first and third series represent two different selections from the same anthology. Weisshäupl recognized that 7.507–29 (a partially alphabetical grouping of epigrams by Simonides, Callimachus, and others, corresponding to 6.133–57) was not structured in the same manner as 7.406–506, and so did not come to Cephalas from the same source as the Meleagrian sequences.[147] But he mistakenly accepted as Meleagrian in structure 7.657–65, a mixed series of poems by Leonidas and Theocritus. Studies on Theocritus have now shown that the Theocritean epigrams in this group were inserted, probably by Cephalas, from the collection transmitted in the bucolic manuscripts.[148]

I divide the sepulchral book into four major sections differentiated by reputation of the deceased, social status, gender, and type of death (Table V). The first section concerns famous persons of the past, almost all literary figures, and concludes with a kind of appendix of enigmatic epitaphs. The second section is devoted to men—mostly war dead or men of good character. This section flows without a definite break into the third section on women (first old women and then younger ones), adolescents, children, and old or lower-status men (including philosophers). The final section deals with deaths at sea. The general movement from upper-class persons to women to men of lower status resembles the overall pattern found in the dedicatory book. Meleager's arrangement in the last two sections displays, as well, an interesting parallelism with the new Posidippus collection. The funereal section on the papyrus has first epigrams on old women, then epigrams on younger women (mothers, virgins, and children mixed), and last epitaphs for old men.[149] There follows, after two intervening groups on other topics, a section on shipwrecks. Since the great majority of the

146. Weisshäupl (1896).
147. Wiesshäupl (1889) 25–26, (1896) 185–86.
148. Smutny 63–65; Gow (1952) II 524–27; Gow-Page (1965) I xx–xxi, II 525.
149. Private correspondence from Guido Bastianini, April 10, 1995.

Posidippus epigrams on the Milan papyrus have not descended to us through the *Anthology*, it is unlikely that Meleager was directly influenced by that collection. The similarities we have identified suggest, then, some standardized methods of arrangement for epigram sylloges of the Hellenistic period.

Meleager's initial section on famous literary figures (7.406–20, 7.707–19) has been decimated by Cephalas' removal of numerous epigrams to his own opening section at the beginning of *AP* 7. As a result, no clue remains about the introduction to Meleager's epitaphic book, although it is tempting to speculate that he began, as Cephalas does, with epigrams on Homer, perhaps even with the very poems by Alcaeus and Antipater (7.1–2) that now head *AP* 7. Another candidate, since Leonidas will emerge as the dominating model for Meleager's epitaphic book, is 9.24, where Leonidas compares Homer, preeminent among poets, to the sun outshining the stars—a statement that could well function to introduce a section on literary greats. It is quite likely that many if not all of the Meleagrian poems on literary figures in *AP* 9, though not formally epitaphic, were originally part of the funereal book. But despite the disappearance of the introductory poems, some traces of Meleager's arrangement in the first section are still visible. Dioscorides' epitaph for Thespis (7.410) stands next to its companion piece for Aeschylus (Θέσπιδος εὕρεμα τοῦτο, 7.411), while his epitaph for Sositheus (7.707) appears beside the Machon epigram (7.708) in the third long sequence of *AP* 7. We may reasonably conclude that, together with the epitaph for Sophocles (7.37) now removed to the Cephalan section, these five poems by Dioscorides formed a short sequence within Meleager's longer first section. The conclusion to the section is fairly well preserved as well: Callimachus' self-epitaph leads directly to an anonymous epitaph for Meleager and then a series of three self-epitaphs composed by the editor himself (7.415–19; cf. 7.421, another Meleagrian self-epitaph). This multiplicity of self-identifications not only plays up Meleager's editorial awareness of the earlier convention of self-epitaph in epigram collections but also looks back, humorously, to the multiple poems on single authors that must once have existed in this section. If other poets had yet to write epigrams on Meleager himself (the anonymous poem must be either another self-epitaph with its ascription now lost or a later intruder), then Meleager chose to compose a series of them for his own anthology. Through repetition of key words and purposeful self-variation (Μενιππείοις ... Χάρισιν, 7.417.4, 418.6), Meleager manages to suggest that his own literary career, from the composition of the Menippean *Charites* to his erotic epigrams, was consistently characterized by the quality of charm, or χάρις: "Rejoice (χαῖρε) even among the dead, you who fitted the Muse of Eros and the Graces into one art (Χάριτας σοφίαν εἰς μίαν)" (7.421). The poems for literary greats in the third Meleagrian sequence (7.707–19) confirm the initial position of this category within Meleager's poetry book; there seem, however, to be some intruders. 7.717, on an elderly rustic, is clearly misplaced. But since Meleager's desire to group by theme often prevailed over strict categorization, it is more doubtful whether 7.710–12 are also intrusive. Meleager may have chosen to place the epitaphs for Baucis (7.710, 712) beside Antipater's poem on Erinna (7.713), although the presence of an epitaph for a girl who perished on her wedding day (7.711), picking up the theme of the Baucis poems, suggests that all three poems may have been moved here *en bloc* by a later editor.[150]

The structure of the appendix on enigmatic epitaphs has been previously analyzed. Here it suffices to comment on the position of the poems within the funereal book, a position that has nothing to do with the character of the deceased individuals or the manner of their deaths. Rather, this series of epigrams forms a natural extension of the previous section commenting on earlier literary figures, because it calls the reader's attention to the process of reading and composition. Meleager picks up and reiterates, through his own interpretation of Antipater's interpretion of Leonidas (7.428), Antipater's point that the composer is first of all a reader of texts composed by others. In this fashion, the enigmatic epitaphs form a suitable bridge between Meleager's catalogue of earlier poets and his body of more commonplace epitaphs.

The second long section of the sepulchral book (7.430–54, 7.720–25) is concerned with men of good character, first war dead and then others, though the latter part of the section contains a couple of contrary examples. My division of Meleager's various epigram books into longer sections and shorter sequences, while useful for analysis, remains my own attempt to bring order to the transmitted material. There is no evidence that Meleager provided the sorts of internal headings that we find in the Milan papyrus (although the four books were probably given generic titles at the beginning of their respective rolls), and his method of linking thematically, sometimes even between one long section and another, indicate that he was primarily concerned with the effects of a linear reading. Yet the opening portion of the second section, on war dead, presents unambiguous groupings. A sequence of eight epitaphs for Spartan warriors (7.430–37) begins with three poems on the famous sixth-century battle between the Spartans and the Argives at Thyrea, to which must be added two poems on the topic from the third Meleagrian sequence (7.720–21). 7.229, which repeats after 7.721 in its original Meleagrian context, concerns a Spartan killed by Argives, and its position in the *Garland* may have suggested a reference to Thyrea. The quotation from the father's funeral speech in this poem would provide an excellent transition to 7.433–34, a pair in which a Spartan mother slays and curses a cowardly son and another proclaims her willing sacrifice of eight sons for the fatherland. Another repetition, of 7.231 on an Ambracian patriot after 7.438, increases the pool of epigrams on non-Spartan warriors, apparently contemporaries of their epigrammatists (7.438, 7.722, 7.724). A nonsepulchral anonymous poem lamenting the destruction of Laconia by the Achaeans (ἁ πάρος ἄδμητος καὶ ἀνέμβατος,

150. Cf. Weisshäupl (1896) 187.

ὦ Λακεδαῖμον, καπνὸν ἐπ' Εὐρώτᾳ δέρκεαι Ὠλένιον, "Lacedaemon, before unconquered and never invaded, you see Olenian smoke upon the Eurotas," 7.723.1–2) provides a pathetic link between the epigrams on Sparta's past glory and those on Hellenistic warriors. Overall, we may judge this segment of the sepulchral book an excellent example of Meleager's ability to create literary effect through "mere" editing.

Gow-Page suggest that 7.439–40, on good men but not necessarily war dead, are misplaced,[151] but we may note that the remainder of Meleager's second long section is not as tightly ordered as the initial sequence on warriors. The group on multiple burials (7.441–45) begins with noble youths and men who died in battle but ends with two poems on more commonplace individuals. 7.446–47 form a pair on men buried in foreign soil (Ἑρμιονεὺς ὁ ξεῖνος; σύντομος ἦν ὁ ξεῖνος, linking to the conventional ξεῖνε in 7.445), and 7.448–49 are copy and model, both epitaphs for a Pratalidas equally skilled in love, war, hunting, and dance; the two pairs are themselves linked by Κρής in 7.447 and Κρῆτα in 7.448. The reference to love in the Pratalidas pair apparently triggered the anomalous intrusion of the epitaph in which Philaenis defends herself against charges that she wrote sex manuals (7.450). If the position of this poem is truly Meleagrian (which is doubtful, given the gender anomaly), the connection to the general theme of nobility of character must reside in Philaenis' attempt to clear her name. The section concluded with a series of couplets (7.451–54). The last, a Callimachean epitaph for a man who died from excessive drinking, couples with 7.725, another Callimachean epitaph on the same topic. Together, they offer counter examples to the previous section on noble men and provide transition to the third section, which begins with Leonidas' epitaph for Maronis, a "wine-loving" old woman (7.455).

The next section of Meleager's sepulchral book is longer and more varied than the other three. Given the need to include a large number of epitaphs for commonplace people, young and old, male and female, Meleager chose to provide unity not so much through similarity in social status or type of death (though short sequences linked in these ways remain) but rather by focusing in the center of this long section on philosophical speculation about the meaning of death for all human beings. A lower-class view of death's harsh potential to level the inequality between rich and poor dominates the remaining portion of the sepulchral book and seems to derive ultimately from Leonidas' epigram collection.

The first portion of this section divides easily into short sequences—on elderly women (7.455–59, 7.726, 7.728) with the change in gender signaling a new section, poor but good men (7.460–61), women who died in childbirth (7.462–65, 7.729–30), and sons lamented by their parents (7.466–69). The only problem

---

151. Gow-Page (1965) I xxiii.

in the sequence involves 7.727, Theaetetus' epitaph for a man admired for his intelligence with a lesson on the uselessness of fame (δόξα) in the underworld. In its present position it falls between two epitaphs for elderly women but is not too distant in general sentiment from 7.460–61 on men who deserve whatever kindly treatment death may afford.

The central portion of the third section is occupied by a substantial sequence (7.470–80, 7.731–32), which provides the philosophical framework for reading the sepulchral book as a whole. Meleager may signal his interest in this portion of the collection by beginning with one of his own compositions:[152]

> – εἶπον ἀνειρομένῳ τίς καὶ τίνος ἐσσί. Φ. Φίλαυλος
>   Εὐκρατίδεω. – ποδαπὸς δ' εὔχεαι · · · · · ·
> – ἔζησας δὲ τίνα στέργων βίον; Φ. οὐ τὸν ἀρότρου
>   οὐδὲ τὸν ἐκ νηῶν, τὸν δὲ σοφοῖς ἕταρον.
> – γήραϊ δ' ἢ νούσῳ βίον ἔλλιπες; Φ. ἤλυθον Ἅιδην
>   αὐτοθελεί Κείων γευσάμενος κυλίκων.
> – ἦ πρέσβυς; Φ. καὶ κάρτα. – λάβοι νύ σε βῶλος ἐλαφρή
>   σύμφωνον πινυτῷ σχόντα λόγῳ βίοτον.

$$(130 \text{ G-P} = AP \text{ 7.470})$$

> – Tell me, I ask, your name and your father's name. Ph. Philaulus,
>   Eucratides' son. – And where were you from? · · · · · · ·
> – What sort of livelihood did you choose to follow? – Ph. Not plowing
>   nor sailing, but I was a companion of wise men.
> – Did you die from old age or illness? – Ph. I came to Hades
>   of my own free will, by tasting the Cean cups.
> – Were you old? Ph. Very. – May the earth be light upon you
>   since you lived a life commensurate with wise judgment.

The poet adopts a sympathetic tone toward Philaulus, who rejected the material rewards to be obtained on land or sea in favor of philosophical inquiry. The old philosopher's decision to end his life by drinking hemlock (Cean cups) leads directly to Callimachus' epitaph for Cleombrotus, who committed suicide after reading a Platonic treatise on the soul (7.471). Other poems on the thoughtful choice of suicide (7.472b–73, 7.731–32) then followed or, possibly in the case of 7.731–32, preceded Leonidas' nonepitaphic meditation on death (7.472). This long poem, discussed more fully in the Leonidas chapter, provides justification for a voluntary act of self-destruction by arguing that human striving for achievement is meaningless in comparison with the physical reality of death's power to dissolve the tissue of our bodies. Three poems on disturbed burials

152. The ascription is, however, disputed. It is attributed to Meleager in the Palatine but to Antipater (without ethnic) by Planudes. Stadtmüller preferred the Sidonian on the basis of comparison with 7.413 (which is similar only in its reference to Cynicism) and 7.164, 7.165 (where the dialogues with the dead are imitative of Leonidas). Later editors (Waltz, Beckby, and Gow-Page) follow the Palatine authorship.

and exposed corpses (7.478–80), two by Leonidas himself, reflect back upon Leonidas' powerful description of the body's decay. They also grant to the intervening poems—one on a couple who lost all their children in a single day, one on a bride who died of grief for her bridegroom, and Meleager's tender epitaph for his beloved Heliodora (7.474–76)[153]—a special poignancy, the suggestion that consolation for grief of this magnitude can come only by contemplating the essential meaninglessness of existence. Such a pessimistic view is clearly unsuitable for the earlier portion of the sepulchral book, which celebrated the lives of persons who received recognition after death, especially for literary or military achievement. But when placed among epitaphs for commonplace individuals, whose often short lives had meaning only to those who loved them, Leonidas' philosophical poem provides an intellectual premise for the acceptance of death's pain. We may imagine that the poem had a similar function in Leonidas' own collection.

Under the shadow of this philosophical perspective, the remainder of the long third section concentrates on familial relationships, especially the grief of parents for their offspring. Easiest to recognize are a sequence of four pathetic epitaphs for children (7.481–83 with 7.170, which repeats after 7.481 in the Palatine manuscript) and a longer sequence of epitaphs for girls who died before marriage (7.486–93, 7.649). Two poems that give the dying words of a girl to her father or to her mother (7.646–47) may have been transitional between the two groups. Other poems are less closely integrated but yet reflect on the general theme of relationships between parents and children. An epigram for a woman who outlived five daughters and five sons (7.484) invites the reader to contemplate the enormity of her grief through the lens of her own epitaph. Though an epitaph for a male follower of Bacchus (7.485) seems off the topic, it may yet connect to an epitaph for two priestesses, twin sisters who died in their eightieth year having buried neither husbands nor offspring (7.733). This happier possibility for a human life repeats in a corrupt epitaph for a man buried by his "good children" (7.734). Somewhere in the vicinity belong the dying words of Aristocrates (7.648), who, contrary to his own example, bids even a poor man to acquire a wife and descendants. In this section on familial relationships, the acquisition of loved ones, despite the grief that may result, remains a desirable aspect of human existence.

In all likelihood, 7.735–37 formed the conclusion to the third section, repackaging its themes as transition to the fourth section on deaths at sea. Perhaps directly following the sequence on girls dead before marriage appeared Damagetus' epitaph for Theano, who dies as she calls upon her husband absent on a sea voyage (7.735). To point up the moral, we next find Leonidas' nonsepulchral warning that even the most poverty-stricken existence is preferable to a life

---

153. For a literary analysis of this last poem, see S. Small, "The Composition of *Anth. Pal.*, VII, 476 (Meleager)," *AJP* 72 (1951) 47–56.

of travel (μὴ φθείρευ, ὤνθρωπε, περιπλάνιον βίον ἕλκων, "don't wear yourself
out, my man, leading a vagabond life," 7.736.1). As a succinct illustration of
the Leonidean moral, this anonymous couplet then concludes the section:

ἐνθάδ' ἐγὼ ληστῆρος ὁ τρισδείλαιος ἄρη
    ἐδμήθην, κεῖμαι δ' οὐδενὶ κλαιόμενος.

(45 G-P = *AP* 7.737)

Here met I my death, utterly unfortunate, through the violence
    of a brigand. And I lie mourned by no one.

The circumstances implied—death at the hands of a robber in a for-
eign land—suggest a sea voyage without directly mentioning one. After
all the pitiable permutations of family grief comes this even more pitiable
happenstance—to lie forever unmourned.

Remnants of the last section of the sepulchral book are divided among the
three longer Meleagrian sequences (7.494–506, 7.650–54, 7.738–39). Since
7.270 repeats after 7.650, we may assume that the poems on shipwrecks by
Meleagrian authors in the Cephalan sequence at 7.263–73 also appeared in the
final section of the sepulchral book. As a result of these dispersions to four
different locations in the *AP*, it is now difficult to observe the patterns of linkage
and the internal groupings that likely characterized this fairly homogeneous
section of the epitymbia. But important observations on structure can still be
made. The poem that most likely signaled the opening of the sea-faring section
was Phalaecus' nonepitaphic admonition (balancing Leonidas 7.736) to avoid
a career on the sea (φεῦγε θαλάσσια ἔργα) in favor of farming:

ἠπείρῳ γὰρ ἔνεστι μακρὸς βίος, εἰν ἁλὶ δ' οὔ πως
    εὔμαρὲς εἰς πολιὴν ἀνδρὸς ἰδεῖν κεφαλήν.

(5.3–4 G-P = *AP* 7.650.3–4)

On land you may have a long life. But on the sea
    it's never easy to find a man with grey hair.

I like to think that this introductory ναυηγοῦ παραίνεσις (so the lemmatist) was
directly followed by a fine anonymous epitaph (note the aptness of ἐν πόντῳ)
for a fisherman, whose skill and love of the sea could not protect him from its
dangers:

ἐν πόντῳ Σώδαμος ὁ Κρὴς θάνεν, ᾦ φίλα, Νηρεῦ,
    δίκτυα καὶ τὸ σὸν ἦν κεῖνο σύνηθες ὕδωρ,
ἰχθυβολεὺς ὁ περισσὸς ἐν ἀνδράσιν. ἀλλὰ θάλασσα
    οὔτι διακρίνει χείματος οὐδ' ἁλιεῖς.[154]

(51 G-P = *AP* 7.494)

154. In line 1 I print Hecker's φίλα in place of φίλε found in the mss.

Sodamus the Cretan died on the sea. He loved your nets,
  Nereus, and felt at home on your waters—
A consummate catcher of fish. But the sea in storm makes
  no distinction between fishermen and others.

All three sequences indicate that there then followed a good number of poems on travelers and merchants lost at sea. The recurring moral is that desire for wealth compels men to court disaster in sea travel, and the recurring pathos of the epitaphs is the separation of the drowned from the family that mourns, often separation even from the tombstone that bears the inscription. It is likely that the last three poems of the first Meleagrian sequence (7.504–6), again on fishermen, formed the conclusion to the section. The final epitaph, Leonidas' poem for a man half-eaten by a shark and so buried both on land and sea (κἠν γῇ κἠν πόντῳ, 7.506.1; perhaps balancing 7.494.1), cleverly effects the transition from the watery realm of the fourth section back to the solid earth of standard burials.

Wifstrand pointed out that Leonidas' epitaph for Crethon must be the final poem among the epitymbia "because it contains a warning about the perishability of wealth":[155]

αὕτα ἐπὶ Κρήθωνος ἐγὼ λίθος οὔνομα κείνου
  δηλοῦσα, Κρήθων δ᾽ ἐγχθόνιος σποδιά,
ὁ πρὶν καὶ Γύγῃ παρισεύμενος ὄλβον, ὁ τὸ πρὶν
  βουπάμων, ὁ πρὶν πλούσιος αἰπολίοις,
ὁ πρίν—τί πλείω μυθεῦμ᾽ ἔτι; πᾶσι μακαρτός,
  φεῦ, γαίης ὅσσης ὅσσον ἔχει μόριον.

(75 G-P = AP 7.740)

I, the stone that stands here, reveal the name of famous Crethon,
  but Crethon himself is ash under the earth,
He who once equaled Gyges in wealth, who once possessed
  many herds of cattle and was rich in goats,
Who once—But why say more? Judged fortunate by all,
  alas, what a small portion of earth he now holds.

We may add as its companion pieces a poem by Alexander Aetolus, 7.507a,[156] and two other epitaphs by Leonidas, 7.655–56. In the epigram by the Aetolian a poor man points out to the passerby that his grave is not that of the wealthy Croesus: "only a small tomb for a laboring man, but sufficient for me." In the first of the Leonidean poems the deceased requests that his body be covered by just a little dust in preference to a rich monument, while in the second another

---

155. Wifstrand 25.
156. For the Planudean ascription of 7.507a to "Alexander," who in a Meleagrian sequence must be the Aetolian, and the separation from 7.507b, which belongs to the Simonidean series, see Page (1981) 4.

poor man requests a salutation despite the fact that thorns and brambles hide the name engraved on his humble tombstone. To certify the vanity of the wealthy Crethon, we hear the voices of these poor, who have a truer understanding of death's nothingness. The concluding sequence, because it is clearly not part of the fourth section on deaths at sea, reaches back to color our perception of the entire book of epitymbia. A linear reading of Meleager's anthology of sepulchral epigrams must have been a moving experience, effected through its compelling structure. Drawing upon patterns of arrangement such as that in the Milan papyrus and upon Leonidas' ideological thematizing, Meleager created an epigram book that likely seemed both conventional in pattern and novel in its comprehensiveness, a culmination of literary tradition. Though the collection included comment on the literary past and commemoration of the noble, it was dominated, through its linear movement and key philosophical statements, by a more democratic, even lower-class view of death. The last brief sequence of four poems, by the authority of its position, undercuts the various claims to glory in the earlier sections of the book and reinforces Leonidas' preference for a simple life—as a philosophy shared by the editor. It is no surprise that Meleager should prove a sympathetic reader of Leonidas' Cynic-inspired poetry book, since in his earlier years he had been an avid imitator of an important Cynic writer of the third century, his countryman Menippus.

The epideictic poems, concentrated in a single Meleagrian sequence in *AP* 9 (313–38), have gone essentially unanalyzed. To my knowledge, no one has bothered even to list the topics and themes in the sequence, so that the characteristics of this group of epigrams as the remnants of a poetry book remain unrecognized. Wifstrand believed that many of the Meleagrian epigrams in *AP* 9 were placed there by Cephalas from their original home in the dedicatory section.[157] While Cephalas does seem to have removed various epigrams, erotic and funereal as well as dedicatory, from their original Meleagrian books because he perceived their formal character to be epideictic, the opposite process seems to have taken place within the Meleagrian sequence in *AP* 9. Here Cephalas took epigrams from their epideictic context to place them within *his own* thematically organized groupings in other books. The repetition of 6.334 after 9.328, where it is thematically suited, provides concrete evidence for this, while we may feel confident that 6.163, Meleager's imitation of Leonidas 9.322 and Antipater 9.323, once stood beside its models. Cameron is surely right to argue that the epideictica formed one of the four books in the *Garland*, as shown by the usual Meleagrian technique of organization by thematic linkage and alternation of authors in 9.313–38. The twenty-six epigrams in the sequence may represent, however, no more than about one-fifth of the original Meleagrian book. Other epigrams

157. Wifstrand 27–28.

from that collection are to be found among the fifty-eight or so Meleagrian poems elsewhere in *AP* 9 and among the fifty-six or so Meleagrian epigrams preserved only by Planudes (now in *AP* 16). Meleager's epideictic book could, then, have consisted of 140 or more epigrams, a collection rivaling in size the dedicatory book.

The grouping of epideictic epigrams as a class apparently goes back to Meleager, and was repeated in Agathias' *Cycle*, although we have no way to know whether those editors used the term *epideictica* as a title or heading.[158] Epideictic epigrams are notoriously difficult to define. Related most often to dedications and less often to sepulchral or even erotic epigrams, they tend to set a scene or to describe an object. In general, they are composed simply for exhibition, not for inscription, and so those epigrams that are considered pure "Buchpoesie" are likely to be classified as epideictic. Meleager's epideictica are rich in conversational tones, providing personalized rather than objective perspectives. Deities are addressed or address passersby, dedicated objects speak or are spoken to, the poet calls upon the reader to share an experience, dialogues are common. Meleager constructed his epideictic collection by applying (though not strictly of course) a classificatory standard of this sort, but he also sought coherence by concentrating on pastoral and erotic themes. This much is clear even from the skeletal remains that are now preserved in *AP* 9. While a series of topics can still be discerned in 9.313–38, the short sequences tend to be severely truncated and some must have completely disappeared; as a result, only bits of the thematic linkage can be discerned. It is, however, sometimes rather easy to surmise which poems may have completed certain thematic sequences.

The Meleagrian sequence opens with Anyte's invitation to rest in a laurel grove and to drink sweet water (ἵζε', ἁδύ, ἀμπαύσῃς, πνοιᾷ ... Ζεφύρου, 9.313). It has already been argued that this poem together with 9.314 on a statue of Hermes (ἄμπαυσιν) and 16.228 (ἀνάπαυσον, ἁδύ, ἄμπαυμα) formed an opening sequence in Anyte's epigram collection. Meleager added to this series a similar poem by Nicias, one of Anyte's imitators (9.315, ἵζευ). Other epigrams that Meleager may have placed here to supplement his borrowings from Anyte include 16.11 (ἵζευ, Ζέφυρος πνεύματι), 16.12 (ἵζευ, Ζεφύρους), 16.13 (καθίζεο, Ζεφύροις), 16.227 (ἄμπαυσον, Ζεφύροιο), and 16.230. As Meleager reuses Posidippus' call for a Bacchic bedewing to begin his erotic book, so he opens his epideictic book with a reuse of Anyte, who was likely the first poet to issue a collection of her own inscriptional epigrams and so the first to illustrate the declamatory tone.

On the model of 9.314 spoken by Hermes, Meleager continues with a series of four epigrams on statues of gods set up in rural locations (9.316–19), the first

---

158. On the meaning of the term, see Beckby III 10–11; A. Kambylis, "Das griechische Epigramm in Byzantinischer Zeit," *WJA* 20 (1994/95) 22 with n. 9, where he quotes a remark by scribe A in the heading to *AP* 9: οὐδὲ τοῖς παλαιοῖς ἠμέληται τὸ ἐπιδεικτικὸν εἶδος.

two on dual statues (Hermes and Heracles, Hermaphroditus and Silenus) and the second two on statues of Hermes alone. 16.188 and 16.190, both on rural statues of Hermes, are possible additions to this sequence (note λελογχώς in both 9.318.1 and 16.188.1). Two epigrams on Aphrodite, unarmed in one (9.320) and bearing the arms of Ares in the other (note λέλογχας, 9.321.1), continue the motif of divine images, while pointing up the erotic theme already broached by the sexually explicit conversation between Hermaphroditus, Silenus, and a goatherd in 9.317. Leonidas' epigram on an armed Aphrodite (16.171), forming a contrasting pair with 9.320 by the same poet, must have once been part of this short sequence. The transition to the next two epigrams, on Ares' discontentment with a dedication of unused weapons (9.322–23), is an easy one, and Meleager's variation of the Ares topic (6.163) must have stood here as well. The thread of Meleager's thematic sequencing breaks off at this point, though the next epigram seems to have a programmatic relationship to the overarching themes of the collection:

ἀ σῦριγξ, τί τοι ὧδε παρ' Ἀφρογένειαν ὄρουσας;
  τίπτ' ἀπό ποιμενίου χείλεος ὧδε πάρει;
οὔ τοι πρῶνες ἔθ' ὧδ' οὔτ' ἄγκεα, πάντα δ' Ἔρωτες
  καὶ Πόθος· ἀ δ' ἀγρία Μοῦσ' ἐν ὄρει μενέτω.

(Mnasalces 16 G-P = AP 9.324)

Syrinx, why have you hastened here to the Form-Born goddess?
  Why have you come here away from the shepherd's lips?
Promontories and glens now mean nothing to you, and all is Passion
  and Desire. But let the rustic Muse stay on the mountain.

The apparently inappropriate dedication of a syrinx to Aphrodite raises the question of the connecton between the pastoral and the erotic—the two thematic axes of Meleager's epideictic book.[159] Another now isolated epigram, on a shell engraved with an image of Eros (9.325), also seems to symbolize the link between the erotic and the natural.[160]

A series of five dedications to Nymphs—9.326–28, 6.334, 9.329—(which repeats after 9.328), forms another clearly recognizable sequence, perhaps to be supplemented with 16.291, Anyte's dedication to Pan and the Nymphs. Celebrating the refreshment provided by the cool water of the Nymphs' springs, the poems provide a link back to the opening of the epideictic book. An obscene conversation in which Pan threatens a personal attack on a person who desires to drink from the spring he guards (9.330) suggests a missing section on Pan (such as 16.226, 16.231) and perhaps on Priapus (such as 16.236–37, 16.261). The

159. Reitzenstein (1893) 130–31 suggested that Mnasalces here characterizes himself as a herdsman and his poetry as syrinx music—in the manner of post-Theocritean bucolic poets.

160. We may speculate that other ecphrastic epigrams on plastic images of Eros (such as 9.179, 16.14, 16.196–97) once filled out this portion of the book.

motif of the Nymphs washing the newborn Bacchus (9.331) as the precipitating event for the mixing of water and wine continues the underlying erotic theme, since the fire kindled by drinking unmixed wine is clearly sexual in nature. Epigrams on temples of Aphrodite by Nossis and by Mnasalces (9.332–33) are linked by first person plural verbs (ἰδώμεθα, στῶμεν); Anyte's 9.144, which served as inspiration for Mnasalces, was surely once here as well. Next come three poems on humble dedications to male deities (9.334–36), linked by clever verbal repetition (σμικροῖς, Μικαλίωνος, μικρῷ μικρός).

The Meleagrian sequence in *AP* 9 comes to a close with two epigrams on Pan. The first, spoken by Pan as patron of hunters (9.337), is unproblematic. The second (9.338), attributed to Theocritus, I would normally exclude from the sequence, since Meleager seems not to have known the Theocritean collection that was transmitted through the bucolic manuscripts and was later integrated into the *Anthology*. But the poem looks remarkably like a closure piece:

εὔδεις φυλλοστρῶτι πέδῳ, Δάφνι, σῶμα κεκμακός
    ἀμπαύων, στάλικες δ' ἀρτιπαγεῖς ἀν' ὄρη·
ἀγρεύει δέ τυ Πὰν καὶ ὁ τὸν κροκόεντα Πρίηπος
    κισσὸν ἐφ' ἱμερτῷ κρατὶ καθαπτόμενος,
ἄντρον ἔσω στείχοντες ὁμόρροθοι. ἀλλὰ τὺ φεῦγε,
    φεῦγε μεθεὶς ὕπνου κῶμα †καταγρόμενον.

(19 G-P = AP 9.338)

You sleep on the leaf-strewn ground, Daphnis, to rest
    your weary body, having just fixed your stakes on the mountains.
And you are stalked by Pan and Priapus, whose lovely head
    is wreathed with the ivy's yellow berries,
As they advance side by side into the the the cave. But flee,
    flee, shaking off the deep slumber that holds you.

The theme of hunting, carried over from the preceding poem (εὐάγρει, συνα-γρεύω, 9.337; ἀγρεύει, 9.338), has now turned erotic, while Daphnis' restful sleep (note ἀμπαύων) looks back to the series of invitations that open the epideictic anthology. The warning to Daphnis to flee, shaking off his deep slumber, arouses the reader, too, from the peaceful reverie of Meleager's pastoral-erotic epideictica (cf. *ite domum*, . . . *ite*, Verg. *Ecl.* 10.77). In this instance, then, Meleager may have acquired a Theocritean epigram from some unknown source, or the poem may have received its ascription to Theocritus at a later date from an editor who knew the bucolic collection.

If one final speculation may be allowed, I would here suggest that Meleager's paired epigrams addressed to insects, one to a grasshopper and one to a cicada, originally occupied key positions in the epideictic book, most likely in a beginning sequence:

ἀκρίς, ἐμῶν ἀπάτημα πόθων, παραμύθιον ὕπνου,
    ἀκρίς, ἀρουραίη Μοῦσα λιγυπτέρυγε,

αὐτοφυὲς μίμημα λύρας, κρέκε μοί τι ποθεινόν
ἐγκρούουσα φίλοις ποσσὶ λάλους πτέρυγας,
ὥς με πόνων ῥύσαιο παναγρύπνοιο μερίμνης,
ἀκρί, μιτωσαμένη φθόγγον ἐρωτοπλάνον·
δῶρα δέ σοι γήτειον ἀειθαλὲς ὀρθρινὰ δώσω
καὶ δροσερὰς στόμασι σχιζομένας ψακάδας.

(12 G-P = AP 7.195)

Grasshopper, deceiver of my desires, inducer of sleep,
   grasshopper, you shrill-winged rustic Muse,
Nature's imitation of the lyre, play for me a lovely tune
   by striking your feet against your vocal wings,
So as to release me from the pains of my all-wakeful cares,
   grasshopper, as you weave your love-beguiling sound.
As payment I will give you in the morning fresh greens
   and drops of dew sprayed from the mouth.

ἀχήεις τέττιξ, δροσεραῖς σταγόνεσσι μεθυσθείς
   ἀγρονόμαν μέλπεις μοῦσαν ἐρημολάλον,
ἄκρα δ' ἐφεζόμενος πετάλοις πριονώδεσι κώλοις
   αἰθίοπι κλάζεις χρωτὶ μέλισμα λύρας·
ἀλλά, φίλος, φθέγγου τι νέον δενδρώδεσι Νύμφαις
   παίγνιον, ἀντῳδὸν Πανὶ κρέκων κέλαδον,
ὄφρα φυγὼν τὸν Ἔρωτα μεσημβρινὸν ὕπνον ἀγρεύσω
   ἐνθάδ' ὑπὸ σκιερᾷ κεκλιμένος πλατάνῳ.

(13 G-P = AP 7.196)

Echoing cicada, drunk on the moisture of dew, you sing
   a country song that babbles in the wild,
And sitting on the leaf's edge, you strike your serrated limbs
   against your dark skin to produce a lyrelike song.
Now dear friend, sound out some new tune for the Nymphs
   of the trees, sending an echoing response to Pan,
So that escaping Eros I may hunt down the sleep of noon
   reclining here in the shade of the plane.

In the *AP* these poems appear in a long sequence of animal epitaphs (7.189–216), apparently arranged by Cephalas. Yet neither of the epigrams is in fact sepulchral, and so there is no reason to assume they were grouped by Meleager with his funereal poems.[161] As imaginary conversations without any inscriptional context, they fit well into the epideictic classification, and their rustic subject

---

161. R. B. Egan, "Two Complementary Epigrams of Meleager (*A.P.* vii 195 and 196)," *JHS* 108 (1988) 24–32 argues that the insect poems are in fact sepulchral and that the cicada and grasshopper address each other from the grave to request musical relief from love longing. But the argument presupposes that Meleager placed both epigrams in his sepulchral section, for which we have no evidence.

matter matches flawlessly the thematics of Meleager's epideictic book. Various features in each seem programmatic. Both the grasshopper and the cicada are traditional symbols for the poet, and here each is asked by the epigrammatist to perform a song. At the beginning of an epigram book the insects' songs would of course prefigure the contents of the collection.[162] In each case the soothing song is to produce sleep as an escape from, or cessation of, erotic desire. We will remember that at the close of the amatory book Meleager asks Eros to put to sleep his wakeful passion for Heliodora (τὸν ἄγρυπνον ἐμοὶ πόθον Ἡλιοδώρας κοίμισον, 5.215.1–2), as here he requests that the grasshopper's song release him from the pain of all-wakeful care (πόνων ῥύσαιο παναγρύπνοιο μερίμνης, 7.195.5). Verbal echos link the insect poems to the opening of the amatory book as well. There, in a poem addressed to Pan, Zenophila's sweet lyre-playing is described in pastoral-sounding terms (ἁδὺ κρέκεις τι μέλος, 5.139.2) remarkably like those in Meleager's insect poems (κρέκε μοί τι ποθεινόν, 7.195.3; φθέγγου τι νέον ... παίγνιον, ἀντῳδὸν Πανὶ κρέκων κέλαδον, 7.196.5–6).[163] And as Meleager asks how he may escape his desire for Zenophila (ποῖ σε φύγω; 5.139.3), so he requests from the cicada escape from Eros (φυγὸν τὸν Ἔρωτα, 7.196.7) through noon sleep in the shade of a plane tree. Finally, we may note how well the two insect poems, if they did appear in the opening sequence of the epideictic book, would prepare for the Daphnis poem at the end. The pastoral repose that Meleager hunts for (ἀγρεύσω, 7.196.7) as he enters a world of restful song is transformed at the book's conclusion into the sleep that Daphnis must shake off as he flees (φεῦγε) the erotic hunting (ἀγρεύει) of Pan and Priapus. Although the position of these two epigrams cannot be conclusively known without the lucky find of some papyrus, verbal echoes and thematic connections indicate that they would have made a striking transition from the amatory into the epideictic book. Vergil's prominent interest in Meleager's

162. An important influence on Meleager's choice of subject was surely Anyte's lament for a grasshopper and a cicada (20 G-P = *AP* 7.190), a poem that has implications for her own poetry. The programmatic use of epigrams about animals descends as well from Leonidas' mouse poem (37 G-P = *AP* 6.302), which contains the seal of the poet's name and announces the theme of his poverty. In Latin poetry a parallel is offered by Catullus' *passer* poems (2 and 3), which as a pair are directly indebted to Meleager's paired insect poems. In poem 2 not only does Catullus imitate Meleager's general structure and some of his vocabulary (see J. D. Bishop, "Catullus 2 and its Hellenistic Antecedents," *CP* 61 [1966] 158–61), but his prayer to the sparrow to lessen his love anguish (*tristis animi levare curas*, 2.10) also has the same kind of anticipatory relationship to his *libellus*. The position of the sparrow poems within Catullus' collection (whatever its length) also parallels the position I suggest for 7.195 and 196 in Meleager's book. These arguments have been presented in fuller form in Gutzwiller (1996b) 96–97.

163. For the pastoral ambiance of these phrases, cf. Theoc. *Id.* 1.1–2, *Epigr.* 5.1–2; [Bion] 2.1. De Venuto 287–91, noting the parallel language linking 5.139 with 7.195 and 196, has concluded that Zenophila is identified with the grasshopper.

cicada poem, which he echoes twice in the first two lines of the first *Eclogue* (cf. *patulae recubans sub tegmine fagi* with ὑπὸ σκιερᾷ κεκλιμένος πλατάνῳ and *silvestrem ... Musam meditaris* with ἀγρονόμαν μέλπεις μοῦσαν), adds further support to the supposition that this epigram had an important programmatic function in the *Garland*.

Even apart from such speculation, it is clear that the Meleagrian epideictica, like the erotica, epitymbia, and anathematica, formed a carefully designed poetry book fitted out with opening and closing poems, short thematically linked sequences, and probably (though not now visible) longer organizational sections as well. As other Meleagrian books were given structural focus through the placement of key thematizing epigrams at points of opening, closing, and transition, so the epideictic book was structured along the intersecting axes of the pastoral and erotic worlds.   Among the epideictic epigrams now placed elsewhere in *AP* 9 or surviving in Planudes (*AP* 16) are found several topics that would reinforce the thematic coherence of Meleager's poetry book: the sequence on Myron's *Cow* (9.719–24, 728, 734), poems on rural animals (9.99, 9.743–45), on Daphnis and Pan (9.341), on famous statues of Aphrodite and Eros (16.160–61, 167, 170, 172, 206), on Apelles' portrait of Aphrodite rising from the sea (16.178, 182), as well as the epitaphs for animals (7.190–203), which were perhaps considered epideictic because not truly inscriptional.   In particular, the Meleagrian poems on a locust and a cicada may once have served, programmatically, to reinforce the pastoral-erotic focus of the epideictic book. Given the resurgence of interest in bucolic poetry toward the end of the second century B.C., in the poetry of Bion and the bucolic collection of Artemidorus, it is not surprising that Meleager would devote a substantial portion of his *Garland* to pastoral themes.   The combination of pastoral and erotic in such Roman collections as Vergil's *Eclogues* and Tibullus' love elegies thus acquires a precedent in Meleager's epideictic book.

Meleager's *Garland* was not just a useful compendium of Greek literary epigram, but a work of art in its own right, the aesthetic quality of its carefully selected poetry matched by the aesthetic quality of its artistically designed structure. The *Garland* served as the culmination of a whole literary tradition by selecting from both the poetry and the structure of earlier epigram books. Meleager drew the organizing themes for the individual books within his anthology from the collections of major third-century epigrammatists: the symposium theme from Posidippus and Asclepiades, the equation of poetic subjects with flowers from Nossis, the leveling of class distinction through death from Leonidas, a pastoral setting from Anyte. His prooemial poem exceeding normal epigram length finds parallel in the Arsinoe poem opening the *Symmeikta Epigrammata*. Dividing a collection by formal types probably had numerous precedents, ranging from short sections on rather specific subjects such as appear on the new Posidippus papyrus to broader categories such as the divisions on which Meleager's four books are based. Structuring in short sequences by grouping models with copies remains without demonstrable precedent, although Antipater's variations were clearly the impetus for the trend. If there is no evidence that Antipater himself pointed the way in anthologizing, he more certainly demonstrated the possibility of enhancing meaning through juxtaposition by constructing such sequences as that on Myron's *Cow*. Meleager's own sequences of self-variations on a given topic clearly look back to Antipater.

Within its own historical horizon, the *Garland* must have had an immediate appeal as an artistic encapsulation of the Hellenic past, a summary of an entire genre in a literary mode, an original work of art made out of known poetic icons. In producing a work so suited to contemporary needs and tastes, Meleager's talents as composer coalesced with his talents as editor. His method of composing variations, to combine vocabulary and themes from more than one model to produce a highly original epigram, is directly connected to his method of editing, to link poems through multiple associations so that the intertextuality of model and copy becomes part of the contextual fabric of the anthology. The result was a literary work of such high artistic merit that the *Garland* eventually came to replace the various epigram books it excerpted, by repackaging both old and new material for an audience of late Hellenistic, and Roman, tastes.

Tables

TABLE I

Structure of Cephalan Books from *AP* Containing Meleagrian Material

	1	2	3	4	5	6	7	8	9
Erotica AP 5	Rufinus and others 1–103	Philip 104–33	Meleager 134–215	Agathias 216–302	miscellaneous 303–9				
Anathematica AP 6	thematic arrangement 1–53	Agathias 54–86	Philip 87–108	Meleager 110–32	misc. 133–57 + 158–78	thematic arrangement 179–226	Philip 227–61	Meleager 262–313	misc. 314–58
Epitymbia AP 7	thematic arrangement 1–363	Philip 364–405	Meleager 406–507a	misc. 507b–29 + 530–50	Agathias 551–614	Diogenes Laertius 615–20	Philip 622–45	Meleager 646–56	misc. 657–748
Epideictica AP 9	thematic arrangement 1–214	Philip 215–312	Meleager 313–38	misc. 339–63	Agathias 364–401	misc. 402–583	lacuna of c. 450 epigrams	thematic arrangement 584–827	
Paederastica AP 12	Strato 1–11	misc. 12–36	Meleager 37–168	misc. 169–74	Strato 175–255	concluding poems 256–58			

TABLE II
Meleager's Amatory Book (*AP* 5 and 12)

5.134–215	*12.37–168*

Opening sequence (5.134–49, 12.49–51)

5.134–49	12.49–51
5.134–37 – wine	12.49–51 – wine
5.138–41 – song	
5.142–49 – garlands and *charis*	

Transitional male-female section (12.52–53)

	12.52–53 – contrasting male/female pair

Section on boys (12.54–97, 12.37–44, 9.15–16)

	12.54–97, 12.37–44, 9.15–16
	12.54 – transitional
	12.55–62 – cities (single boys)
	12.63–70 – Zeus (single boys)
	12.71–78 – epigram pairs (single boys)
	12.79–87, 9.15 – flame of love
	12.88–95, 9.16 – multiple loves
	12.96–97, 12.37–41 – physical qualities of boys
	12.41 – women preferred to boys
	12.42–44 – negative qualities of boys
	12.44 – farewell to boy love

Mixed male-female section (5.150–91, 12.45–48, 12.98–160)

	12.98–101, 12.45–48 – poets and the power of love
5.150–68	12.102–120
	12.102–6 – promiscuity vs. fidelity
5.150, 5.6–8 – oaths	
	12.107–8 – nature analogy
5.151–52 – mosquito pair	
5.153 – lightning	12.109–10 – lightning
5.154–57 – couplets	12.111–14 – couplets
5.158–63 – pain caused by hetairas	
5.164–68 – komos	12.115–20 – komos

5.169–87
  5.169–71 – sweetness of love

  5.172–75 – sleeping and waking

  5.176–80 – Eros personified
  5.181–87 – mimes
5.188–91 – sea of love

12.121–54
  12.121–35 – sweetness,
    various themes
  12.136–38 – sleeping and waking
  12.139–44 – awakening of desire
  12.145–54 – various themes

12.155 – mime
12.156–60 – sea of love

Section on women (5.192–208, 12.161)

5.192–208
  5.193–96 – single women
  5.197–98 – multiple women
  5.199–207 – dedications by women
    5.199–201 – dedications after love making
    5.202–4 – parodic epigrams on women
    5.205–7 – marginal women
  5.208 – women preferred to men

12.161
  12.161 – single woman

Transitional male-female section (5.209–10, 12.162–65)

5.209–10 – mutual love

12.162–65 – mutual love

Concluding sequence (5.211–15, 12.166–68)

5.211–15
  5.211–12 – love never ceases
  5.213–14 – plea for reception
  5.215 – prayer for end to desire

12.166–68
  12.166 – love never ceases
  12.167 – plea for reception

  12.168 – cup of love

TABLE III

Structure of Meleager's Amatory Book (*AP* 5 and 12)

Opening sequence (5.134–49, 12.49–51) – symposium themes

   Transitional (male-female) (12.52–53)

      Boys (12.54–97, 12.37–44, 9.15–16)

         Heterogeneous section (5.150–91, 12.45–48, 12.98–160)

      Women (5.192–208, 12.161)

   Transitional (male-female) (5.209–10, 12.162–65)

Concluding sequence (5.211–215, 12.166–68) – release from love and cup of love

---

TABLE IV
Meleager's Dedicatory Book (*AP* 6)

6.110–132	6.262–313	6.351–358

Dedications by men, mostly noble (6.110–32, 6.262–64, 6.351)

6.110–16 – by heroic hunters	6.262–63 – by heroic hunters	
6.110–12 – hinds		
6.113 – ibex		
6.114–16 – bull		
	6.262 – unnamed animal	
	6.263 – lion	
6.117–120 – miscellaneous items		
6.117 – hammer		
6.118 – lyre, bow, and nets		
6.119 – grapes		
6.120 – cicada		
6.121–32 – weapons	6.264 – weapon	6.351 – weapon
		6.351 – club
6.121 – bow		
6.122–23 – spear		
6.124–32 – shields	6.264 – shield	

Dedications primarily to goddesses, primarily by women (6.265–92, 6.352–58, 6.146)

	6.265–92, 6.146	6. 352–58
	6.265 – robe to Hera	
	6.266–69 – to Artemis	
	6.270–74, 6.146 – for childbirth	
	6.275–82 – of adolescents	
	6.283–85 – weaving and sex	
	6.286–89 – by weavers	
	6.290–92 – miscellaneous items by women	

Dedications by lower-class men and by children (6.293–312)

	6.293–98 – by old men	
	6.299–303 – on poverty	
	6.304–7 – on food, gluttony, and poverty	
	6.308–12 – by children (except 311)	

Conclusion (6.313)

| | 6.313 – Bacchylides' victory epigram | |

TABLE V
Meleager's Sepulchral Book (*AP* 7)

7.406–507a	7.646–656	7.707–740

Epitaphs for famous persons and enigmatic epitaphs (7.406–29, 7.707–19)

7.406–507a	7.646–656	7.707–740
7.406–20 – famous persons		7.707–19 (except 711, 717) – famous persons
7.421–29 – enigmatic epitaphs		

Epitaphs for noble men (7.430–54, 7.720–25, with 7.229, 231)

7.406–507a	7.646–656	7.707–740
7.430–38, 7.231, 7.441–43 – war dead		7.720–21, 7.229, 7.722–24 – war dead
7.430–37 – Spartans		7.720–21, 7.229, 7.723 – Spartans
7.430–32 – battle at Thyrea		7.720–721 – Thyrea
7.438, 7.231 – other warriors		7.722, 7.724 – other warriors
7.441–45 – multiple burials		
7.446–54 – deceased men		
7.446–47 – strangers		
7.448–49 – pair on Pratalidas		
7.451–54 – couplets		
7.454 – drunkard (transitional)		7.725 – drunkard

Epitaphs for commonplace individuals (7.455–93, 7.646–49, 7.726–37 with 7.170)

7.406–507a	7.646–656	7.707–740
7.455–59 – old women		7.726, 7.728 – old women
7.460–61 – common men		
7.462–65 – women who died in childbirth		7.729–730 – childbirth
7.466–69 – sons mourned by parents		
7.470–80 – meaninglessness of life in comparison with death		
7.470–71 – philosophers who commit suicide		
7.472 – meditation on death		
7.472b–73 – suicides		7.731–32 – suicides
7.474–77 – miscellaneous deaths		
7.478–80 – exposed bodies		
7.481–93 – familial relationships	7.646–49 – fam. rel.	7.733–34 – fam. rel.
7.481, 7.170, 7.482–83 – children		
7.484 – parent and child	7.646–48 – parent and child	7.733–34 – parent and child
7.486–93 – girls dead	7.649 – girl dead before marriage	
		7.735–37 – avoid vagabond life

Deaths at sea (7.494–506, 7.650–54, 7.738–39 with 7.270)

7.494–506 – deaths at sea	7.650, 7.270, 7.652–54 – deaths at sea 7.650 – avoid the sea	7.738–39 – deaths at sea
7.494 – even fishermen drown 7.495–503 – travelers and merchants 7.504–6 – fishermen again	7.270, 7.652–54 – travelers and merchants	7.738–39 – travelers and merchants

Concluding sequence (7.507a, 7.655–56, 7.740)

7.507a – poor versus wealthy	7.655–56 – unimportance of grave marker	7.740 – perishability of wealth

TABLE VI
Meleager's Epideictic Book (*AP* 9)

9.313–38

9.313–15	opening sequence: invitations to rest in grove
9.316–19	statues of gods in rural locations
9.320–21	Aphrodite armed or not armed
9.322–23	arms inappropriately dedicated to Ares
9.324	dedication of pipe to Aphrodite
9.325	shell engraved with image of Eros
9.326–28, 6.334, 9.329	dedications to Nymphs
9.330	Pan guarding spring
9.331	Nymphs bathing newborn Bacchus
9.332–33	temples of Aphrodite
9.334–36	humble dedications to male deities
9.337–38	Pan, Daphnis fleeing from sleep

SELECT BIBLIOGRAPHY

Anderson, Graham. 1993. *The Second Sophistic: A Cultural Phenomenon in the Roman Empire.* London.

Aubreton, Robert, F. Buffière, and J. Irigoin, eds. 1994. *Anthologie grecque: Anthologie Palatine.* Vol. 11. Paris.

Baale, Maria. 1903. *Studia in Anytes poetriae vitam et carminum reliquias.* Haarlem.

Barbantani, S. 1993. "I poeti lirici del canone alessandrino nell'epigrammatistica." *Aevum Antiquum* 6: 5–97.

Barigazzi, A. 1968. "Il testamento di Posidippo di Pella." *Hermes* 96: 190–216.

——— . 1973. "Amore e poetica in Callimaco (ep. 28 e 6)." *RFIC* 101: 186–94.

——— . 1985. "Leonida, A. P. 7.472: l'uomo e la ragnetela." *Prometheus* 11: 193–210.

Barnard, S. 1991. "Anyte: Poet of Children and Animals." *Rose di Pieria.* Edited by Francesco de Martino. Bari. Pp. 165–76.

Barns, J. 1950, 1951. "A New Gnomologium." *CQ* 44: 126–37, 45: 1–19.

Bastianini, Guido, and C. Gallazzi. 1993a. "Il poeta ritrovato." *Rivista 'Ca' de Sass'* 121: 28–39.

——— . 1993b. *Posidippo: epigrammi.* Milan.

Beckby, Hermann, ed. 1957–58. *Anthologia Graeca.* 4 vols. Munich.

Bing, Peter. 1988a. "Theocritus' Epigrams on the Statues of Ancient Poets." *A&A* 34: 117–23.

——— . 1988b. *The Well-Read Muse: Present and Past in Callimachus and the Hellenistic Poets.* Hypomnemata, 90. Göttingen.

——— . 1995. "Ergänzungsspiel in the Epigrams of Callimachus." *A&A* 41: 115–31.

Birt, Theodor. 1882. *Das antike Buchwesen in seinem Verhältniss zur Litteratur.* Berlin.

Blum, Rudolf. 1991. *Kallimachos: The Alexandrian Library and the Origins of Bibliography.* Translated by H. H. Wellisch. Madison.

Boas, Marcus. 1905. *De epigrammatis Simonideis.* Groningen.

Braun, L. 1985. "L'arte di Callimaco negli epigrammi funerari." *SCO* 35: 57–70.

Brecht, F. J. 1930. *Motiv- und Typengeschichte des griechischen Spottepigramms.* Philologus Supplementband, 22. Heft 2. Leipzig.

Bulloch, A. W. 1985. "Hellenistic Poetry." *The Cambridge History of Classical Literature* I. Edited by P. E. Easterling and B. M. W. Knox. Cambridge. Pp. 541–621.

Bulloch, A. W., E. S. Gruen, A. A. Long, and A. Stewart, eds. 1993. *Images and Ideologies: Self-Definition in the Hellenistic World*. Berkeley.

Burton, Joan B. 1995. *Theocritus's Urban Mimes: Mobility, Gender, and Patronage*. Berkeley.

Cahen, É., ed. 1922. *Callimaque*. Paris.

———. 1929. *Callimaque et son oeuvre poétique*. Paris.

Calderini, I. G. Galli. 1982. "Su alcuni epigrammi dell'*Antologia Palatina* corredati di lemmi alternativi." *AAP* 31: 239–80.

———. 1983. "Edilo epigrammista." *AAP* 32: 363–76.

———. 1984. "Gli epigrammi di Edilo: interpretazione ed esegesi." *AAP* 33: 79–118.

Cameron, Alan. 1968. "The *Garlands* of Meleager and Philip." *GRBS* 9: 323–49.

———. 1980. "The *Garland* of Philip." *GRBS* 21: 43–62.

———. 1981. "Asclepiades' Girl Friends." *Reflections of Women in Antiquity*. Edited by H. P. Foley. New York. Pp. 275–302. Reprinted in revised form in Cameron 1995. Pp. 494–519.

———. 1982. "Strato and Rufinus." *CQ* 32: 162–73.

———. 1990. "Two Mistresses of Ptolemy Philadelphus." *GRBS* 31: 287–311.

———. 1993. *The Greek Anthology from Meleager to Planudes*. Oxford.

———. 1995. *Callimachus and His Critics*. Princeton.

Cavallini, E. 1991. "Due poetesse greche." *Rose di Pieria*. Edited by Francesco de Martino. Bari. Pp. 97–135.

Clairmont, Christoph W. 1970. *Gravestone and Epigram: Greek Memorials from the Archaic and Classical Period*. Mainz.

Clayman, D. L. 1980. *Callimachus' "Iambi"*. Leiden.

Coco, Luigi, ed. 1988. *Callimaco: epigrammi*. Manduria.

Courtney, Edward, ed. 1993. *The Fragmentary Latin Poets*. Oxford.

Daly, Lloyd W. 1967. *Contributions to a History of Alphabetization in Antiquity and the Middle Ages*. Brussels.

Dawson, C. M. 1950. "The *Iambi* of Callimachus." *YCL* 11: 1–168.

Day, J. W. 1989. "Rituals in Stone: Early Greek Grave Epigrams and Monuments." *JHS* 109: 16–28.

Degani, E. 1981. "Nosside." *GFF* 4: 43–52.

del Re, R. 1965. "Un epigramma di Leonida." *RFIC* 93: 430–37.

De Venuto, D. 1968. "Alcuni aspetti della tecnica letteraria di Meleagro." *RCCM* 10: 287–98.

Dudley, Donald R. 1937. *A History of Cynicism*. London.

Easterling, P. E. 1985. "Books and Readers in the Greek World: The Hellenistic and Imperial Periods." *The Cambridge History of Classical Literature* I. Edited by P. E. Easterling and B. M. W. Knox. Cambridge. Pp. 16–41.

Ferguson, J. 1970. "The Epigrams of Callimachus." *G&R* 17: 64–80.

Fernández-Galiano, Emilio. 1987. *Posidipo de Pela*. Madrid.

Figueira, Thomas, and G. Nagy, eds. 1985. *Theognis of Megara: Poetry and the Polis*. Baltimore.

Fowler, Barbara H. 1989. *The Hellenistic Aesthetic*. Madison.

Fowler, D. P. 1995. "Martial and the Book." *Ramus* 24: 31–58.

Fraistat, N. 1986. "Introduction." *Poems in Their Place: The Intertextuality and Order of Poetic Collections*. Edited by Neil Fraistat. Chapel Hill. Pp. 3–17.

Fraser, P. M. 1972. *Ptolemaic Alexandria*. 3 vols. Oxford.

Friedländer, Paul, with Herbert Hoffleit. 1948. *Epigrammata: Greek Inscriptions in Verse from the Beginnings to the Persian Wars*. Berkeley.

Gabathuler, Mathäus. 1937. *Hellenistische Epigramme auf Dichter*. St. Gallen.

Garrison, Daniel H. 1978. *Mild Frenzy: A Reading of the Hellenistic Love Epigram*. Hermes Einzelschriften. Heft 41. Wiesbaden.

Geffcken, Johannes. 1896. *Leonidas von Tarent*. *Jahrbücher für classische Philologie*, Suppl. 23. Leipzig.

——— . 1909. *Kynika und Verwandtes*. Heidelberg.

——— . 1917. "Studien zum griechischen Epigramm." *NJA* 39: 88–117. Reprinted in shortened form in *Das Epigramm: Zur Geschichte einer inschriftlicher und literarischen Gattung*. Edited by Gerhard Pfohl. Darmstadt, 1969. Pp. 21–46.

——— . 1925. "Leonidas von Tarent." *RE* 24 HB: 2021–31.

Gentili, B. 1968. "Epigramma ed elegia." *L'épigramme grecque*. Entretiens sur l'antiquité classique, 14. Geneva. Pp. 39–90.

Geoghegan, D. 1979. *Anyte: The Epigrams*. Rome.

Giangrande, G. 1968. "Sympotic Literature and Epigram." *L'épigramme grecque*. Entretiens sur l'antiquité classique, 14. Geneva. Pp. 91–177.

——— . 1969. "Interpretationen Hellenistischer Dichter." *Hermes* 97: 440–54.

Gigante, Marcello. 1971. *L'edera di Leonida*. Naples.

——— . 1974. "Nosside." *PP* 29: 22–39.

Goldhill, Simon. 1994. "The Naive and Knowing Eye: Ecphrasis and the Culture of Viewing in the Hellenistic World." *Art and Text in Ancient Greek Culture*. Edited by Simon Goldhill and R. Osborne. Cambridge. Pp. 197–223.

Gow, A. S. F. 1954. "Antipater of Sidon: Notes and Queries." *CR* 4: 1–6.

——— . 1958a. *The Greek Anthology, Sources and Ascriptions*. London.

——— . 1958b. "Leonidas of Tarentum." *CQ* 8: 113–23.

Gow, A. S. F., ed. 1952. *Theocritus*. 2 vols. 2nd ed. Cambridge.

——— , ed. 1965. *Machon: The Fragments*. Cambridge.

Gow, A. S. F., and D. L. Page, eds. 1965. *The Greek Anthology: Hellenistic Epigrams*. 2 vols. Cambridge.

——— . 1968. *The Greek Anthology: The Garland of Philip*. 2 vols. Cambridge.

Grainger, John D. 1991. *Hellenistic Phoenicia*. Oxford.

Green, Peter. 1990. *Alexander to Actium: The Historical Evolution of the Hellenistic Age*. Berkeley.

Gronewald, M. 1985. "Epigramme des Mnasalkes." *Kölner Papyri* V. Edited by Michael Gronewald, K. Maresch, and W. Schäfer. Opladen. Pp. 22–32.

Gutzwiller, Kathryn J. 1991. *Theocritus' Pastoral Analogies: The Formation of a Genre*. Madison.

——— . 1992. "The Nautilus, the Halcyon, and Selenaia: Callimachus's *Epigram* 5 Pf. = 14 G.-P." *CA* 11: 194–209.

——— . 1993. "Callimachus and Hedylus: A Note on Catullus 66.13–14." *Mnemosyne* 46: 530–32.

——— . 1995. "Cleopatra's Ring." *GRBS* 36: 383–98.

———. 1996a. "The Evidence for Theocritean Poetry Books." *Theocritus*. Hellenistica Groningana, 2. Edited by M. A. Harder, R. F. Regtuit, and G. C. Wakker. Groningen. Pp. 119–38.

———. 1996b. "Vergil and the Date of the Theocritean Epigram Book." *Philologus* 140: 92–99.

———. 1997. "The Poetics of Editing in Meleager's *Garland*." *TAPA* 127: 169–200.

Hansen, Bernhard. 1914. *De Leonida Tarentino*. Diss. Leipzig.

Hansen, Peter Allan. 1983. *Carmina epigraphica Graeca saeculorum VII–V a. Chr. n.* Berlin.

———. 1989. *Carmina epigraphica Graeca saeculi IV a. Chr. n.* Berlin.

Harder, A. 1993. "Aspects of the Structure of Callimachus' *Aetia*." *Callimachus*. Hellenistica Groningana, 1. Edited by M. A. Harder, R. F. Regtuit, and G. C. Wakker. Groningen. Pp. 99–110.

Harris, William V. 1989. *Ancient Literacy*. Cambridge, Mass.

Hauvette, Amédée. 1907. *Les épigrammes de Callimaque: étude critique et littéraire*. Paris. Also printed in *REG* 20 (1907) 295–357.

Hunter, R. 1992. "Callimachus and Heraclitus." *MD* 28: 113–23.

Hutchinson, G. O. 1988. *Hellenistic Poetry*. Oxford.

Jacobs, Friedrich. 1794–1814. *Anthologia Graeca*. 13 vols. Leipzig.

———. 1813–17. *Anthologia Graeca ad fidem codicis olim Palatini nunc Parisini*. 4 vols. Leipzig.

Kaibel, G. 1896. "Zu den Epigrammen des Kallimachos." *Hermes* 31: 264–70.

Kaibel, Georg, ed. 1878. *Epigrammata Graeca ex lapidibus conlecta*. Berlin.

Kindstrand, Jan F. 1976. *Bion of Borysthenes: A Collection of the Fragments*. Uppsala.

Knauer, Otto. 1935. *Die Epigramme des Asklepiades v. Samos*. Diss. Tübingen.

Knox, B. M. W. 1985. "Books and Readers in the Greek World: From the Beginnings to Alexandria." *The Cambridge History of Classical Literature* I. Edited by P. E. Easterling and B. M. W. Knox. Cambridge. Pp. 1–16.

Köhnken, A. 1993. "Gattungstypik in kallimacheischen Weihepigrammen." *Religio Graeco-Romana: Festschrift für Walter Pötscher*. Edited by Joachim Dalfen, G. Petersmann, and F. Schwarz. Horn. Pp. 119–30.

Körte, A. 1927. "Lynkeus von Samos." *RE* 26 HB: 2472–73.

Krevans, Nita. 1984. *The Poet as Editor: Callimachus, Virgil, Horace, Propertius and the Development of the Poetic Book*. Diss. Princeton.

Kroll, Wilhelm. 1924. *Studien zum Verständnis der römischen Literatur*. Stuttgart.

Lattimore, Richmond. 1962. *Themes in Greek and Latin Epitaphs*. Urbana.

Laurens, Pierre. 1989. *L'abeille dans l'ambre: célébration de l'épigramme*. Paris.

Lausberg, Marion. 1982. *Das Einzeldistichon: Studien zum antiken Epigramm*. Munich.

Lazzarini, Maria L. 1976. *Le formule delle dediche votive nella Grecia arcaica*. Rome.

Lenzinger, Franz. 1965. *Zur griechischen Anthologie*. Zurich.

Livrea, E. 1989. "Due epigrammi Callimachei." *Prometheus* 15: 199–206.

———. 1990. "Tre epigrammi funerari Callimachei." *Hermes* 118: 314–24.

———. 1995. "From Pittacus to Byzantium: The History of a Callimachean Epigram." *CQ* 45: 474–80.

Lloyd-Jones, H. 1963. "The Seal of Posidippus." *JHS* 83: 75–99. Reprinted in *Greek Comedy, Hellenistic Literature, Greek Religion, and Miscellanea*. Oxford, 1990. Pp. 158–95.

Lloyd-Jones, Hugh, and Peter Parsons, eds. 1983. *Supplementum Hellenisticum*. Berlin.

Luck, G. 1954. "Die Dichterinnen der griechischen Anthologie." *MH* 11: 170–87.

————. 1967. Review of Gow/Page, *Hellenistic Epigrams*. *GGA* 219: 23–61.

Ludwig, W. 1963. "Plato's Love Epigrams." *GRBS* 4: 59–82.

————. 1966. Review of Gow/Page, *Hellenistic Epigrams*. *Gnomon* 38: 20–25.

————. 1968. "Die Kunst der Variation im hellenistischen Liebesepigramm." *L'épigramme grecque*. Entretiens sur l'antiquité classique, 14. Geneva. Pp. 299–348.

Marvin, M. 1993. "Copying in Roman Sculpture: The Replica Series." *Roman Art in Context: An Anthology*. Edited by Eve d'Ambra. Englewood Cliffs, N.J. Pp. 161–88.

Mattsson, Axel. 1942. *Untersuchungen zur Epigrammsammlung des Agathias*. Lund. Reprinted in *The Greek Anthology* II. Edited by Sonya L. Tarán. New York, 1987.

Meillier, Claude. 1979. *Callimaque et son temps*. Lille.

Meyer, D. 1993. "Die Einbeziehung des Lesers in den Epigrammen des Kallimachos." *Callimachus*. Hellenistica Groningana, 1. Edited by M. A. Harder, R. F. Regtuit, and G. C. Wakker. Groningen. Pp. 161–75.

Ouvré, Henri. 1894. *Méléagre de Gadara*. Paris.

Pack, Roger A. 1965. *The Greek and Latin Literary Texts from Greco-Roman Egypt*. 2nd ed. Ann Arbor.

Page, Denys L., ed. 1942. *Greek Literary Papyri* I. Loeb Classical Series. Cambridge, Mass.

————. 1975. *Epigrammata Graeca*. Oxford.

————. 1978. *The Epigrams of Rufinus*. Cambridge.

————. 1981. *Further Greek Epigrams*. Cambridge.

Paton, W. R., ed. and trans. 1916–18. *The Greek Anthology*. 5 vols. Loeb Classical Library. Cambridge, Mass.

Peek, Werner. 1953. "Poseidippus von Pella." *RE* 43 HB: 428–46.

Peek, Werner, ed. 1955. *Griechische Vers-Inschriften I: Grab-Epigramme*. Berlin.

————. 1960. *Griechische Grabgedichte*. Berlin.

Pfeiffer, Rudolf, ed. 1949–51. *Callimachus*. 2 vols. Oxford.

Pfuhl, Ernst, and H. Möbius. 1977–79. *Die ostgriechischen Grabreliefs*. 2 vols. Mainz.

Pollitt, J. J. 1986. *Art in the Hellenistic Age*. Cambridge.

Pontani, Filippo Maria, ed. 1978. *Antologia Palatina*. Turin.

Powell, John U., ed. 1925. *Collectanea Alexandrina*. Oxford.

Preisendanz, Karl, ed. 1911. *Anthologia Palatina: Codex Palatinus et Codex Parisinus phototypice editi*. Lugduni Batavorum.

Puelma, M. 1996. "Ἐπίγραμμα—*epigramma*: Aspekte einer Wortgeschichte." *MH* 53: 123–39.

Radice, G. Lombardo. 1965. "Leonida Tarentino, poeta 'ricco.' " *Maia* 17: 141–57.

Radinger, Carl. 1895. *Meleagros von Gadara: Eine litterargeschichtliche Skizze*. Innsbruck. Reprinted in *The Greek Anthology* II. Edited by Sonya L. Tarán. New York, 1987.

Raubitschek, A. E. 1968. "Das Denkmal-Epigramm." *L'épigramme grecque*. Entretiens sur l'antiquité classique, 14. Geneva. Pp. 3–36.

Reitzenstein, Richard. 1893. *Epigramm und Skolion: Ein Beitrag zur Geschichte der alexandrinischen Dichtung*. Giessen.

Riedweg, C. 1994. "Reflexe hellenistischer Dichtungstheorie im griechischen Epigramm." *ICS* 19: 123–50.

Russell, D. A. 1979. "De imitatione." *Creative Imitation and Latin Literature*. Edited by David West and T. Woodman. Cambridge. Pp. 1–16.

————. 1983. *Greek Declamation*. Cambridge.

Santirocco, Matthew. 1986. *Unity and Design in Horace's "Odes."* Chapel Hill.

Schneider, Otto, ed. 1870–73. *Callimachea.* 2 vols. Leipzig.

Schott, Paul. 1905. *Posidippi epigrammata collecta et illustrata.* Diss. Berlin.

Schwarz, Gerda. 1971. *Die griechische Kunst des 5. und 4. Jahrhunderts v. Chr. im Spiegel der Anthologia Graeca.* Diss. Graz.

Seelbach, Wilhelm. 1964. *Die Epigramme des Mnasalkes von Sikyon und des Theodoridas von Syrakus.* Klassisch-philologische Studien, 28. Wiesbaden.

Setti, Giovanni. 1890. *Studi sulla Antologia Greca: gli epigrammi degli Antipatri.* Turin.

Sider, David. 1987. "The Love Poetry of Philodemus." *AJP* 108: 311–24.

———. 1997. *The Epigrams of Philodemus: Introduction, Text, and Commentary.* Oxford.

Skiadas, Aristoxenos D. 1965. *Homer im griechischen Epigramm.* Athens.

Skinner, Marilyn B. 1989. "Sapphic Nossis." *Arethusa* 22: 5–18.

———. 1991a. "Aphrodite Garlanded: Eros and Poetic Creativity in Sappho and Nossis." *Rose di Pieria.* Edited by Francesco de Martino. Bari. Pp. 79–96.

———. 1991b. "Nossis *Thelyglossos*: The Private Text and the Public Book." *Women's History and Ancient History.* Edited by Sarah B. Pomeroy. Chapel Hill. Pp. 20–47.

Smith, Barbara Herrnstein. 1968. *Poetic Closure: A Study of How Poems End.* Chicago.

Smutny, Robert J. 1955. "The Text History of the Epigrams of Theocritus." *University of California Publications in Classical Philology*, 15.2. Berkeley.

Snyder, Jane McIntosh. 1989. *The Woman and the Lyre: Women Writers in Classical Greece and Rome.* Carbondale, Ill.

Stadtmüller, Hugo, ed. 1894–1906. *Anthologia Graeca epigrammatum Palatina cum Planudea.* 3 vols. Leipzig.

Stella, Luigia A. 1949. *Cinque poeti dell'Antologia Palatina.* Bologna.

Svenbro, Jesper. 1993. *Phrasikleia: An Anthropology of Reading in Ancient Greece.* Translated by Janet Lloyd. Ithaca.

Tarán, Sonya L. 1979. *The Art of Variation in the Hellenistic Epigram.* Leiden.

Tarditi, G. 1988. "Per una lettura degli epigrammatisti greci." *Aevum Antiquum* 1: 5–75.

Thomas, Rosalind. 1989. *Oral Tradition and Written Record in Classical Athens.* Cambridge.

Turner, E. G. 1952. *Athenian Books in the Fifth and Fourth Centuries B.C.* London.

Van Hoorn, G. 1951. *Choes and Anthesteria.* Leiden.

Van Sickle, J. 1980. "The Book-Roll and Some Conventions of the Poetic Book." *Arethusa* 13: 5–42.

———. 1981. "Poetics of Opening and Closure in Meleager, Catullus, and Gallus." *CW* 75: 65–75.

Vetta, Massimo. 1980. *Theognis elegiarum liber secundus.* Rome.

Wallace, William, and Mary Wallace. 1941. *Asklepiades of Samos.* Oxford.

Walsh, G. B. 1990. "Surprised by Self: Audible Thought in Hellenistic Poetry." *CP* 85: 1–21.

———. 1991. "Callimachean Passages: The Rhetoric of Epitaph in Epigram." *Arethusa* 24: 77–103.

Waltz, Pierre, *et al.*, eds. 1928–94. *Anthologie grecque.* 13 vols. Paris.

Webster, T. B. L. 1964. *Hellenistic Poetry and Art.* London.

Weisshäupl, Rudolf. 1889. *Die Grabgedichte der griechischen Anthologie.* Vienna. Reprinted in *The Greek Anthology* I. Edited by Sonya L. Tarán. New York, 1987.

———. 1896. "Zu den Quellen der Anthologia Palatina." *Serta Harteliana*. Vienna. Pp. 184–88.

West, Martin L. 1974. *Studies in Greek Elegy and Iambus*. Berlin.

White, Heather. 1985. *New Essays in Hellenistic Poetry*. Amsterdam.

Wifstrand, Albert. 1926. *Studien zur griechischen Anthologie*. Diss. Lund. Reprinted in *The Greek Anthology* I. Edited by Sonya L. Tarán. New York, 1987.

Wilamowitz-Moellendorff, Ulrich v. 1906. *Die Textgeschichte der griechischen Bukoliker*. Berlin.

———. 1913. *Sappho und Simonides: Untersuchungen über griechische Lyriker*. Berlin.

———. 1924. *Hellenistische Dichtung in der Zeit des Kallimachos*. 2 vols. Berlin.

Wiseman, T. P. 1969. *Catullan Questions*. Leicester.

Zanker, G. 1987. *Realism in Alexandrian Poetry*. London.

Zanker, P. 1993. "The Hellenistic Grave Stelai from Smyrna: Identity and Self-Image in the Polis." *Images and Ideologies: Self-Definition in the Hellenistic World*. Edited by A. W. Bulloch, E. S. Gruen, A. A. Long, and A. Stewart. Berkeley. Pp. 212–30.

GENERAL INDEX

Aelian, 231

Aesthetic evaluation: of epigram, 2, 47–48; of variation, 227–28, 233–35. *See also* Literariness

Agathias: principles of arrangement in, 36n.68, 284; *Cycle*, 15, 28, 284, 316

Agis, 37

Alcaeus (lyric poet), 10

Alcaeus of Messene (epigrammatist): composed epitaphs for literary greats, 259, 261–62; enigmatic epitaph of, 268–69; erotic epigram of, 288; found on papyrus, 34; included in Meleager's *Garland*, 228

Alexander Aetolus, 37n.73, 314

Alexander Peloplaton, 234

Alphabetization: in *AP* sequence, 37–39; in Meleager's *Garland* (false), 36n.68, 277–78, 301; in Philip's *Garland*, 38–39, 277, 301; in scholarly editions, 38, 45, 51–52; in Theocritus, 38

Amyntas: found on papyrus, 34–35, 240; varied others, 232, 240

Anacreon: Alexandrian edition of, 51–53; in *AP* sequence, 37–38, 51, 301; assignment of epigrams to, 49; in epigram, 263–65; forerunner of epigrammatists, 5; lyric poetry of, 131, 132, 144; model for Hellenistic epigrammatists, 56–57, 92–93, 102

Anacreontic anthology, 10n.32

Animals, in epigram, 54–55, 60–68, 110–13, 319–21. *See also* Insects

Anonymous erotic epigrammatist, 288, 300

Anthologies: Byzantine, 6, 15–16; and canonization of epigram, 227; effect of, on hermeneutics, 6; possibility of, before Meleager, 33–35, 46; typical of epigram, 13–14

Anthology, as word, 79

Antimachus: in epigram, 163, 219–20; forerunner of epigrammatists, 5; praised by Antipater of Sidon, 261; precedent for Callimachus' *Aetia*, 186

Antipater of Sidon: and anthologies, 239–40, 276; composed epigram variations, 228–29, 236–37, 240–57, 276; composed epitaphs for literary greats, 260–65; connection of, with Rome, 231–32, 236, 238–39, 257–59; date of, 236n.20; enigmatic epigrams of, 269–73; epigram collection of, 236, 239–76; epitaph for, 273–76; found on papyrus, 34–35; improviser, 4–5, 231–32, 234, 239; inscriptions by, 229–31, 239; scholarly opinion of, 237–38; varied Leonidas, 236, 240–43, 246–50; varied by others, 235

Antipater of Thessalonica, 163, 236–37

Antiphanes, 87

Antisthenes of Paphos, 229–30

Anyte: epigram collection of, 45, 53–74; in *AP* sequence, 37; model for other epigrammatists, 112, 113, 228; opening poem of, 71–73, 158, 316

Aphrodite, as inspiratory deity, 76, 78–79, 110, 127–28

Apollonius of Rhodes, 20, 131, 144

Aratus: in epigram, 89, 226; epigrams of, 17; indebted to Hesiod, 76

Arcadia, 53, 54, 57, 69–70, 103

Compositor: Humanities Typsetting & Graphics
Text: Baskerville 10/12
Display: Baskerville
Greek: Ibycus by Silvio Levy
   modified by Pierre A. MacKay
Printer & Binder: Thomson-Shore, Inc.